FREQUENTLY USED SYMBOLS AND ABBREVIATIONS

AAI	Average Age of Inventory		EOQ	Economic Order Quantity
ACH	Automated Clearinghouse		EPS	Earnings per Share
ACP	Average Collection Period		ERP	Enterprise Resource Planning
AF_j	Amount of Funds Available from Financing Source j at a Given Cost		EU	European Union
ANPV	Annualized Net Present Value		EVA	Economic Value Added
A/P	Accounts Payable		FC	Fixed Operating Cost
APP	Average Payment Period		FCF	Free Cash Flow
APR	Annual Percentage Rate		FDI	Foreign Direct Investment
APY	Annual Percentage Yield		FLM	Financial Leverage Multiplier
A/R	Accounts Receivable		FV	Future Value
β_j	Beta Coefficient or Index of Nondiversifiable Risk for Asset j		GAAP	Generally accepted accounting principles
β_p	Portfolio Beta		GATT	General Agreement on Tariffs and Trade
B_0	Value of a Bond		g	Growth Rate
C	Carrying Cost per Unit per Period		I	Interest Payment
CAPM	Capital Asset Pricing Model		IP	Inflation Premium
CCC	Cash Conversion Cycle		IPO	Initial Public Offering
CD	Stated Cash Discount in Percentage Terms		IRR	Internal Rate of Return
CF_0	Initial Investment		JIT	Just-In-Time System
CF_t	Cash Inflow in Period t		LBO	Leveraged Buyout
CV	Coefficient of Variation		m	Number of times per year interest is compounded
D_p	Preferred Stock Dividend		M	Bond's Par Value
D_t	• Per-Share Dividend Expected at the End of Year t		M/B	Market/Book Ratio
	• Depreciation Expense in Year t		MACRS	Modified Accelerated Cost Recovery System
DFL	Degree of Financial Leverage		MNC	Multinational Company
DIP	Debtor in Possession		MP	Market Price per Share
DOL	Degree of Operating Leverage		MPR	Market Price Ratio of Exchange
DPS	Dividends per Share		MRP	Materials Requirement Planning
DTC	Depository Transfer Check		n	• Number of Outcomes Considered
DTL	Degree of Total Leverage			• Number of Periods—Typically, Years
e	Exponential Function = 2.7183			• Years to Maturity
E	Exercise Price of the Warrant		N	• Number of Days Payment Can Be Delayed by Giving up the Cash Discount
EAR	Effective Annual Rate			• Number of Shares of Common Stock Obtainable With One Warrant
EBIT	Earnings Before Interest and Taxes		N_d	Net Proceeds from the Sale of Debt (Bond)
EOM	End of the Month			

STUDENT VALUE EDITION

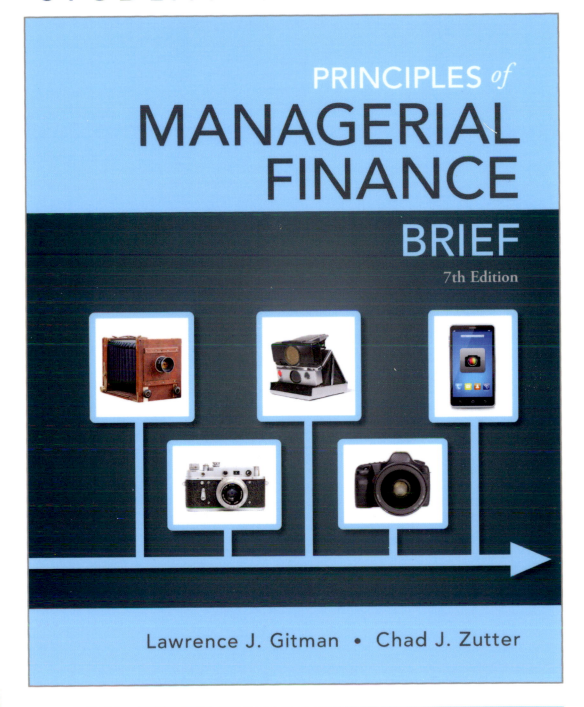

Principles *of*
MANAGERIAL FINANCE

BRIEF

7th Edition

Lawrence J. Gitman • Chad J. Zutter

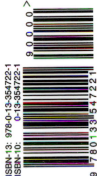

ISBN-13: 978-0-13-354722-1
ISBN-10: 0-13-354722-1

ALWAYS LEARNING

PEARSON

N_n	Net Proceeds from the Sale of New Common Stock
N_p	Net Proceeds from the Sale of Preferred Stock
NAFTA	North American Free Trade Agreement
NCAI	Net Current Asset Investment
NFAI	Net Fixed Asset Investment
NOPAT	Net operating profits after taxes
NPV	Net Present Value
O	Order Cost Per Order
OC	Operating Cycle
OCF	Operating Cash Flow
P	Price (value) of asset
P_0	Value of Common Stock
$PBDT_t$	Profits Before Depreciation and Taxes in year t
PD	Preferred Stock Dividend
P/E	Price/Earnings Ratio
PI	Profitability Index
PMT	Amount of Payment
Pr	Probability
PV	Present Value
Q	• Order Quantity in Units
	• Sales Quantity in Units
r	• Actual, Expected ($\bar{r}$), or Required Rate of Return
	• Annual Rate of Interest
	• Cost of Capital
r^*	Real Rate of Interest
r_a	Weighted Average Cost of Capital
r_d	• Required Return on Bond
	• Before-Tax Cost of Debt
r_i	After-Tax Cost of Debt
r_j	Required Return on Asset j
r_m	• Market Return
	• Return on the Market Portfolio of Assets
r_p	• Cost of Preferred Stock
	• Portfolio Return

r_r	Cost of Retained Earnings
r_s	• Required Return on Common Stock
	• Cost of Common Stock Equity
R_F	Risk-Free Rate of Interest
RADR	Risk-Adjusted Discount Rate
RE	Ratio of Exchange
ROA	Return on Total Assets
ROE	Return on Common Equity
S	• Usage in Units per Period
	• Sales in Dollars
SML	Security Market Line
t	Time
T	Firm's Marginal Tax Rate
TVW	Theoretical Value of a Warrant
V	• Value of an Asset or Firm
	• Venture Capital
V_C	Value of Entire Company
V_D	Value of All Debt
V_P	Value of Preferred Stock
V_S	Value of Common Stock
VC	Variable Operating Cost per Unit
w_j	• Proportion of the Portfolio's Total Dollar Value Represented by Asset j
	• Proportion of a Specific Source of Financing j in the Firm's Capital Structure
WACC	Weighted Average Cost of Capital
WTO	World Trade Organization
YTM	Yield to Maturity
ZBA	Zero Balance Account
σ	Standard Deviation
Σ	Summation Sign

Principles of
Managerial Finance
BRIEF

Seventh Edition

Lawrence J. Gitman
San Diego State University

Chad J. Zutter
University of Pittsburgh

PEARSON

Boston   Columbus   Indianapolis   New York   San Francisco   Upper Saddle River
Amsterdam   Cape Town   Dubai   London   Madrid   Milan   Munich   Paris   Montréal   Toronto
Delhi   Mexico City   São Paulo   Sydney   Hong Kong   Seoul   Singapore   Taipei   Tokyo

Editor in Chief: Donna Battista
Editorial Project Manager: Mary Kate Murray
Editorial Assistant: Elissa Senra-Sargent
Executive Marketing Manager: Anne Fahlgren
Managing Editor: Jeff Holcomb
Production Project Manager: Alison Eusden
Operations Specialist: Carol Melville
Art Director: Jonathan Boylan
Cover Designer: Jonathan Boylan

Cover Art: Dja65/Shutterstock; Ensuper/Shutterstock;
   Steven Chang/Shutterstock; Deamles for Sale/Shutter-
   stock; Yasnaten/Fotolia; SP-PIC/Fotolia
Content Lead, MyFinanceLab: Miguel Leonarte
Senior Media Producer: Melissa Honig
Permissions Associate Project Manager: Samantha Graham
Full-Service Project Management, Composition, and Interior
   Design: Cenveo Publisher Services/Nesbitt
Printer/Binder: LSC Communications
Cover Printer: LSC Communications
Text Font: Sabon LT Std

Credits and acknowledgments borrowed from other sources and reproduced, with permission, in this textbook appear on the appropriate page within the text.

Library of Congress Cataloging-in-Publication Data is on file.

5 17

PEARSON

ISBN: 10: 0-13-354640-3
ISBN: 13: 978-0-13-354640-8

The Pearson Series in Finance

Bekaert/Hodrick
International Financial Management

Berk/DeMarzo
*Corporate Finance**
*Corporate Finance: The Core**

Berk/DeMarzo/Harford
*Fundamentals of Corporate Finance**

Brooks
*Financial Management: Core Concepts**

Copeland/Weston/Shastri
Financial Theory and Corporate Policy

Dorfman/Cather
Introduction to Risk Management and Insurance

Eakins/McNally
*Corporate Finance Online**

Eiteman/Stonehill/Moffett
Multinational Business Finance

Fabozzi
Bond Markets: Analysis and Strategies

Fabozzi/Modigliani
Capital Markets: Institutions and Instruments

Fabozzi/Modigliani/Jones
Foundations of Financial Markets and Institutions

Finkler
Financial Management for Public, Health, and Not-for-Profit Organizations

Foerster
*Financial Management: Concepts and Applications**

Frasca
Personal Finance

Gitman/Zutter
*Principles of Managerial Finance**
*Principles of Managerial Finance—Brief Edition**

Haugen
The Inefficient Stock Market: What Pays Off and Why
The New Finance: Overreaction, Complexity, and Uniqueness

Holden
Excel Modeling in Corporate Finance
Excel Modeling in Investments

Hughes/MacDonald
International Banking: Text and Cases

Hull
Fundamentals of Futures and Options Markets
Options, Futures, and Other Derivatives

Keown
*Personal Finance: Turning Money into Wealth**

Keown/Martin/Petty
*Foundations of Finance: The Logic and Practice of Financial Management**

Kim/Nofsinger
Corporate Governance

Madura
*Personal Finance**

Marthinsen
Risk Takers: Uses and Abuses of Financial Derivatives

McDonald
Derivatives Markets
Fundamentals of Derivatives Markets

Mishkin/Eakins
Financial Markets and Institutions

Moffett/Stonehill/Eiteman
Fundamentals of Multinational Finance

Nofsinger
Psychology of Investing

Pennacchi
Theory of Asset Pricing

Rejda
Principles of Risk Management and Insurance

Smart/Gitman/Joehnk
*Fundamentals of Investing**

Solnik/McLeavey
Global Investments

Titman/Keown/Martin
*Financial Management: Principles and Applications**

Titman/Martin
Valuation: The Art and Science of Corporate Investment Decisions

Weston/Mitchel/Mulherin
Takeovers, Restructuring, and Corporate Governance

*Dedicated to the memory
of my mother, Dr. Edith Gitman,
who instilled in me the importance
of education and hard work.*
LJG

*Dedicated to my wonderful children,
Logan, Henry, Evelyn, and Oliver, who provide me with
constant commotion, fun, and affection.*
CJZ

Our Proven Teaching and Learning System

Users of *Principles of Managerial Finance, Brief* have praised the effectiveness of the book's Teaching and Learning System, which they hail as one of its hallmarks. The system, driven by a set of carefully developed learning goals, has been retained and polished in this seventh edition. The "walkthrough" on the pages that follow illustrates and describes the key elements of the Teaching and Learning System. We encourage both students and instructors to acquaint themselves at the start of the semester with the many useful features the book offers.

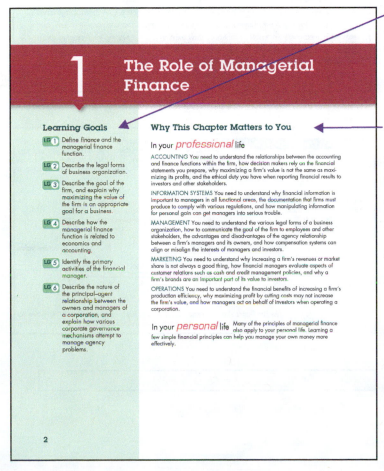

Six **Learning Goals** at the start of the chapter highlight the most important concepts and techniques in the chapter. Students are reminded to think about the learning goals while working through the chapter by strategically placed **learning goal icons**.

Every chapter opens with a feature, titled **Why This Chapter Matters to You**, that helps motivate student interest by highlighting both professional and personal benefits from achieving the chapter learning goals.

Its first part, **In Your Professional Life**, discusses the intersection of the finance topics covered in the chapter with the concerns of other major business disciplines. It encourages students majoring in accounting, information systems, management, marketing, and operations to appreciate how financial acumen will help them achieve their professional goals.

The second part, **In Your Personal Life**, identifies topics in the chapter that will have particular application to personal finance. This feature also helps students appreciate the tasks performed in a business setting by pointing out that the tasks are not necessarily different from those that are relevant in their personal lives.

Learning goal icons tie chapter content to the learning goals and appear next to related text sections and again in the chapter-end summary, end-of-chapter homework materials, and supplements such as the *Study Guide, Test Item File,* and MyFinanceLab.

For help in study and review, boldfaced **key terms** and their definitions appear in the margin where they are first introduced. These terms are also boldfaced in the book's index and appear in the end-of-book glossary.

Matter of Fact boxes provide interesting empirical facts that add background and depth to the material covered in the chapter.

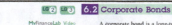

6.2 Corporate Bonds

MyFinanceLab Video

corporate bond
A long-term debt instrument indicating that a corporation has borrowed a certain amount of money and promises to repay it in the future under clearly defined terms.

A corporate bond is a long-term debt instrument indicating that a corporation has borrowed a certain amount of money and promises to repay it in the future under clearly defined terms. Most bonds are issued with maturities of 10 to 30 years and with a par value, or face value, of $1,000. The coupon interest rate on a bond represents the percentage of the bond's par value that will be paid annually, typically in two equal semiannual payments, as interest. The bondholders, who are the lenders, are promised the semiannual interest payments and, at maturity, repayment of the principal amount.

Corporations

corporation
An entity created by law.

stockholders
The owners of a corporation, whose ownership, or *equity,* takes the form of common stock or, less frequently, preferred stock.

A corporation is an entity created by law. A corporation has the legal powers of an individual in that it can sue and be sued, make and be party to contracts, and acquire property in its own name. Although only about 20 percent of all U.S. businesses are incorporated, the largest businesses nearly always are; corporations account for roughly 80 percent of total business revenues. Although corporations engage in all types of businesses, manufacturing firms account for the largest portion of corporate business receipts and net profits. Table 1.1 lists the key strengths and weaknesses of corporations.

Matter of fact

Bond Yields Hit Record Lows

On July 25, 2012, the 10-year Treasury note and 30-year Treasury bond yields reached all-time lows of 1.43% and 2.46%. That was good news for the housing market. Many mortgage rates are linked to rates on Treasury securities. For example, the traditional 30-year mortgage rate is typically linked to the yield on 10-year Treasury notes. With mortgage rates reaching new lows, potential buyers found that they could afford more expensive homes, and existing homeowners were able to refinance their existing loans, lowering their monthly mortgage payments and leaving them with more money to spend on other things. This kind of activity is precisely what the Federal Reserve hoped to stimulate by keeping interest rates low during the economic recovery.

Personal Finance Examples demonstrate how students can apply managerial finance concepts, tools, and techniques to their personal financial decisions.

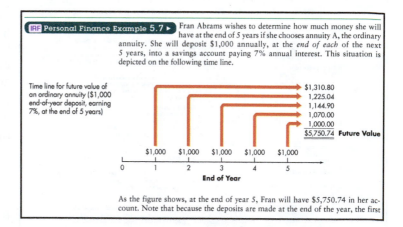

IRF Personal Finance Example 5.7 ▶ Fran Abrams wishes to determine how much money she will have at the end of 5 years if she chooses annuity A, the ordinary annuity. She will deposit $1,000 annually, at the *end of each* of the next 5 years, into a savings account paying 7% annual interest. This situation is depicted on the following time line.

Time line for future value of an ordinary annuity ($1,000 end-of-year deposit, earning 7%, at the end of 5 years)

$1,310.80
1,225.04
1,144.90
1,070.00
1,000.00
$5,750.74 **Future Value**

$1,000 $1,000 $1,000 $1,000 $1,000

0   1   2   3   4   5
End of Year

As the figure shows, at the end of year 5, Fran will have $5,750.74 in her account. Note that because the deposits are made at the end of the year, the first

Key Equations appear in blue boxes throughout the text to help readers identify the most important mathematical relationships. The variables used in these equations are, for convenience, printed on the *front endpapers* of the book.

$$PV = CF \div r \qquad (5.7)$$

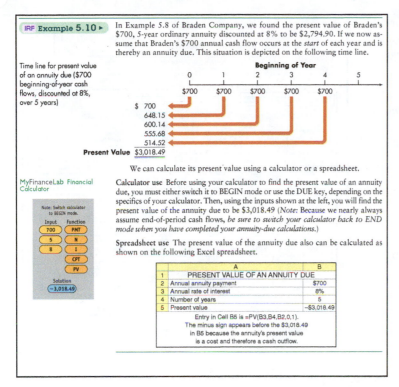

IRF Example 5.10 ▶

In Example 5.8 of Braden Company, we found the present value of Braden's $700, 5-year ordinary annuity discounted at 8% to be $2,794.90. If we now assume that Braden's $700 annual cash flow occurs at the *start* of each year and is thereby an annuity due. This situation is depicted on the following time line.

Time line for present value of an annuity due ($700 beginning-of-year cash flows, discounted at 8%, over 5 years)

Beginning of Year

	0	1	2	3	4	5
	$700	$700	$700	$700	$700	

$ 700
648.15
600.14
555.68
514.52

Present Value $3,018.49

We can calculate its present value using a calculator or a spreadsheet.

MyFinanceLab Financial Calculator

Note: Switch calculator to BEGIN mode.

Input	Function
700	PMT
5	N
8	I
	CPT
	PV

Solution
−3,018.49

Calculator use Before using your calculator to find the present value of an annuity due, you must either switch it to BEGIN mode or use the DUE key, depending on the specifics of your calculator. Then, using the inputs shown at the left, you will find the present value of the annuity due to be $3,018.49 (*Note: Because* we nearly always assume end-of-period cash flows, *be sure to switch your calculator back to END mode when you have completed your annuity-due calculations.*)

Spreadsheet use The present value of the annuity due also can be calculated as shown on the following Excel spreadsheet.

	A	B
1	PRESENT VALUE OF AN ANNUITY DUE	
2	Annual annuity payment	$700
3	Annual rate of interest	8%
4	Number of years	5
5	Present value	−$3,018.49

Entry in Cell B5 is =PV(B3,B4,B2,0,1).
The minus sign appears before the $3,018.49
in B5 because the annuity's present value
is a cost and therefore a cash outflow.

Examples are an important component of the book's learning system. Numbered and clearly set off from the text, they provide an immediate and concrete demonstration of how to apply financial concepts, tools, and techniques.

Some examples demonstrate time-value-of-money techniques. These examples often show the use of time lines, equations, financial calculators, and spreadsheets (with cell formulas).

New! An IRF icon, which appears with some examples, indicates that the example can be solved using the interest rate factors. The reader can access the *Interest Rate Factor Supplement* at MyFinanceLab. The *Interest Rate Factor Supplement* is a self-contained supplement that explains how the reader should use the interest rate factors and documents how the in-chapter examples can be solved by using them.

MyFinanceLab contains additional resources to demonstrate the examples. **New!** The MyFinanceLab Financial Calculator reference indicates that the reader can use the finance calculator tool in MyFinanceLab to find the solution for an example by inputting the keystrokes shown in the calculator screenshot. **New!** The MyFinanceLab Solution Video reference indicates that the reader can watch a video in MyFinanceLab of the author discussing or solving the example. **New!** The MyFinanceLab Video reference indicates that the reader can watch a video on related core topical areas.

→ REVIEW QUESTIONS

5-10 What is the difference between an *ordinary annuity* and an *annuity due*? Which is more valuable? Why?

5-11 What are the most efficient ways to calculate the present value of an ordinary annuity?

5-12 How can the formula for the future value of an annuity be modified to find the future value of an annuity due?

5-13 How can the formula for the present value of an ordinary annuity be modified to find the present value of an annuity due?

5-14 What is a *perpetuity*? Why is the present value of a perpetuity equal to the annual cash payment divided by the interest rate?

→ EXCEL REVIEW QUESTIONS MyFinanceLab

5-15 Since tax time comes around every year you smartly decide to make equal contributions to your IRA at the end of every year. Based on the information provided at MFL, calculate the future value of annual IRA contributions grown until retirement.

5-16 You have just graduated from college, begun your new career, and now it is time to buy your first home. Based on the information provided at MFL, determine how much you can spend for your new dream home.

5-17 Rather than making contributions to an IRA at the end of each year, you decide to make equal contributions at the beginning of each year. Based on the information provided at MFL, solve for the future value of beginning-of-year annual IRA contributions grown until retirement.

Review Questions appear at the end of each major text section. These questions challenge readers to stop and test their understanding of key concepts, tools, techniques, and practices before moving on to the next section.

New! Excel Review Questions ask readers to complete problems using a simulated Excel spreadsheet in MyFinanceLab that resemble the examples demonstrated in the corresponding section. These problems allow students to gain experience building Excel spreadsheet solutions and developing valuable business skill.

In Practice boxes offer insights into important topics in managerial finance through the experiences of real companies, both large and small. There are three categories of In Practice boxes:

Focus on Ethics boxes in every chapter help readers understand and appreciate important ethical issues and problems related to managerial finance.

Focus on Practice boxes take a corporate focus that relates a business event or situation to a specific financial concept or technique.

Both types of In Practice boxes end with one or more *critical thinking questions* to help readers broaden the lesson from the content of the box.

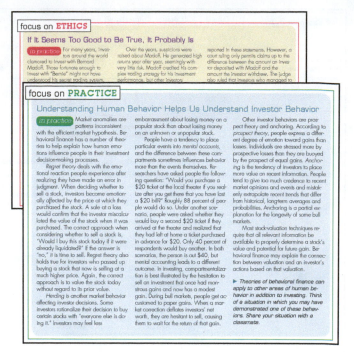

The end-of-chapter **Summary** consists of two sections. The first section, **Focus on Value**, explains how the chapter's content relates to the firm's goal of maximizing owner wealth. This feature helps reinforce understanding of the link between the financial manager's actions and share value.

The second part of the Summary, the **Review of Learning Goals**, restates each learning goal and summarizes the key material that was presented to support mastery of the goal. This review provides students with an opportunity to reconcile what they have learned with the learning goal and to confirm their understanding before moving forward.

Summary

FOCUS ON VALUE

Time value of money is an important tool that financial managers and other market participants use to assess the effects of proposed actions. Because firms have long lives and some decisions affect their long-term cash flows, the effective application of time-value-of-money techniques is extremely important. These techniques enable financial managers to evaluate cash flows occurring at different times so as to combine, compare, and evaluate them and link them to the firm's

REVIEW OF LEARNING GOALS

LG 1 **Discuss the role of time value in finance, the use of computational tools, and the basic patterns of cash flow.** Financial managers and investors use time-value-of-money techniques when assessing the value of expected cash flow streams. Alternatives can be assessed by either compounding to find future value or discounting to find present value. Financial managers rely primarily on present value techniques. Financial calculators, electronic spreadsheets, and financial tables can streamline the application of time value techniques. The cash flow of a firm can be described by its pattern: single amount, annuity, or mixed stream.

Self-Test Problems, keyed to the learning goals, give readers an opportunity to strengthen their understanding of topics by doing a sample problem. For reinforcement, solutions to the Self-Test Problems appear in the appendix at the back of the book. An IRF icon indicates that the Self-Test Problem can be solved using the interest rate factors. The reader can access the Interest Rate Factor Supplement at MyFinanceLab.

Warm-Up Exercises follow the Self-Test Problems. These short, numerical exercises give students practice in applying tools and techniques presented in the chapter.

Comprehensive Problems, keyed to the learning goals, are longer and more complex than the Warm-Up Exercises. In this section, instructors will find multiple problems that address the important concepts, tools, and techniques in the chapter.

A short descriptor identifies the essential concept or technique of the problem. Problems labeled as **Integrative** tie together related topics.

Personal Finance Problem

 P4–10 **Preparation of cash budget** Sam and Suzy Sizeman need to prepare a cash budget for the last quarter of 2016 to make sure they can cover their expenditures during the period. Sam and Suzy have been preparing budgets for the past several years and have been able to establish specific percentages for most of their cash outflows. These percentages are based on their take-home pay (that is, monthly utilities normally run 5% of monthly take-home pay). The information in the following table can be used to create their fourth-quarter budget for 2016.

 P4–21 **ETHICS PROBLEM** The SEC is trying to get companies to notify the investment community more quickly when a "material change" will affect their forthcoming financial results. In what sense might a financial manager be seen as "more ethical" if he or she follows this directive and issues a press release indicating that sales will not be as high as previously anticipated?

Personal Finance Problems specifically relate to personal finance situations and Personal Finance Examples in each chapter. These problems will help students see how they can apply the tools and techniques of managerial finance in managing their own finances.

The last item in the chapter Problems is an **Ethics Problem**. The ethics problem gives students another opportunity to think about and apply ethics principles to managerial financial situations.

All exercises and problems are available in MyFinanceLab.

Spreadsheet Exercise

CSM Corporation has a bond issue outstanding at the end of 2015. The bond has 15 years remaining to maturity and carries a coupon interest rate of 6%. Interest on the bond is compounded on a semiannual basis. The par value of the CSM bond is $1,000, and it is currently selling for $874.42.

Every chapter includes a **Spreadsheet Exercise**. This exercise gives students an opportunity to use Excel software to create one or more spreadsheets with which to analyze a financial problem. The spreadsheet to be created is often modeled on a table or Excel screenshot located in the chapter. Students can access working versions of the Excel screenshots in MyFinanceLab.

Brief Contents

Contents

Part 1 ▶ **Introduction to Managerial Finance** 1

1
The Role of Managerial Finance
page 2

4
Cash Flow and Financial Planning
page 109

Part 3 Valuation of Securities 211

Part 4 ▶ **Risk and the Required Rate of Return** 293

Part 6 | Long-Term Financial Decisions 463

Part 7 ▸ Short-Term Financial Decisions 549

About the Authors

Lawrence J. Gitman is an emeritus professor of finance at San Diego State University. Dr. Gitman has published more than 50 articles in scholarly journals as well as textbooks covering undergraduate- and graduate-level corporate finance, investments, personal finance, and introduction to business. He is past president of the Academy of Financial Services, the San Diego Chapter of the Financial Executives Institute, the Midwest Finance Association, and the FMA National Honor Society. Dr. Gitman served as Vice-President of Financial Education of the Financial Management Association, as a director of the San Diego MIT Enterprise Forum, and on the CFP® Board of Standards. He received his B.S.I.M. from Purdue University, his M.B.A. from the University of Dayton, and his Ph.D. from the University of Cincinnati. He and his wife have two children and live in La Jolla, California, where he is an avid bicyclist, having twice competed in the coast-to-coast Race Across America.

Chad J. Zutter is the Joseph P. and Angela A. Campolo Faculty Fellow and an associate professor of finance at the University of Pittsburgh. His research has a practical, applied focus and has been the subject of feature stories in, among other prominent outlets, *The Economist* and *CFO Magazine*. His papers have been cited in arguments before the U.S. Supreme Court and in consultation with companies such as Google and Intel. Dr. Zutter won the Jensen Prize for the best paper published in the *Journal of Financial Economics* and also won a best paper award from the *Journal of Corporate Finance*. Dr. Zutter has also won teaching awards at Indiana University and the University of Pittsburgh. He received his B.B.A. from the University of Texas at Arlington and his Ph.D. from Indiana University. He and his wife have four children and live in Pittsburgh, Pennsylvania. Prior to his career in academics, Dr. Zutter was a submariner in the U.S. Navy.

Preface

The desire to write *Principles of Managerial Finance, Brief* came from the experience of teaching the introductory managerial finance course. Those who have taught the introductory course many times can appreciate the difficulties that some students have absorbing and applying financial concepts. Students want a book that speaks to them in plain English and a book that ties concepts to reality. These students want more than just description; they also want demonstration of concepts, tools, and techniques. This book is written with the needs of students in mind, and it effectively delivers the resources that students need to succeed in the introductory finance course.

Courses and students have changed since the first edition of this book, but the goals of the text have not changed. The conversational tone and wide use of examples set off in the text still characterize *Principles of Managerial Finance, Brief*. Building on those strengths, 7 editions, numerous translations, and well over half a million U.S. users, *Principles* has evolved based on feedback from both instructors and students, from adopters, nonadopters, and practitioners. In this edition, Larry and I have worked to ensure that the book reflects contemporary thinking and pedagogy to further strengthen the delivery of the classic topics that our users have come to expect.

CHANGES TO THE SEVENTH EDITION

As we made plans to publish the seventh edition, we carefully assessed feedback from users of the sixth edition as well as instructors not currently using our text about content changes that would improve this teaching and learning tool.

In every chapter, our changes were designed to make the material more up to date and more relevant for students. A number of new topics have been added at appropriate places, and new features appear in each chapter:

- The Matter of Fact feature provides additional detail and interesting empirical facts that help students understand the practical implications of financial concepts. Many of these features have been updated or replaced in the seventh edition.

- The new MyFinanceLab Financial Calculator allows students to find the solution for an example by inputting the keystrokes shown in the calculator screenshot.

- The new MyFinanceLab Solution Videos allow the student to watch a video of the author discussing or solving the example. There are also MyFinanceLab Videos on related core topical areas.

- The new Interest Rate Factor (IRF) Supplement is a self-contained supplement which explains to the student how to use the interest rate factors, and works seamlessly with the textbook, so the student can go directly to the IRF Supplement and see the in-chapter example solved using the interest rate factors.

- We also made changes to many of the problems at the end of each chapter.

The chapter sequence is essentially unchanged from the prior edition, but there are some noteworthy changes within each chapter. This edition contains 15 chapters divided into seven parts. Each part is introduced by a brief overview, which is intended to give students an advance sense for the collective value of the chapters included in the part.

Part 1 contains two chapters. The first provides an overview of the role of managerial finance in a business enterprise. The second describes the financial market context in which firms operate and provides expanded and updated coverage of the recent financial crisis and its lingering consequences. This chapter not only explores the root causes and effects of the financial crisis, but it also discusses the changing regulatory landscape within which financial institutions and markets function.

Part 2 contains three chapters focused on basic financial skills such as financial statement analysis, cash flow analysis, and time-value-of-money calculations.

Part 3 focuses on bond and stock valuation. We placed these two chapters just ahead of the risk and return chapter to provide students with exposure to basic material on bonds and stocks that is easier to grasp than some of the more theoretical concepts in the next part.

Part 4 contains the risk and return chapter as well as the chapter on the cost of capital. We believe that following the risk and return chapter with the cost of capital material helps students understand the important principle that the expectations of a firm's investors shape how the firm should approach major investment decisions (which are covered in Part 5). In other words, Part 4 is designed to help students understand where a project "hurdle rate" comes from before they start using hurdle rates in capital budgeting problems.

Part 5 contains two chapters on various capital budgeting topics. The first of these chapters focuses on capital budgeting methods such as payback and net present value analysis. The second chapter in this part explains how financial analysts construct cash flow projections, which are a required component of net present value analysis, and describes how firms analyze the risks associated with capital investments.

Parts 6 deals with the topics of capital structure and payout policy. These two chapters contain updated material on trends in firms' use of leverage and their payout practices.

Finally, Part 7 contains two chapters centered on working capital issues. A major development in business has been the extent to which firms have found new ways to economize on working capital investments. The first chapter in Part 7 explains why and how firms work hard to squeeze resources from their investments in current assets such as cash and inventory. The second chapter in this part focuses more on management of current liabilities.

Although the text content is sequential, instructors can assign almost any chapter as a self-contained unit, enabling instructors to customize the text to various teaching strategies and course lengths.

Like the previous editions, the seventh edition incorporates a proven learning system, which integrates pedagogy with concepts and practical applications. It concentrates on the knowledge that is needed to make keen financial decisions in an increasingly competitive business environment. The strong pedagogy and generous use of examples—including personal finance examples—make the text an easily accessible resource for in-class learning or out-of-class learning, such as online courses and self-study programs.

ORGANIZATION

The text's organization conceptually links the firm's actions and its value as determined in the financial market. Each major decision area is presented in terms of both risk and return factors and their potential impact on owners' wealth. A Focus on Value element in each chapter's Summary helps reinforce the student's understanding of the link between the financial manager's actions and the firm's share value.

In organizing each chapter, we have adhered to a managerial decision-making perspective, relating decisions to the firm's overall goal of wealth maximization. Once a particular concept has been developed, its application is illustrated by an example, which is a hallmark feature of this book. These examples demonstrate, and solidify in the student's thought, financial decision-making considerations and their consequences.

INTERNATIONAL CONSIDERATIONS

We live in a world where international considerations cannot be divorced from the study of business in general and finance in particular. As in prior editions, discussions of international dimensions of chapter topics are integrated throughout the book. International material is integrated into learning goals and end-of-chapter materials.

PERSONAL FINANCE LINKAGES

The seventh edition contains several features designed to help students see the value of applying financial principles and techniques in their personal lives. At the start of each chapter, the Why This Chapter Matters to You feature helps motivate student interest by discussing how the topic of the chapter relates to the concerns of other major business disciplines and to personal finance. Within the chapter, Personal Finance Examples explicitly link the concepts, tools, and techniques of each chapter to personal finance applications. Throughout the homework material, the book provides numerous personal finance problems. The purpose of these personal finance materials is to demonstrate to students the usefulness of managerial finance knowledge in both business and personal financial dealings.

ETHICAL ISSUES

The need for ethics in business remains as important as ever. Students need to understand the ethical issues that financial managers face as they attempt to maximize shareholder value and to solve business problems. Thus, half the chapters include an In Practice box that focuses on current ethical issues.

HOMEWORK OPPORTUNITIES

Of course, practice is essential for students' learning of managerial finance concepts, tools, and techniques. To meet that need, the book offers a rich and varied menu of homework assignments: short, numerical Warm-Up Exercises; a comprehensive set of Problems, including more than one problem for each important concept or technique and personal finance problems; an Ethics Problem for each chapter; and a Spreadsheet Exercise. In addition, the end-of-section Excel Review Questions and the end-of-chapter problems are available in algorithmic form in MyFinanceLab. These materials (see pages viii through x for detailed descriptions) offer students solid learning opportunities, and they offer instructors opportunities to expand and enrich the classroom environment.

From classroom to boardroom, the seventh edition of *Principles of Managerial Finance, Brief* can help users get to where they want to be. We believe that it is the best edition yet: more relevant, more accurate, and more effective than ever.

Lawrence J. Gitman
La Jolla, California

Chad J. Zutter
Pittsburgh, Pennsylvania

Supplements to the Seventh Edition

The *Principles of Managerial Finance, Brief* Teaching and Learning System includes a variety of useful supplements for teachers and for students.

TEACHING TOOLS FOR INSTRUCTORS

The key teaching tools available to instructors are the *Instructor's Manual,* testing materials, and *PowerPoint Lecture Presentations.*

Instructor's Manual   This comprehensive resource pulls together the teaching tools so that instructors can use the textbook easily and effectively in the classroom. Each chapter provides an overview of key topics and detailed answers and solutions to all review questions, Warm-Up Exercises, end-of-chapter problems, and chapter cases, plus suggested answers to all critical thinking questions in chapter boxes, Ethics Problems, and Group Exercises. At the end of the manual are practice quizzes and solutions. The complete *Instructor's Manual,* including Spreadsheet Exercises, is available online at the Instructor's Resource Center (www.pearsonhighered.com/irc).

Test Item File   Thoroughly revised to accommodate changes in the text, the *Test Item File* consists of a mix of true/false, multiple-choice, and essay questions. Each test question includes identifiers for type of question, skill tested by learning goal, and key topic tested plus, where appropriate, the formulas or equations used in deriving the answer.

   The *Test Item File* is also available in *Test Generator Software (TestGen)* for either Windows or Macintosh. The *Test Item File* and *TestGen* are available online at the Instructor's Resource Center (www.pearsonhighered.com/irc).

PowerPoint Lecture Presentation   *Revised by Kate Demarest, Carroll Community College.* This presentation combines lecture notes with all the art from the textbook. The *PowerPoint Lecture Presentation* is available online at the Instructor's Resource Center (www.pearsonhighered.com/irc).

LEARNING TOOLS FOR STUDENTS

Beyond the book itself, students have access to valuable resources, such as MyFinanceLab and the *Study Guide,* that if taken advantage of can help ensure their success.

MyFinanceLab   *MyFinanceLab*   MyFinanceLab opens the door to a powerful Web-based diagnostic testing and tutorial system designed specifically for the Gitman/Zutter, *Principles of Managerial Finance, Brief.* With MyFinanceLab, instructors can create, edit, and assign online homework and test and track all student work in the online gradebook. MyFinanceLab allows students to take practice tests correlated to the textbook and receive a customized study plan based on the test results. Most end-of-chapter problems are available in MyFinanceLab, and because the problems have algorithmically generated values, no student will have the same homework as another; there is an unlimited opportunity for practice and testing. Students get the help they need, when they need it, from the robust tutorial options, including "View an Example" and "Help Me Solve This," which breaks the problem into its steps and links to the relevant textbook page.

This fully integrated online homework system gives students the hands-on practice and tutorial help they need to learn finance efficiently. There are ample opportunities for online practice and assessment that is automatically graded in MyFinanceLab (www.myfinancelab.com).

Advanced reporting features in MyFinanceLab also allow you to easily report on AACSB accreditation and assessment in just a few clicks.

Chapter Cases with automatically graded assessment are also provided in MyFinanceLab. These cases have students apply the concepts they have learned to a more complex and realistic situation. These cases help strengthen practical application of financial tools and techniques.

MyFinanceLab also has Group Exercises that students can work together in the context of an ongoing company. Each group creates a company and follows it through the various managerial finance topics and business activities presented in the textbook.

An online glossary, digital flashcards, financial calculator tutorials, videos, Spreadsheet Use examples from the text in Excel, and numerous other premium resources are available in MyFinanceLab.

Study Guide   *Revised by Shannon Donovan, Bridgewater State University.* The *Study Guide* is an integral component of the *Principles of Managerial Finance, Brief* Teaching and Learning System. It offers many tools for studying finance. Each chapter contains the following features: chapter summary enumerated by learning goals; topical chapter outline, also broken down by learning goals for quick review; sample problem solutions; study tips; and a full sample exam with the answers at the end of the chapter. A financial dictionary of key terms is located at the end of the *Study Guide,* along with an appendix with tips on using financial calculators.

NEW! *Interest Rate Factor (IRF) Supplement*   This self-contained supplement explains to the student how to use the interest rate factors and works seamlessly with the textbook, so the student can go directly to the IRF Supplement and see the in-chapter example solved using the interest rate factors. All examples which appear in the IRF Supplement are indicated in the text with an IRF icon.

Acknowledgments

TO OUR COLLEAGUES, FRIENDS, AND FAMILY

Pearson sought the advice of a great many excellent reviewers, all of whom influenced the revisions of this book. The following individuals provided extremely thoughtful and useful comments for the preparation of the seventh edition:

Steven L. Beach, *Radford University*
Denis O. Boudreaux, *University of Louisiana Lafayette*
Shannon Donovan, *Bridgewater State University*
Hsing Fang, *California State University–Los Angeles*
John Gonzales, *University of San Francisco*
Adina Schwartz, *Lakeland College*
Tammie Simmons-Mosley, *California State University–East Bay*
Charlene Sullivan, *Purdue University, Krannert School of Management*
Toby White, *Drake University*
David Wilhelm, *Metropolitan Community College*

Our special thanks go to the following individuals who analyzed the manuscript in previous editions:

Saul W. Adelman
M. Fall Ainina
Gary A. Anderson
Ronald F. Anderson
James M. Andre
Gene L. Andrusco
Antonio Apap
David A. Arbeit
Allen Arkins
Saul H. Auslander
Peter W. Bacon
Richard E. Ball
Thomas Bankston
Alexander Barges
Charles Barngrover
Michael Becker
Omar Benkato
Scott Besley
Douglas S. Bible
Charles W. Blackwell
Russell L. Block
Calvin M. Boardman
Paul Bolster
Robert J. Bondi
Jeffrey A. Born
Jerry D. Boswell
Denis O. Boudreaux

Kenneth J. Boudreaux
Wayne Boyet
Ron Braswell
Christopher Brown
William Brunsen
Samuel B. Bulmash
Francis E. Canda
Omer Carey
Patrick A. Casabona
Johnny C. Chan
Robert Chatfield
K. C. Chen
Roger G. Clarke
Terrence M. Clauretie
Mark Cockalingam
Kent Cofoid
Boyd D. Collier
Thomas Cook
Maurice P. Corrigan
Mike Cudd
Donnie L. Daniel
Prabir Datta
Joel J. Dauten
Lee E. Davis
Irv DeGraw
Richard F. DeMong
Peter A. DeVito

R. Gordon Dippel
James P. D'Mello
Carleton Donchess
Thomas W. Donohue
Lorna Dotts
Vincent R. Driscoll
Betty A. Driver
David R. Durst
Dwayne O. Eberhardt
Ronald L. Ehresman
Ted Ellis
F. Barney English
Greg Filbeck
Ross A. Flaherty
Rich Fortin
Timothy J. Gallagher
George W. Gallinger
Sharon Garrison
Gerald D. Gay
Deborah Giarusso
R. H. Gilmer
Anthony J. Giovino
Michael Giuliano
Philip W. Glasgo
Jeffrey W. Glazer
Joel Gold
Ron B. Goldfarb

Dennis W. Goodwin
David A. Gordon
J. Charles Granicz
C. Ramon Griffin
Reynolds Griffith
Arthur Guarino
Lewell F. Gunter
Melvin W. Harju
John E. Harper
Phil Harrington
George F. Harris
George T. Harris
John D. Harris
Mary Hartman
R. Stevenson Hawkey
Roger G. Hehman
Harvey Heinowitz
Glenn Henderson
Russell H. Hereth
Kathleen T. Hevert
J. Lawrence Hexter
Douglas A. Hibbert
Roger P. Hill
Linda C. Hittle
James Hoban
Hugh A. Hobson
Keith Howe
Kenneth M. Huggins
Jerry G. Hunt
Mahmood Islam
James F. Jackson
Stanley Jacobs
Dale W. Janowsky
Jeannette R. Jesinger
Nalina Jeypalan
Timothy E. Johnson
Roger Juchau
Ashok K. Kapoor
Daniel J. Kaufman Jr.
Joseph K. Kiely
Terrance E. Kingston
Raj K. Kohli
Thomas M. Krueger
Lawrence Kryzanowski
Harry R. Kuniansky
William R. Lane
Richard E. La Near
James Larsen
Rick LeCompte
B. E. Lee
Scott Lee
Suk Hun Lee
Michael A. Lenarcic
A. Joseph Lerro

Thomas J. Liesz
Hao Lin
Alan Lines
Larry Lynch
Christopher K. Ma
James C. Ma
Dilip B. Madan
Judy Maese
James Mallet
Inayat Mangla
Bala Maniam
Timothy A. Manuel
Brian Maris
Daniel S. Marrone
William H. Marsh
John F. Marshall
Linda J. Martin
Stanley A. Martin
Charles E. Maxwell
Timothy Hoyt McCaughey
Lee McClain
Jay Meiselman
Vincent A. Mercurio
Joseph Messina
John B. Mitchell
Daniel F. Mohan
Charles Mohundro
Gene P. Morris
Edward A. Moses
Tarun K. Mukherjee
William T. Murphy
Randy Myers
Lance Nail
Donald A. Nast
Vivian F. Nazar
G. Newbould
Charles Ngassam
Alvin Nishimoto
Gary Noreiko
Dennis T. Officer
Kathleen J. Oldfather
Kathleen F. Oppenheimer
Richard M. Osborne
Jerome S. Osteryoung
Prasad Padmanabahn
Roger R. Palmer
Don B. Panton
John Park
Ronda S. Paul
Bruce C. Payne
Gerald W. Perritt
Gladys E. Perry
Stanley Piascik
Gregory Pierce

Mary L. Piotrowski
D. Anthony Plath
Jerry B. Poe
Gerald A. Pogue
Suzanne Polley
Ronald S. Pretekin
Fran Quinn
Rich Ravichandran
David Rayone
Walter J. Reinhart
Jack H. Reubens
Benedicte Reyes
William B. Riley Jr.
Ron Rizzuto
Gayle A. Russell
Patricia A. Ryan
Murray Sabrin
Kanwal S. Sachedeva
R. Daniel Sadlier
Hadi Salavitabar
Gary Sanger
Mukunthan
   Santhanakrishnan
William L. Sartoris
William Sawatski
Steven R. Scheff
Michael Schellenger
Michael Schinski
Tom Schmidt
Carl J. Schwendiman
Carl Schweser
Jim Scott
John W. Settle
Richard A. Shick
A. M. Sibley
Sandeep Singh
Surendra S. Singhvi
Stacy Sirmans
Barry D. Smith
Gerald Smolen
Ira Smolowitz
Jean Snavely
Joseph V. Stanford
John A. Stocker
Lester B. Strickler
Gordon M. Stringer
Elizabeth Strock
Donald H. Stuhlman
Sankar Sundarrajan
Philip R. Swensen
S. Tabriztchi
John C. Talbott
Gary Tallman
Harry Tamule

Richard W. Taylor
Rolf K. Tedefalk
Richard Teweles
Kenneth J. Thygerson
Robert D. Tollen
Emery A. Trahan
Barry Uze
Pieter A. Vandenberg
Nikhil P. Varaiya
Oscar Varela
Kenneth J. Venuto
Sam Veraldi
James A. Verbrugge

Ronald P. Volpe
John M. Wachowicz Jr.
Faye (Hefei) Wang
William H. Weber III
Herbert Weinraub
Jonathan B. Welch
Grant J. Wells
Larry R. White
Peter Wichert
C. Don Wiggins
Howard A. Williams
Richard E. Williams
Glenn A. Wilt Jr.

Bernard J. Winger
Tony R. Wingler
I. R. Woods
John C. Woods
Robert J. Wright
Richard H. Yanow
Seung J. Yoon
Charles W. Young
Philip J. Young
Joe W. Zeman
John Zietlow
J. Kenton Zumwalt
Tom Zwirlein

Special thanks go to Thomas J. Boulton of Miami University for his work on the Focus on Ethics boxes and to Alan Wolk of the University of Georgia for accuracy checking the quantitative content in the textbook. We are pleased by and proud of all their efforts.

No textbook would be complete, let alone usable, if not for the accompanying instructor and student supplements. We are grateful to two individuals for their work creating, revising, and accuracy checking all the valuable instructor and student resources that support the use of *Principles:* Kate Demarest, Carroll Community College for revising the *PowerPoint Lecture Presentation* and Shannon Donovan of Bridgewater State University for revising the *Study Guide.*

A hearty round of applause also goes to the publishing team assembled by Pearson—including Donna Battista, Elissa Senra-Sargent, Mary Kate Murray, Alison Eusden, Melissa Honig, Miguel Leonarte, and others who worked on the book—for the inspiration and the perspiration that define teamwork. Also, special thanks to the formidable Pearson sales force in finance, whose ongoing efforts keep the business fun!

Finally, and most important, many thanks to our families for patiently providing support, understanding, and good humor throughout the revision process. To them we will be forever grateful.

Lawrence J. Gitman
La Jolla, California

Chad J. Zutter
Pittsburgh, Pennsylvania

Part 1 ▶ Introduction to Managerial Finance

Part 1 of *Principles of Managerial Finance* discusses the role that financial managers play in businesses and the financial market environment in which firms operate. We argue that the goal of managers should be to maximize the value of the firm and by doing so maximize the wealth of its owners. Financial managers act on behalf of the firm's owners by making operating and investment decisions whose benefits exceed their costs. These decisions create wealth for shareholders. Maximizing shareholder wealth is important because firms operate in a highly competitive financial market environment that offers shareholders many alternatives for investing their funds. To raise the financial resources necessary to fund the firm's ongoing operations and future investment opportunities, managers have to deliver value to the firm's investors. Without smart financial managers and access to financial markets, firms are unlikely to survive, let alone achieve the long-term goal of maximizing the value of the firm.

1

The Role of Managerial Finance

Learning Goals

LG 1 Define *finance* and the managerial finance function.

LG 2 Describe the legal forms of business organization.

LG 3 Describe the goal of the firm, and explain why maximizing the value of the firm is an appropriate goal for a business.

LG 4 Describe how the managerial finance function is related to economics and accounting.

LG 5 Identify the primary activities of the financial manager.

LG 6 Describe the nature of the principal–agent relationship between the owners and managers of a corporation, and explain how various corporate governance mechanisms attempt to manage agency problems.

Why This Chapter Matters to You

In your *professional* life

ACCOUNTING You need to understand the relationships between the accounting and finance functions within the firm, how decision makers rely on the financial statements you prepare, why maximizing a firm's value is not the same as maximizing its profits, and the ethical duty you have when reporting financial results to investors and other stakeholders.

INFORMATION SYSTEMS You need to understand why financial information is important to managers in all functional areas, the documentation that firms must produce to comply with various regulations, and how manipulating information for personal gain can get managers into serious trouble.

MANAGEMENT You need to understand the various legal forms of a business organization, how to communicate the goal of the firm to employees and other stakeholders, the advantages and disadvantages of the agency relationship between a firm's managers and its owners, and how compensation systems can align or misalign the interests of managers and investors.

MARKETING You need to understand why increasing a firm's revenues or market share is not always a good thing, how financial managers evaluate aspects of customer relations such as cash and credit management policies, and why a firm's brands are an important part of its value to investors.

OPERATIONS You need to understand the financial benefits of increasing a firm's production efficiency, why maximizing profit by cutting costs may not increase the firm's value, and how managers act on behalf of investors when operating a corporation.

In your *personal* life

Many of the principles of managerial finance also apply to your personal life. Learning a few simple financial principles can help you manage your own money more effectively.

1.1 Finance and Business

The field of finance is broad and dynamic. Finance influences everything that firms do, from hiring personnel to building factories to launching new advertising campaigns. Because there are important financial dimensions to almost any aspect of business, there are many financially oriented career opportunities for those who understand the principles of finance described in this textbook. Even if you do not see yourself pursuing a career in finance, you'll find that an understanding of a few key ideas in finance will help make you a smarter consumer and a wiser investor with your own money.

WHAT IS FINANCE?

finance
The science and art of managing money.

Finance can be defined as the science and art of managing money. At the personal level, finance is concerned with individuals' decisions about how much of their earnings they spend, how much they save, and how they invest their savings. In a business context, finance involves the same types of decisions: how firms raise money from investors, how firms invest money in an attempt to earn a profit, and how they decide whether to reinvest profits in the business or distribute them back to investors. The keys to good financial decisions are much the same for businesses and individuals, which is why most students will benefit from an understanding of finance regardless of the career path they plan to follow. Learning the techniques of good financial analysis will not only help you make better financial decisions as a consumer, but it will also help you understand the financial consequences of the important business decisions you will face no matter what career path you follow.

CAREER OPPORTUNITIES IN FINANCE

Careers in finance typically fall into one of two broad categories: (1) financial services and (2) managerial finance. Workers in both areas rely on a common analytical "tool kit," but the types of problems to which that tool kit is applied vary a great deal from one career path to the other.

Financial Services

financial services
The area of finance concerned with the design and delivery of advice and financial products to individuals, businesses, and governments.

Financial services is the area of finance concerned with the design and delivery of advice and financial products to individuals, businesses, and governments. It involves a variety of interesting career opportunities within the areas of banking, personal financial planning, investments, real estate, and insurance.

Managerial Finance

managerial finance
Concerns the duties of the *financial manager* in a business.

financial manager
Actively manages the financial affairs of all types of businesses, whether private or public, large or small, profit seeking or not for profit.

Managerial finance is concerned with the duties of the *financial manager* working in a business. **Financial managers** administer the financial affairs of all types of businesses: private and public, large and small, profit seeking and not for profit. They perform such varied tasks as developing a financial plan or budget, extending credit to customers, evaluating proposed large expenditures, and raising money to fund the firm's operations. In recent years, a number of factors have increased the importance and complexity of the financial manager's duties. These factors include the recent global financial crisis and subsequent responses by regulators, increased competition, and technological change. For example, globalization has led U.S. corporations to increase their transactions in other countries, and foreign corporations have done likewise in the United States. These changes increase demand for financial experts who can manage cash flows in different currencies and protect against the risks that arise from international transactions. These changes increase the finance function's complexity, but they also create opportunities for a more rewarding career. The increasing complexity of the financial manager's duties has increased the popularity of a variety of professional certification programs. Financial managers today actively develop and implement corporate strategies aimed at helping the firm grow and improve its competitive position. As a result, many corporate presidents and chief executive officers (CEOs) rose to the top of their organizations by first demonstrating excellence in the finance function.

LEGAL FORMS OF BUSINESS ORGANIZATION

One of the most important decisions all businesses confront is how to choose a legal form of organization. This decision has very important financial implications because how a business is organized legally influences the risks that the firm's owners must bear, how the firm can raise money, and how the firm's profits will be taxed. The three most common legal forms of business organization are the *sole proprietorship,* the *partnership,* and the *corporation.* More businesses are organized as sole proprietorships than any other legal form, but the largest businesses are almost always organized as corporations. Even so, each type of organization has its advantages and disadvantages.

Sole Proprietorships

sole proprietorship
A business owned by one person and operated for his or her own profit.

A **sole proprietorship** is a business owned by one person who operates it for his or her own profit. About 61 percent of all businesses are sole proprietorships. The typical sole proprietorship is small, such as a bike shop, personal trainer, or plumber. The majority of sole proprietorships operate in the wholesale, retail, service, and construction industries.

Typically, the owner (proprietor), along with a few employees, operates the proprietorship. The proprietor raises capital from personal resources or by borrowing, and he or she is responsible for all business decisions. As a result, this form of organization appeals to entrepreneurs who enjoy working independently.

unlimited liability
The condition of a sole proprietorship (or general partnership), giving creditors the right to make claims against the owner's personal assets to recover debts owed by the business.

A major drawback to the sole proprietorship is **unlimited liability,** which means that liabilities of the business are the entrepreneur's responsibility and that creditors can make claims against the entrepreneur's personal assets if the business fails to pay its debts. The key strengths and weaknesses of sole proprietorships are summarized in Table 1.1.

Partnerships

partnership
A business owned by two or more people and operated for profit.

A **partnership** consists of two or more owners doing business together for profit. Partnerships account for about 8 percent of all businesses, and they are typically larger than sole proprietorships. Partnerships are common in the finance, insurance, and real estate industries. Public accounting and law partnerships often have large numbers of partners.

articles of partnership
The written contract used to formally establish a business partnership.

Most partnerships are established by a written contract known as **articles of partnership.** In a *general* (or *regular*) *partnership,* all partners have unlimited liability, and each partner is legally liable for *all* of the debts of the partnership. Table 1.1 summarizes the strengths and weaknesses of partnerships.

Matter of fact

BizStats.com Total Receipts by Type of U.S. Firm

Although there are vastly more sole proprietorships than there are partnerships and corporations combined, they generate the lowest level of receipts. In total, sole proprietorships generated more than $1.3 trillion in receipts, but this number hardly compares to the more than $50 trillion in receipts generated by corporations.

BizStats.com Total Receipts by Type of U.S. Firm			
	Sole proprietorships	Partnerships	Corporations
Number of firms (millions)	23.1	3.1	7.7
Percentage of all firms	61%	8%	20%
Total receipts ($ billions)	1,324	4,244	50,757
Percentage of all receipts	2%	7%	80%

Corporations

corporation
An entity created by law.

A **corporation** is an entity created by law. A corporation has the legal powers of an individual in that it can sue and be sued, make and be party to contracts, and acquire property in its own name. Although only about 20 percent of all U.S. businesses are incorporated, the largest businesses nearly always are; corporations account for roughly 80 percent of total business revenues. Although

| TABLE 1.1 | Strengths and Weaknesses of the Common Legal Forms of Business Organization |

	Sole proprietorship	Partnership	Corporation
Strengths	• Owner receives all profits (and sustains all losses) • Low organizational costs • Income included and taxed on proprietor's personal tax return • Independence • Secrecy • Ease of dissolution	• Can raise more funds than sole proprietorships • Borrowing power enhanced by more owners • More available brain power and managerial skill • Income included and taxed on partner's personal tax return	• Owners have *limited liability*, which guarantees that they cannot lose more than they invested • Can achieve large size via sale of ownership (stock) • Ownership (stock) is readily transferable • Long life of firm • Can hire professional managers • Has better access to financing
Weaknesses	• Owner has *unlimited liability* in that total wealth can be taken to satisfy debts • Limited fund-raising power tends to inhibit growth • Proprietor must be jack-of-all-trades • Difficult to give employees long-run career opportunities • Lacks continuity when proprietor dies	• Owners have *unlimited liability* and may have to cover debts of other partners • Partnership is dissolved when a partner dies • Difficult to liquidate or transfer partnership	• Taxes are generally higher because corporate income is taxed, and dividends paid to owners are also taxed at a maximum 15% rate • More expensive to organize than other business forms • Subject to greater government regulation • Lacks secrecy because regulations require firms to disclose financial results

stockholders
The owners of a corporation, whose ownership, or *equity*, takes the form of common stock or, less frequently, preferred stock.

limited liability
A legal provision that limits stockholders' liability for a corporation's debt to the amount they initially invested in the firm by purchasing stock.

common stock
The purest and most basic form of corporate ownership.

dividends
Periodic distributions of cash to the stockholders of a firm.

corporations engage in all types of businesses, manufacturing firms account for the largest portion of corporate business receipts and net profits. Table 1.1 lists the key strengths and weaknesses of corporations.

The owners of a corporation are its **stockholders,** whose ownership, or *equity,* takes the form of common stock or, less frequently, preferred stock. Unlike the owners of sole proprietorships or partnerships, stockholders of a corporation enjoy **limited liability,** meaning that they are not personally liable for the firm's debts. Their losses are limited to the amount they invested in the firm when they purchased shares of stock. In Chapter 7, you will learn more about common stock, but for now it is enough to say that **common stock** is the purest and most basic form of corporate ownership. Stockholders expect to earn a return by receiving **dividends**—periodic distributions of cash—or by realizing gains through increases in share price. Because the money to pay dividends generally comes from the profits that a firm earns, stockholders are sometimes referred to as *residual claimants,* meaning that stockholders are paid last, after employees, suppliers, tax authorities, and lenders receive what they are owed. If the firm does not generate enough cash to pay everyone else, there is nothing available for stockholders.

As noted in the upper portion of Figure 1.1, control of the corporation functions a little like a democracy. The stockholders (owners) vote periodically to elect

FIGURE 1.1

Corporate Organization
The general organization of a corporation and the finance function (which is shown in yellow)

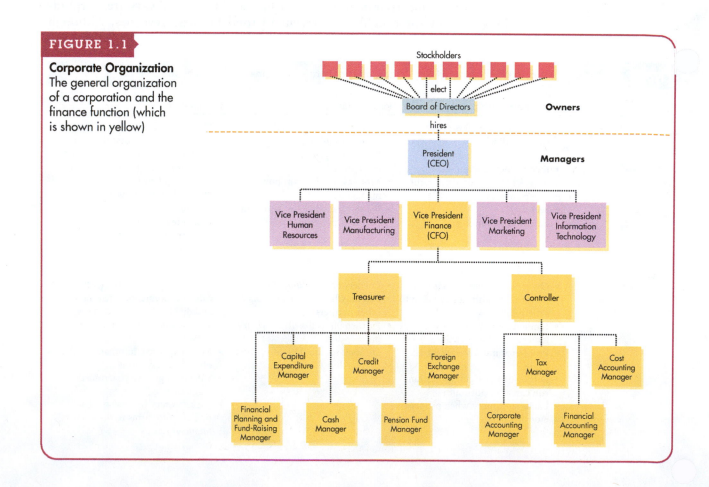

board of directors
Group elected by the firm's stockholders and typically responsible for approving strategic goals and plans, setting general policy, guiding corporate affairs, and approving major expenditures.

president or chief executive officer (CEO)
Corporate official responsible for managing the firm's day-to-day operations and carrying out the policies established by the board of directors.

Limited partnership (LP)
A partnership in which one or more partners have limited liability as long as at least one partner (the general partner) has unlimited liability. The limited partners are passive investors that cannot take an active role in the firm's management.

S corporation (S corp)
A tax-reporting entity that allows certain corporations with 100 or fewer stockholders to choose to be taxed as partnerships. Its stockholders receive the organizational benefits of a corporation and the tax advantages of a partnership.

Limited liability company (LLC)
Permitted in most states, the LLC gives its owners limited liability and taxation as a partnership. But unlike an S corp, the LLC can own more than 80% of another corporation, and corporations, partnerships, or non-U.S. Residents can own LLC shares.

Limited liability partnership (LLP)
Permitted in most states, LLP partners are liable for their own acts of malpractice, but not for those of other partners. The LLP is taxed as a partnership and is frequently used by legal and accounting professionals.

members of the *board of directors* and to decide other issues such as amending the corporate charter. The **board of directors** is typically responsible for approving strategic goals and plans, setting general policy, guiding corporate affairs, and approving major expenditures. Most importantly, the board decides when to hire or fire top managers and establishes compensation packages for the most senior executives. The board consists of "inside" directors, such as key corporate executives, and "outside" or "independent" directors, such as executives from other companies, major shareholders, and national or community leaders. Outside directors for major corporations receive compensation in the form of cash, stock, and stock options. This compensation often totals $100,000 per year or more.

The **president or chief executive officer (CEO)** is responsible for managing day-to-day operations and carrying out the policies established by the board of directors. The CEO reports periodically to the firm's directors.

It is important to note the division between owners and managers in a large corporation, as shown by the dashed horizontal line in Figure 1.1. This separation and some of the issues surrounding it will be addressed in the discussion of *the agency issue* later in this chapter.

Other Limited Liability Organizations

A number of other organizational forms provide owners with limited liability. The most popular are **limited partnership (LP)**, **S corporation (S corp)**, **limited liability company (LLC)**, and **limited liability partnership (LLP)**. Each represents a specialized form or blending of the characteristics of the organizational forms described previously. What they have in common is that their owners enjoy limited liability, and they typically have fewer than 100 owners.

WHY STUDY MANAGERIAL FINANCE?

An understanding of the concepts, techniques, and practices of managerial finance will fully acquaint you with the financial manager's activities and decisions. Because the consequences of most business decisions are measured in financial terms, the financial manager plays a key operational role. People in all areas of responsibility—accounting, information systems, management, marketing, operations, and so forth—need a general awareness of finance so that they will understand how to quantify the consequences of their actions.

OK, so you're not planning to major in finance! To improve your chance of success in your chosen business career, you still will need to understand how financial managers think. Managers in the firm, regardless of their job descriptions, usually have to provide financial justification for the resources they need to do their job. Whether you are hiring new workers, negotiating an advertising budget, or upgrading the technology used in a manufacturing process, understanding the financial aspects of your actions will help you gain the resources you need to be successful. The "Why This Chapter Matters to You" section that appears on each chapter-opening page should help you understand the importance of each chapter in both your professional and personal life.

As you study, you will learn about the career opportunities in managerial finance, which are briefly described in Table 1.2 below. Although we focus on publicly held profit-seeking firms, the principles presented are equally applicable to private and not-for-profit organizations. The decision-making principles developed can also be applied to personal financial decisions. We hope that this first

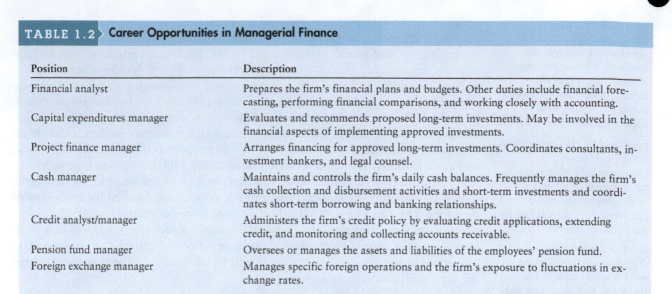

TABLE 1.2 **Career Opportunities in Managerial Finance**

Position	Description
Financial analyst	Prepares the firm's financial plans and budgets. Other duties include financial forecasting, performing financial comparisons, and working closely with accounting.
Capital expenditures manager	Evaluates and recommends proposed long-term investments. May be involved in the financial aspects of implementing approved investments.
Project finance manager	Arranges financing for approved long-term investments. Coordinates consultants, investment bankers, and legal counsel.
Cash manager	Maintains and controls the firm's daily cash balances. Frequently manages the firm's cash collection and disbursement activities and short-term investments and coordinates short-term borrowing and banking relationships.
Credit analyst/manager	Administers the firm's credit policy by evaluating credit applications, extending credit, and monitoring and collecting accounts receivable.
Pension fund manager	Oversees or manages the assets and liabilities of the employees' pension fund.
Foreign exchange manager	Manages specific foreign operations and the firm's exposure to fluctuations in exchange rates.

exposure to the exciting field of finance will provide the foundation and initiative for further study and possibly even a future career.

→ REVIEW QUESTIONS

1–1 What is *finance*? Explain how this field affects all the activities in which businesses engage.

1–2 What is the *financial services* area of finance? Describe the field of *managerial finance*.

1–3 Which legal form of business organization is most common? Which form is dominant in terms of business revenues?

1–4 Describe the roles and the relationships among the major parties in a corporation: stockholders, board of directors, and managers. How are corporate owners rewarded for the risks they take?

1–5 Briefly name and describe some organizational forms other than corporations that provide owners with limited liability.

1–6 Why is the study of managerial finance important to your professional life regardless of the specific area of responsibility you may have within the business firm? Why is it important to your personal life?

LG ③ **1.2 Goal of the Firm**

What goal should managers pursue? There is no shortage of possible answers to this question. Some might argue that managers should focus entirely on satisfying customers. Progress toward this goal could be measured by the market share attained by each of the firm's products. Others suggest that managers must first inspire and motivate employees; in that case, employee turnover might be the key success metric.

to watch. Clearly, the goal managers select will affect many of the decisions they make, so choosing an objective is a critical determinant of how businesses operate.

MAXIMIZE SHAREHOLDER WEALTH

Finance teaches that managers' primary goal should be to maximize the wealth of the firm's owners, the stockholders. The simplest and best measure of stockholder wealth is the firm's share price, so most textbooks (ours included) instruct managers to take actions that increase the firm's share price. A common misconception is that when firms strive to make their shareholders happy, they do so at the expense of other constituencies such as customers, employees, or suppliers. This line of thinking ignores that in most cases, to enrich shareholders, managers must first satisfy the demands of these other interest groups. Dividends that stockholders receive ultimately come from the firm's profits. It is unlikely that a firm whose customers are unhappy with its products, whose employees are looking for jobs at other firms, or whose suppliers are reluctant to ship raw materials will make shareholders rich because such a firm will likely be less profitable in the long run than one that better manages its relations with these stakeholder groups.

Therefore, we argue that the goal of the firm, and also of managers, should be *to maximize the wealth of the owners for whom it is being operated*, which in most instances is equivalent to *maximize the stock price*. This goal translates into a straightforward decision rule for managers: *Only take actions that are expected to increase the wealth of shareholders*. Although that goal sounds simple, implementing it is not always easy. To determine whether a particular course of action will increase or decrease shareholders' wealth, managers have to assess what return (that is, cash inflows net of cash outflows) the action will bring and how risky that return might be. Figure 1.2 depicts this process. In fact, we can say that *the key variables that managers must consider when making business decisions are return (cash flows) and risk*.

MAXIMIZE PROFIT?

It might seem intuitive that maximizing a firm's share price is equivalent to maximizing its profits. That thought is not always correct, however.

Corporations commonly measure profits in terms of **earnings per share (EPS)**, which represent the amount earned during the period on behalf of each

earnings per share (EPS)
The amount earned during the period on behalf of each outstanding share of common stock, calculated by dividing the period's total earnings available for the firm's common stockholders by the number of shares of common stock outstanding.

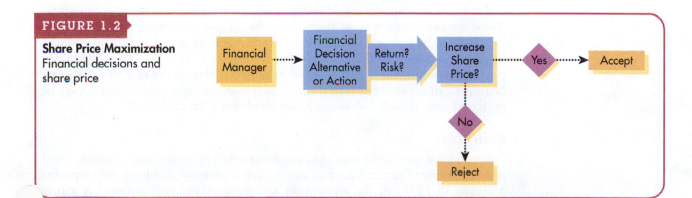

FIGURE 1.2

Share Price Maximization
Financial decisions and share price

outstanding share of common stock. EPS are calculated by dividing the period's total earnings available for the firm's common stockholders by the number of shares of common stock outstanding.

| Example 1.1 ▶ | Nick Dukakis, the financial manager of Neptune Manufacturing, a producer of marine engine components, is choosing between two investments, Rotor and Valve. The following table shows the EPS that each investment is expected to have over its 3-year life. |

MyFinanceLab Solution
Video

Investment	Earnings per share (EPS)			
	Year 1	Year 2	Year 3	Total for years 1, 2, and 3
Rotor	$1.40	$1.00	$0.40	$2.80
Valve	0.60	1.00	1.40	3.00

In terms of the profit maximization goal, Valve would be preferred over Rotor because it results in higher total earnings per share over the 3-year period ($3.00 EPS compared with $2.80 EPS).

Does profit maximization lead to the highest possible share price? For at least three reasons, the answer is often no. First, timing is important. An investment that provides a lower profit overall may be preferable to one that earns a lower profit in the short run. Second, profits and cash flows are not identical. The profit that a firm reports is simply an estimate of how it is doing, an estimate that is influenced by many different accounting choices firms make when assembling their financial reports. Cash flow is a more straightforward measure of the money flowing into and out of the company than profit is. Companies have to pay their bills with cash, not earnings, so cash flow is what matters most to financial managers. Third, risk matters a great deal. A firm that earns a low but reliable profit might be more valuable than another firm with profits that fluctuate a great deal (and therefore can be very high or very low at different times).

Timing

Because the firm can earn a return on funds it receives, *the receipt of funds sooner rather than later is preferred.* In our example, even though the total earnings from Rotor are smaller than those from Valve, Rotor provides much greater earnings per share in the first year. It's possible that by investing in Rotor, Neptune Manufacturing can reinvest the earnings that it receives in year 1 to generate higher profits overall than if it had invested in project Valve. If the rate of return that Neptune can earn on reinvested earnings is high enough, project Rotor may be preferred even though it does not alone maximize total profits.

Cash Flows

Profits do *not* necessarily result in cash flows available to the stockholders. There is no guarantee that the board of directors will increase dividends when profits increase. In addition, the accounting assumptions and techniques that a firm adopts can sometimes allow a firm to show a positive profit even when its cash outflows exceed its cash inflows.

Furthermore, higher earnings do not necessarily translate into a higher stock price. Only when earnings increases are accompanied by increased future cash flows is a higher stock price expected. For example, a firm with a high-quality product sold in a very competitive market could increase its earnings by significantly reducing its equipment maintenance expenditures. The firm's expenses would be reduced, thereby increasing its profits. If the reduced maintenance results in lower product quality, however, the firm may impair its competitive position, and its stock price could drop as many well-informed investors sell the stock in anticipation of lower future cash flows. In this case, the earnings increase was accompanied by lower future cash flows and therefore a lower stock price.

Risk

risk
The chance that actual outcomes may differ from those expected.

Profit maximization also fails to account for **risk,** the chance that actual outcomes may differ from those expected. A basic premise in managerial finance is that a trade-off exists between return (cash flow) and risk. *Return and risk are, in fact, the key determinants of share price, which represents the wealth of the owners in the firm.*

Cash flow and risk affect share price differently: Holding risk fixed, higher cash flow is generally associated with a higher share price. In contrast, holding cash flow fixed, higher risk tends to result in a lower share price because the stockholders do not like risk. In general, stockholders are **risk averse,** which means that they are only willing to bear risk if they expect compensation for doing so. In other words, investors expect to earn higher returns on riskier investments, and they will accept lower returns on relatively safe investments. The key point, which will be fully developed in Chapter 5, is that differences in risk can significantly affect the value of different investments.

risk averse
Requiring compensation to bear risk.

WHAT ABOUT STAKEHOLDERS?

stakeholders
Groups such as employees, customers, suppliers, creditors, owners, and others who have a direct economic link to the firm.

Although maximization of shareholder wealth is the primary goal, many firms broaden their focus to include the interests of *stakeholders* as well as shareholders. **Stakeholders** are groups such as employees, customers, suppliers, creditors, owners, and others who have a direct economic link to the firm. A firm with a *stakeholder focus* consciously avoids actions that would prove detrimental to stakeholders. The goal is not to maximize stakeholder well-being but to preserve it.

The stakeholder view does not alter the goal of maximizing shareholder wealth. Such a view is often considered part of the firm's "social responsibility." It is expected to provide long-run benefit to shareholders by maintaining positive relationships with stakeholders. Such relationships should minimize stakeholder turnover, conflicts, and litigation. Clearly, the firm can better achieve its goal of shareholder wealth maximization by fostering cooperation with its other stakeholders rather than conflict with them.

THE ROLE OF BUSINESS ETHICS

business ethics
Standards of conduct or moral judgment that apply to persons engaged in commerce.

Business ethics are the standards of conduct or moral judgment that apply to persons engaged in commerce. Violations of these standards in finance involve a variety of actions: "creative accounting," earnings management, misleading financial forecasts, insider trading, fraud, excessive executive compensation, options

Matter of fact

Firms Accelerate Dividends So That Shareholders Save on Taxes

One way firms can take actions that maximize the wealth of shareholders is by thinking carefully about the taxes their shareholders must pay on dividend payments. Starting with the Bush tax cuts in 2003, shareholders faced a modest 15 percent tax rate on most dividends. However, absent congressional action to extend the 2003 tax cuts, the tax rate on dividends would jump dramatically in 2013. With a political compromise looking unlikely in the 2012 election year, many firms announced plans to accelerate dividend payments that they had planned to make in early 2013 to late 2012. Washington Post Company, for example, announced that on December 27, 2012, it would pay out the entire $9.80 per share dividend that they had planned to distribute in 2013. What was the stock market's reaction to that announcement? Washington Post shares rose $5. By accelerating their dividend payments, companies such as Washington Post, Expedia, Inc., and luxury goods producer Coach, Inc., were increasing the wealth of their shareholders by helping them save taxes.

backdating, bribery, and kickbacks. The financial press has reported many such violations in recent years, involving such well-known companies as JP Morgan and Capital One. As a result, the financial community is developing and enforcing ethical standards. The goal of these ethical standards is to motivate business and market participants to adhere to both the letter and the spirit of laws and regulations concerned with business and professional practice. Most business leaders believe that businesses actually strengthen their competitive positions by maintaining high ethical standards.

Considering Ethics

Robert A. Cooke, a noted ethicist, suggests that the following questions be used to assess the ethical viability of a proposed action.[1]

1. Is the action arbitrary or capricious? Does it unfairly single out an individual or group?
2. Does the action violate the moral or legal rights of any individual or group?
3. Does the action conform to accepted moral standards?
4. Are there alternative courses of action that are less likely to cause actual or potential harm?

Clearly, considering such questions before taking an action can help ensure its ethical viability.

Today, many firms are addressing the issue of ethics by establishing corporate ethics policies that outline a set of fundamental principles that guide what firms' employees must do or what they must not do. Some firms go further and make their ethical standards a centerpiece of their corporate image. For example, Google famously adopted the motto, "Don't be evil." Even for Google, however, ethical dilemmas are unavoidable in business. The *Focus on Ethics* box provides an example of ethical concerns raised by a new Google product, Google Glass.

---

1. Robert A. Cooke, "Business Ethics: A Perspective," in *Arthur Andersen Cases on Business Ethics* (Chicago: Arthur Andersen, September 1991), pp. 2 and 5.

A major impetus toward the development of ethics policies has been the Sarbanes-Oxley Act of 2002. The act requires firms to disclose whether they have a code of ethics in place, and firms must report any waivers of those codes for senior management. Companies that do not have a code of ethics must explain why they have not adopted one. Many firms require their employees to sign a formal pledge to uphold the firm's ethics policies. Such policies typically apply to employee actions in dealing with all corporate stakeholders, including the public.

ETHICS AND SHARE PRICE

An effective ethics program can enhance corporate value by producing a number of positive benefits. It can reduce potential litigation and judgment costs, maintain a positive corporate image, build shareholder confidence, and gain the loyalty, commitment, and respect of the firm's stakeholders. Such actions, by maintaining and enhancing cash flow and reducing perceived risk, can positively affect the firm's share price. *Ethical behavior is therefore viewed as necessary for achieving the firm's goal of owner wealth maximization.*

focus on ETHICS

Critics See Ethical Dilemmas in Google Glass?

in practice On June 27, 2012, at the Google I/O conference, Google introduced an exciting new product called Glass. Essentially a computer that users wear like a pair of eyeglasses, Google Glass performs many of the functions of a smart phone without requiring people to use their hands. To demonstrate the new product's capabilities, Google cofounder Sergey Brin parachuted out of a zeppelin wearing Glass and transmitted his descent live to those attending the conference.

Google offers an interesting case study on value maximization and corporate ethics. In 2004, Google's founders provided "An Owner's Manual" for shareholders, which stated that "Google is not a conventional company" and that the company's ultimate goal "is to develop services that significantly improve the lives of as many people as possible." The founders stressed that it was not enough for Google to run a successful business; they also want to use the company to make the world a better place. Brin's skydiving stunt made it clear that Google had come up with yet another product that would thrill customers. But what effect would Google Glass have on the general public? Reporters who wrote about high-tech products quickly shifted the focus of their stories from what it would be like to wear Google Glass to what it would be like to be around someone else wearing the product. The device obviously raised big concerns about the privacy of nonusers. One Twitter user posted: "There is a kid using Google Glasses at this restaurant, which, until just now, used to be my favorite spot."

Google's famous corporate motto, "Don't Be Evil," is intended to convey Google's willingness to do the right thing even when doing so requires the firm to sacrifice in the short run. Google's approach does not appear to be limiting its ability to maximize value, as the company's share price increased more than 700 percent from 2004 to 2013! As this book was going to press, however, it remained unclear how Google might respond to critics of its Glass device.

▶ *Is the goal of maximization of shareholder wealth necessarily ethical or unethical?*

▶ *What responsibility, if any, does Google have to protect the privacy of those who interact with other people wearing Glass?*

Sources: **Creativegood.com**, "The Google Glass Feature No One Is Talking About," February 28, 2013; **slog.thestranger.com**, "The Closer Google Glass Gets, the More Ethical Dilemmas Appear," March 5, 2013.

→ **REVIEW QUESTIONS**

1–7 What is the goal of the firm and, therefore, of all managers and employees? Discuss how one measures achievement of this goal.

1–8 For what three main reasons is profit maximization inconsistent with wealth maximization?

1–9 What is *risk*? Why must risk as well as return be considered by the financial manager who is evaluating a decision alternative or action?

1–10 Describe the role of corporate ethics policies and guidelines, and discuss the relationship that is believed to exist between ethics and share price.

  ## 1.3 Managerial Finance Function

People in all areas of responsibility within the firm must interact with finance personnel and procedures to get their jobs done. For financial personnel to make useful forecasts and decisions, they must be willing and able to talk to individuals in other areas of the firm. For example, when considering a new product, the financial manager needs to obtain sales forecasts, pricing guidelines, and advertising and promotion budget estimates from marketing personnel. The managerial finance function can be broadly described by considering its role within the organization, its relationship to economics and accounting, and the primary activities of the financial manager.

ORGANIZATION OF THE FINANCE FUNCTION

The size and importance of the managerial finance function depend on the size of the firm. In small firms, the finance function is generally performed by the accounting department. As a firm grows, the finance function typically evolves into a separate department linked directly to the company president or CEO through the chief financial officer (CFO). The lower portion of the organizational chart in Figure 1.1 on page 6 shows the structure of the finance function in a typical medium- to large-size firm.

Reporting to the CFO are the treasurer and the controller. The **treasurer** (the chief financial manager) typically manages the firm's cash, investing surplus funds when available and securing outside financing when needed. The treasurer also oversees a firm's pension plans and manages critical risks related to movements in foreign currency values, interest rates, and commodity prices. The **controller** (the chief accountant) typically handles the accounting activities, such as corporate accounting, tax management, financial accounting, and cost accounting. The treasurer's focus tends to be more external, whereas the controller's focus is more internal.

If international sales or purchases are important to a firm, it may well employ one or more finance professionals whose job is to monitor and manage the firm's exposure to loss from currency fluctuations. A trained financial manager can "hedge," or protect against such a loss, at a reasonable cost by using a variety of financial instruments. These **foreign exchange managers** typically report to the firm's treasurer.

treasurer
The firm's chief financial manager, who manages the firm's cash, oversees its pension plans, and manages key risks.

controller
The firm's chief accountant, who is responsible for the firm's accounting activities, such as corporate accounting, tax management, financial accounting, and cost accounting.

foreign exchange manager
The manager responsible for managing and monitoring the firm's exposure to loss from currency fluctuations.

RELATIONSHIP TO ECONOMICS

The field of finance is closely related to economics. Financial managers must understand the economic framework and be alert to the consequences of varying levels of economic activity and changes in economic policy. They must also be able to use economic theories as guidelines for efficient business operation. Examples include supply-and-demand analysis, profit-maximizing strategies, and price theory. The primary economic principle used in managerial finance is **marginal cost–benefit analysis,** the principle that financial decisions should be made and actions taken only when the added benefits exceed the added costs. Nearly all financial decisions ultimately come down to an assessment of their marginal benefits and marginal costs.

marginal cost–benefit analysis
Economic principle that states that financial decisions should be made and actions taken only when the added benefits exceed the added costs.

Example 1.2 ▶ Jamie Teng is a financial manager for Nord Department Stores, a large chain of upscale department stores operating primarily in the western United States. She is currently trying to decide whether to replace one of the firm's computer servers with a new, more sophisticated one that would both speed processing and handle a larger volume of transactions. The new computer would require a cash outlay of $8,000, and the old computer could be sold to net $2,000. The total benefits from the new server (measured in today's dollars) would be $10,000. The benefits over a similar time period from the old computer (measured in today's dollars) would be $3,000. Applying marginal cost–benefit analysis, Jamie organizes the data as follows:

Benefits with new computer	$10,000
Less: Benefits with old computer	3,000
(1) Marginal (added) benefits	$ 7,000
Cost of new computer	$ 8,000
Less: Proceeds from sale of old computer	2,000
(2) Marginal (added) costs	$ 6,000
Net benefit [(1) − (2)]	$ 1,000

Because the marginal (added) benefits of $7,000 exceed the marginal (added) costs of $6,000, Jamie recommends that the firm purchase the new computer to replace the old one. The firm will experience a net benefit of $1,000 as a result of this action.

RELATIONSHIP TO ACCOUNTING

The firm's finance and accounting activities are closely related and generally overlap. In small firms, accountants often carry out the finance function; in large firms, financial analysts often help compile accounting information. There are, however, two differences between finance and accounting; one is related to the emphasis on cash flows, and the other is related to decision making.

Emphasis on Cash Flows

accrual basis
In preparation of financial statements, recognizes revenue at the time of sale and recognizes expenses when they are incurred.

cash basis
Recognizes revenues and expenses only with respect to actual inflows and outflows of cash.

The accountant's primary function is to develop and report data for measuring the performance of the firm, assess its financial position, comply with and file reports required by securities regulators, and file and pay taxes. Using generally accepted accounting principles, the accountant prepares financial statements that recognize revenue at the time of sale (whether payment has been received or not) and recognize expenses when they are incurred. This approach is referred to as the **accrual basis.**

The financial manager, on the other hand, places primary emphasis on *cash flows,* the intake and outgo of cash. He or she maintains the firm's solvency by planning the cash flows necessary to satisfy its obligations and to acquire assets needed to achieve the firm's goals. The financial manager uses this **cash basis** to recognize the revenues and expenses only with respect to actual inflows and outflows of cash. Whether a firm earns a profit or experiences a loss, *it must have a sufficient flow of cash to meet its obligations as they come due.*

Example 1.3 ▶

MyFinanceLab Solution Video

Nassau Corporation, a small yacht dealer, sold one yacht for $100,000 in the calendar year just ended. Nassau originally purchased the yacht for $80,000. Although the firm paid in full for the yacht during the year, at year-end it has yet to collect the $100,000 from the customer. The accounting view and the financial view of the firm's performance during the year are given by the following income and cash flow statements, respectively.

Accounting view (accrual basis)		Financial view (cash basis)	
Nassau Corporation income statement for the year ended 12/31		Nassau Corporation cash flow statement for the year ended 12/31	
Sales revenue	$100,000	Cash inflow	$ 0
Less: Costs	80,000	Less: Cash outflow	80,000
Net profit	$ 20,000	Net cash flow	($80,000)

In an accounting sense, Nassau Corporation is profitable, but in terms of actual cash flow, it is a financial failure. Its lack of cash flow resulted from the uncollected accounts receivable of $100,000. Without adequate cash inflows to meet its obligations, the firm will not survive, regardless of its level of profits.

As the example shows, accrual accounting data do not fully describe the circumstances of a firm. Thus, the financial manager must look beyond financial statements to obtain insight into existing or developing problems. Of course, accountants are well aware of the importance of cash flows, and financial managers use and understand accrual-based financial statements. Nevertheless, the financial manager, by concentrating on cash flows, should be able to avoid insolvency and achieve the firm's financial goals.

Personal Finance Example 1.4 ▶ Individuals do not use accrual concepts. Rather, they rely solely on cash flows to measure their financial outcomes. Generally, individuals plan, monitor, and assess their financial activities using cash flows over a given period, typically a month or a year. Ann Bach projects her cash flows during October 2015 as follows:

	Amount	
Item	Inflow	Outflow
Net pay received	$4,400	
Rent		−$1,200
Car payment		−450
Utilities		−300
Groceries		−800
Clothes		−750
Dining out		−650
Gasoline		−260
Interest income	220	
Misc. expense		−425
Totals	$4,620	−$4,835

Ann subtracts her total outflows of $4,835 from her total inflows of $4,620 and finds that her *net cash flow* for October will be −$215. To cover the $215 shortfall, Ann will have to either borrow $215 (putting it on a credit card is a form of borrowing) or withdraw $215 from her savings. Alternatively, she may decide to reduce her outflows in areas of discretionary spending such as clothing purchases, dining out, or areas that make up the $425 of miscellaneous expense.

Decision Making

The second major difference between finance and accounting has to do with decision making. Accountants devote most of their attention to the *collection and presentation of financial data.* Financial managers evaluate the accounting statements, develop additional data, and *make decisions* on the basis of their assessment of the associated returns and risks. Of course, it does not mean that accountants never make decisions or that financial managers never gather data but rather that the primary focuses of accounting and finance are distinctly different.

PRIMARY ACTIVITIES OF THE FINANCIAL MANAGER

In addition to ongoing involvement in financial analysis and planning, the financial manager's primary activities are making investment and financing decisions. Investment decisions determine what types of assets the firm holds. Financing decisions determine how the firm raises money to pay for the assets in which it invests. One way to visualize the difference between a firm's investment and financing decisions is to refer to the balance sheet shown in Figure 1.3. Investment decisions generally refer to the items that appear on the left-hand side of the

FIGURE 1.3

Financial Activities
Primary activities of the
financial manager

<table>
<tr><th colspan="2">Balance Sheet</th></tr>
<tr><td>Current
Assets</td><td>Current
Liabilities</td></tr>
<tr><td>Fixed
Assets</td><td>Long-Term
Funds</td></tr>
</table>

Making Investment Decisions

Making Financing Decisions

balance sheet, and financing decisions relate to the items on the right-hand side. Keep in mind, though, that financial managers make these decisions based on their effect on the value of the firm, not on the accounting principles used to construct a balance sheet.

→ **REVIEW QUESTIONS**

1–11 In what financial activities does a corporate treasurer engage?

1–12 What is the primary economic principle used in managerial finance?

1–13 What are the major differences between accounting and finance with respect to emphasis on cash flows and decision making?

1–14 What are the two primary activities of the financial manager that are related to the firm's balance sheet?

 1.4 Governance and Agency

The majority of owners of a corporation are normally distinct from its managers. Managers are nevertheless entrusted to only take actions or make decisions that are in the best interests of the firm's owners, its shareholders. In most cases, if managers fail to act on the behalf of the shareholders, they will also fail to achieve the goal of maximizing shareholder wealth. To help ensure that managers act in ways that are consistent with the interests of shareholders and mindful of obligations to other stakeholders, firms aim to establish sound corporate governance practices.

CORPORATE GOVERNANCE

corporate governance
The rules, processes, and laws by which companies are operated, controlled, and regulated.

Corporate governance refers to the rules, processes, and laws by which companies are operated, controlled, and regulated. It defines the rights and responsibilities of the corporate participants such as the shareholders, board of directors, officers and managers, and other stakeholders as well as the rules and procedures for making corporate decisions. A well-defined corporate governance structure is intended to benefit all corporate stakeholders by ensuring that the firm is run in a lawful and ethical fashion, in accordance with best practices, and subject to all corporate regulations.

A firm's corporate governance is influenced by both internal factors such as the shareholders, board of directors, and officers as well as external forces such as clients, creditors, suppliers, competitors, and government regulations. The corporate organization, depicted in Figure 1.1 on page 6, helps shape a firm's corporate governance structure. In particular, the stockholders elect a board of directors, who in turn hire officers or managers to operate the firm in a manner consistent with the goals, plans, and policies established and monitored by the board on behalf of the shareholders.

Individual versus Institutional Investors

individual investors
Investors who own relatively small quantities of shares so as to meet personal investment goals.

To better understand the role that shareholders play in shaping a firm's corporate governance, it is helpful to differentiate between the two broad classes of owners: individuals and institutions. Generally, **individual investors** own relatively few shares and as a result do not typically have sufficient means to influence a firm's corporate governance. To influence the firm, individual investors often find it necessary to act as a group by voting collectively on corporate matters. The most important corporate matter individual investors vote on is the election of the firm's board of directors. The corporate board's first responsibility is to the shareholders. The board not only sets policies that specify ethical practices and provide for the protection of stakeholder interests, but it also monitors managerial decision making on behalf of investors.

institutional investors
Investment professionals such as banks, insurance companies, mutual funds, and pension funds that are paid to manage and hold large quantities of securities on behalf of others.

Although they also benefit from the presence of the board of directors, institutional investors have advantages over individual investors when it comes to influencing the corporate governance of a firm. **Institutional investors** are investment professionals that are paid to manage and hold large quantities of securities on behalf of individuals, businesses, and governments. Institutional investors include banks, insurance companies, mutual funds, and pension funds. Unlike individual investors, institutional investors often monitor and directly influence a firm's corporate governance by exerting pressure on management to perform or communicating their concerns to the firm's board. These large investors can also threaten to exercise their voting rights or liquidate their holdings if the board does not respond positively to their concerns. Because individual and institutional investors share the same goal, individual investors benefit from the shareholder activism of institutional investors.

Government Regulation

Unlike the effect that clients, creditors, suppliers, or competitors can have on a particular firm's corporate governance, government regulation generally shapes the corporate governance of all firms. During the past decade, corporate governance has received increased attention due to several high-profile corporate scandals involving abuse of corporate power and, in some cases, alleged criminal activity by corporate officers. The misdeeds derived from two main types of issues: (1) false disclosures in financial reporting and other material information releases and (2) undisclosed conflicts of interest between corporations and their analysts, auditors, and attorneys and between corporate directors, officers, and shareholders.

Sarbanes-Oxley Act of 2002 (SOX)
An act aimed at eliminating corporate disclosure and conflict of interest problems. Contains provisions about corporate financial disclosures and the relationships among corporations, analysts, auditors, attorneys, directors, officers, and shareholders.

Asserting that an integral part of an effective corporate governance regime is provisions for civil or criminal prosecution of individuals who conduct unethical or illegal acts in the name of the firm, in July 2002 the U.S. Congress passed the **Sarbanes-Oxley Act of 2002** (commonly called **SOX**). Sarbanes-Oxley is intended to eliminate many of the disclosure and conflict of interest problems that can arise when corporate managers are not held personally accountable for their firm's financial decisions and disclosures. SOX accomplished the following: established an oversight board to monitor the accounting industry, tightened audit regulations and controls, toughened penalties against executives who commit corporate fraud, strengthened accounting disclosure requirements and ethical guidelines for corporate officers, established corporate board structure and membership guidelines, established guidelines with regard to analyst conflicts of interest, mandated instant disclosure of stock sales by corporate executives, and increased securities regulation authority and budgets for auditors and investigators.

THE AGENCY ISSUE

We know that the duty of the financial manager is to maximize the wealth of the firm's owners. Shareholders give managers decision-making authority over the firm; thus, managers can be viewed as the *agents* of the firm's shareholders. Technically, any manager who owns less than 100 percent of the firm is an agent acting on behalf of other owners. This separation of owners and managers is shown by the dashed horizontal line in Figure 1.1 on page 6, and it is representative of the classic **principal–agent relationship**, where the shareholders are the principals. In general, a contract is used to specify the terms of a principal–agent relationship. This arrangement works well when the agent makes decisions that are in the principal's best interest but doesn't work well when the interests of the principal and agent differ.

In theory, most financial managers would agree with the goal of shareholder wealth maximization. In reality, however, managers are also concerned with their personal wealth, job security, and fringe benefits. Such concerns may cause managers to make decisions that are not consistent with shareholder wealth maximization. For example, financial managers may be reluctant or unwilling to take more than moderate risk if they perceive that taking too much risk might jeopardize their job or reduce their personal wealth.

The Agency Problem

An important theme of corporate governance is to ensure the accountability of managers in an organization through mechanisms that try to reduce or eliminate the principal–agent problem; when these mechanisms fail, however, agency problems arise. **Agency problems** arise when managers deviate from the goal of maximization of shareholder wealth by placing their personal goals ahead of the goals of shareholders. These problems in turn give rise to agency costs. **Agency costs** are costs borne by shareholders due to the presence or avoidance of agency problems and in either case represent a loss of shareholder wealth. For example, shareholders incur agency costs when managers fail to make the best investment decision or when managers have to be monitored to ensure that the best investment decision is made because either situation is likely to result in a lower stock price.

Management Compensation Plans

In addition to the roles played by corporate boards, institutional investors, and government regulations, corporate governance can be strengthened by ensuring that managers' interests are aligned with those of shareholders. A common approach

---

principal–agent relationship
An arrangement in which an agent acts on the behalf of a principal. For example, shareholders of a company (principals) elect management (agents) to act on their behalf.

agency problems
Problems that arise when managers place personal goals ahead of the goals of shareholders.

agency costs
Costs arising from agency problems that are borne by shareholders and represent a loss of shareholder wealth.

incentive plans
Management compensation plans that tie management compensation to share price; one example involves the granting of *stock options.*

stock options
Options extended by the firm that allow management to benefit from increases in stock prices over time.

performance plans
Plans that tie management compensation to measures such as EPS or growth in EPS. *Performance shares, cash bonuses,* or both are used as compensation under these plans.

performance shares
Shares of stock given to management for meeting stated performance goals.

cash bonuses
Cash paid to management for chieving certain performance oals.

is to *structure management compensation* to correspond with firm performance. In addition to combating agency problems, the resulting performance-based compensation packages allow firms to compete for and hire the best managers available. The two key types of managerial compensation plans are incentive plans and performance plans.

Incentive plans tie management compensation to share price. One incentive plan grants **stock options** to management. If the firm's stock price rises over time, managers will be rewarded by being able to purchase stock at the market price in effect at the time of the grant and then to resell the shares at the prevailing higher market price.

Many firms also offer **performance plans** that tie management compensation to performance measures such as earnings per share (EPS) or growth in EPS. Compensation under these plans is often in the form of performance shares or cash bonuses. **Performance shares** are shares of stock given to management as a result of meeting the stated performance goals, whereas **cash bonuses** are cash payments tied to the achievement of certain performance goals.

The execution of many compensation plans has been closely scrutinized in light of the past decade's corporate scandals and financial woes. Both individual and institutional stockholders as well as the Securities and Exchange Commission (SEC) and other government entities continue to publicly question the appropriateness of the multimillion-dollar compensation packages that many corporate executives receive. The total compensation in 2012 for the chief executive officers of the 500 largest U.S. companies is considerable. For example, the three highest-paid CEOs in 2012 were Larry Ellison of Oracle Corp., who earned $96.2 million; Richard Bracken of HCA, who earned $38.6 million; and Robert Iger of Disney, who earned $37.1 million.

Matter of fact

How Closely Are Pay and Performance Linked?

A quick look at the compensation awarded to some of the highest paid CEOs in 2012 reveals that the link between pay and performance is not as strong as one might think. Oracle CEO Larry Ellison earned the highest pay during a year in which Oracle stock lost 22 percent of its value. Whirlpool's chairman, Jeff Fettig, earned less than one-seventh as much as Ellison, but Whirlpool's stock earned a return of almost 120 percent in 2012 (not shown in the table).

Chief Executive	Company	2012 Compensation ($ millions)	2012 Stock Return (Rank)
Larry Ellison	Oracle Corp.	$96.2	−22% (99)
Richard Bracken	HCA	$38.6	+66% (10)
Robert Iger	Disney	$37.1	+75% (7)
Mark Parker	Nike	$35.2	+30% (26)
Philippe Dauman	Viacom	$33.4	+41% (16)
John Donahoe	eBay	$29.7	+68% (9)
Howard Schulz	Starbucks	$28.9	+38% (19)
Stephen Chazen	Occidental Petroleum	$28.5	−16% (97)
Paul Jacobs	Qualcomm	$20.7	+30% (25)

(continued)

Most studies have failed to find a strong relationship between the performance that companies achieve and the compensation that CEOs receive. From 2007 to 2010, publicity surrounding these large compensation packages combined with weakness in the overall economy put downward pressure on executive compensation. Among the 500 largest U.S. companies, average CEO pay fell roughly 50 percent during this period. Contributing to negative publicity surrounding the pay-for-performance issue is the SEC requirement that publicly traded companies disclose to shareholders and others the amount of compensation paid to their CEO, CFO, three other highest-paid executives, and directors; the method used to determine it; and a narrative discussion regarding the underlying compensation policies. At the same time, new compensation plans that better link managers' performance to their compensation are being developed and implemented. As evidence of this trend, a survey of 50 large companies revealed that in 2009 only 35 percent of the compensation paid to CEOs was tied to company performance, but by 2012, those same 50 companies reported that 51 percent of CEO pay was linked to performance.

The Threat of Takeover

When a firm's internal corporate governance structure is unable to keep agency problems in check, it is likely that rival managers will try to gain control of the firm. Because agency problems represent a misuse of the firm's resources and impose agency costs on the firm's shareholders, the firm's stock is generally depressed, making the firm an attractive takeover target. The *threat of takeover* by another firm that believes it can enhance the troubled firm's value by restructuring its management, operations, and financing can provide a strong source of external corporate governance. The constant threat of a takeover tends to motivate management to act in the best interests of the firm's owners.

Unconstrained, managers may have other goals in addition to share price maximization, but much of the evidence suggests that share price maximization—the focus of this text—is the primary goal of most firms.

→ REVIEW QUESTIONS

1-15 What is *corporate governance*? How has the Sarbanes-Oxley Act of 2002 affected it? Explain.

1-16 Define *agency problems*, and describe how they give rise to *agency costs*. Explain how a firm's *corporate governance structure* can help avoid agency problems.

1-17 How can the firm *structure management compensation* to minimize agency problems? What is the current view with regard to the execution of many compensation plans?

1-18 How do market forces—both shareholder activism and the threat of takeover—act to prevent or minimize the *agency problem*? What role do *institutional investors* play in shareholder activism?

Summary

FOCUS ON VALUE

This chapter established the primary goal of the firm: **to maximize the wealth of the owners for whom the firm is being operated.** For public companies, value at any time is reflected in the stock price. Therefore, management should act only on those opportunities that are expected to create value for owners by increasing the stock price. Doing so requires management to consider the returns (magnitude and timing of cash flows), the risk of each proposed action, and their combined effect on value.

REVIEW OF LEARNING GOALS

LG 1 **Define finance and the managerial finance function.** Finance is the science and art of managing money. It affects virtually all aspects of business. Managerial finance is concerned with the duties of the *financial manager* working in a business. Financial managers administer the financial affairs of all types of businesses: private and public, large and small, profit seeking and not for profit. They perform such varied tasks as developing a financial plan or budget, extending credit to customers, evaluating proposed large expenditures, and raising money to fund the firm's operations.

LG 2 **Describe the legal forms of business organization.** The legal forms of business organization are the sole proprietorship, the partnership, and the corporation. The corporation is dominant in terms of business receipts, and its owners are its stockholders. Stockholders expect to earn a return by receiving dividends or by realizing gains through increases in share price.

LG 3 **Describe the goal of the firm, and explain why maximizing the value of the firm is an appropriate goal for a business.** The goal of the firm is to maximize its value and therefore the wealth of its shareholders. Maximizing the value of the firm means running the business in the interest of those who own it, the shareholders. Because shareholders are paid after other stakeholders, it is generally necessary to satisfy the interests of other stakeholders to enrich shareholders.

LG 4 **Describe how the managerial finance function is related to economics and accounting.** All areas of responsibility within a firm interact with finance personnel and procedures. The financial manager must understand the economic environment and rely heavily on the economic principle of marginal cost–benefit analysis to make financial decisions. Financial managers use accounting but concentrate on cash flows and decision making.

LG 5 **Identify the primary activities of the financial manager.** The primary activities of the financial manager, in addition to ongoing involvement in financial analysis and planning, are making investment decisions and making financing decisions.

LG 6 Describe the nature of the principal–agent relationship between the owners and managers of a corporation, and explain how various corporate governance mechanisms attempt to manage agency problems. This separation of owners and managers of the typical firm is representative of the classic principal–agent relationship, where the shareholders are the principals and managers are the agents. This arrangement works well when the agent makes decisions that are in the principal's best interest, but it can lead to agency problems when the interests of the principal and agent differ. A firm's corporate governance structure is intended to help ensure that managers act in the best interests of the firm's shareholders and other stakeholders, and it is usually influenced by both internal and external factors.

Self-Test Problem (Solution in Appendix)

ST1–1   **Emphasis on Cash Flows** Worldwide Rugs is a rug importer located in the United States that resells its import products to local retailers. Last year, Worldwide Rugs imported $2.5 million worth of rugs from around the world, all of which were paid for prior to shipping. On receipt of the rugs, the importer immediately resold them to local retailers for $3 million. To allow its retail clients time to resell the rugs, Worldwide Rugs sells to retailers on credit. Prior to the end of its business year, Worldwide Rugs collected 85 percent of its outstanding accounts receivable.

    a. What is the accounting profit that Worldwide Rugs generated for the year?
    b. Did Worldwide Rugs have a successful year from an accounting perspective?
    c. What is the financial cash flow that Worldwide Rugs generated for the year?
    d. Did Worldwide Rugs have a successful year from a financial perspective?
    e. If the current pattern persists, what is your expectation for the future success of Worldwide Rugs?

Warm-Up Exercises   All problems are available in *MyFinanceLab*.

E1–1   Ann and Jack have been partners for several years. Their firm, A & J Tax Preparation, has been very successful, as the pair agree on most business-related questions. One disagreement, however, concerns the legal form of their business. Ann has tried for the past 2 years to get Jack to agree to incorporate. She believes that there is no downside to incorporating and sees only benefits. Jack strongly disagrees; he thinks that the business should remain a partnership forever.

    First, take Ann's side, and explain the positive side to incorporating the business. Next, take Jack's side, and state the advantages to remaining a partnership. Last, what information would you want if you were asked to make the decision for Ann and Jack?

E1–2   As chief financial officer, it is your responsibility to weigh the finanical pros and cons of the many investment opportunities developed by your company's research and development division. You are currently evaluating two competing 15-year projects that differ in several ways. Relative to your firm's current EPS, the first project is expected to generate above-average EPS during the first 5 years, average EPS during the second five years, and then below-average EPS during the last 5 years. The second project is expected to generate below-average EPS during the first 5 years, average EPS during the second 5 years, and then well-above-average EPS during the last 5 years.

Is the choice obvious if you expect that the second investment will result in a larger overall earnings increase? Given the goal of the firm, what issues will you consider before making a final decision?

LG 4 **E1–3** The end-of-year parties at Yearling, Inc., are known for their extravagance. Management provides the best food and entertainment to thank the employees for their hard work. During the planning for this year's bash, a disagreement broke out between the treasurer's staff and the controller's staff. The treasurer's staff contended that the firm was running low on cash and might have trouble paying its bills over the coming months; they requested that cuts be made to the budget for the party. The controller's staff believed that any cuts were unwarranted, as the firm continued to be very profitable.

Can both sides be correct? Explain your answer.

LG 5 **E1–4** You have been made treasurer for a day at AIMCO, Inc. AIMCO develops technology for video conferencing. A manager of the satellite division has asked you to authorize a capital expenditure in the amount of $10,000. The manager states that this expenditure is necessary to continue a long-running project designed to use satellites to allow video conferencing anywhere on the planet. The manager admits that the satellite concept has been surpassed by recent technological advances in telephony, but he believes that AIMCO should continue the project because $2.5 million has already been spent over the past 15 years on this project. Although the project has little chance to be viable, the manager believes that it would be a shame to waste the money and time already spent.

Use *marginal cost–benefit analysis* to make your decision regarding whether you should authorize the $10,000 expenditure to continue the project.

LG 6 **E1–5** Recently, some branches of Donut Shop, Inc., have dropped the practice of allowing employees to accept tips. Customers who once said, "Keep the change," now have to get used to waiting for their nickels. Management even instituted a policy of requiring that the change be thrown out if a customer drives off without it. As a frequent customer who gets coffee and doughnuts for the office, you notice that the lines are longer and that more mistakes are being made in your order.

Explain why tips could be viewed as similar to stock options and why the delays and incorrect orders could represent a case of *agency costs*. If tips are gone forever, how could Donut Shop reduce these agency costs?

Problems All problems are available in MyFinanceLab.

LG 2 **P1–1** **Liability comparisons** Merideth Harper has invested $25,000 in Southwest Development Company. The firm has recently declared bankruptcy and has $60,000 in unpaid debts. Explain the nature of payments, if any, by Merideth in each of the following situations.
a. Southwest Development Company is a *sole proprietorship* owned by Ms. Harper.
b. Southwest Development Company is a *50–50 partnership* of Merideth Harper and Christopher Black.
c. Southwest Development Company is a *corporation*.

P1–2 **Accrual income versus cash flow for a period** Thomas Book Sales, Inc., supplies textbooks to college and university bookstores. The books are shipped with a proviso that they must be paid for within 30 days but can be returned for a full refund credit within 90 days. In 2014, Thomas shipped and billed book titles totaling $760,000. Collections, net of return credits, during the year totaled $690,000. The company spent $300,000 acquiring the books that it shipped.

a. Using accrual accounting and the preceding values, show the firm's net profit for the past year.

b. Using cash accounting and the preceding values, show the firm's net cash flow for the past year.

c. Which of these statements is more useful to the financial manager? Why?

Personal Finance Problem

 P1–3 **Cash flows** It is typical for Jane to plan, monitor, and assess her financial position using cash flows over a given period, typically a month. Jane has a savings account, and her bank loans money at 6 percent per year while it offers short-term investment rates of 5 percent. Jane's cash flows during August were as follows:

Item	Cash inflow	Cash outflow
Clothes		−$1,000
Interest received	$ 450	
Dining out		−500
Groceries		−800
Salary	4,500	
Auto payment		−355
Utilities		−280
Mortgage		−1,200
Gas		−222

a. Determine Jane's total cash inflows and cash outflows.

b. Determine the *net cash flow* for the month of August.

c. If there is a shortage, what are a few options open to Jane?

d. If there is a surplus, what would be a prudent strategy for her to follow?

  P1–4 **Marginal cost–benefit analysis and the goal of the firm** Ken Allen, capital budgeting analyst for Bally Gears, Inc., has been asked to evaluate a proposal. The manager of the automotive division believes that replacing the robotics used on the heavy truck gear line will produce total benefits of $560,000 (in today's dollars) over the next 5 years. The existing robotics would produce benefits of $400,000 (also in today's dollars) over that same time period. An initial cash investment of $220,000 would be required to install the new equipment. The manager estimates that the existing robotics can be sold for $70,000. Show how Ken will apply *marginal cost–benefit analysis* techniques to determine the following:

a. The marginal (added) benefits of the proposed new robotics.

b. The marginal (added) cost of the proposed new robotics.

c. The net benefit of the proposed new robotics.

d. What should Ken recommend that the company do? Why?

e. What factors besides the costs and benefits should be considered before the final decision is made?

P1–5 **Identifying agency problems, costs, and resolutions** Explain why each of the following situations is an agency problem and what costs to the firm might result from it. Suggest how the problem might be handled short of firing the individual(s) involved.

a. The front desk receptionist routinely takes an extra 20 minutes of lunch time to run personal errands.

b. Division managers are padding cost estimates so as to show short-term efficiency gains when the costs come in lower than the estimates.

c. The firm's chief executive officer has had secret talks with a competitor about the possibility of a merger in which she would become the CEO of the combined firms.

d. A branch manager lays off experienced full-time employees and staffs customer service positions with part-time or temporary workers to lower employment costs and raise this year's branch profit. The manager's bonus is based on profitability.

P1–6 **ETHICS PROBLEM** What does it mean to say that managers should maximize shareholder wealth "subject to ethical constraints"? What ethical considerations might enter into decisions that result in cash flow and stock price effects that are less than they might otherwise have been?

Spreadsheet Exercise

Assume that Monsanto Corporation is considering the replacement of some of its older and outdated carpet-manufacturing equipment. Its objective is to improve the efficiency of operations in terms of both speed and reduction in the number of defects. The company's finance department has compiled pertinent data that will allow it to conduct a *marginal cost–benefit analysis* for the proposed equipment replacement.

The cash outlay for new equipment would be approximately $600,000. The net book value of the old equipment and its potential net selling price add up to $250,000. The total benefits from the new equipment (measured in today's dollars) would be $900,000. The benefits of the old equipment over a similar period of time (measured in today's dollars) would be $300,000.

TO DO

Create a spreadsheet to conduct a *marginal cost–benefit analysis* for Monsanto Corporation, and determine the following:

a. The marginal (added) benefits of the proposed new equipment.
b. The marginal (added) cost of the proposed new equipment.
c. The net benefit of the proposed new equipment.
d. What would you recommend that the firm do? Why?

MyFinanceLab Visit **www.myfinancelab.com** for **Chapter Case: *Assessing the Goal of Sports Products, Inc.,*** Group Exercises, and numerous online resources.

2

The Financial Market Environment

Learning Goals

LG 1 Understand the role that financial institutions play in managerial finance.

LG 2 Contrast the functions of financial institutions and financial markets.

LG 3 Describe the differences between the capital markets and the money markets.

LG 4 Explain the root causes and subsequent effects of the 2008 financial crisis and recession.

LG 5 Understand the major regulations and regulatory bodies that affect financial institutions and markets.

LG 6 Discuss business taxes and their importance in financial decisions.

Why This Chapter Matters to You

In your *professional* life

ACCOUNTING You need to understand how business income is taxed and the difference between average and marginal tax rates.

INFORMATION SYSTEMS You need to understand how information flows between the firm and financial markets.

MANAGEMENT You need to understand why healthy financial institutions are an integral part of a healthy economy and how a crisis in the financial sector can spread and affect almost any type of business.

MARKETING You need to understand why it is important for firms to communicate about their operating results with external investors and how regulations constrain the types of communication that occur.

OPERATIONS You need to understand why external financing is, for most firms, an essential aspect of ongoing operations.

In your *personal* life
Making financial transactions will be a regular occurrence throughout your entire life. These transactions may be as simple as depositing your paycheck in a bank or as complex as deciding how to allocate the money you save for retirement among different investment options. Many of these transactions have important tax consequences, which vary over time and from one type of transaction to another. The content in this chapter will help you make better decisions when you engage in any of these transactions.

2.1 Financial Institutions and Markets

Most successful firms have ongoing needs for funds. They can obtain funds from external sources in three ways. The first source is through a *financial institution* that accepts savings and transfers them to those that need funds. A second source is through *financial markets,* organized forums in which the suppliers and demanders of various types of funds can make transactions. A third source is through *private placement.* Because of the unstructured nature of private placements, here we focus primarily on the role of financial institutions and financial markets in facilitating business financing.

FINANCIAL INSTITUTIONS

financial institution
An intermediary that channels the savings of individuals, businesses, and governments into loans or investments.

Financial institutions serve as intermediaries by channeling the savings of individuals, businesses, and governments into loans or investments. Many financial institutions directly or indirectly pay savers interest on deposited funds; others provide services for a fee (for example, checking accounts for which customers pay service charges). Some financial institutions accept customers' savings deposits and lend this money to other customers or to firms, others invest customers' savings in earning assets such as real estate or stocks and bonds, and some do both. Financial institutions are required by the government to operate within established regulatory guidelines.

Key Customers of Financial Institutions

For financial institutions, the key suppliers of funds and the key demanders of funds are individuals, businesses, and governments. The savings that individual consumers place in financial institutions provide these institutions with a large portion of their funds. Individuals not only supply funds to financial institutions but also demand funds from them in the form of loans. However, individuals as a group are the *net suppliers* for financial institutions: They save more money than they borrow.

Business firms also deposit some of their funds in financial institutions, primarily in checking accounts with various commercial banks. Like individuals, firms borrow funds from these institutions, but firms are *net demanders* of funds: They borrow more money than they save.

Governments maintain deposits of temporarily idle funds, certain tax payments, and Social Security payments in commercial banks. They do not borrow funds *directly* from financial institutions, although by selling their debt securities to various institutions, governments indirectly borrow from them. The government, like business firms, is typically a *net demander* of funds: It typically borrows more than it saves. We've all heard about the federal budget deficit.

Major Financial Institutions

The major financial institutions in the U.S. economy are commercial banks, savings and loans, credit unions, savings banks, insurance companies, mutual funds, and pension funds. These institutions attract funds from individuals, businesses, and governments, combine them, and make loans available to individuals and businesses.

COMMERCIAL BANKS, INVESTMENT BANKS, AND THE SHADOW BANKING SYSTEM

commercial banks
Institutions that provide savers with a secure place to invest their funds and that offer loans to individual and business borrowers.

Commercial banks are among the most important financial institutions in the economy because they provide savers with a secure place to invest funds and they offer both individuals and companies loans to finance investments, such as the purchase of a new home or the expansion of a business. **Investment banks** are institutions that (1) assist companies in raising capital, (2) advise firms on major transactions such as mergers or financial restructurings, and (3) engage in trading and market making activities.

investment banks
Institutions that assist companies in raising capital, advise firms on major transactions such as mergers or financial restructurings, and engage in trading and market making activities.

The traditional business model of a commercial bank—taking in and paying interest on deposits and investing or lending those funds back out at higher interest rates—works to the extent that depositors believe that their investments are secure. Since the 1930s, the U.S. government has given some assurance to depositors that their money is safe by providing deposit insurance (currently up to $250,000 per depositor). Deposit insurance was put in place in response to the banking runs or panics that were part of the Great Depression. The same act of Congress that introduced deposit insurance, the **Glass-Steagall Act,** also created a separation between commercial banks and investment banks, meaning that an institution engaged in taking in deposits could not also engage in the somewhat riskier activities of securities underwriting and trading.

Glass-Steagall Act
An act of Congress in 1933 that created the federal deposit insurance program and separated the activities of commercial and investment banks.

Commercial and investment banks remained essentially separate for more than 50 years, but Congress, with the approval of President Bill Clinton, decided to repeal Glass-Steagall in 1999. Companies that had formerly engaged only in the traditional activities of a commercial bank began competing with investment banks for underwriting and other services. In addition, the 1990s witnessed tremendous growth in what has come to be known as the shadow banking system. The **shadow banking system** describes a group of institutions that engage in lending activities, much like traditional banks, but these institutions do not accept deposits and are therefore not subject to the same regulations as traditional banks. For example, an institution such as a pension fund might have excess cash to invest, and a large corporation might need short-term financing to cover seasonal cash flow needs. A business like Lehman Brothers, which filed for bankruptcy in the early days of the 2008 financial crisis, acted as an intermediary between these two parties and helped facilitate a loan, thereby becoming part of the shadow banking system. In March 2010, Treasury Secretary Timothy Geithner noted that at its peak the shadow banking system financed roughly $8 trillion in assets and was roughly as large as the traditional banking system.

shadow banking system
A group of institutions that engage in lending activities, much like traditional banks, but do not accept deposits and therefore are not subject to the same regulations as traditional banks.

Matter of fact

Consolidation in the U.S. Banking Industry

The U.S. banking industry has been going through a long period of consolidation. According to the Federal Deposit Insurance Corporation (FDIC), the number of commercial banks in the United States declined from 11,463 in 1992 to 6,048 as of March 2013, a decline of 47 percent. The decline is concentrated among small community banks, which larger institutions have been acquiring at a rapid pace.

FINANCIAL MARKETS

financial markets
Forums in which suppliers of funds and demanders of funds can transact business directly.

Financial markets are forums in which suppliers of funds and demanders of funds can transact business directly. Whereas the loans made by financial institutions are granted without the direct knowledge of the suppliers of funds (savers), suppliers in the financial markets know where their funds are being lent or invested. The two key financial markets are the money market and the capital market. Transactions in short-term debt instruments, or marketable securities, take place in the *money market*. Long-term securities—bonds and stocks—are traded in the *capital market*.

private placement
The sale of a new security directly to an investor or group of investors.

To raise money, firms can use either private placements or public offerings. A **private placement** involves the sale of a new security directly to an investor or group of investors, such as an insurance company or pension fund. Most firms, however, raise money through a **public offering** of securities, which is the sale of either bonds or stocks to the general public.

public offering
The sale of either bonds or stocks to the general public.

When a company or government entity sells stocks or bonds to investors and receives cash in return, it is said to have sold securities in the **primary market.** After the primary market transaction occurs, any further trading in the security does not involve the issuer directly, and the issuer receives no additional money from these subsequent transactions. Once the securities begin to trade between investors, they become part of the **secondary market.** On large stock exchanges, billions of shares may trade between buyers and sellers on a single day, and these trades are all secondary market transactions. Money flows from the investors buying stocks to the investors selling them, and the company whose stock is being traded is largely unaffected by the transactions. The primary market is the one in which "new" securities are sold. The secondary market can be viewed as a "preowned" securities market.

primary market
Financial market in which securities are initially issued; the only market in which the issuer is directly involved in the transaction.

secondary market
Financial market in which preowned securities (those that are not new issues) are traded.

THE RELATIONSHIP BETWEEN INSTITUTIONS AND MARKETS

Financial institutions actively participate in the financial markets as both suppliers and demanders of funds. Figure 2.1 depicts the general flow of funds through and between financial institutions and financial markets as well as the mechanics of private placement transactions. Domestic or foreign individuals, businesses,

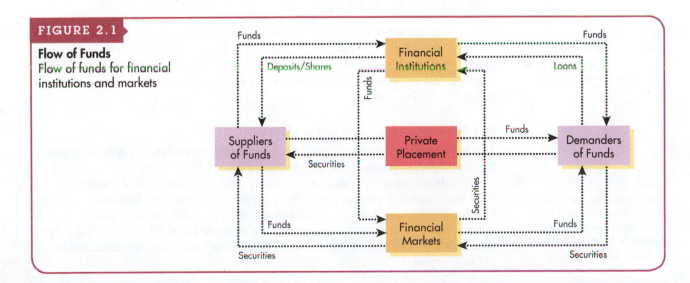

FIGURE 2.1

Flow of Funds
Flow of funds for financial institutions and markets

and governments may supply and demand funds. We next briefly discuss the money market, including its international equivalent: the *Eurocurrency market*. We then end this section with a discussion of the capital market, which is of key importance to the firm.

THE MONEY MARKET

money market
A financial relationship created between suppliers and demanders of *short-term funds*.

The **money market** is created by a financial relationship between suppliers and demanders of *short-term funds* (funds with maturities of 1 year or less). The money market exists because some individuals, businesses, governments, and financial institutions have temporarily idle funds that they wish to invest in a relatively safe, interest-bearing asset. At the same time, other individuals, businesses, governments, and financial institutions find themselves in need of seasonal or temporary financing. The money market brings together these suppliers and demanders of short-term funds.

marketable securities
Short-term debt instruments, such as U.S. Treasury bills, commercial paper, and negotiable certificates of deposit issued by government, business, and financial institutions, respectively.

Most money market transactions are made in **marketable securities**, which are short-term debt instruments such as U.S. Treasury bills, commercial paper, and negotiable certificates of deposit issued by government, business, and financial institutions, respectively. Investors generally consider marketable securities to be among the least risky investments available. Marketable securities are described in Chapter 14.

Eurocurrency market
International equivalent of the domestic money market.

The international equivalent of the domestic money market is called the **Eurocurrency market.** This market for short-term bank deposits is denominated in U.S. dollars or other major currencies. Eurocurrency deposits arise when a corporation or individual makes a bank deposit in a currency other than the local currency of the country where the bank is located. For example, if a multinational corporation were to deposit U.S. dollars in a London bank, this action would create a Eurodollar deposit (a dollar deposit at a bank in Europe). Nearly all Eurodollar deposits are *time deposits,* which means that the bank would promise to repay the deposit, with interest, at a fixed date in the future, in 6 months, for example. During the interim, the bank is free to lend this dollar deposit to creditworthy corporate or government borrowers. If the bank cannot find a borrower on its own, it may lend the deposit to another international bank.

THE CAPITAL MARKET

capital market
A market that enables suppliers and demanders of *long-term funds* to make transactions.

The **capital market** is a market that enables suppliers and demanders of *long-term funds* to make transactions. Included are securities issues of business and government. The backbone of the capital market is formed by the broker and dealer markets that provide a forum for bond and stock transactions. International capital markets also exist.

Key Securities Traded: Bonds and Stocks

The key capital market securities are *bonds* (long-term debt) and both *common stock* and *preferred stock* (equity, or ownership).

bond
Long-term debt instrument used by business and government to raise large sums of money, generally from a diverse group of lenders.

Bonds are long-term debt instruments used by business and government to raise large sums of money, generally from a diverse group of lenders. *Corporate bonds* typically pay interest *semiannually* (every 6 months) at a stated *coupon interest rate*. They have an initial *maturity* of from 10 to 30 years, and a *par*, or *face, value* of $1,000 that must be repaid at maturity. Bonds are described in detail in Chapter 7.

Example 2.1 ▶

MyFinanceLab Solution Video

Lakeview Industries, a major microprocessor manufacturer, has issued a 9% coupon interest rate, 20-year bond with a $1,000 par value that pays interest semiannually. Investors who buy this bond receive the contractual right to $90 annual interest (9% coupon interest rate $\times$ $1,000 par value) distributed as $45 at the end of each 6 months (1/2 $\times$ $90) for 20 years, plus the $1,000 par value at the end of year 20.

As noted earlier, shares of *common stock* are units of ownership, or equity, in a corporation. Common stockholders earn a return by receiving dividends—periodic distributions of cash—or by realizing increases in share price. **Preferred stock** is a special form of ownership that has features of both a bond and common stock. Preferred stockholders are promised a fixed periodic dividend that must be paid prior to payment of any dividends to common stockholders. In other words, preferred stock has "preference" over common stock. Preferred stock and common stock are described in detail in Chapter 8. See the *Focus on Practice* box for the story of one legendary stock price and the equally legendary man who brought it about.

Broker Markets and Dealer Markets

By far, the vast majority of trades made by individual investors take place in the secondary market. Trading mechanisms and processes in the secondary market have evolved rapidly in recent years. In the past, it was possible to classify the secondary market into two segments *on the basis of how securities were traded.* Those two segments were broker markets and dealer markets. Those segments are still relevant today, but the distinctions between them are not as sharp as they once were.

The key difference between broker and dealer markets is a technical point dealing with the way trades are executed. That is, when a trade occurs in a **broker market,** the two sides to the transaction, the buyer and the seller, are brought together, and the trade takes place at that point: Party A sells his or her securities directly to the buyer, Party B. In a sense, with the help of a *broker,* the securities effectively change hands, perhaps literally on the floor of the exchange. The broker market consists of national and regional **securities exchanges,** which are organizations that provide a marketplace in which firms can raise funds through the sale of new securities and purchasers can resell securities.

In contrast, when trades are made in a **dealer market,** the buyer and the seller are never brought together directly. Instead, **market makers** execute the buy/sell orders. Market makers are *securities dealers* who "make markets" by offering to buy or sell certain securities at stated prices. Essentially, two separate trades are made: Party A sells his or her securities (in, say, Dell) to a dealer, and Party B buys his or her securities (in Dell) from another, or possibly even the same, dealer. Thus, there is always a dealer (*market maker*) on one side of a dealer–market transaction. The dealer market is made up of both the **Nasdaq market,** an all-electronic trading platform used to execute securities trades, and the **over-the-counter (OTC) market,** where smaller, unlisted securities are traded.

In recent years, the distinctions between broker and dealer markets have blurred. Electronic trading platforms using sophisticated algorithms place buy and sell orders very rapidly (so-called high-frequency trading), often without any human intervention. These algorithms may be used to speculate on a stock's price movements, or they may be used to take a single, large buy or sell order and break

preferred stock
A special form of ownership having a fixed periodic dividend that must be paid prior to payment of any dividends to common stockholders.

broker market
The securities exchanges on which the two sides of a transaction, the buyer and seller, are brought together to trade securities.

securities exchanges
Organizations that provide the marketplace in which firms can raise funds through the sale of new securities and purchasers can resell securities.

dealer market
The market in which the buyer and seller are not brought together directly but instead have their orders executed by securities dealers that "make markets" in the given security.

market makers
Securities dealers who "make markets" by offering to buy or sell certain securities at stated prices.

Nasdaq market
An all-electronic trading platform used to execute securities trades.

over-the-counter (OTC) market
Market where smaller, unlisted securities are traded.

focus on PRACTICE

Berkshire Hathaway: Can Buffett Be Replaced?

in practice In early 1980, investors could buy one share of Berkshire Hathaway Class A common stock (stock symbol: BRKA) for $285. That may have seemed expensive at the time, but by May 2013 the price of just one share had climbed to $169,700. The wizard behind such phenomenal growth in shareholder value is the chairman of Berkshire Hathaway, Warren Buffett, nicknamed the Oracle of Omaha.

With his partner, Vice-Chairman Charlie Munger, Buffett runs a large conglomerate of dozens of subsidiaries with 288,000 employees and more than $162 billion in annual revenues. He makes it look easy. In his words, "I've taken the easy route, just sitting back and working through great managers who run their own shows. My only tasks are to cheer them on, sculpt and harden our corporate culture, and make major capital-allocation decisions. Our managers have returned this trust by working hard and effectively."[a]

Buffett's style of corporate leadership seems rather laid back, but behind that "aw-shucks" manner is one of the best analytical minds in business. He believes in aligning managerial incentives with performance. Berkshire employs many different incentive arrangements, with their terms depending on such elements as the economic potential or capital intensity of a CEO's business. Whatever the compensation arrangement, Buffett tries to keep it both simple and fair. Buffett himself receives an annual salary of $100,000, which isn't much in this age of supersized CEO compensation packages. Listed for many years among the world's wealthiest people, Buffett has donated most of his Berkshire stock to the Bill and Melinda Gates Foundation.

Berkshire's annual report is a must-read for many investors due to the popularity of Buffett's annual letter to shareholders with his homespun take on such topics as investing, corporate governance, and corporate leadership. Shareholder meetings in Omaha, Nebraska, have turned into cultlike gatherings, with thousands traveling to listen to Buffett answer questions from shareholders. One question that has been firmly answered is that of Buffett's ability to create shareholder value.

The next question that needs to be answered is whether Berkshire Hathaway can successfully replace Buffett (age 83) and Munger (age 89). In October 2010, Berkshire hired hedge fund manager Todd Combs to handle a significant portion of the firm's investments. In May 2013, Buffett announced that members of Berkshire's board of directors were solidly in agreement as to whom the next chief executive should be, but he didn't mention any names. Berkshire shareholders hope that Buffett's special wisdom applies as well to identifying new managerial talent as it does to making strategic investment decisions.

▶ *The share price of BRKA has never been split. Why might the company refuse to split its shares to make them more affordable to average investors?*

[a]Berkshire Hathaway, Inc., "Letter to Shareholders of Berkshire Hathaway, Inc.," *2006 Annual Report*, p. 4.

it into many smaller orders to try to minimize the price effect of buying or selling a large quantity of shares. An increasing amount of trading takes place today "off exchange," often in private trading venues known as "dark pools." Roughly one-third of secondary market trading occurs in these off-exchange environments.

Broker Markets If you are like most people, when you think of the "stock market," the first name to come to mind is the New York Stock Exchange, known currently as the NYSE Euronext after a series of mergers that expanded the exchange's global reach. In point of fact, the NYSE Euronext is the dominant broker market. Several *regional exchanges* are also broker markets. In 2012, the NYSE Euronext accounted for a little more than 25 percent of the *total dollar volume* of all shares traded in the U.S. stock market.

Most exchanges are modeled to some degree after the NYSE Euronext. For a firm's securities to be listed for trading on a stock exchange, a firm must file an application for listing and meet a number of requirements. For example, to be eligible for listing on the NYSE Euronext, a firm must have at least 400 stock-holders owning 100 or more shares; a minimum of 1.1 million shares of publicly held stock outstanding; pretax earnings of at least $10 million over the previous 3 years, with at least $2 million in each of the previous 2 years; and a minimum market value of public shares of $100 million. Clearly, a firm has to reach a certain level of success to be listed on the NYSE Euronext.

Once placed, an order to buy or sell on the NYSE Euronext can be executed in minutes, thanks to sophisticated telecommunication devices. New Internet-based brokerage systems enable investors to place their buy and sell orders electronically. Information on publicly traded securities is reported in various media, both print, such as the *Wall Street Journal*, and electronic, such as MSN Money (**www.moneycentral.msn.com**).

Dealer Markets One of the key features of the *dealer market* is that it has no centralized trading floors. Instead, it is made up of a large number of *market makers* who are linked together via a mass-telecommunications network.

Each market maker is actually a securities dealer who makes a market in one or more securities by offering to buy or sell them at stated bid/ask prices. The **bid price** and **ask price** represent, respectively, the highest price offered to purchase a given security and the lowest price at which the security is offered for sale. In effect, an investor pays the ask price when buying securities and receives the bid price when selling them.

As described earlier, the dealer market is made up of both the *Nasdaq market* and the *over-the-counter (OTC) market,* which together account for about 22 percent of all shares traded in the U.S. market, with the Nasdaq accounting for the overwhelming majority of those trades. (As an aside, the *primary market* is also a dealer market because all new issues are sold to the investing public by securities dealers, acting on behalf of the investment banker.)

The largest dealer market consists of a select group of stocks that are listed and traded on the *National Association of Securities Dealers Automated Quotation System,* typically referred to as *Nasdaq*. Founded in 1971, Nasdaq had its origins in the OTC market but is today considered a *totally separate entity that's no longer a part of the OTC market*. In fact, in 2006 Nasdaq was formally recognized by the SEC as a "listed exchange," essentially giving it the same stature and prestige as the NYSE.

International Capital Markets

Although U.S. capital markets are by far the world's largest, there are important debt and equity markets outside the United States. In the **Eurobond market,** corporations and governments typically issue bonds denominated in dollars and sell

bid price
The highest price offered to purchase a security.

ask price
The lowest price at which a security is offered for sale.

Eurobond market
The market in which corporations and governments typically issue bonds denominated in dollars and sell them to investors located outside the United States.

Matter of fact

NYSE Euronext is the World's Largest Stock Exchange

According to the World Federation of Exchanges, the largest stock market in the world in 2012, as measured by the total market value of securities listed on that market, is the NYSE Euronext, with listed securities worth more than $14.1 trillion in the United States and $2.8 trillion in Europe. The next largest is the Nasdaq at $4.6 trillion, with exchanges in Tokyo and London not far behind at $3.5 billion and $3.3 billion respectively.

them to investors located outside the United States. A U.S. corporation might, for example, issue dollar-denominated bonds that would be purchased by investors in Belgium, Germany, or Switzerland. Through the Eurobond market, issuing firms and governments can tap a much larger pool of investors than would be generally available in the local market.

foreign bond
A bond that is issued by a foreign corporation or government and is denominated in the investor's home currency and sold in the investor's home market.

The *foreign bond market* is an international market for long-term debt securities. A **foreign bond** is a bond issued by a foreign corporation or government that is denominated in the investor's home currency and sold in the investor's home market. A bond issued by a U.S. company that is denominated in Swiss francs and sold in Switzerland is a foreign bond. Although the foreign bond market is smaller than the Eurobond market, many issuers have found it to be an attractive way of tapping debt markets around the world.

international equity market
A market that allows corporations to sell blocks of shares to investors in a number of different countries simultaneously.

Finally, the **international equity market** allows corporations to sell blocks of shares to investors in a number of different countries simultaneously. This market enables corporations to raise far larger amounts of capital than they could in any single market. International equity sales have been indispensable to governments that have sold state-owned companies to private investors.

The Role of Capital Markets

From a firm's perspective, the role of a capital market is to be a liquid market where firms can interact with investors to obtain valuable external financing resources. From investors' perspectives, the role of a capital market is to be an **efficient market** that establishes correct prices for the securities that firms sell and allocates funds to their most productive uses. This role is especially true for securities that are actively traded in broker or dealer markets, where intense competition among investors determines the prices of securities.

efficient market
A market that establishes correct prices for the securities that firms sell and allocates funds to their most productive uses.

The price of an individual security is determined by the interaction between buyers and sellers in the market. If the market is efficient, the price of a stock is an unbiased estimate of its true value. Investors compete with one another for information about a stock's true value, so at any given time, a stock's price reflects all the information that is known about the stock. Changes in the price reflect new information that investors learn about and act on. For example, suppose that a certain stock currently trades at $40 per share. If this company announces that sales of a new product have been higher than expected, and if investors have not already anticipated that announcement, investors will raise their estimate of what the stock is truly worth. At $40, the stock is a relative bargain, so there will temporarily be more buyers than sellers wanting to trade the stock, and its price will have to rise to restore equilibrium in the market. The more efficient the market is, the more rapidly this whole process works. In theory, even information known only to insiders may become incorporated in stock prices.

New information is, almost by definition, unpredictable. For example, it is well known that retail companies in the United States have a spike in sales near the end of the calendar year as the holiday season approaches. When a firm reports higher sales near the end of the year, it is not new information because investors in the market are aware of the seasonal pattern and anticipate that sales will be higher in the fourth quarter than at any other time of year. To the market, new information would be a report from a retailer that its sales were higher (or lower) in the fourth quarter than investors had already expected. Because it is unanticipated, new information has a random quality (that is, sometimes firms announce better-than-expected results, and sometimes they announce worse-than-expected results). As new information arrives, stock prices quickly respond, and those price movements will appear to occur at random. Therefore, one sign that a stock market is efficient is that changes in stock prices are nearly impossible to predict, even by professional investors.

Not everyone agrees that prices in financial markets are as efficient as described in the preceding paragraph. Advocates of *behavioral finance,* an emerging field that blends ideas from finance and psychology, argue that stock prices and prices of other securities can deviate from their true values for extended periods and that these deviations may lead to predictable patterns in stock prices. These people point to episodes such as the huge run-up and subsequent collapse of the prices of Internet stocks in the late 1990s and the failure of markets to accurately assess the risk of mortgage-backed securities in the more recent financial crisis as examples of the principle that stock prices sometimes can be wildly inaccurate measures of value.

Just how efficient are the prices in financial markets? That question will be debated for a long time. It is clear that prices do move in response to new information, and for most investors and corporate managers, the best advice is probably to be cautious when betting against the market. Identifying securities that the market has over- or undervalued is extremely difficult, and very few people have demonstrated an ability to bet against the market correctly for an extended time.

→ REVIEW QUESTIONS

2–1 Who are the key participants in the transactions of financial institutions? Who are *net suppliers,* and who are *net demanders*?

2–2 What role do *financial markets* play in our economy? What are *primary* and *secondary* markets? What relationship exists between financial institutions and financial markets?

2–3 What is the *money market*? What is the *Eurocurrency market*?

2–4 What is the *capital market*? What are the primary securities traded in it?

2–5 What are *broker markets*? What are *dealer markets*? How do they differ?

2–6 Briefly describe the international capital markets, particularly the *Eurobond market* and the *international equity market.*

2–7 What are *efficient markets*? What determines the price of an individual security in such a market?

 ## 2.2 The Financial Crisis

In the summer and fall of 2008, the U.S. financial system, and financial systems around the world, appeared to be on the verge of collapse. Troubles in the financial sector spread to other industries, and a severe global recession ensued. In this section, we outline some of the main causes and consequences of that crisis.

FINANCIAL INSTITUTIONS AND REAL ESTATE FINANCE

In the classic film *It's a Wonderful Life,* the central character is George Bailey, who runs a financial institution called the Bailey Building and Loan Association. In a key scene in that movie, a bank run is about to occur, and depositors demand that George return the money that they had invested in the Building and Loan. George pleads with one man to keep his funds at the bank, saying:

> You're thinking of this place all wrong, as if I have the money back in a safe. The money's not here. Your money is in Joe's house. That's right next to yours—and then the Kennedy house, and Mrs. Maklin's house, and a hundred others. You're

lending them the money to build, and then they're going to pay it back to you as best they can. What are you going to do, foreclose on them?

This scene offers a relatively realistic portrayal of the role that financial institutions played in allocating credit for investments in residential real estate for many years. Local banks took deposits and made loans to local borrowers. However, since the 1970s, a process called securitization has changed the way that mortgage finance works. **Securitization** refers to the process of pooling mortgages or other types of loans and then selling claims or securities against that pool in a secondary market. These securities, called **mortgage-backed securities,** can be purchased by individual investors, pension funds, mutual funds, or virtually any other investor. As homeowners repay their loans, those payments eventually make their way into the hands of investors who hold the mortgage-backed securities. Therefore, a primary risk associated with mortgage-backed securities is that homeowners may not be able to, or may choose not to, repay their loans. Banks today still lend money to individuals who want to build or purchase new homes, but they typically bundle those loans together and sell them to organizations that securitize them and pass them on to investors all over the world.

securitization
The process of pooling mortgages or other types of loans and then selling claims or securities against that pool in the secondary market.

mortgage-backed securities
Securities that represent claims on the cash flows generated by a pool of mortgages.

FALLING HOME PRICES AND DELINQUENT MORTGAGES

Prior to the 2008 financial crisis, most investors viewed mortgage-backed securities as relatively safe investments. Figure 2.2 illustrates one of the main reasons for this view. The figure shows the behavior of the Standard & Poor's Case-Shiller Index, a barometer of home prices in ten major U.S. cities, in each

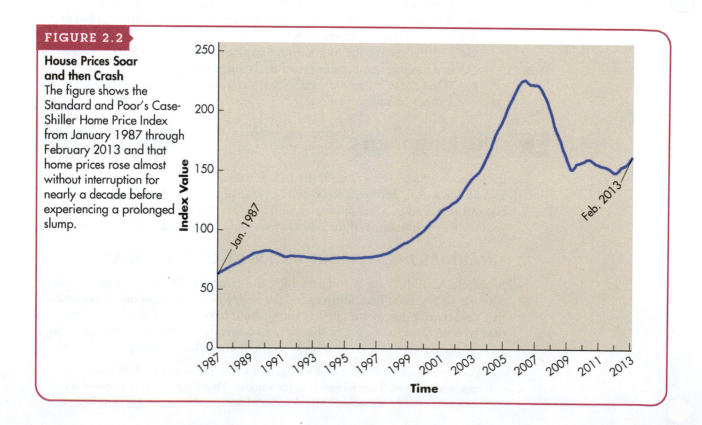

FIGURE 2.2

House Prices Soar and then Crash
The figure shows the Standard and Poor's Case-Shiller Home Price Index from January 1987 through February 2013 and that home prices rose almost without interruption for nearly a decade before experiencing a prolonged slump.

month from January 1987 to February 2013. Historically, declines in the index were relatively infrequent, and between July 1995 and April 2006 the index rose continuously without posting even a single monthly decline. When house prices are rising, the gap between what a borrower owes on a home and what the home is worth widens. Lenders will allow borrowers who have difficulty making payments on their mortgages to tap this built-up home equity to refinance their loans and lower their payments. Therefore, rising home prices helped keep mortgage default rates low from the mid-1990s through 2006. Investing in real estate and mortgage-backed securities seemed to involve very little risk during this period.

In part because real estate investments appeared to be relatively safe, lenders began relaxing their standards for borrowers. This change led to tremendous growth in a category of loans called subprime mortgages. Subprime mortgages are mortgage loans made to borrowers with lower incomes and poorer credit histories as compared to "prime" borrowers. Loans granted to subprime borrowers often have adjustable, rather than fixed, interest rates, which makes subprime borrowers particularly vulnerable if interest rates rise. Many of these borrowers (and lenders) assumed that rising home prices would allow borrowers to refinance their loans if they had difficulties making payments. Partly through the growth of subprime mortgages, banks and other financial institutions gradually increased their investments in real estate loans. In 2000, real estate loans accounted for less than 40 percent of the total loan portfolios of large banks. By 2007, real estate loans grew to more than half of all loans made by large banks, and the fraction of these loans in the subprime category increased as well.

Unfortunately, as Figure 2.2 shows, home prices fell almost without interruption from May 2006 through May 2009. Over that 3-year period, home prices fell on average by more than 30 percent. Not surprisingly, when homeowners had difficulty making their mortgage payments, refinancing was no longer an option, and delinquency rates and foreclosures began to climb. By 2009, nearly 25 percent of subprime borrowers were behind schedule on their mortgage payments. Some borrowers, recognizing that the value of their homes was far less than the amount they owed on their mortgages, simply walked away from their homes and let lenders repossess them.

CRISIS OF CONFIDENCE IN BANKS

With delinquency rates rising, the value of mortgage-backed securities began to fall and so, too, did the fortunes of financial institutions that had invested heavily in real estate assets. In March 2008, the Federal Reserve provided financing for the acquisition (that is, the rescue) of Bear Stearns by JPMorgan Chase. Later that year, Lehman Brothers filed for bankruptcy. Throughout 2008 and 2009, the Federal Reserve, the George W. Bush administration, and finally the administration of Barack Obama took unprecedented steps to try to shore up the banking sector and stimulate the economy, but these measures could not completely avert the crisis.

Figure 2.3 shows the behavior of the Standard & Poor's Banking Index, an index that tracks bank stocks. Bank stocks fell 81 percent between January 2008 and March 2009, and the number of bank failures skyrocketed. According to the FDIC, only three banks failed in 2007. In 2008, that number rose by a factor of eight to 25 failed banks, and the number increased nearly six times to 140 failures in 2009. While the economy began to recover in 2010, bank failures

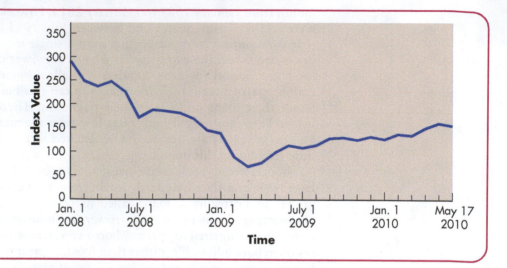

FIGURE 2.3

Bank Stocks Plummet During Financial Crisis
The graph shows the Standard and Poor's Banking Stock Index from January 2008 to May 2010. Concerns about the health of U.S. financial institutions drove bank stocks down by 81 percent in just over a year.

continued at a rapid pace, with 157 institutions failing that year followed by 92 more failures in 2011.

SPILLOVER EFFECTS AND THE GREAT RECESSION

As banks came under intense financial pressure in 2008, they began to tighten their lending standards and dramatically reduce the quantity of loans they mad In the aftermath of the Lehman Brothers bankruptcy, lending in the money ma ket contracted very sharply. Corporations that had relied on the money market as a source of short-term funding found that they could no longer raise money in this market or could do so only at extraordinarily high rates.

As a consequence, businesses began to hoard cash and cut back on expenditures, and economic activity contracted. Gross domestic product (GDP) declined in five out of six quarters starting in the first quarter of 2008, and the economy shed more than 8 million jobs in 2008–2009 as the unemployment rate reached 10 percent. Congress passed an $862 billion stimulus package to try to revive the economy, and the Federal Reserve pushed short-term interest rates close to 0 percent. Although the economy began to recover in 2009, the recovery was very slow. As late as May 2013, total employment was still just 2 percent lower than it had been prior to the start of the recession.

Perhaps the most important lesson from this episode is how important financial institutions are to a modern economy. By some measures, the 2008–2009 recession was the worst experienced in the United States since the Great Depression. Indeed, there many parallels between those two economic contractions. Both were preceded by a period of rapid economic growth, rising stock prices, and movements by banks into new lines of business, and both involved a major crisis in the financial sector. Recessions associated with a banking crisis tend to be more severe than other recessions because so many businesses rely on credit to operate. When financial institutions contract borrowing, activity in most other industries slows down too.

→ REVIEW QUESTIONS

2–8 What is securitization, and how does it facilitate investment in real estate assets?

2–9 What is a mortgage-backed security? What is the basic risk associated with mortgage-backed securities?

2–10 How do rising home prices contribute to low mortgage delinquencies?

2–11 Why do falling home prices create an incentive for homeowners to default on their mortgages even if they can afford to make the monthly payments?

2–12 Why does a crisis in the financial sector spill over into other industries?

LG 5 2.3 Regulation of Financial Institutions and Markets

The previous section discussed just how vulnerable modern economies are when financial institutions are in a state of crisis. Partly to avoid these types of problems, governments typically regulate financial institutions and markets as much or more than almost any other sector in the economy. This section provides an overview of the financial regulatory landscape in the United States.

REGULATIONS GOVERNING FINANCIAL INSTITUTIONS

Federal Deposit Insurance Corporation (FDIC)
An agency created by the Glass-Steagall Act that provides insurance for deposits at banks and monitors banks to ensure their safety and soundness.

As mentioned in Section 2.1, Congress passed the Glass-Steagall Act in 1933 during the depths of the Great Depression. The early 1930s witnessed a series of banking panics that caused almost one-third of the nation's banks to fail. Troubles within the banking sector and other factors contributed to the worst economic contraction in U.S. history, in which industrial production fell by more than 50 percent, the unemployment rate peaked at almost 25 percent, and stock prices dropped roughly 86 percent. The Glass-Steagall Act attempted to calm the public's fears about the banking industry by establishing the **Federal Deposit Insurance Corporation (FDIC)**, which provided deposit insurance, effectively guaranteeing that individuals would not lose their money if they held it in a bank that failed. The FDIC was also charged with examining banks on a regular basis to ensure that they were "safe and sound." The Glass-Steagall Act also prohibited institutions that took deposits from engaging in activities such as securities underwriting and trading, thereby effectively separating commercial banks from investment banks.

Over time, U.S. financial institutions faced competitive pressures from both domestic and foreign businesses that engaged in facilitating loans or making loans directly. Because these competitors either did not accept deposits or were located outside the United States, they were not subject to the same regulations as domestic banks. As a result, domestic banks began to lose market share in their core businesses. Pressure mounted to repeal the Glass-Steagall Act to enable U.S. banks to compete more effectively, and in 1999 Congress enacted and President Bill Clinton signed the **Gramm-Leach-Bliley Act,** which allows commercial banks, investment banks, and insurance companies to consolidate and compete for business in a wider range of activities.

Gramm-Leach-Bliley Act
An act that allows business combinations (that is, mergers) between commercial banks, investment banks, and insurance companies and thus permits these institutions to compete in markets that prior regulations prohibited them from entering.

In the aftermath of the recent financial crisis and recession, Congress passed the Dodd-Frank Wall Street Reform and Consumer Protection Act in July 2010. In print, the new law runs for hundreds of pages and calls for the creation of several new agencies, including the Financial Stability Oversight Council, the Office of Financial Research, and the Bureau of Consumer Financial Protection. The act also realigns the duties of several existing agencies and requires existing and new agencies to report to Congress regularly. Three years after Dodd-Frank became law, the various agencies affected or created by the new law were still writing rules specifying how the new law's provisions would be implemented. Exactly how the new legislation will affect financial institutions and markets remains unclear.

REGULATIONS GOVERNING FINANCIAL MARKETS

Securities Act of 1933
An act that regulates the sale of securities to the public via the primary market.

Two other pieces of legislation were passed during the Great Depression that had an enormous effect on the regulation of financial markets. The **Securities Act of 1933** imposed new regulations governing the sale of new securities. That is, the 1933 act was intended to regulate activity in the primary market in which securities are initially issued to the public. The act was designed to ensure that the sellers of new securities provided extensive disclosures to the potential buyers of those securities.

Securities Exchange Act of 1934
An act that regulates the trading of securities such as stocks and bonds in the secondary market.

Securities and Exchange Commission (SEC)
The primary government agency responsible for enforcing federal securities laws.

The **Securities Exchange Act of 1934** regulates the secondary trading of securities such as stocks and bonds. The Securities Exchange Act of 1934 also created the **Securities and Exchange Commission (SEC)**, which is the primary agency responsible for enforcing federal securities laws. In addition to the one-time disclosures required of security issuers by the Securities Act of 1933, the Securities Exchange Act of 1934 requires ongoing disclosure by companies whose securities trade in secondary markets. Companies must make a 10-Q filing every quarter and a 10-K filing annually. The 10-Q and 10-K forms contain detailed information about the financial performance of the firm during the relevant period. Today, these forms are available online through the SEC's website known as EDGAR (Electronic Data Gathering, Analysis, and Retrieval). The 1934 act also imposes limits on the extent to which corporate "insiders," such as senior managers, can trade in their firm's securities.

Although the type and level of government regulation will always be debatable, the idea that we need and, in fact, benefit from some level of government regulation of financial institutions and markets is quite reasonable. The biggest benefits of government regulation are the resulting trust and confidence in the financial institutions and markets derived by society. Such trust and confidence are necessary to ensure society's participation in the financial market environment that nearly every individual in one way or another hopes to benefit from.

→ REVIEW QUESTIONS

2-13 Why do you think that so many pieces of important legislation related to financial markets and institutions were passed during the Great Depression?

2-14 What different aspects of financial markets do the Securities Act of 1933 and the Securities Exchange Act of 1934 regulate?

LG 6 2.4 Business Taxes

Taxes are a fact of life, and businesses, like individuals, must pay taxes on income. The income of sole proprietorships and partnerships is taxed as the income of the individual owners; corporate income is subject to corporate taxes.

Regardless of their legal form, all businesses can earn two types of income, ordinary and capital gains. Under current law, these two types of income are treated differently in the taxation of individuals; they are not treated differently for entities subject to corporate taxes. However, frequent amendments are made to the tax code, particularly as economic conditions change and when party control of the legislative and executive branches of government shifts.

ORDINARY INCOME

ordinary income
Income earned through the sale of a firm's goods or services.

The **ordinary income** of a corporation is income earned through the sale of goods or services. Ordinary income in 2012 was taxed subject to the rates depicted in the corporate tax rate schedule in Table 2.1.

Example 2.2 ▶

Webster Manufacturing, Inc., a small manufacturer of kitchen knives, has before-tax earnings of $250,000. The tax on these earnings can be found by using the tax rate schedule in Table 2.1:

$$\text{Total taxes due} = \$22,250 + [0.39 \times (\$250,000 - \$100,000)]$$
$$= \$22,250 + (0.39 \times \$150,000)$$
$$= \$22,250 + \$58,500 = \underline{\$80,750}$$

From a financial point of view, it is important to understand the difference between average and marginal tax rates, the treatment of interest and dividend income, and the effects of tax deductibility.

Marginal versus Average Tax Rates

marginal tax rate
The rate at which *additional income* is taxed.

The **marginal tax rate** represents the rate at which the *next dollar of income* is taxed. In the current corporate tax structure, the marginal tax rate is 15 percent if the firm earns less than $50,000. If a firm earns more than $50,000 but less than $75,000, the marginal tax rate is 25 percent. As a firm's income rises, the marginal tax rate that it faces changes as shown in Table 2.1. In the example above, if Webster Manufacturing's earnings increase to $250,001, the last $1 in income would be taxed at the marginal rate of 39 percent.

TABLE 2.1 Corporate Tax Rate Schedule							
			Tax calculation				
Range of taxable income		**Base tax**	**+**	**(Marginal rate**	**×**	**amount over base bracket)**	
$ 0 to $ 50,000	$	0	+	(15%	×	amount over $	0)
50,000 to 75,000		7,500	+	(25	×	amount over	50,000)
75,000 to 100,000		13,750	+	(34	×	amount over	75,000)
100,000 to 335,000		22,250	+	(39	×	amount over	100,000)
335,000 to 10,000,000		113,900	+	(34	×	amount over	335,000)
10,000,000 to 15,000,000		3,400,000	+	(35	×	amount over	10,000,000)
15,000,000 to 18,333,333		5,150,000	+	(38	×	amount over	15,000,000)
Over 18,333,333		6,416,667	+	(35	×	amount over	18,333,333)

average tax rate
A firm's taxes divided by its taxable income.

The **average tax rate** paid on the firm's ordinary income can be calculated by dividing its taxes by its taxable income. For most firms, the average tax rate does not equal the marginal tax rate because tax rates change with income levels. In the example above, Webster Manufacturing's marginal tax rate is 39 percent, but its average tax rate is 32.3 percent ($80,750 ÷ $250,000). For very large corporations with earnings in the hundreds of millions or even billions of dollars, the average tax rate is very close to the 35 percent marginal rate in the top bracket because most of the firm's income is taxed at that rate.

In most of the business decisions that managers make, *it's the marginal tax rate that really matters*. To keep matters simple, the examples in this text will use a *flat 40 percent tax rate*. That means that *both the average tax rate and the marginal tax rate equal 40 percent*.

Interest and Dividend Income

double taxation
Situation that occurs when after-tax corporate earnings are distributed as cash dividends to stockholders, who then must pay personal taxes on the dividend amount.

In the process of determining taxable income, any *interest received* by the corporation is included as ordinary income. Dividends, on the other hand, are treated differently. This different treatment moderates the effect of **double taxation,** which occurs when the already once-taxed earnings of a corporation are distributed as cash dividends to stockholders, who must pay taxes on dividends up to a maximum rate of 15 percent. Dividends that the firm receives on common and preferred stock held in other corporations are subject to a 70 percent exclusion for tax purposes.[1] The dividend exclusion in effect eliminates most of the potential tax liability from the dividends received by the second and any subsequent corporations.

Tax-Deductible Expenses

In calculating their taxes, corporations are allowed to deduct operating expenses, as well as interest expense. The tax deductibility of these expenses reduces their after-tax cost. The following example illustrates the benefit of tax deductibility.

Example 2.3 ▶

MyFinanceLab Solution Video

Two companies, Debt Co. and No-Debt Co., both expect in the coming year to have earnings before interest and taxes of $200,000. During the year, Debt Co. will have to pay $30,000 in interest. No-Debt Co. has no debt and therefore will have no interest expense. Calculation of the earnings after taxes for these two firms is as follows:

	Debt Co.	No-Debt Co.
Earnings before interest and taxes	$200,000	$200,000
Less: Interest expense	30,000	0
Earnings before taxes	$170,000	$200,000
Less: Taxes (40%)	68,000	80,000
Earnings after taxes	$102,000	$120,000
Difference in earnings after taxes		$18,000

---

1. The 70 percent exclusion applies if the firm receiving dividends owns less than 20 percent of the shares of the firm paying the dividends. The exclusion is 80 percent if the corporation owns between 20 percent and 80 percent of the stock in the corporation paying it dividends; 100 percent of the dividends received are excluded if it owns more than 80 percent of the corporation paying it dividends. For convenience, we are assuming here that the ownership interest in the dividend-paying corporation is less than 20 percent.

Debt Co. had $30,000 more interest expense than No-Debt Co., but Debt Co.'s earnings after taxes are only $18,000 less than those of No-Debt Co. This difference is attributable to Debt Co.'s $30,000 interest expense deduction providing a tax savings of $12,000 ($68,000 for Debt Co. versus $80,000 for No-Debt Co.). This amount can be calculated directly by multiplying the tax rate by the amount of interest expense (0.40 × $30,000 = $12,000). Similarly, the $18,000 *after-tax cost* of the interest expense can be calculated directly by multiplying 1 minus the tax rate by the amount of interest expense [(1 − 0.40) × $30,000 = $18,000].

The tax deductibility of expenses reduces their actual (after-tax) cost to the firm as long as the firm is profitable. If a firm experiences a net loss in a given year, its tax liability is already zero. Even in this case, losses in one year can be used to offset taxes paid on profits in prior years, and in some cases losses can be "carried forward" to offset income and lower taxes in subsequent years. Note that both for accounting and tax purposes *interest is a tax-deductible expense, whereas dividends are not.* Because dividends are not tax deductible, their after-tax cost is equal to the amount of the dividend. Thus, a $30,000 cash dividend has an after-tax cost of $30,000.

CAPITAL GAINS

capital gain
The amount by which the sale price of an asset exceeds the asset's purchase price.

If a firm sells a capital asset (such as stock held as an investment) for more than it paid for the asset, the difference between the sale price and purchase price is called a **capital gain.** For corporations, capital gains are added to ordinary corporate income and taxed at the regular corporate rates.

Example 2.4 ▶

Ross Company, a manufacturer of pharmaceuticals, has pretax operating earnings of $500,000 and has just sold for $150,000 an asset that was purchased 2 years ago for $125,000. Because the asset was sold for more than its initial purchase price, there is a capital gain of $25,000 ($150,000 sale price − $125,000 initial purchase price). The corporation's taxable income will total $525,000 ($500,000 ordinary income plus $25,000 capital gain). Multiplying its taxable income by 40% produces Ross Company's tax liability of $210,000.

→ **REVIEW QUESTIONS**

2–15 Describe the tax treatment of *ordinary income* and that of *capital gains.* What is the difference between the *average tax rate* and the *marginal tax rate?*

2–16 How does the tax treatment of dividend income by the corporation moderate the effects of *double taxation?*

2–17 What benefit results from the tax deductibility of certain corporate expenses?

Summary

THE ROLE OF FINANCIAL INSTITUTIONS AND MARKETS

This chapter described why financial institutions and markets are an integral part of managerial finance. Companies cannot get started or survive without raising capital, and financial institutions and markets give firms access to the money they need to grow. As we have seen in recent years, however, financial markets can be quite turbulent, and when large financial institutions get into trouble, access to capital is reduced and firms throughout the economy suffer as a result. Taxes are an important part of this story as well because the rules governing how business income is taxed shape the incentives of firms to make new investments.

REVIEW OF LEARNING GOALS

LG 1 **Understand the role that financial institutions play in managerial finance.** Financial institutions bring net suppliers of funds and net demanders together to help translate the savings of individuals, businesses, and governments into loans and other types of investments. The net suppliers of funds are generally individuals or households who save more money than they borrow. Businesses and governments are generally net demanders of funds, meaning that they borrow more money than they save.

LG 2 **Contrast the functions of financial institutions and financial markets.** Both financial institutions and financial markets help businesses raise the money that they need to fund new investments for growth. Financial institutions collect the savings of individuals and channel those funds to borrowers such as businesses and governments. Financial markets provide a forum in which savers and borrowers can transact business directly. Businesses and governments issue debt and equity securities directly to the public in the primary market. Subsequent trading of these securities between investors occurs in the secondary market.

LG 3 **Describe the differences between the capital markets and the money markets.** In the money market, savers who want a temporary place to deposit funds where they can earn interest interact with borrowers who have a short-term need for funds. Marketable securities, including Treasury bills, commercial paper, and other instruments, are the primary securities traded in the money market. The Eurocurrency market is the international equivalent of the domestic money market.

In contrast, the capital market is the forum in which savers and borrowers interact on a long-term basis. Firms issue either debt (bonds) or equity (stock) securities in the capital market. Once issued, these securities trade on secondary markets that are either broker markets or dealer markets. An important function of the capital market is to determine the underlying value of the securities issued by businesses. In an efficient market, the price of a security is an unbiased estimate of its true value.

LG 4 **Explain the root causes of the 2008 financial crisis and recession.** The financial crisis was caused by several factors related to investments in real estate. Financial institutions lowered their standards for lending to prospective homeowners, and institutions also invested heavily in mortgage-backed securities. When home prices fell and mortgage delinquencies rose, the value of the mortgage-backed securities held by banks plummeted, causing some banks to fail and many others to restrict the flow of credit to business. That, in turn, contributed to a severe recession in the United States and abroad.

LG 5 **Understand the major regulations and regulatory bodies that affect financial institutions and markets.** The Glass-Steagall Act created the FDIC and imposed a separation between commercial and investment banks. The act was designed to limit the risks that banks could take and to protect depositors. More recently, the Gramm-Leach-Bliley Act essentially repealed the elements of Glass-Steagall pertaining to the separation of commercial and investment banks. After the recent financial crisis, much debate has occurred regarding the proper regulation of large financial institutions. The Dodd-Frank Act was passed in 2010 and contained a host of new regulatory requirements, the effects of which are yet to be determined.

The Securities Act of 1933 and the Securities Exchange Act of 1934 are the major pieces of legislation shaping the regulation of financial markets. The 1933 act focuses on regulating the sale of securities in the primary market, whereas the 1934 act deals with regulations governing transactions in the secondary market. The 1934 act also created the Securities and Exchange Commission, the primary body responsible for enforcing federal securities laws.

LG 6 **Discuss business taxes and their importance in financial decisions.** Corporate income is subject to corporate taxes. Corporate tax rates apply to both ordinary income (after deduction of allowable expenses) and capital gains. The average tax rate paid by a corporation ranges from 15 to 35 percent. Corporate taxpayers can reduce their taxes through certain provisions in the tax code: dividend income exclusions and tax-deductible expenses. A capital gain occurs when an asset is sold for more than its initial purchase price; gains are added to ordinary corporate income and taxed at regular corporate tax rates. (For convenience, we assume a 40 percent marginal tax rate throughout.)

Self-Test Problem (Solution in Appendix)

 ST2–1 **Corporate taxes** Montgomery Enterprises, Inc., had operating earnings of $280,000 for the year just ended. During the year, the firm sold stock that it held in another company for $180,000, which was $30,000 above its original purchase price of $150,000, paid 1 year earlier.

a. What is the amount, if any, of capital gains realized during the year?

b. How much total taxable income did the firm earn during the year?

c. Use the corporate tax rate schedule given in Table 2.1 to calculate the firm's total taxes due.

d. Calculate both the *average tax rate* and the *marginal tax rate* on the basis of your findings.

Warm-Up Exercises

All problems are available in MyFinanceLab.

LG 1   **E2–1**   What does it mean to say that individuals as a group are net suppliers of funds for financial institutions? What do you think the consequences might be in financial markets if individuals consumed more of their incomes and thereby reduced the supply of funds available to financial institutions?

LG 2   **E2–2**   You are the chief financial officer (CFO) of Gaga Enterprises, an edgy fashion design firm. Your firm needs $10 million to expand production. How do you think the process of raising this money will vary if you raise it with the help of a financial institution versus raising it directly in the financial markets?

LG 3   **E2–3**   For what kinds of needs do you think a firm would issue securities in the money market versus the capital market?

LG 4   **E2–4**   Your broker calls to offer you the investment opportunity of a lifetime, the chance to invest in mortgage-backed securities. The broker explains that these securities are entitled to the principal and interest payments received from a pool of residential mortgages. List some of the questions you would ask your broker so as to assess the risk of this investment opportunity.

LG 5   **E2–5**   Over the past 100 years, the level of government regulation of financial institutions and markets has ebbed and flowed or, as some economists might argue, has ebbed and flooded. Although the laws and regulatory agencies created by the government have various defined and not-so-well defined goals, what might you argue is the single biggest benefit of government regulation?

LG 6   **E2–6**   Reston, Inc., has asked your corporation, Pruro, Inc., for financial assistance. As a long-time customer of Reston, your firm has decided to give that assistance. The question you are debating is whether Pruro should take Reston stock with a 5% annual dividend or a promissory note paying 5% annual interest.

Assuming payment is guaranteed and the dollar amounts for annual interest and dividend income are identical, which option will result in greater after-tax income for the first year?

Problems

All problems are available in MyFinanceLab.

LG 6   **P2–1**   **Corporate taxes**   Tantor Supply, Inc., is a small corporation acting as the exclusive distributor of a major line of sporting goods. During 2013, the firm earned $92,500 before taxes.
   a. Calculate the firm's tax liability using the corporate tax rate schedule given in Table 2.1.
   b. How much are Tantor Supply's 2013 after-tax earnings?
   c. What was the firm's *average tax rate,* based on your findings in part a?
   d. What was the firm's *marginal tax rate,* based on your findings in part a?

LG 6 **P2–2** **Average corporate tax rates** Using the corporate tax rate schedule given in Table 2.1, perform the following:

a. Calculate the tax liability, after-tax earnings, and average tax rates for the following levels of corporate earnings before taxes: $10,000; $80,000; $300,000; $500,000; $1.5 million; $10 million; and $20 million.

b. Plot the *average tax rates* (measured on the *y* axis) against the pretax income levels (measured on the *x* axis). What generalization can be made concerning the relationship between these variables?

LG 6 **P2–3** **Marginal corporate tax rates** Using the corporate tax rate schedule given in Table 2.1, perform the following:

a. Find the marginal tax rate for the following levels of corporate earnings before taxes: $15,000; $60,000; $90,000; $200,000; $400,000; $1 million; and $20 million.

b. Plot the *marginal tax rates* (measured on the *y* axis) against the pretax income levels (measured on the *x* axis). Explain the relationship between these variables.

LG 6 **P2–4** **Interest versus dividend income** During the year just ended, Shering Distributors, Inc., had pretax earnings from operations of $490,000. In addition, during the year it received $20,000 in income from interest on bonds it held in Zig Manufacturing and received $20,000 in income from dividends on its 5% common stock holding in Tank Industries, Inc. Shering is in the 40% tax bracket and is eligible for a 70% dividend exclusion on its Tank Industries stock.

a. Calculate the firm's tax on its operating earnings only.

b. Find the tax and the after-tax amount attributable to the interest income from Zig Manufacturing bonds.

c. Find the tax and the after-tax amount attributable to the dividend income from the Tank Industries, Inc., common stock.

d. Compare, contrast, and discuss the after-tax amounts resulting from the interest income and dividend income calculated in parts **b** and **c**.

e. What is the firm's total tax liability for the year?

LG 6 **P2–5** **Interest versus dividend expense** Michaels Corporation expects earnings before interest and taxes to be $50,000 for the current period. Assuming an ordinary tax rate of 35%, compute the firm's earnings after taxes and earnings available for common stockholders (earnings after taxes and preferred stock dividends, if any) under the following conditions:

a. The firm pays $12,000 in interest.

b. The firm pays $12,000 in preferred stock dividends.

LG 6 **P2–6** **Capital gains taxes** Perkins Manufacturing is considering the sale of two nondepreciable assets, X and Y. Asset X was purchased for $2,000 and will be sold today for $2,250. Asset Y was purchased for $30,000 and will be sold today for $35,000. The firm is subject to a 40% tax rate on capital gains.

a. Calculate the amount of capital gain, if any, realized on each of the assets.

b. Calculate the tax on the sale of each asset.

LG 6 **P2–7** **Capital gains taxes** As part of its operations, Ferguson's Plumbing has bought and sold several nondepreciable capital assets. The purchase and sale prices for these assets are contained in the following table. Assuming that Fergurson's pays a 40% capital gains tax, complete the table by filling in the last two columns.

Asset	Sale price	Purchase price	Capital gain	Tax
A	$ 3,400	$ 3,000		
B	12,000	12,000		
C	80,000	62,000		
D	45,000	41,000		
E	18,000	16,500		

 P2–8   **ETHICS PROBLEM** The Securities Exchange Act of 1934 limits, but does not prohibit, corporate insiders from trading in their own firm's shares. What ethical issues might arise when a corporate insider wants to buy or sell shares in the firm where he or she works?

Spreadsheet Exercise

 Hemingway Corporation is considering expanding its operations to boost its income, but before making a final decision, it has asked you to calculate the corporate tax consequences of its decision. Currently, Hemingway generates before-tax yearly income of $200,000 and has no debt outstanding. Expanding operations would allow Hemingway to increase before-tax yearly income to $350,000. Hemingway can use either cash reserves or debt to finance its expansion. If Hemingway uses debt, it will have yearly interest expense of $70,000.

TO DO

Create a spreadsheet to conduct a *tax analysis* for Hemingway Corporation and determine the following:

a. What is Hemingway's current annual corporate tax liability?
b. What is Hemingway's current average tax rate?
c. If Hemingway finances its expansion using cash reserves, what will be its new corporate tax liability and average tax rate?
d. If Hemingway finances its expansion using debt, what will be its new corporate tax liability and average tax rate?
e. What would you recommend that the firm do? Why?

MyFinanceLab Visit **www.myfinancelab.com** for **Chapter Case: *The Pros and Cons of Being Publicly Listed,*** Group Exercises, and numerous online resources.

Part 2 > Financial Tools

In this part, you will learn about some of the basic analytical tools that financial managers use almost every day. Chapter 3 reviews the main financial statements that are the primary means by which firms communicate with investors, analysts, and the rest of the business community. It also illustrates some simple tools that managers use to analyze the information contained in financial statements to identify and diagnose financial problems.

Firms create financial statements using the accrual principles of accounting; in finance, though, it is cash flow that really matters. Chapter 4 shows how to use financial statements to determine how much cash flow a firm is generating and how it is spending that cash flow. It also explains how firms develop short-term and long-term financial plans.

Managers have to decide whether the up-front costs of investments are justified by the subsequent cash that those investments are likely to produce. Chapter 5 illustrates techniques that firms use to evaluate these sorts of trade-offs.

3 Financial Statements and Ratio Analysis

Learning Goals

LG 1 Review the contents of the stockholders' report and the procedures for consolidating international financial statements.

LG 2 Understand who uses financial ratios and how.

LG 3 Use ratios to analyze a firm's liquidity and activity.

LG 4 Discuss the relationship between debt and financial leverage and the ratios used to analyze a firm's debt.

LG 5 Use ratios to analyze a firm's profitability and its market value.

LG 6 Use a summary of financial ratios and the DuPont system of analysis to perform a complete ratio analysis.

Why This Chapter Matters to You

In your *professional* life

ACCOUNTING You need to understand the stockholders' report and preparation of the four key financial statements, how firms consolidate international financial statements, and how to calculate and interpret financial ratios for decision making.

INFORMATION SYSTEMS You need to understand what data are included in the firm's financial statements so as to design systems that will supply such data to those who prepare the statements and to those in the firm who use the data for ratio calculations.

MANAGEMENT You need to understand what parties are interested in the stockholders' report and why, how the financial statements will be analyzed by those both inside and outside the firm to assess various aspects of performance, the caution that should be exercised in using financial ratio analysis, and how the financial statements affect the value of the firm.

MARKETING You need to understand the effects your decisions will have on the financial statements, particularly the income statement and the statement of cash flows, and how analysis of ratios, especially those involving sales figures, will affect the firm's decisions about levels of inventory, credit policies, and pricing decisions.

OPERATIONS You need to understand how the costs of operations are reflected in the firm's financial statements and how analysis of ratios—particularly those involving assets, cost of goods sold, or inventory—may affect requests for new equipment or facilities.

In your *personal* life

A routine step in personal financial planning is to prepare and analyze personal financial statements so that you can monitor progress toward your financial goals. Also, to build and monitor your investment portfolio, you need to understand and analyze corporate financial statements.

LG ① ## 3.1 The Stockholders' Report

generally accepted accounting principles (GAAP)
The practice and procedure guidelines used to prepare and maintain financial records and reports; authorized by the Financial Accounting Standards Board (FASB).

Financial Accounting Standards Board (FASB)
The accounting profession's rule-setting body, which authorizes generally accepted accounting principles (GAAP).

Public Company Accounting Oversight Board (PCAOB)
A not-for-profit corporation established by the Sarbanes-Oxley Act of 2002 to protect the interests of investors and further the public interest in the preparation of informative, fair, and independent audit reports.

stockholders' report
Annual report that publicly owned corporations must provide to stockholders; it summarizes and documents the firm's financial activities during the past year.

letter to stockholders
Typically, the first element of the annual stockholders' report and the primary communication from management.

income statement
Provides a financial summary of the firm's operating results during a specified period.

Every corporation has many and varied uses for the standardized records and reports of its financial activities. Periodically, reports must be prepared for regulators, creditors (lenders), owners, and management. The guidelines used to prepare and maintain financial records and reports are known as **generally accepted accounting principles (GAAP)**. These accounting practices and procedures are authorized by the accounting profession's rule-setting body, the **Financial Accounting Standards Board (FASB)**.

In addition, the *Sarbanes-Oxley Act of 2002,* enacted in an effort to eliminate the many disclosure and conflict-of-interest problems of corporations, established the **Public Company Accounting Oversight Board (PCAOB)**, a not-for-profit corporation that oversees auditors of public corporations. The PCAOB is charged with protecting the interests of investors and furthering the public interest in the preparation of informative, fair, and independent audit reports. The expectation is that it will instill confidence in investors with regard to the accuracy of the audited financial statements of public companies.

Publicly owned corporations with more than $5 million in assets and 500 or more stockholders are required by the U.S. Securities and Exchange Commission (SEC)—the federal regulatory body that governs the sale and listing of securities—to provide their stockholders with an annual **stockholders' report.** The stockholders' report summarizes and documents the firm's financial activities during the past year. It begins with a letter to the stockholders from the firm's chief executive officer or chairman of the board.

THE LETTER TO STOCKHOLDERS

The **letter to stockholders** is the primary communication from management. It describes the events that are considered to have had the greatest effect on the firm during the year. It also typically discusses management philosophy, corporate governance issues, strategies, and actions as well as plans for the coming year.

THE FOUR KEY FINANCIAL STATEMENTS

The four key financial statements required by the SEC for reporting to shareholders are (1) the income statement, (2) the balance sheet, (3) the statement of stockholders' equity, and (4) the statement of cash flows. The financial statements from the 2015 stockholders' report of Bartlett Company, a manufacturer of metal fasteners, are presented and briefly discussed in this section. Most likely, you have studied these four financial statements in an accounting course, so the purpose of looking at them here is to refresh your memory of the basics rather than provide an exhaustive review.

Income Statement

The **income statement** provides a financial summary of the firm's operating results during a specified period. Most common are income statements covering a 1-year period ending at a specified date, ordinarily December 31 of the calendar year.

focus on **ETHICS**

Taking Earnings Reports at Face Value

in practice   Near the end of each quarter, Wall Street's much anticipated "earnings season" arrives. During earnings season, many companies unveil their quarterly performance. Interest is high, as media outlets rush to report the latest announcements, analysts slice and dice the numbers, and investors buy and sell based on the news. The most anticipated performance metric for most companies is earnings per share (EPS), which is typically compared to the estimates of the analysts who cover a firm. Firms that beat analyst estimates often see their share prices jump, whereas those that miss estimates, by even a small amount, tend to suffer price declines.

Many investors are aware of the pitfalls of judging firms based on reported earnings. Specifically, the complexity of financial reports makes it easy for managers to mislead investors. Sometimes, the methods used to mislead investors are within the rules, albeit not the spirit, of acceptable accounting practices. Other times, firms break the rules to make their numbers. The practice of manipulating earnings to mislead investors is known as earnings management.

Some firms are notorious for consistently beating analysts' estimates. For example, for one 10-year period (1995–2004), General Electric Co. (GE) beat Wall Street earnings estimates every quarter, often by only a penny or two per share. However, in 2009, the Securities and Exchange Commission (SEC) fined GE $50 million for improper accounting practices, including recording sales that had not yet occurred. When GE went back to correct the problems identified by the SEC, it found that net earnings between 2001 and 2007 were a total of $280 million lower than originally reported.

In one of his famous letters to the shareholders of Berskshire Hathaway, Warren Buffett offers three bits of advice regarding financial reporting.[a] First, he warns that weak visible accounting practices are typically a sign of bigger problems. Second, he suggests that, when you can't understand management, the reason is probably that management doesn't want you to understand them. Third, he warns that investors should be suspicious of projections because earnings and growth do not typically progress in an orderly fashion. Finally, Buffett notes that "Managers that always promise to 'make the numbers' will at some point be tempted to *make up* the numbers."

▶ *Why might financial managers be tempted to manage earnings?*

▶ *Is it unethical for managers to manage earnings if they disclose their activities to investors?*

[a] www.berkshirehathaway.com/letters/2002pdf.pdf

Many large firms, however, operate on a 12-month financial cycle, or *fiscal year,* that ends at a time other than December 31. In addition, monthly income statements are typically prepared for use by management, and quarterly statements must be made available to the stockholders of publicly owned corporations.

Table 3.1 presents Bartlett Company's income statements for the years ended December 31, 2015 and 2014. The 2015 statement begins with *sales revenue*—the total dollar amount of sales during the period—from which the *cost of goods sold* is deducted. The resulting *gross profit* of $986,000 represents the amount remaining to satisfy operating, financial, and tax costs. Next, *operating expenses*—which include selling expense, general and administrative expense, lease expense, and depreciation expense—are deducted from gross profits. The resulting *operating profits* of $418,000 represent the profits earned from producing and selling products; this amount does not consider financial and tax costs. (Operating profit is often called *earnings before interest and taxes,* or *EBIT.*) Next, the financial cost—*interest expense*—is subtracted from operating profits to find *net profits* (or *earnings*) *before taxes.* After subtracting $93,000 in 2015 interest, Bartlett Company had $325,000 of net profits before taxes.

TABLE 3.1	Bartlett Company Income Statements ($000)	
	For the years ended December 31	
	2015	**2014**
Sales revenue	$3,074	$2,567
Less: Cost of goods sold	2,088	1,711
Gross profits	$ 986	$ 856
Less: Operating expenses		
Selling expense	$ 100	$ 108
General and administrative expenses	194	187
Lease expense[a]	35	35
Depreciation expense	239	223
Total operating expense	$ 568	$ 553
Operating profits	$ 418	$ 303
Less: Interest expense	93	91
Net profits before taxes	$ 325	$ 212
Less: Taxes	94	64
Net profits after taxes	$ 231	$ 148
Less: Preferred stock dividends	10	10
Earnings available for common stockholders	$ 221	$ 138
Earnings per share (EPS)[b]	$2.90	$1.81
Dividend per share (DPS)[c]	$1.29	$0.75

[a]Lease expense is shown here as a separate item rather than being included as part of interest expense as specified by the FASB for financial reporting purposes. The approach used here is consistent with tax reporting rather than financial reporting procedures.

[b]Calculated by dividing the earnings available for common stockholders by the number of shares of common stock outstanding: 76,262 in 2015 and 76,244 in 2014. Earnings per share in 2015: $221,000 ÷ 76,262 = $2.90 ; in 2014: $138,000 ÷ 76,244 = $1.81.

[c]Calculated by dividing the dollar amount of dividends paid to common stockholders by the number of shares of common stock outstanding. Dividends per share in 2015: $98,000 ÷ 76,262 = $1.29; in 2014: $57,183 ÷ 76,244 = $0.75.

Next, taxes are calculated at the appropriate tax rates and deducted to determine *net profits* (or *earnings*) *after taxes,* also referred to as *net income.* Bartlett Company's net profits after taxes for 2015 were $231,000. Any preferred stock dividends must be subtracted from net profits after taxes to arrive at *earnings available for common stockholders,* which is the amount earned by the firm on behalf of the common stockholders during the period.

Dividing earnings available for common stockholders by the number of shares of common stock outstanding results in *earnings per share (EPS).* EPS represent the number of dollars earned during the period on behalf of each outstanding share of common stock. In 2015, Bartlett Company earned $221,000 for its common stockholders, which represents $2.90 for each outstanding share. The actual cash **dividend per share (DPS)**, which is the dollar amount of cash distributed during the period on behalf of each outstanding share of common stock, paid in 2015 was $1.29.

dividend per share (DPS)
The dollar amount of cash distributed during the period on behalf of each outstanding share of common stock.

Personal Finance Example 3.1 ▶ Jan and Jon Smith, a mid-30s married couple with no children, prepared a personal income and expense statement, which is similar to a corporate income statement. A condensed version of their income and expense statement follows.

Jan and Jon Smith's Income and Expense Statement for the Year Ended December 31, 2015	
Income	
Salaries	$72,725
Interest received	195
Dividends received	120
(1) Total income	73,040
Expenses	
Mortgage payments	$16,864
Auto loan payments	2,520
Utilities	2,470
Home repairs and maintenance	1,050
Food	5,825
Car expense	2,265
Health care and insurance	1,505
Clothes, shoes, accessories	1,700
Insurance	1,380
Taxes	16,430
Appliance and furniture payments	1,250
Recreation and entertainment	4,630
Tuition and books for Jan	1,400
Personal care and other items	2,415
(2) Total expenses	$61,704
(3) Cash surplus (or deficit) [(1) − (2)]	$11,336

During the year, the Smiths had total income of $73,040 and total expenses of $61,704, which left them with a cash surplus of $11,336. They can use the surplus to increase their savings and investments.

Balance Sheet

The **balance sheet** presents a summary statement of the firm's financial position at a given time. The statement balances the firm's *assets* (what it owns) against its financing, which can be either *debt* (what it owes) or *equity* (what was provided by owners). Bartlett Company's balance sheets as of December 31 of 2015 and 2014 are presented in Table 3.2. They show a variety of asset, liability (debt), and equity accounts.

An important distinction is made between short-term and long-term assets and liabilities. The **current assets** and **current liabilities** are *short-term* assets a

balance sheet
Summary statement of the firm's financial position at a given point in time.

current assets
Short-term assets, expected to be converted into cash within 1 year or less.

current liabilities
Short-term liabilities, expected to be paid within 1 year or less.

TABLE 3.2	Bartlett Company Balance Sheets ($000)

	December 31	
Assets	2015	2014
Cash	$ 363	$ 288
Marketable securities	68	51
Accounts receivable	503	365
Inventories	289	300
Total current assets	$1,223	$1,004
Land and buildings	$2,072	$1,903
Machinery and equipment	1,866	1,693
Furniture and fixtures	358	316
Vehicles	275	314
Other (includes financial leases)	98	96
Total gross fixed assets (at cost)	$4,669	$4,322
Less: Accumulated depreciation	2,295	2,056
Net fixed assets	$2,374	$2,266
Total assets	$3,597	$3,270
Liabilities and Stockholders' Equity		
Accounts payable	$ 382	$ 270
Notes payable	79	99
Accruals	159	114
Total current liabilities	$ 620	$ 483
Long-term debt (includes financial leases)	1,023	967
Total liabilities	$1,643	$1,450
Preferred stock: cumulative 5%, $100 par, 2,000 shares authorized and issued	$ 200	$ 200
Common stock: $2.50 par, 100,000 shares authorized, shares issued and outstanding in 2015: 76,262; in 2014: 76,244	191	190
Paid-in capital in excess of par on common stock	428	418
Retained earnings	1,135	1,012
Total stockholders' equity	$1,954	$1,820
Total liabilities and stockholders' equity	$3,597	$3,270

liabilities, which means that they are expected to be converted into cash (current assets) or paid (current liabilities) within 1 year or less. All other assets and liabilities, along with stockholders' equity, which is assumed to have an infinite life, are considered *long-term,* or *fixed,* because they are expected to remain on the firm's books for more than 1 year.

As is customary, the assets are listed from the most liquid—*cash*—down to the least liquid. *Marketable securities* are very liquid short-term investments, such as U.S. Treasury bills or certificates of deposit, held by the firm. Because they are highly liquid, marketable securities are viewed as a form of cash ("near cash"). *Accounts receivable* represent the total monies owed the firm by its customers on credit sales. *Inventories* include raw materials, work in process (partially finished goods), and finished goods held by the firm. The entry for *gross fixed assets* is the original cost of all fixed (long-term) assets owned by the firm.[1] *Net fixed assets* represent the difference between gross fixed assets and *accumulated depreciation,* the total expense recorded for the depreciation of fixed assets. The net value of fixed assets is called their *book value.*

Like assets, the liabilities and equity accounts are listed from short-term to long-term. Current liabilities include *accounts payable,* amounts owed for credit purchases by the firm; *notes payable,* outstanding short-term loans, typically from commercial banks; and *accruals,* amounts owed for services for which a bill may not or will not be received. Examples of accruals include taxes due the government and wages due employees. **Long-term debt** represents debt for which payment is not due in the current year. *Stockholders' equity* represents the owners' claims on the firm. The *preferred stock* entry shows the historical proceeds from the sale of preferred stock ($200,000 for Bartlett Company).

Next, the amount paid by the original purchasers of common stock is shown by two entries, common stock and paid-in capital in excess of par on common stock. The *common stock* entry is the *par value* of common stock. **Paid-in capital in excess of par** represents the amount of proceeds in excess of the par value received from the original sale of common stock. The sum of the common stock and paid-in capital accounts divided by the number of shares outstanding represents the original price per share received by the firm on a single issue of common stock. Bartlett Company therefore received about $8.12 per share [($191,000 par + $428,000 paid-in capital in excess of par) ÷ 76,262 shares] from the sale of its common stock.

Finally, **retained earnings** represent the cumulative total of all earnings, net of dividends, that have been retained and reinvested in the firm since its inception. It is important to recognize that retained earnings are not cash but rather have been used to finance the firm's assets.

Bartlett Company's balance sheets in Table 3.2 show that the firm's total assets increased from $3,270,000 in 2014 to $3,597,000 in 2015. The $327,000 increase was due primarily to the $219,000 increase in current assets. The asset increase, in turn, appears to have been financed primarily by

long-term debt
Debt for which payment is not due in the current year.

paid-in capital in excess of par
The amount of proceeds in excess of the par value received from the original sale of common stock.

retained earnings
The cumulative total of all earnings, net of dividends, that have been retained and reinvested in the firm since its inception.

---

1. For convenience, the term *fixed assets* is used throughout this text to refer to what, in a strict accounting sense, is captioned "property, plant, and equipment." This simplification of terminology permits certain financial concepts to be more easily developed.

an increase of $193,000 in total liabilities. Better insight into these changes can be derived from the statement of cash flows, which we will discuss shortly.

Personal Finance Example 3.2 ▶	The following personal balance sheet for Jan and Jon Smith—the couple introduced earlier, who are married, in their mid-30s, and have no children—is similar to a corporate balance sheet.

Jan and Jon Smith's Balance Sheet: December 31, 2015			
Assets		**Liabilities and Net Worth**	
Cash on hand	$ 90	Credit card balances	$ 665
Checking accounts	575	Utility bills	120
Savings accounts	760	Medical bills	75
Money market funds	800	Other current liabilities	45
Total liquid assets	$ 2,225	Total current liabilities	$ 905
Stocks and bonds	$ 2,250	Real estate mortgage	$ 92,000
Mutual funds	1,500	Auto loans	4,250
Retirement funds, IRA	2,000	Education loan	3,800
Total investments	$ 5,750	Personal loan	4,000
Real estate	$120,000	Furniture loan	800
Cars	14,000	Total long-term liabilities	$104,850
Household furnishings	3,700	Total liabilities	$105,755
Jewelry and artwork	1,500	Net worth (N/W)	41,420
Total personal property	$139,200	Total liabilities	
Total assets	$147,175	and net worth	$147,175

The Smiths have total assets of $147,175 and total liabilities of $105,755. Personal net worth (N/W) is a "plug figure"—the difference between total assets and total liabilities—which in the case of Jan and Jon Smith is $41,420.

statement of stockholders' equity
Shows all equity account transactions that occurred during a given year.

statement of retained earnings
Reconciles the net income earned during a given year, and any cash dividends paid, with the change in retained earnings between the start and the end of that year. An abbreviated form of the *statement of stockholders' equity.*

Statement of Retained Earnings

The *statement of retained earnings* is an abbreviated form of the statement of stockholders' equity. Unlike the **statement of stockholders' equity,** which shows all equity account transactions that occurred during a given year, the **statement of retained earnings** reconciles the net income earned during a given year, and any cash dividends paid, with the change in retained earnings between the start and the end of that year. Table 3.3 presents this statement for Bartlett Company for the year ended December 31, 2015. The statement shows that the company began the year with $1,012,000 in retained earnings and had net profits after taxes of $231,000, from which it paid a total of $108,000 in dividends, resulting in year-end retained earnings of $1,135,000. Thus, the net increase for Bartlett Company was $123,000 ($231,000 net profits after taxes minus $108,000 in dividends) during 2015.

TABLE 3.3	Bartlett Company Statement of Retained Earnings ($000) for the Year Ended December 31, 2015
Retained earnings balance (January 1, 2015)	$1,012
Plus: Net profits after taxes (for 2015)	231
Less: Cash dividends (paid during 2015)	
Preferred stock	10
Common stock	98
Total dividends paid	$ 108
Retained earnings balance (December 31, 2015)	$1,135

Statement of Cash Flows

statement of cash flows
Provides a summary of the firm's operating, investment, and financing cash flows and reconciles them with changes in its cash and marketable securities during the period.

The **statement of cash flows** is a summary of the cash flows over the period of concern. The statement provides insight into the firm's operating, investment, and financing cash flows and reconciles them with changes in its cash and marketable securities during the period. Bartlett Company's statement of cash flows for the year ended December 31, 2015, is presented in Table 3.4. Further insight into this statement is included in the discussion of cash flow in Chapter 4.

TABLE 3.4	Bartlett Company Statement of Cash Flows ($000) for the Year Ended December 31, 2015
Cash Flow from Operating Activities	
Net profits after taxes	$ 231
Depreciation	239
Increase in accounts receivable	(138)[a]
Decrease in inventories	11
Increase in accounts payable	112
Increase in accruals	45
Cash provided by operating activities	$ 500
Cash Flow from Investment Activities	
Increase in gross fixed assets	(347)
Change in equity investments in other firms	0
Cash provided by investment activities	($ 347)
Cash Flow from Financing Activities	
Decrease in notes payable	(20)
Increase in long-term debts	56
Changes in stockholders' equity[b]	11
Dividends paid	(108)
Cash provided by financing activities	($ 61)
Net increase in cash and marketable securities	$ 92

[a]As is customary, parentheses are used to denote a negative number, which in this case is a cash outflow.

[b]Retained earnings are excluded here because their change is actually reflected in the combination of the "net profits after taxes" and "dividends paid" entries.

NOTES TO THE FINANCIAL STATEMENTS

notes to the financial statements
Explanatory notes keyed to relevant accounts in the statements; they provide detailed information on the accounting policies, procedures, calculations, and transactions underlying entries in the financial statements.

Included with published financial statements are explanatory notes keyed to the relevant accounts in the statements. These **notes to the financial statements** provide detailed information on the accounting policies, procedures, calculations, and transactions underlying entries in the financial statements. Common issues addressed by these notes include revenue recognition, income taxes, breakdowns of fixed asset accounts, debt and lease terms, and contingencies. Since passage of Sarbanes-Oxley, notes to the financial statements have also included some details about compliance with that law. Professional securities analysts use the data in the statements and notes to develop estimates of the value of securities that the firm issues, and these estimates influence the actions of investors and therefore the firm's share value.

CONSOLIDATING INTERNATIONAL FINANCIAL STATEMENTS

Financial Accounting Standards Board (FASB) Standard No. 52
Mandates that U.S.–based companies translate their foreign-currency-denominated assets and liabilities into U.S. dollars, for consolidation with the parent company's financial statements. This process is done by using the *current rate (translation) method.*

current rate (translation) method
Technique used by U.S.–based companies to translate their foreign-currency-denominated assets and liabilities into U.S. dollars, for consolidation with the parent company's financial statements, using the year-end (current) exchange rate.

So far, we've discussed financial statements involving only one currency, the U.S. dollar. The issue of how to consolidate a company's foreign and domestic financial statements has bedeviled the accounting profession for many years. The current policy is described in **Financial Accounting Standards Board (FASB) Standard No. 52**, which mandates that U.S.–based companies translate their foreign-currency-denominated assets and liabilities into U.S. dollars for consolidation with the parent company's financial statements. This process is done by using a technique called the **current rate (translation) method,** under which all a U.S. parent company's foreign-currency-denominated assets and liabilities are converted into dollar values using the exchange rate prevailing at the fiscal year ending date (the current rate). Income statement items are treated similarly. Equity accounts, on the other hand, are translated into dollars by using the exchange rate that prevailed when the parent's equity investment was made (the historical rate). Retained earnings are adjusted to reflect each year's operating profits or losses.

→ **REVIEW QUESTIONS**

3–1 What roles do GAAP, the FASB, and the PCAOB play in the financial reporting activities of public companies?

3–2 Describe the purpose of each of the four major financial statements.

3–3 Why are the notes to the financial statements important to professional securities analysts?

3–4 How is the *current rate (translation) method* used to consolidate a firm's foreign and domestic financial statements?

 ## 3.2 Using Financial Ratios

The information contained in the four basic financial statements is of major significance to a variety of interested parties who regularly need to have relative measures of the company's performance. *Relative* is the key word here, because the analysis of financial statements is based on the use of *ratios* or *relative values.*

ratio analysis
Involves methods of calculating and interpreting financial ratios to analyze and monitor the firm's performance.

Ratio analysis involves methods of calculating and interpreting financial ratios to analyze and monitor the firm's performance. The basic inputs to ratio analysis are the firm's income statement and balance sheet.

INTERESTED PARTIES

Ratio analysis of a firm's financial statements is of interest to shareholders, creditors, and the firm's own management. Both current and prospective shareholders are interested in the firm's current and future level of risk and return, which directly affect share price. The firm's creditors are interested primarily in the short-term liquidity of the company and its ability to make interest and principal payments. A secondary concern of creditors is the firm's profitability; they want assurance that the business is healthy. Management, like stockholders, is concerned with all aspects of the firm's financial situation, and it attempts to produce financial ratios that will be considered favorable by both owners and creditors. In addition, management uses ratios to monitor the firm's performance from period to period.

TYPES OF RATIO COMPARISONS

Ratio analysis is not merely the calculation of a given ratio. More important is the *interpretation* of the ratio value. A meaningful basis for comparison is needed to answer such questions as "Is it too high or too low?" and "Is it good or bad?" Both cross-sectional and time-series ratio comparisons can be made.

Cross-Sectional Analysis

cross-sectional analysis
Comparison of different firms' financial ratios at the same point in time; involves comparing the firm's ratios with those of other firms in its industry or with industry averages.

benchmarking
A type of *cross-sectional analysis* in which the firm's ratio values are compared with those of a key competitor or with a group of competitors that it wishes to emulate.

Cross-sectional analysis involves the comparison of different firms' financial ratios at the same point in time. Analysts are often interested in how well a firm has performed in relation to other firms in its industry. Frequently, a firm will compare its ratio values with those of a key competitor or with a group of competitors that it wishes to emulate. This type of cross-sectional analysis, called **benchmarking,** has become very popular.

Comparison to industry averages is also popular. These figures can be found in the *Almanac of Business and Industrial Financial Ratios, Dun & Bradstreet's Industry Norms and Key Business Ratios, RMA Annual Statement Studies, Value Line,* and industry sources. It is also possible to derive financial ratios for yourself using financial information reported in financial databases, such as Compustat. Table 3.5 illustrates a brief cross-sectional ratio analysis by comparing several ratios for pairs of firms that compete with each other as well as for the industry median value.

Analysts have to be very careful when drawing conclusions from ratio comparisons. It's tempting to assume that if one ratio for a particular firm is above the industry norm, it is a sign that the firm is performing well, at least along the dimension measured by that ratio. However, ratios may be above or below the industry norm for both positive and negative reasons, and it is necessary to determine why a firm's performance differs from its industry peers. *Thus, ratio analysis on its own is probably most useful in highlighting areas for further investigation.*

TABLE 3.5	Financial Ratios for Select Firms and Their Industry Median Values								
	Current ratio	Quick ratio	Inventory turnover	Average collection period (days)	Total asset turnover	Debt ratio	Net profit margin (%)	Return on total assets (%)	Return on common equity (%)
Dell	1.3	1.2	40.5	58.9	1.6	0.8	2.7	4.3	25.4
Hewlett-Packard	1.2	1.1	13.8	80.6	1.0	0.6	6.7	6.7	18.9
Computers	2.5	2.1	5.8	61.3	0.9	0.4	−3.1	−2.2	−2.6
Home Depot	1.3	0.4	4.3	5.3	1.6	0.5	4.0	6.5	13.7
Lowe's	1.3	0.2	3.7	0.0	1.4	0.4	3.7	5.4	9.3
Building materials	2.8	0.8	3.7	5.3	1.6	0.3	4.0	6.5	13.7
Kroger	1.0	0.3	12.0	4.3	3.3	0.8	0.1	0.3	1.4
Whole Foods Market	1.3	1.0	25.6	7.0	3.6	0.4	2.3	8.0	14.5
Grocery stores	1.3	0.7	11.1	7.5	2.4	0.6	2.1	3.1	9.8
Sears	1.3	0.3	3.7	5.4	1.8	0.6	0.5	0.9	2.6
Walmart	0.9	0.3	9.0	3.7	2.4	0.6	3.5	8.4	20.3
Merchandise stores	1.7	0.6	4.1	3.7	2.3	0.5	1.5	4.9	10.8

The data used to calculate these ratios are drawn from the Compustat North American database.

Example 3.3 ▶

MyFinanceLab Solution Video

In early 2016, Mary Boyle, the chief financial analyst at Caldwell Manufacturing, a producer of heat exchangers, gathered data on the firm's financial performance during 2015, the year just ended. She calculated a variety of ratios and obtained industry averages. She was especially interested in inventory turnover, which reflects the speed with which the firm moves its inventory from raw materials through production into finished goods and to the customer as a completed sale. Generally, higher values of this ratio are preferred because they indicate a quicker turnover of inventory and more efficient inventory management. Caldwell Manufacturing's calculated inventory turnover for 2015 and the industry average inventory turnover were as follows:

	Inventory Turnover, 2015
Caldwell Manufacturing	14.8
Industry average	9.7

Mary's initial reaction to these data was that the firm had managed its inventory significantly *better than* the average firm in the industry. The turnover was nearly 53% faster than the industry average. On reflection, however, she realized that a very high inventory turnover could be a sign that the firm is not holding enough inventories. The consequence of low inventory could be excessive stockouts (insufficient inventory to meet customer needs). Discussions with people in the manufacturing and marketing departments did, in fact, uncover such a problem: Inventories during the year were extremely low, resulting in numerous production delays that hindered the firm's ability to meet demand and resulted in disgruntled customers and lost sales. A ratio that initially appeared to reflect extremely efficient inventory management was actually the symptom of a major problem.

Time-Series Analysis

time-series analysis
Evaluation of the firm's financial performance over time using financial ratio analysis.

Time-series analysis evaluates performance over time. Comparison of current to past performance, using ratios, enables analysts to assess the firm's progress. Developing trends can be seen by using multiyear comparisons. Any significant year-to-year changes may be symptomatic of a problem, especially if the same trend is not an industry-wide phenomenon.

Combined Analysis

The most informative approach to ratio analysis combines cross-sectional and time-series analyses. A combined view makes it possible to assess the trend in the behavior of the ratio in relation to the trend for the industry. Figure 3.1 depicts this type of approach using the average collection period ratio of Bartlett Company over the years 2012–2015. This ratio reflects the average amount of time (in days) it takes the firm to collect bills, and lower values of this ratio generally are preferred. The figure quickly discloses that (1) Bartlett's effectiveness in collecting its receivables is poor in comparison to the industry, and (2) Bartlett's trend is toward longer collection periods. Clearly, Bartlett needs to shorten its collection period.

CAUTIONS ABOUT USING RATIO ANALYSIS

Before discussing specific ratios, we should consider the following cautions about their use:

1. Ratios that reveal large deviations from the norm merely indicate *the possibility* of a problem. Additional analysis is typically needed to determine whether there is a problem and to isolate the *causes* of the problem.

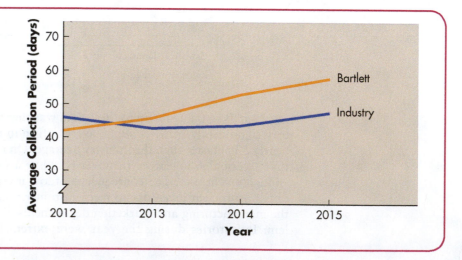

FIGURE 3.1

Combined Analysis
Combined cross-sectional and time-series view of Bartlett Company's average collection period, 2012–2015

2. A single ratio does not generally provide sufficient information from which to judge the *overall* performance of the firm. However, if an analysis is concerned only with certain *specific* aspects of a firm's financial position, one or two ratios may suffice.

3. The ratios being compared should be calculated using financial statements dated at the same point in time during the year. If they are not, the effects of *seasonality* may produce erroneous conclusions and decisions.

4. It is preferable to use *audited financial statements* for ratio analysis. If they have not been audited, the data in them may not reflect the firm's true financial condition.

5. The financial data being compared should have been developed in the same way. The use of differing accounting treatments—especially relative to inventory and depreciation—can distort the results of ratio comparisons, regardless of whether cross-sectional or time-series analysis is used.

6. Results can be distorted by *inflation,* which can cause the book values of inventory and depreciable assets to differ greatly from their replacement values. Additionally, inventory costs and depreciation write-offs can differ from their true values, thereby distorting profits. Without adjustment, inflation tends to cause older firms (older assets) to appear more efficient and profitable than newer firms (newer assets). Clearly, in using ratios, you must be careful when comparing older with newer firms or comparing a firm to itself over a long period of time.

CATEGORIES OF FINANCIAL RATIOS

Financial ratios can be divided for convenience into five general categories: liquidity, activity, debt, profitability, and market ratios. Liquidity, activity, and debt ratios primarily measure risk. Profitability ratios measure return. Market ratios capture both risk and return.

As a rule, the inputs necessary for an effective financial analysis include, at a minimum, the income statement and the balance sheet. We will use the 2015 and 2014 income statements and balance sheets for Bartlett Company, presented earlier in Tables 3.1 and 3.2, to demonstrate ratio calculations. Note, however, that the ratios presented in the remainder of this chapter can be applied to almost any company. Of course, many companies in different industries use ratios that focus on aspects peculiar to their industry.

→ REVIEW QUESTIONS

3–5 With regard to financial ratio analysis, how do the viewpoints held by the firm's present and prospective shareholders, creditors, and management differ?

3–6 What is the difference between *cross-sectional* and *time-series* ratio analysis? What is *benchmarking*?

3–7 To what types of deviations from the norm should the analyst pay primary attention when performing cross-sectional ratio analysis? Why?

3–8 Why is it preferable to compare ratios calculated using financial statements that are dated at the same point in time during the year?

LG ③   ## 3.3 Liquidity Ratios

liquidity
A firm's ability to satisfy its short-term obligations *as they come due.*

The **liquidity** of a firm is measured by its ability to satisfy its short-term obligations *as they come due.* Liquidity refers to the solvency of the firm's *overall* financial position, or the ease with which it can pay its bills. Because a common precursor to financial distress and bankruptcy is low or declining liquidity, these ratios can provide early signs of cash flow problems and impending business failure. Clearly, it is desirable that a firm is able to pay its bills, so having enough liquidity for day-to-day operations is important. However, liquid assets, like cash held at banks and marketable securities, do not earn a particularly high rate of return, so shareholders will not want a firm to *overinvest* in liquidity. Firms have to balance the need for safety that liquidity provides against the low returns that liquid assets generate for investors. The two basic measures of liquidity are the current ratio and the quick (acid-test) ratio.

CURRENT RATIO

current ratio
A measure of liquidity calculated by dividing the firm's current assets by its current liabilities.

The **current ratio,** one of the most commonly cited financial ratios, measures the firm's ability to meet its short-term obligations. It is expressed as

$$\text{Current ratio} = \text{Current assets} \div \text{Current liabilities} \qquad (3.1)$$

The current ratio for Bartlett Company in 2015 is

$$\$1,223,000 \div \$620,000 = 1.97$$

A higher current ratio indicates a greater degree of liquidity. How much liquidity a firm needs depends on a variety of factors, including the firm's size, its access to short-term financing sources like bank credit lines, and the volatility of its business. For example, a grocery store whose revenues are relatively predictable may not need as much liquidity as a manufacturing firm who faces sudden and unexpected shifts in demand for its products. The more predictable a firm's cash flows, the lower the acceptable current ratio. Because Bartlett Company is in a business with a relatively predictable annual cash flow, its current ratio of 1.97 should be quite acceptable.

Matter of fact

Determinants of Liquidity Needs

Glance back at the first column of data in Table 3.5 which shows the current ratio for a variety of companies and industries. Notice that the industry with the highest current ratio (that is, most liquidity) is building materials, a business that is notoriously sensitive to business cycle swings. The current ratio for that industry is 2.8, indicating that the typical firm in that business has almost three times as much in current assets as in current liabilities. Two of the largest competitors in that industry, The Home Depot and Lowe's, operate with a current ratio of 1.3, less than half the industry average. Does this ratio mean that these firms have a liquidity problem? Not necessarily. Large enterprises generally have well-established relationships with banks that can provide lines of credit and other short-term loan products in the event that the firm has a need for liquidity. Smaller firms may not have the same access to credit and therefore tend to operate with more liquidity.

Personal Finance Example 3.4 ▶

MyFinanceLab Solution
Video

Individuals, like corporations, can use financial ratios to analyze and monitor their performance. Typically, personal finance ratios are calculated using the personal income and expense statement and personal balance sheet for the period of concern. Here we use these statements, presented in the preceding personal finance examples, to demonstrate calculation of Jan and Jon Smith's liquidity ratio for calendar year 2015.

The personal *liquidity ratio* is calculated by dividing total liquid assets by total current debt. It indicates the percent of annual debt obligations that an individual can meet using current liquid assets. The Smiths' total liquid assets were $2,225. Their total current debts are $21,539 (total current liabilities of $905 + mortgage payments of $16,864 + auto loan payments of $2,520 + appliance and furniture payments of $1,250). Substituting these values into the ratio formula, we get

$$\text{Liquidity ratio} = \frac{\text{Total liquid assets}}{\text{Total current debts}} = \frac{\$2,225}{\$21,539} = 0.103, \text{ or } 10.3\%$$

That ratio indicates that the Smiths can cover only about 10% of their existing 1-year debt obligations with their current liquid assets. Clearly, the Smiths plan to meet these debt obligations from their income, but this ratio suggests that their liquid funds do not provide a large cushion. One of their goals should probably be to build up a larger fund of liquid assets to meet unexpected expenses.

QUICK (ACID-TEST) RATIO

quick (acid-test) ratio
A measure of liquidity calculated by dividing the firm's current assets minus inventory by its current liabilities.

The **quick (acid-test) ratio** is similar to the current ratio except that it excludes inventory, which is generally the least liquid current asset. The generally low liquidity of inventory results from two primary factors: (1) Many types of inventory cannot be easily sold because they are partially completed items, special-purpose items, and the like; and (2) inventory is typically sold on credit, which means that it becomes an account receivable before being converted into cash. An additional problem with inventory as a liquid asset is that the times when companies face the most dire need for liquidity, when business is bad, are precisely the times when it is most difficult to convert inventory into cash by selling it. The quick ratio is calculated as

$$\text{Quick ratio} = \frac{\text{Current assets} - \text{Inventory}}{\text{Current liabilities}} \qquad (3.2)$$

The quick ratio for Bartlett Company in 2015 is

$$\frac{\$1,223,000 - \$289,000}{\$620,000} = \frac{\$934,000}{\$620,000} = 1.51$$

As with the current ratio, the quick ratio level that a firm should strive to achieve depends largely on the nature of the business in which it operates. The quick ratio provides a better measure of overall liquidity only when a firm's inventory cannot be easily converted into cash. If inventory is liquid, the current ratio is a preferred measure of overall liquidity.

Matter of fact

The Importance of Inventories

Turn again to Table 3.5 and examine the columns listing current and quick ratios for different firms and industries. Notice that Dell has a current ratio of 1.3, as do The Home Depot and Lowe's. However, although the quick ratios for The Home Depot and Lowe's are dramatically lower than their current ratios, for Dell the current and quick ratios have nearly the same value. Why? For many years, Dell operated on a "built-to-order" business model that allowed it to hold very little inventory. In contrast, all it takes is a trip to your local Home Depot or Lowe's store to see that the business model in this industry requires a massive investment in inventory, which implies that the quick ratio will be much less than the current ratio for building materials firms.

→ **REVIEW QUESTIONS**

3–9 Under what circumstances would the current ratio be the preferred measure of overall firm liquidity? Under what circumstances would the quick ratio be preferred?

3–10 In Table 3.5, most of the specific firms listed have current ratios that fall below the industry average. Why? The exception to this general pattern is Whole Foods Market, which competes at the very high end of the retail grocery market. Why might Whole Foods Market operate with greater-than-average liquidity?

LG 3   ## 3.4 Activity Ratios

activity ratios
Measure the speed with which various accounts are converted into sales or cash, or inflows or outflows.

Activity ratios measure the speed with which various accounts are converted into sales or cash, or inflows or outflows. In a sense, activity ratios measure how efficiently a firm operates along a variety of dimensions such as inventory management, disbursements, and collections. A number of ratios are available for measuring the activity of the most important current accounts, which include inventory, accounts receivable, and accounts payable. The efficiency with which total assets are used can also be assessed.

INVENTORY TURNOVER

inventory turnover
Measures the activity, or liquidity, of a firm's inventory.

Inventory turnover commonly measures the activity, or liquidity, of a firm's inventory. It is calculated as

$$\text{Inventory turnover} = \text{Cost of goods sold} \div \text{Inventory} \qquad (3.3)$$

Applying this relationship to Bartlett Company in 2015 yields

$$\$2,088,000 \div \$289,000 = 7.2$$

The resulting turnover is meaningful only when it is compared with that of other firms in the same industry or to the firm's past inventory turnover. An inventory turnover of 20 would not be unusual for a grocery store, whose goods are highly perishable and must be sold quickly, whereas an aircraft manufacturer might turn its inventory just four times per year.

average age of inventory
Average number of days' sales
in inventory.

Another inventory activity ratio measures how many days of inventory the firm has on hand. Inventory turnover can be easily converted into an **average age of inventory** by dividing it into 365. For Bartlett Company, the average age of inventory in 2015 is 50.7 days (365 ÷ 7.2). This value can also be viewed as the average number of days' sales in inventory.

AVERAGE COLLECTION PERIOD

average collection period
The average amount of time
needed to collect accounts
receivable.

The **average collection period,** or average age of accounts receivable, is useful in evaluating credit and collection policies. It is arrived at by dividing the average daily sales into the accounts receivable balance:[2]

$$
\begin{aligned}
\text{Average collection period} &= \frac{\text{Accounts receivable}}{\text{Average sales per day}} \\
&= \frac{\text{Accounts receivable}}{\dfrac{\text{Annual sales}}{365}}
\end{aligned}
\tag{3.4}
$$

The average collection period for Bartlett Company in 2015 is

$$
\frac{\$503{,}000}{\dfrac{\$3{,}074{,}000}{365}} = \frac{\$503{,}000}{\$8{,}422} = 59.7 \text{ days}
$$

On average, it takes the firm 59.7 days to collect an account receivable.

The average collection period is meaningful only in relation to the firm's credit terms. If Bartlett Company extends 30-day credit terms to customers, an average collection period of 59.7 days may indicate a poorly managed credit department, collection department, or both. It is also possible that the lengthened collection period resulted from an intentional relaxation of credit-term enforcement in response to competitive pressures. If the firm had extended 60-day credit terms, the 59.7-day average collection period would be quite acceptable. Clearly, additional information is needed to evaluate the effectiveness of the firm's credit and collection policies.

Matter of fact

Who Gets Credit?

Notice in Table 3.5 the vast differences across industries in the average collection periods. Companies in the building materials, grocery, and merchandise store industries collect in just a few days, whereas firms in the computer industry take roughly 2 months to collect on their sales. The difference is primarily because these industries serve very different customers. Grocery and retail stores serve individuals who pay cash or use credit cards (which, to the store, are essentially the same as cash). Computer manufacturers sell to retail chains, businesses, and other large organizations that negotiate agreements that allow them to pay for the computers they order well after the sale is made.

---

2. The formula as presented assumes, for simplicity, that all sales are made on a credit basis. If that is not the case, *average credit sales per day* should be substituted for average sales per day.

AVERAGE PAYMENT PERIOD

average payment period
The average amount of time needed to pay accounts payable.

The **average payment period,** or average age of accounts payable, is calculated in the same manner as the average collection period:

$$\text{Average payment period} = \frac{\text{Accounts payable}}{\text{Average purchases per day}}$$
$$= \frac{\text{Accounts payable}}{\dfrac{\text{Annual purchases}}{365}} \quad \text{(3.5)}$$

The difficulty in calculating this ratio stems from the need to find annual purchases,[3] a value not available in published financial statements. Ordinarily, purchases are estimated as a given percentage of cost of goods sold. If we assume that Bartlett Company's purchases equaled 70 percent of its cost of goods sold in 2015, its average payment period is

$$\frac{\$382,000}{\dfrac{0.70 \times \$2,088,000}{365}} = \frac{\$382,000}{\$4,004} = 95.4 \text{ days}$$

The 95.4 days is meaningful only in relation to the average credit terms extended to the firm. If Bartlett Company's suppliers have extended, on average, 30-day credit terms, an analyst would give Bartlett a low credit rating because it was taking too long to pay its bills. Prospective lenders and suppliers of trade credit are interested in the average payment period because it provides insight into the firm's bill-paying patterns.

TOTAL ASSET TURNOVER

total asset turnover
Indicates the efficiency with which the firm uses its assets to generate sales.

The **total asset turnover** indicates the efficiency with which the firm uses its assets to generate sales. Total asset turnover is calculated as

$$\text{Total asset turnover} = \text{Sales} \div \text{Total assets} \quad \text{(3.6)}$$

The value of Bartlett Company's total asset turnover in 2015 is

$$\$3,074,000 \div \$3,597,000 = 0.85$$

which means that the company turns over its assets 0.85 times per year.

---

3. Technically, annual *credit* purchases—rather than annual purchases—should be used in calculating this ratio. For simplicity, this refinement is ignored here.

Matter of fact

Sell It Fast

Observe in Table 3.5 that the grocery business turns over assets faster than any of the other industries listed. That makes sense because inventory is among the most valuable assets held by these firms, and grocery stores have to sell baked goods, dairy products, and produce quickly or throw such items away when they spoil. It's true that some items in a grocery store have a shelf life longer than anyone really wants to know (think Twinkies), but on average a grocery store has to replace its entire inventory in just a few days or weeks, and that practice contributes to the rapid turnover of the firm's total assets.

Generally, the higher a firm's total asset turnover, the more efficiently its assets have been used. This measure is probably of greatest interest to management because it indicates whether the firm's operations have been financially efficient.

→ REVIEW QUESTION

3–11 To assess the firm's average collection period and average payment period ratios, what additional information is needed, and why?

LG 4 3.5 Debt Ratios

The *debt position* of a firm indicates the amount of other people's money being used to generate profits. In general, the financial analyst is most concerned with long-term debts because these commit the firm to a stream of contractual payments over the long run. The more debt a firm has, the greater its risk of being unable to meet its contractual debt payments. Because creditors' claims must be satisfied before the earnings can be distributed to shareholders, current and prospective shareholders pay close attention to the firm's ability to repay debts. Lenders are also concerned about the firm's indebtedness.

financial leverage
The magnification of risk and return through the use of fixed-cost financing, such as debt and preferred stock.

In general, the more debt a firm uses in relation to its total assets, the greater its *financial leverage*. **Financial leverage** is the magnification of risk and return through the use of fixed-cost financing, such as debt and preferred stock. The more fixed-cost debt a firm uses, the greater will be its expected risk and return.

Example 3.5 ► Patty Akers is in the process of incorporating her new business. After much analysis, she determined that an initial investment of $50,000—$20,000 in current assets and $30,000 in fixed assets—is necessary. These funds can be obtained in either of two ways. The first is the *no-debt plan,* under which she would invest the full $50,000 without borrowing. The other alternative, the *debt plan,* involves investing $25,000 and borrowing the balance of $25,000 at 12% annual interest.

Patty expects $30,000 in sales, $18,000 in operating expenses, and a 40% tax rate. Projected balance sheets and income statements associated with the two plans are summarized in Table 3.6. The no-debt plan results in after-tax profits of $7,200, which represent a 14.4% rate of return on Patty's $50,000 investment.

TABLE 3.6	Financial Statements Associated with Patty's Alternatives	
Balance sheets	No-debt plan	Debt plan
Current assets	$20,000	$20,000
Fixed assets	30,000	30,000
Total assets	$50,000	$50,000
Debt (12% interest)	$ 0	$25,000
(1) Equity	50,000	25,000
Total liabilities and equity	$50,000	$50,000
Income Statements		
Sales	$30,000	$30,000
Less: Operating expenses	18,000	18,000
Operating profits	$12,000	$12,000
Less: Interest expense	0	$0.12 \times \$25,000 =$ 3,000
Net profits before taxes	$12,000	$ 9,000
Less: Taxes (rate = 40%)	4,800	3,600
(2) Net profits after taxes	$ 7,200	$ 5,400
Return on equity [(2) ÷ (1)]	$\dfrac{\$7,200}{\$50,000} = 14.4\%$	$\dfrac{\$5,400}{\$25,000} = 21.6\%$

The debt plan results in $5,400 of after-tax profits, which represent a 21.6% rate of return on Patty's investment of $25,000. The debt plan provides Patty with a higher rate of return, but the risk of this plan is also greater because the annual $3,000 of interest must be paid whether Patty's business is profitable or not.

The previous example demonstrates that *with increased debt comes greater risk as well as higher potential return.* Therefore, the greater the financial leverage, the greater the potential risk and return. A detailed discussion of the effect of debt on the firm's risk, return, and value is included in Chapter 11. Here, we emphasize the use of financial leverage ratios to assess externally a firm's debt position.

There are two general types of leverage measures: measures of the degree of indebtedness and measures of the ability to service debts. The **degree of indebtedness** measures the amount of debt relative to other significant balance sheet amounts. Two popular measures of the degree of indebtedness are the debt ratio and the debt-to-equity ratio.

The second type of leverage measures, the **ability to service debts,** reflect a firm's ability to make the payments required on a scheduled basis over the life of a debt. The term *to service debts* simply means to pay debts on time. The firm's ability to pay certain fixed charges is measured using **coverage ratios.** Typically, higher coverage ratios are preferred (especially by the firm's lenders), but a very high ratio might indicate that the firm's management is too conservative and might be able to earn higher returns by borrowing more. In general, the lower the firm's coverage ratios, the less certain it is to be able to pay fixed obligations. If a firm is unable to pay these obligations, its creditors may seek immediate repayment, which in most instances would force a firm into bankruptcy. Two popular coverage ratios are the times interest earned ratio and the fixed-payment coverage ratio.

degree of indebtedness
Measures the amount of debt relative to other significant balance sheet amounts.

ability to service debts
The ability of a firm to make the payments required on a scheduled basis over the life of a debt.

coverage ratios
Ratios that measure the firm's ability to pay certain fixed charges.

DEBT RATIO

debt ratio
Measures the proportion of total assets financed by the firm's creditors.

The **debt ratio** measures the proportion of total assets financed by the firm's creditors. The higher this ratio, the greater the amount of other people's money being used to generate profits. The ratio is calculated as

$$\text{Debt ratio} = \text{Total liabilities} \div \text{Total assets} \qquad (3.7)$$

The debt ratio for Bartlett Company in 2015 is

$$\$1,643,000 \div \$3,597,000 = 0.457 = 45.7\%$$

This value indicates that the company has financed close to half of its assets with debt. The higher this ratio, the greater the firm's degree of indebtedness and the more financial leverage it has.

DEBT-TO-EQUITY RATIO

debt-to-equity ratio
Measures the relative proportion of total liabilities and common stock equity used to finance the firm's total assets.

The **debt-to-equity ratio** measures the relative proportion of total liabilties to common stock equity used to finance the firm's assets. As with debt ratio, the higher this ratio, the greater the firm's use of financial leverage. The debt-to-equity ratio is calculated as

$$\text{Debt to equity ratio} = \text{Total liabilities} \div \text{Common stock equity} \qquad (3.8)$$

The debt-to-equity ratio for Bartlett Company in 2015 is

$$\$1,643,000 \div \$1,754,000 = 0.937 = 93.7\%$$

This result tells us that for every $1.00 common stockholders have invested in Bartlett Company, the company owes about 94 cents to creditors. The value for common stock equity ($1,754,000) was found by subtracting the $200,000 of preferred stock equity from the total stockholders' equity of $1,954,000. It is important to note that several methods exist for calculating the debt-to-equity ratio. A common alternative uses only long-term debt in the numerator. In that case, the ratio in 2015 for Bartlett Company is

$$\$1,023,000 \div \$1,754,000 = 0.583 = 58.3\%$$

When conducting ratio analyses, some financial analysts choose to focus on all stockholders rather than only common stockholders, in which case they use values relevant to all stockholders such as net profits after taxes (instead of earnings available for common stockholders) and total stockholders' equity (instead of common stock equity). Clearly, different methods can lead to very different results. Regardless of which method is used, however, a low debt-to-equity ratio is often viewed as an indication that a company is not taking sufficient advantage of financial leverage to increase profits, whereas a high debt-to-equity ratio is often viewed as an indication that a company may not be able to generate enough cash to satisfy its debt obligations.

TIMES INTEREST EARNED RATIO

times interest earned ratio
Measures the firm's ability to make contractual interest payments; sometimes called the *interest coverage ratio.*

The **times interest earned ratio,** sometimes called the *interest coverage ratio,* measures the firm's ability to make contractual interest payments. The higher its value, the better able the firm is to fulfill its interest obligations. The times interest earned ratio is calculated as

$$\text{Times interest earned ratio} = \text{Earnings before interest and taxes} \div \text{Interest} \quad (3.9)$$

The figure for *earnings before interest and taxes (EBIT)* is the same as that for *operating profits* shown in the income statement. Applying this ratio to Bartlett Company yields the 2015 value of

$$\text{Time interest earned ratio} = \$418{,}000 \div \$93{,}000 = 4.49$$

The times interest earned ratio for Bartlett Company seems acceptable. A value of at least 3.0—and preferably closer to 5.0—is often suggested. The firm's earnings before interest and taxes could shrink by as much as 78 percent [(4.49 − 1.0) ÷ 4.49] and the firm would still be able to pay the $93,000 in interest it owes. Thus, the firm has a large margin of safety.

FIXED-PAYMENT COVERAGE RATIO

fixed-payment coverage ratio
Measures the firm's ability to meet all fixed-payment obligations.

The **fixed-payment coverage ratio** measures the firm's ability to meet all fixed-payment obligations such as loan interest and principal, lease payments, and preferred stock dividends. As is true of the times interest earned ratio, the higher this value, the better. The formula for the fixed-payment coverage ratio is

$$\frac{\text{Fixed-payment coverage ratio}}{} = \frac{\text{Earnings before interest and taxes} + \text{Lease payments}}{\text{Interest} + \text{Lease payments} + \{(\text{Principal payments} + \text{Preferred stock dividends}) \times [1/(1-T)]\}} \quad (3.10)$$

where T is the corporate tax rate applicable to the firm's income. The term $1/(1 - T)$ is included to adjust the after-tax principal and preferred stock dividend payments back to a before-tax equivalent that is consistent with the before-tax values of all other terms. Applying the formula to Bartlett Company's 2015 data yields

$$\frac{\text{Fixed-payment coverage ratio}}{} = \frac{\$418{,}000 + \$35{,}000}{\$93{,}000 + \$35{,}000 + \{(\$71{,}000 + \$10{,}000) \times [1/(1-0.29)]\}}$$

$$= \frac{\$453{,}000}{\$242{,}000} = 1.87$$

Because the earnings available are nearly twice as large as its fixed-payment obligations, the firm appears safely able to meet the latter.

Like the times interest earned ratio, the fixed-payment coverage ratio measures risk. The lower the ratio, the greater the risk to both lenders and owners, and the greater the ratio, the lower the risk. This ratio allows interested parties to assess the firm's ability to meet additional fixed-payment obligations without being driven into bankruptcy.

→ REVIEW QUESTIONS

3–12 What is *financial leverage?*

3–13 What ratio measures the firm's *degree of indebtedness?* What ratios assess the firm's *ability to service debts?*

There are many measures of profitability. As a group, these measures enable analysts to evaluate the firm's profits with respect to a given level of sales, a certain level of assets, or the owners' investment. Without profits, a firm could not attract outside capital. Owners, creditors, and management pay close attention to boosting profits because of the great importance the market places on earnings.

COMMON-SIZE INCOME STATEMENTS

common-size income statement
An income statement in which each item is expressed as a percentage of sales.

A useful tool for evaluating profitability in relation to sales is the **common-size income statement**. Each item on this statement is expressed as a percentage of sales. Common-size income statements are especially useful when comparing performance across years because it is easy to see if certain categories of expenses are trending up or down as a percentage of the total volume of business that the company transacts. Three frequently cited ratios of profitability that come directly from the common-size income statement are (1) the gross profit margin, (2) the operating profit margin, and (3) the net profit margin.

Common-size income statements for 2015 and 2014 for Bartlett Company are presented and evaluated in Table 3.7 on page 76. These statements reveal that the firm's cost of goods sold increased from 66.7 percent of sales in 2014 to 67.9 percent in 2015, resulting in a worsening gross profit margin. However, thanks to a decrease in total operating expenses, the firm's net profit margin rose from 5.4 percent of sales in 2014 to 7.2 percent in 2015. The decrease in expenses more than compensated for the increase in the cost of goods sold. A decrease in the firm's 2015 interest expense (3.0 percent of sales versus 3.5 percent in 2014) added to the increase in 2015 profits.

GROSS PROFIT MARGIN

gross profit margin
Measures the percentage of each sales dollar remaining after the firm has paid for its goods.

The **gross profit margin** measures the percentage of each sales dollar remaining after the firm has paid for its goods. The higher the gross profit margin, the better (that is, the lower the relative cost of merchandise sold). The gross profit margin is calculated as

$$\text{Gross profit margin} = \frac{\text{Sales} - \text{Cost of goods sold}}{\text{Sales}} = \frac{\text{Gross profits}}{\text{Sales}} \quad (3.11)$$

Bartlett Company's gross profit margin for 2015 is

$$\frac{\$3,074,000 - \$2,088,000}{\$3,074,000} = \frac{\$986,000}{\$3,074,000} = 0.321 = 32.1\%$$

This value is labeled (1) on the common-size income statement in Table 3.7.

OPERATING PROFIT MARGIN

operating profit margin
Measures the percentage of each sales dollar remaining after all costs and expenses *other than* interest, taxes, and preferred stock dividends are deducted; the "pure profits" earned on each sales dollar.

The **operating profit margin** measures the percentage of each sales dollar remaining after all costs and expenses *other than* interest, taxes, and preferred stock dividends are deducted. It represents the "pure profits" earned on each sales dollar. Operating profits are "pure" because they measure only the profits earned

TABLE 3.7 Bartlett Company Common-Size Income Statements

	For the years ended December 31		Evaluation[a]
	2015	2014	2014–2015
Sales revenue	100.0%	100.0%	Same
Less: Cost of goods sold	67.9	66.7	Worse
(1) Gross profit margin	32.1%	33.3%	Worse
Less: Operating expenses			
Selling expense	3.3%	4.2%	Better
General and administrative expenses	6.8	6.7	Worse
Lease expense	1.1	1.3	Better
Depreciation expense	7.3	9.3	Better
Total operating expense	18.5%	21.5%	Better
(2) Operating profit margin	13.6%	11.8%	Better
Less: Interest expense	3.0	3.5	Better
Net profits before taxes	10.6%	8.3%	Better
Less: Taxes	3.1	2.5	Worse[b]
Net profits after taxes	7.5%	5.8%	Better
Less: Preferred stock dividends	0.3	0.4	Better
(3) Net profit margin	7.2%	5.4%	Better

[a]Subjective assessments based on data provided.

[b]Taxes as a percentage of sales increased noticeably between 2014 and 2015 because of differing costs and expenses, whereas the average tax rates (taxes ÷ net profits before taxes) for 2014 and 2015 remained about the same: 30% and 29%, respectively.

on operations and ignore interest, taxes, and preferred stock dividends. A high operating profit margin is preferred. The operating profit margin is calculated as

$$\text{Operating profit margin} = \text{Operating profits} \div \text{Sales} \qquad (3.12)$$

Bartlett Company's operating profit margin for 2015 is

$$\$418{,}000 \div \$3{,}074{,}000 = 0.136 = 13.6\%$$

This value is labeled (2) on the common-size income statement in Table 3.7.

NET PROFIT MARGIN

net profit margin
Measures the percentage of each sales dollar remaining after all costs and expenses, *including* interest, taxes, and preferred stock dividends, have been deducted.

The **net profit margin** measures the percentage of each sales dollar remaining after all costs and expenses, *including* interest, taxes, and preferred stock dividends, have been deducted. The higher the firm's net profit margin, the better. The net profit margin is calculated as

$$\text{Net profit margin} = \text{earnings available for common stockholders} \div \text{Sales} \quad (3.13)$$

Bartlett Company's net profit margin for 2015 is

$$\$221{,}000 \div \$3{,}074{,}000 = 0.072 = 7.2\%$$

This value is labeled (3) on the common-size income statement in Table 3.7.

The net profit margin is a commonly cited measure of the firm's success with respect to earnings on sales. "Good" net profit margins differ considerably across industries. A net profit margin of 1 percent or less would not be unusual for a grocery store, whereas a net profit margin of 10 percent would be low for a retail jewelry store.

EARNINGS PER SHARE (EPS)

The firm's *earnings per share (EPS)* is generally of interest to present or prospective stockholders and management. As we noted earlier, EPS represents the number of dollars earned during the period on behalf of each outstanding share of common stock. Earnings per share is calculated as

$$\text{Earnings per share} = \frac{\text{Earnings available for common stockholders}}{\text{Number of shares of common stock outstanding}} \tag{3.14}$$

Bartlett Company's earnings per share in 2015 is

$$\$221{,}000 \div 76{,}262 = \$2.90$$

This figure represents the dollar amount earned *on behalf of* each outstanding share of common stock. The dollar amount of cash *actually distributed* to each shareholder is the *dividend per share (DPS)*, which, as noted in Bartlett Company's income statement (Table 3.1), rose to $1.29 in 2015 from $0.75 in 2014. EPS is closely watched by the investing public and is considered an important indicator of corporate success.

RETURN ON TOTAL ASSETS (ROA)

return on total assets (ROA)
Measures the overall effectiveness of management in generating profits with its available assets; also called the *return on investment (ROI)*.

The **return on total assets** (**ROA**), often called the *return on investment (ROI)*, measures the overall effectiveness of management in generating profits with its available assets. The higher the firm's return on total assets, the better. The return on total assets is calculated as

$$\text{ROA} = \text{Earnings available for common stockholders} \div \text{Total assets} \tag{3.15}$$

Bartlett Company's return on total assets in 2015 is

$$\$221{,}000 \div \$3{,}597{,}000 = 0.061 = 6.1\%$$

This value indicates that the company earned 6.1 cents on each $1.00 of common stockholders' asset investment. When a firm has preferred stock outstanding, the return on assets can be calculated for all stockholders by dividing the net profits after taxes by total assets. In this case, you would arrive at an ROA of 6.4 percent.

RETURN ON EQUITY (ROE)

return on equity (ROE)
Measures the return earned on the common stockholders' investment in the firm.

The **return on equity** (**ROE**) measures the return earned on the common stockholders' investment in the firm. Generally, the owners are better off the higher is this return. Return on equity is calculated as

$$\text{ROE} = \text{Earnings available for common stockholders} \div \text{Common stock equity} \tag{3.16}$$

The ROE for Bartlett Company in 2015 is

$$\$221,000 \div \$1,754,000 = 0.126 = 12.6\%$$

The calculated ROE of 12.6 percent indicates that during 2015 Bartlett earned 12.6 cents on each $1.00 of common stock equity. Here again, some analysts will elect to calculate ROE across stockholders when preferred stock is outstanding. In this case, net profits after taxes ($231,000) is divided by total stockholders' equity ($1,954,000) to arrive at return on total stockholders' equity of 11.8 percent. More often than not, publicly traded companies will not have preferred stock, so the return on total stockholders' equity will, more often than not, be the same as the ROE for common equity. The same can be said for the ROA calculations.

→ REVIEW QUESTIONS

3–14 What three ratios of profitability are found on a *common-size income statement?*

3–15 What would explain a firm's having a high gross profit margin and a low net profit margin?

3–16 Which measure of profitability is probably of greatest interest to the investing public? Why?

3.7 Market Ratios

market ratios
Relate a firm's market value, as measured by its current share price, to certain accounting values.

Market ratios relate the firm's market value, as measured by its current share price, to certain accounting values. These ratios give insight into how investors in the marketplace believe that the firm is doing in terms of risk and return. They tend to reflect, on a relative basis, the common stockholders' assessment of all aspects of the firm's past and expected future performance. Here we consider two widely quoted market ratios, one that focuses on earnings and another that considers book value.

PRICE/EARNINGS (P/E) RATIO

price/earnings (P/E) ratio
Measures the amount that investors are willing to pay for each dollar of a firm's earnings; the higher the P/E ratio, the greater the investor confidence.

The **price/earnings (P/E) ratio** is commonly used to assess the owners' appraisal of share value. The P/E ratio measures the amount that investors are willing to pay for each dollar of a firm's earnings. The level of this ratio indicates the degree of confidence that investors have in the firm's future performance. The higher the P/E ratio, the greater the investor confidence. The P/E ratio is calculated as

P/E ratio = Market price per share of common stock ÷ Earnings per share   (3.17)

If Bartlett Company's common stock at the end of 2015 was selling at $32.25, the P/E ratio, using the EPS of $2.90, at year-end 2015 is

$$\$32.25 \div \$2.90 = 11.12$$

This figure indicates that investors were paying $11.12 for each $1.00 of earnings. The P/E ratio is most informative when applied in cross-sectional analysis using an industry average P/E ratio or the P/E ratio of a benchmark firm.

MARKET/BOOK (M/B) RATIO

market/book (M/B) ratio
Provides an assessment of how investors view the firm's performance. Firms expected to earn high returns relative to their risk typically sell at higher M/B multiples.

The **market/book (M/B) ratio** provides an assessment of how investors view the firm's performance. It relates the market value of the firm's shares to its book—strict accounting—value. To calculate the firm's M/B ratio, we first need to find the *book value per share of common stock:*

$$\text{Book value per share of common stock} = \frac{\text{Common stock equity}}{\text{Number of shares of common stock outstanding}} \tag{3.18}$$

Substituting the appropriate values for Bartlett Company from its 2015 balance sheet, we get

$$\text{Book value per share of common stock} = \frac{\$1,754,000}{76,262} = \$23.00$$

The formula for the market/book ratio is

$$\text{Market/book (M/B) ratio} = \frac{\text{Market price per share of common stock}}{\text{Book value per share of common stock}} \tag{3.19}$$

Substituting Bartlett Company's end of 2015 common stock price of $32.25 and its $23.00 book value per share of common stock (calculated above) into the M/B ratio formula, we get

$$\$32.25 \div \$23.00 = 1.40$$

This M/B ratio means that investors are currently paying $1.40 for each $1.00 of book value of Bartlett Company's stock.

The stocks of firms that are expected to perform well—improve profits, increase their market share, or launch successful products—typically sell at higher M/B ratios than the stocks of firms with less attractive outlooks. Simply stated, firms expected to earn high returns relative to their risk typically sell at higher M/B multiples. Clearly, Bartlett's future prospects are being viewed favorably by investors, who are willing to pay more than their book value for the firm's shares. Like P/E ratios, M/B ratios are typically assessed cross-sectionally to get a feel for the firm's return and risk compared to peer firms.

→ **REVIEW QUESTION**

3–17 How do the *price/earnings (P/E) ratio* and the *market/book (M/B) ratio* provide a feel for the firm's return and risk?

LG 6 3.8 A Complete Ratio Analysis

Analysts frequently wish to take an overall look at the firm's financial performance and status. Here we consider two popular approaches to a complete ratio analysis: (1) summarizing all ratios and (2) the DuPont system of analysis. The summary analysis approach tends to view *all aspects* of the firm's financial activities to isolate key areas of responsibility. The DuPont system acts as a search technique aimed at finding the *key areas* responsible for the firm's financial condition.

SUMMARIZING ALL RATIOS

We can use Bartlett Company's ratios to perform a complete ratio analysis using both cross-sectional and time-series analysis approaches. The 2015 ratio values calculated earlier and the ratio values calculated for 2013 and 2014 for Bartlett Company, along with the industry average ratios for 2015, are summarized in Table 3.8 (see pages 82 and 83), which also shows the formula used to calculate each ratio. Using these data, we can discuss the five key aspects of Bartlett's performance: liquidity, activity, debt, profitability, and market.

Liquidity

The overall liquidity of the firm seems to exhibit a reasonably stable trend, having been maintained at a level that is relatively consistent with the industry average in 2015. The firm's liquidity seems to be good.

Activity

Bartlett Company's inventory appears to be in good shape. Its inventory management seems to have improved, and in 2015 it performed at a level above that of the industry. The firm may be experiencing some problems with accounts receivable. The average collection period seems to have crept up above that of the industry. Bartlett also appears to be slow in paying its bills; it pays nearly 30 days slower than the industry average, which could adversely affect the firm's credit standing. Although overall liquidity appears to be good, the management of receivables and payables should be examined. Bartlett's total asset turnover reflects a decline in the efficiency of total asset utilization between 2013 and 2014. Although in 2015 it rose to a level considerably above the industry average, it appears that the pre-2014 level of efficiency has not yet been achieved.

Debt

Bartlett Company's indebtedness increased over the 2013–2015 period and is currently above the industry average. Although this increase in the debt ratio could be cause for alarm, the firm's ability to meet interest and fixed-payment obligations improved, from 2014 to 2015, to a level that outperforms the industry. The firm's increased indebtedness in 2014 apparently caused deterioration in its ability to pay debt adequately. However, Bartlett has evidently improved its income in 2015 so that it is able to meet its interest and fixed-payment obligations at a level consistent with the average in the industry. In summary, it appears that although 2014 was an off year, the company's improved ability to pay debts in 2015 compensates for its increased degree of indebtedness.

Profitability

Bartlett's profitability relative to sales in 2015 was better than the average company in the industry, although it did not match the firm's 2013 performance. Although the *gross* profit margin was better in 2014 and 2015 than in 2013, higher levels of operating and interest expenses in 2014 and 2015 appear to have caused the 2015 *net* profit margin to fall below that of 2013. However, Bartlett Company's 2015 net profit margin is quite favorable when compared with the industry average.

The firm's earnings per share, return on total assets, and return on common equity behaved much as its net profit margin did over the 2013–2015 period. Bartlett appears to have experienced either a sizable drop in sales between 2013 and 2014 or a rapid expansion in assets during that period. The exceptionally high 2015 level of return on common equity suggests that the firm is performing quite well. The firm's above-average returns—net profit margin, EPS, ROA, and ROE—may be attributable to it being more risky than average. A look at market ratios is helpful in assessing risk.

Market

Investors have greater confidence in the firm in 2015 than in the prior 2 years, as reflected in the price/earnings (P/E) ratio of 11.1. However, this ratio is below the industry average. The P/E ratio suggests that the firm's risk has declined but remains above that of the average firm in its industry. The firm's market/book (M/B) ratio has increased over the 2013–2015 period, and in 2015 it exceeds the industry average, which implies that investors are optimistic about the firm's future performance. The P/E and M/B ratios reflect the firm's increased profitability over the 2013–2015 period: Investors expect to earn high future returns as compensation for the firm's above-average risk.

In summary, the firm appears to be growing and has recently undergone an expansion in assets, financed primarily through the use of debt. The 2014–2015 period seems to reflect a phase of adjustment and reco very from the rapid growth in assets. Bartlett's sales, profits, and other performance factors seem to be growing with the increase in the size of the operation. In addition, the market response to these accomplishments appears to have been positive. In short, the firm seems to have done well in 2015.

DUPONT SYSTEM OF ANALYSIS

DuPont system of analysis
System used to dissect the firm's financial statements and to assess its financial condition.

The **DuPont system of analysis** is used to dissect the firm's financial statements and to assess its financial condition. It merges the income statement and balance sheet into two summary measures of profitability, return on total assets (ROA) and return on common equity (ROE). Figure 3.2 depicts the basic DuPont system with Bartlett Company's 2015 monetary and ratio values. The upper portion of the chart summarizes the income statement activities, and the lower portion summarizes the balance sheet activities.

DuPont Formula

DuPont formula
Multiplies the firm's *net profit margin* by its *total asset turnover* to calculate the firm's *return on total assets (ROA)*.

The DuPont system first brings together the *net profit margin,* which measures the firm's profitability on sales, with its *total asset turnover,* which indicates how efficiently the firm has used its assets to generate sales. In the **DuPont formula,** the product of these two ratios results in the *return on total assets (ROA):*

$$ROA = \text{Net profit margin} \times \text{Total asset turnover}$$

Substituting the appropriate formulas for net profit margin and total asset turnover into the equation and simplifying results in the formula for ROA given earlier,

$$ROA = \frac{\text{Earnings available for common stockholders}}{\text{Sales}} \times \frac{\text{Sales}}{\text{Total assets}} = \frac{\text{Earnings available for common stockholders}}{\text{Total assets}}$$

When the 2015 values of the net profit margin and total asset turnover for Bartlett Company, calculated earlier, are substituted into the DuPont formula, the result is

$$ROA = 7.2\% \times 0.85 = 6.1\%$$

TABLE 3.8　Summary of Bartlett Company Ratios (2010–2015, Including 2015 Industry Averages)

Ratio	Formula	Year 2013[a]	Year 2014[b]	Year 2015[b]	Industry average 2015[c]	Evaluation[d] Cross-sectional 2015	Evaluation[d] Time-series 2013–2015	Evaluation[d] Overall
Liquidity								
Current ratio	$\dfrac{\text{Current assets}}{\text{Current liabilities}}$	2.04	2.08	1.97	2.05	OK	OK	OK
Quick (acid-test) ratio	$\dfrac{\text{Current assets} - \text{Inventory}}{\text{Current liabilities}}$	1.32	1.46	1.51	1.43	OK	Good	Good
Activity								
Inventory turnover	$\dfrac{\text{Cost of goods sold}}{\text{Inventory}}$	5.1	5.7	7.2	6.6	Good	Good	Good
Average collection period	$\dfrac{\text{Accounts receivable}}{\text{Average sales per day}}$	43.9 days	51.2 days	59.7 days	44.3 days	Poor	Poor	Poor
Average payment period	$\dfrac{\text{Accounts payable}}{\text{Average purchases per day}}$	75.8 days	81.2 days	95.4 days	66.5 days	Poor	Poor	Poor
Total assets turnover	$\dfrac{\text{Sales}}{\text{Total assets}}$	0.94	0.79	0.85	0.75	OK	OK	OK
Debt								
Debt ratio	$\dfrac{\text{Total liabilities}}{\text{Total assets}}$	36.8%	44.3%	45.7%	40.0%	OK	OK	OK
Times interest earned ratio	$\dfrac{\text{Earnings before interest and taxes}}{\text{Interest}}$	5.6	3.3	4.5	4.3	Good	OK	OK
Fixed-payment coverage ratio	$\dfrac{\text{Earnings before interest and taxes} + \text{Lease payments}}{\text{Int.} + \text{Lease pay.} + \{(\text{Prin.} + \text{Pref. div.}) \times [1/(1 - T)]\}}$	2.4	1.4	1.9	1.5	Good	Good	Good
Profitability								
Gross profit margin	$\dfrac{\text{Gross profits}}{\text{Sales}}$	31.4%	33.3%	32.1%	30.0%	OK	OK	OK
Operating profit margin	$\dfrac{\text{Operating profits}}{\text{Sales}}$	14.6%	11.8%	13.6%	11.0%	Good	OK	Good
Net profit margin	$\dfrac{\text{Earnings available for common stockholders}}{\text{Sales}}$	8.2%	5.4%	7.2%	6.2%	Good	OK	Good

Ratio	Formula	Year			Industry average	Evaluation[d]		
		2013[a]	2014[b]	2015[b]	2015[c]	Cross-sectional 2015	Time-series 2013–2015	Overall
Profitability (cont.)								
Earnings per share (EPS)	Earnings available for common stockholders / Number of shares of common stock outstanding	$3.26	$1.81	$2.90	$2.26	Good	OK	Good
Return on total assets (ROA)	Earnings available for common stockholders / Total assets	7.8%	4.2%	6.1%	4.6%	Good	OK	Good
Return on equity (ROE)	Earnings available for common stockholders / Common stock equity	13.7%	8.5%	12.6%	8.5%	Good	OK	Good
Market								
Price/earnings (P/E) ratio	Market price per share of common stock / Earnings per share	10.5	10.0[e]	11.1	12.5	OK	OK	OK
Market/book (M/B) ratio	Market price per share of common stock / Book value per share of common stock	1.25	0.85[e]	1.40	1.30	OK	OK	OK

[a]Calculated from data not included in this chapter.
[b]Calculated by using the financial statements presented in Tables 3.1 and 3.2.
[c]Obtained from sources not included in this chapter.
[d]Subjective assessments based on data provided.
[e]The market price per share at the end of 2014 was $18.06.

FIGURE 3.2

DuPont System of Analysis
The DuPont system of analysis with application to Bartlett Company (2015)

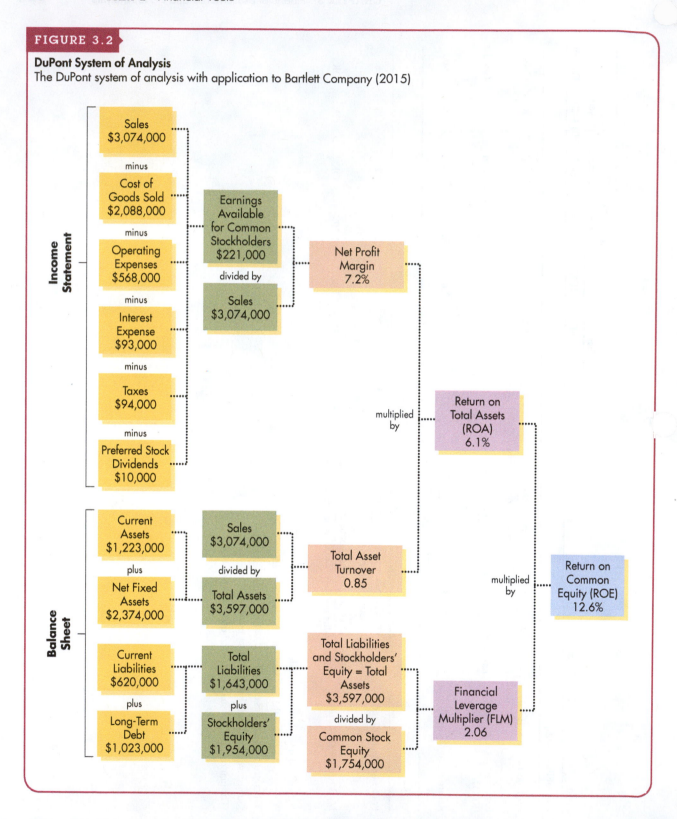

This value is the same as that calculated directly in Section 3.6 (page 77). The DuPont formula enables the firm to break down its return into profit-on-sales and efficiency-of-asset-use components. Typically, a firm with a low net profit margin has a high total asset turnover, which results in a reasonably good return on total assets. Often, the opposite situation exists.

Modified DuPont Formula

modified DuPont formula
Relates the firm's *return on total assets (ROA)* to its *return on equity (ROE)* using the *financial leverage multiplier (FLM)*.

financial leverage multiplier (FLM)
The ratio of the firm's total assets to its common stock equity.

The second step in the DuPont system employs the **modified DuPont formula.** This formula relates the firm's *return on total assets (ROA)* to its *return on equity (ROE)*. The latter is calculated by multiplying the return on total assets (ROA) by the **financial leverage multiplier (FLM)**, which is the ratio of total assets to common stock equity:

$$ROE = ROA \times FLM$$

Substituting the appropriate formulas for ROA and FLM into the equation and simplifying results in the formula for ROE given earlier:

$$ROE = \frac{\text{Earnings available for common stockholders}}{\text{Total assets}} \times \frac{\text{Total assets}}{\text{Common stock equity}} = \frac{\text{Earnings available for common stockholders}}{\text{Common stock equity}}$$

Use of the FLM to convert the ROA into the ROE reflects the effect of financial leverage on owners' return. Substituting the values for Bartlett Company's ROA of 6.1 percent, calculated earlier, and Bartlett's FLM of 2.051 ($3,597,000 total assets ÷ $1,754,000 common stock equity) into the modified DuPont formula yields

$$ROE = 6.1\% \times 2.06 = 12.6\%$$

The 12.6 percent ROE calculated by using the modified DuPont formula is the same as that calculated directly (page 78).

The FLM is also often referred to as the equity multiplier, and it is sometimes calculated using total stockholder's equity in the denominator. Regardless of whether one chooses to use common stock equity or total stockholders' equity, it is important to realize that the multiplier, the debt ratio, and debt-to-equity ratio are all related such that any one of them can be directly calculated from the other two. For example, using the debt-to-equity and debt ratios shown on page 73, we can calculate the multiplier as

$$0.937 \div 0.457 = 2.05$$

In this case, we see that the debt-to-equity ratio divided by the debt ratio provides us with the financial leverage multiplier. Just be sure that your choices of liabilities and stockholder equity are consistent across the three measures when relating them to one another.

Matter of fact

Dissecting ROA

Return to Table 3.5, and examine the total asset turnover figures for Dell and The Home Depot. Both firms turn their assets 1.6 times per year. Now look at the return on assets column. Dell's ROA is 4.3 percent, but The Home Depot's is significantly higher at 6.5 percent. If the two firms are equal in terms of the efficiency with which they manage their assets (that is, equal asset turns), why is The Home Depot more profitable relative to assets? The answer lies in the DuPont formula. Notice that Home Depot's net profit margin is 4.0 percent compared with Dell's 2.7 percent. That difference drives the superior ROA figures for The Home Depot.

Applying the DuPont System

The advantage of the DuPont system is that it allows the firm to break its return on equity into a profit-on-sales component (net profit margin), an efficiency-of-asset-use component (total asset turnover), and a use-of-financial-leverage component (financial leverage multiplier). The total return to owners can therefore be analyzed in these important dimensions.

The use of the DuPont system of analysis as a diagnostic tool is best explained using Figure 3.2. Beginning with the rightmost value—the ROE—the financial analyst moves to the left, dissecting and analyzing the inputs to the formula to isolate the probable cause of the resulting above-average (or below-average) value.

Example 3.6 ▶	For the sake of demonstration, let's ignore all industry average data in Table 3.8 and assume that Bartlett's ROE of 12.6% is actually below the industry average. Moving to the left in Figure 3.2, we would examine the inputs to the ROE—the ROA and the FLM—relative to the industry averages. Let's assume that the FLM is in line with the industry average but the ROA is below the industry average. Moving farther to the left, we examine the two inputs to the ROA, the net profit margin and total asset turnover. Assume that the net profit margin is in line with the industry average but the total asset turnover is below the industry average. Moving still farther to the left, we find that whereas the firm's sales are consistent with the industry value, Bartlett's total assets have grown significantly during the past year. Looking farther to the left, we would review the firm's activity ratios for current assets. Let's say that whereas the firm's inventory turnover is in line with the industry average, its average collection period is well above the industry average.
MyFinanceLab Solution Video	

We can readily trace the possible problem back to its cause: Bartlett's low ROE is primarily the consequence of slow collections of accounts receivable, which resulted in high levels of receivables and therefore high levels of total assets. The high total assets slowed Bartlett's total asset turnover, driving down its ROA, which then drove down its ROE. By using the DuPont system of analysis to dissect Bartlett's overall returns as measured by its ROE, we found that slow collections of receivables caused the below-industry-average ROE. Clearly, the firm needs to manage its credit operations better.

→ REVIEW QUESTIONS

3–18 Financial ratio analysis is often divided into five areas: *liquidity, activity, debt, profitability,* and *market* ratios. Differentiate each of these areas of analysis from the others. Which is of the greatest concern to creditors?

3–19 Describe how you would use a large number of ratios to perform a complete ratio analysis of the firm.

3–20 What three areas of analysis are combined in the *modified DuPont formula?* Explain how the *DuPont system of analysis* is used to dissect the firm's results and isolate their causes.

Summary

FOCUS ON VALUE

Financial managers review and analyze the firm's financial statements periodically, both to uncover developing problems and to assess the firm's progress toward achieving its goals. These actions are aimed at **preserving and creating value for the firm's owners.** Financial ratios enable financial managers to monitor the pulse of the firm and its progress toward its strategic goals. Although financial statements and financial ratios rely on accrual concepts, they can provide useful insights into important aspects of risk and return (cash flow) that affect share price.

REVIEW OF LEARNING GOALS

LG 1 **Review the contents of the stockholders' report and the procedures for consolidating international financial statements.** The annual stockholders' report, which publicly owned corporations must provide to stockholders, documents the firm's financial activities of the past year. It includes the letter to stockholders and various subjective and factual information. It also contains four key financial statements: the income statement, the balance sheet, the statement of stockholders' equity (or its abbreviated form, the statement of retained earnings), and the statement of cash flows. Notes describing the technical aspects of the financial statements follow. Financial statements of companies that have operations whose cash flows are denominated in one or more foreign currencies must be translated into U.S. dollars in accordance with *FASB Standard No. 52.*

LG 2 **Understand who uses financial ratios and how.** Ratio analysis enables stockholders, lenders, and the firm's managers to evaluate the firm's financial performance. It can be performed on a cross-sectional or a time-series basis. Benchmarking is a popular type of cross-sectional analysis. Users of ratios should understand the cautions that apply to their use.

LG 3 **Use ratios to analyze a firm's liquidity and activity.** Liquidity, or the ability of the firm to pay its bills as they come due, can be measured by the current ratio and the quick (acid-test) ratio. Activity ratios measure the speed with which accounts are converted into sales or cash, or inflows or outflows. The activity of inventory can be measured by its turnover: that of accounts receivable by the average collection period and that of accounts payable by the average payment period. Total asset turnover measures the efficiency with which the firm uses its assets to generate sales.

LG 4 **Discuss the relationship between debt and financial leverage and the ratios used to analyze a firm's debt.** The more debt a firm uses, the greater its financial leverage, which magnifies both risk and return. Financial debt ratios measure both the degree of indebtedness and the ability to service debts. A common measure of indebtedness is the debt ratio. The ability to pay fixed charges can be measured by times interest earned and fixed-payment coverage ratios.

LG 5 **Use ratios to analyze a firm's profitability and its market value.** The common-size income statement, which shows each item as a percentage of sales, can be used to determine gross profit margin, operating profit margin, and net profit margin. Other measures of profitability include earnings per share, return on total assets, and return on common equity. Market ratios include the price/earnings ratio and the market/book ratio.

LG 6 **Use a summary of financial ratios and the DuPont system of analysis to perform a complete ratio analysis.** A summary of all ratios can be used to perform a complete ratio analysis using cross-sectional and time-series analysis. The DuPont system of analysis is a diagnostic tool used to find the key areas responsible for the firm's financial performance. It enables the firm to break the return on common equity into three components: profit on sales, efficiency of asset use, and use of financial leverage.

Self-Test Problems   (Solutions in Appendix)

LG 3 **LG 4**   **ST3–1**   **Ratio formulas and interpretations**   Without referring to the text, indicate for each
LG 5   of the following ratios the formula for calculating it and the kinds of problems, if any, the firm may have if that ratio is too high relative to the industry average. What if the ratio is too low relative to the industry average? Create a table similar to the one that follows and fill in the empty blocks.

Ratio	Too high	Too low
Current ratio =		
Inventory turnover =		
Times interest earned =		
Gross profit margin =		
Return on total assets =		
Price/earnings (P/E) ratio =		

LG 3 **LG 4**   **ST3–2**   **Balance sheet completion using ratios**   Complete the 2015 balance sheet for O'Keefe
LG 5   Industries using the information that follows it.

O'Keefe Industries Balance Sheet December 31, 2015			
Assets		**Liabilities and Stockholders' Equity**	
Cash	$32,720	Accounts payable	$120,000
Marketable securities	25,000	Notes payable	_____
Accounts receivable	_____	Accruals	20,000
Inventories	_____	Total current liabilities	_____
Total current assets	_____	Long-term debt	_____
Net fixed assets	_____	Stockholders' equity	$600,000
Total assets	$_____	Total liabilities and stockholders' equity	$_____

The following financial data for 2015 are also available:

1. Sales totaled $1,800,000.
2. The gross profit margin was 25%.
3. Inventory turnover was 6.0.
4. There are 365 days in the year.
5. The average collection period was 40 days.

6. The current ratio was 1.60.
7. The total asset turnover ratio was 1.20.
8. The debt ratio was 60%.

Warm-Up Exercises

All problems are available in MyFinanceLab.

LG 1 **E3–1** You are a summer intern at the office of a local tax preparer. To test your basic knowledge of financial statements, your manager, who graduated from your alma mater 2 years ago, gives you the following list of accounts and asks you to prepare a simple income statement using those accounts.

Accounts	($000,000)
Depreciation	25
General and administrative expenses	22
Sales	345
Sales expenses	18
Cost of goods sold	255
Lease expense	4
Interest expense	3

a. Arrange the accounts into a well-labeled income statement. Make sure you label and solve for gross profit, operating profit, and net profit before taxes.
b. Using a 35% tax rate, calculate taxes paid and net profit after taxes.
c. Assuming a dividend of $1.10 per share with 4.25 million shares outstanding, calculate EPS and additions to retained earnings.

LG 1 **E3–2** Explain why the income statement can also be called a "profit-and-loss statement." What exactly does the word *balance* mean in the title of the balance sheet? Why do we balance the two halves?

LG 1 **E3–3** Cooper Industries, Inc., began 2015 with retained earnings of $25.32 million. During the year, it paid four quarterly dividends of $0.35 per share to 2.75 million common stockholders. Preferred stockholders, holding 500,000 shares, were paid two semiannual dividends of $0.75 per share. The firm had a net profit after taxes of $5.15 million. Prepare the statement of retained earnings for the year ended December 31, 2015.

LG 3 **E3–4** Bluestone Metals, Inc., is a metal fabrication firm that manufactures prefabricated metal parts for customers in a variety of industries. The firm's motto is "If you need it, we can make it." The CEO of Bluestone recently held a board meeting during which he extolled the virtues of the corporation. The company, he stated confidently, had the capability to build any product and could do so using a lean manufacturing model. The firm would soon be profitable, claimed the CEO, because the company used state-of-the-art technology to build a variety of products while keeping inventory levels low. As a business press reporter, you have calculated some ratios to analyze the financial health of the firm. Bluestone's current ratios and quick ratios for the past 6 years are shown in the following table:

	2010	2011	2012	2013	2014	2015
Current ratio	1.2	1.4	1.3	1.6	1.8	2.2
Quick ratio	1.1	1.3	1.2	0.8	0.6	0.4

What do you think of the CEO's claim that the firm is lean and soon to be profitable? (*Hint:* Is there a possible warning sign in the relationship between the two ratios?)

 E3–5 If we know that a firm has a net profit margin of 4.5%, total asset turnover of 0.72, and a financial leverage multiplier of 1.43, what is its ROE? What is the advantage to using the DuPont system to calculate ROE over the direct calculation of earnings available for common stockholders divided by common stock equity?

Problems   All problems are available in MyFinanceLab.

 P3–1 **Reviewing basic financial statements** The income statement for the year ended December 31, 2015, the balance sheets for December 31, 2015 and 2014, and the statement of retained earnings for the year ended December 31, 2015, for Technica, Inc., are given below and on the following page. Briefly discuss the form and informational content of each of these statements.

Technica, Inc., Income Statement for the Year Ended December 31, 2015	
Sales revenue	$600,000
Less: Cost of goods sold	460,000
Gross profits	$140,000
Less: Operating expenses	
General and administrative expenses	$ 30,000
Depreciation expense	30,000
Total operating expense	$ 60,000
Operating profits	$ 80,000
Less: Interest expense	10,000
Net profits before taxes	$ 70,000
Less: Taxes	27,100
Earnings available for common stockholders	$ 42,900
Earnings per share (EPS)	$2.15

Technica, Inc., Balance Sheets		
	December 31	
Assets	2015	2014
Cash	$ 15,000	$ 16,000
Marketable securities	7,200	8,000
Accounts receivable	34,100	42,200
Inventories	82,000	50,000
Total current assets	$138,300	$116,200
Land and buildings	$150,000	$150,000
Machinery and equipment	200,000	190,000
Furniture and fixtures	54,000	50,000
Other	11,000	10,000
Total gross fixed assets	$415,000	$400,000
Less: Accumulated depreciation	145,000	115,000
Net fixed assets	$270,000	$285,000
Total assets	$408,000	$401,200
Liabilities and Stockholders' Equity		
Accounts payable	$ 57,000	$ 49,000
Notes payable	13,000	16,000
Accruals	5,000	6,000
Total current liabilities	$ 75,000	$ 71,000
Long-term debt	$150,000	$160,000
Common stock equity (shares outstanding: 19,500 in 2015 and 20,000 in 2014)	$110,200	$120,000
Retained earnings	73,100	50,200
Total stockholders' equity	$183,300	$170,200
Total liabilities and stockholders' equity	$408,300	$401,200

Technica, Inc., Statement of Retained Earnings for the Year Ended December 31, 2015	
Retained earnings balance (January 1, 2015)	$50,200
Plus: Net profits after taxes (for 2015)	42,900
Less: Cash dividends (paid during 2015)	20,000
Retained earnings balance (December 31, 2015)	$73,100

 P3–2 Financial statement account identification Mark each of the accounts listed in the following table as follows:
   a. In column (1), indicate in which statement—income statement (IS) or balance sheet (BS)—the account belongs.
   b. In column (2), indicate whether the account is a current asset (CA), current liability (CL), expense (E), fixed asset (FA), long-term debt (LTD), revenue (R), or stockholders' equity (SE).

Account name	(1) Statement	(2) Type of account
Accounts payable	_____	_____
Accounts receivable	_____	_____
Accruals	_____	_____
Accumulated depreciation	_____	_____
Administrative expense	_____	_____
Buildings	_____	_____
Cash	_____	_____
Common stock (at par)	_____	_____
Cost of goods sold	_____	_____
Depreciation	_____	_____
Equipment	_____	_____
General expense	_____	_____
Interest expense	_____	_____
Inventories	_____	_____
Land	_____	_____
Long-term debts	_____	_____
Machinery	_____	_____
Marketable securities	_____	_____
Notes payable	_____	_____
Operating expense	_____	_____
Paid-in capital in excess of par	_____	_____
Preferred stock	_____	_____
Preferred stock dividends	_____	_____
Retained earnings	_____	_____
Sales revenue	_____	_____
Selling expense	_____	_____
Taxes	_____	_____
Vehicles	_____	_____

LG 1   **P3–3**   **Income statement preparation**   On December 31, 2015, Cathy Chen, a self-employed certified public accountant (CPA), completed her first full year in business. During the year, she billed $360,000 for her accounting services. She had two employees, a bookkeeper and a clerical assistant. In addition to her *monthly* salary of $8,000, Ms. Chen paid *annual* salaries of $48,000 and $36,000 to the bookkeeper and the clerical assistant, respectively. Employment taxes and benefit costs for Ms. Chen and her employees totaled $34,600 for the year. Expenses for office supplies, including postage, totaled $10,400 for the year. In addition, Ms. Chen spent $17,000 during the year on tax-deductible travel and entertainment associated with client visits and new business development. Lease payments for the office space rented (a tax-deductible expense) were $2,700 *per month*. Depreciation expense on the office furniture and fixtures was $15,600 for the year. During the year, Ms. Chen paid interest of $15,000 on the $120,000 borrowed to start the business. She paid an average tax rate of 30% during 2015.

a. Prepare an income statement for Cathy Chen, CPA, for the year ended December 31, 2015.

b. Evaluate her 2015 financial performance.

Personal Finance Problem

LG 1   **P3–4 Income statement preparation** Adam and Arin Adams have collected their personal income and expense information and have asked you to put together an income and expense statement for the year ended December 31, 2015. The following information is received from the Adams family.

Adam's salary	$45,000	Utilities	$ 3,200
Arin's salary	30,000	Groceries	2,200
Interest received	500	Medical	1,500
Dividends received	150	Property taxes	1,659
Auto insurance	600	Income tax, Social Security	13,000
Home insurance	750	Clothes and accessories	2,000
Auto loan payment	3,300	Gas and auto repair	2,100
Mortgage payment	14,000	Entertainment	2,000

a. Create a personal *income and expense statement* for the period ended December 31, 2015. It should be similar to a corporate income statement.
b. Did the Adams family have a cash surplus or cash deficit?
c. If the result is a surplus, how can the Adams family use that surplus?

LG 1   **P3–5 Calculation of EPS and retained earnings** Everdeen Mining, Inc., ended 2015 with a net profit *before* taxes of $436,000. The company is subject to a 40% tax rate and must pay $64,000 in preferred stock dividends before distributing any earnings on the 170,000 shares of common stock currently outstanding.
a. Calculate Everdeen's 2015 earnings per share (EPS).
b. If the firm paid common stock dividends of $0.80 per share, how many dollars would go to retained earnings?

LG 1   **P3–6 Balance sheet preparation** Use the *appropriate items* from the following list to prepare in good form Mellark's Baked Goods balance sheet at December 31, 2015.

Item	Value ($000) at December 31, 2015	Item	Value ($000) at December 31, 2015
Accounts payable	$ 220	Inventories	$ 375
Accounts receivable	450	Land	100
Accruals	55	Long-term debts	420
Accumulated depreciation	265	Machinery	420
Buildings	225	Marketable securities	75
Cash	215	Notes payable	475
Common stock (at par)	90	Paid-in capital in excess	
Cost of goods sold	2,500	of par	360
Depreciation expense	45	Preferred stock	100
Equipment	140	Retained earnings	210
Furniture and fixtures	170	Sales revenue	3,600
General expense	320	Vehicles	25

Personal Finance Problem

 P3–7 **Balance sheet preparation** Adam and Arin Adams have collected their personal asset and liability information and have asked you to put together a balance sheet as of December 31, 2015. The following information is received from the Adams family.

Cash	$ 300	Retirement funds, IRA	$ 2,000
Checking	3,000	2014 Sebring	15,000
Savings	1,200	2010 Jeep	8,000
IBM stock	2,000	Money market funds	1,200
Auto loan	8,000	Jewelry and artwork	3,000
Mortgage	100,000	Net worth	76,500
Medical bills payable	250	Household furnishings	4,200
Utility bills payable	150	Credit card balance	2,000
Real estate	150,000	Personal loan	3,000

a. Create a personal balance sheet as of December 31, 2015. It should be similar to a corporate balance sheet.
b. What must the total assets of the Adams family be equal to by December 31, 2015?
c. What was their *net working capital (NWC)* for the year? (*Hint:* NWC is the difference between total liquid assets and total current liabilities.)

 P3–8 **Effect of net income on a firm's balance sheet** Conrad Air, Inc., reported net income of $1,365,000 for the year ended December 31, 2016. Show how Conrad's balance sheet would change from 2015 to 2016 depending on how Conrad "spent" those earnings as described in the scenarios that appear below.

Conrad Air, Inc., Balance Sheet as of December 31, 2015			
Assets		**Liabilities and Stockholders' Equity**	
Cash	$ 120,000	Accounts payable	$ 170,000
Marketable securities	35,000	Short-term notes	$ 55,000
Accounts receivable	45,000	Current liabilities	$ 125,000
Inventories	$ 130,000	Long-term debt	$2,700,000
Current assets	$ 330,000	Total liabilities	$2,825,000
Equipment	$2,970,000	Common stock	$ 500,000
Buildings	$1,600,000	Retained earnings	$1,575,000
Fixed assets	$4,570,000	Stockholders' equity	$2,075,000
Total assets	$4,900,000	Total liabilities and equity	$4,900,000

a. Conrad paid no dividends during the year and invested the funds in marketable securities.
b. Conrad paid dividends totaling $500,000 and used the balance of the net income to retire (pay off) long-term debt.
c. Conrad paid dividends totaling $500,000 and invested the balance of the net income in building a new hangar.
d. Conrad paid out all $1,365,000 as dividends to its stockholders.

P3–9 **Initial sale price of common stock** Haymitch Brewing Corporation has one issue of preferred stock and one issue of common stock outstanding. Given Haymitch's stockholders' equity account that follows, determine the original price per share at which the firm sold its single issue of common stock.

Stockholders' Equity ($000)	
Preferred stock	$ 225
Common stock ($0.50 par, 400,000 shares outstanding)	200
Paid-in capital in excess of par on common stock	2,600
Retained earnings	800
Total stockholders' equity	$3,825

 P3–10 **Statement of retained earnings** Hayes Enterprises began 2015 with a retained earnings balance of $928,000. During 2015, the firm earned $377,000 after taxes. From this amount, preferred stockholders were paid $47,000 in dividends. At year-end 2015, the firm's retained earnings totaled $1,048,000. The firm had 140,000 shares of common stock outstanding during 2015.
a. Prepare a statement of retained earnings for the year ended December 31, 2015, for Hayes Enterprises. (*Note:* Be sure to calculate and include the amount of cash dividends paid in 2015.)
b. Calculate the firm's 2015 earnings per share (EPS).
c. How large a per-share cash dividend did the firm pay on common stock during 2015?

 P3–11 **Changes in stockholders' equity** Listed are the equity sections of balance sheets for years 2014 and 2015 as reported by Mountain Air Ski Resorts, Inc. The overall value of stockholders' equity has risen from $2,000,000 to $7,500,000. Use the statements to discover how and why that happened.

Mountain Air Ski Resorts, Inc. Balance Sheets (partial)		
Stockholders' equity	**2014**	**2015**
Common stock ($1.00 par)		
Authorized: 5,000,000 shares		
Outstanding: 1,500,000 shares 2015		$1,500,000
500,000 shares 2014	$ 500,000	
Paid-in capital in excess of par	500,000	4,500,000
Retained earnings	1,000,000	1,500,000
Total stockholders' equity	$2,000,000	$7,500,000

The company paid total dividends of $200,000 during fiscal 2015.
a. What was Mountain Air's net income for fiscal 2015?
b. How many new shares did the corporation issue and sell during the year?
c. At what average price per share did the new stock sold during 2015 sell?
d. At what price per share did Mountain Air's original 500,000 shares sell?

P3–12   **Ratio comparisons**   Robert Arias recently inherited a stock portfolio from his uncle.
   Wishing to learn more about the companies in which he is now invested, Robert performs a ratio analysis on each one and decides to compare them to one another. Some of his ratios are listed below.

Ratio	Island Electric Utility	Burger Heaven	Fink Software	Roland Motors
Current ratio	1.10	1.3	6.8	4.5
Quick ratio	0.90	0.82	5.2	3.7
Debt ratio	0.68	0.46	0.0	0.35
Net profit margin	6.2%	14.3%	28.5%	8.4%

Assuming that his uncle was a wise investor who assembled the portfolio with care, Robert finds the wide differences in these ratios confusing. Help him out.
a. What problems might Robert encounter in comparing these companies to one another on the basis of their ratios?
b. Why might the current and quick ratios for the electric utility and the fast-food stock be so much lower than the same ratios for the other companies?
c. Why might it be all right for the electric utility to carry a large amount of debt, but not the software company?
d. Why wouldn't investors invest all their money in software companies instead of in less profitable companies? (Focus on risk and return.)

 P3–13   **Liquidity management**   Bauman Company's total current assets, total current liabilities, and inventory for each of the past 4 years follow:

Item	2012	2013	2014	2015
Total current assets	$16,950	$21,900	$22,500	$27,000
Total current liabilities	9,000	12,600	12,600	17,400
Inventory	6,000	6,900	6,900	7,200

a. Calculate the firm's current and quick ratios for each year. Compare the resulting time series for these measures of liquidity.
b. Comment on the firm's liquidity over the 2012–2013 period.
c. If you were told that Bauman Company's inventory turnover for each year in the 2012–2015 period and the industry averages were as follows, would this information support or conflict with your evaluation in part **b**? Why?

Inventory turnover	2012	2013	2014	2015
Bauman Company	6.3	6.8	7.0	6.4
Industry average	10.6	11.2	10.8	11.0

Personal Finance Problem

 P3–14 **Liquidity ratio** Josh Smith has compiled some of his personal financial data to determine his liquidity position. The data are as follows.

Account	Amount
Cash	$3,200
Marketable securities	1,000
Checking account	800
Credit card payables	1,200
Short-term notes payable	900

a. Calculate Josh's *liquidity ratio*.
b. Several of Josh's friends have told him that they have liquidity ratios of about 1.8. How would you analyze Josh's liquidity relative to his friends?

 P3–15 **Inventory management** Wilkins Manufacturing has annual sales of $4 million and a gross profit margin of 40%. Its *end-of-quarter inventories* are

Quarter	Inventory
1	$ 400,000
2	800,000
3	1,200,000
4	200,000

a. Find the average quarterly inventory and use it to calculate the firm's inventory turnover and the average age of inventory.
b. Assuming that the company is in an industry with an average inventory turnover of 2.0, how would you evaluate the activity of Wilkins' inventory?

P3–16 **Accounts receivable management** An evaluation of the books of Blair Supply, which follows, gives the end-of-year accounts receivable balance, which is believed to consist of amounts originating in the months indicated. The company had annual sales of $2.4 million. The firm extends 30-day credit terms.

Month of origin	Accounts receivable
July	$ 3,875
August	2,000
September	34,025
October	15,100
November	52,000
December	193,000
Year-end accounts receivable	$300,000

a. Use the year-end total to evaluate the firm's collection system.
b. If 70% of the firm's sales occur between July and December, would this information affect the validity of your conclusion in part a? Explain.

P3–17 **Interpreting liquidity and activity ratios** The new owners of Bluegrass Natural Foods, Inc., have hired you to help them diagnose and cure problems that the company has had in maintaining adequate liquidity. As a first step, you perform a liquidity analysis. You then do an analysis of the company's short-term activity ratios. Your calculations and appropriate industry norms are listed.

Ratio	Bluegrass	Industry norm
Current ratio	4.5	4.0
Quick ratio	2.0	3.1
Inventory turnover	6.0	10.4
Average collection period	73 days	52 days
Average payment period	31 days	40 days

a. What recommendations relative to the amount and the handling of inventory could you make to the new owners?
b. What recommendations relative to the amount and the handling of accounts receivable could you make to the new owners?
c. What recommendations relative to the amount and the handling of accounts payable could you make to the new owners?
d. What results, overall, would you hope your recommendations would achieve? Why might your recommendations not be effective?

 P3–18 **Debt analysis** Springfield Bank is evaluating Creek Enterprises, which has requested a $4,000,000 loan, to assess the firm's financial leverage and financial risk. On the basis of the debt ratios for Creek, along with the industry averages (see the top of the next page) and Creek's recent financial statements (following), evaluate and recommend appropriate action on the loan request.

Creek Enterprises Income Statement for the Year Ended December 31, 2015	
Sales revenue	$30,000,000
Less: Cost of goods sold	21,000,000
Gross profits	$ 9,000,000
Less: Operating expenses	
Selling expense	$ 3,000,000
General and administrative expenses	1,800,000
Lease expense	200,000
Depreciation expense	1,000,000
Total operating expense	$ 6,000,000
Operating profits	$ 3,000,000
Less: Interest expense	1,000,000
Net profits before taxes	$ 2,000,000
Less: Taxes (rate = 40%)	800,000
Net profits after taxes	$ 1,200,000
Less: Preferred stock dividends	100,0000
Earnings available for common stockholders	$ 1,100,000

Creek Enterprises Balance Sheet December 31, 2015			
Assets		**Liabilities and Stockholders' Equity**	
Cash	$ 1,000,000	Accounts payable	$ 8,000,000
Marketable securities	3,000,000	Notes payable	8,000,000
Accounts receivable	12,000,000	Accruals	500,000
Inventories	7,500,000	Total current liabilities	$16,500,000
Total current assets	$23,500,000	Long-term debt (includes	
Land and buildings	$11,000,000	financial leases)[b]	$20,000,000
Machinery and equipment	20,500,000	Preferred stock (25,000	
Furniture and fixtures	8,000,000	shares, $4 dividend)	$ 2,500,000
Gross fixed assets (at cost)[a]	$39,500,000	Common stock (1 million	
Less: Accumulated depreciation	13,000,000	shares at $5 par)	5,000,000
Net fixed assets	$26,500,000	Paid-in capital in excess of	
Total assets	$50,000,000	par value	4,000,000
		Retained earnings	2,000,000
		Total stockholders' equity	$13,500,000
		Total liabilities and	
		stockholders' equity	$50,000,000

Industry averages	
Debt ratio	0.51
Times interest earned ratio	7.30
Fixed-payment coverage ratio	1.85

[a]The firm has a 4-year financial lease requiring annual beginning-of-year payments of $200,000. Three years of the lease have yet to run.

[b]Required annual principal payments are $800,000.

LG 5 **P3–19** **Profitability analysis** In early 2013, Pepsi reported revenues of $65.64 billion with earnings available for common stockholders of $6.12 billion. Pepsi's total assets at the time were $74.64 billion. Meanwhile, one of Pepsi's competitors, Dr. Pepper, reported sales of $6.01 billion with earnings of $0.63 billion. Dr. Pepper had assets of $8.87 billion. Which company was more profitable? Why is it hard to get a clear answer to this question?

LG 5 **P3–20** **Common-size statement analysis** A common-size income statement for Creek Enterprises' 2014 operations follows. Using the firm's 2015 income statement presented in Problem 3–18, develop the 2015 common-size income statement and compare it with the 2014 statement. Which areas require further analysis and investigation?

Creek Enterprises Common-Size Income Statement for the Year Ended December 31, 2014	
Sales revenue ($35,000,000)	100.0%
Less: Cost of goods sold	65.9
Gross profits	34.1%
Less: Operating expenses	
Selling expense	12.7%
General and administrative expenses	6.3
Lease expense	0.6
Depreciation expense	3.6
Total operating expense	23.2
Operating profits	10.9%
Less: Interest expense	1.5
Net profits before taxes	9.4%
Less: Taxes (rate = 40%)	3.8
Net profits after taxes	5.6%
Less: Preferred stock dividends	0.1
Earnings available for common stockholders	5.5%

P3–21 **The relationship between financial leverage and profitability** Pelican Paper, Inc., and Timberland Forest, Inc., are rivals in the manufacture of craft papers. Some financial statement values for each company follow. Use them in a ratio analysis that compares the firms' financial leverage and profitability.

Item	Pelican Paper, Inc.	Timberland Forest, Inc.
Total assets	$10,000,000	$10,000,000
Total equity (all common)	9,000,000	5,000,000
Total debt	1,000,000	5,000,000
Annual interest	100,000	500,000
Total sales	25,000,000	25,000,000
EBIT	6,250,000	6,250,000
Earnings available for common stockholders	3,690,000	3,450,000

a. Calculate the following debt and coverage ratios for the two companies. Discuss their financial risk and ability to cover the costs in relation to each other.
1. Debt ratio
2. Times interest earned ratio
b. Calculate the following profitability ratios for the two companies. Discuss their profitability relative to one another.
1. Operating profit margin
2. Net profit margin
3. Return on total assets
4. Return on common equity
c. In what way has the larger debt of Timberland Forest made it more profitable than Pelican Paper? What are the risks that Timberland's investors undertake when they choose to purchase its stock instead of Pelican's?

 P3–22 **Ratio proficiency** McDougal Printing, Inc., had sales totaling $40,000,000 in fiscal year 2015. Some ratios for the company are listed below. Use this information to determine the dollar values of various income statement and balance sheet accounts as requested.

McDougal Printing, Inc. Year Ended December 31, 2015	
Sales	$40,000,000
Gross profit margin	80%
Operating profit margin	35%
Net profit margin	8%
Return on total assets	16%
Return on common equity	20%
Total asset turnover	2
Average collection period	62.2 days

Calculate values for the following:
a. Gross profits
b. Cost of goods sold

c. Operating profits
d. Operating expenses
e. Earnings available for common stockholders
f. Total assets
g. Total common stock equity
h. Accounts receivable

LG 6 **P3–23** **Cross-sectional ratio analysis** Use the financial statements below and on the next page for Fox Manufacturing Company for the year ended December 31, 2015, along with the industry average ratios below to do the following:

a. Prepare and interpret a complete ratio analysis of the firm's 2015 operations.
b. Summarize your findings and make recommendations.

Fox Manufacturing Company Income Statement for the Year Ended December 31, 2015	
Sales revenue	$600,000
Less: Cost of goods sold	460,000
Gross profits	$140,000
Less: Operating expenses	
General and administrative expenses	$ 30,000
Depreciation expense	30,000
Total operating expense	60,000
Operating profits	$ 80,000
Less: Interest expense	10,000
Net profits before taxes	$ 70,000
Less: Taxes	27,100
Net profits after taxes (*Hint:* Earnings available for common stockholders as there are no preferred stockholders)	$ 42,900
Earnings per share (EPS)	$2.15

Ratio	Industry average, 2015
Current ratio	2.35
Quick ratio	0.87
Inventory turnover[a]	4.55
Average collection period[a]	35.8 days
Total asset turnover	1.09
Debt ratio	0.300
Times interest earned ratio	12.3
Gross profit margin	0.202
Operating profit margin	0.135
Net profit margin	0.091
Return on total assets (ROA)	0.099
Return on common equity (ROE)	0.167
Earnings per share (EPS)	$3.10

[a]Based on a 365-day year and on end-of-year figures.

Fox Manufacturing Company Balance Sheet
December 31, 2015

Assets

Cash	$ 15,000
Marketable securities	7,200
Accounts receivable	34,100
Inventories	82,000
Total current assets	$138,300
Net fixed assets	270,000
Total assets	$408,300

Liabilities and Stockholders' Equity

Accounts payable	$ 57,000
Notes payable	13,000
Accruals	5,000
Total current liabilities	$ 75,000
Long-term debt	$150,000
Common stock equity (20,000 shares outstanding)	$110,200
Retained earnings	73,100
Total stockholders' equity	$183,300
Total liabilities and stockholders' equity	$408,300

LG 6   **P3–24   Financial statement analysis**   The financial statements of Zach Industries for the year ended December 31, 2015, follow.

Zach Industries Income Statement
for the Year Ended December 31, 2015

Sales revenue	$160,000
Less: Cost of goods sold	106,000
Gross profits	$ 54,000
Less: Operating expenses	
Selling expense	$ 16,000
General and administrative expenses	10,000
Lease expense	1,000
Depreciation expense	10,000
Total operating expense	$ 37,000
Operating profits	$ 17,000
Less: Interest expense	6,100
Net profits before taxes	$ 10,900
Less: Taxes	4,360
Net profits after taxes	$ 6,540

Zach Industries Balance Sheet December 31, 2015	
Assets	
Cash	$ 500
Marketable securities	1,000
Accounts receivable	25,000
Inventories	45,500
Total current assets	$ 72,000
Land	$ 26,000
Buildings and equipment	90,000
Less: Accumulated depreciation	38,000
Net fixed assets	$ 78,000
Total assets	$150,000
Liabilities and Stockholders' Equity	
Accounts payable	$ 22,000
Notes payable	47,000
Total current liabilities	$ 69,000
Long-term debt	22,950
Common stock[a]	31,500
Retained earnings	26,550
Total liabilities and stockholders' equity	$ 150,000

[a]The firm's 3,000 outstanding shares of common stock closed 2015 at a price of $25 per share.

a. Use the preceding financial statements to complete the following table. Assume that the industry averages given in the table are applicable for both 2014 and 2015.

Ratio	Industry average	Actual 2014	Actual 2015
Current ratio	1.80	1.84	_____
Quick ratio	0.70	0.78	_____
Inventory turnover[a]	2.50	2.59	_____
Average collection period[a]	37.5 days	36.5 days	_____
Debt ratio	65%	67%	_____
Times interest earned ratio	3.8	4.0	_____
Gross profit margin	38%	40%	_____
Net profit margin	3.5%	3.6%	_____
Return on total assets	4.0%	4.0%	_____
Return on common equity	9.5%	8.0%	_____
Market/book ratio	1.1	1.2	_____

[a]Based on a 365-day year and on end-of-year figures.

b. Analyze Zach Industries' financial condition as it is related to (1) liquidity, (2) activity, (3) debt, (4) profitability, and (5) market. Summarize the company's overall financial condition.

P3–25 **Integrative: Complete ratio analysis** Given the following financial statements (following and on the next page), historical ratios, and industry averages, calculate Sterling Company's financial ratios for the most recent year. (Assume a 365-day year.)

Sterling Company Income Statement for the Year Ended December 31, 2015	
Sales revenue	$ 10,000,000
Less: Cost of goods sold	7,500,000
Gross profits	$ 2,500,000
Less: Operating expenses	
Selling expense	$ 300,000
General and administrative expenses	650,000
Lease expense	50,000
Depreciation expense	200,000
Total operating expense	$ 1,200,000
Operating profits	$ 1,300,000
Less: Interest expense	200,000
Net profits before taxes	$ 1,100,000
Less: Taxes (rate = 40%)	440,000
Net profits after taxes	$ 660,000
Less: Preferred stock dividends	50,000
Earnings available for common stockholders	$ 610,000
Earnings per share (EPS)	$3.05

Sterling Company Balance Sheet December 31, 2015			
Assets		**Liabilities and Stockholders' Equity**	
Cash	$ 200,000	Accounts payable[a]	$ 900,000
Marketable securities	50,000	Notes payable	200,000
Accounts receivable	800,000	Accruals	100,000
Inventories	950,000	Total current liabilities	$ 1,200,000
Total current assets	$ 2,000,000	Long-term debt (includes	
Gross fixed assets (at cost)	$12,000,000	financial leases)	$ 3,000,000
Less: Accumulated depreciation	3,000,000	Preferred stock (25,000 shares,	
Net fixed assets	$ 9,000,000	$2 dividend)	$ 1,000,000
Other assets	1,000,000	Common stock (200,000	
Total assets	$12,000,000	shares at $3 par)[b]	600,000
		Paid-in capital in excess of par value	5,200,000
		Retained earnings	1,000,000
		Total stockholders' equity	$ 7,800,000
		Total liabilities and stockholders' equity	$12,000,000

[a]Annual credit purchases of $6,200,000 were made during the year.
[b]On December 31, 2015, the firm's common stock closed at $39.50 per share.

Analyze its overall financial situation from both a cross-sectional and a time-series viewpoint. Break your analysis into evaluations of the firm's liquidity, activity, debt, profitability, and market.

Historical and Industry Average Ratios for Sterling Company			
Ratio	Actual 2013	Actual 2014	Industry average, 2015
Current ratio	1.40	1.55	1.85
Quick ratio	1.00	0.92	1.05
Inventory turnover	9.52	9.21	8.60
Average collection period	45.6 days	36.9 days	35.5 days
Average payment period	59.3 days	61.6 days	46.4 days
Total asset turnover	0.74	0.80	0.74
Debt ratio	0.20	0.20	0.30
Times interest earned ratio	8.2	7.3	8.0
Fixed-payment coverage ratio	4.5	4.2	4.2
Gross profit margin	0.30	0.27	0.25
Operating profit margin	0.12	0.12	0.10
Net profit margin	0.062	0.062	0.053
Return on total assets (ROA)	0.045	0.050	0.040
Return on common equity (ROE)	0.061	0.067	0.066
Earnings per share (EPS)	$1.75	$2.20	$1.50
Price/earnings (P/E) ratio	12.0	10.5	11.2
Market/book (M/B) ratio	1.20	1.05	1.10

LG 6 **P3–26** **DuPont system of analysis** Use the following ratio information for Johnson International and the industry averages for Johnson's line of business to:
a. Construct the DuPont system of analysis for both Johnson and the industry.
b. Evaluate Johnson (and the industry) over the 3-year period.
c. Indicate in which areas Johnson requires further analysis. Why?

Johnson	2013	2014	2015
Financial leverage multiplier	1.75	1.75	1.85
Net profit margin	0.059	0.058	0.049
Total asset turnover	2.11	2.18	2.34
Industry averages			
Financial leverage multiplier	1.67	1.69	1.64
Net profit margin	0.054	0.047	0.041
Total asset turnover	2.05	2.13	2.15

LG 6 **P3–27** **Complete ratio analysis, recognizing significant differences** Home Health, Inc., has come to Jane Ross for a yearly financial checkup. As a first step, Jane has prepared a complete set of ratios for fiscal years 2014 and 2015. She will use them to look for significant changes in the company's situation from one year to the next.

Home Health, Inc., Financial Ratios		
Ratio	2014	2015
Current ratio	3.25	3.00
Quick ratio	2.50	2.20
Inventory turnover	12.80	10.30
Average collection period	42.6 days	31.4 days
Total asset turnover	1.40	2.00
Debt ratio	0.45	0.62
Times interest earned ratio	4.00	3.85
Gross profit margin	68%	65%
Operating profit margin	14%	16%
Net profit margin	8.3%	8.1%
Return on total assets	11.6%	16.2%
Return on common equity	21.1%	42.6%
Price/earnings ratio	10.7	9.8
Market/book ratio	1.40	1.25

a. To focus on the degree of change, calculate the year-to-year proportional change by subtracting the year 2014 ratio from the year 2015 ratio and then dividing the difference by the year 2014 ratio. Multiply the result by 100. Preserve the positive or negative sign. The result is the percentage change in the ratio from 2014 to 2015. Calculate the proportional change for the ratios shown here.

b. For any ratio that shows a year-to-year difference of 10% or more, state whether the difference is in the company's favor or not.

c. For the most significant changes (25% or more), look at the other ratios and cite at least one other change that may have contributed to the change in the ratio that you are discussing.

 P3–28 **ETHICS PROBLEM** Do some reading in periodicals or on the Internet to find out more about the Sarbanes-Oxley Act's provisions for companies. Select one of those provisions, and indicate why you think financial statements will be more trustworthy if company financial executives implement this provision of SOX.

Spreadsheet Exercise

 The income statement and balance sheet are the primary reports that a firm constructs for use by management and for distribution to stockholders, regulatory bodies, and the general public. They are the primary sources of historical financial information about the firm. Dayton Products, Inc., is a moderate-sized manufacturer. The company's management has asked you to perform a detailed financial statement analysis of the firm.

The income statements for the years ending December 31, 2015 and 2014, respectively, are presented in the following table.

Annual Income Statements (Values in Millions)		
	For the year ended	
	December 31, 2015	December 31, 2014
Sales	$178,909	$187,510
Cost of goods sold	109,701	111,631
Selling, general, and administrative expenses	12,356	12,900
Other tax expense	33,572	33,377
Depreciation and amortization	12,103	7,944
Other income (add to EBIT to arrive at EBT)	3,147	3,323
Interest expense	398	293
Income tax rate (average)	35.324%	37.945%
Dividends paid per share	$1.13	$0.91
Basic EPS from total operations	$1.34	$2.25

You also have the following balance sheet information as of December 31, 2015 and 2014, respectively.

Annual Balance Sheets (Values in Millions)		
	December 31, 2015	December 31, 2014
Cash	$ 7,229	$ 6,547
Receivables	21,163	19,549
Inventories	8,068	7,904
Other current assets	1,831	1,681
Property, plant, and equipment, gross	204,960	187,519
Accumulated depreciation and depletion	110,020	97,917
Other noncurrent assets	19,413	17,891
Accounts payable	13,792	22,862
Short-term debt payable	4,093	3,703
Other current liabilities	15,290	3,549
Long-term debt payable	6,655	7,099
Deferred income taxes	16,484	16,359
Other noncurrent liabilities	21,733	16,441
Retained earnings	74,597	73,161
Total common shares outstanding	6.7 billion	6.8 billion

TO DO

a. Create a spreadsheet similar to Table 3.1 to model the following:
   (1) A multiple-step comparative income statement for Dayton, Inc., for the periods ending December 31, 2015 and 2014. You must calculate the cost of goods sold for the year 2015.
   (2) A common-size income statement for Dayton, Inc., covering the years 2015 and 2014.

b. Create a spreadsheet similar to Table 3.2 to model the following:
   (1) A detailed, comparative balance sheet for Dayton, Inc., for the years ended December 31, 2015 and 2014.
   (2) A common-size balance sheet for Dayton, Inc., covering the years 2015 and 2014.

c. Create a spreadsheet similar to Table 3.8 to perform the following analysis:
   (1) Create a table that reflects both 2015 and 2014 operating ratios for Dayton, Inc., segmented into (a) liquidity, (b) activity, (c) debt, (d) profitability, and (e) market. Assume that the current market price for the stock is $90.
   (2) Compare the 2015 ratios to the 2014 ratios. Indicate whether the results "outperformed the prior year" or "underperformed relative to the prior year."

MyFinanceLab   Visit www.myfinancelab.com for **Chapter Case: *Assessing Martin Manufacturing's Current Financial Position,*** Group Exercises, and numerous online resources.

4

Cash Flow and Financial Planning

Learning Goals

LG 1 Understand tax depreciation procedures and the effect of depreciation on the firm's cash flows.

LG 2 Discuss the firm's statement of cash flows, operating cash flow, and free cash flow.

LG 3 Understand the financial planning process, including long-term (strategic) financial plans and short-term (operating) financial plans.

LG 4 Discuss the cash-planning process and the preparation, evaluation, and use of the cash budget.

LG 5 Explain the simplified procedures used to prepare and evaluate the pro forma income statement and the pro forma balance sheet.

LG 6 Evaluate the simplified approaches to pro forma financial statement preparation and the common uses of pro forma statements.

Why This Chapter Matters to You

In your *professional* life

ACCOUNTING You need to understand how depreciation is used for both tax and financial reporting purposes; how to develop the statement of cash flows; the primary focus on cash flows, rather than accruals, in financial decision making; and how pro forma financial statements are used within the firm.

INFORMATION SYSTEMS You need to understand the data that must be kept to record depreciation for tax and financial reporting, the information needed for strategic and operating plans, and what data are needed as inputs for preparing cash plans and profit plans.

MANAGEMENT You need to understand the difference between strategic and operating plans, and the role of each; the importance of focusing on the firm's cash flows; and how use of pro forma statements can head off trouble for the firm.

MARKETING You need to understand the central role that marketing plays in formulating the firm's long-term strategic plans and the importance of the sales forecast as the key input for both cash planning and profit planning.

OPERATIONS You need to understand how depreciation affects the value of the firm's plant assets, how the results of operations are captured in the statement of cash flows, that operations provide key inputs into the firm's short-term financial plans, and the distinction between fixed and variable operating costs.

In your *personal* life

Individuals, like corporations, should focus on cash flow when planning and monitoring finances. You should establish short- and long-term financial goals (destinations) and develop personal financial plans (road maps) that will guide their achievement. Cash flows and financial plans are as important for individuals as for corporations.

4.1 Analyzing the Firm's Cash Flow

"Cash is king" is an old saying in finance. Cash flow, the lifeblood of the firm, is the primary ingredient in any financial valuation model. Whether an analyst wants to put a value on an investment that a firm is considering or the objective is to value the firm itself, estimating cash flow is central to the valuation process. This chapter explains where the cash flow numbers used in valuations come from.

DEPRECIATION

depreciation
A portion of the costs of fixed assets charged against annual revenues over time.

For tax and financial reporting purposes, businesses generally cannot deduct as an expense the full cost of an asset that will be in use for several years. Instead, each year firms are required to charge a portion of the costs of fixed assets against revenues. This allocation of historical cost over time is called **depreciation**. Depreciation deductions, like any other business expenses, reduce the income that a firm reports on its income statement and therefore reduce the taxes that the firm must pay. However, depreciation deductions are not associated with any cash outlay. That is, when a firm deducts depreciation expense, it is allocating a portion of an asset's original cost (that the firm has already paid for) as a charge against that year's income. The net effect is that *depreciation deductions increase a firm's cash flow because they reduce a firm's tax bill.*

For tax purposes, the depreciation of business assets is regulated by the Internal Revenue Code. Because the objectives of financial reporting sometimes differ from those of tax legislation, firms often use different depreciation methods for financial reporting than those required for tax purposes. Keeping two different sets of records for these two purposes is legal in the United States.

modified accelerated cost recovery system (MACRS)
System used to determine the depreciation of assets for tax purposes.

Depreciation for tax purposes is determined by using the **modified accelerated cost recovery system (MACRS)**; a variety of depreciation methods are available for financial reporting purposes. All depreciation methods require you to know an asset's depreciable value and its depreciable life.

Depreciable Value of an Asset

Under the basic MACRS procedures, the depreciable value of an asset (the amount to be depreciated) is its *full* cost, including outlays for installation. Even if the asset is expected to have some salvage value at the end of its useful life, the firm can still take depreciation deductions equal to the asset's full initial cost.

Example 4.1 ▶

MyFinanceLab Solution
Video

Baker Corporation acquired a new machine at a cost of $38,000, with installation costs of $2,000. When the machine is retired from service, Baker expects to sell it for scrap metal and receive $1,000. Regardless of its expected salvage value, the depreciable value of the machine is $40,000: $38,000 cost + $2,000 installation cost.

Depreciable Life of an Asset

depreciable life
Time period over which an asset is depreciated.

The time period over which an asset is depreciated is called its **depreciable life**. The shorter the depreciable life, the larger the annual depreciation deductions will be, and the larger will be the tax savings associated with those deductions, all other things being equal. Accordingly, firms generally would like to depreciate

TABLE 4.1	First Four Property Classes under MACRS
Property class (recovery period)	Definition
3 years	Research equipment and certain special tools
5 years	Computers, printers, copiers, duplicating equipment, cars, light-duty trucks, qualified technological equipment, and similar assets
7 years	Office furniture, fixtures, most manufacturing equipment, railroad track, and single-purpose agricultural and horticultural structures
10 years	Equipment used in petroleum refining or in the manufacture of tobacco products and certain food products

recovery period
The appropriate depreciable life of a particular asset as determined by MACRS.

their assets as rapidly as possible. However, the firm must abide by certain Internal Revenue Service (IRS) requirements for determining depreciable life. These MACRS standards, which apply to both new and used assets, require the taxpayer to use as an asset's depreciable life the appropriate MACRS **recovery period**. There are six MACRS recovery periods—3, 5, 7, 10, 15, and 20 years—excluding real estate. It is customary to refer to the property classes as 3-, 5-, 7-, 10-, 15-, and 20-year property. The first four property classes—those routinely used by business—are defined in Table 4.1.

DEPRECIATION METHODS

For *financial reporting purposes,* companies can use a variety of depreciation methods (straight-line, double-declining balance, and sum-of-the-years'-digits). For *tax purposes,* assets in the first four MACRS property classes are depreciated by the double-declining balance method, using a half-year convention (meaning that a half-year's depreciation is taken in the year the asset is purchased) and switching to straight-line when advantageous. The *approximate percentages* (rounded to the nearest whole percent) written off each year for the first four property classes are shown in Table 4.2. Rather than using the percentages in the table, the firm can either use straight-line depreciation over the asset's recovery period with the half-year convention or use the alternative depreciation system. For purposes of this text, we will use the MACRS depreciation percentages because they generally provide for the fastest write-off and therefore the best cash flow effects for the profitable firm.

Because MACRS requires use of the half-year convention, assets are assumed to be acquired in the middle of the year; therefore, only one-half of the first year's depreciation is recovered in the first year. As a result, the final half-year of depreciation is recovered in the year immediately following the asset's stated recovery period. In Table 4.2, the depreciation percentages for an n-year class asset are given for $n + 1$ years. For example, a 5-year asset is depreciated over 6 recovery years. The application of the tax depreciation percentages given in Table 4.2 can be demonstrated by a simple example.

TABLE 4.2	Rounded Depreciation Percentages by Recovery Year Using MACRS for First Four Property Classes

	Percentage by recovery year[a]			
Recovery year	3 years	5 years	7 years	10 years
1	33%	20%	14%	10%
2	45	32	25	18
3	15	19	18	14
4	7	12	12	12
5		12	9	9
6		5	9	8
7			9	7
8			4	6
9				6
10				6
11				4
Totals	100%	100%	100%	100%

[a]These percentages have been rounded to the nearest whole percent to simplify calculations while retaining realism. To calculate the *actual* depreciation for tax purposes, be sure to apply the actual unrounded percentages or directly apply double-declining balance depreciation using the half-year convention.

Example 4.2 ▶   Baker Corporation acquired, for an installed cost of $40,000, a machine having a recovery period of 5 years. Using the applicable percentages from Table 4.2, Baker calculates the depreciation in each year as follows:

Year	Cost (1)	Percentages (from Table 4.2) (2)	Depreciation [(1) × (2)] (3)
1	$40,000	20%	$ 8,000
2	40,000	32	12,800
3	40,000	19	7,600
4	40,000	12	4,800
5	40,000	12	4,800
6	40,000	5	2,000
Totals		100%	$40,000

Column 3 shows that the full cost of the asset is written off over 6 recovery years.

Because financial managers focus primarily on cash flows, *only tax depreciation methods will be used throughout this text.*

DEVELOPING THE STATEMENT OF CASH FLOWS

The *statement of cash flows*, introduced in Chapter 3, summarizes the firm's cash flow over a given period. Keep in mind that analysts typically lump cash and marketable securities together when assessing the firm's liquidity because both

cash flow from operating activities
Cash flows directly related to sale and production of the firm's products and services.

cash flow from investment activities
Cash flows associated with purchase and sale of both fixed assets and equity investments in other firms.

cash flow from financing activities
Cash flows that result from debt and equity financing transactions; include incurrence and repayment of debt, cash inflow from the sale of stock, and cash outflows to repurchase stock or pay cash dividends.

Matter of fact

Apple's Cash Flows

In its 2012 annual report, Apple reported more than $50 billion in cash from its operating activities. In the same year, Apple used $48.2 billion in cash to invest in marketable securities and other investments. By comparison, its financing cash flows were minor, resulting in a cash outflow of about $1.7 billion, mostly from stock issued to employees as part of Apple's compensation plans.

---

cash and marketable securities represent a reservoir of liquidity. That reservoir is *increased by cash inflows* and *decreased by cash outflows*.

Also note that the firm's cash flows fall into three categories: (1) cash flow from operating activities, (2) cash flow from investment activities, and (3) cash flow from financing activities. **Cash flow from operating activities** include the cash inflows and outflows directly related to the sale and production of the firm's products and services. **Cash flow from investment activities** include the cash flows associated with the purchase and sale of both fixed assets and equity investments in other firms. Clearly, purchase transactions would result in cash outflows, whereas sales transactions would generate cash inflows. **Cash flow from financing activities** results from debt and equity financing transactions. Incurring either short-term or long-term debt would result in a corresponding cash inflow; repaying debt would result in an outflow. Similarly, the sale of the company's stock would result in a cash inflow; the repurchase of stock or payment of cash dividends would result in an outflow.

Classifying Inflows and Outflows of Cash

The statement of cash flows, in effect, summarizes the inflows and outflows of cash during a given period. Table 4.3 classifies the basic inflows (sources) and outflows (uses) of cash. For example, if a firm's accounts payable balance increased by $1,000 during the year, the change would be an *inflow of cash*. The change would be an *outflow of cash* if the firm's inventory increased by $2,500.

A few additional points can be made with respect to the classification scheme in Table 4.3:

1. A *decrease* in an asset, such as the firm's cash balance, is an *inflow of cash*. Why? It is because cash that has been tied up in the asset is released and can be used for some other purpose, such as repaying a loan. On the other hand, an *increase* in the firm's cash balance is an *outflow of cash* because additional cash is being tied up in the firm's cash balance.

   The classification of decreases and increases in a firm's cash balance is difficult for many to grasp. To clarify, imagine that you store all your cash in a bucket. Your cash balance is represented by the amount of cash in the bucket. When you need cash, you withdraw it from the bucket, which *decreases your cash balance and provides an inflow* of cash to you. Conversely, when you have excess cash, you deposit it in the bucket, which *increases your cash balance and represents an outflow* of cash from you. Focus on the movement of funds *in and out of your pocket*: Clearly, a decrease in cash (from the bucket) is an inflow (to your pocket); an increase in cash (in the bucket) is an outflow (from your pocket).

TABLE 4.3 ▷ **Inflows and Outflows of Cash**

Inflows (sources)	Outflows (uses)
Decrease in any asset	Increase in any asset
Increase in any liability	Decrease in any liability
Net profits after taxes	Net loss after taxes
Depreciation and other noncash charges	Dividends paid
Sale of stock	Repurchase or retirement of stock

noncash charge
An expense that is deducted on the income statement but does not involve the actual outlay of cash during the period; includes depreciation, amortization, and depletion.

2. Depreciation (like amortization and depletion) is a **noncash charge**, an expense that is deducted on the income statement but does not involve an actual outlay of cash. Therefore, when measuring the amount of cash flow generated by a firm, we have to add depreciation back to net income; if we don't, we will understate the cash that the firm has truly generated. For this reason, depreciation appears as a source of cash in Table 4.3.

3. Because depreciation is treated as a separate cash inflow, only *gross* rather than *net* changes in fixed assets appear on the statement of cash flows. The change in net fixed assets is equal to the change in gross fixed assets minus the depreciation charge. Therefore, if we treated depreciation as a cash inflow as well as the reduction in net (rather than gross) fixed assets, we would be double counting depreciation.

4. Direct entries of changes in retained earnings are not included on the statement of cash flows. Instead, entries for items that affect retained earnings appear as net profits or losses after taxes and dividends paid.

Preparing the Statement of Cash Flows

The statement of cash flows uses data from the income statement, along with the beginning- and end-of-period balance sheets. The income statement for the year ended December 31, 2015, and the December 31 balance sheets for 2014 and 2015 for Baker Corporation are given in Tables 4.4 and 4.5 (see facing page), respectively. The statement of cash flows for the year ended December 31, 2015, for Baker Corporation is presented in Table 4.6 (see page 116). Note that all cash inflows as well as net profits after taxes and depreciation are treated as positive

TABLE 4.4	Baker Corporation 2015 Income Statement ($000)
Sales revenue	$1,700
Less: Cost of goods sold	1,000
Gross profits	$ 700
Less: Operating expenses	
Selling, general, and administrative expense	$ 230
Depreciation expense	100
Total operating expense	$ 330
Earnings before interest and taxes (EBIT)	$ 370
Less: Interest expense	70
Net profits before taxes	$ 300
Less: Taxes (rate = 40%)	120
Net profits after taxes	$ 180
Less: Preferred stock dividends	10
Earnings available for common stockholders	$ 170
Earnings per share (EPS)[a]	$1.70

[a]Calculated by dividing the earnings available for common stockholders by the number of shares of common stock outstanding ($170,000 ÷ 100,000 shares = $1.70 per share).

TABLE 4.5	Baker Corporation Balance Sheets ($000)		

		December 31	
Assets		**2015**	**2014**
Cash and marketable securities		$1,000	$ 500
Accounts receivable		400	500
Inventories		600	900
Total current assets		$2,000	$1,900
Land and buildings		$1,200	$1,050
Machinery and equipment, furniture and fixtures, vehicles, and other		1,300	1,150
Total gross fixed assets (at cost)		$2,500	$2,200
Less: Accumulated depreciation		1,300	1,200
Net fixed assets		$1,200	$1,000
Total assets		$3,200	$2,900
Liabilities and stockholders' equity			
Accounts payable		$ 700	$ 500
Notes payable		600	700
Accruals		100	200
Total current liabilities		$1,400	$1,400
Long-term debt		600	400
Total liabilities		$2,000	$1,800
Preferred stock		$ 100	$ 100
Common stock: $1.20 par, 100,000 shares outstanding in 2015 and 2014		120	120
Paid-in capital in excess of par on common stock		380	380
Retained earnings		600	500
Total stockholders' equity		$1,200	$1,100
Total liabilities and stockholders' equity		$3,200	$2,900

values. All cash outflows, any losses, and dividends paid are treated as negative values. The items in each category—operating, investment, and financing—are totaled, and the three totals are added to get the "Net increase (decrease) in cash and marketable securities" for the period. As a check, this value should reconcile with the actual change in cash and marketable securities for the year, which is obtained from the beginning- and end-of-period balance sheets.

Interpreting the Statement

The statement of cash flows allows the financial manager and other interested parties to analyze the firm's cash flow. The manager should pay special attention both to the major categories of cash flow and to the individual items of cash inflow and outflow, to assess whether any developments have occurred that are contrary to the company's financial policies. In addition, the statement can be used to evaluate progress toward projected goals or to isolate inefficiencies. The

TABLE 4.6	Baker Corporation Statement of Cash Flows ($000) for the Year Ended December 31, 2015	
Cash flow from operating activities		
Net profits after taxes		$180
Depreciation		100
Decrease in accounts receivable		100
Decrease in inventories		300
Increase in accounts payable		200
Decrease in accruals		(100)[a]
Cash provided by operating activities		$780
Cash flow from investment activities		
Increase in gross fixed assets		($300)
Changes in equity investments in other firms		0
Cash provided by investment activities		($300)
Cash flow from financing activities		
Decrease in notes payable		($100)
Increase in long-term debt		200
Changes in stockholders' equity[b]		0
Dividends paid		(80)
Cash provided by financing activities		$ 20
Net increase in cash and marketable securities		$500

[a]As is customary, parentheses are used to denote a negative number, which in this case is a cash outflow.

[b]Retained earnings are excluded here because their change is actually reflected in the combination of the "Net profits after taxes" and "Dividends paid" entries.

financial manager also can prepare a statement of cash flows developed from projected financial statements to determine whether planned actions are desirable in view of the resulting cash flows.

operating cash flow (OCF)
The cash flow a firm generates from its normal operations; calculated as *net operating profits after taxes (NOPAT)* plus depreciation.

Operating Cash Flow A firm's **operating cash flow** (OCF) is the cash flow it generates from its normal operations: producing and selling its output of goods or services. A variety of definitions of OCF can be found in the financial literature. The definition introduced here excludes the impact of interest on cash flow. We exclude those effects because we want a measure that captures the cash flow generated by the firm's operations, not by how those operations are financed and taxed. The first step is to calculate **net operating profits after taxes (NOPAT)**, which represent the firm's earnings before interest and after taxes. Letting T equal the applicable corporate tax rate, NOPAT is calculated as

net operating profits after taxes (NOPAT)
A firm's earnings before interest and after taxes, EBIT $\times (1 - T)$.

$$NOPAT = EBIT \times (1 - T) \qquad (4.1)$$

To convert NOPAT to operating cash flow (OCF), we merely add back depreciation:

$$\text{OCF} = \text{NOPAT} + \text{Depreciation} \qquad (4.2)$$

We can substitute the expression for NOPAT from Equation 4.1 into Equation 4.2 to get a single equation for OCF:

$$\text{OCF} = [\text{EBIT} \times (1 - T)] + \text{Depreciation} \qquad (4.3)$$

Example 4.3 ►

MyFinanceLab Solution
Video

Substituting the values for Baker Corporation from its income statement (Table 4.4) into Equation 4.3, we get

$$\text{OCF} = [\$370 \times (1.00 - 0.40)] + \$100 = \$222 + \$100 = \$322$$

During 2015, Baker Corporation generated $322,000 of cash flow from producing and selling its output. Therefore, we can conclude that Baker's operations are generating positive cash flows.

FREE CASH FLOW

free cash flow (FCF)
The amount of cash flow available to investors (creditors and owners) after the firm has met all operating needs and paid for investments in net fixed assets and net current assets.

The firm's **free cash flow (FCF)** represents the cash available to investors—the providers of debt (creditors) and equity (owners)—after the firm has met all operating needs and paid for net investments in fixed assets and current assets. Free cash flow can be defined as

$$\begin{aligned} \text{FCF} = \text{OCF} &- \text{Net fixed asset investment (NFAI)} \\ &- \text{Net current asset investment (NCAI)} \end{aligned} \qquad (4.4)$$

The *net fixed asset investment (NFAI)* is the *net investment* that the firm makes in fixed assets and refers to purchases minus sales of fixed assets. You can calculate the NFAI using

$$\text{NFAI} = \text{Change in net fixed assets} + \text{Depreciation} \qquad (4.5)$$

The NFAI is also equal to the change in gross fixed assets from one year to the next.

Example 4.4 ►

Using the Baker Corporation's balance sheets in Table 4.5, we see that its change in net fixed assets between 2014 and 2015 was $200 ($1,200 in 2015 − $1,000 in 2014). Substituting this value and the $100 of depreciation for 2015 into Equation 4.5, we get Baker's net fixed asset investment (NFAI) for 2015:

$$\text{NFAI} = \$200 + \$100 = \$300$$

Baker Corporation therefore invested a net $300,000 in fixed assets during 2015. This amount would, of course, represent a cash outflow to acquire fixed assets during 2015.

Looking at Equation 4.5, we can see that if net fixed assets decline by an amount exceeding the depreciation for the period, the NFAI would be negative. A negative NFAI represents a net cash *inflow* attributable to the firm selling more assets than it acquired during the year.

The *net current asset investment (NCAI)* represents the net investment made by the firm in its current (operating) assets. "Net" refers to the difference between current assets and the sum of accounts payable and accruals. Notes payable are not included in the NCAI calculation because they represent a negotiated creditor claim on the firm's free cash flow. The NCAI calculation is

$$\text{NCAI} = \text{Change in current assets} - \text{Change in (accounts payable} + \text{accruals)}$$
(4.6)

Example 4.5 ▶ Looking at the Baker Corporation's balance sheets for 2014 and 2015 in Table 4.5, we see that the change in current assets between 2014 and 2015 is $100 ($2,000 in 2015 − $1,900 in 2014). The difference between Baker's accounts payable plus accruals of $800 in 2015 ($700 in accounts payable + $100 in accruals) and of $700 in 2014 ($500 in accounts payable + $200 in accruals) is $100 ($800 in 2015 − $700 in 2014). Substituting into Equation 4.6 the change in current assets and the change in the sum of accounts payable plus accruals for Baker Corporation, we get its 2015 NCAI:

$$\text{NCAI} = \$100 - \$100 = \$0$$

So, during 2015 Baker Corporation made no investment ($0) in its current asset net of accounts payable and accruals.

Now we can substitute Baker Corporation's 2015 operating cash flow (OCF) of $322, its net fixed asset investment (NFAI) of $300, and its net current asset investment (NCAI) of $0 into Equation 4.4 to find its free cash flow (FCF):

$$\text{FCF} = \$322 - \$300 - \$0 = \$22$$

We can see that during 2015 Baker generated $22,000 of free cash flow, which it can use to pay its investors: creditors (payment of interest) and owners (payment of dividends). Thus, the firm generated adequate cash flow to cover all its operating costs and investments and had free cash flow available to pay investors. However, Baker's interest expense in 2015 was $70,000, so the firm is not generating enough FCF to provide a sufficient return to its investors.

Clearly, cash flow is the lifeblood of the firm. The *Focus on Practice* box discusses Cisco System's free cash flow. In the next section, we consider various aspects of financial planning for cash flow and profit.

→ **REVIEW QUESTIONS**

4–1 Briefly describe the first four *modified accelerated cost recovery system (MACRS)* property classes and recovery periods. Explain how the depreciation percentages are determined by using the MACRS recovery periods.

4–2 Describe the overall cash flow through the firm in terms of cash flow from operating activities, cash flow from investment activities, and cash flow from financing activities.

focus on **PRACTICE**

Free Cash Flow at Cisco Systems

in practice On May 13, 2010, Cisco Systems issued what at first glance appeared to be a favorable earnings report, saying that it had achieved earnings per share of $0.42 for the most recent quarter, ahead of the expectations of Wall Street experts who had projected EPS of $0.39. Oddly, though, Cisco stock began to fall after the earnings announcement.

In subsequent analysis, one analyst observed that of the three cents by which Cisco beat the street's forecast, one cent could be attributed to the fact that the quarter was 14 weeks rather than the more typical 13 weeks. Another penny was attributable to unusual tax gains, and the third was classified with the somewhat vague label, "other income." Other analysts were even more skeptical. One noted that Cisco's free cash flow in the prior three quarters had been $6.24 billion, but $5.55 billion of that had been spent to buy shares to offset dilution from the stock options that Cisco granted its employees. The analyst complained, "Cisco is being run for the benefit of its employees and not its public shareholders."

▶ *Free cash flow is often considered a more reliable measure of a company's income than reported earnings. What are some possible ways that corporate accountants might be able to change their earnings to portray a more favorable earnings statement?*

Source: "Update Cisco Systems (CSCO)," May 13, 2010, **http://jubakpicks.com**; Eric Savitz, "Cisco Shares Off Despite Strong FYQ3; Focus on Q4 Guidance," May 13, 2010, **http://blogs.barrons.com**.

4–3 Explain why a decrease in cash is classified as a *cash inflow (source)* and why an increase in cash is classified as a *cash outflow (use)* in preparing the statement of cash flows.

4–4 Why is depreciation (as well as amortization and depletion) considered a *noncash charge?*

4–5 Describe the general format of the statement of cash flows. How are cash inflows differentiated from cash outflows on this statement?

4–6 Why do we exclude interest expense and taxes from operating cash flow?

4–7 From a strict financial perspective, define and differentiate between a firm's *operating cash flow (OCF)* and its *free cash flow (FCF)*.

LG 3   4.2 The Financial Planning Process

Financial planning is an important aspect of the firm's operations because it provides road maps for guiding, coordinating, and controlling the firm's actions to achieve its objectives. Two key aspects of the financial planning process are *cash planning* and *profit planning*. Cash planning involves preparation of the firm's cash budget. Profit planning involves preparation of pro forma statements. Both the cash budget and the pro forma statements are useful for internal financial planning. They also are routinely required by existing and prospective lenders.

The **financial planning process** begins with long-term, or *strategic,* financial plans. These plans, in turn, guide the formulation of short-term, or *operating,* plans and budgets. Generally, the short-term plans and budgets implement the firm's long-term strategic objectives. Although the remainder of this chapter places primary emphasis on short-term financial plans and budgets, a few preliminary comments on long-term financial plans are in order.

financial planning process
Planning that begins with long-term, or *strategic,* financial plans that in turn guide the formulation of short-term, or *operating,* plans and budgets.

LONG-TERM (STRATEGIC) FINANCIAL PLANS

long-term (strategic) financial plans
Plans that lay out a company's planned financial actions and the anticipated impact of those actions over periods ranging from 2 to 10 years.

Long-term (strategic) financial plans lay out a company's planned financial actions and the anticipated effect of those actions over periods ranging from 2 to 10 years. Five-year strategic plans, which are revised as significant new information becomes available, are common. Generally, firms that are subject to high degrees of operating uncertainty, relatively short production cycles, or both tend to use shorter planning horizons.

Long-term financial plans are part of an integrated strategy that, along with production and marketing plans, guides the firm toward strategic goals. Those long-term plans consider proposed outlays for fixed assets, research and development activities, marketing and product development actions, capital structure, and major sources of financing. Also included would be termination of existing projects, product lines, or lines of business; repayment or retirement of outstanding debts; and any planned acquisitions. Such plans tend to be supported by a series of annual budgets.

SHORT-TERM (OPERATING) FINANCIAL PLANS

short-term (operating) financial plans
Specify short-term financial actions and the anticipated impact of those actions.

Short-term (operating) financial plans specify short-term financial actions and the anticipated effect of those actions. These plans most often cover a 1- to 2-year period. Key inputs include the sales forecast and various forms of operating and financial data. Key outputs include a number of operating budgets, the cash budget, and pro forma financial statements. The entire short-term financial planning process is outlined in Figure 4.1 below. Here we focus solely on cash and prof planning from the financial manager's perspective.

Short-term financial planning begins with the sales forecast. From it, companies develop production plans that take into account lead (preparation) times and include estimates of the required raw materials. Using the production plans, the

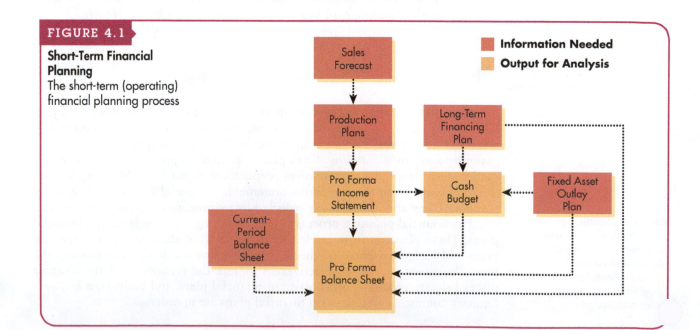

FIGURE 4.1

Short-Term Financial Planning
The short-term (operating) financial planning process

firm can estimate direct labor requirements, factory overhead outlays, and operating expenses. Once these estimates have been made, the firm can prepare a pro forma income statement and cash budget. With these basic inputs, the firm can finally develop a pro forma balance sheet.

Personal Finance Example 4.6 ▶ The first step in personal financial planning requires you to define your goals. Whereas in a corporation the goal is to maximize owner wealth (that is, share price), individuals typically have a number of major goals.

Generally, personal goals can be short-term (1 year), intermediate-term (2 to 5 years), or long-term (6 or more years). The short- and intermediate-term goals support the long-term goals. Clearly, types of long-term personal goals depend on the individual's or family's age, and goals will continue to change with one's life situation.

You should set your personal financial goals carefully and realistically. Each goal should be clearly defined and have a priority, time frame, and cost estimate. For example, a college senior's intermediate-term goal in 2015 might include earning a master's degree at a cost of $40,000 by 2017, and his or her long-term goal might be to buy a condominium at a cost of $125,000 by 2019.

Throughout the remainder of this chapter, we will concentrate on the key outputs of the short-term financial planning process: the cash budget, the pro forma income statement, and the pro forma balance sheet.

→ REVIEW QUESTIONS

4–8 What is the *financial planning process*? Contrast *long-term (strategic) financial plans* and *short-term (operating) financial plans*.

4–9 Which three statements result as part of the short-term (operating) financial planning process?

LG④   ## 4.3 Cash Planning: Cash Budgets

cash budget (cash forecast)
A statement of the firm's planned inflows and outflows of cash that is used to estimate its short-term cash requirements.

The **cash budget,** or **cash forecast,** is a statement of the firm's planned inflows and outflows of cash. It is used by the firm to estimate its short-term cash requirements, with particular attention being paid to planning for surplus cash and for cash shortages.

Typically, the cash budget is designed to cover a 1-year period, divided into smaller time intervals. The number and type of intervals depend on the nature of the business. The more seasonal and uncertain a firm's cash flows, the greater the number of intervals. Because many firms are confronted with a seasonal cash flow pattern, the cash budget is quite often presented on a *monthly basis.* Firms with stable patterns of cash flow may use quarterly or annual time intervals.

THE SALES FORECAST

sales forecast
The prediction of the firm's sales over a given period, based on external and/or internal data; used as the key input to the short-term financial planning process.

The key input to the short-term financial planning process is the firm's **sales forecast.** This prediction of the firm's sales over a given period is ordinarily prepared by the marketing department. On the basis of the sales forecast, the financial manager estimates the monthly cash flows that will result from projected sales and from outlays related to production, inventory, and sales. The manager also determines the level of fixed assets required and the amount of financing, if any, needed to support the forecast level of sales and production. In practice, obtaining good data is the most difficult aspect of forecasting. The sales forecast may be based on an analysis of external data, internal data, or a combination of the two.

external forecast
A sales forecast based on the relationships observed between the firm's sales and certain key external economic indicators.

An **external forecast** is based on the relationships observed between the firm's sales and certain key external economic indicators such as the gross domestic product (GDP), new housing starts, consumer confidence, and disposable personal income. Forecasts containing these indicators are readily available.

internal forecast
A sales forecast based on a buildup, or consensus, of sales forecasts through the firm's own sales channels.

Internal forecasts are based on a consensus of sales forecasts through the firm's own sales channels. Typically, the firm's salespeople in the field are asked to estimate how many units of each type of product they expect to sell in the coming year. These forecasts are collected and totaled by the sales manager, who may adjust the figures using knowledge of specific markets or of the salesperson's forecasting ability. Finally, adjustments may be made for additional internal factors, such as production capabilities.

Firms generally use a combination of external and internal forecast data to make the final sales forecast. The internal data provide insight into sales expectations, and the external data provide a means of adjusting these expectations to take into account general economic factors. The nature of the firm's product also often affects the mix and types of forecasting methods used.

PREPARING THE CASH BUDGET

The general format of the cash budget is presented in Table 4.7. The following discussion along with Tables 4.8 and 4.9 illustrates each of its components individually. Table 4.10 presents the completed cash budget for Coulson Industries.

TABLE 4.7	The General Format of the Cash Budget				
	Jan.	Feb.	. . .	Nov.	Dec.
Total cash receipts	$XXA	$XXH		$XXN	$XXU
Less: Total cash disbursements	XXB	XXI	. . .	XXO	XXV
Net cash flow	$XXC	$XXJ		$XXP	$XXW
Add: Beginning cash	XXD	XXE	XXK	XXQ	XXR
Ending cash	$XXE	$XXK		$XXR	$XXX
Less: Minimum cash balance	XXF	XXL	. . .	XXS	XXY
Required total financing		$XXM		$XXT	
Excess cash balance	$XXG				$XXZ

Total Cash Receipts

total cash receipts
All of a firm's inflows of cash during a given financial period.

Total cash receipts include all a firm's inflows of cash during a given financial period. The most common components of cash receipts are cash sales, collections of accounts receivable, and other cash receipts.

Example 4.7 ▶

Coulson Industries, a defense contractor, is developing a cash budget for October, November, and December. Coulson's sales in August and September were $100,000 and $200,000, respectively. Sales of $400,000, $300,000, and $200,000 have been forecast for October, November, and December, respectively. Historically, 20% of the firm's sales have been for cash, 50% have generated accounts receivable collected after 1 month, and the remaining 30% have generated accounts receivable collected after 2 months. Bad-debt expenses (uncollectible accounts) have been negligible. In December, the firm will receive a $30,000 dividend from stock in a subsidiary. The schedule of expected cash receipts for the company is presented in Table 4.8. It contains the following:

Forecast sales This initial entry is *merely informational.* It is provided as an aid in calculating other sales-related items.

Cash sales The cash sales shown for each month represent 20% of the total sales forecast for that month.

Collections of A/R These entries represent the collection of accounts receivable (A/R) resulting from sales in earlier months.

Lagged 1 month These figures represent sales made in the preceding month that generated accounts receivable collected in the current month. Because 50% of the current month's sales are collected 1 month later, the collections of A/R with a 1-month lag shown for September represent 50% of the sales in August, collections for October represent 50% of September sales, and so on.

Lagged 2 months These figures represent sales made 2 months earlier that generated accounts receivable collected in the current month. Because 30% of sales are collected 2 months later, the collections with a 2-month lag shown for October represent 30% of the sales in August, and so on.

Other cash receipts These are cash receipts expected from sources other than sales. Interest received, dividends received, proceeds from the sale of equipment, stock and bond sale proceeds, and lease receipts may show up here. For Coulson Industries, the only other cash receipt is the $30,000 dividend due in December.

TABLE 4.8	A Schedule of Projected Cash Receipts for Coulson Industries ($000)				
	Aug.	Sept.	Oct.	Nov.	Dec.
Sales forecast	$100	$200	$400	$300	$200
Cash sales (0.20)	$20	$40	$ 80	$ 60	$ 40
Collections of A/R:					
Lagged 1 month (0.50)		50	100	200	150
Lagged 2 months (0.30)			30	60	120
Other cash receipts	—	—	—	—	30
Total cash receipts	$20	$90	$210	$320	$340

Total cash receipts This figure represents the total of all the cash receipts listed for each month. For Coulson Industries, we are concerned only with October, November, and December, as shown in Table 4.8.

Total Cash Disbursements

total cash disbursements
All outlays of cash by the firm during a given financial period.

Total cash disbursements include all outlays of cash by the firm during a given financial period. The most common cash disbursements are

Cash purchases	Fixed-asset outlays
Payments of accounts payable	Interest payments
Rent (and lease) payments	Cash dividend payments
Wages and salaries	Principal payments (loans)
Tax payments	Repurchases or retirements of stock

It is important to recognize that *depreciation and other noncash charges are NOT included in the cash budget* because they merely represent a scheduled write-off of an earlier cash outflow. The impact of depreciation, as we noted earlier, is reflected in the reduced cash outflow for tax payments.

Example 4.8 ▶ Coulson Industries has gathered the following data needed for the preparation of a cash disbursements schedule for October, November, and December.

Purchases The firm's purchases represent 70% of sales. Of this amount, 10% is paid in cash, 70% is paid in the month immediately following the month of purchase, and the remaining 20% is paid 2 months following the month of purchase.

Rent payments Rent of $5,000 will be paid each month.

Wages and salaries Fixed salaries for the year are $96,000, or $8,000 per month. In addition, wages are estimated as 10% of monthly sales.

Tax payments Taxes of $25,000 must be paid in December.

Fixed-asset outlays New machinery costing $130,000 will be purchased and paid for in November.

Interest payments An interest payment of $10,000 is due in December.

Cash dividend payments Cash dividends of $20,000 will be paid in October.

Principal payments (loans) A $20,000 principal payment is due in December.

Repurchases or retirements of stock No repurchase or retirement of stock is expected between October and December.

The firm's cash disbursements schedule, using the preceding data, is shown in Table 4.9. Some items in the table are explained in greater detail as follows:

Purchases This entry is *merely informational*. The figures represent 70% of the forecast sales for each month. They have been included to facilitate calculation of the cash purchases and related payments.

Cash purchases The cash purchases for each month represent 10% of the month's purchases.

Payments of A/P These entries represent the payment of accounts payable (A/P) resulting from purchases in earlier months.

TABLE 4.9	A Schedule of Projected Cash Disbursements for Coulson Industries ($000)				
Purchases (0.70 × sales)	Aug. $70	Sept. $140	Oct. $280	Nov. $210	Dec. $140
Cash purchases (0.10)	$7	$14	$ 28	$ 21	$ 14
Payments of A/P:					
Lagged 1 month (0.70)		49	98	196	147
Lagged 2 months (0.20)			14	28	56
Rent payments			5	5	5
Wages and salaries			48	38	28
Tax payments					25
Fixed-asset outlays				130	
Interest payments					10
Cash dividend payments			20		
Principal payments					20
Total cash disbursements	$7	$63	$213	$418	$305

Lagged 1 month These figures represent purchases made in the preceding month that are paid for in the current month. Because 70% of the firm's purchases are paid for 1 month later, the payments with a 1-month lag shown for September represent 70% of the August purchases, payments for October represent 70% of September purchases, and so on.

Lagged 2 months These figures represent purchases made 2 months earlier that are paid for in the current month. Because 20% of the firm's purchases are paid for 2 months later, the payments with a 2-month lag for October represent 20% of the August purchases, and so on.

Wages and salaries These amounts were obtained by adding $8,000 to 10% of the *sales* in each month. The $8,000 represents the salary component; the rest represents wages.

The remaining items on the cash disbursements schedule are self-explanatory.

Net Cash Flow, Ending Cash, Financing, and Excess Cash

Look back at the general-format cash budget in Table 4.7 on page 122. We have inputs for the first two entries, and we now continue calculating the firm's cash needs. The firm's **net cash flow** is found by subtracting the cash disbursements from cash receipts in each period. Then we add beginning cash to the firm's net cash flow to determine the **ending cash** for each period.

Finally, we subtract the desired minimum cash balance from ending cash to find the **required total financing** or the **excess cash balance**. If the ending cash is less than the minimum cash balance, *financing* is required. Such financing is typically viewed as short-term and is therefore represented by notes payable. If the ending cash is greater than the minimum cash balance, *excess cash* exists. Any excess cash is assumed to be invested in a liquid, short-term, interest-paying vehicle, that is, in marketable securities.

net cash flow
The mathematical difference between the firm's cash receipts and its cash disbursements in each period.

ending cash
The sum of the firm's beginning cash and its net cash flow for the period.

required total financing
Amount of funds needed by the firm if the ending cash for the period is less than the desired minimum cash balance; typically represented by notes payable.

excess cash balance
The (excess) amount available for investment by the firm if the period's ending cash is greater than the desired minimum cash balance; assumed to be invested in marketable securities.

Example 4.9 ▶   Table 4.10 presents Coulson Industries' cash budget. The company wishes to maintain, as a reserve for unexpected needs, a minimum cash balance of $25,000. For Coulson Industries to maintain its required $25,000 ending cash balance, it will need total borrowing of $76,000 in November and $41,000 in December. In October, the firm will have an excess cash balance of $22,000, which can be held in an interest-earning marketable security. The required total financing figures in the cash budget refer to *how much will be owed at the end of the month;* they do *not* represent the monthly changes in borrowing.

The monthly changes in borrowing and in excess cash can be found by further analyzing the cash budget. In October, the $50,000 beginning cash, which becomes $47,000 after the $3,000 net cash outflow, results in a $22,000 excess cash balance once the $25,000 minimum cash is deducted. In November, the $76,000 of required total financing resulted from the $98,000 net cash outflow less the $22,000 of excess cash from October. The $41,000 of required total financing in December resulted from reducing November's $76,000 of required total financing by the $35,000 of net cash inflow during December. Summarizing, the *financial activities for each month* would be as follows:

October: **Invest the $22,000** excess cash balance in marketable securities.

November: Liquidate the $22,000 of marketable securities and **borrow $76,000** (notes payable).

December: **Repay $35,000** of notes payable to leave $41,000 of outstanding required total financing.

TABLE 4.10 ▷ A Cash Budget for Coulson Industries ($000)			
	Oct.	**Nov.**	**Dec.**
Total cash receipts[a]	$210	$ 320	$ 340
Less: Total cash disbursements[b]	213	418	305
Net cash flow	($ 3)	($ 98)	$ 35
Add: Beginning cash	50	47	(51)
Ending cash	$ 47	($ 51)	($ 16)
Less: Minimum cash balance	25	25	25
Required total financing (notes payable)[c]		$ 76	$ 41
Excess cash balance (marketable securities)[d]	$ 22		

[a]From Table 4.8.

[b]From Table 4.9.

[c]Values are placed in this line when the ending cash is less than the desired minimum cash balance. These amounts are typically financed short-term and therefore are represented by notes payable.

[d]Values are placed in this line when the ending cash is greater than the desired minimum cash balance. These amounts are typically assumed to be invested short-term and therefore are represented by marketable securities.

EVALUATING THE CASH BUDGET

The cash budget indicates whether a cash shortage or surplus is expected in each of the months covered by the forecast. Each month's figure is based on the internally imposed requirement of a minimum cash balance and *represents the total balance at the end of the month.*

At the end of each of the 3 months, Coulson expects the following balances in cash, marketable securities, and notes payable:

	End-of-month balance ($000)		
Account	Oct.	Nov.	Dec.
Cash	$25	$25	$25
Marketable securities	22	0	0
Notes payable	0	76	41

Note that the firm is assumed first to liquidate its marketable securities to meet deficits and then to borrow with notes payable if additional financing is needed. As a result, it will not have marketable securities and notes payable on its books at the same time. Because it may be necessary to borrow up to $76,000 for the 3-month period, the financial manager should be certain that some arrangement is made to ensure the availability of these funds.

Personal Finance Example 4.10 ▶ Because individuals receive only a finite amount of income (cash inflow) during a given period, they need to prepare budgets to make sure they can cover their expenses (cash outflows) during the period. The *personal budget* is a short-term financial planning report that helps individuals or families achieve short-term financial goals. Personal budgets typically cover a 1-year period, broken into months.

A condensed version of a personal budget for the first quarter (3 months) is shown below.

	Jan.	Feb.	Mar.
Income			
Take-home pay	$4,775	$4,775	$4,775
Investment income			90
(1) Total income	$4,775	$4,775	$4,865
Expenses			
(2) Total expenses	$4,026	$5,291	$7,396
Cash surplus or deficit [(1)−(2)]	$ 749	($ 516)	($2,531)
Cumulative cash surplus or deficit	$ 749	$ 233	($2,298)

The personal budget shows a cash surplus of $749 in January followed by monthly deficits in February and March of $516 and $2,531, resulting in a cumulative deficit of $2,298 through March. Clearly, to cover the deficit, some action—such as increasing income, reducing expenses, drawing down savings, or borrowing—will be necessary to bring the budget into balance. Borrowing by using credit can offset a deficit in the short term but can lead to financial trouble if done repeatedly.

COPING WITH UNCERTAINTY IN THE CASH BUDGET

Aside from careful estimation of cash budget inputs, there are two ways of coping with uncertainty in the cash budget. One is to prepare several cash budgets, based on pessimistic, most likely, and optimistic forecasts. From this range of cash flows, the financial manager can determine the amount of financing necessary to cover the most adverse situation. The use of several cash budgets, based on differing scenarios, also should give the financial manager a sense of the riskiness of the various alternatives. This *scenario analysis,* or "what if" approach, is often used to analyze cash flows under a variety of circumstances. Clearly, the use of electronic spreadsheets simplifies the process of performing scenario analysis.

Example 4.11 ▶ Table 4.11 presents the summary of Coulson Industries' cash budget prepared for each month using pessimistic, most likely, and optimistic estimates of total cash receipts and disbursements. The most likely estimate is based on the expected outcomes presented earlier.

During October, Coulson will, at worst, need a maximum of $15,000 of financing and, at best, will have a $62,000 excess cash balance. During November, its financing requirement will be between $0 and $185,000, or it could experience an excess cash balance of $5,000. The December projections show maximum borrowing of $190,000 with a possible excess cash balance of $107,000. By considering the extreme values in the pessimistic and optimistic outcomes, Coulson Industries should be better able to plan its cash requirements. For the 3-month period, the peak borrowing requirement under the worst circumstances would be $190,000, which happens to be considerably greater than the most likely estimate of $76,000 for this period.

TABLE 4.11 ⟩ **A Scenario Analysis of Coulson Industries' Cash Budget ($000)**

	October			November			December		
	Pessi-mistic	Most likely	Opti-mistic	Pessi-mistic	Most likely	Opti-mistic	Pessi-mistic	Most likely	Opti-mistic
Total cash receipts	$ 160	$210	$285	$ 210	$320	$410	$ 275	$340	$422
Less: Total cash disbursements	200	213	248	380	418	467	280	305	320
Net cash flow	($ 40)	($ 3)	$ 37	($170)	($ 98)	($ 57)	($ 5)	$ 35	$102
Add: Beginning cash	50	50	50	10	47	87	(160)	(51)	30
Ending cash	$ 10	$ 47	$ 87	($160)	($ 51)	$ 30	($165)	($ 16)	$132
Less: Minimum cash balance	25	25	25	25	25	25	25	25	25
Required total financing	$ 15			$ 185	$ 76		$ 190	$ 41	
Excess cash balance		$ 22	$ 62			$ 5			$107

A second and much more sophisticated way of coping with uncertainty in the cash budget is *simulation* (discussed in Chapter 11). By simulating the occurrence of sales and other uncertain events, the firm can develop a probability distribution of its ending cash flows for each month. The financial decision maker can then use the probability distribution to determine the amount of financing needed to protect the firm adequately against a cash shortage.

CASH FLOW WITHIN THE MONTH

Because the cash budget shows cash flows only on a total monthly basis, the information provided by the cash budget is not necessarily adequate for ensuring solvency. A firm must look more closely at its pattern of daily cash receipts and cash disbursements to ensure that adequate cash is available for paying bills as they come due.

The synchronization of cash flows in the cash budget at month-end does not ensure that the firm will be able to meet its daily cash requirements. Because a firm's cash flows are generally quite variable when viewed on a daily basis, effective cash planning requires a look *beyond* the cash budget. The financial manager must therefore plan and monitor cash flow more frequently than on a monthly basis. The greater the variability of cash flows from day to day, the greater the amount of attention required.

→ **REVIEW QUESTIONS**

4–10 What is the purpose of the *cash budget?* What role does the sales forecast play in its preparation?

4–11 Briefly describe the basic format of the cash budget.

4–12 How can the two "bottom lines" of the cash budget be used to determine the firm's short-term borrowing and investment requirements?

4–13 What is the cause of uncertainty in the cash budget, and what two techniques can be used to cope with this uncertainty?

LG 5 | 4.4 Profit Planning: Pro Forma Statements

pro forma statements
Projected, or forecast, income statements and balance sheets.

Whereas cash planning focuses on forecasting cash flows, *profit planning* relies on accrual concepts to project the firm's profit and overall financial position. Shareholders, creditors, and the firm's management pay close attention to the **pro forma statements,** which are projected income statements and balance sheets. The basic steps in the short-term financial planning process were shown in the flow diagram of Figure 4.1. The approaches for estimating the pro forma statements are all based on the belief that the financial relationships reflected in the firm's past financial statements will not change in the coming period. The commonly used simplified approaches are presented in subsequent discussions.

Two inputs are required for preparing pro forma statements: (1) financial statements for the preceding year and (2) the sales forecast for the coming year. A variety of assumptions must also be made. The company that we will use to illustrate the simplified approaches to pro forma preparation is Vectra

Manufacturing, which manufactures and sells one product. It has two basic product models, X and Y, which are produced by the same process but require different amounts of raw material and labor.

PRECEDING YEAR'S FINANCIAL STATEMENTS

The income statement for the firm's 2015 operations is given in Table 4.12. It indicates that Vectra had sales of $100,000, total cost of goods sold of $80,000, net profits before taxes of $9,000, and net profits after taxes of $7,650. The firm paid $4,000 in cash dividends, leaving $3,650 to be transferred to retained earnings. The firm's balance sheet for 2015 is given in Table 4.13.

SALES FORECAST

Just as for the cash budget, the key input for pro forma statements is the sales forecast. Vectra Manufacturing's sales forecast for the coming year (2016), based on both external and internal data, is presented in Table 4.14. The unit sale prices of the products reflect an increase from $20 to $25 for model X and from $40 to $50 for model Y. These increases are necessary to cover anticipated increases in costs.

→ REVIEW QUESTION

4–14 What is the purpose of *pro forma statements?* What inputs are required for preparing them using the simplified approaches?

TABLE 4.12	Vectra Manufacturing's Income Statement for the Year Ended December 31, 2015
Sales revenue	
Model X (1,000 units at $20/unit)	$ 20,000
Model Y (2,000 units at $40/unit)	80,000
Total sales	$100,000
Less: Cost of goods sold	
Labor	$ 28,500
Material A	8,000
Material B	5,500
Overhead	38,000
Total cost of goods sold	$ 80,000
Gross profits	$ 20,000
Less: Operating expenses	10,000
Operating profits	$ 10,000
Less: Interest expense	1,000
Net profits before taxes	$ 9,000
Less: Taxes (0.15 × $9,000)	1,350
Net profits after taxes	$ 7,650
Less: Common stock dividends	4,000
To retained earnings	$ 3,650

TABLE 4.13	Vectra Manufacturing's Balance Sheet, December 31, 2015		
Assets		**Liabilities and stockholders' equity**	
Cash	$ 6,000	Accounts payable	$ 7,000
Marketable securities	4,000	Taxes payable	300
Accounts receivable	13,000	Notes payable	8,300
Inventories	16,000	Other current liabilities	3,400
Total current assets	$39,000	Total current liabilities	$19,000
Net fixed assets	51,000	Long-term debt	18,000
Total assets	$90,000	Total liabilities	$37,000
		Common stock	30,000
		Retained earnings	23,000
		Total liabilities and stockholders' equity	$90,000

TABLE 4.14	2016 Sales Forecast for Vectra Manufacturing		
Unit sales		Dollar sales	
Model X	1,500	Model X ($25/unit)	$ 37,500
Model Y	1,950	Model Y ($50/unit)	97,500
		Total	$135,000

LG 5 4.5 Preparing the Pro Forma Income Statement

percent-of-sales method
A simple method for developing the pro forma income statement; it forecasts sales and then expresses the various income statement items as percentages of projected sales.

A simple method for developing a pro forma income statement is the **percent-of-sales method.** It forecasts sales and then expresses the various income statement items as percentages of projected sales. The percentages used are likely to be the percentages of sales for those items in the previous year. By using dollar values taken from Vectra's 2015 income statement (Table 4.12), we find that these percentages are

$$\frac{\text{Cost of goods sold}}{\text{Sales}} = \frac{\$80,000}{\$100,000} = 0.800 = 80.0\%$$

$$\frac{\text{Operating expenses}}{\text{Sales}} = \frac{\$10,000}{\$100,000} = 0.100 = 10.0\%$$

$$\frac{\text{Interest expense}}{\text{Sales}} = \frac{\$1,000}{\$100,000} = 0.010 = 1.0\%$$

Applying these percentages to the firm's forecast sales of $135,000 (developed in Table 4.14), we get the 2016 pro forma income statement shown in Table 4.15. We have assumed that Vectra will pay $4,000 in common stock dividends, so the expected contribution to retained earnings is $6,327. This represents a considerable increase over $3,650 in the preceding year (see Table 4.12).

CONSIDERING TYPES OF COSTS AND EXPENSES

The technique that is used to prepare the pro forma income statement in Table 4.15 assumes that all the firm's costs and expenses are *variable*. That is, for a

TABLE 4.15	A Pro Forma Income Statement, Using the Percent-of-Sales Method, for Vectra Manufacturing for the Year Ended December 31, 2016
Sales revenue	$135,000
Less: Cost of goods sold (0.80)	108,000
Gross profits	$ 27,000
Less: Operating expenses (0.10)	13,500
Operating profits	$ 13,500
Less: Interest expense (0.01)	1,350
Net profits before taxes	$ 12,150
Less: Taxes (0.15 × $12,150)	1,823
Net profits after taxes	$ 10,327
Less: Common stock dividends	4,000
To retained earnings	$ 6,327

given percentage increase in sales, the same percentage increase in cost of goods sold, operating expenses, and interest expense would result. For example, as Vectra's sales increased by 35 percent, we assumed that its costs of goods sold also increased by 35 percent. On the basis of this assumption, the firm's net profits before taxes also increased by 35 percent.

Because this approach assumes that all costs are variable, it may understate the increase in profits that will occur when sales increase if some of the firm's costs are fixed. Similarly, if sales decline, the percentage-of-sales method may overstate profits if some costs are fixed and do not fall when revenues decline. Therefore, a pro forma income statement constructed using the percentage-of-sales method generally tends to *understate profits when sales are increasing* and *overstate profits when sales are decreasing*. The best way to adjust for the presence of fixed costs when preparing a pro forma income statement is to break the firm's historical costs and expenses into *fixed* and *variable* components. The potential returns as well as risks resulting from use of fixed (operating and financial) costs to create "leverage" are discussed in Chapter 12. The key point to recognize is that fixed costs make a firm's profits more variable than its revenues. That is, when both profits and sales are rising, profits tend to increase at a faster rate, but when profits and sales are in decline, the percentage drop in profits is often greater than the rate of decline in sales.

Example 4.12 ▶   Vectra Manufacturing's 2015 actual and 2016 pro forma income statements, broken into fixed and variable cost and expense components are shown at the top of the next page.

Breaking Vectra's costs and expenses into fixed and variable components provides a more accurate projection of its pro forma profit. By assuming that *all* costs are variable (as shown in Table 4.15), we find that projected net profits before taxes would continue to equal 9 percent of sales (in 2015, $9,000 net profits before taxes ÷ $100,000 sales). Therefore, the 2016 net profits before taxes would have been $12,150 (0.09 × $135,000 projected sales)

Vectra Manufacturing Income Statements		
	2015 Actual	2016 pro forma
Sales revenue	$100,000	$135,000
Less: Cost of goods sold		
Fixed cost	40,000	40,000
Variable cost (0.40 × sales)	40,000	54,000
Gross profits	$ 20,000	$ 41,000
Less: Operating expenses		
Fixed expense	$ 5,000	$ 5,000
Variable expense (0.05 × sales)	5,000	6,750
Operating profits	$ 10,000	$ 29,250
Less: Interest expense (all fixed)	1,000	1,000
Net profits before taxes	$ 9,000	$ 28,250
Less: Taxes (0.15 × net profits before taxes)	1,350	4,238
Net profits after taxes	$ 7,650	$ 24,012

instead of the $28,250 obtained by using the firm's fixed-cost–variable-cost breakdown.

Clearly, when using a simplified approach to prepare a pro forma income statement, we should break down costs and expenses into fixed and variable components.

→ **REVIEW QUESTIONS**

4–15 How is the *percent-of-sales method* used to prepare pro forma income statements?

4–16 Why does the presence of fixed costs cause the percent-of-sales method of pro forma income statement preparation to fail? What is a better method?

LG 5 4.6 Preparing the Pro Forma Balance Sheet

judgmental approach
A simplified approach for preparing the pro forma balance sheet under which the firm estimates the values of certain balance sheet accounts and uses its external financing as a balancing, or "plug," figure.

A number of simplified approaches are available for preparing the pro forma balance sheet. One involves estimating all balance sheet accounts as a strict percentage of sales. A better and more popular approach is the **judgmental approach,** under which the firm estimates the values of certain balance sheet accounts and uses its external financing as a balancing, or "plug," figure. The judgmental approach represents an improved version of the percent-of-sales approach to pro forma balance sheet preparation. Because the judgmental approach requires only slightly more information and should yield better estimates than the somewhat naive percent-of-sales approach, it is presented here.

To apply the judgmental approach to prepare Vectra Manufacturing's 2016 pro forma balance sheet, a number of assumptions must be made about levels of various balance sheet accounts:

1. A minimum cash balance of $6,000 is desired.
2. Marketable securities will remain unchanged from their current level of $4,000.
3. Accounts receivable on average represent about 45 days of sales (about 1/8 of a year). Because Vectra's annual sales are projected to be $135,000, accounts receivable should average $16,875 (1/8 × $135,000).
4. The ending inventory should remain at a level of about $16,000, of which 25 percent (approximately $4,000) should be raw materials and the remaining 75 percent (approximately $12,000) should consist of finished goods.
5. A new machine costing $20,000 will be purchased. Total depreciation for the year is $8,000. Adding the $20,000 acquisition to the existing net fixed assets of $51,000 and subtracting the depreciation of $8,000 yields net fixed assets of $63,000.
6. Purchases will represent approximately 30 percent of annual sales, which in this case is approximately $40,500 (0.30 × $135,000). The firm estimates that it can take 73 days on average to satisfy its accounts payable. Thus accounts payable should equal one-fifth (73 days ÷ 365 days) of the firm's purchases, or $8,100 (1/5 × $40,500).
7. Taxes payable will equal one-fourth of the current year's tax liability, which equals $455 (one-fourth of the tax liability of $1,823 shown in the pro forma income statement in Table 4.15).
8. Notes payable will remain unchanged from their current level of $8,300.
9. No change in other current liabilities is expected. They remain at the level of the previous year: $3,400.
10. The firm's long-term debt and its common stock will remain unchanged at $18,000 and $30,000, respectively; no issues, retirements, or repurchases of bonds or stocks are planned.
11. Retained earnings will increase from the beginning level of $23,000 (from the balance sheet dated December 31, 2015, in Table 4.13) to $29,327. The increase of $6,327 represents the amount of retained earnings calculated in the year-end 2016 pro forma income statement in Table 4.15.

external financing required ("plug" figure)
Under the judgmental approach for developing a pro forma balance sheet, the amount of external financing needed to bring the statement into balance. It can be either a positive or a negative value.

A 2016 pro forma balance sheet for Vectra Manufacturing based on these assumptions is presented in Table 4.16. A **"plug" figure**—called the **external financing required**—of $8,293 is needed to bring the statement into balance. This means that the firm will have to obtain about $8,300 of additional external financing to support the increased sales level of $135,000 for 2016.

A *positive* value for "external financing required," like that shown in Table 4.16, means that, based on its plans, the firm will not generate enough internal financing to support its forecast growth in assets. To support the forecast level of operation, the firm must raise funds externally by using debt and/or equity financing or by reducing dividends. Once the form of financing is determined, the pro forma balance sheet is modified to replace "external financing required" with the planned increases in the debt and/or equity accounts.

A *negative* value for "external financing required" indicates that, based on its plans, the firm will generate more financing internally than it needs t

TABLE 4.16	A Pro Forma Balance Sheet, Using the Judgmental Approach, for Vectra Manufacturing (December 31, 2016)			
Assets			**Liabilities and stockholders' equity**	
Cash		$ 6,000	Accounts payable	$ 8,100
Marketable securities		4,000	Taxes payable	455
Accounts receivable		16,875	Notes payable	8,300
Inventories			Other current liabilities	3,400
Raw materials	$ 4,000		Total current liabilities	$ 20,255
Finished goods	12,000		Long-term debt	18,000
Total inventory		16,000	Total liabilities	$ 38,255
Total current assets		$ 42,875	Common stock	30,000
Net fixed assets		63,000	Retained earnings	29,327
Total assets		$105,875	Total	$ 97,582
			External financing required[a]	8,293
			Total liabilities and stockholders' equity	$105,875

[a]The amount of external financing needed to force the firm's balance sheet to balance. Because of the nature of the judgmental approach, the balance sheet is not expected to balance without some type of adjustment.

support its forecast growth in assets. In this case, funds are available for use in repaying debt, repurchasing stock, or increasing dividends. Once the specific actions are determined, "external financing required" is replaced in the pro forma balance sheet with the planned reductions in the debt and/or equity accounts. Obviously, besides being used to prepare the pro forma balance sheet, the judgmental approach is frequently used specifically to estimate the firm's financing requirements.

→ REVIEW QUESTIONS

4–17 Describe the *judgmental approach* for simplified preparation of the pro forma balance sheet.

4–18 What is the significance of the "plug" figure, *external financing required?* Differentiate between strategies associated with positive values and with negative values for external financing required.

LG 6 ## 4.7 Evaluation of Pro Forma Statements

It is difficult to forecast the many variables involved in preparing pro forma statements. As a result, investors, lenders, and managers frequently use the techniques presented in this chapter to make rough estimates of pro forma financial statements. It is nonetheless important to recognize the basic weaknesses of these simplified approaches. The weaknesses lie in two assumptions: (1) that the firm's past financial condition is an accurate indicator of its future and (2) that certain variables (such as cash, accounts receivable, and inventories) can be forced to take on certain "desired" values. These assumptions cannot be justified solely on the basis of their ability to simplify the calculations involved. However, despite their weaknesses, the simplified approaches to pro forma statement preparation are likely to remain popular because of their relative simplicity. The widespread use of spreadsheets certainly helps to streamline the financial planning process.

However pro forma statements are prepared, analysts must understand how to use them to make financial decisions. Both financial managers and lenders can use pro forma statements to analyze the firm's inflows and outflows of cash, as well as its liquidity, activity, debt, profitability, and market value. Various ratios can be calculated from the pro forma income statement and balance sheet to evaluate performance. Cash inflows and outflows can be evaluated by preparing a pro forma statement of cash flows. After analyzing the pro forma statements, the financial manager can take steps to adjust planned operations to achieve short-term financial goals. For example, if projected profits on the pro forma income statement are too low, a variety of pricing and/or cost-cutting actions might be initiated. If the projected level of accounts receivable on the pro forma balance sheet is too high, changes in credit or collection policy may be called for. Pro forma statements are therefore of great importance in solidifying the firm's financial plans for the coming year.

→ **REVIEW QUESTIONS**

4–19 What are the two basic weaknesses of the simplified approaches to preparing pro forma statements?

4–20 What is the financial manager's objective in evaluating pro forma statements?

Summary

FOCUS ON VALUE

Cash flow, the lifeblood of the firm, is a key determinant of the value of the firm. The financial manager must plan and manage the firm's cash flow. The goal is to ensure the firm's solvency and to generate positive cash flow for the firm's owners. Both the magnitude and the risk of the cash flows generated on behalf of the owners determine the firm's value.

To carry out the responsibility to create value for owners, the financial manager uses tools such as cash budgets and pro forma financial statements as part of the process of generating positive cash flow. Good financial plans should result in large free cash flows. Clearly, the financial manager must deliberately and carefully plan and manage the firm's cash flows to achieve the firm's goal of maximizing share price.

REVIEW OF LEARNING GOALS

LG 1 Understand tax depreciation procedures and the effect of depreciation on the firm's cash flows. Depreciation is an important factor affecting a firm's cash flow. An asset's depreciable value and depreciable life are determined by using the MACRS standards in the federal tax code. MACRS groups assets (excluding real estate) into six property classes based on length of recovery period.

LG 2 **Discuss the firm's statement of cash flows, operating cash flow, and free cash flow.** The statement of cash flows is divided into cash flow from operating, investment, and financing activities. It reconciles changes in the firm's cash flows with changes in cash and marketable securities for the period. Interpreting the statement of cash flows involves both the major categories of cash flow and the individual items of cash inflow and outflow. From a strict financial point of view, a firm's operating cash flow is defined to exclude interest. Of greater importance is a firm's free cash flow, which is the amount of cash flow available to creditors and owners.

LG 3 **Understand the financial planning process, including long-term (strategic) financial plans and short-term (operating) financial plans.** The two key aspects of the financial planning process are cash planning and profit planning. Cash planning involves the cash budget or cash forecast. Profit planning relies on the pro forma income statement and balance sheet. Long-term (strategic) financial plans act as a guide for preparing short-term (operating) financial plans. Long-term plans tend to cover periods ranging from 2 to 10 years; short-term plans most often cover a 1- to 2-year period.

LG 4 **Discuss the cash-planning process and the preparation, evaluation, and use of the cash budget.** The cash-planning process uses the cash budget, based on a sales forecast, to estimate short-term cash surpluses and shortages. The cash budget is typically prepared for a 1-year period divided into months. It nets cash receipts and disbursements for each period to calculate net cash flow. Ending cash is estimated by adding beginning cash to the net cash flow. By subtracting the desired minimum cash balance from the ending cash, the firm can determine required total financing or the excess cash balance. To cope with uncertainty in the cash budget, scenario analysis or simulation can be used. A firm must also consider its pattern of daily cash receipts and cash disbursements.

LG 5 **Explain the simplified procedures used to prepare and evaluate the pro forma income statement and the pro forma balance sheet.** A pro forma income statement can be developed by calculating past percentage relationships between certain cost and expense items and the firm's sales and then applying these percentages to forecasts. Because this approach implies that all costs and expenses are variable, it tends to understate profits when sales are increasing and to overstate profits when sales are decreasing. This problem can be avoided by breaking down costs and expenses into fixed and variable components. In this case, the fixed components remain unchanged from the most recent year, and the variable costs and expenses are forecast on a percent-of-sales basis.

Under the judgmental approach, the values of certain balance sheet accounts are estimated and the firm's external financing is used as a balancing, or "plug," figure. A positive value for "external financing required" means that the firm will not generate enough internal financing to support its forecast growth in assets and will have to raise funds externally or reduce dividends. A negative value for "external financing required" indicates that the firm will generate more financing internally than it needs to support its forecast growth in assets and funds will be available for use in repaying debt, repurchasing stock, or increasing dividends.

LG 6 Evaluate the simplified approaches to pro forma financial statement preparation and the common uses of pro forma statements. Simplified approaches for preparing pro forma statements assume that the firm's past financial condition is an accurate indicator of the future. Pro forma statements are commonly used to forecast and analyze the firm's level of profitability and overall financial performance so that adjustments can be made to planned operations to achieve short-term financial goals.

Self-Test Problems (Solutions in Appendix)

  ST4–1   **Depreciation and cash flow** A firm expects to have earnings before interest and taxes (EBIT) of $160,000 in each of the next 6 years. It pays annual interest of $15,000. The firm is considering the purchase of an asset that costs $140,000, requires $10,000 in installation cost, and has a recovery period of 5 years. It will be the firm's only asset, and the asset's depreciation is already reflected in its EBIT estimates.

a. Calculate the annual depreciation for the asset purchase using the MACRS depreciation percentages in Table 4.2 on page 112.

b. Calculate the firm's operating cash flows for each of the 6 years, using Equation 4.3. Assume that the firm is subject to a 40% tax rate on all the profit that it earns.

c. Suppose that the firm's net fixed assets, current assets, accounts payable, and accruals had the following values at the start and end of the final year (year 6). Calculate the firm's free cash flow (FCF) for that year.

Account	Year 6 start	Year 6 end
Net fixed assets	$ 7,500	$ 0
Current assets	90,000	110,000
Accounts payable	40,000	45,000
Accruals	8,000	7,000

d. Compare and discuss the significance of each value calculated in parts **b** and **c**.

  ST4–2   **Cash budget and pro forma balance sheet inputs** Jane McDonald, a financial analyst for Carroll Company, has prepared the following sales and cash disbursement estimates for the period February–June of the current year.

Month	Sales	Cash disbursements
February	$500	$400
March	600	300
April	400	600
May	200	500
June	200	200

McDonald notes that, historically, 30% of sales have been for cash. Of *credit sales,* 70% are collected 1 month after the sale, and the remaining 30% are collected 2 months after the sale. The firm wishes to maintain a minimum ending balance in its cash account of $25. Balances above this amount would be invested in short-term government securities (marketable securities), whereas any deficits would be financed through short-term bank borrowing (notes payable). The beginning cash balance at April 1 is $115.

a. Prepare cash budgets for April, May, and June.
b. How much financing, if any, at a maximum would Carroll Company require to meet its obligations during this 3-month period?
c. A pro forma balance sheet dated at the end of June is to be prepared from the information presented. Give the size of each of the following: cash, notes payable, marketable securities, and accounts receivable.

LG 5 **ST4–3** **Pro forma income statement** Euro Designs, Inc., expects sales during 2016 to rise from the 2015 level of $3.5 million to $3.9 million. Because of a scheduled large loan payment, the interest expense in 2016 is expected to drop to $325,000. The firm plans to increase its cash dividend payments during 2016 to $320,000. The company's year-end 2015 income statement follows.

Euro Designs, Inc., Income Statement for the Year Ended December 31, 2015	
Sales revenue	$3,500,000
Less: Cost of goods sold	1,925,000
Gross profits	$1,575,000
Less: Operating expenses	420,000
Operating profits	$1,155,000
Less: Interest expense	400,000
Net profits before taxes	$ 755,000
Less: Taxes (rate = 40%)	302,000
Net profits after taxes	$ 453,000
Less: Cash dividends	250,000
To retained earnings	$ 203,000

a. Use the *percent-of-sales method* to prepare a 2016 pro forma income statement for Euro Designs, Inc.
b. Explain why the statement may underestimate the company's actual 2016 pro forma income.

Warm-Up Exercises

All problems are available in MyFinanceLab.

LG 1 **E4–1** The installed cost of a new computerized controller was $65,000. Calculate the depreciation schedule by year assuming a recovery period of 5 years and using the appropriate MACRS depreciation percentages given in Table 4.2 on page 112.

LG 2 **E4–2** Classify the following changes in each of the accounts as either an *inflow* or an *outflow* of cash. During the year (a) marketable securities increased, (b) land and buildings decreased, (c) accounts payable increased, (d) vehicles decreased, (e) accounts receivable increased, and (f) dividends were paid.

LG 2 **E4–3** Determine the *operating cash flow (OCF)* for Kleczka, Inc., based on the following data. (All values are in thousands of dollars.) During the year the firm had sales of $2,500, cost of goods sold totaled $1,800, operating expenses totaled $300, and depreciation expenses were $200. The firm is in the 35% tax bracket.

LG 2 **E4–4** During the year, Xero, Inc., experienced an increase in net fixed assets of $300,000 and had depreciation of $200,000. It also experienced an increase in current assets of $150,000 and an increase in accounts payable and accruals of $75,000. If operating cash flow (OCF) for the year was $700,000, calculate the firm's *free cash flow (FCF)* for the year.

LG 5 **E4–5** Rimier Corp. forecasts sales of $650,000 for 2016. Assume that the firm has fixed costs of $250,000 and variable costs amounting to 35% of sales. Operating expenses are estimated to include fixed costs of $28,000 and a variable portion equal to 7.5% of sales. Interest expenses for the coming year are estimated to be $20,000. Estimate Rimier's net profits before taxes for 2016.

Problems   All problems are available in MyFinanceLab.

LG 1 **P4–1** **Depreciation** On March 20, 2015, Norton Systems acquired two new assets. Asset A was research equipment costing $17,000 and having a 3-year recovery period. Asset B was duplicating equipment having an installed cost of $45,000 and a 5-year recovery period. Using the MACRS depreciation percentages in Table 4.2 on page 112, prepare a depreciation schedule for each of these assets.

LG 1 **P4–2** **Depreciation** In early 2015, Sosa Enterprises purchased a new machine for $10,000 to make cork stoppers for wine bottles. The machine has a 3-year recovery period and is expected to have a salvage value of $2,000. Develop a depreciation schedule for this asset using the MACRS depreciation percentages in Table 4.2.

LG 1 LG 2 **P4–3** **MACR depreciation expense and accounting cash flow** Pavlovich Instruments, Inc., a maker of precision telescopes, expects to report pretax income of $430,000 this year. The company's financial manager is considering the timing of a purchase of new computerized lens grinders. The grinders will have an installed cost of $80,000 and a cost recovery period of 5 years. They will be depreciated using the MACRS schedule.
a. If the firm purchases the grinders before year-end, what depreciation expense will it be able to claim this year? (Use Table 4.2 on page 112.)
b. If the firm reduces its reported income by the amount of the depreciation expense calculated in part a, what tax savings will result?

LG 1 LG 2 **P4–4** **Depreciation and accounting cash flow** A firm in the third year of depreciating its only asset, which originally cost $180,000 and has a 5-year MACRS recovery period, has gathered the following data relative to the current year's operations.
a. Use the *relevant data* to determine the operating cash flow (see Equations 4.2 and 4.3) for the current year.
b. Explain the impact that depreciation, as well as any other noncash charges, has on a firm's cash flows.

Accruals	$ 15,000
Current assets	120,000
Interest expense	15,000
Sales revenue	400,000
Inventory	70,000
Total costs before depreciation, interest, and taxes	290,000
Tax rate on ordinary income	40%

P4–5 **Classifying inflows and outflows of cash** Classify each of the following items as an inflow (I) or an outflow (O) of cash, or as neither (N).

Item	Change ($)	Item	Change ($)
Cash	+100	Accounts receivable	−700
Accounts payable	−1,000	Net profits	+600
Notes payable	+500	Depreciation	+100
Long-term debt	−2,000	Repurchase of stock	+600
Inventory	+200	Cash dividends	+800
Fixed assets	+400	Sale of stock	+1,000

P4–6 **Finding operating and free cash flows** Consider the following balance sheets and selected data from the income statement of Keith Corporation.

Keith Corporation Balance Sheets		
	December 31	
Assets	2015	2014
Cash	$ 1,500	$ 1,000
Marketable securities	1,800	1,200
Accounts receivable	2,000	1,800
Inventories	2,900	2,800
Total current assets	$ 8,200	$ 6,800
Gross fixed assets	$29,500	$28,100
Less: Accumulated depreciation	14,700	13,100
Net fixed assets	$14,800	$15,000
Total assets	$23,000	$21,800
Liabilities and stockholders' equity		
Accounts payable	$ 1,600	$ 1,500
Notes payable	2,800	2,200
Accruals	200	300
Total current liabilities	$ 4,600	$ 4,000
Long-term debt	5,000	5,000
Total liabilities	$ 9,600	$ 9,000
Common stock	$10,000	$10,000
Retained earnings	3,400	2,800
Total stockholders' equity	$13,400	$12,800
Total liabilities and stockholders' equity	$23,000	$21,800

Keith Corporation Income Statement Data (2015)	
Depreciation expense	$1,600
Earnings before interest and taxes (EBIT)	2,700
Interest expense	367
Net profits after taxes	1,400
Tax rate	40%

a. Calculate the firm's *net operating profit after taxes (NOPAT)* for the year ended December 31, 2015, using Equation 4.1.

b. Calculate the firm's *operating cash flow (OCF)* for the year ended December 31, 2015, using Equation 4.3.

c. Calculate the firm's *free cash flow (FCF)* for the year ended December 31, 2015, using Equation 4.4.

d. Interpret, compare, and contrast your cash flow estimates in parts **b** and **c**.

 P4–7   **Cash receipts**   A firm has actual sales of $65,000 in April and $60,000 in May. It expects sales of $70,000 in June and $100,000 in July and in August. Assuming that sales are the only source of cash inflows and that half of them are for cash and the remainder are collected evenly over the following 2 months, what are the firm's expected cash receipts for June, July, and August?

 P4–8   **Cash disbursements schedule**   Maris Brothers, Inc., needs a cash disbursement schedule for the months of April, May, and June. Use the format of Table 4.9 on page 125 and the following information in its preparation.

Sales: February = $500,000; March = $500,000; April = $560,000; May = $610,000; June = $650,000; July = $650,000

Purchases: Purchases are calculated as 60% of the next month's sales, 10% of purchases are made in cash, 50% of purchases are paid for 1 month after purchase, and the remaining 40% of purchases are paid for 2 months after purchase.

Rent: The firm pays rent of $8,000 per month.

Wages and salaries: Base wage and salary costs are fixed at $6,000 per month plus a variable cost of 7% of the current month's sales.

Taxes: A tax payment of $54,500 is due in June.

Fixed asset outlays: New equipment costing $75,000 will be bought and paid for in April.

Interest payments: An interest payment of $30,000 is due in June.

Cash dividends: Dividends of $12,500 will be paid in April.

Principal repayments and retirements: No principal repayments or retirements are due during these months.

 P4–9   **Cash budget: Basic**   Grenoble Enterprises had sales of $50,000 in March and $60,000 in April. Forecast sales for May, June, and July are $70,000, $80,000, and $100,000, respectively. The firm has a cash balance of $5,000 on May 1 and wishes to maintain a minimum cash balance of $5,000. Given the following data, prepare and interpret a cash budget for the months of May, June, and July.

(1) The firm makes 20% of sales for cash, 60% are collected in the next month, and the remaining 20% are collected in the second month following sale.

(2) The firm receives other income of $2,000 per month.

(3) The firm's actual or expected purchases, all made for cash, are $50,000, $70,000, and $80,000 for the months of May through July, respectively.

(4) Rent is $3,000 per month.

(5) Wages and salaries are 10% of the previous month's sales.

(6) Cash dividends of $3,000 will be paid in June.

(7) Payment of principal and interest of $4,000 is due in June.

(8) A cash purchase of equipment costing $6,000 is scheduled in July.

(9) Taxes of $6,000 are due in June.

Personal Finance Problem

 P4–10 **Preparation of cash budget** Sam and Suzy Sizeman need to prepare a cash budget for the last quarter of 2016 to make sure they can cover their expenditures during the period. Sam and Suzy have been preparing budgets for the past several years and have been able to establish specific percentages for most of their cash outflows. These percentages are based on their take-home pay (that is, monthly utilities normally run 5% of monthly take-home pay). The information in the following table can be used to create their fourth-quarter budget for 2016.

Income	
Monthly take-home pay	$4,900
Expenses	
Housing	30%
Utilities	5%
Food	10%
Transportation	7%
Medical/dental	.5%
Clothing for October and November	3%
Clothing for December	$440
Property taxes (November only)	11.5%
Appliances	1%
Personal care	2%
Entertainment for October and November	6%
Entertainment for December	$1,500
Savings	7.5%
Other	5%
Excess cash	4.5%

a. Prepare a quarterly cash budget for Sam and Suzy covering the months October through December 2016.

b. Are there individual months that incur a deficit?

c. What is the cumulative cash surplus or deficit by the end of December 2016?

 P4–11 **Cash budget: Advanced** The actual sales and purchases for Xenocore, Inc., for September and October 2015, along with its forecast sales and purchases for the period November 2015 through April 2016, follow.

The firm makes 20% of all sales for cash and collects on 40% of its sales in each of the 2 months following the sale. Other cash inflows are expected to be $12,000 in September and April, $15,000 in January and March, and $27,000 in February. The firm pays cash for 10% of its purchases. It pays for 50% of its purchases in the following month and for 40% of its purchases 2 months later.

Year	Month	Sales	Purchases
2015	September	$210,000	$120,000
2015	October	250,000	150,000
2015	November	170,000	140,000
2015	December	160,000	100,000
2016	January	140,000	80,000
2016	February	180,000	110,000
2016	March	200,000	100,000
2016	April	250,000	90,000

Wages and salaries amount to 20% of the preceding month's sales. Rent of $20,000 per month must be paid. Interest payments of $10,000 are due in January and April. A principal payment of $30,000 is also due in April. The firm expects to pay cash dividends of $20,000 in January and April. Taxes of $80,000 are due in April. The firm also intends to make a $25,000 cash purchase of fixed assets in December.

a. Assuming that the firm has a cash balance of $22,000 at the beginning of November, determine the end-of-month cash balances for each month, November through April.

b. Assuming that the firm wishes to maintain a $15,000 minimum cash balance, determine the required total financing or excess cash balance for each month, November through April.

c. If the firm were requesting a line of credit to cover needed financing for the period November to April, how large would this line have to be? Explain your answer.

 P4–12 Cash flow concepts The following represent financial transactions that Johnsfield & Co. will be undertaking in the next planning period. For each transaction, check the statement or statements that will be affected immediately.

Transaction	Cash budget	Pro forma income statement	Pro forma balance sheet
Cash sale			
Credit sale			
Accounts receivable are collected			
Asset with 5-year life is purchased			
Depreciation is taken			
Amortization of goodwill is taken			
Sale of common stock			
Retirement of outstanding bonds			
Fire insurance premium is paid for the next 3 years			

P4–13   **Cash budget: Scenario analysis** Trotter Enterprises, Inc., has gathered the following data to plan for its cash requirements and short-term investment opportunities for October, November, and December. All amounts are shown in thousands of dollars.

	October			November			December		
	Pessi- mistic	Most likely	Opti- mistic	Pessi- mistic	Most likely	Opti- mistic	Pessi- mistic	Most likely	Opti- mistic
Total cash receipts	$260	$342	$462	$200	$287	$366	$191	$294	$353
Total cash disbursements	285	326	421	203	261	313	287	332	315

a. Prepare a *scenario analysis* of Trotter's cash budget using −$20,000 as the beginning cash balance for October and a minimum required cash balance of $18,000.
b. Use the analysis prepared in part **a** to predict Trotter's financing needs and investment opportunities over the months of October, November, and December. Discuss how knowledge of the timing and amounts involved can aid the planning process.

 P4–14   **Multiple cash budgets: Scenario analysis** Brownstein, Inc., expects sales of $100,000 during each of the next 3 months. It will make monthly purchases of $60,000 during this time. Wages and salaries are $10,000 per month plus 5% of sales. Brownstein expects to make a tax payment of $20,000 in the next month and a $15,000 purchase of fixed assets in the second month and to receive $8,000 in cash from the sale of an asset in the third month. All sales and purchases are for cash. Beginning cash and the minimum cash balance are assumed to be zero.
a. Construct a cash budget for the next 3 months.
b. Brownstein is unsure of the sales levels, but all other figures are certain. If the most pessimistic sales figure is $80,000 per month and the most optimistic is $120,000 per month, what are the monthly minimum and maximum ending cash balances that the firm can expect for each of the 1-month periods?
c. Briefly discuss how the financial manager can use the data in parts **a** and **b** to plan for financing needs.

 P4–15   **Pro forma income statement** The marketing department of Metroline Manufacturing estimates that its sales in 2016 will be $1.5 million. Interest expense is expected to remain unchanged at $35,000, and the firm plans to pay $70,000 in cash dividends during 2016. Metroline Manufacturing's income statement for the year ended December 31, 2015, and a breakdown of the firm's cost of goods sold and operating expenses into their fixed and variable components are given below.
a. Use the *percent-of-sales method* to prepare a pro forma income statement for the year ended December 31, 2016.
b. Use *fixed and variable cost data* to develop a pro forma income statement for the year ended December 31, 2016.
c. Compare and contrast the statements developed in parts **a** and **b**. Which statement probably provides the better estimate of 2016 income? Explain why.

Metroline Manufacturing Income Statement for the Year Ended December 31, 2015	
Sales revenue	$1,400,000
Less: Cost of goods sold	910,000
Gross profits	$ 490,000
Less: Operating expenses	120,000
Operating profits	$ 370,000
Less: Interest expense	35,000
Net profits before taxes	$ 335,000
Less: Taxes (rate = 40%)	134,000
Net profits after taxes	$ 201,000
Less: Cash dividends	66,000
To retained earnings	$ 135,000

Metroline Manufacturing Breakdown of Costs and Expenses into Fixed and Variable Components for the Year Ended December 31, 2015	
Cost of goods sold	
Fixed cost	$210,000
Variable cost	700,000
Total costs	$910,000
Operating expenses	
Fixed expenses	$ 36,000
Variable expenses	84,000
Total expenses	$120,000

LG 5   P4–16   Pro forma income statement: Scenario analysis Allen Products, Inc., wants to do a *scenario analysis* for the coming year. The pessimistic prediction for sales is $900,000; the most likely amount of sales is $1,125,000; and the optimistic prediction is $1,280,000. Allen's income statement for the most recent year follows.

Allen Products, Inc., Income Statement for the Year Ended December 31, 2015	
Sales revenue	$937,500
Less: Cost of goods sold	421,875
Gross profits	$515,625
Less: Operating expenses	234,375
Operating profits	$281,250
Less: Interest expense	30,000
Net profits before taxes	$251,250
Less: Taxes (rate = 25%)	62,813
Net profits after taxes	$188,437

a. Use the *percent-of-sales method,* the income statement for December 31, 2015, and the sales revenue estimates to develop pessimistic, most likely, and optimistic pro forma income statements for the coming year.
b. Explain how the percent-of-sales method could result in an overstatement of profits for the pessimistic case and an understatement of profits for the most likely and optimistic cases.
c. Restate the pro forma income statements prepared in part **a** to incorporate the following assumptions about the 2015 costs:

$250,000 of the cost of goods sold is fixed; the rest is variable.
$180,000 of the operating expenses is fixed; the rest is variable.
All the interest expense is fixed.

d. Compare your findings in part **c** to your findings in part **a**. Do your observations confirm your explanation in part **b**?

LG 5 **P4–17** **Pro forma balance sheet: Basic** Leonard Industries wishes to prepare a pro forma balance sheet for December 31, 2016. The firm expects 2016 sales to total $3,000,000. The following information has been gathered:

(1) A minimum cash balance of $50,000 is desired.

(2) Marketable securities are expected to remain unchanged.

(3) Accounts receivable represent 10% of sales.

(4) Inventories represent 12% of sales.

(5) A new machine costing $90,000 will be acquired during 2016. Total depreciation for the year will be $32,000.

(6) Accounts payable represent 14% of sales.

(7) Accruals, other current liabilities, long-term debt, and common stock are expected to remain unchanged.

(8) The firm's net profit margin is 4%, and it expects to pay out $70,000 in cash dividends during 2016.

(9) The December 31, 2015, balance sheet follows.

Leonard Industries Balance Sheet December 31, 2015			
Assets		**Liabilities and stockholders' equity**	
Cash	$ 45,000	Accounts payable	$ 395,000
Marketable securities	15,000	Accruals	60,000
Accounts receivable	255,000	Other current liabilities	30,000
Inventories	340,000	Total current liabilities	$ 485,000
Total current assets	$ 655,000	Long-term debt	350,000
Net fixed assets	600,000	Total liabilities	$ 835,000
Total assets	$ 1,255,000	Common stock	200,000
		Retained earnings	220,000
		Total liabilities and stockholders' equity	$1,255,000

a. Use the *judgmental approach* to prepare a pro forma balance sheet dated December 31, 2016, for Leonard Industries.

b. How much, if any, additional financing will Leonard Industries require in 2016? Discuss.

c. Could Leonard Industries adjust its planned 2016 dividend to avoid the situation described in part **b?** Explain how.

LG 5 **P4–18** **Pro forma balance sheet** Peabody & Peabody has 2015 sales of $10 million. It wishes to analyze expected performance and financing needs for 2017, which is 2 years ahead. Given the following information, respond to parts a and **b.**

(1) The percents of sales for items that vary directly with sales are as follows:

　　Accounts receivable, 12%
　　Inventory, 18%
　　Accounts payable, 14%
　　Net profit margin, 3%

(2) Marketable securities and other current liabilities are expected to remain unchanged.

(3) A minimum cash balance of $480,000 is desired.

(4) A new machine costing $650,000 will be acquired in 2016, and equipment costing $850,000 will be purchased in 2017. Total depreciation in 2016 is forecast as $290,000, and in 2017 $390,000 of depreciation will be taken.

(5) Accruals are expected to rise to $500,000 by the end of 2017.

(6) No sale or retirement of long-term debt is expected.

(7) No sale or repurchase of common stock is expected.

(8) The dividend payout of 50% of net profits is expected to continue.

(9) Sales are expected to be $11 million in 2016 and $12 million in 2017.

(10) The December 31, 2015, balance sheet follows.

Peabody & Peabody Balance Sheet December 31, 2015 ($000)			
Assets		**Liabilities and stockholders' equity**	
Cash	$ 400	Accounts payable	$1,400
Marketable securities	200	Accruals	400
Accounts receivable	1,200	Other current liabilities	80
Inventories	1,800	Total current liabilities	$1,880
Total current assets	$3,600	Long-term debt	2,000
Net fixed assets	4,000	Total liabilities	3,880
Total assets	$7,600	Common equity	3,720
		Total liabilities and stockholders' equity	$7,600

a. Prepare a pro forma balance sheet dated December 31, 2017.

b. Discuss the financing changes suggested by the statement prepared in part **a**.

 P4–19 **Integrative: Pro forma statements** Red Queen Restaurants wishes to prepare financial plans. Use the financial statements and the other information provided below to prepare the financial plans.

The following financial data are also available:

(1) The firm has estimated that its sales for 2016 will be $900,000.

(2) The firm expects to pay $35,000 in cash dividends in 2016.

(3) The firm wishes to maintain a minimum cash balance of $30,000.

(4) Accounts receivable represent approximately 18% of annual sales.

(5) The firm's ending inventory will change directly with changes in sales in 2016.

(6) A new machine costing $42,000 will be purchased in 2016. Total depreciation for 2016 will be $17,000.

(7) Accounts payable will change directly in response to changes in sales in 2016.

(8) Taxes payable will equal one-fourth of the tax liability on the pro forma income statement.

(9) Marketable securities, other current liabilities, long-term debt, and common stock will remain unchanged.

a. Prepare a pro forma income statement for the year ended December 31, 2016, using the *percent-of-sales method.*

b. Prepare a pro forma balance sheet dated December 31, 2016, using the *judgmental approach.*

c. Analyze these statements, and discuss the resulting *external financing required.*

Red Queen Restaurants Income Statement for the Year Ended December 31, 2015	
Sales revenue	$800,000
Less: Cost of goods sold	600,000
Gross profits	$200,000
Less: Operating expenses	100,000
Net profits before taxes	$100,000
Less: Taxes (rate = 40%)	40,000
Net profits after taxes	$ 60,000
Less: Cash dividends	20,000
To retained earnings	$ 40,000

Red Queen Restaurants Balance Sheet December 31, 2015			
Assets		**Liabilities and stockholders' equity**	
Cash	$ 32,000	Accounts payable	$100,000
Marketable securities	18,000	Taxes payable	20,000
Accounts receivable	150,000	Other current liabilities	5,000
Inventories	100,000	Total current liabilities	$125,000
Total current assets	$300,000	Long-term debt	200,000
Net fixed assets	350,000	Total liabilities	$325,000
Total assets	$650,000	Common stock	150,000
		Retained earnings	175,000
		Total liabilities and stockholders' equity	$650,000

LG 5 **P4–20** **Integrative: Pro forma statements** Provincial Imports, Inc., has assembled past (2015) financial statements (income statement and balance sheet below) and financial projections for use in preparing financial plans for the coming year (2016).

Provincial Imports, Inc., Income Statement for the Year Ended December 31, 2015	
Sales revenue	$5,000,000
Less: Cost of goods sold	2,750,000
Gross profits	$2,250,000
Less: Operating expenses	850,000
Operating profits	$1,400,000
Less: Interest expense	200,000
Net profits before taxes	$1,200,000
Less: Taxes (rate = 40%)	480,000
Net profits after taxes	$ 720,000
Less: Cash dividends	288,000
To retained earnings	$ 432,000

Information related to financial projections for the year 2016 is as follows:

Provincial Imports, Inc., Balance Sheet December 31, 2015			
Assets		**Liabilities and stockholders' equity**	
Cash	$ 200,000	Accounts payable	$ 700,000
Marketable securities	225,000	Taxes payable	95,000
Accounts receivable	625,000	Notes payable	200,000
Inventories	500,000	Other current liabilities	5,000
Total current assets	$1,550,000	Total current liabilities	$1,000,000
Net fixed assets	1,400,000	Long-term debt	500,000
Total assets	$2,950,000	Total liabilities	$1,500,000
		Common stock	75,000
		Retained earnings	1,375,000
		Total liabilities and equity	$2,950,000

(1) Projected sales are $6,000,000.
(2) Cost of goods sold in 2015 includes $1,000,000 in fixed costs.
(3) Operating expense in 2015 includes $250,000 in fixed costs.
(4) Interest expense will remain unchanged.
(5) The firm will pay cash dividends amounting to 40% of net profits after taxes.
(6) Cash and inventories will double.
(7) Marketable securities, notes payable, long-term debt, and common stock will remain unchanged.
(8) Accounts receivable, accounts payable, and other current liabilities will change in direct response to the change in sales.
(9) A new computer system costing $356,000 will be purchased during the year. Total depreciation expense for the year will be $110,000.
(10) The tax rate will remain at 40%.

a. Prepare a pro forma income statement for the year ended December 31, 2016, using the *fixed cost data* given to improve the accuracy of the *percent-of-sales method*.

b. Prepare a pro forma balance sheet as of December 31, 2016, using the information given and the *judgmental approach*. Include a reconciliation of the retained earnings account.

c. Analyze these statements, and discuss the resulting *external financing required*.

LG 3   **P4–21 ETHICS PROBLEM** The SEC is trying to get companies to notify the investment community more quickly when a "material change" will affect their forthcoming financial results. In what sense might a financial manager be seen as "more ethical" if he or she follows this directive and issues a press release indicating that sales will not be as high as previously anticipated?

Spreadsheet Exercise

You have been assigned the task of putting together a statement for the ACME Company that shows its expected inflows and outflows of cash over the months of July 2016 through December 2016.

You have been given the following data for ACME Company:

(1) Expected gross sales for May through December, respectively, are $300,000, $290,000, $425,000, $500,000, $600,000, $625,000, $650,000, and $700,000.

(2) 12% of the sales in any given month are collected during that month. However, the firm has a credit policy of 3/10 net 30, so factor a 3% discount into the current month's sales collection.

(3) 75% of the sales in any given month are collected during the following month after the sale.

(4) 13% of the sales in any given month are collected during the second month following the sale.

(5) The expected purchases of raw materials in any given month are based on 60% of the expected sales during the following month.

(6) The firm pays 100% of its current month's raw materials purchases in the following month.

(7) Wages and salaries are paid on a monthly basis and are based on 6% of the current month's expected sales.

(8) Monthly lease payments are 2% of the current month's expected sales.

(9) The monthly advertising expense amounts to 3% of sales.

(10) R&D expenditures are expected to be allocated to August, September, and October at the rate of 12% of sales in those months.

(11) During December a prepayment of insurance for the following year will be made in the amount of $24,000.

(12) During the months of July through December, the firm expects to have miscellaneous expenditures of $15,000, $20,000, $25,000, $30,000, $35,000, and $40,000, respectively.

(13) Taxes will be paid in September in the amount of $40,000 and in December in the amount of $45,000.

(14) The beginning cash balance in July is $15,000.

(15) The target cash balance is $15,000.

TO DO

a. Prepare a cash budget for July 2016 through December 2016 by creating a combined spreadsheet that incorporates spreadsheets similar to those in Tables 4.8, 4.9, and 4.10. Divide your spreadsheet into three sections:

(1) Total cash receipts

(2) Total cash disbursements

(3) Cash budget covering the period of July through December

The cash budget should reflect the following:

(1) Beginning and ending monthly cash balances

(2) The required total financing in each month required

(3) The excess cash balance in each month with excess

b. Based on your analysis, briefly describe the outlook for this company over the next 6 months. Discuss its specific obligations and the funds available to meet them. What could the firm do in the case of a cash deficit? (Where could it get the money?) What should the firm do if it has a cash surplus?

MyFinanceLab Visit www.myfinancelab.com for **Chapter Case: Preparing Martin Manufacturing's 2016 Pro Forma Financial Statements,** Group Exercises, and numerous online resources.

5

Time Value of Money

Learning Goals

LG 1 Discuss the role of time value in finance, the use of computational tools, and the basic patterns of cash flow.

LG 2 Understand the concepts of future value and present value, their calculation for single amounts, and the relationship between them.

LG 3 Find the future value and the present value of both an ordinary annuity and an annuity due, and find the present value of a perpetuity.

LG 4 Calculate both the future value and the present value of a mixed stream of cash flows.

LG 5 Understand the effect that compounding interest more frequently than annually has on future value and on the effective annual rate of interest.

LG 6 Describe the procedures involved in (1) determining deposits needed to accumulate a future sum, (2) loan amortization, (3) finding interest or growth rates, and (4) finding an unknown number of periods.

Why This Chapter Matters to You

In your *professional* life

ACCOUNTING You need to understand time-value-of-money calculations to account for certain transactions such as loan amortization, lease payments, and bond interest rates.

INFORMATION SYSTEMS You need to understand time-value-of-money calculations to design systems that accurately measure and value the firm's cash flows.

MANAGEMENT You need to understand time-value-of-money calculations so that you can manage cash receipts and disbursements in a way that will enable the firm to receive the greatest value from its cash flows.

MARKETING You need to understand time value of money because funding for new programs and products must be justified financially using time-value-of-money techniques.

OPERATIONS You need to understand time value of money because the value of investments in new equipment, in new processes, and in inventory will be affected by the time value of money.

In your *personal* life

Time-value-of-money techniques are widely used in personal financial planning. You can use them to calculate the value of savings at given future dates and to estimate the amount you need now to accumulate a given amount at a future date. You also can apply them to value lump-sum amounts or streams of periodic cash flows and to the interest rate or amount of time needed to achieve a given financial goal.

LG ① ## 5.1 The Role of Time Value in Finance

The *time value of money* refers to the observation that it is better to receive money sooner than later. Money that you have in hand today can be invested to earn a positive rate of return, producing more money tomorrow. For that reason, a dollar today is worth more than a dollar in the future. In business, managers constantly face trade-offs in situations in which actions that require outflows of cash today may produce inflows of cash later. Because the cash that comes in the future is worth less than the cash that firms spend up front, managers need a set of tools to help them compare cash inflows and outflows that occur at different times. This chapter introduces you to those tools.

FUTURE VALUE VERSUS PRESENT VALUE

Suppose that a firm has an opportunity to spend $15,000 today on some investment that will produce $17,000 spread out over the next 5 years as follows:

Year 1	$3,000
Year 2	$5,000
Year 3	$4,000
Year 4	$3,000
Year 5	$2,000

Is this investment a wise one? It might seem that the obvious answer is yes because the firm spends $15,000 and receives $17,000. Remember, though, that the value of the dollars the firm receives in the future is less than the value of the dollars that they spend today. Therefore, it is not clear whether the $17,000 inflows are enough to justify the initial investment.

Time-value-of-money analysis helps managers answer questions like this one. The idea is that managers need a way to compare cash today versus cash in the future. There are two ways of doing so. One way is to ask the question, What amount of money in the future is equivalent to $15,000 today? In other words, what is the *future value* of $15,000? The other approach asks, What amount today is equivalent to $17,000 paid out over the next 5 years as outlined above? In other words, what is the *present value* of the stream of cash flows coming in the next 5 years?

time line
A horizontal line on which time zero appears at the leftmost end and future periods are marked from left to right; can be used to depict investment cash flows.

A **time line** depicts the cash flows associated with a given investment. It is a horizontal line on which time zero appears at the leftmost end and future periods are marked from left to right. A time line illustrating our hypothetical investment problem appears in Figure 5.1. The cash flows occurring at time zero (today) and

---

FIGURE 5.1

Time Line
Time line depicting an investment's cash flows

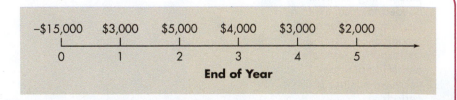

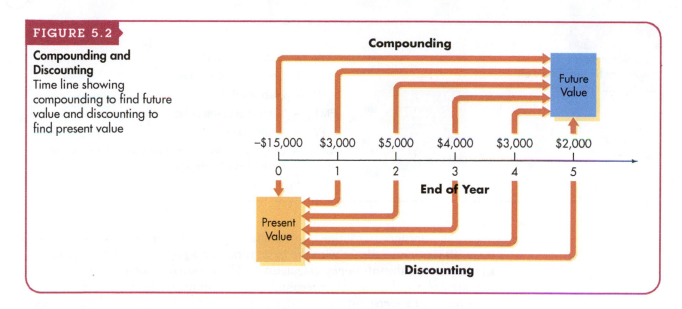

FIGURE 5.2

Compounding and Discounting
Time line showing compounding to find future value and discounting to find present value

at the end of each subsequent year are above the line; the negative values represent *cash outflows* ($15,000 invested today at time zero), and the positive values represent *cash inflows* ($3,000 inflow in 1 year, $5,000 inflow in 2 years, and so on).

To make the correct investment decision, managers need to compare the cash flows depicted in Figure 5.1 at a single point in time. Typically, that point is either the end or the beginning of the investment's life. The future value technique uses *compounding* to find the *future value* of each cash flow at the end of the investment's life and then sums these values to find the investment's future value. This approach is depicted above the time line in Figure 5.2. The figure shows that the future value of each cash flow is measured at the end of the investment's 5-year life. Alternatively, the present value technique uses *discounting* to find the *present value* of each cash flow at time zero and then sums these values to find the investment's value today. Application of this approach is depicted below the time line in Figure 5.2. In practice, when making investment decisions, *managers usually adopt the present value approach.*

COMPUTATIONAL TOOLS

Finding present and future values can involve time-consuming calculations. Although you should understand the concepts and mathematics underlying these calculations, financial calculators and spreadsheets streamline the application of time value techniques.

Financial Calculators

Financial calculators include numerous preprogrammed financial routines. Learning how to use these routines can make present and future values calculations a breeze.

We focus primarily on the keys pictured in Figure 5.3. We typically use four of the first five keys shown in the left column, along with the compute (**CPT**) key. One of the four keys represents the unknown value being calculated. The keystrokes on some of the more sophisticated calculators are menu-driven: After you

FIGURE 5.3

Calculator Keys
Important financial keys on
the typical calculator

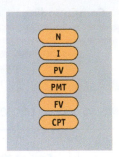

N —	Number of periods
I —	Interest rate per period
PV —	Present value
PMT —	Amount of payment (used only for annuities)
FV —	Future value
CPT —	Compute key used to initiate financial calculation once all values are input

select the appropriate routine, the calculator prompts you to input each value. Regardless, any calculator with the basic future and present value functions can simplify time-value-of-money calculations. The keystrokes for financial calculators are explained in the reference guides that accompany them.

Once you understand the underlying concepts, you probably will want to use a calculator to streamline calculations. With a little practice, you can increase both the speed and the accuracy of your financial computations. Remember that *conceptual understanding of the material is the objective.* An ability to solve problems with the aid of a calculator does not necessarily reflect such an understanding, so don't just settle for answers. Work with the material until you are sure that you also understand the concepts.

Electronic Spreadsheets

Like financial calculators, electronic spreadsheets have built-in routines that simplify time-value calculations. We provide in the text a number of spreadsheet solutions that identify the cell entries for calculating time values. The value for each variable is entered in a cell in the spreadsheet, and the calculation is programmed using an equation that links the individual cells. Changing any of the input variables automatically changes the solution as a result of the equation linking the cells.

Cash Flow Signs

To provide a correct answer, financial calculators and electronic spreadsheets require that a calculation's relevant cash flows be entered accurately as either cash inflows or cash outflows. Cash inflows are indicated by entering positive values, and cash outflows are indicated by entering negative values. By entering the cash flows correctly, you are providing the financial calculator or electronic spreadsheet the calculation's time line. With accurate cash flows entered, answers provided by financial calculators or electronic spreadsheets will indicate the proper result.

BASIC PATTERNS OF CASH FLOW

The cash flow—both inflows and outflows—of a firm can be described by its general pattern. It can be defined as a single amount, an annuity, or a mixed stream.

Single amount: A lump-sum amount either currently held or expected at some future date. Examples include $1,000 today and $650 to be received at the end of 10 years.

Annuity: A level periodic stream of cash flow. For our purposes, we'll work primarily with *annual* cash flows. Examples include either paying out or receiving $800 at the end of each of the next 7 years.

Mixed stream: A stream of cash flow that is *not* an annuity; a stream of unequal periodic cash flows that reflect no particular pattern. Examples include the following two cash flow streams A and B.

End of year	Mixed cash flow stream	
	A	B
1	$ 100	−$ 50
2	800	100
3	1,200	80
4	1,200	−60
5	1,400	
6	300	

Note that neither cash flow stream has equal, periodic cash flows and that A is a 6-year mixed stream and B is a 4-year mixed stream.

In the next three sections of this chapter, we develop the concepts and techniques for finding future and present values of single amounts, annuities, and mixed streams, respectively. Detailed demonstrations of these cash flow patterns are included.

→ **REVIEW QUESTIONS**

5–1 What is the difference between *future value* and *present value*? Which approach is generally preferred by financial managers? Why?

5–2 Define and differentiate among the three basic patterns of cash flow: (1) a single amount, (2) an annuity, and (3) a mixed stream.

LG 2 5.2 Single Amounts

Imagine that at age 25 you began investing $2,000 per year in an investment that earns 5 percent interest. At the end of 40 years, at age 65, you would have invested a total of $80,000 (40 years × $2,000 per year). How much would you have accumulated at the end of the fortieth year? $100,000? $150,000? $200,000? No, your $80,000 would have grown to $242,000! Why? Because the time value of money allowed your investments to generate returns that built on each other over the 40 years.

FUTURE VALUE OF A SINGLE AMOUNT

The most basic future value and present value concepts and computations concern single amounts, either present or future amounts. We begin by considering problems that involve finding the future value of cash that is on hand immediately. Then we will use the underlying concepts to solve problems that determine the value today of cash that will be received or paid in the future.

We often need to find the value at some future date of a given amount of money placed on deposit today. For example, if you deposit $500 today into an account that pays 5 percent annual interest, how much would you have in the account in 10 years? **Future value** is the value at a given future date of an amount placed on deposit today and earning interest at a specified rate. The future value depends on the rate of interest earned and the length of time the money is left on deposit. Here we explore the future value of a single amount.

future value
The value at a given future date of an amount placed on deposit today and earning interest at a specified rate. Found by applying *compound interest* over a specified period of time.

compound interest
Interest that is earned on a given deposit and has become part of the *principal* at the end of a specified period.

principal
The amount of money on which interest is paid.

The Concept of Future Value

We speak of **compound interest** to indicate that the amount of interest earned on a given deposit has become part of the *principal* at the end of a specified period. The term **principal** refers to the amount of money on which the interest is paid. Annual compounding is the most common type.

The *future value* of a present amount is found by applying *compound interest* over a specified period of time. Savings institutions advertise compound interest returns at a rate of x percent, or x percent interest, compounded annually, semiannually, quarterly, monthly, weekly, daily, or even continuously. The concept of future value with annual compounding can be illustrated by a simple example.

Personal Finance Example 5.1 ▶

MyFinanceLab Solution
Video

If Fred Moreno places $100 in a savings account paying 8% interest compounded annually, at the end of 1 year he will have $108 in the account, which is the initial principal of $100 plus 8% ($8) in interest. The future value at the end of the first year is

$$\text{Future value at end of year 1} = \$100 \times (1 + 0.08) = \$108$$

If Fred were to leave this money in the account for another year, he would be paid interest at the rate of 8% on the new principal of $108. At the end of this second year, there would be $116.64 in the account. This amount would represent the principal at the beginning of year 2 ($108) plus 8% of the $108 ($8.64) in interest. The future value at the end of the second year is

$$\text{Future value at end of year 2} = \$108 \times (1 + 0.08)$$
$$= \$116.64$$

Substituting the expression $100 × (1 + 0.08) from the first-year calculation for the $108 value in the second-year calculation gives us

$$\text{Future value at end of year 2} = \$100 \times (1 + 0.08) \times (1 + 0.08)$$
$$= \$100 \times (1 + 0.08)^2$$
$$= \$116.64$$

The equations in the preceding example lead to a more general formula for calculating future value.

The Equation for Future Value

The basic relationship illustrated in Example 5.1 can be generalized to find the future value after any number of periods. We use the following notation for the various inputs:

FV_n = future value at the end of period n

PV = initial principal, or present value

r = annual rate of interest paid. (*Note*: On financial calculators, **I** is typically used to represent this rate.)

n = number of periods (typically years) that the money is left on deposit

The general equation for the future value at the end of period n is

$$FV_n = PV \times (1 + r)^n \tag{5.1}$$

A simple example will illustrate how to apply Equation 5.1.

IRF Personal Finance Example 5.2 ▶ Jane Farber places $800 in a savings account paying 6% interest compounded annually. She wants to know how much money will be in the account at the end of 5 years. Substituting $PV = \$800$, $r = 0.06$, and $n = 5$ into Equation 5.1 gives the amount at the end of year 5:

$$FV_5 = \$800 \times (1 + 0.06)^5 = \$800 \times (1.33823) = \$1{,}070.58$$

This analysis can be depicted on a time line as follows:

Time line for future value of a single amount ($800 initial principal, earning 6%, at the end of 5 years)

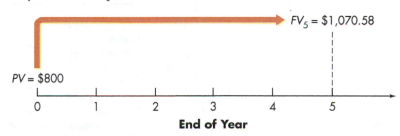

Solving the equation in the preceding example involves raising 1.06 to the fifth power. Using a financial calculator or electronic spreadsheet greatly simplifies the calculation.

Personal Finance Example 5.3 ▶ In Personal Finance Example 5.2, Jane Farber placed $800 in her savings account at 6% interest compounded annually and wishes to find out how much will be in the account at the end of 5 years.

MyFinanceLab Financial Calculator

Calculator use[1] The financial calculator can be used to calculate the future value directly. First enter −800 and depress **PV**; next enter 5 and depress **N**; then enter 6 and depress **I** (which is equivalent to "r" in our notation); finally, to calculate the future value, depress **CPT** and then **FV**. The future value of

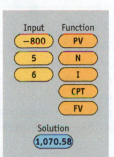

1. Many calculators allow the user to set the number of payments per year. Most of these calculators are preset for monthly payments, or 12 payments per year. Because we work primarily with annual payments—one payment per year—it is important to *be sure that your calculator is set for one payment per year*. Although most calculators are preset to recognize that all payments occur at the end of the period, it is also important to *make sure that your calculator is correctly set on the END mode*. To avoid including previous data in current calculations, *always clear all registers of your calculator before inputting values and making each computation*. The known values *can be punched into the calculator in any order*; the order specified in this as well as other demonstrations of calculator use included in this text merely reflects convenience and personal preference.

$1,070.58 should appear on the calculator display as shown on the previous page. Remember that the calculator differentiates inflows from outflows by preceding the outflows with a negative sign. For example, in the problem just demonstrated, the $800 present value (PV), because it was keyed as a negative number, is considered an outflow. Therefore, the calculated future value (FV) of 1,070.58 is shown as a positive number to indicate that it is the resulting inflow. Had the $800 present value been keyed as a positive number (800), the future value of $1,070.58 would have been displayed as a negative number (–1,070.58). Simply stated, *the cash flows—present value (PV) and future value (FV)—will have opposite signs.* (*Note:* In future examples of calculator use, we will use only a display similar to that shown here. If you need a reminder of the procedures involved, review this paragraph.)

Spreadsheet use Excel offers a mathematical function that makes the calculation of future values easy. The format of that function is FV(rate,nper,pmt,pv,type). The terms inside the parentheses are inputs that Excel requires to calculate the future value. The terms *rate* and *nper* refer to the interest rate and the number of time periods, respectively. The term *pv* represents the lump sum (or present value) that you are investing today. For now, we will ignore the other two inputs, *pmt* and *type,* and enter a value of zero. The future value of the single amount also can be calculated as shown on the following Excel spreadsheet.

	A	B
1	FUTURE VALUE OF A SINGLE AMOUNT	
2	Present value	–$800
3	Annual rate of interest	6%
4	Number of years	5
5	Future value	$1,070.58

Entry in Cell B5 is =FV(B3,B4,0,B2,0).
The minus sign appears before the $800
in B2 because the cost of the investment
is treated as a cash outflow.

Changing any of the values in cells B2, B3, or B4 automatically changes the result shown in cell B5 because the formula in that cell links back to the others. As with the calculator, Excel reports cash inflows as positive numbers and cash outflows as negative numbers. In the example here, we have entered the $800 present value as a negative number, which causes Excel to report the future value as a positive number. Logically, Excel treats the $800 present value as a cash outflow, as if you are paying for the investment you are making, and it treats the future value as a cash inflow when you reap the benefits of your investment 5 years later.

A Graphical View of Future Value

Remember that we measure future value at the *end* of the given period. Figure 5.4 illustrates how the future value depends on the interest rate and the number of periods that money is invested. It shows that (1) the higher the interest rate, the higher the future value, and (2) the longer the period of time, the higher the future value. Note that for an interest rate of 0 percent, the future value always equals the present value ($1.00). For any interest rate greater than zero, however, the future value is greater than the present value of $1.00.

FIGURE 5.4

FIGURE 5.4

Future Value Relationship
Interest rates, time periods, and future value of one dollar

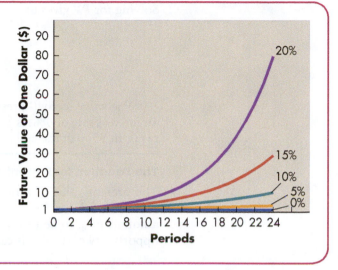

PRESENT VALUE OF A SINGLE AMOUNT

It is often useful to determine the value today of a future amount of money. For example, how much would I have to deposit today into an account paying 7 percent annual interest to accumulate $3,000 at the end of 5 years? **Present value** is the current dollar value of a future amount, or the amount of money that would have to be invested today at a given interest rate over a specified period to equal the future amount. Like future value, the present value depends largely on the interest rate and the point in time at which the amount is to be received. This section explores the present value of a single amount.

present value
The current dollar value of a future amount; the amount of money that would have to be invested today at a given interest rate over a specified period to equal the future amount.

The Concept of Present Value

The process of finding present values is often referred to as **discounting cash flows.** It is concerned with answering the following question: If I can earn r percent on my money, what is the most I would be willing to pay now for an opportunity to receive FV_n dollars n periods from today?

discounting cash flows
The process of finding present values; the inverse of compounding interest.

This process is actually the inverse of compounding interest. Instead of finding the future value of present dollars invested at a given rate, discounting determines the present value of a future amount, assuming an opportunity to earn a certain return on the money. This annual rate of return is variously referred to as the *discount rate, required return, cost of capital,* and *opportunity cost.* These terms will be used interchangeably in this text.

Personal Finance Example 5.4 ▶ Paul Shorter has an opportunity to receive $300 one year from now. If he can earn 6% on his investments in the normal course of events, what is the most he should pay now for this opportunity? To answer this question, Paul must determine how many dollars he would have to invest at 6% today to have $300 one year. Letting *PV* equal this unknown amount and using the same notation as in the future value discussion, we have

$$PV \times (1 + 0.06) = \$300$$

Solving for PV gives us

$$PV = \frac{\$300}{(1 + 0.06)}$$
$$= \$283.02$$

The value today ("present value") of $300 received 1 year from today, given an interest rate of 6%, is $283.02. That is, investing $283.02 today at 6% would result in $300 at the end of 1 year.

The Equation for Present Value

The present value of a future amount can be found mathematically by solving Equation 5.1 for PV. In other words, the present value, PV, of some future amount, FV_n, to be received n periods from now, assuming an interest rate (or opportunity cost) of r, is calculated as

$$PV = \frac{FV_n}{(1 + r)^n} \tag{5.2}$$

IRF **Personal Finance Example 5.5** ▶ Pam Valenti wishes to find the present value of $1,700 that she will receive 8 years from now. Pam's opportunity cost is 8%. Substituting $FV_8 = \$1{,}700$, $n = 8$, and $r = 0.08$ into Equation 5.2 yields

$$PV = \frac{\$1{,}700}{(1 + 0.08)^8} = \frac{\$1{,}700}{1.85093} = \$918.46$$

The following time line shows this analysis.

Time line for present value of a single amount ($1,700 future amount, discounted at 8%, from the end of 8 years)

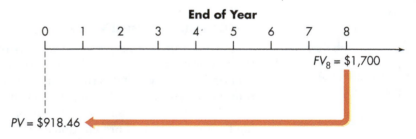

End of Year

0   1   2   3   4   5   6   7   8

$FV_8 = \$1{,}700$

$PV = \$918.46$

MyFinanceLab Financial Calculator

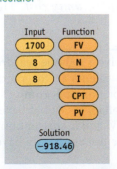

Input	Function
1700	FV
8	N
8	I
	CPT
	PV

Solution
−918.46

Calculator use Using the calculator's financial functions and the inputs shown at the left, you should find the present value to be $918.46. Notice that the calculator result is shown as a negative value to indicate that the present value is a cash outflow (that is, the investment's cost).

Spreadsheet use The format of Excel's present value function is very similar to the future value function covered earlier. The appropriate syntax is PV(rate,nper,pmt,fv,type). The input list inside the parentheses is the same as in Excel's future value function with one exception. The present value function contains the term *fv*, which represents the future lump sum payment (or receipt) whose present value you are trying to calculate. The present value of the single future amount also can be calculated as shown on the following Excel spreadsheet.

	A	B
1	PRESENT VALUE OF A SINGLE AMOUNT	
2	Future value	$1,700
3	Annual rate of interest	8%
4	Number of years	8
5	Present value	–$918.46
	Entry in Cell B5 is =PV(B3,B4,0,B2,0). The minus sign appears before the $918.46 in B5 because the cost of the investment is treated as a cash outflow.	

A Graphical View of Present Value

Remember that present value calculations assume that the future values are measured at the *end* of the given period. The relationships among the factors in a present value calculation are illustrated in Figure 5.5. The figure clearly shows that, everything else being equal, (1) the higher the discount rate, the lower the present value, and (2) the longer the period of time, the lower the present value. Also note that given a discount rate of 0 percent, the present value always equals the future value ($1.00). But for any discount rate greater than zero, the present value is less than the future value of $1.00.

→ REVIEW QUESTIONS

5–3 How is the *compounding process* related to the payment of interest on savings? What is the general equation for future value?

5–4 What effect would a *decrease* in the interest rate have on the future value of a deposit? What effect would an *increase* in the holding period have on future value?

5–5 What is meant by "the present value of a future amount"? What is the general equation for present value?

5–6 What effect does *increasing* the required return have on the present value of a future amount? Why?

5–7 How are present value and future value calculations related?

FIGURE 5.5

Present Value Relationship
Discount rates, time periods, and present value of one dollar

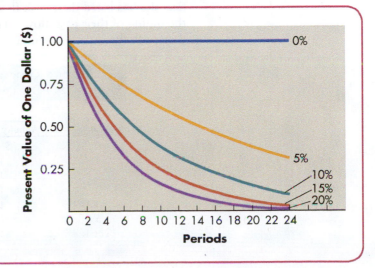

→ EXCEL REVIEW QUESTIONS MyFinanceLab

5–8 It is tax time and you would like to make a tax deductible contribution to an Individual Retirement Account (IRA). Based on the information provided at MFL, find the future value of an IRA contribution grown until retirement.

5–9 It is never too soon to begin investing for a child's college education. Based on the information provided at MFL, determine the present value you would need to invest today to ensure that your child gets the college education she deserves.

LG3 5.3 Annuities

annuity
A stream of equal periodic cash flows over a specified time period. These cash flows can be *inflows* of returns earned on investments or *outflows* of funds invested to earn future returns.

ordinary annuity
An annuity for which the cash flow occurs at the *end* of each period.

annuity due
An annuity for which the cash flow occurs at the *beginning* of each period.

How much would you pay today, given that you can earn 7 percent on low-risk investments, to receive a guaranteed $3,000 at the end of *each* of the next 20 years? How much will you have at the end of 5 years if your employer withholds and invests $1,000 of your bonus at the end of *each* of the next 5 years, guaranteeing you a 9 percent annual rate of return? To answer these questions, you need to understand the application of the time value of money to *annuities*.

An **annuity** is a stream of equal periodic cash flows, over a specified time period. These cash flows are usually annual but can occur at other intervals, such as monthly rent or car payments. The cash flows in an annuity can be *inflows* (the $3,000 received at the end of each of the next 20 years) or *outflows* (the $1,000 invested at the end of each of the next 5 years).

TYPES OF ANNUITIES

There are two general types of annuities. For an **ordinary annuity,** the cash flow occurs at the *end* of each period. For an **annuity due,** the cash flow occurs at the *beginning* of each period.

Personal Finance Example 5.6 ▶ Fran Abrams is evaluating two annuities. Both are 5-year, $1,000 annuities; annuity A is an ordinary annuity, and annuity B is an annuity due. To better understand the difference between these annuities, she has listed their cash flows in Table 5.1. The two annuities differ only in the timing of their cash flows: The cash flows occur sooner with the annuity due than with the ordinary annuity.

TABLE 5.1 Comparison of Ordinary Annuity and Annuity Due Cash Flows ($1,000, 5 Years)

	Annual cash flows	
Year	Annuity A (*ordinary*)	Annuity B (*annuity due*)
0	$ 0	$1,000
1	1,000	1,000
2	1,000	1,000
3	1,000	1,000
4	1,000	1,000
5	1,000	0
Totals	$5,000	$5,000

Although the cash flows of both annuities in Table 5.1 total $5,000, the annuity due would have a higher future value than the ordinary annuity because each of its five annual cash flows can earn interest for 1 year more than each of the ordinary annuity's cash flows. In general, as will be demonstrated later in this chapter, *the value (present or future) of an annuity due is always greater than the value of an otherwise identical ordinary annuity.*

Because ordinary annuities are more frequently used in finance, *unless otherwise specified, the term* annuity *is intended throughout this book to refer to ordinary annuities.*

FINDING THE FUTURE VALUE OF AN ORDINARY ANNUITY

One way to find the future value of an ordinary annuity is to calculate the future value of each of the individual cash flows and then add up those figures. Fortunately, there are several shortcuts to get to the answer. You can calculate the future value of an ordinary annuity that pays an annual cash flow equal to *CF* by using Equation 5.3:

$$FV_n = CF \times \left\{ \frac{\left[(1 + r)^n - 1 \right]}{r} \right\} \tag{5.3}$$

As before, in this equation *r* represents the interest rate, and *n* represents the number of payments in the annuity (or, equivalently, the number of years over which the annuity is spread). The calculations required to find the future value of an ordinary annuity are illustrated in the following example.

IRF **Personal Finance Example 5.7 ▶**   Fran Abrams wishes to determine how much money she will have at the end of 5 years if she chooses annuity A, the ordinary annuity. She will deposit $1,000 annually, at the *end of each* of the next 5 years, into a savings account paying 7% annual interest. This situation is depicted on the following time line.

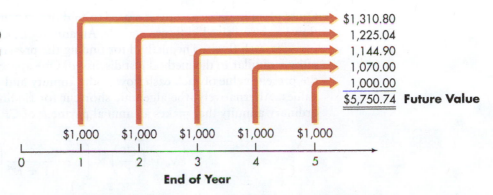

Time line for future value of an ordinary annuity ($1,000 end-of-year deposit, earning 7%, at the end of 5 years)

As the figure shows, at the end of year 5, Fran will have $5,750.74 in her account. Note that because the deposits are made at the end of the year, the first deposit will earn interest for 4 years, the second for 3 years, and so on. Plugging the relevant values into Equation 5.3, we have

$$FV_5 = \$1,000 \times \left\{ \frac{[(1 + 0.07)^5 - 1]}{0.07} \right\} = \$5,750.74$$

MyFinanceLab Financial Calculator

Input	Function
−1000	PMT
5	N
7	I
	CPT
	FV

Solution
5,750.74

Calculator use Using the calculator inputs shown at the left, you can confirm that the future value of the ordinary annuity equals $5,750.74. In this example, the $1,000 annuity payment is entered as a negative value because it is cash outflow, which in turn causes the calculator to correctly treat the resulting future value as a cash inflow (that is, the investment's payoff).

Spreadsheet use To calculate the future value of an annuity in Excel, we will use the same future value function that we used to calculate the future value of a lump sum, but we will add two new input values. Recall that the future value function's syntax is FV(rate,nper,pmt,pv,type). We have already explained the terms *rate*, *nper*, and *pv* in this function. The term *pmt* refers to the annual payment that the annuity offers. The term *type* is an input that lets Excel know whether the annuity being valued is an ordinary annuity (in which case the input value for *type* is 0 or omitted) or an annuity due (in which case the correct input value for *type* is 1). In this particular problem, the input value for *pv* is 0 or omitted because there is no up-front money received. The only cash flows are those that are part of the annuity stream. The future value of the ordinary annuity can be calculated as shown on the following Excel spreadsheet.

	A	B
1	FUTURE VALUE OF AN ORDINARY ANNUITY	
2	Annual annuity payment	−$1,000
3	Annual rate of interest	7%
4	Number of years	5
5	Future value	$5,750.74

Entry in Cell B5 is =FV(B3,B4,B2,0,0).
The minus sign appears before the $1,000
in B2 because the annuity's payments
are cash outflows.

FINDING THE PRESENT VALUE OF AN ORDINARY ANNUITY

Quite often in finance, there is a need to find the present value of a *stream* of cash flows to be received in future periods. An annuity is, of course, a stream of equal periodic cash flows. The method for finding the present value of an ordinary annuity is similar to the method just discussed. One approach would be to calculate the present value of each cash flow in the annuity and then add up those present values. Alternatively, the algebraic shortcut for finding the present value of an ordinary annuity that makes an annual payment of CF for n years looks like

$$PV_n = \left(\frac{CF}{r}\right) \times \left[1 - \frac{1}{(1 + r)^n} \right] \qquad (5.4)$$

Of course, the simplest approach is to solve problems like this one with a financial calculator or spreadsheet program.

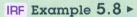 **Example 5.8** ►

MyFinanceLab Solution Video

Braden Company, a small producer of plastic toys, wants to determine the most it should pay to purchase a particular ordinary annuity. The annuity consists of cash flows of $700 at the end of each year for 5 years. The firm requires the annuity to provide a minimum return of 8%. This situation is depicted on the following time line.

Time line for present value of an ordinary annuity ($700 end-of-year cash flows, discounted at 8%, over 5 years)

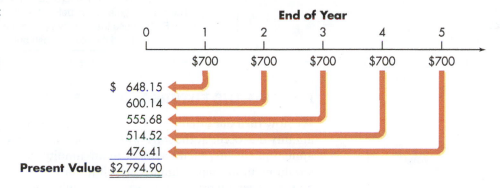

MyFinanceLab Financial Calculator

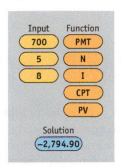

Table 5.2 shows that one way to find the present value of the annuity is to simply calculate the present values of all the cash payments using the present value equation (Equation 5.2 on page 162) and sum them. This procedure yields a present value of $2,794.90. Calculators and spreadsheets offer streamlined methods for arriving at this figure.

Calculator use Using the calculator's inputs shown at the left, you will find the present value of the ordinary annuity to be $2,794.90. Because the present value in this example is a cash outflow representing the cost of the annuity, it is shown as a negative value in the calculator display.

Spreadsheet use The present value of the ordinary annuity also can be calculated as shown on the following Excel spreadsheet.

TABLE 5.2	Long Method for Finding the Present Value of an Ordinary Annuity		
Year (n)	Cash flow	Present value calculation	Present value
1	$700	$\dfrac{700}{(1 + 0.08)^1} =$	$ 648.15
2	700	$\dfrac{700}{(1 + 0.08)^2} =$	600.14
3	700	$\dfrac{700}{(1 + 0.08)^3} =$	555.68
4	700	$\dfrac{700}{(1 + 0.08)^4} =$	514.52
5	700	$\dfrac{700}{(1 + 0.08)^5} =$	476.41
		Present value of annuity	$2,794.90

	A	B
1	PRESENT VALUE OF AN ORDINARY ANNUITY	
2	Annual annuity payment	$700
3	Annual rate of interest	8%
4	Number of years	5
5	Present value	−$2,794.90

Entry in Cell B5 is =PV(B3,B4,B2,0,0).
The minus sign appears before the $2,794.90
in B5 because the annuity's present value
is a cost and therefore a cash outflow.

FINDING THE FUTURE VALUE OF AN ANNUITY DUE

We now turn our attention to annuities due. Remember that the cash flows of an annuity due occur at the *start of the period*. In other words, if we are dealing with annual payments, each payment in an annuity due comes 1 year earlier than it would in an ordinary annuity, which in turn means that each payment can earn an extra year's worth of interest. That is why the future value of an annuity due exceeds the future value of an otherwise identical ordinary annuity.

The algebraic shortcut for the future value of an annuity due that makes annual payments of *CF* for *n* years is

$$FV_n = CF \times \left\{ \frac{[(1+r)^n - 1]}{r} \right\} \times (1+r) \qquad (5.5)$$

Compare this equation with Equation 5.3 on page 165, which shows how to calculate the future value of an ordinary annuity. The two equations are nearly identical, but Equation 5.5 has an added term, $(1+r)$, at the end. In other words, the value obtained from Equation 5.5 will be $(1+r)$ times greater than the value in Equation 5.3 if the other inputs (*CF* and *n*) are the same, and that makes sense because all the payments in the annuity due earn 1 more year's worth of interest compared with the ordinary annuity.

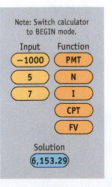

IRF **Personal Finance Example 5.9** ▶

MyFinanceLab Financial
Calculator

Note: Switch calculator
to BEGIN mode.

Input	Function
−1000	PMT
5	N
7	I
	CPT
	FV

Solution
6,153.29

Recall from an earlier example, illustrated in Table 5.1 on page 164, that Fran Abrams wanted to choose between an ordinary annuity and an annuity due, both offering similar terms except for the timing of cash flows. We calculated the future value of the ordinary annuity in Example 5.7, but we now want to calculate the future value of the annuity due. This situation is depicted on the time line on the following page. We can calculate its future value using a calculator or a spreadsheet.

Calculator use Before using your calculator to find the future value of an annuity due, you must either switch it to BEGIN mode or use the DUE key, depending on the specific calculator. Then, using the inputs shown at the left, you will find the future value of the annuity due to be $6,153.29. (*Note:* Because we nearly always assume end-of-period cash flows, *be sure to switch your calculator back to END mode when you have completed your annuity-due calculations.*)

Time line for future value of an annuity due ($1,000 beginning-of-year deposit, earning 7%, at the end of 5 years)

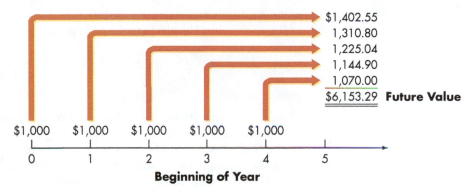

Spreadsheet use The future value of the annuity due also can be calculated as shown on the following Excel spreadsheet. Remember that for an annuity due the *type* input value must be set to 1, and we must also specify the *pv* input value as 0 because the inputs are in an ordered series.

	A	B
1	FUTURE VALUE OF AN ANNUITY DUE	
2	Annual annuity payment	−$1,000
3	Annual rate of interest	7%
4	Number of years	5
5	Future value	$6,153.29
	Entry in Cell B5 is =FV(B3,B4,B2,0,1). The minus sign appears before the $1,000 in B2 because the annuity's payments are cash outflows.	

Comparison of an Annuity Due with an Ordinary Annuity Future Value

The future value of an annuity due is *always greater* than the future value of an otherwise identical ordinary annuity. We can see that by comparing the future values at the end of year 5 of Fran Abrams's two annuities:

Ordinary annuity = $5,750.74   versus   Annuity due = $6,153.29

Because the cash flow of the annuity due occurs at the beginning of the period rather than at the end (that is, each payment comes 1 year sooner in the annuity due), its future value is greater. How much greater? It is interesting to calculate the percentage difference between the value of the annuity and the value of the annuity due:

($6,153.29 − $5,750.74) ÷ $5,750.74 = 0.07 = 7%

Recall that the interest rate in this example is 7 percent. It is no coincidence that the annuity due is 7 percent more valuable than the annuity. An extra year's interest on each of the annuity due's payments make the annuity due 7 percent more valuable than the annuity.

FINDING THE PRESENT VALUE OF AN ANNUITY DUE

We can also find the present value of an annuity due. This calculation can be easily performed by adjusting the ordinary annuity calculation. Because the cash flows of an annuity due occur at the beginning rather than the end of the period, to find their present value each annuity due cash flow is discounted back 1 less year than for an ordinary annuity. The algebraic formula for the present value of an annuity due is

$$PV_n = \left(\frac{CF}{r}\right) \times \left[1 - \frac{1}{(1+r)^n}\right] \times (1+r) \qquad (5.6)$$

Notice the similarity between this equation and Equation 5.4 on page 166. The two equations are identical except that Equation 5.6 has an extra term at the end, $(1+r)$. The reason for this extra term is the same as in the case when we calculated the future value of the annuity due. In the annuity due, each payment arrives 1 year earlier (compared to the annuity), so each payment is worth a little more, 1 year's interest more.

IRF Example 5.10 ▶

In Example 5.8 of Braden Company, we found the present value of Braden's $700, 5-year ordinary annuity discounted at 8% to be $2,794.90. If we now assume that Braden's $700 annual cash flow occurs at the *start* of each year and is thereby an annuity due. This situation is depicted on the following time line.

Time line for present value of an annuity due ($700 beginning-of-year cash flows, discounted at 8%, over 5 years)

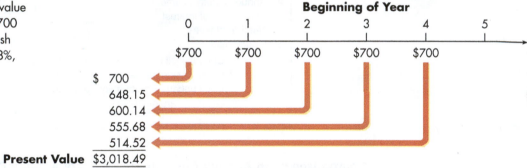

We can calculate its present value using a calculator or a spreadsheet.

MyFinanceLab Financial Calculator

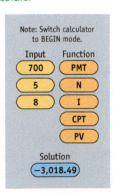

Note: Switch calculator to BEGIN mode.

Input	Function
700	PMT
5	N
8	I
	CPT
	PV

Solution
−3,018.49

Calculator use Before using your calculator to find the present value of an annuity due, you must either switch it to BEGIN mode or use the DUE key, depending on the specifics of your calculator. Then, using the inputs shown at the left, you will find the present value of the annuity due to be $3,018.49 (*Note:* Because we nearly always assume end-of-period cash flows, *be sure to switch your calculator back to END mode when you have completed your annuity-due calculations.*)

Spreadsheet use The present value of the annuity due also can be calculated as shown on the following Excel spreadsheet.

	A	B
1	PRESENT VALUE OF AN ANNUITY DUE	
2	Annual annuity payment	$700
3	Annual rate of interest	8%
4	Number of years	5
5	Present value	−$3,018.49

Entry in Cell B5 is =PV(B3,B4,B2,0,1).
The minus sign appears before the $3,018.49
in B5 because the annuity's present value
is a cost and therefore a cash outflow.

Comparison of an Annuity Due with an Ordinary Annuity Present Value

The present value of an annuity due is always greater than the present value of an otherwise identical ordinary annuity. We can verify this statement by comparing the present values of the Braden Company's two annuities:

Ordinary annuity = $2,794.90   versus   Annuity due = $3,018.49

Because the cash flow of the annuity due occurs at the beginning of the period rather than at the end, its present value is greater. If we calculate the percentage difference in the values of these two annuities, we will find that the annuity due is 8 percent more valuable than the annuity:

$$(\$3,018.49 - \$2,794.90) \div \$2,794.90 = 0.08 = 8\%$$

Matter of fact

Getting Your (Annuity) Due

Kansas truck driver Donald Damon got the surprise of his life when he learned that he held the winning ticket for the Powerball lottery drawing held November 11, 2009. The advertised lottery jackpot was $96.6 million. Damon could have chosen to collect his prize in 30 annual payments of $3,220,000 (30 × $3.22 million = $96.6 million), but instead he elected to accept a lump sum payment of $48,367,329.08, roughly half the stated jackpot total.

FINDING THE PRESENT VALUE OF A PERPETUITY

perpetuity
An annuity with an infinite life, providing continual annual cash flow.

A **perpetuity** is an annuity with an infinite life. In other words, it is an annuity that never stops providing its holder with a cash flow at the end of each year (for example, the right to receive $500 at the end of each year forever).

It is sometimes necessary to find the present value of a perpetuity. Fortunately, the calculation for the present value of a perpetuity is one of the easiest in finance. If a perpetuity pays an annual cash flow of *CF*, starting 1 year from now, the present value of the cash flow stream is

$$PV = CF \div r \qquad\qquad (5.7)$$

IRF Personal Finance Example 5.11 ▶ Ross Clark wishes to endow a chair in finance at his alma mater. The university indicated that it requires $200,000 per year to support the chair, and the endowment would earn 10% per year. To determine the amount Ross must give the university to fund the chair, we must determine the present value of a $200,000 perpetuity discounted at 10%. Using Equation 5.7, we can determine that the present value of a perpetuity paying $200,000 per year is $2 million when the interest rate is 10%:

$$PV = \$200,000 \div 0.10 = \$2,000,000$$

In other words, to generate $200,000 every year for an indefinite period requires $2,000,000 today if Ross Clark's alma mater can earn 10% on its investments. If the university earns 10% interest annually on the $2,000,000, it can withdraw $200,000 per year indefinitely.

→ REVIEW QUESTIONS

5-10 What is the difference between an *ordinary annuity* and an *annuity due*? Which is more valuable? Why?

5-11 What are the most efficient ways to calculate the present value of an ordinary annuity?

5-12 How can the formula for the future value of an annuity be modified to find the future value of an annuity due?

5-13 How can the formula for the present value of an ordinary annuity be modified to find the present value of an annuity due?

5-14 What is a *perpetuity*? Why is the present value of a perpetuity equal to the annual cash payment divided by the interest rate?

→ EXCEL REVIEW QUESTIONS MyFinanceLab

5-15 Since tax time comes around every year you smartly decide to make equal contributions to your IRA at the end of every year. Based on the information provided at MFL, calculate the future value of annual IRA contributions grown until retirement.

5-16 You have just graduated from college, begun your new career, and now it is time to buy your first home. Based on the information provided at MFL, determine how much you can spend for your new dream home.

5-17 Rather than making contributions to an IRA at the end of each year, you decide to make equal contributions at the beginning of each year. Based on the information provided at MFL, solve for the future value of beginning-of-year annual IRA contributions grown until retirement.

 5.4 Mixed Streams

mixed stream
A stream of unequal periodic cash flows that reflect no particular pattern.

Two types of cash flow streams are possible, the annuity and the mixed stream. Whereas an *annuity* is a pattern of equal periodic cash flows, a **mixed stream** is a stream of unequal periodic cash flows that reflect no particular pattern. Financial managers frequently need to evaluate opportunities that are expected to provide mixed streams of cash flows. Here we consider both the future value and the present value of mixed streams.

FUTURE VALUE OF A MIXED STREAM

Determining the future value of a mixed stream of cash flows is straightforward. We determine the future value of each cash flow at the specified future date and then add all the individual future values to find the total future value.

IRF **Example 5.12 ▶**   Shrell Industries, a cabinet manufacturer, expects to receive the following mixed stream of cash flows over the next 5 years from one of its small customers.

End of year	Cash flow
1	$11,500
2	14,000
3	12,900
4	16,000
5	18,000

If Shrell expects to earn 8% on its investments, how much will it accumulate by the end of year 5 if it immediately invests these cash flows when they are received? This situation is depicted on the following time line.

Time line for future value of a mixed stream (end-of-year cash flows, compounded at 8% to the end of year 5)

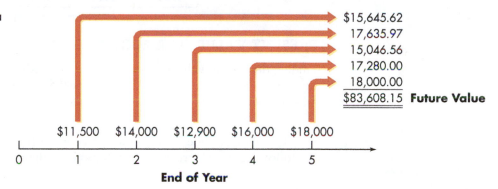

Calculator use Unfortunately, unless you can program your calculator or have one of the more advanced financial calculators, most calculators lack a function that would allow you to input *all the cash flows,* specify the interest rate, and directly calculate the future value of the entire cash flow stream. Fortunately, there is a way to overcome this limitation. Use your calculator to find the future value of each individual cash flow, as demonstrated earlier (in Personal Finance Example 5.3 on page 159), and then sum the individual future values to get the future value of the entire cash flow stream. Summing the individual future values of Shrell Industries' mixed cash flow stream results in a future value of $83,608.15 at the end of year 5.

Spreadsheet use A relatively simple way to use Excel to calculate the future value of a mixed stream is to use the Excel net present value (NPV) function combined with the future value (FV) function discussed on page 160. The syntax of the NPV function is NPV(rate, value1, value2, value 3, . . .). The rate argument is the interest rate, and value1, value2, value3, . . . represent a stream of cash flows. The NPV function assumes that the first payment in the stream arrives 1 year in the future and that all subsequent payments arrive at 1-year intervals.

   To find the future value of a mixed stream, the trick is to use the NPV function to first find the present value of the mixed stream and then find the future of this present value lump sum amount. The Excel spreadsheet at the top of the next page illustrates this approach (notice that the NPV is shown as an outflow because it represents the net present value of the stream of investment costs).

	A	B
1	FUTURE VALUE OF A MIXED STREAM	
2	Year	Cash Flow
3	1	–$11,500
4	2	–$14,000
5	3	–$12,900
6	4	–$16,000
7	5	–$18,000
8	Annual rate of interest	8%
9	NPV	–$56,902.30
10	Number of years	5
11	Future value	$83,608.15

Entry in Cell B9 is =NPV(B8,B3:B7).
Entry in Cell B11 is =FV(B8,B10,0,B9,0).
The minus sign appears before the values
in B3:B7 because they are cash outflows.

PRESENT VALUE OF A MIXED STREAM

Finding the present value of a mixed stream of cash flows is similar to finding the future value of a mixed stream. We determine the present value of each future amount and then add all the individual present values together to find the total present value.

IRF Example 5.13 ▶

MyFinanceLab Solution
Video

Frey Company, a shoe manufacturer, has been offered an opportunity to receive the following mixed stream of cash flows over the next 5 years.

End of year	Cash flow
1	$400
2	800
3	500
4	400
5	300

If the firm must earn at least 9% on its investments, what is the most it should pay for this opportunity? This situation is depicted on the following time line.

Time line for present value of a mixed stream (end-of-year cash flows, discounted at 9% over the corresponding number of years)

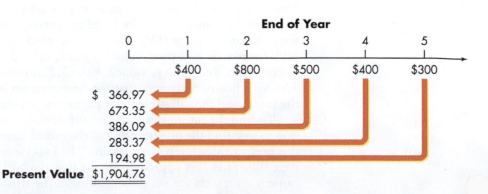

Calculator use You can use a calculator to find the present value of each individual cash flow, as demonstrated earlier (on page 162), and then sum the present values to get the present value of the stream. However, most financial calculators have a function that allows you to punch in *all cash flows*, specify the discount rate, and then directly calculate the present value of the entire cash flow stream. You can refer to your calculator's manual for the procedure to enter a stream of cash flows (the typical financial calculator will have a cash flow register). The present value of Frey Company's cash flow stream found using a calculator is $1,904.76.

Spreadsheet use To calculate the present value of a mixed stream in Excel, we will use the NPV function. The present value of the mixed stream of future cash flows can be calculated as shown on the following Excel spreadsheet.

	A	B
1	PRESENT VALUE OF A MIXED STREAM	
2	Year	Cash Flow
3	1	$400
4	2	$800
5	3	$500
6	4	$400
7	5	$300
8	Annual rate of interest	9%
9	Present value	$1,904.76
	Entry in Cell B9 is =NPV(B8,B3:B7).	

→ **REVIEW QUESTION**

5-18 How is the future value of a mixed stream of cash flows calculated? How is the present value of a mixed stream of cash flows calculated?

→ **EXCEL REVIEW QUESTION** MyFinanceLab

5-19 To give yourself a financial head start after college you have decided to work summer jobs and invest the money you earn until after graduation. You expect that your earnings each summer will vary depending on the job you get. Based on the information provided at MFL, find the value of your financial head start after graduation.

LG⑤ **5.5 Compounding Interest More Frequently Than Annually**

Interest is often compounded more frequently than once a year. Savings institutions compound interest semiannually, quarterly, monthly, weekly, daily, or even continuously. This section discusses various issues and techniques related to these more frequent compounding intervals.

SEMIANNUAL COMPOUNDING

semiannual compounding
Compounding of interest over two periods within the year.

Semiannual compounding of interest involves two compounding periods within the year. Instead of the stated interest rate being paid once a year, one-half of the stated interest rate is paid twice a year.

IRF Personal Finance Example 5.14 ▶ Fred Moreno has decided to invest $100 in a savings account paying 8% interest *compounded semiannually*. If he leaves his money in the account for 24 months (2 years), he will be paid 4% interest compounded over four periods, each of which is 6 months long. Table 5.3 shows that at the end of 12 months (1 year) with 8% semiannual compounding, Fred will have $108.16; at the end of 24 months (2 years), he will have $116.99.

TABLE 5.3	Future Value from Investing $100 at 8% Interest Compounded Semiannually over 24 Months (2 Years)		
Period	Beginning principal	Future value calculation	Future value at end of period
6 months	$100.00	100.00 × (1 + 0.04) =	$104.00
12 months	104.00	104.00 × (1 + 0.04) =	108.16
18 months	108.16	108.16 × (1 + 0.04) =	112.49
24 months	112.49	112.49 × (1 + 0.04) =	116.99

QUARTERLY COMPOUNDING

quarterly compounding
Compounding of interest over four periods within the year.

Quarterly compounding of interest involves four compounding periods within the year. One-fourth of the stated interest rate is paid four times a year.

IRF Personal Finance Example 5.15 ▶ Fred Moreno has found an institution that will pay him 8% interest *compounded quarterly*. If he leaves his money in this account for 24 months (2 years), he will be paid 2% interest compounded over eight periods, each of which is 3 months long. Table 5.4 shows the amount Fred will have at the end of each period. At the end of 12 months (1 year), with 8% quarterly compounding, Fred will have $108.24; at the end of 24 months (2 years), he will have $117.17.

TABLE 5.4	Future Value from Investing $100 at 8% Interest Compounded Quarterly over 24 Months (2 Years)		
Period	Beginning principal	Future value calculation	Future value at end of period
3 months	$100.00	100.00 × (1 + 0.02) =	$102.00
6 months	102.00	102.00 × (1 + 0.02) =	104.04
9 months	104.04	104.04 × (1 + 0.02) =	106.12
12 months	106.12	106.12 × (1 + 0.02) =	108.24
15 months	108.24	108.24 × (1 + 0.02) =	110.41
18 months	110.41	110.41 × (1 + 0.02) =	112.62
21 months	112.62	112.62 × (1 + 0.02) =	114.87
24 months	114.87	114.87 × (1 + 0.02) =	117.17

TABLE 5.5	Future Value at the End of Years 1 and 2 from Investing $100 at 8% Interest, Given Various Compounding Periods

	Compounding period		
End of year	Annual	Semiannual	Quarterly
1	$108.00	$108.16	$108.24
2	116.64	116.99	117.17

Table 5.5 compares values for Fred Moreno's $100 at the end of years 1 and 2 given annual, semiannual, and quarterly compounding periods at the 8 percent rate. The table shows that *the more frequently interest is compounded, the greater the amount of money accumulated.* This statement is true for *any interest rate for any period of time.*

A GENERAL EQUATION FOR COMPOUNDING MORE FREQUENTLY THAN ANNUALLY

The future value formula (Equation 5.1) can be rewritten for use when compounding takes place more frequently. If m equals the number of times per year interest is compounded, the formula for the future value of a lump sum becomes

$$FV_n = PV \times \left(1 + \frac{r}{m}\right)^{m \times n} \tag{5.8}$$

If $m = 1$, Equation 5.8 reduces to Equation 5.1. Thus, if interest compounds annually, Equation 5.8 will provide the same result as Equation 5.1. The general use of Equation 5.8 can be illustrated with a simple example.

IRF Personal Finance Example 5.16 ▶ The preceding examples calculated the amount that Fred Moreno would have at the end of 2 years if he deposited $100 at 8% interest compounded semiannually and compounded quarterly. For semiannual compounding, m would equal 2 in Equation 5.8; for quarterly compounding, m would equal 4. Substituting the appropriate values for semiannual and quarterly compounding into Equation 5.7, we find that

1. *For semiannual compounding:*

$$FV_2 = \$100 \times \left(1 + \frac{0.08}{2}\right)^{2 \times 2} = \$100 \times (1 + 0.04)^4 = \$116.99$$

2. *For quarterly compounding:*

$$FV_2 = \$100 \times \left(1 + \frac{0.08}{4}\right)^{4 \times 2} = \$100 \times (1 + 0.02)^8 = \$117.17$$

These results agree with the values for FV_2 in Tables 5.4 and 5.5.

If the interest were compounded monthly, weekly, or daily, m would equal 12, 52, or 365, respectively.

USING COMPUTATIONAL TOOLS FOR COMPOUNDING MORE FREQUENTLY THAN ANNUALLY

As before, we can simplify the process of doing the calculations by using a calculator or spreadsheet program.

Personal Finance Example 5.17 ▶ Fred Moreno wished to find the future value of $100 invested at 8% interest compounded both semiannually and quarterly for 2 years.

MyFinanceLab Financial Calculator

Input | Function
-100 | PV
4 | N
4 | I
| CPT
| FV

Solution
116.99

Input | Function
-100 | PV
8 | N
2 | I
| CPT
| FV

Solution
117.17

Calculator use If the calculator were used for the semiannual compounding calculation, the number of periods would be 4, and the interest rate would be 4%. The future value of $116.99 will appear on the calculator display as shown at the top left.

For the quarterly compounding case, the number of periods would be 8 and the interest rate would be 2%. The future value of $117.17 will appear on the calculator display as shown in the second display at the left.

Spreadsheet use The future value of the single amount with semiannual and quarterly compounding also can be calculated as shown on the following Excel spreadsheet.

	A	B
1	FUTURE VALUE OF A SINGLE AMOUNT WITH SEMIANNUAL AND QUARTERLY COMPOUNDING	
2	Present value	−$100
3	Annual rate of interest	8%
4	Compounding frequency - semiannual	2
5	Number of years	2
6	Future value with semiannual compounding	$116.99
7	Present value	−$100
8	Annual rate of interest	8%
9	Compounding frequency - quarterly	4
10	Number of years	2
11	Future value with quarterly compounding	$117.17

Entry in Cell B6 is =FV(B3/B4,B5*B4,0,B2,0).
Entry in Cell B11 is =FV(B8/B9,B10*B9,0,B7,0).
The minus sign appears before the $100 in B2 and B7 because the cost of the investment is treated as a cash outflow.

CONTINUOUS COMPOUNDING

continuous compounding
Compounding interest literally all the time. Equivalent to compounding interest an infinite number of times per year.

In the extreme case, interest can be compounded continuously. In this case interest is compounded every second (or even every nanosecond)—literally, interest compounds all the time. In this case, m in Equation 5.8 would approach infinity. Through the use of calculus, we know that as m approaches infinity, Equation 5.8 converges to

$$FV_n = (PV) \times (e^{r \times n}) \tag{5.9}$$

where e is the exponential function,[2] which has a value of approximately 2.7183.

---

2. Most calculators have the exponential function, typically noted by e^x, built into them. The use of this key is especially helpful in calculating future value when interest is compounded continuously.

IRF Personal Finance Example 5.18 ▶ To find the value at the end of 2 years ($n = 2$) of Fred Moreno's $100 deposit ($PV = \$100$) in an account paying 8% annual interest ($r = 0.08$) compounded continuously, we can substitute into Equation 5.9:

$$FV_2 \text{ (continuous compounding)} = \$100 \times e^{0.08 \times 2}$$
$$= \$100 \times 2.7183^{0.16}$$
$$= \$100 \times 1.1735 = \$117.35$$

MyFinanceLab Financial Calculator

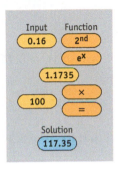

Input	Function
0.16	2nd
	e^x
1.1735	
100	×
	=

Solution
117.35

Calculator use To find this value using the calculator, you need first to find the value of $e^{0.16}$ by punching in 0.16 and then pressing **2nd** and then e^x to get 1.1735. Next multiply this value by $100 to get the future value of $117.35 as shown at the left. (*Note:* On some calculators, you may not have to press **2nd** before pressing e^x.)

Spreadsheet use The future value of the single amount with continuous compounding of Fred's deposit also can be calculated as shown on the following Excel spreadsheet.

	A	B
	FUTURE VALUE OF A SINGLE AMOUNT	
1	WITH CONTINUOUS COMPOUNDING	
2	Present value	$100
3	Annual rate of interest, compounded continuously	8%
4	Number of years	2
5	Future value with continuous compounding	$117.35
	Entry in Cell B5 is =B3*EXP(B3*B4).	

The future value with continuous compounding therefore equals $117.35. As expected, the continuously compounded value is larger than the future value of interest compounded semiannually ($116.99) or quarterly ($117.17). In fact, continuous compounding produces a greater future value than any other compounding frequency.

NOMINAL AND EFFECTIVE ANNUAL RATES OF INTEREST

nominal (stated) annual rate
Contractual annual rate of interest charged by a lender or promised by a borrower.

effective (true) annual rate (EAR)
The annual rate of interest actually paid or earned.

Both businesses and investors need to make objective comparisons of loan costs or investment returns over different compounding periods. To put interest rates on a common basis, so as to allow comparison, we distinguish between nominal and effective annual rates. The **nominal, or stated, annual rate** is the contractual annual rate of interest charged by a lender or promised by a borrower. The **effective, or true, annual rate (EAR)** is the annual rate of interest actually paid or earned. The effective annual rate reflects the effects of compounding frequency, whereas the nominal annual rate does not.

Using the notation introduced earlier, we can calculate the effective annual rate, *EAR*, by substituting values for the nominal annual rate, *r*, and the compounding frequency, *m*, into the equation

$$EAR = \left(1 + \frac{r}{m}\right)^m - 1 \tag{5.10}$$

We can apply Equation 5.10 using data from preceding examples.

Personal Finance Example 5.19 ▸   Fred Moreno wishes to find the effective annual rate associated with an 8% nominal annual rate ($r = 0.08$) when interest is compounded (1) annually ($m = 1$), (2) semiannually ($m = 2$), and (3) quarterly ($m = 4$). Substituting these values into Equation 5.10, we get

1. *For annual compounding:*

$$EAR = \left(1 + \frac{0.08}{1}\right)^1 - 1 = (1 + 0.08)^1 - 1 = 1 + 0.08 - 1 = 0.08 = 8\%$$

2. *For semiannual compounding:*

$$EAR = \left(1 + \frac{0.08}{2}\right)^2 - 1 = (1 + 0.04)^2 - 1 = 1.0816 - 1 = 0.0816 = 8.16\%$$

3. *For quarterly compounding:*

$$EAR = \left(1 + \frac{0.08}{4}\right)^4 - 1 = (1 + 0.02)^4 - 1 = 1.0824 - 1 = 0.0824 = 8.24\%$$

Calculator use To find the *EAR* using the calculator, you first need to enter the nominal annual rate and the compounding frequency per year. Most financial calculators have a NOM key for entering the nominal rate and either a P/Y or C/Y key for entering the compounding frequency per year. Once these inputs are entered, the EFF or CPT key is depressed to display the corresponding effective annual rate.

Spreadsheet use Interest rate conversions are easily done using Excel using the EFFECT and NOMINAL functions. To find the *EAR*, the EFFECT function requires you to input nominal annual rate and the compounding frequency, whereas if you input an *EAR* and the compounding frequency, the NOMINAL function provides the nominal annual rate or *APR*. Interest rate conversions from the 8% *APR* to the semiannual *EAR* and from the quarterly *EAR* back to the 8% *APR* are shown on the following Excel spreadsheet.

	A	B
	INTEREST RATE CONVERSION	
1	NOMINAL VS. EFFECTIVE ANNUAL RATE	
2	Nominal annual rate of interest	8%
3	Compounding frequency - semiannual	2
4	Effective annual rate of interest	8.16%
5	Nominal annual rate of interest	8%
6	Compounding frequency - quarterly	4
7	Effective annual rate of interest	8.24%
	Entry in Cell B4 is =EFFECT(B2,B3).	
	Entry in Cell B5 is =NOMINAL(B7,B6).	

These values demonstrate two important points. First, nominal and effective annual rates are equivalent for annual compounding. Second, the effective annual rate increases w ith increasing compounding frequency, up to a limit that occurs with *continuous compounding.*[3]

annual percentage rate (APR)
The *nominal annual rate* of interest, found by multiplying the periodic rate by the number of periods in one year, that must be disclosed to consumers on credit cards and loans as a result of "truth-in-lending laws."

At the consumer level, "truth-in-lending laws" require disclosure on credit card and loan agreements of the **annual percentage rate** (**APR**). The APR is the *nominal annual rate,* which is found by multiplying the periodic rate by the number of periods in 1 year. For example, a bank credit card that charges 1.5 percent per month (the periodic rate) would have an APR of 18 percent (1.5% per month $\times$ 12 months per year).

annual percentage yield (APY)
The *effective annual rate* of interest that must be disclosed to consumers by banks on their savings products as a result of "truth-in-savings laws."

"Truth-in-savings laws," on the other hand, require banks to quote the **annual percentage yield** (**APY**) on their savings products. The APY is the *effective annual rate* a savings product pays. For example, a savings account that pays 0.5 percent per month would have an APY of 6.17 percent $[(1.005)^{12} - 1]$.

Quoting loan interest rates at their lower nominal annual rate (the APR) and savings interest rates at the higher effective annual rate (the APY) offers two advantages. First, it tends to standardize disclosure to consumers. Second, it enables financial institutions to quote the most attractive interest rates: low loan rates and high savings rates.

→ REVIEW QUESTIONS

5-20 What effect does compounding interest more frequently than annually have on (**a**) future value and (**b**) the *effective annual rate (EAR)?* Why?

5-21 How does the future value of a deposit subject to continuous compounding compare to the value obtained by annual compounding?

5-22 Differentiate between a *nominal annual rate* and an *effective annual rate (EAR).* Define *annual percentage rate (APR)* and *annual percentage yield (APY).*

→ EXCEL REVIEW QUESTIONS   MyFinanceLab

5-23 You are responsible for managing your company's short term investments and you know that the compounding frequency of investment opportunities is quite important. Based on the information provided at MFL, calculate the future value of an investment opportunity based on various compounding frequencies.

5-24 What if your short term investments provide continuous compounding? Based on the information provided at MFL, determine the future value of an investment opportunity based on continuous compounding.

5-25 Rather than comparing future values, you often compare the effective annual rates of various investment opportunities with differing compounding frequencies. Based on the information provided at MFL, solve for the effective annual rates of several investment opportunities with different compounding frequencies.

---

3. The effective annual rate for this extreme case can be found by using the equation
$$EAR \text{ (continuous compounding)} = e^r - 1 \qquad (5.10a)$$
For the 8% nominal annual rate ($r = 0.08$), substitution into Equation 5.10a results in an effective annual rate of
$$e^{0.08} - 1 = 1.0833 - 1 = 0.0833 = 8.33\%$$
in the case of continuous compounding. This result is the highest effective annual rate attainable with an 8% nominal rate.

5.6 Special Applications of Time Value

Future value and present value techniques have a number of important applications in finance. We'll study four of them in this section: (1) determining deposits needed to accumulate a future sum, (2) loan amortization, (3) finding interest or growth rates, and (4) finding an unknown number of periods.

DETERMINING DEPOSITS NEEDED TO ACCUMULATE A FUTURE SUM

Suppose that you want to buy a house 5 years from now, and you estimate that an initial down payment of $30,000 will be required at that time. To accumulate the $30,000, you will wish to make equal annual end-of-year deposits into an account paying annual interest of 6 percent. The solution to this problem is closely related to the process of finding the future value of an annuity. You must determine what size annuity will result in a single amount equal to $30,000 at the end of year 5.

Earlier in the chapter, Equation 5.3 was provided for the future value of an ordinary annuity that made a payment, *CF*, each year. In the current problem, we know the future value we want to achieve, $30,000, but we want to solve for the annual cash payment that we'd have to save to achieve that goal. Solving Equation 5.3 for *CF* gives

$$CF = FV_n \div \left\{ \frac{\left[(1 + r)^n - 1 \right]}{r} \right\} \tag{5.11}$$

As a practical matter, to solve problems like this one, analysts nearly always use a calculator or Excel as demonstrated in the following example.

Personal Finance Example 5.20 ▶   As just stated, you want to determine the equal annual end-of-year deposits required to accumulate $30,000 at the end of 5 years, given an interest rate of 6%.

MyFinanceLab Financial Calculator

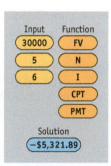

Input	Function
30000	FV
5	N
6	I
	CPT
	PMT

Solution
−$5,321.89

Calculator use Using the calculator inputs shown at the left, you will find the annual deposit amount to be $5,321.89. Thus, if $5,321.89 is deposited at the end of each year for 5 years at 6% interest, there will be $30,000 in the account at the end of 5 years.

Spreadsheet use In Excel (see the spreadsheet below), solving for the annual cash flow that helps you reach the $30,000 means using the payment function. Its

	A	B
1	ANNUAL DEPOSITS AMOUNT TO ACCUMULATE A FUTURE SUM	
2	Future value	$30,000
3	Annual rate of interest	6%
4	Number of years	5
5	Annual annuity payment	−$5,321.89

Entry in Cell B5 is =PMT(B3,B4,0,B2,0).
The minus sign appears before the annuity payment in B5 because deposit amounts are cash outflows for the investor.

syntax is PMT (rate,nper,pv, fv,type). All the inputs in this function have been discussed previously. The Excel spreadsheet illustrates how to use this function to find the annual payment required to save $30,000.

LOAN AMORTIZATION

loan amortization
The determination of the equal periodic loan payments necessary to provide a lender with a specified interest return and to repay the loan principal over a specified period.

loan amortization schedule
A schedule of equal payments to repay a loan. It shows the allocation of each loan payment to interest and principal.

The term **loan amortization** refers to the determination of equal periodic loan payments. These payments provide a lender with a specified interest return and repay the loan principal over a specified period. The loan amortization process involves finding the future payments, over the term of the loan, whose present value at the loan interest rate equals the amount of initial principal borrowed. Lenders use a **loan amortization schedule** to determine these payment amounts and the allocation of each payment to interest and principal. In the case of home mortgages, these tables are used to find the equal *monthly* payments necessary to *amortize*, or pay off, the mortgage at a specified interest rate over a 15- to 30-year period.

Amortizing a loan actually involves creating an annuity out of a present amount. For example, say you borrow $6,000 at 10 percent and agree to make equal annual end-of-year payments over 4 years. To find the size of the payments, the lender determines the amount of a 4-year annuity discounted at 10 percent that has a present value of $6,000.

Earlier in the chapter, Equation 5.4 demonstrated how to find the present value of an ordinary annuity given information about the number of time periods, the interest rate, and the annuity's periodic payment. We can rearrange that equation to solve for the payment, our objective in this problem:

$$CF = (PV \times r) \div \left[1 - \frac{1}{(1 + r)^n} \right] \qquad (5.12)$$

Personal Finance Example 5.21 ▶ As just stated, you want to determine the equal annual end-of-year payments necessary to amortize fully a $6,000, 10% loan over 4 years.

Calculator use Using the calculator inputs shown at the left, you will find the annual payment amount to be $1,892.82. Thus, to repay the interest and principal on a $6,000, 10%, 4-year loan, equal annual end-of-year payments of $1,892.82 are necessary.

MyFinanceLab Financial Calculator

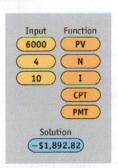

The allocation of each loan payment to interest and principal can be seen in columns 3 and 4 of the *loan amortization schedule* in Table 5.6. The portion of each payment that represents interest (column 3) declines over the repayment period, and the portion going to principal repayment (column 4) increases. This pattern is typical of amortized loans; as the principal is reduced, the interest component declines, leaving a larger portion of each subsequent loan payment to repay principal.

Spreadsheet use The annual payment to repay the loan also can be calculated as shown on the first Excel spreadsheet shown on page 184. The amortization schedule, shown in Table 5.6, allocating each loan payment to interest and principal can be calculated precisely as shown on the second Excel spreadsheet on page 184.

TABLE 5.6 Loan Amortization Schedule ($6,000 Principal, 10% Interest, 4-Year Repayment Period)

End-of-year	Beginning-of-year principal (1)	Loan payment (2)	Payments Interest [0.10 × (1)] (3)	Payments Principal [(2) − (3)] (4)	End-of-year principal [(1) − (4)] (5)
1	$6,000.00	$1,892.82	$600.00	$1,292.82	$4,707.18
2	4,707.18	1,892.82	470.72	1,422.10	3,285.08
3	3,285.08	1,892.82	328.51	1,564.31	1,720.77
4	1,720.77	1,892.82	172.08	1,720.74	—[a]

[a]Because of rounding, a slight difference ($0.03) exists between the beginning-of-year-4 principal (in column 1) and the year-4 principal payment (in column 4).

	A	B
1	ANNUAL PAYMENT AMOUNT TO REPAY A LOAN	
2	Present value	$6,000
3	Annual rate of interest	10%
4	Number of years	4
5	Annual loan payment	−$1,892.82

Entry in Cell B5 is =PMT(B3,B4,B2,0,0).
The minus sign appears before the loan
payment in B5 because loan payments
are cash outflows for the borrower.

	A	B	C	D	E
1		LOAN AMORTIZATION SCHEDULE			
2		Loan principal		$6,000	
3		Annual rate of interest		10%	
4		Number of years		4	
5		Annual annuity payments			
6	Year	Total	To Interest	To Principal	Year-End Principal
7	0				$6,000.00
8	1	−$1,892.82	−$600.00	−$1,292.82	$4,707.18
9	2	−$1,892.82	−$470.72	−$1,422.11	$3,285.07
10	3	−$1,892.82	−$328.51	−$1,564.32	$1,720.75
11	4	−$1,892.82	−$172.07	−$1,720.75	$0.00

Key Cell Entries
Cell B8 is =PMT(D3,D4,D2,0,0), copy to B9:B11
Cell C8 is =PMT(D3,D4,D2,0,0), copy to C9:C11
Cell D8 is =PMT(D3,D4,D2,0,0), copy to D9:D11
Cell E8 is =E7-D8, copy to E9:E11
The minus sign appears before the loan payments
because these are cash outflows for the borrower.

To attract buyers who could not immediately afford 15- to 30-year mortgages of equal annual payments, lenders offered mortgages whose interest rates adjusted at certain points. The *Focus on Practice* box discusses how such mortgages have worked out for some "subprime" borrowers.

focus on **PRACTICE**

New Century Brings Trouble for Subprime Mortgages

in practice As the housing market began to boom at the end of the twentieth century and into the early twenty-first, the market share of subprime mortgages climbed from near 0 percent in 1997 to about 20 percent of mortgage originations in 2006. Several factors combined to fuel the rapid growth of lending to borrowers with tarnished credit, including a low interest rate environment, loose underwriting standards, and innovations in mortgage financing such as "affordability programs" to increase rates of homeownership among lower-income borrowers.

Particularly attractive to new home buyers was the hybrid adjustable rate mortgage (ARM), which featured a low introductory interest rate that reset upward after a preset period of time. Interest rates began a steady upward trend beginning in late 2004. In 2006, some $300 billion worth of adjustable ARMs were reset to higher rates. In a market with rising home values, a borrower has the option to refinance the mortgage, using some of the equity created by the home's increasing value to reduce the mortgage payment. After 2006, however, home prices started a 3-year slide, so refinancing was not an

option for many subprime borrowers. Instead, borrowers in trouble could try to convince their lenders to allow a "short sale," in which the borrower sells the home for whatever the market will bear and the lender agrees to accept the proceeds from that sale as settlement for the mortgage debt. For lenders and borrowers alike, foreclosure is the last, worst option.

▶ *As a reaction to problems in the subprime area, lenders tightened lending standards. What effect do you think this change had on the housing market?*

FINDING INTEREST OR GROWTH RATES

It is often necessary to calculate the compound annual interest or *growth rate* (that is, the annual rate of change in values) of a series of cash flows. Examples include finding the interest rate on a loan, the rate of growth in sales, and the rate of growth in earnings. In doing so, we again make use of Equation 5.1. In this case, we want to solve for the interest rate (or growth rate) representing the increase in value of some investment between two time periods. Solving Equation 5.1 for r, we have

$$r = \left(\frac{FV_n}{PV}\right)^{1/n} - 1 \tag{5.13}$$

The simplest situation is one in which an investment's value has increased over time, and you want to know the annual rate of growth (that is, interest) that is represented by the increase in the investment.

Personal Finance Example 5.22 ▶ Ray Noble purchased an investment 4 years ago for $1,250. Now it is worth $1,520. What compound annual rate of return has Ray earned on this investment? Plugging the appropriate values into Equation 5.13, we have

$$r = (\$1{,}520 \div \$1{,}250)^{(1/4)} - 1 = 0.0501 = 5.01\% \text{ per year}$$

Calculator use Using the calculator to find the interest or growth rate, we treat the earliest value as a present value, PV, and the latest value as a future value, FV_n. (*Note:* Most calculators require *either* the PV or the FV value to be input as a negative value to calculate an unknown interest or growth rate. That approach

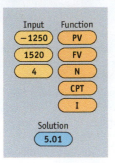

is used here.) Using the inputs shown at the left, you will find the interest or growth rate to be 5.01%.

Spreadsheet use   The interest or growth rate for the series of cash flows also can be calculated as shown on the following Excel spreadsheet.

	A	B
1	SOLVING FOR INTEREST OR GROWTH RATE OF A SINGLE AMOUNT INVESTMENT	
2	Present value	– $1,250
3	Number of years	4
4	Future value	$1,520.00
5	Annual rate of interest	5.01%
	Entry in Cell B5 is =RATE(B3,0,B2,B4,0). The minus sign appears before the $1,250 in B2 because the cost of the investment is treated as a cash outflow.	

Another type of interest-rate problem involves finding the interest rate associated with an *annuity,* or equal-payment loan.

Personal Finance Example 5.23 ▶   Jan Jacobs can borrow $2,000 to be repaid in equal annual end-of-year amounts of $514.14 for the next 5 years. She wants to find the interest rate on this loan.

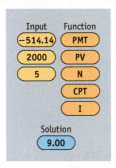

Calculator use   (*Note:* Most calculators require *either* the *PMT* or the *PV* value to be input as a negative number to calculate an unknown interest rate on an equal-payment loan. That approach is used here.) Using the inputs shown at the left, you will find the interest rate to be 9.00%.

Spreadsheet use   The interest or growth rate for the annuity also can be calculated as shown on the following Excel spreadsheet.

	A	B
1	SOLVING FOR INTEREST OR GROWTH RATE OF AN ORDINARY ANNUITY	
2	Present value	$2,000
3	Number of years	5
4	Annual annuity amount	–$514.14
5	Annual rate of interest	9.00%
	Entry in Cell B5 is =RATE(B3,B4,B2,0,0). The minus sign appears before the $514.14 in B4 because the loan payment is treated as a cash outflow.	

FINDING AN UNKNOWN NUMBER OF PERIODS

Sometimes it is necessary to calculate the number of time periods needed to generate a given amount of cash flow from an initial amount. Here we briefly consider this calculation for both single amounts and annuities. This simplest case is when a person wishes to determine the number of periods, n, it will take for an initial deposit, PV, to grow to a specified future amount, FV_n, given a stated interest rate, r.

Personal Finance Example 5.24 ▶

Ann Bates wishes to determine the number of years it will take for her initial $1,000 deposit, earning 8% annual interest, to grow to equal $2,500. Simply stated, at an 8% annual rate of interest, how many years, n, will it take for Ann's $1,000, PV, to grow to $2,500, FV_n?

MyFinanceLab Financial Calculator

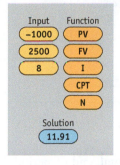

Calculator use Using the calculator, we treat the initial value as the present value, PV, and the latest value as the future value, FV_n. (*Note:* Most calculators require *either* the PV or the FV value to be input as a negative number to calculate an unknown number of periods. That approach is used here.) Using the inputs shown at the left, we find the number of periods to be 11.91 years.

Spreadsheet use The number of years for the present value to grow to a specified future value can be calculated as shown on the following Excel spreadsheet.

	A	B
1	SOLVING FOR THE YEARS OF A SINGLE AMOUNT INVESTMENT	
2	Present value	−$1,000
3	Annual rate of interest	8%
4	Future value	$2,500
5	Number of years	11.91
	Entry in Cell B5 is =NPER(B3,0,B2,B4,0). The minus sign appears before the $1,000 in B2 because the initial deposit is treated as a cash outflow.	

Another type of number-of-periods problem involves finding the number of periods associated with an *annuity*. Occasionally, we wish to find the unknown life, n, of an annuity that is intended to achieve a specific objective, such as repaying a loan of a given amount.

Personal Finance Example 5.25 ▶

Bill Smart can borrow $25,000 at an 11% annual interest rate; equal, annual, end-of-year payments of $4,800 are required. He wishes to determine how long it will take to fully repay the loan. In other words, he wishes to determine how many years, n, it will take to repay the $25,000, 11% loan, PV_n, if the payments of $4,800 are made at the end of each year.

MyFinanceLab Financial Calculator

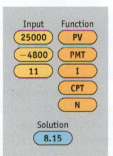

Calculator use (*Note:* Most calculators require *either* the PV or the PMT value to be input as a negative number to calculate an unknown number of periods. That approach is used here.) Using the inputs shown at the left, you will find the number of periods to be 8.15 years. So, after making 8 payments of $4,800, Bill will still have a small outstanding balance.

Spreadsheet use The number of years to pay off the loan also can be calculated as shown on the following Excel spreadsheet.

	A	B
1	SOLVING FOR THE YEARS TO REPAY A SINGLE LOAN AMOUNT	
2	Present value	$25,000
3	Annual rate of interest	11%
4	Annual payment amount	−$4,800.00
5	Number of years	8.15

Entry in Cell B5 is =NPER(B3,B4,B2,0,0).
The minus sign appears before the $4,800
in B4 because the loan payments
are treated as cash outflows.

→ REVIEW QUESTIONS

5-26 How can you determine the size of the equal, annual, end-of-period deposits necessary to accumulate a certain future sum at the end of a specified future period at a given annual interest rate?

5-27 Describe the procedure used to amortize a loan into a series of equal periodic payments.

5-28 How can you determine the unknown number of periods when you know the present and future values—single amount or annuity—and the applicable rate of interest?

→ EXCEL REVIEW QUESTIONS   MyFinanceLab

5-29 You want to buy a new car as a graduation present for yourself, but before finalizing a purchase you need to consider the monthly payment amount. Based on the information provided at MFL, find the monthly payment amount for the car you are considering.

5-30 As a savvy finance major you realize that you can quickly estimate your retirement age by knowing how much you need to retire, how much you can contribute each month to your retirement account, and what rate of return you can earn on your retirement investment and solving for the number of years it will take to get there. Based on the information provided at MFL, estimate the age at which you will be able to retire.

Summary

FOCUS ON VALUE

Time value of money is an important tool that financial managers and other market participants use to assess the effects of proposed actions. Because firms have long lives and some decisions affect their long-term cash flows, the effective application of time-value-of-money techniques is extremely important. These techniques enable financial managers to evaluate cash flows occurring at different times so as to combine, compare, and evaluate them and link them to the firm's overall goal of share price maximization. It will become clear in Chapters 6 and 7 that the application of time value techniques is a key part of the value determination process needed to make intelligent value-creating decisions.

REVIEW OF LEARNING GOALS

LG 1 **Discuss the role of time value in finance, the use of computational tools, and the basic patterns of cash flow.** Financial managers and investors use time-value-of-money techniques when assessing the value of expected cash flow streams. Alternatives can be assessed by either compounding to find future value or discounting to find present value. Financial managers rely primarily on present value techniques. Financial calculators, electronic spreadsheets, and financial tables can streamline the application of time value techniques. The cash flow of a firm can be described by its pattern: single amount, annuity, or mixed stream.

LG 2 **Understand the concepts of future value and present value, their calculation for single amounts, and the relationship between them.** Future value (FV) relies on compound interest to measure future amounts. The initial principal or deposit in one period, along with the interest earned on it, becomes the beginning principal of the following period.

The present value (PV) of a future amount is the amount of money today that is equivalent to the given future amount, considering the return that can be earned. Present value is the inverse of future value.

LG 3 **Find the future value and the present value of both an ordinary annuity and an annuity due, and find the present value of a perpetuity.** An annuity is a pattern of equal periodic cash flows. For an ordinary annuity, the cash flows occur at the end of the period. For an annuity due, cash flows occur at the beginning of the period.

The future or present value of an ordinary annuity can be found by using algebraic equations, a financial calculator, or a spreadsheet program. The value of an annuity due is always $r\%$ greater than the value of an identical annuity. The present value of a perpetuity—an infinite-lived annuity—equals the annual cash payment divided by the discount rate.

LG 4 **Calculate both the future value and the present value of a mixed stream of cash flows.** A mixed stream of cash flows is a stream of unequal periodic cash flows that reflect no particular pattern. The future value of a mixed stream of cash flows is the sum of the future values of each individual cash flow. Similarly, the present value of a mixed stream of cash flows is the sum of the present values of the individual cash flows.

LG 5 **Understand the effect that compounding interest more frequently than annually has on future value and on the effective annual rate of interest.** Interest can be compounded at intervals ranging from annually to daily and even continuously. The more often interest is compounded, the larger the future amount that will be accumulated, and the higher the effective, or true, annual rate (EAR).

The annual percentage rate (APR)—a nominal annual rate—is quoted on credit cards and loans. The annual percentage yield (APY)—an effective annual rate—is quoted on savings products.

LG 6 **Describe the procedures involved in (1) determining deposits needed to accumulate a future sum, (2) loan amortization, (3) finding interest or growth rates, and (4) finding an unknown number of periods.** (1) The periodic deposit to accumulate a given future sum can be found by solving the equation for the future value of an annuity for the annual payment. (2) A loan can be amortized into equal periodic payments by solving the equation for the present value of an annuity for the periodic payment. (3) Interest or growth rates can be estimated by finding the unknown interest rate in the equation for the present value of a single amount or an annuity. (4) The number of periods can be estimated by finding the unknown number of periods in the equation for the present value of a single amount or an annuity.

Self-Test Problems (Solutions in Appendix)

LG 2 **LG 5**   **ST5–1**   **Future values for various compounding frequencies** Delia Martin has $10,000 that she can deposit in any of three savings accounts for a 3-year period. Bank A compounds interest on an annual basis, bank B compounds interest twice each year, and bank C compounds interest each quarter. All three banks have a stated annual interest rate of 4%.

IRF

    a. What amount would Ms. Martin have at the end of the third year, leaving all interest paid on deposit, in each bank?

    b. What *effective annual rate (EAR)* would she earn in each of the banks?

    c. On the basis of your findings in parts **a** and **b**, which bank should Ms. Martin deal with? Why?

    d. If a fourth bank (bank D), also with a 4% stated interest rate, compounds interest continuously, how much would Ms. Martin have at the end of the third year? Does this alternative change your recommendation in part **c**? Explain why or why not.

LG 3   **ST5–2**   **Future values of annuities** Ramesh Abdul wishes to choose the better of two equally costly cash flow streams: annuity X and annuity Y. X is an *annuity due* with a cash inflow of $9,000 for each of 6 years. Y is an *ordinary annuity* with a cash inflow of $10,000 for each of 6 years. Assume that Ramesh can earn 15% on his investments.

IRF

    a. On a purely subjective basis, which annuity do you think is more attractive? Why?

    b. Find the future value at the end of year 6 for both annuities.

    c. Use your finding in part **b** to indicate which annuity is more attractive. Why? Compare your finding to your subjective response in part **a**.

LG 2 **LG 3** **LG 4**   **ST5–3**   **Present values of single amounts and streams** You have a choice of accepting either of two 5-year cash flow streams or single amounts. One cash flow stream is an ordinary annuity, and the other is a mixed stream. You may accept alternative A or B, either as a cash flow stream or as a single amount. Given the cash flow stream and single amounts associated with each (see the following table), and assuming a 9% opportunity cost, which alternative (A or B) and in which form (cash flow stream or single amount) would you prefer?

IRF

	Cash flow stream	
End of year	Alternative A	Alternative B
1	$700	$1,100
2	700	900
3	700	700
4	700	500
5	700	300
	Single amount	
At time zero	$2,825	$2,800

ST5–4 Deposits needed to accumulate a future sum Judi Janson wishes to accumulate $8,000 by the end of 5 years by making equal, annual, end-of-year deposits over the next 5 years. If Judi can earn 7% on her investments, how much must she deposit at the *end of each year* to meet this goal?

Warm-Up Exercises   All problems are available in MyFinanceLab.

LG 2 E5–1 Assume that a firm makes a $2,500 deposit into its money market account. If this account is currently paying 0.7% (yes, that's right, less than 1%!), what will the account balance be after 1 year?

LG 2 LG 5 E5–2 If Bob and Judy combine their savings of $1,260 and $975, respectively, and deposit this amount into an account that pays 2% annual interest, compounded monthly, what will the account balance be after 4 years?

LG 3 E5–3 Gabrielle just won $2.5 million in the state lottery. She is given the option of receiving a total of $1.3 million now, or she can elect to be paid $100,000 at the end of each of the next 25 years. If Gabrielle can earn 5% annually on her investments, from a strict economic point of view which option should she take?

LG 4 E5–4 Your firm has the option of making an investment in new software that will cost $130,000 today and is estimated to provide the savings shown in the following table over its 5-year life.

Year	Savings estimate
1	$35,000
2	50,000
3	45,000
4	25,000
5	15,000

Should the firm make this investment if it requires a minimum annual return of 9% on all investments?

E5–5 Joseph is a friend of yours. He has plenty of money but little financial sense. He received a gift of $12,000 for his recent graduation and is looking for a bank in which to deposit the funds. Partners' Savings Bank offers an account with an annual interest rate of 3% compounded semiannually, whereas Selwyn's offers an account with a 2.75% annual interest rate compounded continuously. Calculate the value of the two accounts at the end of 1 year, and recommend to Joseph which account he should choose.

E5–6 Jack and Jill have just had their first child. If college is expected to cost $150,000 per year in 18 years, how much should the couple begin depositing annually at the end of each year to accumulate enough funds to pay the first year's tuition at the beginning of the nineteenth year? Assume that they can earn a 6% annual rate of return on their investment.

Problems   All problems are available in MyFinanceLab.

P5–1 **Using a time line** The financial manager at Starbuck Industries is considering an investment that requires an initial outlay of $25,000 and is expected to result in cash inflows of $3,000 at the end of year 1, $6,000 at the end of years 2 and 3, $10,000 at the end of year 4, $8,000 at the end of year 5, and $7,000 at the end of year 6.
  a. Draw and label a time line depicting the cash flows associated with Starbuck Industries' proposed investment.
  b. Use arrows to demonstrate, on the time line in part **a,** how compounding to find future value can be used to measure all cash flows at the end of year 6.
  c. Use arrows to demonstrate, on the time line in part **b,** how discounting to find present value can be used to measure all cash flows at time zero.
  d. Which of the approaches—*future value* or *present value*—do financial managers rely on most often for decision making? Why?

P5–2 **Future value calculation** *Without referring to the preprogrammed function on your financial calculator,* use the basic formula for future value along with the given interest rate, r, and the number of periods, n, to calculate the future value of $1 in each of the cases shown in the following table.

Case	Interest rate, r	Number of periods, n
A	12%	2
B	6	3
C	9	2
D	3	4

P5–3 **Future value** You have $100 to invest. If you can earn 12% interest, about how long does it take for your $100 investment to grow to $200? Suppose that the interest rate is just half that, at 6%. At half the interest rate, does it take twice as long to double your money? Why or why not? How long does it take?

P5–4 **Future values** For each of the cases shown in the following table, calculate the future value of the single cash flow deposited today at the end of the deposit period if the interest is compounded annually at the rate specified.

Case	Single cash flow	Interest rate	Deposit period (years)
A	$ 200	5%	20
B	4,500	8	7
C	10,000	9	10
D	25,000	10	12
E	37,000	11	5
F	40,000	12	9

Personal Finance Problem

 P5–5 **Time value** You have $1,500 to invest today at 7% interest compounded annually.

  a. Find how much you will have accumulated in the account at the end of (1) 3 years, (2) 6 years, and (3) 9 years.

  b. Use your findings in part **a** to calculate the amount of interest earned in (1) the first 3 years (years 1 to 3), (2) the second 3 years (years 4 to 6), and (3) the third 3 years (years 7 to 9).

  c. Compare and contrast your findings in part **b**. Explain why the amount of interest earned increases in each succeeding 3-year period.

Personal Finance Problem

 P5–6 **Time value** As part of your financial planning, you wish to purchase a new car exactly 5 years from today. The car you wish to purchase costs $14,000 today, and your research indicates that its price will increase by 2% to 4% per year over the next 5 years.

  a. Estimate the price of the car at the end of 5 years if inflation is (1) 2% per year and (2) 4% per year.

  b. How much more expensive will the car be if the rate of inflation is 4% rather than 2%?

  c. Estimate the price of the car if inflation is 2% for the next 2 years and 4% for 3 years after that.

Personal Finance Problem

 P5–7 **Time value** You can deposit $10,000 into an account paying 9% annual interest either today or exactly 10 years from today. How much better off will you be at the end of 40 years if you decide to make the initial deposit today rather than 10 years from today?

Personal Finance Problem

 P5–8 **Time value** Misty needs to have $15,000 at the end of 5 years to fulfill her goal of purchasing a small sailboat. She is willing to invest a lump sum today and leave the money untouched for 5 years until it grows to $15,000, but she wonders what sort of investment return she will need to earn to reach her goal. Use your calculator or spreadsheet to figure out the approximate annually compounded rate of return needed in each of these cases:

a. Misty can invest $10,200 today.
b. Misty can invest $8,150 today.
c. Misty can invest $7,150 today.

Personal Finance Problem

LG 2   **P5–9**   **Single-payment loan repayment** A person borrows $200 to be repaid in 8 years with 14% annually compounded interest. The loan may be repaid at the end of any earlier year with no prepayment penalty.

a. What amount will be due if the loan is repaid at the end of year 1?
b. What is the repayment at the end of year 4?
c. What amount is due at the end of the eighth year?

LG 2   **P5–10**   **Present value calculation** *Without referring to the preprogrammed function on your financial calculator,* use the basic formula for present value, along with the given opportunity cost, *r*, and the number of periods, *n*, to calculate the present value of $1 in each of the cases shown in the following table.

Case	Opportunity cost, r	Number of periods, n
A	2%	4
B	10	2
C	5	3
D	13	2

LG 2   **P5–11**   **Present values** For each of the cases shown in the following table, calculate the present value of the cash flow, discounting at the rate given and assuming that the cash flow is received at the end of the period noted.

Case	Single cash flow	Discount rate	End of period (years)
A	$ 7,000	12%	4
B	28,000	8	20
C	10,000	14	12
D	150,000	11	6
E	45,000	20	8

LG 2   **P5–12**   **Present value concept** Answer each of the following questions.

a. What single investment made today, earning 12% annual interest, will be worth $6,000 at the end of 6 years?
b. What is the present value of $6,000 to be received at the end of 6 years if the discount rate is 12%?
c. What is the most you would pay today for a promise to repay you $6,000 at the end of 6 years if your opportunity cost is 12%?
d. Compare, contrast, and discuss your findings in parts a through c.

Personal Finance Problem

P5–13   Time value Jim Nance has been offered an investment that will pay him $500 three years from today.

    a. If his opportunity cost is 7% compounded annually, what value should he place on this opportunity today?

    b. What is the most he should pay to purchase this payment today?

    c. If Jim can purchase this investment for less than the amount calculated in part **a,** what does that imply about the rate of return that he will earn on the investment?

P5–14   Time value An Iowa state savings bond can be converted to $100 at maturity 6 years from purchase. If the state bonds are to be competitive with U.S. savings bonds, which pay 8% annual interest (compounded annually), at what price must the state sell its bonds? Assume no cash payments on savings bonds prior to redemption.

Personal Finance Problem

P5–15   Time value and discount rates You just won a lottery that promises to pay you $1,000,000 exactly 10 years from today. Because the $1,000,000 payment is guaranteed by the state in which you live, opportunities exist to sell the claim today for an immediate single cash payment.

    a. What is the least you will sell your claim for if you can earn the following rates of return on similar-risk investments during the 10-year period?

        (1) 6%

        (2) 9%

        (3) 12%

    b. Rework part a under the assumption that the $1,000,000 payment will be received in 15 rather than 10 years.

    c. On the basis of your findings in parts **a** and **b,** discuss the effect of both the size of the rate of return and the time until receipt of payment on the present value of a future sum.

Personal Finance Problem

P5–16   Time value comparisons of single amounts In exchange for a $20,000 payment today, a well-known company will allow you to choose *one* of the alternatives shown in the following table. Your opportunity cost is 11%.

Alternative	Single amount
A	$28,500 at end of 3 years
B	$54,000 at end of 9 years
C	$160,000 at end of 20 years

    a. Find the value today of each alternative.

    b. Are all the alternatives acceptable? That is, are they worth $20,000 today?

    c. Which alternative, if any, will you take?

Personal Finance Problem

LG 2 **P5–17** **Cash flow investment decision** Tom Alexander has an opportunity to purchase any of the investments shown in the following table. The purchase price, the amount of the single cash inflow, and its year of receipt are given for each investment. Which purchase recommendations would you make, assuming that Tom can earn 10% on his investments?

Investment	Price	Single cash inflow	Year of receipt
A	$18,000	$30,000	5
B	600	3,000	20
C	3,500	10,000	10
D	1,000	15,000	40

LG 2 **P5–18** **Calculating deposit needed** You put $10,000 in an account earning 5%. After 3 years, you make another deposit into the same account. Four years later (that is, 7 years after your original $10,000 deposit), the account balance is $20,000. What was the amount of the deposit at the end of year 3?

LG 3 **P5–19** **Future value of an annuity** For each case in the accompanying table, answer the questions that follow.

Case	Amount of annuity	Interest rate	Deposit period (years)
A	$ 2,500	8%	10
B	500	12	6
C	30,000	20	5
D	11,500	9	8
E	6,000	14	30

a. Calculate the future value of the annuity, assuming that it is
(1) An ordinary annuity.
(2) An annuity due.
b. Compare your findings in parts a(1) and a(2). All else being identical, which type of annuity—ordinary or annuity due—is preferable? Explain why.

LG 3 **P5–20** **Present value of an annuity** Consider the following cases.

Case	Amount of annuity	Interest rate	Period (years)
A	$ 12,000	7%	3
B	55,000	12	15
C	700	20	9
D	140,000	5	7
E	22,500	10	5

a. Calculate the present value of the annuity, assuming that it is
   (1) An ordinary annuity.
   (2) An annuity due.
b. Compare your findings in parts a(1) and a(2). All else being identical, which type of annuity—ordinary or annuity due—is preferable? Explain why.

Personal Finance Problem

LG 3 **P5–21** **Time value: Annuities** Marian Kirk wishes to select the better of two 10-year annuities, C and D. Annuity C is an *ordinary annuity* of $2,500 per year for 10 years. Annuity D is an *annuity due* of $2,200 per year for 10 years.
a. Find the *future value* of both annuities at the end of year 10 assuming that Marian can earn (1) 10% annual interest and (2) 20% annual interest.
b. Use your findings in part a to indicate which annuity has the greater future value at the end of year 10 for both the (1) 10% and (2) 20% interest rates.
c. Find the *present value* of both annuities, assuming that Marian can earn (1) 10% annual interest and (2) 20% annual interest.
d. Use your findings in part c to indicate which annuity has the greater present value for both (1) 10% and (2) 20% interest rates.
e. Briefly compare, contrast, and explain any differences between your findings using the 10% and 20% interest rates in parts b and d.

Personal Finance Problem

LG 3 **P5–22** **Retirement planning** Hal Thomas, a 25-year-old college graduate, wishes to retire at age 65. To supplement other sources of retirement income, he can deposit $2,000 each year into a tax-deferred individual retirement arrangement (IRA). The IRA will earn a 10% return over the next 40 years.
a. If Hal makes annual end-of-year $2,000 deposits into the IRA, how much will he have accumulated by the end of his sixty-fifth year?
b. If Hal decides to wait until age 35 to begin making annual end-of-year $2,000 deposits into the IRA, how much will he have accumulated by the end of his sixty-fifth year?
c. Using your findings in parts a and b, discuss the impact of delaying making deposits into the IRA for 10 years (age 25 to age 35) on the amount accumulated by the end of Hal's sixty-fifth year.
d. Rework parts a, b, and c, assuming that Hal makes all deposits at the beginning, rather than the end, of each year. Discuss the effect of beginning-of-year deposits on the future value accumulated by the end of Hal's sixty-fifth year.

Personal Finance Problem

LG 3 **P5–23** **Value of a retirement annuity** An insurance agent is trying to sell you an immediate-retirement annuity, which for a single amount paid today will provide you with $12,000 at the end of each year for the next 25 years. You currently earn 9% on low-risk investments comparable to the retirement annuity. Ignoring taxes, what is the most you would pay for this annuity?

Personal Finance Problem

LG 2 **LG 3** **P5–24** **Funding your retirement** You plan to retire in exactly 20 years. Your goal is to create a fund that will allow you to receive $20,000 at the end of each year for the 30 years between retirement and death (a psychic told you that you would die exactly

30 years after you retire). You know that you will be able to earn 11% per year during the 30-year retirement period.

a. How large a fund will you need *when you retire* in 20 years to provide the 30-year, $20,000 retirement annuity?

b. How much will you need *today* as a single amount to provide the fund calculated in part a if you earn only 9% per year during the 20 years preceding retirement?

c. What effect would an increase in the rate you can earn both during and prior to retirement have on the values found in parts a and b? Explain.

d. Now assume that you will earn 10% from now through the end of your retirement. You want to make 20 end-of-year deposits into your retirement account that will fund the 30-year stream of $20,000 annual annuity payments. How large do your annual deposits have to be?

Personal Finance Problem

  P5–25 **Value of an annuity versus a single amount** Assume that you just won the state lottery. Your prize can be taken either in the form of $40,000 at the end of each of the next 25 years (that is, $1,000,000 over 25 years) or as a single amount of $500,000 paid immediately.

a. If you expect to be able to earn 5% annually on your investments over the next 25 years, ignoring taxes and other considerations, which alternative should you take? Why?

b. Would your decision in part a change if you could earn 7% rather than 5% on your investments over the next 25 years? Why?

c. On a strictly economic basis, at approximately what earnings rate would you be indifferent between the two plans?

 P5–26 **Perpetuities** Consider the data in the following table.

Perpetuity	Annual amount	Discount rate
A	$ 20,000	8%
B	100,000	10
C	3,000	6
D	60,000	5

Determine the present value of each perpetuity.

Personal Finance Problem

 P5–27 **Creating an endowment** On completion of her introductory finance course, Marla Lee was so pleased with the amount of useful and interesting knowledge she gained that she convinced her parents, who were wealthy alumni of the university she was attending, to create an endowment. The endowment is to allow three needy students to take the introductory finance course each year in perpetuity. The guaranteed annual cost of tuition and books for the course is $600 per student. The endowment will be created by making a single payment to the university. The university expects to earn exactly 6% per year on these funds.

a. How large an initial single payment must Marla's parents make to the university to fund the endowment?
b. What amount would be needed to fund the endowment if the university could earn 9% rather than 6% per year on the funds?

LG 4   **P5–28**   **Value of a mixed stream** For each of the mixed streams of cash flows shown in the following table, determine the future value at the end of the final year if deposits are made into an account paying annual interest of 12%, assuming that no withdrawals are made during the period and that the deposits are made

a. At the *end* of each year.
b. At the *beginning* of each year.

	Cash flow stream		
Year	A	B	C
1	$ 900	$30,000	$1,200
2	1,000	25,000	1,200
3	1,200	20,000	1,000
4		10,000	1,900
5		5,000	

Personal Finance Problem

LG 4   **P5–29**   **Value of a single amount versus a mixed stream** Gina Vitale has just contracted to sell a small parcel of land that she inherited a few years ago. The buyer is willing to pay $24,000 at the closing of the transaction or will pay the amounts shown in the following table at the *beginning* of each of the next 5 years. Because Gina doesn't really need the money today, she plans to let it accumulate in an account that earns 7% annual interest. Given her desire to buy a house at the end of 5 years after closing on the sale of the lot, she decides to choose the payment alternative—$24,000 single amount or the mixed stream of payments in the following table—that provides the higher future value at the end of 5 years. Which alternative will she choose?

Mixed stream	
Beginning of year	Cash flow
1	$ 2,000
2	4,000
3	6,000
4	8,000
5	10,000

P5–30 **Value of mixed streams** Find the present value of the streams of cash flows shown in the following table. Assume that the firm's opportunity cost is 12%.

	A		B		C
Year	Cash flow	Year	Cash flow	Year	Cash flow
1	−$2,000	1	$10,000	1–5	$10,000/yr
2	3,000	2–5	5,000/yr	6–10	8,000/yr
3	4,000	6	7,000		
4	6,000				
5	8,000				

 P5–31 **Present value: Mixed streams** Consider the mixed streams of cash flows shown in the following table.

	Cash flow stream	
Year	A	B
1	$ 50,000	$ 10,000
2	40,000	20,000
3	30,000	30,000
4	20,000	40,000
5	10,000	50,000
Totals	$150,000	$150,000

a. Find the present value of each stream using a 15% discount rate.
b. Compare the calculated present values and discuss them in light of the undiscounted cash flows totaling $150,000 in each case.

  P5–32 **Value of a mixed stream** Harte Systems, Inc., a maker of electronic surveillance equipment, is considering selling to a well-known hardware chain the rights to market its home security system. The proposed deal calls for the hardware chain to pay Harte $30,000 and $25,000 at the end of years 1 and 2 and to make annual year-end payments of $15,000 in years 3 through 9. A final payment to Harte of $10,000 would be due at the end of year 10.
a. Lay out the cash flows involved in the offer on a time line.
b. If Harte applies a required rate of return of 12% to them, what is the present value of this series of payments?
c. A second company has offered Harte an immediate one-time payment of $100,000 for the rights to market the home security system. Which offer should Harte accept?

Personal Finance Problem

 P5–33 **Funding budget shortfalls** As part of your personal budgeting process, you have determined that in each of the next 5 years you will have budget shortfalls. In other words, you will need the amounts shown in the following table at the end of the given year to balance your budget, that is, to make inflows equal outflows. You expect to be able to earn 8% on your investments during the next 5 years and wish to fund the budget shortfalls over the next 5 years with a single amount.

End of year	Budget shortfall
1	$ 5,000
2	4,000
3	6,000
4	10,000
5	3,000

a. How large must the single deposit today into an account paying 8% annual interest be to provide for full coverage of the anticipated budget shortfalls?
b. What effect would an increase in your earnings rate have on the amount calculated in part a? Explain.

 P5–34 **Relationship between future value and present value: Mixed stream** Using the information in the accompanying table, answer the questions that follow.

Year (t)	Cash flow
1	$ 800
2	900
3	1,000
4	1,500
5	2,000

a. Determine the *present value* of the mixed stream of cash flows using a 5% discount rate.
b. How much would you be willing to pay for an opportunity to buy this stream, assuming that you can at best earn 5% on your investments?
c. What effect, if any, would a 7% rather than a 5% opportunity cost have on your analysis? (Explain verbally.)

 P5–35 **Relationship between future value and present value: Mixed stream** The table below shows a mixed cash flow stream except that the cash flow for year 3 is missing.

Year 1	$10,000
Year 2	5,000
Year 3	
Year 4	20,000
Year 5	3,000

Suppose that somehow you know that the present value of the entire stream is $32,911.03 and that the discount rate is 4%. What is the amount of the missing cash flow in year 3?

LG 5 **P5–36** **Changing compounding frequency** Using annual, semiannual, and quarterly compounding periods for each of the following, (1) calculate the future value if $5,000 is deposited initially, and (2) determine the *effective annual rate (EAR)*.
a. At 12% annual interest for 5 years.
b. At 16% annual interest for 6 years.
c. At 20% annual interest for 10 years.

LG 5 **P5–37** **Compounding frequency, time value, and effective annual rates** For each of the cases in the following table:
a. Calculate the future value at the end of the specified deposit period.
b. Determine the *effective annual rate, EAR*.
c. Compare the nominal annual rate, r, to the effective annual rate, EAR. What relationship exists between compounding frequency and the nominal and effective annual rates?

Case	Amount of initial deposit	Nominal annual rate, r	Compounding frequency, m (times/year)	Deposit period (years)
A	$ 2,500	6%	2	5
B	50,000	12	6	3
C	1,000	5	1	10
D	20,000	16	4	6

LG 5 **P5–38** **Continuous compounding** For each of the cases in the following table, find the future value at the end of the deposit period, assuming that interest is compounded continuously at the given nominal annual rate.

Case	Amount of initial deposit	Nominal annual rate, r	Deposit period (years), n
A	$1,000	9%	2
B	600	10	10
C	4,000	8	7
D	2,500	12	4

Personal Finance Problem

LG 5 **P5–39** **Compounding frequency and time value** You plan to invest $2,000 in an individual retirement arrangement (IRA) today at a *nominal annual rate* of 8%, which is expected to apply to all future years.

a. How much will you have in the account at the end of 10 years if interest is compounded (1) annually, (2) semiannually, (3) daily (assume a 365-day year), and (4) continuously?

b. What is the *effective annual rate (EAR)* for each compounding period in part **a**?

c. How much greater will your IRA balance be at the end of 10 years if interest is compounded continuously rather than annually?

d. How does the compounding frequency affect the future value and effective annual rate for a given deposit? Explain in terms of your findings in parts **a** through **c**.

Personal Finance Problem

 P5–40   **Comparing compounding periods**   René Levin wishes to determine the future value at the end of 2 years of a $15,000 deposit made today into an account paying a nominal annual rate of 12%.

a. Find the future value of René's deposit, assuming that interest is compounded (1) annually, (2) quarterly, (3) monthly, and (4) continuously.

b. Compare your findings in part **a**, and use them to demonstrate the relationship between compounding frequency and future value.

c. What is the maximum future value obtainable given the $15,000 deposit, the 2-year time period, and the 12% nominal annual rate? Use your findings in part **a** to explain.

Personal Finance Problem

LG 3 **LG 5** **P5–41**   **Annuities and compounding**   Janet Boyle intends to deposit $300 per year in a credit union for the next 10 years, and the credit union pays an annual interest rate of 8%.

a. Determine the future value that Janet will have at the end of 10 years, given that end-of-period deposits are made and no interest is withdrawn, if

(1) $300 is deposited annually and the credit union pays interest annually.

(2) $150 is deposited semiannually and the credit union pays interest semiannually.

(3) $75 is deposited quarterly and the credit union pays interest quarterly.

b. Use your findings in part **a** to discuss the effect of more frequent deposits and compounding of interest on the future value of an annuity.

LG 6 **P5–42**   **Deposits to accumulate future sums**   For each of the cases shown in the following table, determine the amount of the equal, annual, end-of-year deposits necessary to accumulate the given sum at the end of the specified period, assuming the stated annual interest rate.

Case	Sum to be accumulated	Accumulation period (years)	Interest rate
A	$ 5,000	3	12%
B	100,000	20	7
C	30,000	8	10
D	15,000	12	8

Personal Finance Problem

 P5–43   **Creating a retirement fund**   To supplement your planned retirement in exactly 42 years, you estimate that you need to accumulate $220,000 by the end of 42 years from today. You plan to make equal, annual, end-of-year deposits into an account paying 8% annual interest.

a. How large must the annual deposits be to create the $220,000 fund by the end of 42 years?

b. If you can afford to deposit only $600 per year into the account, how much will you have accumulated by the end of the forty-second year?

Personal Finance Problem

LG 6   **P5–44**   **Accumulating a growing future sum**   A retirement home at Deer Trail Estates now costs $185,000. Inflation is expected to cause this price to increase at 6% per year over the 20 years before C. L. Donovan retires. How large an equal, annual, end-of-year deposit must be made each year into an account paying an annual interest rate of 10% for him to have the cash needed to purchase a home at retirement?

Personal Finance Problem

LG 3   **LG 6**   **P5–45**   **Deposits to create a perpetuity**   You have decided to endow your favorite university with a scholarship. It is expected to cost $6,000 per year to attend the university into perpetuity. You expect to give the university the endowment in 10 years and will accumulate it by making equal annual (end-of-year) deposits into an account. The rate of interest is expected to be 10% for all future time periods.

a. How large must the endowment be?

b. How much must you deposit at the end of each of the next 10 years to accumulate the required amount?

Personal Finance Problem

LG 2   **LG 3**   **P5–46**   **Inflation, time value, and annual deposits**   While vacationing in Florida, John Kelley saw the vacation home of his dreams. It was listed with a sale price of $200,000. The only catch is that John is 40 years old and plans to continue working until he is 65. Still, he believes that prices generally increase at the overall rate of inflation. John believes that he can earn 9% annually after taxes on his investments. He is willing to invest a fixed amount at the end of each of the next 25 years to fund the cash purchase of such a house (one that can be purchased today for $200,000) when he retires.

LG 6

a. Inflation is expected to average 5% per year for the next 25 years. What will John's dream house cost when he retires?

b. How much must John invest at the *end* of each of the next 25 years to have the cash purchase price of the house when he retires?

c. If John invests at the *beginning* instead of at the end of each of the next 25 years, how much must he invest each year?

LG 6   **P5–47**   **Loan payment**   Determine the equal, annual, end-of-year payment required each year over the life of the loans shown in the following table to repay them fully during the stated term of the loan.

Loan	Principal	Interest rate	Term of loan (years)
A	$12,000	8%	3
B	60,000	12	10
C	75,000	10	30
D	4,000	15	5

Personal Finance Problem

LG 6 **P5–48** **Loan amortization schedule** Joan Messineo borrowed $15,000 at a 14% annual rate of interest to be repaid over 3 years. The loan is amortized into three equal, annual, end-of-year payments.

a. Calculate the annual, end-of-year loan payment.

b. Prepare a loan amortization schedule showing the interest and principal breakdown of each of the three loan payments.

c. Explain why the interest portion of each payment declines with the passage of time.

LG 6 **P5–49** **Loan interest deductions** Liz Rogers just closed a $10,000 business loan that is to be repaid in three equal, annual, end-of-year payments. The interest rate on the loan is 13%. As part of her firm's detailed financial planning, Liz wishes to determine the annual interest deduction attributable to the loan. (Because it is a business loan, the interest portion of each loan payment is tax-deductible to the business.)

a. Determine the firm's annual loan payment.

b. Prepare an amortization schedule for the loan.

c. How much interest expense will Liz's firm have in *each* of the next 3 years as a result of this loan?

Personal Finance Problem

LG 6 **P5–50** **Monthly loan payments** Tim Smith is shopping for a used car. He has found one priced at $4,500. The dealer has told Tim that if he can come up with a down payment of $500, the dealer will finance the balance of the price at a 12% annual rate over 2 years (24 months).

a. Assuming that Tim accepts the dealer's offer, what will his *monthly* (end-of-month) payment amount be?

b. Use a financial calculator or spreadsheet to help you figure out what Tim's *monthly* payment would be if the dealer were willing to finance the balance of the car price at a 9% annual rate.

LG 6 **P5–51** **Growth rates** You are given the series of cash flows shown in the following table.

	Cash flows		
Year	A	B	C
1	$500	$1,500	$2,500
2	560	1,550	2,600
3	640	1,610	2,650
4	720	1,680	2,650
5	800	1,760	2,800
6		1,850	2,850
7		1,950	2,900
8		2,060	
9		2,170	
10		2,280	

a. Calculate the compound annual growth rate between the first and last payment in each stream.

b. If year-1 values represent initial deposits in a savings account paying annual interest, what is the annual rate of interest earned on each account?

c. Compare and discuss the growth rate and interest rate found in parts **a** and **b**, respectively.

Personal Finance Problem

LG 6   **P5–52**   **Rate of return** Rishi Singh has $1,500 to invest. His investment counselor suggests an investment that pays no stated interest but will return $2,000 at the end of 3 years.

a. What annual rate of return will Rishi earn with this investment?

b. Rishi is considering another investment, of equal risk, that earns an annual return of 8%. Which investment should he make, and why?

Personal Finance Problem

LG 6   **P5–53**   **Rate of return and investment choice** Clare Jaccard has $5,000 to invest. Because she is only 25 years old, she is not concerned about the length of the investment's life. What she is sensitive to is the rate of return she will earn on the investment. With the help of her financial advisor, Clare has isolated four equally risky investments, each providing a single amount at the end of its life, as shown in the following table. All the investments require an initial $5,000 payment.

Investment	Single amount	Investment life (years)
A	$ 8,400	6
B	15,900	15
C	7,600	4
D	13,000	10

a. Calculate, to the nearest 1%, the rate of return on each of the four investments available to Clare.

b. Which investment would you recommend to Clare, given her goal of maximizing the rate of return?

LG 6   **P5–54**   **Rate of return: Annuity** What is the rate of return on an investment of $10,606 if the company will receive $2,000 each year for the next 10 years?

Personal Finance Problem

LG 6   **P5–55**   **Choosing the best annuity** Raina Herzig wishes to choose the best of four immediate-retirement annuities available to her. In each case, in exchange for paying a single premium today, she will receive equal, annual, end-of-year cash benefits for a specified number of years. She considers the annuities to be equally risky and is not concerned about their differing lives. Her decision will be based solely on the rate of return she will earn on each annuity. The key terms of the four annuities are shown in the following table.

Annuity	Premium paid today	Annual benefit	Life (years)
A	$30,000	$3,100	20
B	25,000	3,900	10
C	40,000	4,200	15
D	35,000	4,000	12

a. Calculate to the nearest 1% the rate of return on each of the four annuities Raina is considering.
b. Given Raina's stated decision criterion, which annuity would you recommend?

Personal Finance Problem

 P5–56 **Interest rate for an annuity** Anna Waldheim was seriously injured in an industrial accident. She sued the responsible parties and was awarded a judgment of $2,000,000. Today, she and her attorney are attending a settlement conference with the defendants. The defendants have made an initial offer of $156,000 per year for 25 years. Anna plans to counteroffer at $255,000 per year for 25 years. Both the offer and the counteroffer have a present value of $2,000,000, the amount of the judgment. Both assume payments at the end of each year.
a. What interest rate assumption have the defendants used in their offer (rounded to the nearest whole percent)?
b. What interest rate assumption have Anna and her lawyer used in their counteroffer (rounded to the nearest whole percent)?
c. Anna is willing to settle for an annuity that carries an interest rate assumption of 9%. What annual payment would be acceptable to her?

Personal Finance Problem

 P5–57 **Loan rates of interest** John Flemming has been shopping for a loan to finance the purchase of a used car. He has found three possibilities that seem attractive and wishes to select the one with the lowest interest rate. The information available with respect to each of the three $5,000 loans is shown in the following table.

Loan	Principal	Annual payment	Term (years)
A	$5,000	$1,352.81	5
B	5,000	1,543.21	4
C	5,000	2,010.45	3

a. Determine the interest rate associated with each of the loans.
b. Which loan should John take?

 P5–58 **Number of years to equal future amount** For each of the following cases, determine the number of years it will take for the initial deposit to grow to equal the future amount at the given interest rate.

Case	Initial deposit	Future amount	Interest rate
A	$ 300	$ 1,000	7%
B	12,000	15,000	5
C	9,000	20,000	10
D	100	500	9
E	7,500	30,000	15

Personal Finance Problem

 P5–59 **Time to accumulate a given sum** Manuel Rios wishes to determine how long it will take an initial deposit of $10,000 to double.

    a. If Manuel earns 10% annual interest on the deposit, how long will it take for him to double his money?

    b. How long will it take if he earns only 7% annual interest?

    c. How long will it take if he can earn 12% annual interest?

    d. Reviewing your findings in parts **a, b,** and **c,** indicate what relationship exists between the interest rate and the amount of time it will take Manuel to double his money.

P5–60 **Number of years to provide a given return** In each of the following cases, determine the number of years that the given annual *end-of-year* cash flow must continue to provide the given rate of return on the given initial amount.

Case	Initial amount	Annual cash flow	Rate of return
A	$ 1,000	$ 250	11%
B	150,000	30,000	15
C	80,000	10,000	10
D	600	275	9
E	17,000	3,500	6

Personal Finance Problem

 P5–61 **Time to repay installment loan** Mia Salto wishes to determine how long it will take to repay a loan with initial proceeds of $14,000 where annual *end-of-year* installment payments of $2,450 are required.

    a. If Mia can borrow at a 12% annual rate of interest, how long will it take for her to repay the loan fully?

    b. How long will it take if she can borrow at a 9% annual rate?

    c. How long will it take if she has to pay 15% annual interest?

    d. Reviewing your answers in parts **a, b,** and **c,** describe the general relationship between the interest rate and the amount of time it will take Mia to repay the loan fully.

P5–62 **ETHICS PROBLEM** A manager at a "Check Into Cash" business defends his business practice as simply "charging what the market will bear." "After all," says the manager, "we don't force people to come in the door." How would you respond to this ethical defense of the payday-advance business?

Spreadsheet Exercise

At the end of 2015, Uma Corporation is considering undertaking a major long-term project in an effort to remain competitive in its industry. The production and sales departments have determined the potential annual cash flow savings that could accrue to the firm if it acts soon. Specifically, they estimate that a mixed stream of future cash flow savings will occur at the end of the years 2016 through 2021. The years 2022 through 2026 will see consecutive and equal cash flow savings at the end of each year. The firm estimates that its discount rate over the first 6 years will be 7%. The expected discount rate over the years 2022 through 2026 will be 11%.

The project managers will find the project acceptable if it results in present cash flow savings of at least $860,000. The following cash flow savings data are supplied to the finance department for analysis.

End of year	Cash flow savings
2016	$110,000
2017	120,000
2018	130,000
2019	150,000
2020	160,000
2021	150,000
2022	90,000
2023	90,000
2024	90,000
2025	90,000
2026	90,000

TO DO

Create spreadsheets similar to Table 5.2, and then answer the following questions.

a. Determine the value (at the beginning of 2016) of the future cash flow savings expected to be generated by this project.
b. Based solely on the one criterion set by management, should the firm undertake this specific project? Explain.
c. What is the "interest rate risk," and how might it influence the recommendation made in part **b**? Explain.

MyFinanceLab Visit **www.myfinancelab.com** for **Chapter Case: *Funding Jill Moran's Retirement Annuity,*** Group Exercises, and numerous online resources.

In Part 2, you learned how to use time-value-of-money tools to compare cash flows at different times. In the next two chapters, you'll put those tools to use valuing the two most common types of securities: bonds and stocks.

Chapter 6 introduces you to the world of interest rates and bonds. Although bonds are among the safest investments available, they are not without risk. The primary risk that bond investors face is the risk that market interest rates will fluctuate. Those fluctuations cause bond prices to move, and those movements affect the returns that bond investors earn. Chapter 6 explains why interest rates vary from one bond to another and the factors that cause interest rates to move.

Chapter 7 focuses on stock valuation. It explains the characteristics of stock that distinguish it from debt and describes how companies issue stock to investors. You'll have another chance to practice time-value-of-money techniques as Chapter 7 illustrates how to value stocks by discounting either (1) the dividends that stockholders receive or (2) the free cash flows that the firm generates over time.

6 Interest Rates and Bond Valuation

Why This Chapter Matters to You

In your *professional* life

ACCOUNTING You need to understand interest rates and the various types of bonds to be able to account properly for amortization of bond premiums and discounts and for bond issues and retirements.

INFORMATION SYSTEMS You need to understand the data that is necessary to track bond valuations and bond amortization schedules.

MANAGEMENT You need to understand the behavior of interest rates and how they affect the types of funds the firm can raise and the timing and cost of bond issues and retirements.

MARKETING You need to understand how the interest rate level and the firm's ability to issue bonds may affect the availability of financing for marketing research projects and new-product development.

OPERATIONS You need to understand how the interest rate level may affect the firm's ability to raise funds to maintain and grow the firm's production capacity.

In your *personal* life

Interest rates have a direct impact on personal financial planning. Movements in interest rates occur frequently and affect the returns from and values of savings and investments. The rate of interest you are charged on credit cards and loans can have a profound effect on your personal finances. Understanding the basics of interest rates is important to your personal financial success.

6.1 Interest Rates and Required Returns

As noted in Chapter 2, financial institutions and markets create the mechanism through which funds flow between savers (funds suppliers) and borrowers (funds demanders). All else being equal, savers would like to earn as much interest as possible, and borrowers would like to pay as little as possible. The interest rate prevailing in the market at any given time reflects the equilibrium between savers and borrowers.

INTEREST RATE FUNDAMENTALS

interest rate
Usually applied to debt instruments such as bank loans or bonds; the compensation paid by the borrower of funds to the lender; from the borrower's point of view, the cost of borrowing funds.

required return
Usually applied to equity instruments such as common stock; the cost of funds obtained by selling an ownership interest.

inflation
A rising trend in the prices of most goods and services.

liquidity preference
A general tendency for investors to prefer short-term (that is, more liquid) securities.

The *interest rate* or *required return* represents the cost of money. It is the compensation that a supplier of funds expects and a demander of funds must pay. Usually the term **interest rate** is applied to debt instruments such as bank loans or bonds, whereas the term **required return** may be applied to almost any kind of investment, including common stock, which gives the investor an ownership stake in the issuer. In fact, the meaning of these two terms is quite similar because in both cases the supplier is compensated for providing funds to the demander.

A variety of factors can influence the equilibrium interest rate. One factor is **inflation,** a rising trend in the prices of most goods and services. Typically, savers demand higher returns (that is, higher interest rates) when inflation is high because they want their investments to more than keep pace with rising prices. A second factor influencing interest rates is risk. When people perceive that a particular investment is riskier, they will expect a higher return on that investment as compensation for bearing the risk. A third factor that can affect the interest rate is a **liquidity preference** among investors. The term *liquidity preference* refers to the general tendency of investors to prefer short-term securities (that is, securities that are more liquid). If, all other things being equal, investors would prefer to buy short-term rather than long-term securities, interest rates on short-term instruments such as Treasury bills will be lower than rates on longer-term securities. Investors will hold these securities, despite the relatively low return that they offer, because they meet investors' preferences for liquidity.

Matter of fact

Fear Turns T-Bill Rates Negative

Near the height of the financial crisis in December 2008, interest rates on Treasury bills briefly turned negative, meaning that investors paid more to the Treasury than the Treasury promised to pay back. Why would anyone put their money into an investment that they *know* will lose money? Remember that 2008 saw the demise of Lehman Brothers, and fears that other commercial banks and investments banks might fail were rampant. Evidently, some investors were willing to pay the U.S. Treasury to keep their money safe for a short time.

real rate of interest
The rate that creates equilibrium between the supply of savings and the demand for investment funds in a perfect world, without inflation, where suppliers and demanders of funds have no liquidity preferences and there is no risk.

The Real Rate of Interest

Imagine a *perfect world* in which there is no inflation, in which investors have no liquidity preferences, and in which there is no risk. In this world, there would be one cost of money: the **real rate of interest.** The real rate of interest

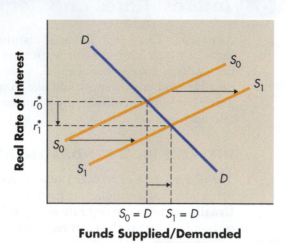

$$S_0 = D \quad S_1 = D$$

Funds Supplied/Demanded

creates equilibrium between the supply of savings and the demand for funds. It represents the most basic cost of money. Historically, the real rate of interest in the United States has averaged about 1 percent per year, but that figure does fluctuate over time. This supply–demand relationship is shown in Figure 6.1 by the supply function (labeled S_0) and the demand function (labeled D). An equilibrium between the supply of funds and the demand for funds ($S_0 = D$) occurs at a rat of interest r_0^*, the real rate of interest.

Clearly, the real rate of interest changes with changing economic conditions, tastes, and preferences. To combat a recession, the Board of Governors of the Federal Reserve System might initiate actions to increase the supply of credit in the economy, causing the supply function in Figure 6.1 to shift to, say, S_1. The result could be a lower real rate of interest, r_1^*, at equilibrium ($S_1 = D$). With a lower cost of money, firms might find that investments that were previously unattractive are now worth undertaking, and as firms hire more workers and spend more on plant and equipment, the economy begins to expand again.

Nominal or Actual Rate of Interest (Return)

nominal rate of interest
The actual rate of interest charged by the supplier of funds and paid by the demander.

The **nominal rate of interest** is the actual rate of interest charged by the supplier of funds and paid by the demander. *Throughout this book, interest rates and required rates of return are nominal rates unless otherwise noted.* The nominal rate of interest differs from the real rate of interest, r^*, as a result of two factors, inflation and risk. When people save money and invest it, they are sacrificing consumption today (that is, they are spending less than they could) in return for higher future consumption. When investors expect inflation to occur, they believe that the price of consuming goods and services will be higher in the future than in the present. Therefore, they will be reluctant to sacrifice today's consumption unless the return they can earn on the money they save (or invest) will be high enough to allow them to purchase the goods and services they desire at a higher future price. That is, *investors will demand a higher nominal rate of return if they expect inflation*. The additional return that investors require to compensate them for inflation is called the expected inflation premium (*IP*).

Similarly, investors generally demand higher rates of return on risky investments as compared to safe ones. Otherwise, there is little incentive for investors to bear the additional risk. Therefore, *investors will demand a higher nominal rate of return on risky investments.* The additional return that investors require to compensate them for bearing risk is called the risk premium (*RP*). Therefore, the nominal rate of interest for security 1, r_1, is given by

$$r_1 = \underbrace{r^* + IP}_{\substack{\text{risk-free} \\ \text{rate, } R_F}} + \underbrace{RP_1}_{\substack{\text{risk} \\ \text{premium}}} \tag{6.1}$$

As the horizontal braces below the equation indicate, the nominal rate, r_1, can be viewed as having two basic components: a risk-free rate of return, R_F, and a risk premium, RP_1:

$$r_1 = R_F + RP_1 \tag{6.2}$$

For the moment, ignore the risk premium, RP_1, and focus exclusively on the risk-free rate. Equation 6.1 says that the risk-free rate can be represented as

$$R_F = r^* + IP \tag{6.3}$$

The risk-free rate (as shown in Equation 6.3) embodies the real rate of interest plus the expected inflation premium. The inflation premium is driven by investors' expectations about inflation: The more inflation they expect, the higher will be the inflation premium, and the higher will be the nominal interest rate.

Three-month *U.S. Treasury bills (T-bills)* are short-term IOUs issued by the U.S. Treasury, and they are widely regarded as the safest investments in the world. They are as close as we can get in the real world to a risk-free investment. To estimate the real rate of interest, analysts typically try to determine what rate of inflation investors expect over the coming 3 months. Next, *they subtract the expected inflation rate from the nominal rate on the 3-month T-bill to arrive at the underlying real rate of interest.* For the risk-free asset in Equation 6.3, the real rate of interest, r^*, would equal $R_F - IP$. A simple personal finance example can demonstrate the practical distinction between nominal and real rates of interest.

Personal Finance Example 6.1 ▶

MyFinanceLab Solution
Video

Marilyn Carbo has $10 that she can spend on candy costing $0.25 per piece. She could buy 40 pieces of candy ($10.00 ÷ $0.25) today. The nominal rate of interest on a 1-year investment is currently 7%, and the expected rate of inflation over the coming year is 4%. Instead of buying the 40 pieces of candy today, Marilyn could invest the $10. After 1 year, she would have $10.70 because she would have earned 7% interest—an additional $0.70 (0.07 × $10.00)—on her $10 investment. During that year, inflation would have increased the cost of the candy by 4%—an additional $0.01 (0.04 × $0.25)—to $0.26 per piece. As a result, at the end of the 1-year period Marilyn would be able to buy about 41.2 pieces of candy ($10.70 ÷ $0.26), or roughly 3% more (41.2 ÷ 40.0 = 1.03). The 3% increase in Marilyn's buying power represents her real rate of return. The nominal rate of return on her investment (7%) is partly eroded by inflation (4%), so her real return during the year is the difference between the nominal rate and the inflation rate (7% − 4% = 3%).

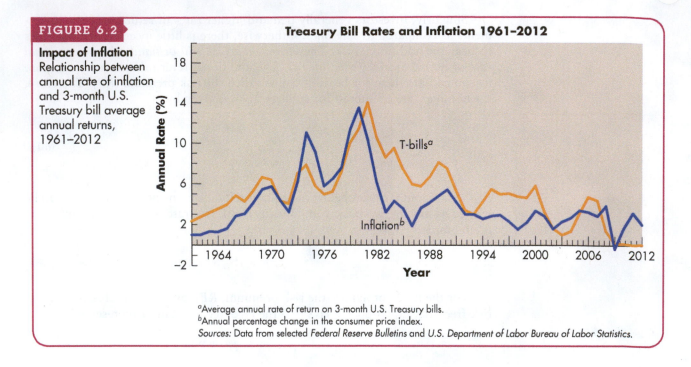

FIGURE 6.2

Impact of Inflation
Relationship between annual rate of inflation and 3-month U.S. Treasury bill average annual returns, 1961–2012

Treasury Bill Rates and Inflation 1961–2012

[a]Average annual rate of return on 3-month U.S. Treasury bills.
[b]Annual percentage change in the consumer price index.
Sources: Data from selected *Federal Reserve Bulletins* and *U.S. Department of Labor Bureau of Labor Statistics.*

The premium for *expected inflation* in Equation 6.3 represents the avera rate of *inflation* expected over the life of an investment. It is *not* the rate of infl tion experienced over the immediate past, although investors' inflation expectations are undoubtedly influenced by the rate of inflation that has occurred in the recent past. Even so, the inflation premium reflects the expected rate of inflation. The expected inflation premium changes over time in response to many factors, such as changes in monetary and fiscal policies, currency movements, and international political events.

Figure 6.2 illustrates the annual movement of the rate of inflation and the risk-free rate of return from 1961 through 2012. During this period, the two rates tended to move in a similar fashion. Note that T-bill rates were slightly above the inflation rate most of the time, meaning that T-bills generally offered a small positive real return. Between 1978 and the early 1980s, inflation and interest rates were quite high, peaking at more than 13 percent in 1980–1981. Since then, rates have gradually declined. To combat a severe recession, the Federal Reserve pushed interest rates down to almost 0% in 2009 and kept them there for several years. Note that over this entire period, the inflation rate was negative only once (in 2009). Even though the economy experienced a positive inflation rate each year from 2010 to 2012, the Fed kept interest rates near zero, so the real interest rate in those years was actually negative.

TERM STRUCTURE OF INTEREST RATES

term structure of interest rates
The relationship between the maturity and rate of return for bonds with similar levels of risk.

yield curve
A graphic depiction of the term structure of interest rates.

The **term structure of interest rates** is the relationship between the maturity and rate of return for bonds with similar levels of risk. A graph of this relationship is called the **yield curve.** A quick glance at the yield curve tells analysts how rates vary between short-, medium-, and long-term bonds, but it may also provi information on where interest rates and the economy in general are headed in the future. Usually, when analysts examine the term structure of interest rates, they focus on Treasury securities because they are generally considered to be free of default risk.

Yield Curves

yield to maturity (YTM)
Compound annual rate of return earned on a debt security purchased on a given day and held to maturity.

A bond's **yield to maturity (YTM)** (discussed later in this chapter) represents the compound annual rate of return that an investor earns on the bond, assuming that the bond makes all promised payments and the investor holds the bond to maturity. In a yield curve, the yield to maturity is plotted on the vertical axis and time to maturity is plotted on the horizontal axis. Figure 6.3 shows three yield curves for U.S. Treasury securities: one at May 22, 1981, a second at September 29, 1989, and a third at May 20, 2013.

Observe that both the position and the shape of the yield curves change over time. The yield curve of May 22, 1981, indicates that short-term interest rates at that time were above longer-term rates. For reasons that a glance at the figure makes obvious, this curve is described as *downward sloping*. Interest rates in May 1981 were also quite high by historical standards, so the overall level of the yield curve is high. Historically, a downward-sloping yield curve, which is sometimes called an **inverted yield curve,** occurs infrequently and is often a sign that the economy is weakening. Most recessions in the United States have been preceded by an inverted yield curve.

inverted yield curve
A *downward-sloping* yield curve indicates that short-term interest rates are generally higher than long-term interest rates.

normal yield curve
An *upward-sloping* yield curve indicates that long-term interest rates are generally higher than short-term interest rates.

Usually, short-term interest rates are lower than long-term interest rates, as they were on May 20, 2013. That is, the **normal yield curve** is *upward sloping*. Notice that the May 2013 yield curve lies entirely beneath the other two curves shown in Figure 6.3. In other words, interest rates in May 2013 were unusually low, largely because at that time the economy was still recovering from a deep recession, and the Federal Reserve was exerting downward pressure on interest rates to stimulate the economy. Sometimes, a **flat yield curve,** similar to that of September 29, 1989, exists. A flat yield curve simply means that rates do not vary much at different maturities.

flat yield curve
A yield curve that indicates that interest rates do not vary much at different maturities.

FIGURE 6.3

Treasury Yield Curves
Yield curves for U.S. Treasury securities: May 22, 1981; September 29, 1989; and May 20, 2013

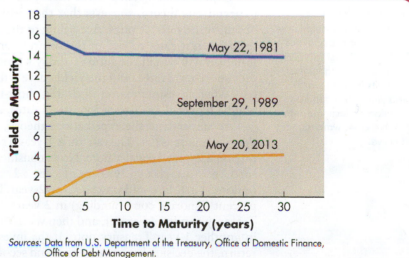

Sources: Data from U.S. Department of the Treasury, Office of Domestic Finance, Office of Debt Management.

The shape of the yield curve may affect the firm's financing decisions. A financial manager who faces a downward-sloping yield curve may be tempted to rely more heavily on cheaper, long-term financing. However, a risk in following this strategy is that interest rates may fall in the future, so long-term rates that seem cheap today may be relatively expensive tomorrow. Likewise, when the yield curve is upward sloping, the manager may believe that it is wise to use cheaper, short-term financing. Relying on short-term financing has its own risks. Firms that borrow on a short-term basis may see their costs rise if interest rates go up. Even more serious is the risk that a firm may not be able to refinance a short-term loan when it comes due. A variety of factors influence the choice of loan maturity, but the shape of the yield curve is something that managers must consider when making decisions about short-term versus long-term borrowing.

Matter of fact

Bond Yields Hit Record Lows

On July 25, 2012, the 10-year Treasury note and 30-year Treasury bond yields reached all-time lows of 1.43% and 2.46%. That was good news for the housing market. Many mortgage rates are linked to rates on Treasury securities. For example, the traditional 30-year mortgage rate is typically linked to the yield on 10-year Treasury notes. With mortgage rates reaching new lows, potential buyers found that they could afford more expensive homes, and existing homeowners were able to refinance their existing loans, lowering their monthly mortgage payments and leaving them with more money to spend on other things. This kind of activity is precisely what the Federal Reserve hoped to stimulate by keeping interest rates low during the economic recovery.

Theories of Term Structure

Three theories are frequently cited to explain the general shape of the yield curve: the expectations theory, the liquidity preference theory, and the market segmentation theory.

expectations theory
The theory that the yield curve reflects investor expectations about future interest rates; an expectation of rising interest rates results in an upward-sloping yield curve, and an expectation of declining rates results in a downward-sloping yield curve.

Expectations Theory   One theory of the term structure of interest rates, the **expectations theory,** suggests that the yield curve reflects investor expectations about future interest rates. According to this theory, when investors expect short-term interest rates to rise in the future (perhaps because investors believe that inflation will rise in the future), today's long-term rates will be higher than current short-term rates, and the yield curve will be upward sloping. The opposite is true when investors expect declining short-term rates: Today's short-term rates will be higher than current long-term rates, and the yield curve will be inverted.

To understand the expectations theory, consider this example. Suppose that the yield curve is flat. The rate on a 1-year Treasury note is 4 percent, and so is the rate on a 2-year Treasury note. Now, consider an investor who has money to place into a low-risk investment for 2 years. The investor has two options. First, he could purchase the 2-year Treasury note and receive a total of 8 percent (ignoring compounding) in 2 years. Second, he could invest in the 1-year Treasury earning 4 percent, and then when that security matures, he could reinvest in another 1-year Treasury note. If the investor wants to maximize his expected return, the decision between the first and second options above depends on whether he expects interest rates to rise, fall, or remain unchanged during the next year.

If the investor believes that interest rates will rise, it means next year's return on a 1-year Treasury note will be greater than 4 percent (that is, greater than the 1-year Treasury rate right now). Let's say the investor believes that the interest rate on a 1-year note next year will be 5 percent. If the investor expects rising rates, his expected return is higher if he follows the second option, buying a 1-year Treasury note now (paying 4 percent) and reinvesting in a new security that pays 5 percent next year. Over 2 years, the investor would expect to earn about 9 percent (ignoring compounding) in interest, compared to just 8 percent earned by holding the 2-year bond.

If the current 1-year rate is 4 percent and investors generally expect that rate to go up to 5 percent next year, what would the 2-year Treasury note rate have to be right now to remain competitive? The answer is 4.5 percent. An investor who buys this security and holds it for 2 years would earn about 9 percent interest (again, ignoring compounding), the same as the expected return from investing in two consecutive 1-year bonds. In other words, *if investors expect interest rates to rise, the 2-year rate today must be higher than the 1-year rate today, and that in turn means that the yield curve must have an upward slope.*

Example 6.2 ▶	Suppose that a 5-year Treasury note currently offers a 3% annual return. Investors believe that interest rates are going to decline, and 5 years from now, they expect the rate on a 5-year Treasury note to be 2.5%. According to the expectations theory, what is the return that a 10-year Treasury note has to offer today? What does this imply about the slope of the yield curve?
	Consider an investor who purchases a 5-year note today and plans to reinvest in another 5-year note in the future. Over the 10-year investment horizon, this investor expects to earn about 27.5%, ignoring compounding (that's 3% per year for the first 5 years and 2.5% per year for the next 5 years). To compete with that return, a 10-year bond today could offer 2.75% per year. That is, a bond that pays 2.75% for each of the next 10 years produces the same 27.5% total return that the series of two 5-year notes is expected to produce. Therefore, the 5-year rate today is 3% and the 10-year rate today is 2.75%, and the yield curve is downward sloping.

Liquidity Preference Theory Most of the time, yield curves are upward sloping, which, according to the expectations theory, means that investors expect interest rates to rise. An alternative explanation for the typical upward slope of the yield curve is the **liquidity preference theory**. This theory holds that, all else being equal, investors generally prefer to buy short-term securities, while issuers prefer to sell long-term securities. For investors, short-term securities are attractive because they are highly liquid and their prices are not particularly volatile.[1] Hence, investors will accept somewhat lower rates on short-term bonds because they are less risky than long-term bonds. Conversely, when firms or governments want to lock in their borrowing costs for a long period of time by selling long-term bonds, those bonds have to offer higher rates to entice investors away from the short-term securities that they prefer. Borrowers are willing to pay somewhat higher rates because long-term debt allows them to eliminate or reduce the risk of not being able to refinance

liquidity preference theory
Theory suggesting that long-term rates are generally higher than short-term rates (hence, the yield curve is upward sloping) because investors perceive short-term investments to be more liquid and less risky than long-term investments. Borrowers must offer higher rates on long-term bonds to entice investors away from their preferred short-term securities.

---

1. Later in this chapter, we demonstrate that debt instruments with longer maturities are more sensitive to changing market interest rates. For a given change in market rates, the price or value of longer-term debts will be more significantly changed (up or down) than the price or value of debts with shorter maturities.

short-term debts when they come due. Borrowing on a long-term basis also reduces uncertainty about future borrowing costs.

Market Segmentation Theory   The **market segmentation theory** suggests that the market for loans is totally segmented on the basis of maturity and that the supply of and demand for loans within each segment determine its prevailing interest rate. In other words, the equilibrium between suppliers and demanders of short-term funds, such as seasonal business loans, would determine prevailing short-term interest rates, and the equilibrium between suppliers and demanders of long-term funds, such as real estate loans, would determine prevailing long-term interest rates. The slope of the yield curve would be determined by the general relationship between the prevailing rates in each market segment. Simply stated, an upward-sloping yield curve indicates greater borrowing demand relative to the supply of funds in the long-term segment of the debt market relative to the short-term segment.

All three term structure theories have merit. From them, we can conclude that at any time the slope of the yield curve is affected by (1) interest rate expectations, (2) liquidity preferences, and (3) the comparative equilibrium of supply and demand in the short- and long-term market segments. Upward-sloping yield curves result from expectations of rising interest rates, lender preferences for shorter-maturity loans, and greater supply of short-term loans than of long-term loans relative to demand. The opposite conditions would result in a downward-sloping yield curve. At any time, the interaction of these three forces determines the prevailing slope of the yield curve.

RISK PREMIUMS: ISSUER AND ISSUE CHARACTERISTICS

So far, we have considered only risk-free U.S. Treasury securities. We now reintroduce the risk premium and assess it in view of risky non-Treasury issues. Recall Equation 6.1:

$$r_1 = \underbrace{r^* + IP}_{\substack{\text{risk-free} \\ \text{rate, } R_F}} + \underbrace{RP_1}_{\substack{\text{risk} \\ \text{premium}}}$$

In words, the nominal rate of interest for security 1 (r_1) is equal to the risk-free rate, consisting of the real rate of interest (r^*) plus the inflation expectation premium (IP), plus the risk premium (RP_1). The *risk premium* varies with specific issuer and issue characteristics.

Example 6.3 ▶

MyFinanceLab Solution
Video

The nominal interest rates on a number of classes of long-term securities in May 2013 were as follows:

Security	Nominal interest rate
U.S. Treasury bonds (average)	3.18%
Corporate bonds (by risk ratings):	
High quality (Aaa–Aa)	3.94%
Medium quality (A–Baa)	4.76%
Speculative (Ba–C)	5.46%

Because the U.S. Treasury bond would represent the risk-free, long-term security, we can calculate the risk premium of the other securities by subtracting the risk-free rate, 3.18%, from each nominal rate (yield):

Security	Risk premium
Corporate bonds (by ratings):	
High quality (Aaa–Aa)	3.94% − 3.18% = 0.76%
Medium quality (A–Baa)	4.76% − 3.18% = 1.58%
Speculative (Ba–C)	5.46% − 3.18% = 2.28%

These risk premiums reflect differing issuer and issue risks. The lower-rated (speculative) corporate issues have a higher risk premium than that of the higher-rated corporate issues (high quality and medium quality), and that risk premium is the compensation that investors demand for bearing the higher default risk of lower quality bonds.

The risk premium consists of a number of issuer- and issue-related components, including business risk, financial risk, interest rate risk, liquidity risk, and tax risk, as well as the purely debt-specific risks—default risk, maturity risk, and contractual provision risk—briefly defined in Table 6.1. In general, the highest risk premiums and therefore the highest returns result from securities issued by firms with a high risk of default and from long-term maturities that have unfavorable contractual provisions.

TABLE 6.1	Debt-Specific Risk Premium Components
Component	**Description**
Default risk	The possibility that the issuer of debt will not pay the contractual interest or principal as scheduled. The greater the uncertainty as to the borrower's ability to meet these payments, the greater the risk premium. High bond ratings reflect low default risk, and low bond ratings reflect high default risk.
Maturity risk	That the longer the maturity, the more the value of a security will change in response to a given change in interest rates. If interest rates on otherwise similar-risk securities suddenly rise, the prices of long-term bonds will decline by more than the prices of short-term bonds and vice versa.[a]
Contractual provision risk	Conditions that are often included in a debt agreement or a stock issue. Some of these reduce risk, whereas others may increase risk. For example, a provision allowing a bond issuer to retire its bonds prior to their maturity under favorable terms increases the bond's risk.

[a]A detailed discussion of the effects of interest rates on the price or value of bonds and other fixed-income securities is presented later in this chapter.

→ **REVIEW QUESTIONS**

6-1 What is the *real rate of interest*? Differentiate it from the *nominal rate of interest* for the risk-free asset, a 3-month U.S. Treasury bill.

6–2 What is the *term structure of interest rates,* and how is it related to the *yield curve*?

6–3 For a given class of similar-risk securities, what does each of the following yield curves reflect about interest rates: (**a**) downward sloping, (**b**) upward sloping, and (**c**) flat? What is the "normal" shape of the yield curve?

6–4 Briefly describe the following theories of the general shape of the yield curve: (**a**) expectations theory, (**b**) liquidity preference theory, and (**c**) market segmentation theory.

6–5 List and briefly describe the potential issuer- and issue-related risk components that are embodied in the risk premium. Which are the purely debt-specific risks?

  ## 6.2 Corporate Bonds

MyFinanceLab Video

corporate bond
A long-term debt instrument indicating that a corporation has borrowed a certain amount of money and promises to repay it in the future under clearly defined terms.

coupon interest rate
The percentage of a bond's par value that will be paid annually, typically in two equal semiannual payments, as interest.

bond indenture
A legal document that specifies both the rights of the bondholders and the duties of the issuing corporation.

standard debt provisions
Provisions in a *bond indenture* specifying certain record-keeping and general business practices that the bond issuer must follow; normally, they do not place a burden on a financially sound business.

restrictive covenants
Provisions in a *bond indenture* that place operating and financial constraints on the borrower.

A **corporate bond** is a long-term debt instrument indicating that a corporation has borrowed a certain amount of money and promises to repay it in the future under clearly defined terms. Most bonds are issued with maturities of 10 to 30 years and with a par value, or face value, of $1,000. The **coupon interest rate** on a bond represents the percentage of the bond's par value that will be paid annually, typically in two equal semiannual payments, as interest. The bondholders, who are the lenders, are promised the semiannual interest payments and, at maturity, repayment of the principal amount.

LEGAL ASPECTS OF CORPORATE BONDS

Certain legal arrangements are required to protect purchasers of bonds. Bondholders are protected primarily through the indenture and the trustee.

Bond Indenture

A **bond indenture** is a legal document that specifies both the rights of the bondholders and the duties of the issuing corporation. Included in the indenture are descriptions of the amount and timing of all interest and principal payments, various standard and restrictive provisions, and, frequently, sinking-fund requirements and security interest provisions. The borrower commonly must (1) *maintain satisfactory accounting records* in accordance with generally accepted accounting principles (GAAP), (2) periodically *supply audited financial statements,* (3) *pay taxes and other liabilities when due,* and (4) *maintain all facilities in good working order.*

Standard Provisions   The **standard debt provisions** in the bond indenture specify certain record-keeping and general business practices that the bond issuer must follow.

Restrictive Provisions   Bond indentures also normally include certain **restrictive covenants,** which place operating and financial constraints on the borrower. These provisions help protect the bondholder against increases in borrower risk. Without them, the borrower could increase the firm's risk but not have to pay increased interest to compensate for the increased risk.

The most common restrictive covenants do the following:

1. Require a *minimum level of liquidity,* to ensure against loan default.
2. *Prohibit the sale of accounts receivable* to generate cash. Selling receivables could cause a long-run cash shortage if proceeds were used to meet current obligations.
3. Impose *fixed-asset restrictions.* The borrower must maintain a specified level of fixed assets to guarantee its ability to repay the bonds.
4. *Constrain subsequent borrowing.* Additional long-term debt may be prohibited, or additional borrowing may be *subordinated* to the original loan. **Subordination** means that subsequent creditors agree to wait until all claims of the *senior debt* are satisfied.
5. *Limit the firm's annual cash dividend payments* to a specified percentage or amount.

Other restrictive covenants are sometimes included in bond indentures.

The violation of any standard or restrictive provision by the borrower gives the bondholders the right to demand immediate repayment of the debt. Generally, bondholders evaluate any violation to determine whether it jeopardizes the loan. They may then decide to demand immediate repayment, continue the loan, or alter the terms of the bond indenture.

subordination
In a bond indenture, the stipulation that subsequent creditors agree to wait until all claims of the *senior debt* are satisfied.

Sinking-Fund Requirements Another common restrictive provision is a **sinking-fund requirement.** Its objective is to provide for the systematic retirement of bonds prior to their maturity. To carry out this requirement, the corporation makes semiannual or annual payments that are used to retire bonds by purchasing them in the marketplace.

sinking-fund requirement
A restrictive provision often included in a bond indenture, providing for the systematic retirement of bonds prior to their maturity.

Security Interest The bond indenture identifies any collateral pledged against the bond and specifies how it is to be maintained. The protection of bond collateral is crucial to guarantee the safety of a bond issue.

Trustee

trustee
A paid individual, corporation, or commercial bank trust department that acts as the third party to a *bond indenture* and can take specified actions on behalf of the bondholders if the terms of the indenture are violated.

A **trustee** is a third party to a *bond indenture*. The trustee can be an individual, a corporation, or (most often) a commercial bank trust department. The trustee is paid to act as a "watchdog" on behalf of the bondholders and can take specified actions on behalf of the bondholders if the terms of the indenture are violated.

COST OF BONDS TO THE ISSUER

The cost of bond financing is generally greater than the issuer would have to pay for short-term borrowing. The major factors that affect the cost, which is the rate of interest paid by the bond issuer, are the bond's maturity, the size of the offering, the issuer's risk, and the basic cost of money.

Impact of Bond Maturity

Generally, as we noted earlier in Section 6.1, long-term debt pays higher interest rates than short-term debt. In a practical sense, the longer the maturity of a bond, the less accuracy there is in predicting future interest rates and therefore the greater the bondholders' risk of giving up an opportunity to lend money at a higher rate. In addition, the longer the term, the greater the chance that the issuer might default.

Impact of Offering Size

The size of the bond offering also affects the interest cost of borrowing but in an inverse manner: Bond flotation and administration costs per dollar borrowed are likely to decrease with increasing offering size. On the other hand, the risk to the bondholders may increase, because larger offerings result in greater risk of default.

Impact of Issuer's Risk

The greater the issuer's *default risk*, the higher the interest rate. Some of this risk can be reduced through inclusion of appropriate restrictive provisions in the bond indenture. Clearly, bondholders must be compensated with higher returns for taking greater risk. Frequently, bond buyers rely on bond ratings (discussed later) to determine the issuer's overall risk.

Impact of the Cost of Money

The cost of money in the capital market is the basis for determining a bond's coupon interest rate. Generally, the rate on U.S. Treasury securities of equal maturity is used as the lowest-risk cost of money. To that basic rate is added a *risk premium* (as described earlier in this chapter) that reflects the factors mentioned above (maturity, offering size, and issuer's risk).

GENERAL FEATURES OF A BOND ISSUE

Three features sometimes included in a corporate bond issue are a conversion feature, a call feature, and stock purchase warrants. These features provide the issuer or the purchaser with certain opportunities for replacing or retiring the bond or supplementing it with some type of equity issue.

conversion feature
A feature of *convertible bonds* that allows bondholders to change each bond into a stated number of shares of common stock.

Convertible bonds offer a **conversion feature** that allows bondholders to change each bond into a stated number of shares of common stock. Bondholders convert their bonds into stock only when the market price of the stock is such that conversion will provide a profit for the bondholder. Inclusion of the conversion feature by the issuer lowers the interest cost and provides for automatic conversion of the bonds to stock if future stock prices appreciate noticeably.

call feature
A feature included in nearly all corporate bond issues that gives the issuer the opportunity to repurchase bonds at a stated *call price* prior to maturity.

The **call feature** is included in nearly all corporate bond issues. It gives the issuer the opportunity to repurchase bonds prior to maturity. The **call price** is the stated price at which bonds may be repurchased prior to maturity. Sometimes the call feature can be exercised only during a certain period. As a rule, the call price exceeds the par value of a bond by an amount equal to 1 year's interest. For example, a $1,000 bond with a 10 percent coupon interest rate would be callable for around $1,100 [$1,000 + (10% × $1,000)]. The amount by which the call price exceeds the bond's par value is commonly referred to as the **call premium**. This premium compensates bondholders for having the bond called away from them; to the issuer, it is the cost of calling the bonds.

call price
The stated price at which a bond may be repurchased, by use of a *call feature*, prior to maturity.

call premium
The amount by which a bond's *call price* exceeds its par value.

The call feature enables an issuer to call an outstanding bond when interest rates fall and issue a new bond at a lower interest rate. When interest rates rise, the call privilege will not be exercised, except possibly to meet *sinking-fund requirements*. Of course, to sell a callable bond in the first place, the issuer must pay a higher interest rate than on noncallable bonds of equal risk, to compensate bondholders for the risk of having the bonds called away from them.

Bonds occasionally have stock purchase warrants attached as "sweeteners" to make them more attractive to prospective buyers. **Stock purchase warrants** are instruments that give their holders the right to purchase a certain number of shares of the issuer's common stock at a specified price over a certain period of time. Their inclusion typically enables the issuer to pay a slightly lower coupon interest rate than would otherwise be required.

stock purchase warrants
Instruments that give their holders the right to purchase a certain number of shares of the issuer's common stock at a specified price over a certain period of time.

BOND YIELDS

The *yield*, or rate of return, on a bond is frequently used to assess a bond's performance over a given period of time, typically 1 year. Because there are a number of ways to measure a bond's yield, it is important to understand popular yield measures. The three most widely cited bond yields are (1) *current yield*, (2) *yield to maturity (YTM)*, and (3) *yield to call (YTC)*. Each of these yields provides a unique measure of the return on a bond.

The simplest yield measure is the **current yield,** the annual interest payment divided by the current price. For example, a $1,000 par value bond with an 8 percent coupon interest rate that currently sells for $970 would have a current yield of 8.25% $[(0.08 \times \$1,000) \div \$970]$. This measure indicates the cash return for the year from the bond. However, because current yield ignores any change in bond value, it does not measure the total return. As we'll see later in this chapter, both the yield to maturity and the yield to call measure the total return.

current yield
A measure of a bond's cash return for the year; calculated by dividing the bond's annual interest payment by its current price.

BOND PRICES

Because most corporate bonds are purchased and held by institutional investors, such as banks, insurance companies, and mutual funds, rather than individual investors, bond trading and price data are not readily available to individuals. Table 6.2 includes some data on the bonds of five companies, noted A through E. Looking at the data for Company C's bond, which is highlighted in the table, we see that the bond has a coupon interest rate of 5.200 percent and a maturity date of January 15, 2017. These data identify a specific bond issued by Company C. (The company could have more than a single bond issue outstanding.) The price represents the final price at which the bond traded on the current day.

Although most corporate bonds are issued with a *par*, or *face value* of $1,000, *all bonds are quoted as a percentage of par*. A $1,000 par-value bond quoted at 94.007 is priced at $940.07 (94.007% $\times$ $1,000). Corporate bonds

TABLE 6.2 Data on Selected Bonds				
Company	Coupon	Maturity	Price	Yield (YTM)
Company A	4.125%	Nov. 15, 2014	998.521	4.28%
Company B	4.000	Oct. 31, 2039	94.007	4.54
Company C	5.200	Jan. 15, 2017	103.143	4.34
Company D	3.150	Jan. 15, 2020	95.140	3.96
Company E	3.850	Jan. 14, 2015	100.876	3.40

are quoted in dollars and cents. Thus, Company C's price of 103.143 for the day was $1,031.43 (that is, 103.143% × $1,000).

The final column of Table 6.2 represents the bond's *yield to maturity (YTM)*, which is the compound annual rate of return that would be earned on the bond if it were purchased and held to maturity. (YTM is discussed in detail later in this chapter.)

BOND RATINGS

Independent agencies such as Moody's, Fitch, and Standard & Poor's assess the riskiness of publicly traded bond issues. These agencies derive their ratings by using financial ratio and cash flow analyses to assess the likely payment of bond interest and principal. Table 6.3 summarizes these ratings. For discussion of ethical issues related to the bond-rating agencies, see the *Focus on Ethics* box.

Normally, an inverse relationship exists between the quality of a bond and the rate of return that it must provide bondholders: High-quality (high-rated) bonds provide lower returns than lower-quality (low-rated) bonds, reflecting the lender's risk–return trade-off. When considering bond financing, the financial manager must be concerned with the expected ratings of the bond issue because these ratings affect salability and cost.

---

focus on ETHICS

Can We Trust the Bond Raters?

in practice Moody's Investors Service, Standard & Poor's, and Fitch Ratings play a crucial role in the financial markets. These credit-rating agencies evaluate and attach ratings to credit instruments (for example, bonds). Historically, bonds that received higher ratings were almost always repaid, whereas lower-rated, more speculative "junk" bonds experienced much higher default rates. The agencies' ratings have a direct impact on firms' costs of raising external capital and investors' appraisals of fixed-income investments.

Recently, the credit-rating agencies have been criticized for their role in the subprime crisis. The agencies attached ratings to complex securities that did not reflect the true risk of the underlying investments. For example, securities backed by mortgages issued to borrowers with bad credit and no documented income often received investment-grade ratings that implied almost zero probability of default. However, when home prices began to decline in 2006, securities backed by risky mortgages did default, including many that had been rated investment grade.

It is not entirely clear why the rating agencies assigned such high ratings to these securities. Did the agencies believe that complex financial engineering could create investment-grade securities out of risky mortgage loans? Did the agencies understand the securities they were rating? Were they unduly influenced by the security issuers, who also happened to pay for the ratings? Apparently, some within the rating agencies were suspicious. In a December 2006 e-mail exchange between colleagues at Standard & Poor's, one individual proclaimed, "Let's hope we are all wealthy and retired by the time this house of cards falters."[a]

▶ *What ethical issues may arise because the companies that issue bonds pay the rating agencies to rate their bonds?*

---

[a] http://oversight.house.gov/images/stories/Hearings/Committee_on_Oversight/E-mail_from_Belinda_Ghetti_to_Nicole_Billick_et_al._December_16_2006.pdf

TABLE 6.3	Moody's and Standard & Poor's Bond Ratings		
Moody's	**Interpretation**	**Standard & Poor's**	**Interpretation**
Aaa	Prime quality	AAA	Investment grade
Aa	High grade	AA	
A	Upper medium grade	A	
Baa	Medium grade	BBB	
Ba	Lower medium grade	BB	Speculative
	or speculative	B	
B	Speculative		
Caa	From very speculative	CCC	
Ca	to near or in default	CC	
C	Lowest grade	C	Income bond
		D	In default

Note: Some ratings may be modified to show relative standing within a major rating category; for example, Moody's uses numerical modifiers (1, 2, 3), whereas Standard & Poor's uses plus (+) and minus (−) signs.

Sources: Moody's Investors Service, Inc., and Standard & Poor's Corporation.

COMMON TYPES OF BONDS

debentures
subordinated debentures
income bonds
mortgage bonds
collateral trust bonds
equipment trust certificates
See Table 6.4.

zero- (or low-) coupon bonds
junk bonds
floating-rate bonds
extendible notes
putable bonds
See Table 6.5.

Bonds can be classified in a variety of ways. Here we break them into traditional bonds (the basic types that have been around for years) and contemporary bonds (newer, more innovative types). The traditional types of bonds are summarized in terms of their key characteristics and priority of lender's claim in Table 6.4. Note that the first three types—**debentures, subordinated debentures,** and **income bonds**—are unsecured, whereas the last three—**mortgage bonds, collateral trust bonds,** and **equipment trust certificates**—are secured.

Table 6.5 (see page 229) describes the key characteristics of five contemporary types of bonds: **zero- (or low-) coupon bonds, junk bonds, floating-rate bonds, extendible notes,** and **putable bonds.** These bonds can be either unsecured or secured. Changing capital market conditions and investor preferences have spurred further innovations in bond financing in recent years and will probably continue to do so.

INTERNATIONAL BOND ISSUES

Eurobond
A bond issued by an international borrower and sold to investors in countries with currencies other than the currency in which the bond is denominated.

Companies and governments borrow internationally by issuing bonds in two principal financial markets: the Eurobond market and the foreign bond market. Both give borrowers the opportunity to obtain large amounts of long-term debt financing quickly, in the currency of their choice and with flexible repayment terms.

A **Eurobond** is issued by an international borrower and sold to investors in countries with currencies other than the currency in which the bond is denominated. An example is a dollar-denominated bond issued by a U.S. corporation and sold to Belgian investors. From the founding of the Eurobond market in the 1960s until the mid-1980s, "blue chip" U.S. corporations were the largest single class of Eurobond issuers. Some of these companies were able to borrow in this market at interest rates below those the U.S. government paid on Treasury bonds. As the market matured, issuers became able to choose the currency in which they borrowed, and European and Japanese borrowers rose to prominence. In more

TABLE 6.4 **Characteristics and Priority of Lender's Claim of Traditional Types of Bonds**

Bond type	Characteristics	Priority of lender's claim
Unsecured bonds		
Debentures	Unsecured bonds that only creditworthy firms can issue. Convertible bonds are normally debentures.	Claims are the same as those of any general creditor. May have other unsecured bonds subordinated to them.
Subordinated debentures	Claims are not satisfied until those of the creditors holding certain (senior) debts have been fully satisfied.	Claim is that of a general creditor but not as good as a senior debt claim.
Income bonds	Payment of interest is required only when earnings are available. Commonly issued in reorganization of a failing firm.	Claim is that of a general creditor. Are not in default when interest payments are missed because they are contingent only on earnings being available.
Secured Bonds		
Mortgage bonds	Secured by real estate or buildings.	Claim is on proceeds from sale of mortgaged assets; if not fully satisfied, the lender becomes a general creditor. The *first-mortgage* claim must be fully satisfied before distribution of proceeds to *second-mortgage* holders and so on. A number of mortgages can be issued against the same collateral.
Collateral trust bonds	Secured by stock and (or) bonds that are owned by the issuer. Collateral value is generally 25% to 35% greater than bond value.	Claim is on proceeds from stock and/or bond collateral; if not fully satisfied, the lender becomes a general creditor.
Equipment trust certificates	Used to finance "rolling stock," such as airplanes, trucks, boats, railroad cars. A trustee buys the asset with funds raised through the sale of trust certificates and then leases it to the firm; after making the final scheduled lease payment, the firm receives title to the asset. A type of leasing.	Claim is on proceeds from the sale of the asset; if proceeds do not satisfy outstanding debt, trust certificate lenders become general creditors.

foreign bond
A bond that is issued by a foreign corporation or government and is denominated in the investor's home currency and sold in the investor's home market.

recent years, the Eurobond market has become much more balanced in terms of the mix of borrowers, total issue volume, and currency of denomination.

In contrast, a **foreign bond** is issued by a foreign corporation or government and is denominated in the investor's home currency and sold in the investor's home market. A Swiss-franc–denominated bond issued in Switzerland by a U.S. company is an example of a foreign bond. The three largest foreign-bond markets are Japan, Switzerland, and the United States.

→ **REVIEW QUESTIONS**

6–6 What are typical maturities, denominations, and interest payments of a corporate bond? What mechanisms protect bondholders?

6–7 Differentiate between *standard debt provisions* and *restrictive covenants* included in a bond indenture. What are the consequences if a bond issuer violates any of these covenants?

TABLE 6.5 > Characteristics of Contemporary Types of Bonds	
Bond type	**Characteristics**[a]
Zero- (or low-) coupon bonds	Issued with no (zero) or a very low coupon (stated interest) rate and sold at a large discount from par. A significant portion (or all) of the investor's return comes from gain in value (that is, par value minus purchase price). Generally callable at par value.
Junk bonds	Debt rated Ba or lower by Moody's or BB or lower by Standard & Poor's. Commonly used by rapidly growing firms to obtain growth capital, most often as a way to finance mergers and takeovers. High-risk bonds with high yields, often yielding 2% to 3% more than the best-quality corporate debt.
Floating-rate bonds	Stated interest rate is adjusted periodically within stated limits in response to changes in specified money market or capital market rates. Popular when future inflation and interest rates are uncertain. Tend to sell at close to par because of the automatic adjustment to changing market conditions. Some issues provide for annual redemption at par at the option of the bondholder.
Extendible notes	Short maturities, typically 1 to 5 years, that can be renewed for a similar period at the option of holders. Similar to a floating-rate bond. An issue might be a series of 3-year renewable notes over a period of 15 years; every 3 years, the notes could be extended for another 3 years, at a new rate competitive with market interest rates at the time of renewal.
Putable bonds	Bonds that can be redeemed at par (typically, $1,000) at the option of their holder either at specific dates after the date of issue and every 1 to 5 years thereafter or when and if the firm takes specified actions, such as being acquired, acquiring another company, or issuing a large amount of additional debt. In return for its conferring the right to "put the bond" at specified times or when the firm takes certain actions, the bond's yield is lower than that of a nonputable bond.

[a] The claims of lenders (that is, bondholders) against issuers of each of these types of bonds vary, depending on the bonds' other features. Each of these bonds can be unsecured or secured.

6–8 How is the cost of bond financing typically related to the cost of short-term borrowing? In addition to a bond's maturity, what other major factors affect its cost to the issuer?

6–9 What is a *conversion feature?* A *call feature?* What are *stock purchase warrants?*

6–10 What is the *current yield* for a bond? How are bond prices quoted? How are bonds rated, and why?

6–11 Compare the basic characteristics of *Eurobonds* and *foreign bonds*.

6.3 Valuation Fundamentals

valuation
The process that links risk and return to determine the worth of an asset.

Valuation is the process that links risk and return to determine the worth of an asset. It is a relatively simple process that can be applied to *expected* streams of benefits from bonds, stocks, income properties, oil wells, and so on. To determine an asset's worth at a given point in time, a financial manager uses the time-value-of-money techniques presented in Chapter 5 and the concepts of risk and return that we will develop in Chapter 8.

KEY INPUTS

There are three key inputs to the valuation process: (1) cash flows (returns), (2) timing, and (3) a measure of risk, which determines the required return. Each is described below.

Cash Flows (Returns)

The value of any asset depends on the cash flow(s) it is *expected* to provide over the ownership period. To have value, an asset does not have to provide an annual cash flow; it can provide an intermittent cash flow or even a single cash flow over the period.

Personal Finance Example 6.4 ▶ Celia Sargent wishes to estimate the value of three assets she is considering investing in: common stock in Michaels Enterprises, an interest in an oil well, and an original painting by a well-known artist. Her cash flow estimates for each are as follows:

Stock in Michaels Enterprises *Expect* to receive cash dividends of $300 per year indefinitely.

Oil well *Expect* to receive cash flow of $2,000 at the end of year 1, $4,000 at the end of year 2, and $10,000 at the end of year 4, when the well is to be sold.

Original painting *Expect* to be able to sell the painting in 5 years for $85,000.

With these cash flow estimates, Celia has taken the first step toward placing a value on each of the assets.

Timing

In addition to making cash flow estimates, we must know the timing of the cash flows.[2] For example, Celia expects the cash flows of $2,000, $4,000, and $10,000 for the oil well to occur at the ends of years 1, 2, and 4, respectively. The combination of the cash flow and its timing fully defines the return expected from the asset.

Risk and Required Return

The level of risk associated with a given cash flow can significantly affect its value. In general, the greater the risk of (or the less certain) a cash flow, the lower its value. Greater risk can be incorporated into a valuation analysis by using a higher required return or discount rate. The higher the risk, the greater the required return, and the lower the risk, the less the required return.

Personal Finance Example 6.5 ▶ Let's return to Celia Sargent's task of placing a value on the original painting and consider two scenarios.

Scenario 1: Certainty A major art gallery has contracted to buy the painting for $85,000 at the end of 5 years. Because this contract is considered a certain

---

2. Although cash flows can occur at any time during a year, for computational convenience as well as custom, we will assume that they occur at the *end of the year* unless otherwise noted.

situation, Celia views this asset as "money in the bank." She thus would use the prevailing risk-free rate of 3% as the required return when calculating the value of the painting.

Scenario 2: High risk The values of original paintings by this artist have fluctuated widely over the past 10 years. Although Celia expects to be able to sell the painting for $85,000, she realizes that its sale price in 5 years could range between $30,000 and $140,000. Because of the high uncertainty surrounding the painting's value, Celia believes that a 15% required return is appropriate.

These two estimates of the appropriate required return illustrate how this rate captures risk. The often subjective nature of such estimates is also evident.

BASIC VALUATION MODEL

Simply stated, the value of any asset is *the present value of all future cash flows it is expected to provide over the relevant time period.* The time period can be any length, even infinity. The value of an asset is therefore determined by discounting the expected cash flows back to their present value, using the required return commensurate with the asset's risk as the appropriate discount rate. Using the present value techniques explained in Chapter 5, we can express the value of any asset at time zero, V_0, as

$$V_0 = \frac{CF_1}{(1 + r)^1} + \frac{CF_2}{(1 + r)^2} + \cdots + \frac{CF_n}{(1 + r)^n} \qquad (6.4)$$

where

$$V_0 = \text{value of the asset at time zero}$$
$$CF_t = \text{cash flow } expected \text{ at the end of year } t$$
$$r = \text{appropriate required return (discount rate)}$$
$$n = \text{relevant time period}$$

We can use Equation 6.4 to determine the value of any asset.

IRF Personal Finance Example 6.6 ▶ Celia Sargent uses Equation 6.4 to calculate the value of each asset. She values Michaels Enterprises stock using Equation 5.7 on page 171, which says that the present value of a perpetuity equals the annual payment divided by the required return. In the case of Michaels stock, the annual cash flow is $300, and Celia decides that a 12% discount rate is appropriate for this investment. Therefore, her estimate of the value of Michaels Enterprises stock is

$$\$300 \div 0.12 = \$2,500$$

Next, Celia values the oil well investment, which she believes is the most risky of the three investments. Using a 20% required return, Celia estimates the oil well's value to be

$$\frac{\$2,000}{(1 + 0.20)^1} + \frac{\$4,000}{(1 + 0.20)^2} + \frac{\$10,000}{(1 + 0.20)^4} = \$9,266.98$$

Finally, Celia estimates the value of the painting by discounting the expected $85,000 lump sum payment in 5 years at 15%:

$$\$85{,}000 \div (1 + 0.15)^5 = \$42{,}260.02$$

Note that, regardless of the pattern of the expected cash flow from an asset, the basic valuation equation can be used to determine its value.

→ REVIEW QUESTIONS

6–12 Why is it important for financial managers to understand the valuation process?

6–13 What are the three key inputs to the valuation process?

6–14 Does the valuation process apply only to assets that provide an annual cash flow? Explain.

6–15 Define and specify the general equation for the value of any asset, V_0.

LG 5   LG 6   ## 6.4 Bond Valuation

The basic valuation equation can be customized for use in valuing specific securities: bonds, common stock, and preferred stock. We describe bond valuation in this chapter, and valuation of common stock and preferred stock are discussed in Chapter 7.

BOND FUNDAMENTALS

As noted earlier in this chapter, *bonds* are long-term debt instruments used by business and government to raise large sums of money, typically from a diverse group of lenders. Most corporate bonds pay interest *semiannually* (every 6 months) at a stated *coupon interest rate*, have an initial *maturity* of 10 to 30 years, and have a *par value*, or *face value*, of $1,000 that must be repaid at maturity.

Example 6.7 ▶ Mills Company, a large defense contractor, on January 1, 2014, issued a 10% coupon interest rate, 10-year bond with a $1,000 par value that pays interest annually. Investors who buy this bond receive the contractual right to two cash flows: (1) $100 annual interest (10% coupon interest rate × $1,000 par value) distributed at the end of each year and (2) the $1,000 par value at the end of the tenth year.

We will use data for Mills's bond issue to look at basic bond valuation.

BASIC BOND VALUATION

The value of a bond is the present value of the payments its issuer is contractually obligated to make, from the current time until it matures. The basic model for the value, B_0, of a bond is given by

$$B_0 = I \times \left[\sum_{t=1}^{n} \frac{1}{(1 + r_d)^t} \right] + M \times \left[\frac{1}{(1 + r_d)^n} \right] \tag{6.5}$$

where

$$
\begin{aligned}
B_0 &= \text{value of the bond at time zero} \\
I &= \textit{annual} \text{ interest paid in dollars} \\
n &= \text{number of years to maturity} \\
M &= \text{par value in dollars} \\
r_d &= \text{required return on the bond}
\end{aligned}
$$

We can calculate bond value by using Equation 6.5 and a financial calculator or by using a spreadsheet.

IRF **Personal Finance Example 6.8** ▶ Tim Sanchez wishes to determine the current value of the Mills Company bond. *Assuming that interest on the Mills Company bond issue is paid annually* and that the required return is equal to the bond's coupon interest rate, $I = \$100, r_d = 10\%, M = \$1,000$, and $n = 10$ years.

The computations involved in finding the bond value are depicted graphically on the following time line.

Time line for bond valuation (Mills Company's 10% coupon interest rate, 10-year maturity, $1,000 par, January 1, 2014, issue date, paying annual interest, and required rate of return of 10%)

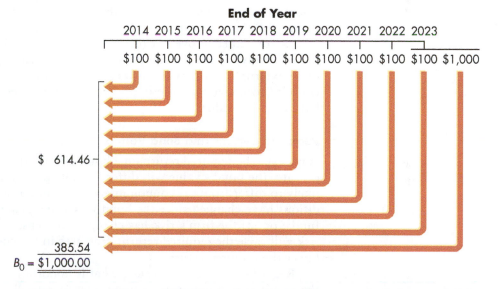

MyFinanceLab Financial Calculator

Input	Function
10	N
10	I
100	PMT
1000	FV
	CPT
	PV

Solution
−1,000

Calculator use using the Mills Company's inputs shown at the left, you should find the bond value to be exactly $1,000. Note that *the calculated bond value is equal to its par value, which will always be the case when the required return is equal to the coupon interest rate.*[3]

Spreadsheet use The value of the Mills Company bond also can be calculated as shown in the following Excel spreadsheet.

---

3. Note that because bonds pay interest in arrears, the prices at which they are quoted and traded reflect their value *plus* any accrued interest. For example, a $1,000 par value, 10% coupon bond paying interest semiannually and having a calculated value of $900 would pay interest of $50 at the end of each 6-month period. If it is now 3 months since the beginning of the interest period, three-sixths of the $50 interest, or $25 (that is, 3/6 × $50), would be accrued. The bond would therefore be quoted at $925: its $900 value plus the $25 in accrued interest. For convenience, *throughout this book, bond values will always be assumed to be calculated at the beginning of the interest period*, thereby avoiding the need to consider accrued interest.

	A	B
1	VALUATION FOR ANNUAL BOND	
2	Par value	$1,000
3	Coupon interest rate	10%
4	Annual Interest payment	$100
5	Required rate of return	10%
6	Number of years to maturity	10
7	Bond value	−$1,000.00

Entry in Cell B7 is =PV(B3,B6,B4,B2,0).
The minus sign appears before the $1,000.00 in B7
because the bond's price is a cost for the investor.

BOND VALUE BEHAVIOR

In practice, the value of a bond in the marketplace is rarely equal to its par value. In the bond data (see Table 6.2 on page 225), you can see that the prices of bonds often differ from their par values of 100 (100 percent of par, or $1,000). Some bonds are valued below par (current price below 100), and others are valued above par (current price above 100). A variety of forces in the economy, as well as the passage of time, tend to affect value. Although these external forces are in no way controlled by bond issuers or investors, it is useful to understand the impact that required return and time to maturity have on bond value.

Required Returns and Bond Values

Whenever the required return on a bond differs from the bond's coupon interest rate, the bond's value will differ from its par value. The required return is likely to differ from the coupon interest rate because either (1) economic conditions have changed since the bond was issued, causing a shift in the cost of funds; or (2) the firm's risk has changed. Increases in the cost of funds or in risk will raise the required return; decreases in the cost of funds or in risk will lower the required return.

Regardless of the exact cause, what is important is the relationship between the required return and the coupon interest rate: When the required return is greater than the coupon interest rate, the bond value, B_0, will be less than its par value, M. In this case, the bond is said to sell at a **discount,** which will equal $M - B_0$. When the required return falls below the coupon interest rate, the bond value will be greater than par. In this situation, the bond is said to sell at a **premium,** which will equal $B_0 - M$.

discount
The amount by which a bond sells below its par value.

premium
The amount by which a bond sells above its par value.

IRF Example 6.9 ▶

MyFinanceLab Solution Video

The preceding example showed that when the required return equaled the coupon interest rate, the bond's value equaled its $1,000 par value. If for the same bond the required return were to rise to 12% or fall to 8%, its value in each case could be found using Equation 6.5 or as follows.

MyFinanceLab Financial Calculator

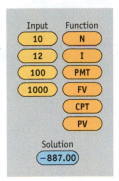

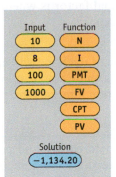

Calculator use Using the inputs shown at the left for the two different required returns, you will find the value of the bond to be below or above par. At a 12% required return, the bond would sell at a *discount* of $113.00 ($1,000 par value − $887.00 value). At the 8% required return, the bond would sell for a *premium* of $134.20 ($1,134.20 value − $1,000 par value). The results of these calculations for Mills Company's bond values are summarized in Table 6.6 and graphically depicted in Figure 6.4. The inverse relationship between bond value and required return is clearly shown in the figure.

Spreadsheet use The values for the Mills Company bond at required returns of 12% and 8% also can be calculated as shown in the following Excel spreadsheet. Once this spreadsheet has been configured, you can compare bond values for any two required returns by simply changing the input values.

	A	B	C
1	VALUATION FOR ANNUAL BOND		
2	Par value	$1,000	$1,000
3	Coupon interest rate	10%	10%
4	Annual Interest payment	$100	$100
5	Required rate of return	12%	8%
6	Number of years to maturity	10	10
7	Bond value	−$887.00	−$1,134.20

Entry in Cell B7 is =PV(B3,B6,B4,B2,0).
Note that the bond trades at a discount
(i.e., below par) because the bond's coupon
rate is below investors' required rate of return.

Entry in Cell C7 is =PV(B3,B6,B4,B2,0).
Note that the bond trades at a premium
(i.e., above par) because the bond's coupon
rate is above investors' required rate of return.

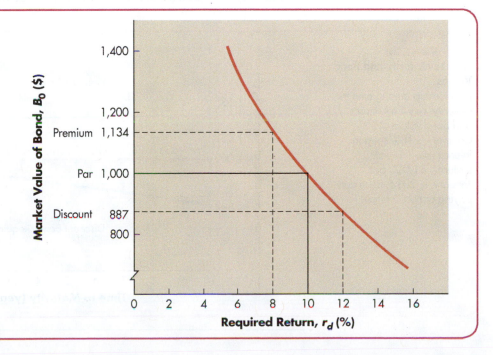

FIGURE 6.4

Bond Values and Required Returns
Bond values and required returns (Mills Company's 10% coupon interest rate, 10-year maturity, $1,000 par, January 1, 2014, issue date, paying annual interest)

TABLE 6.6	Bond Values for Various Required Returns (Mills Company's 10% Coupon Interest Rate, 10-Year Maturity, $1,000 Par, January 1, 2014, Issue Date, Paying Annual Interest)		
Required return, r_d		Bond value, B_0	Status
12%		$ 887.00	Discount
10		1,000.00	Par value
8		1,134.20	Premium

Time to Maturity and Bond Values

Whenever the required return is different from the coupon interest rate, the amount of time to maturity affects bond value. An additional factor is whether required returns are constant or change over the life of the bond.

Constant Required Returns   When the required return is different from the coupon interest rate and is *constant until maturity*, the value of the bond will approach its par value as the passage of time moves the bond's value closer to maturity. (Of course, when the required return *equals* the coupon interest rate, the bond's value will remain at par until it matures.)

Example 6.10 ▶   Figure 6.5 depicts the behavior of the bond values calculated earlier and presented in Table 6.6 for Mills Company's 10% coupon interest rate bond paying annual interest and having 10 years to maturity. Each of the three required returns—12%, 10%, and 8%—is assumed to remain constant over the 10 years to the bond's maturity. The bond's value at both 12% and 8% approaches and ultimately equals the bond's $1,000 par value at its maturity, as the discount (at 12%) or premium (at 8%) declines with the passage of time.

FIGURE 6.5

Time to Maturity and Bond Values
Relationship among time to maturity, required returns, and bond values (Mills Company's 10% coupon interest rate, 10-year maturity, $1,000 par, January 1, 2014, issue date, paying annual interest)

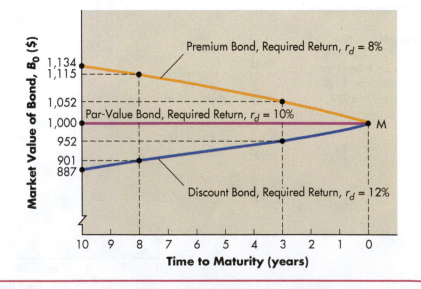

interest rate risk
The chance that interest rates will change and thereby change the required return and bond value. Rising rates, which result in decreasing bond values, are of greatest concern.

Changing Required Returns The chance that interest rates will change and thereby change the required return and bond value is called **interest rate risk**.[4] Bondholders are typically more concerned with rising interest rates because a rise in interest rates, and therefore in the required return, causes a decrease in bond value. The shorter the amount of time until a bond's maturity, the less responsive is its market value to a given change in the required return. In other words, *short maturities have less interest rate risk than long maturities when all other features (coupon interest rate, par value, and interest payment frequency) are the same.* This statement is true because of the mathematics of time value; the present values of short-term cash flows change far less than the present values of longer-term cash flows in response to a given change in the discount rate (required return).

Example 6.11 ▶

MyFinanceLab Solution Video

The effect of changing required returns on bonds with differing maturities can be illustrated by using Mills Company's bond and Figure 6.5. If the required return rises from 10% to 12% when the bond has 8 years to maturity (see the dashed line at 8 years), the bond's value decreases from $1,000 to $901, which is a 9.9% decrease. If the same change in required return had occurred with only 3 years to maturity (see the dashed line at 3 years), the bond's value would have dropped to just $952, only a 4.8% decrease. Similar types of responses can be seen for the change in bond value associated with decreases in required returns. The shorter the time to maturity, the less the impact on bond value caused by a given change in the required return.

YIELD TO MATURITY (YTM)

When investors evaluate bonds, they commonly consider yield to maturity (YTM), which is the compound annual rate of return earned on a debt security purchased on a given day and held to maturity. (The measure assumes, of course, that the issuer makes all scheduled interest and principal payments as promised.)[5] The yield to maturity on a bond with a current price equal to its par value (that is, $B_0 = M$) will always equal the coupon interest rate. When the bond value differs from par, the yield to maturity will differ from the coupon interest rate.

Assuming that interest is paid annually, the yield to maturity on a bond can be found by solving Equation 6.5 for r_d. In other words, the current value, the annual interest, the par value, and the number of years to maturity are known, and the required return must be found. The required return is the bond's yield to maturity. The YTM can be found by using a financial calculator, by using an Excel spreadsheet, or by trial and error. The calculator provides accurate YTM values with minimum effort.

---

4. A more robust measure of a bond's response to interest rate changes is *duration*. Duration measures the sensitivity of a bond's prices to changing interest rates. It incorporates both the interest rate (coupon rate) and the time to maturity into a single statistic. Duration is simply a weighted average of the maturity of the present values of all the contractual cash flows yet to be paid by the bond. Duration is stated in years, so a bond with a 5-year duration will decrease in value by 5 percent if interest rates rise by 1 percent or will increase in value by 5 percent if interest rates fall by 1 percent.

5. Many bonds have a *call feature*, which means that they may not reach maturity if the issuer, after a specified time period, calls them back. Because the call feature typically cannot be exercised until a specific future date, investors often calculate the *yield to call (YTC)*. The yield to call represents the rate of return that investors earn if they buy a callable bond at a specific price and hold it until it is called back and they receive the *call price*, which would be set above the bond's par value. Here our focus is solely on the more general measure of yield to maturity.

IRF **Personal Finance Example 6.12** ▶ Earl Washington wishes to find the YTM on Mills Company's bond. The bond currently sells for $1,080, has a 10% coupon interest rate and $1,000 par value, pays interest annually, and has 10 years to maturity.

MyFinanceLab Financial
Calculator

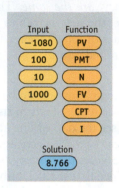

Input	Function
−1080	PV
100	PMT
10	N
1000	FV
	CPT
	I

Solution
8.766

Calculator use Most calculators require *either* the present value (B_0 in this case) or the future values (I and M in this case) to be input as negative numbers to calculate yield to maturity. That approach is employed here. Using the inputs shown at the left, you should find the YTM to be 8.766%.

Spreadsheet use The yield to maturity of Mills Company's bond also can be calculated as shown in the Excel spreadsheet below. First, enter all the bond's cash flows. Note that you begin with the bond's price as an outflow (a negative number). In other words, an investor has to pay the price up front to receive the cash flows over the next 10 years. Next, use Excel's *internal rate of return* function. This function calculates the discount rate that makes the present value of a series of cash flows equal to zero. In this case, when the present value of all cash flows is zero, the present value of the inflows (interest and principal) equals the present value of the outflows (the bond's initial price). In other words, the internal rate of return function is giving us the bond's YTM, the discount rate that equates the bond's price to the present value of its cash flows.

Since the typical bond's interest payments form an annuity stream you can further reduce the work necessary to solve for a bond's yield to maturity using Excel. The second screenshot below shows how to use the RATE function in Excel to determine a bond's yield to maturity.

	A	B
1	YIELD TO MATURITY	
2	Year	Cash Flow
3	0	−$1,080
4	1	$100
5	2	$100
6	3	$100
7	4	$100
8	5	$100
9	6	$100
10	7	$100
11	8	$100
12	9	$100
13	10	$1,100
14	YTM	8.766%

Entry in Cell B14 is =IRR(B3:B13)

	A	B
1	YIELD TO MATURITY	
2	Par value	$1,000
3	Coupon interest rate	10.0%
4	Interest payments per year	1
5	Interest payment	$100.00
6	Number of years to maturity	10
7	Bond current value	−$1,080.00
8	Bond yield to maturity	8.766%

Entry in Cell B14 is =RATE(B6*B4,B5,B7,B2,0).

SEMIANNUAL INTEREST AND BOND VALUES

The procedure used to value bonds paying interest semiannually is similar to that shown in Chapter 5 for compounding interest more frequently than annually, except that here we need to find present value instead of future value. It involves the following changes:

1. Converting annual interest, I, to semiannual interest by dividing I by 2.
2. Converting the number of years to maturity, n, to the number of 6-month periods to maturity by multiplying n by 2.
3. Converting the required stated (rather than effective)[6] annual return for similar-risk bonds that also pay semiannual interest from an annual rate, r_d, to a semiannual rate by dividing r_d by 2.

Substituting these three changes into Equation 6.5 yields

$$B_0 = \frac{I}{2} \times \left[\sum_{t=1}^{2n} \frac{1}{\left(1 + \frac{r_d}{2}\right)^t} \right] + M \times \left[\frac{1}{\left(1 + \frac{r_d}{2}\right)^{2n}} \right] \qquad (6.6)$$

IRF Example 6.13 ▶ Assuming that the Mills Company bond pays interest semiannually and that the required stated annual return, r_d, is 12% for similar-risk bonds that also pay semiannual interest, substituting these values into Equation 6.6 yields

$$B_0 = \frac{\$100}{2} \times \left[\sum_{t=1}^{20} \frac{1}{\left(1 + \frac{0.12}{2}\right)^t} \right] + \$1,000 \times \left[\frac{1}{\left(1 + \frac{0.12}{2}\right)^{20}} \right] = \$885.30$$

MyFinanceLab Financial Calculator

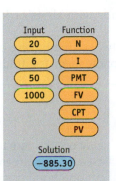

Calculator use In using a calculator to find bond value when interest is paid semiannually, we must double the number of periods and divide both the required stated annual return and the annual interest by 2. For the Mills Company bond, we would use 20 periods (2 × 10 years), a required return of 6% (12% ÷ 2), and an interest payment of $50 ($100 ÷ 2). Using these inputs, you should find the bond value with semiannual interest to be $885.30, as shown at the left.

Spreadsheet use The value of the Mills Company bond paying semiannual interest at a required return of 12% also can be calculated as shown in the Excel spreadsheet at the top of the following page.

---

6. As we noted in Chapter 5, the effective annual rate of interest, EAR, for stated interest rate r, when interest is paid semiannually ($m = 2$), can be found by using Equation 5.10:

$$EAR = \left(1 + \frac{r}{2}\right)^2 - 1$$

For example, a bond with a 12% required stated annual return, r_d, that pays semiannual interest would have an effective annual rate of

$$EAR = \left(1 + \frac{0.12}{2}\right)^2 - 1 = (1.06)^2 - 1 = 1.1236 - 1 = 0.1236 = 12.36\%$$

Because most bonds pay semiannual interest at semiannual rates equal to 50 percent of the stated annual rate, their effective annual rates are generally higher than their stated annual rates.

	A	B
1	VALUATION FOR SEMIANNUAL BOND	
2	Par value	$1,000
3	Coupon interest rate	10%
4	Interest payments per year	2
5	Interest payment	$50
6	Required rate of return	12%
7	Number of years to maturity	10
8	Bond value	−$885.30

Entry in Cell B8 is =PV(B6/B4,B7*B4,B5,B2,0).
The minus sign appears before the $885.30
in B8 because the bond's price
is a cost for the investor.

Comparing this result with the $887.00 value found earlier for annual compounding, we can see that the bond's value is lower when semiannual interest is paid. *This situation will always occur when the bond sells at a discount.* For bonds selling at a premium, the opposite will occur: The value with semiannual interest will be greater than with annual interest.

→ REVIEW QUESTIONS

6–16 What procedure is used to value a bond that pays annual interest? Semi-annual interest?

6–17 What relationship between the required return and the coupon interest rate will cause a bond to sell at a *discount*? At a *premium*? At its *par value*?

6–18 If the required return on a bond differs from its coupon interest rate, describe the behavior of the bond value over time as the bond moves toward maturity.

6–19 As a risk-averse investor, would you prefer bonds with short or long periods until maturity? Why?

6–20 What is a bond's *yield to maturity (YTM)*? Briefly describe the use of a financial calculator and the use of an Excel spreadsheet for finding YTM.

→ EXCEL REVIEW QUESTIONS   MyFinanceLab

6–21 Spreadsheet models can be used to determine the value of a bond based on its provisions and the required rate of return. Based on the information provided at MFL, find the value of an annual coupon bond using a spreadsheet model.

6–22 Some bonds make interest payments more than once per year. Based on the information provided at MFL, develop a spreadsheet capable of comparing bond values for differing payment frequencies.

6–23 As a financial manager it is often helpful to know the yield to maturity of outstanding bonds. Based on the information provided at MFL, use a spreadsheet to compute the yield to maturity for a bond.

Summary

FOCUS ON VALUE

Interest rates and required returns embody the real cost of money, inflationary expectations, and issuer and issue risk. They reflect the level of return required by market participants as compensation for the risk perceived in a specific security or asset investment. Because these returns are affected by economic expectations, they vary as a function of time, typically rising for longer-term maturities. The yield curve reflects such market expectations at any point in time.

The value of an asset can be found by calculating the present value of its expected cash flows, using the required return as the discount rate. Bonds are the easiest financial assets to value; both the amounts and the timing of their cash flows are contractual and therefore known with certainty (at least for high-grade bonds). The financial manager needs to understand how to apply valuation techniques to bonds, stocks, and tangible assets (as we will demonstrate in the following chapters) to make decisions that are consistent with the firm's **share price maximization goal.**

REVIEW OF LEARNING GOALS

LG 1 **Describe interest rate fundamentals, the term structure of interest rates, and risk premiums.** The flow of funds between savers and borrowers is regulated by the interest rate or required return. In a perfect, inflation-free, certain world there would be one cost of money: the real rate of interest. The nominal or actual interest rate is the sum of the risk-free rate and a risk premium reflecting issuer and issue characteristics. The risk-free rate is the real rate of interest plus an inflation premium.

For any class of similar-risk bonds, the term structure of interest rates reflects the relationship between the interest rate or rate of return and the time to maturity. Yield curves can be downward sloping (inverted), upward sloping (normal), or flat. The expectations theory, liquidity preference theory, and market segmentation theory are cited to explain the shape of the yield curve. Risk premiums for non-Treasury debt issues result from business risk, financial risk, interest rate risk, liquidity risk, tax risk, default risk, maturity risk, and contractual provision risk.

LG 2 **Review the legal aspects of bond financing and bond cost.** Corporate bonds are long-term debt instruments indicating that a corporation has borrowed an amount that it promises to repay in the future under clearly defined terms. Most bonds are issued with maturities of 10 to 30 years and a par value of $1,000. The bond indenture, enforced by a trustee, states all conditions of the bond issue. It contains both standard debt provisions and restrictive covenants, which may include a sinking-fund requirement and/or a security interest. The cost of a bond to an issuer depends on its maturity, offering size, and issuer risk and on the basic cost of money.

LG 3 **Discuss the general features, yields, prices, ratings, popular types, and international issues of corporate bonds.** A bond issue may include a conversion feature, a call feature, or stock purchase warrants. The yield, or rate of return, on a bond can be measured by its current yield, yield to maturity (YTM), or yield to call (YTC). Bond prices are typically reported along with their coupon, maturity date, and yield to maturity (YTM). Bond ratings by independent agencies indicate the risk of a bond issue. Various types of traditional and contemporary bonds are available. Eurobonds and foreign bonds enable established creditworthy companies and governments to borrow large amounts internationally.

LG 4 **Understand the key inputs and basic model used in the bond valuation process.** Key inputs to the valuation process include cash flows (returns), timing, and risk and the required return. The value of any asset is equal to the present value of all future cash flows it is *expected* to provide over the relevant time period.

LG 5 **Apply the basic valuation model to bonds, and describe the impact of required return and time to maturity on bond values.** The value of a bond is the present value of its interest payments plus the present value of its par value. The discount rate used to determine bond value is the required return, which may differ from the bond's coupon interest rate. A bond can sell at a discount, at par, or at a premium, depending on whether the required return is greater than, equal to, or less than its coupon interest rate. The amount of time to maturity affects bond values. The value of a bond will approach its par value as the bond moves closer to maturity. The chance that interest rates will change and thereby change the required return and bond value is called interest rate risk. The shorter the amount of time until a bond's maturity, the less responsive is its market value to a given change in the required return.

LG 6 **Explain yield to maturity (YTM), its calculation, and the procedure used to value bonds that pay interest semiannually.** Yield to maturity is the rate of return investors earn if they buy a bond at a specific price and hold it until maturity. YTM can be calculated by using a financial calculator or by using an Excel spreadsheet. Bonds that pay interest semiannually are valued by using the same procedure used to value bonds paying annual interest except that the interest payments are one-half of the annual interest payments, the number of periods is twice the number of years to maturity, and the required return is one-half of the stated annual required return on similar-risk bonds.

Self-Test Problems (Solutions in Appendix)

  ST6–1 **Bond valuation** Lahey Industries has outstanding a $1,000 par-value bond with an 8% coupon interest rate. The bond has 12 years remaining to its maturity date.

IRF

  a. If interest is paid *annually,* find the value of the bond when the required return is (1) 7%, (2) 8%, and (3) 10%.
  b. Indicate for each case in part **a** whether the bond is selling at a discount, at a premium, or at its par value.
  c. Using the 10% required return, find the bond's value when interest is paid *semiannually.*

  ST6–2 **Bond yields** Elliot Enterprises' bonds currently sell for $1,150, have an 11% coupon interest rate and a $1,000 par value, pay interest *annually,* and have 18 years to maturity.

IRF

  a. Calculate the bonds' *current yield.*
  b. Calculate the bonds' *yield to maturity (YTM).*
  c. Compare the YTM calculated in part **b** to the bonds' coupon interest rate and current yield (calculated in part **a**). Use a comparison of the bonds' current price and par value to explain these differences.

Warm-Up Exercises   All problems are available in MyFinanceLab.

LG 1   E6–1   The risk-free rate on T-bills recently was 1.23%. If the real rate of interest is estimated to be 0.80%, what was the expected level of inflation?

LG 1   E6–2   The yields for Treasuries with differing maturities on a recent day were as shown in the table below.

Maturity	Yield
3 months	1.41%
6 months	1.71
2 years	2.68
3 years	3.01
5 years	3.70
10 years	4.51
30 years	5.25

a. Use the information to plot a *yield curve* for this date.
b. If the expectations hypothesis is true, approximately what rate of return do investors expect a 5-year Treasury note to pay 5 years from now?
c. If the expectations hypothesis is true, approximately (ignoring compounding) what rate of return do investors expect a 1-year Treasury security to pay starting 2 years from now?
d. Is it possible that even though the yield curve slopes up in this problem, investors do not expect rising interest rates? Explain.

LG 1   E6–3   The yields for Treasuries with differing maturities, including an estimate of the real rate of interest, on a recent day were as shown in the following table.

Maturity	Yield	Real rate of interest
3 months	1.41%	0.80%
6 months	1.71	0.80
2 years	2.68	0.80
3 years	3.01	0.80
5 years	3.70	0.80
10 years	4.51	0.80
30 years	5.25	0.80

Use the information in the preceding table to calculate the *inflation expectation* for each maturity.

LG 1   E6–4   Recently, the annual inflation rate measured by the Consumer Price Index (CPI) was forecast to be 3.3%. How could a T-bill have had a negative real rate of return over the same period? How could it have had a zero real rate of return? What minimum rate of return must the T-bill have earned to meet your requirement of a 2% real rate of return?

LG 1   E6–5   Calculate the *risk premium* for each of the following rating classes of long-term securities, assuming that the yield to maturity (YTM) for comparable Treasuries is 4.51%.

Rating class	Nominal interest rate
AAA	5.12%
BBB	5.78
B	7.82

LG 4 **E6–6** You have two assets and must calculate their values today based on their different payment streams and appropriate required returns. Asset 1 has a required return of 15% and will produce a stream of $500 at the end of each year indefinitely. Asset 2 has a required return of 10% and will produce an end-of-year cash flow of $1,200 in the first year, $1,500 in the second year, and $850 in its third and final year.

LG 5 **E6–7** A bond with 5 years to maturity and a coupon rate of 6% has a par, or face, value of $20,000. Interest is paid annually. If you required a return of 8% on this bond, what is the value of this bond to you?

LG 5 **E6–8** Assume a 5-year Treasury bond has a coupon rate of 4.5%.
a. Give examples of required rates of return that would make the bond sell at a discount, at a premium, and at par.
b. If this bond's par value is $10,000, calculate the differing values for this bond given the required rates you chose in part **a.**

Problems

All problems are available in MyFinanceLab.

LG 1 **P6–1** **Interest rate fundamentals: The real rate of return** Carl Foster, a trainee at an investment banking firm, is trying to get an idea of what real rate of return investors are expecting in today's marketplace. He has looked up the rate paid on 3-month U.S. Treasury bills and found it to be 5.5%. He has decided to use the rate of change in the Consumer Price Index as a proxy for the inflationary expectations of investors. That annualized rate now stands at 3%. On the basis of the information that Carl has collected, what estimate can he make of the *real rate of return*?

LG 1 **P6–2** **Real rate of interest** To estimate the real rate of interest, the economics division of Mountain Banks—a major bank holding company—has gathered the data summarized in the following table. Because there is a high likelihood that new tax

Amount of funds supplied/demanded ($ billion)	Currently		With passage of tax legislation
	Interest rate required by funds suppliers	Interest rate required by funds demanders	Interest rate required by funds demanders
$ 1	2%	7%	9%
5	3	6	8
10	4	4	7
20	6	3	6
50	7	2	4
100	9	1	3

legislation will be passed in the near future, current data as well as data reflecting the probable impact of passage of the legislation on the demand for funds are also included in the table. (*Note:* The proposed legislation will not affect the supply schedule of funds. Assume a perfect world in which inflation is expected to be zero, funds suppliers and demanders have no liquidity preference, and all outcomes are certain.)

a. Draw the supply curve and the demand curve for funds using the current data. (*Note:* Unlike the functions in Figure 6.1 on page 214, the functions here will not appear as straight lines.)

b. Using your graph, label and note the *real rate of interest* using the current data.

c. Add to the graph drawn in part **a** the new demand curve expected in the event that the proposed tax legislation is passed.

d. What is the new real rate of interest? Compare and analyze this finding in light of your analysis in part **b**.

Personal Finance Problem

P6–3 **Real and nominal rates of interest** Zane Perelli currently has $100 that he can spend today on polo shirts costing $25 each. Alternatively, he could invest the $100 in a risk-free U.S. Treasury security that is expected to earn a 9% nominal rate of interest. The consensus forecast of leading economists is a 5% rate of inflation over the coming year.

a. How many polo shirts can Zane purchase today?

b. How much money will Zane have at the end of 1 year if he forgoes purchasing the polo shirts today?

c. How much would you expect the polo shirts to cost at the end of 1 year in light of the expected inflation?

d. Use your findings in parts **b** and **c** to determine how many polo shirts (fractions are OK) Zane can purchase at the end of 1 year. In percentage terms, how many more or fewer polo shirts can Zane buy at the end of 1 year?

e. What is Zane's *real rate of return* over the year? How is it related to the percentage change in Zane's buying power found in part **d**? Explain.

P6–4 **Yield curve** A firm wishing to evaluate interest rate behavior has gathered yield data on five U.S. Treasury securities, each having a different maturity and all measured at the same point in time. The summarized data follow.

U.S. Treasury security	Time to maturity	Yield
A	1 year	12.6%
B	10 years	11.2
C	6 months	13.0
D	20 years	11.0
E	5 years	11.4

a. Draw the yield curve associated with these data.

b. Describe the resulting yield curve in part **a**, and explain the general expectations embodied in it.

P6–5 **Nominal interest rates and yield curves** A recent study of inflationary expectations has revealed that the consensus among economic forecasters yields the following

average annual rates of inflation expected over the periods noted.
(*Note:* Assume that the risk that future interest rate movements will affect longer maturities more than shorter maturities is zero; that is, assume that there is no *maturity risk.*)

Period	Average annual rate of inflation
3 months	5%
2 years	6
5 years	8
10 years	8.5
20 years	9

a. If the real rate of interest is currently 2.5%, find the *nominal rate of interest* on each of the following U.S. Treasury issues: 20-year bond, 3-month bill, 2-year note, and 5-year bond.
b. If the real rate of interest suddenly dropped to 2% without any change in inflationary expectations, what effect, if any, would it have on your answers in part a? Explain.
c. Using your findings in part a, draw a yield curve for U.S. Treasury securities. Describe the general shape and expectations reflected by the curve.
d. What would a follower of the *liquidity preference theory* say about how the preferences of lenders and borrowers tend to affect the shape of the yield curve drawn in part c? Illustrate that effect by placing on your graph a dotted line that approximates the yield curve without the effect of liquidity preference.
e. What would a follower of the *market segmentation theory* say about the supply and demand for long-term loans versus the supply and demand for short-term loans given the yield curve constructed for part c of this problem?

LG 1   **P6–6**   **Nominal and real rates and yield curves**   A firm wishing to evaluate interest rate behavior has gathered data on the nominal rate of interest and on inflationary expectations for five U.S. Treasury securities, each having a different maturity and each measured at a different point in time during the year just ended. (*Note:* Assume that the risk that future interest rate movements will affect longer maturities more than shorter maturities is zero; that is, assume that there is no *maturity risk.*) These data are summarized in the following table.

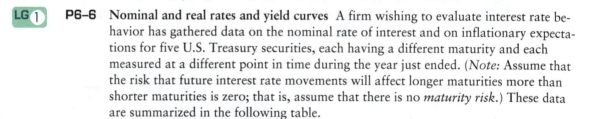

U.S. Treasury security	Point in time	Maturity	Nominal rate of interest	Inflationary expectation
A	Jan. 7	2 years	12.6%	9.5%
B	Mar. 12	10 years	11.2	8.2
C	May 30	6 months	13.0	10.0
D	Aug. 15	20 years	11.0	8.1
E	Dec. 30	5 years	11.4	8.3

a. Using the preceding data, find the *real rate of interest* at each point in time.
b. Describe the behavior of the real rate of interest over the year. What forces might be responsible for such behavior?
c. Draw the yield curve associated with these data, assuming that the nominal rates were measured at the same point in time.
d. Describe the resulting yield curve in part **c**, and explain the general expectations embodied in it.

LG 1 **P6–7** **Term structure of interest rates** The following yield data for a number of highest-quality corporate bonds existed at each of the three points in time noted.

	Yield		
Time to maturity (years)	5 years ago	2 years ago	Today
1	9.1%	14.6%	9.3%
3	9.2	12.8	9.8
5	9.3	12.2	10.9
10	9.5	10.9	12.6
15	9.4	10.7	12.7
20	9.3	10.5	12.9
30	9.4	10.5	13.5

a. On the same set of axes, draw the yield curve at each of the three given times.
b. Label each curve in part **a** with its general shape (downward sloping, upward sloping, flat).
c. Describe the general interest rate expectation existing at each of the three times.
d. Examine the data from 5 years ago. According to the expectations theory, what approximate return did investors expect a 5-year bond to pay as of today?

LG 1 **P6–8** **Risk-free rate and risk premiums** The real rate of interest is currently 3%; the inflation expectation and risk premiums for a number of securities follow.

Security	Inflation expectation Premium	Risk premium
A	6%	3%
B	9	2
C	8	2
D	5	4
E	11	1

a. Find the *risk-free rate of interest, R_F*, that is applicable to each security.
b. Although not noted, what factor must be the cause of the differing risk-free rates found in part **a**?
c. Find the *nominal rate of interest* for each security.

P6–9 **Risk premiums** Eleanor Burns is attempting to find the nominal rate of interest for each of two securities—A and B—issued by different firms at the same point in time. She has gathered the following data.

Characteristic	Security A	Security B
Time to maturity	3 years	15 years
Inflation expectation premium	9.0%	7.0%
Risk premium for:		
Liquidity risk	1.0%	1.0%
Default risk	1.0%	2.0%
Maturity risk	0.5%	1.5%
Other risk	0.5%	1.5%

a. If the real rate of interest is currently 2%, find the *risk-free rate of interest* applicable to each security.
b. Find the total risk premium attributable to each security's issuer and issue characteristics.
c. Calculate the *nominal rate of interest* for each security. Compare and discuss your findings.

 P6–10 **Bond interest payments before and after taxes** Charter Corp. has issued 2,500 debentures with a total principal value of $2,500,000. The bonds have a coupon interest rate of 7%.
a. What dollar amount of interest per bond can an investor expect to receive each year from Charter?
b. What is Charter's total interest expense per year associated with this bond issue?
c. Assuming that Charter is in a 35% corporate tax bracket, what is the company's net after-tax interest cost associated with this bond issue?

LG 4 **P6–11** **Bond prices and yields** Assume that the Financial Management Corporation's $1,000-par-value bond had a 5.700% coupon, matures on May 15, 2023, has a current price quote of 97.708, and has a yield to maturity (YTM) of 6.034%. Given this information, answer the following questions:
a. What was the dollar price of the bond?
b. What is the bond's *current yield?*
c. Is the bond selling at par, at a discount, or at a premium? Why?
d. Compare the bond's current yield calculated in part **b** to its YTM and explain why they differ.

Personal Finance Problem

LG 4 **P6–12** **Valuation fundamentals** Imagine that you are trying to evaluate the economics of purchasing an automobile. You expect the car to provide annual after-tax cash benefits of $1,200 at the end of each year and assume that you can sell the car for after-tax proceeds of $5,000 at the end of the planned 5-year ownership period. All funds for purchasing the car will be drawn from your savings, which are currently earning 6% after taxes.
a. Identify the cash flows, their timing, and the required return applicable to valuing the car.
b. What is the maximum price you would be willing to pay to acquire the car? Explai

P6–13   **Valuation of assets** Using the information provided in the following table, find the value of each asset.

| Asset | Cash flow | | Appropriate required return |
	End of year	Amount	
A	1	$ 5,000	18%
	2	5,000	
	3	5,000	
B	1 through ∞	$ 300	15%
C	1	$ 0	16%
	2	0	
	3	0	
	4	0	
	5	35,000	
D	1 through 5	$ 1,500	12%
	6	8,500	
E	1	$ 2,000	14%
	2	3,000	
	3	5,000	
	4	7,000	
	5	4,000	
	6	1,000	

Personal Finance Problem

 P6–14   **Asset valuation and risk** Laura Drake wishes to estimate the value of an asset expected to provide cash inflows of $3,000 per year at the end of years 1 through 4 and $15,000 at the end of year 5. Her research indicates that she must earn 10% on low-risk assets, 15% on average-risk assets, and 22% on high-risk assets.

a. Determine what is the most Laura should pay for the asset if it is classified as (1) low-risk, (2) average-risk, and (3) high-risk.

b. Suppose that Laura is unable to assess the risk of the asset and wants to be certain she's making a good deal. On the basis of your findings in part **a**, what is the most she should pay? Why?

c. All else being the same, what effect does increasing risk have on the value of an asset? Explain in light of your findings in part **a**.

 P6–15   **Basic bond valuation** Complex Systems has an outstanding issue of $1,000-par-value bonds with a 12% coupon interest rate. The issue pays interest *annually* and has 16 years remaining to its maturity date.

a. If bonds of similar risk are currently earning a 10% rate of return, how much should the Complex Systems bond sell for today?

b. Describe the *two* possible reasons why the rate on similar-risk bonds is below the coupon interest rate on the Complex Systems bond.

c. If the required return were at 12% instead of 10%, what would the current value of Complex Systems' bond be? Contrast this finding with your findings in part **a** and discuss.

P6–16 **Bond valuation: Annual interest** Calculate the value of each of the bonds shown in the following table, all of which pay interest *annually*.

Bond	Par value	Coupon interest rate	Years to maturity	Required return
A	$1,000	14%	20	12%
B	1,000	8	16	8
C	100	10	8	13
D	500	16	13	18
E	1,000	12	10	10

 P6–17 **Bond value and changing required returns** Midland Utilities has outstanding a bond issue that will mature to its $1,000 par value in 12 years. The bond has a coupon interest rate of 11% and pays interest *annually*.

a. Find the value of the bond if the required return is (1) 11%, (2) 15%, and (3) 8%.

b. Plot your findings in part a on a set of "required return (*x* axis)–market value of bond (*y* axis)" axes.

c. Use your findings in parts a and b to discuss the relationship between the coupon interest rate on a bond and the required return and the market value of the bond relative to its par value.

d. What *two* possible reasons could cause the required return to differ from the coupon interest rate?

 P6–18 **Bond value and time: Constant required returns** Pecos Manufacturing has just issued a 15-year, 12% coupon interest rate, $1,000-par bond that pays interest *annually*. The required return is currently 14%, and the company is certain it will remain at 14% until the bond matures in 15 years.

a. Assuming that the required return does remain at 14% until maturity, find the value of the bond with (1) 15 years, (2) 12 years, (3) 9 years, (4) 6 years, (5) 3 years, and (6) 1 year to maturity.

b. Plot your findings on a set of "time to maturity (*x* axis)–market value of bond (*y* axis)" axes constructed similarly to Figure 6.5 on page 236.

c. All else remaining the same, when the required return differs from the coupon interest rate and is assumed to be constant to maturity, what happens to the bond value as time moves toward maturity? Explain in light of the graph in part b.

Personal Finance Problem

 P6–19 **Bond value and time: Changing required returns** Lynn Parsons is considering investing in either of two outstanding bonds. The bonds both have $1,000 par values and 11% coupon interest rates and pay *annual* interest. Bond A has exactly 5 years to maturity, and bond B has 15 years to maturity.

a. Calculate the value of bond A if the required return is (1) 8%, (2) 11%, and (3) 14%.

b. Calculate the value of bond B if the required return is (1) 8%, (2) 11%, and (3) 14%.

c. From your findings in parts **a** and **b,** complete the following table, and discuss the relationship between time to maturity and changing required returns.

Required return	Value of bond A	Value of bond B
8%	?	?
11	?	?
14	?	?

d. If Lynn wanted to minimize *interest rate risk,* which bond should she purchase? Why?

LG 6 **P6–20** **Yield to maturity** The relationship between a bond's yield to maturity and coupon interest rate can be used to predict its pricing level. For each of the bonds listed, state whether the price of the bond will be at a premium to par, at par, or at a discount to par.

Bond	Coupon interest rate	Yield to maturity	Price
A	6%	10%	_____
B	8	8	_____
C	9	7	_____
D	7	9	_____
E	12	10	_____

LG 6 **P6–21** **Yield to maturity** The Salem Company bond currently sells for $955, has a 12% coupon interest rate and a $1,000 par value, pays interest *annually,* and has 15 years to maturity.
a. Calculate the *yield to maturity (YTM)* on this bond.
b. Explain the relationship that exists between the coupon interest rate and yield to maturity and the par value and market value of a bond.

LG 6 **P6–22** **Yield to maturity** Each of the bonds shown in the following table pays interest *annually.*

Bond	Par value	Coupon interest rate	Years to maturity	Current value
A	$1,000	9%	8	$ 820
B	1,000	12	16	1,000
C	500	12	12	560
D	1,000	15	10	1,120
E	1,000	5	3	900

a. Calculate the *yield to maturity (YTM)* for each bond.
b. What relationship exists between the coupon interest rate and yield to maturity and the par value and market value of a bond? Explain.

LG 2 LG 5
LG 6
P6–23 **Bond valuation and yield to maturity** Mark Goldsmith's broker has shown him two bonds. Each has a maturity of 5 years, a par value of $1,000, and a yield to maturity of 12%. Bond A has a coupon interest rate of 6% paid annually. Bond B has a coupon interest rate of 14% paid annually.

a. Calculate the selling price for each of the bonds.

b. Mark has $20,000 to invest. Judging on the basis of the price of the bonds, how many of either one could Mark purchase if he were to choose it over the other? (Mark cannot really purchase a fraction of a bond, but for purposes of this question, pretend that he can.)

c. Calculate the yearly interest income of each bond on the basis of its coupon rate and the number of bonds that Mark could buy with his $20,000.

d. Assume that Mark will reinvest the interest payments as they are paid (at the end of each year) and that his rate of return on the reinvestment is only 10%. For each bond, calculate the value of the principal payment plus the value of Mark's reinvestment account at the end of the 5 years.

e. Why are the two values calculated in part **d** different? If Mark were worried that he would earn less than the 12% yield to maturity on the reinvested interest payments, which of these two bonds would be a better choice?

LG 6
P6–24 **Bond valuation: Semiannual interest** Find the value of a bond maturing in 6 years, with a $1,000 par value and a coupon interest rate of 10% (5% paid semiannually) if the required return on similar-risk bonds is 14% annual interest (7% paid semiannually).

LG 6
P6–25 **Bond valuation: Semiannual interest** Calculate the value of each of the bonds shown in the following table, all of which pay interest *semiannually*.

Bond	Par value	Coupon interest rate	Years to maturity	Required stated annual return
A	$1,000	10%	12	8%
B	1,000	12	20	12
C	500	12	5	14
D	1,000	14	10	10
E	100	6	4	14

LG 6
P6–26 **Bond valuation: Quarterly interest** Calculate the value of a $5,000-par-value bond paying quarterly interest at an annual coupon interest rate of 10% and having 10 years until maturity if the required return on similar-risk bonds is currently a 12% annual rate paid *quarterly*.

LG 1
P6–27 **ETHICS PROBLEM** Bond rating agencies have invested significant sums of money in an effort to determine which quantitative and nonquantitative factors best predict bond defaults. Furthermore, some of the raters invest time and money to meet privately with corporate personnel to get nonpublic information that is used in assigning the issue's bond rating. To recoup those costs, some bond rating agencies have tied their ratings to the purchase of additional services. Do you believe that this is an acceptable practice? Defend your position.

Spreadsheet Exercise

 CSM Corporation has a bond issue outstanding at the end of 2015. The bond has 15 years remaining to maturity and carries a coupon interest rate of 6%. Interest on the bond is compounded on a semiannual basis. The par value of the CSM bond is $1,000, and it is currently selling for $874.42.

TO DO

Create a spreadsheet similar to the Excel spreadsheet examples located in the chapter for yield to maturity and semiannual interest to model the following:

a. Create a spreadsheet similar to the Excel spreadsheet examples located in the chapter to solve for the yield to maturity.

b. Create a spreadsheet similar to the Excel spreadsheet examples located in the chapter to solve for the price of the bond if the yield to maturity is 2% higher.

c. Create a spreadsheet similar to the Excel spreadsheet examples located in the chapter to solve for the price of the bond if the yield to maturity is 2% lower.

d. What can you summarize about the relationship between the price of the bond, the par value, the yield to maturity, and the coupon rate?

MyFinanceLab Visit www.myfinancelab.com for **Chapter Case:** *Evaluating Annie Hegg's Proposed Investment in Atilier Industries Bonds,* Group Exercises, and other numerous resources.

7

Stock Valuation

Learning Goals

LG 1 Differentiate between debt and equity.

LG 2 Discuss the features of both common and preferred stock.

LG 3 Describe the process of issuing common stock, including venture capital, going public, and the investment banker.

LG 4 Understand the concept of market efficiency and basic stock valuation using zero-growth, constant-growth, and variable-growth models.

LG 5 Discuss the free cash flow valuation model and the book value, liquidation value, and price/earnings (P/E) multiple approaches.

LG 6 Explain the relationships among financial decisions, return, risk, and the firm's value.

Why This Chapter Matters to You

In your *professional* life

ACCOUNTING You need to understand the difference between debt and equity in terms of tax treatment; the ownership claims of capital providers, including venture capitalists and stockholders; and the differences between book value per share and other market-based valuations.

INFORMATION SYSTEMS You need to understand the procedures used to issue common stock, the information needed to value stock, how to collect and process the necessary information from each functional area, and how to disseminate information to investors.

MANAGEMENT You need to understand the difference between debt and equity capital, the rights and claims of stockholders, the process of issuing common stock, and the effects each functional area has on the value of the firm's stock.

MARKETING You need to understand that the firm's ideas for products and services will greatly affect investors' beliefs regarding the likely success of the firm's projects and that projects that are viewed as more likely to succeed are also viewed as more valuable and therefore lead to a higher stock value.

OPERATIONS You need to understand that the evaluations of venture capitalists and other would-be investors will in part depend on the efficiency of the firm's operations and that more cost-efficient operations lead to better growth prospects and therefore higher stock valuations.

In your *personal* life
At some point, you are likely to hold stocks as an asset in your retirement program. You may want to estimate a stock's value. If the stock is selling below its estimated value, you may buy the stock; if its market price is above its value, you may sell it. Some individuals rely on financial advisors to make such buy or sell recommendations. Regardless of how you approach investment decisions, it will be helpful for you to understand how stocks are valued.

7.1 Differences between Debt and Equity

Although debt and equity capital are both sources of external financing used by firms, they are very different in several important respects. Most importantly, debt financing is obtained from creditors, and equity financing is obtained from investors who then become part owners of the firm. Creditors (lenders or debtholders) have a legal right to be repaid, whereas investors have only an expectation of being repaid. **Debt** includes all borrowing incurred by a firm, including bonds, and is repaid according to a fixed schedule of payments. **Equity** consists of funds provided by the firm's owners (investors or stockholders), and the stockholders earn a return that is not guaranteed but is tied to the firm's performance. A firm can obtain equity either *internally*, by retaining earnings rather than paying them out as dividends to its stockholders, or *externally*, by selling common or preferred stock. The key differences between debt and equity capital are summarized in Table 7.1 and discussed in the following pages.

debt
Includes all borrowing incurred by a firm, including bonds, and is repaid according to a fixed schedule of payments.

equity
Funds provided by the firm's owners (investors or stockholders) that are repaid subject to the firm's performance.

VOICE IN MANAGEMENT

Unlike creditors, holders of equity (stockholders) are owners of the firm. Stockholders generally have voting rights that permit them to select the firm's directors and vote on special issues. In contrast, debtholders do not receive voting privileges but instead rely on the firm's contractual obligations to them to be their voice.

CLAIMS ON INCOME AND ASSETS

Equityholders' claims on income and assets are secondary to the claims of creditors. Their *claims on income* cannot be paid until the claims of all creditors, including both interest and scheduled principal payments, have been satisfied. After satisfying creditor's claims, the firm's board of directors decides whether to distribute dividends to the owners.

Matter of fact

How Are Assets Divided in Bankruptcy?

According to the U.S. Securities and Exchange Commission, in bankruptcy assets are divided up as follows:

1. **Secured creditors:** Secured bank loans or secured bonds are paid first.
2. **Unsecured creditors:** Unsecured bank loans or unsecured bonds, suppliers, or customers have the next claim.
3. **Equityholders:** Equityholders or the owners of the company have the last claim on assets, and they may not receive anything if the secured and unsecured creditors' claims are not fully repaid.

Equityholders' *claims on assets* also are secondary to the claims of creditors. If the firm fails, its assets are sold, and the proceeds are distributed in this order: secured creditors, unsecured creditors, and equityholders. Because equityholders are the last to receive any distribution of assets, their investment is relatively risky, and they expect greater returns from their investment in the firm's stock than the returns creditors require on the firm's borrowings. The higher rate of

TABLE 7.1	Key Differences between Debt and Equity	
	Type of capital	
Characteristic	Debt	Equity
Voice in management[a]	No	Yes
Claims on income and assets	Senior to equity	Subordinate to debt
Maturity	Stated	None
Tax treatment	Interest deduction	No deduction

[a]Debtholders do not have voting rights, but instead they rely on the firm's contractual obligations to them to be their voice.

return expected by equityholders means that there is a higher cost of equity financing relative to the cost of debt financing for the firm.

MATURITY

Unlike debt, equity is a *permanent form* of financing for the firm. It does not "mature," so repayment is not required. When they purchase shares, stockholders must recognize that, although a ready market may exist for their shares, the price of the shares will fluctuate over time, and there is no way to know what the share price will be when an investor is ready to sell. This fluctuation of the market price of equity makes the overall returns to a firm's stockholders even more risky.

TAX TREATMENT

Interest payments to debtholders are treated as tax-deductible expenses by the issuing firm, whereas dividend payments to a firm's stockholders are not tax deductible. The tax deductibility of interest lowers the corporation's cost of debt financing, which is yet another reason the cost of debt financing is lower than the cost of equity financing.

→ **REVIEW QUESTION**

7–1 What are the key differences between *debt* and *equity*?

 7.2 Common and Preferred Stock

A firm can obtain equity capital by selling either common or preferred stock. All corporations initially issue common stock to raise equity capital. Some of these firms later issue either additional common stock or preferred stock to raise more equity capital. Although both common and preferred stock are forms of equity capital, preferred stock has some similarities to debt that significantly differentiate it from common stock. Here we first consider the features of both common and preferred stock and then describe the process of issuing common stock, including the use of venture capital.

COMMON STOCK

The true owners of a corporate business are the common stockholders. Common stockholders are sometimes referred to as *residual owners* because they receive what is left—the residual—after all other claims on the firm's income and assets have been satisfied. They are assured of only one thing: that they cannot lose any more than they have invested in the firm. As a result of this generally uncertain position, common stockholders expect to earn relatively high returns. Those returns may come in the form of dividends, capital gains, or both.

Ownership

privately owned (stock)
The common stock of a firm is owned by private investors; this stock is not publicly traded.

publicly owned (stock)
The common stock of a firm is owned by public investors; this stock is publicly traded.

closely owned (stock)
The common stock of a firm is owned by an individual or a small group of investors (such as a family); they are usually privately owned companies.

widely owned (stock)
The common stock of a firm is owned by many unrelated individual or institutional investors.

The common stock of a firm can be **privately owned** by private investors or **publicly owned** by public investors. Private companies are usually smaller than public companies and they are often **closely owned** by an individual investor or a small group of private investors (such as a family). Public companies are **widely owned** by many unrelated individual or institutional investors. The shares of privately owned firms generally do not trade actively in the stock market; if the shares are traded, the transactions are among private investors and often require the firm's consent. Large corporations, which are emphasized in the following discussions, are publicly owned, and their shares are generally actively traded in the stock markets described in Chapter 2.

Par Value

par-value common stock
An arbitrary value established for legal purposes in the firm's corporate charter and which can be used to find the total number of shares outstanding by dividing it into the book value of common stock.

The market value of common stock is completely unrelated to its par value. The **par value** of common stock is an arbitrary value established for legal purposes in the firm's corporate charter and is generally set quite low, often an amount of $1 or less. Recall that when a firm sells new shares of common stock, the par value of the shares sold is recorded in the capital section of the balance sheet as part of common stock. One benefit of this recording is that at any time the total number of shares of common stock outstanding can be found by dividing the book value of common stock by the par value.

Setting a low par value is advantageous in states where certain corporate taxes are based on the par value of stock. A low par value is also beneficial in states that have laws against selling stock at a discount to par. For example, a company whose common stock has a par value of $20 per share would be unable to issue stock if investors are unwilling to pay more than $16 per share.

Preemptive Rights

preemptive right
Allows common stockholders to maintain their proportionate ownership in the corporation when new shares are issued, thus protecting them from dilution of their ownership.

dilution of ownership
A reduction in each previous shareholder's fractional ownership resulting from the issuance of additional shares of common stock.

dilution of earnings
A reduction in each previous shareholder's fractional claim on the firm's earnings resulting from the issuance of additional shares of common stock.

rights
Financial instruments that allow stockholders to purchase additional shares at a price below the market price, in direct proportion to their number of owned shares.

The **preemptive right** allows common stockholders to maintain their *proportionate* ownership in the corporation when new shares are issued, thus protecting them from dilution of their ownership. A **dilution of ownership** is a reduction in each previous shareholder's fractional ownership resulting from the issuance of additional shares of common stock. Preemptive rights allow preexisting shareholders to maintain their preissuance voting control and protects them against the dilution of earnings. Preexisting shareholders experience a **dilution of earnings** when their claim on the firm's earnings is *diminished* as a result of new shares being issued.

In a *rights offering*, the firm grants **rights** to its shareholders. These financial instruments allow stockholders to purchase additional shares at a price below the

authorized shares
Shares of common stock that a firm's corporate charter allows it to issue.

outstanding shares
Issued shares of common stock held by investors, including both private and public investors.

treasury stock
Issued shares of common stock held by the firm; often these shares have been repurchased by the firm.

issued shares
Shares of common stock that have been put into circulation; the sum of *outstanding shares* and *treasury stock.*

market price, in direct proportion to their number of owned shares. In these situations, *rights* are an important financing tool without which shareholders would run the risk of losing their proportionate control of the corporation. From the firm's viewpoint, the use of rights offerings to raise new equity capital may be less costly than a public offering of stock.

Authorized, Outstanding, and Issued Shares

A firm's corporate charter indicates how many **authorized shares** it can issue. The firm cannot sell more shares than the charter authorizes without obtaining approval through a shareholder vote. To avoid later having to amend the charter, firms generally attempt to authorize more shares than they initially plan to issue.

Authorized shares become **outstanding shares** when they are issued or sold to investors. If the *firm* repurchases any of its outstanding shares, these shares are recorded as **treasury stock** and are no longer considered to be outstanding shares. **Issued shares** are the shares of common stock that have been put into circulation; they represent the sum of *outstanding shares* and *treasury stock.*

Example 7.1 ▶

Golden Enterprises, a producer of medical pumps, has the following stockholders' equity account on December 31:

Stockholders' Equity

Common stock—$0.80 par value:	
Authorized 35,000,000 shares; issued 15,000,000 shares	$ 12,000,000
Paid-in capital in excess of par	63,000,000
Retained earnings	31,000,000
	$106,000,000
Less: Cost of treasury stock (1,000,000 shares)	4,000,000
Total stockholders' equity	$102,000,000

How many shares of additional common stock can Golden sell without gaining approval from its shareholders? The firm has 35 million authorized shares, 15 million issued shares, and 1 million shares of treasury stock. Thus, 14 million shares are outstanding (15 million issued shares minus 1 million shares of treasury stock), and Golden can issue 21 million additional shares (35 million authorized shares minus 14 million outstanding shares) without seeking shareholder approval. This total includes the treasury shares currently held, which the firm can reissue to the public without obtaining shareholder approval.

Voting Rights

Generally, each share of common stock entitles its holder to one vote in the election of directors and on special issues. Votes are generally assignable and may be cast at the annual stockholders' meeting.

Because most small stockholders do not attend the annual meeting to vote, they may sign a **proxy statement** transferring their votes to another party. The solicitation of proxies from shareholders is closely controlled by the Securities and Exchange Commission to ensure that proxies are not bein

proxy statement
A statement transferring the votes of a stockholder to another party.

solicited on the basis of false or misleading information. Existing management generally receives the stockholders' proxies because it is able to solicit them at company expense.

Occasionally, when the firm is widely owned, outsiders may wage a **proxy battle** to unseat the existing management and gain control of the firm. To win a corporate election, votes from a majority of the shares voted are required. Historically, the odds of an outside group winning a proxy battle were generally slim, but that has changed in recent years. Investors such as Carl Icahn have had repeated success gaining seats on boards of directors and affecting corporate policies in other ways through proxy rights.

proxy battle
The attempt by a nonmanagement group to gain control of the management of a firm by soliciting a sufficient number of proxy votes.

Rather than trying to gain control of the firm through a proxy fight, shareholders can simply make proposals that may be voted on at a shareholders meeting. Even in very large firms, these proposals can sometimes be effective. In 2011, for instance, shareholders of Standard & Poor's 500 firms put forward 347 proposals, of which 16.1% received majority support.

In recent years, many firms, including household names like Google and Facebook, have issued two or more classes of common stock with unequal voting rights. A firm can use different classes of stock as a defense against a *hostile take-over* in which an outside group, without management support, tries to gain voting control of the firm by buying its shares in the marketplace. **Supervoting shares**, which have multiple votes per share, allow "insiders" to maintain control against an outside group whose shares have only one vote each. At other times, a class of **nonvoting common stock** is issued when the firm wishes to raise capital through the sale of common stock but does not want to give up its voting control.

supervoting shares
Stock that carries with it multiple votes per share rather than the single vote per share typically given on regular shares of common stock.

nonvoting common stock
Common stock that carries no voting rights; issued when the firm wishes to raise capital through the sale of common stock but does not want to give up its voting control.

When different classes of common stock are issued on the basis of unequal voting rights, class A common typically—but not universally—has one vote per share, and class B common has supervoting rights. In most cases, the multiple share classes are equal with respect to all other aspects of ownership, although there are some exceptions to this general rule. In particular, there is usually no difference in the distribution of earnings (dividends) and assets. Treasury stock, which is held within the corporation, generally *does not* have voting rights, *does not* earn dividends, and *does not* have a claim on assets in liquidation.

Dividends

The payment of dividends to the firm's shareholders is at the discretion of the company's board of directors. Most corporations that pay dividends pay them quarterly. Dividends may be paid in cash, stock, or merchandise. Cash dividends are the most common, merchandise dividends the least.

Common stockholders are not promised a dividend, but they come to expect certain payments on the basis of the historical dividend pattern of the firm. Before firms pay dividends to common stockholders, they must pay any past due dividends owed to preferred stockholders. The firm's ability to pay dividends can be affected by restrictive debt covenants designed to ensure that the firm can repay its creditors.

Since passage of the *Jobs and Growth Tax Relief Reconciliation Act of 2003*, many firms now pay larger dividends to shareholders, who are subject to a maximum tax rate of 20 percent on dividends rather than the maximum tax rate of 39.6 percent on other forms of income. Because of the importance of the dividend decision to the growth and valuation of the firm, dividends are discussed in greater detail in Chapter 13.

International Stock Issues

Although the international market for common stock is not as large as the international market for bonds, cross-border issuance and trading of common stock have increased dramatically in the past 30 years.

Matter of fact

Did Tax Cuts Stimulate Dividends?

A careful analysis of how firms responded to the dividend tax cuts contained in the 2003 Jobs and Growth Tax Relief Reconciliation Act found that firms dramatically increased dividends soon after that law was passed. One interesting comparison involved the tendency of firms that had never paid dividends to start paying them. In the quarters leading up to the tax cut, only about 4 firms per quarter began paying dividends, but in the quarters immediately following the passage of the new tax law, 29 firms per quarter announced that they would start paying dividends. Similar increases occurred in firms that already paid dividends, with nearly 50 percent of all dividend-paying firms announcing that they would increase their dividend payments by 20 percent or more after the tax cut became law. There was, however, an important confounding factor: Corporate earnings jumped at the same time, so whether dividends rose due to tax policy or due to improving corporate profits remains a matter of debate.

Some corporations *issue stock in foreign markets*. For example, the stock of General Electric trades in Frankfurt, London, Paris, and Tokyo; the stocks of Time Warner and Microsoft trade in Frankfurt and London; and the stock of McDonald's trades in Frankfurt, London, and Paris. The Frankfurt, London, and Tokyo markets are the most popular. Issuing stock internationally broadens the ownership base and helps a company integrate into the local business environment. Having locally traded stock can facilitate corporate acquisitions because shares can be used as an acceptable method of payment.

Foreign corporations have also discovered the benefits of trading their stock in the United States. The disclosure and reporting requirements mandated by the U.S. Securities and Exchange Commission have historically discouraged all but the largest foreign firms from directly listing their shares on the New York Stock Exchange or the American Stock Exchange.

American depositary shares (ADSs)
Dollar-denominated receipts for the stocks of foreign companies that are held by a U.S. financial institution overseas.

American depositary receipts (ADRs)
Securities, backed by *American depositary shares (ADSs)*, that permit U.S. investors to hold shares of non-U.S. companies and trade them in U.S. markets.

As an alternative, most foreign companies choose to tap the U.S. market through **American depositary shares** (**ADSs**). These shares are dollar-denominated receipts for the stocks of foreign companies that are held by a U.S. financial institution overseas. They serve as backing for **American depositary receipts** (**ADRs**), which are securities that permit U.S. investors to hold shares of non-U.S. companies and trade them in U.S. markets. Because ADRs are issued, in dollars, to U.S. investors, they are subject to U.S. securities laws. At the same time, they give investors the opportunity to diversify their portfolios internationally.

PREFERRED STOCK

Most corporations do not issue preferred stock, but preferred shares are common in some industries. *Preferred stock* gives its holders certain privileges that make them senior to common stockholders. Preferred stockholders are promised a fixed periodic dividend, which is stated either as a percentage or as a dollar amount. How the dividend is specified depends on whether the preferred stock has a *par value*

par-value preferred stock
Preferred stock with a stated face value that is used with the specified dividend percentage to determine the annual dollar dividend.

no-par preferred stock
Preferred stock with no stated face value but with a stated annual dollar dividend.

Par-value preferred stock has a stated face value, and its annual dividend is specified as a percentage of this value. **No-par preferred stock** has no stated face value, but its annual dividend is stated in dollars. Preferred stock is most often issued by public utilities, by financial institutions such as banks and insurance companies, by acquiring firms in merger transactions, and by young firms receiving investment funds from venture capital firms. Like the dividends on common stock, preferred dividends are not tax deductible for the firm that pays them.

Basic Rights of Preferred Stockholders

The basic rights of preferred stockholders are somewhat stronger than the rights of common stockholders. Preferred stock is often considered *quasi-debt* because, much like interest on debt, it specifies a fixed periodic payment (dividend). Preferred stock is unlike debt in that it has no maturity date. Because they have a fixed claim on the firm's income that takes precedence over the claim of common stockholders, preferred stockholders are exposed to less risk.

Preferred stockholders are also given *preference over common stockholders in the liquidation of assets* in a legally bankrupt firm, although they must "stand in line" behind creditors. The amount of the claim of preferred stockholders in liquidation is normally equal to the par or stated value of the preferred stock. Preferred stockholders are *not normally given a voting right*, although preferred stockholders are sometimes allowed to elect one member of the board of directors.

Features of Preferred Stock

A preferred stock issue generally includes a number of features. Along with the stock's par value, the amount of dividend payments, the dividend payment dates, and any restrictive covenants, such features are specified in an agreement similar to a *bond indenture*.

Restrictive Covenants   The restrictive covenants in a preferred stock issue focus on ensuring the firm's continued existence and regular payment of the dividend. These covenants include provisions about passing dividends, the sale of senior securities, mergers, sales of assets, minimum liquidity requirements, and repurchases of common stock. The violation of preferred stock covenants usually permits preferred stockholders either to obtain representation on the firm's board of directors or to force the retirement of their stock at or above its par or stated value.

cumulative (preferred stock)
Preferred stock for which all passed (unpaid) dividends in arrears, along with the current dividend, must be paid before dividends can be paid to common stockholders.

noncumulative (preferred stock)
Preferred stock for which passed (unpaid) dividends do not accumulate.

callable feature (preferred stock)
A feature of *callable preferred stock* that allows the issuer to retire the shares within a certain period of time and at a specified price.

Cumulation   Most preferred stock is **cumulative** with respect to any dividends passed. That is, all dividends in arrears, along with the current dividend, must be paid before dividends can be paid to common stockholders. If preferred stock is **noncumulative**, passed (unpaid) dividends do not accumulate. In this case, only the current dividend must be paid before dividends can be paid to common stockholders. Because the common stockholders can receive dividends only after the dividend claims of preferred stockholders have been satisfied, it is in the firm's best interest to pay preferred dividends when they are due.

Other Features   Preferred stock can be *callable* or *convertible*. Preferred stock with a **callable feature** allows the issuer to retire outstanding shares within a certain period of time at a specified price. The call price is normally set above the initial issuance price, but it may decrease as time passes. Making preferred stock callable provides the issuer with a way to bring the fixed-payment commitment of the preferred issue to an end if conditions make it desirable to do so.

conversion feature (preferred stock)
A feature of *convertible preferred stock* that allows holders to change each share into a stated number of shares of common stock.

Preferred stock with a **conversion feature** allows *holders* to change each share into a stated number of shares of common stock, usually anytime after a predetermined date. The conversion ratio can be fixed, or the number of shares of common stock that the preferred stock can be exchanged for changes through time according to a predetermined formula.

ISSUING COMMON STOCK

Because of the high risk associated with a business startup, a firm's initial financing typically comes from its founders in the form of a common stock investment. Until the founders have made an equity investment, it is highly unlikely that others will contribute either equity or debt capital. Early-stage investors in the firm's equity, as well as lenders who provide debt capital, want to be assured that they are taking no more risk than the founders. In addition, they want confirmation that the founders are confident enough in their vision for the firm that they are willing to risk their own money.

Typically, the initial nonfounder financing for business startups with attractive growth prospects comes from private equity investors. Then, as the firm establishes the viability of its product or service offering and begins to generate revenues, cash flow, and profits, it will often "go public" by issuing shares of common stock to a much broader group of investors.

Before we consider the initial *public* sale of equity, let's discuss some of the key aspects of early-stage equity financing in firms that have attractive growth prospects.

Venture Capital

venture capital
Privately raised external equity capital used to fund early-stage firms with attractive growth prospects.

venture capitalists (VCs)
Providers of venture capital; typically, formal businesses that maintain strong oversight over the firms they invest in and that have clearly defined exit strategies.

angel capitalists (angels)
Wealthy individual investors who do not operate as a business but invest in promising early-stage companies in exchange for a portion of the firm's equity.

The initial external equity financing privately raised by firms, typically early-stage firms with attractive growth prospects, is called **venture capital**. Those who provide venture capital are known as **venture capitalists (VCs)**. They typically are formal business entities that maintain strong oversight over the firms they invest in and that have clearly defined exit strategies. Less visible early-stage investors called **angel capitalists** (or **angels**) tend to be investors who do not actually operate as a business; they are often wealthy individual investors who are willing to invest in promising early-stage companies in exchange for a portion of the firm's equity. Although angels play a major role in early-stage equity financing, we will focus on VCs because of their more formal structure and greater public visibility.

Organization and Investment Stages   Venture capital investors tend to be organized in one of four basic ways, as described in Table 7.2. The *VC limited partnership* is by far the dominant structure. These funds have as their sole objective to earn high returns rather than to obtain access to the companies so as to sell or buy other products or services.

VCs can invest in early-stage companies, later-stage companies, or buyouts and acquisitions. Generally, about 40 to 50 percent of VC investments are devoted to early-stage companies (for startup funding and expansion) and a similar percentage to later-stage companies (for marketing, production expansion, and preparation for public offering); the remaining 5 to 10 percent are devoted to the buyout or acquisition of other companies. Generally, VCs look for compound annual rates of return ranging from 20 to 50 percent or more, depending on both the development stage and the attributes of each company. Earlier-stage investments tend to demand higher returns than later-stage investments because of the higher risk associated with the earlier stages of a firm's growth.

TABLE 7.2	Organization of Venture Capital Investors
Organization	Description
Small business investment companies (SBICs)	Corporations chartered by the federal government that can borrow at attractive rates from the U.S. Treasury and use the funds to make venture capital investments in private companies.
Financial VC funds	Subsidiaries of financial institutions, particularly banks, set up to help young firms grow and, it is hoped, become major customers of the institution.
Corporate VC funds	Firms, sometimes subsidiaries, established by nonfinancial firms, typically to gain access to new technologies that the corporation can access to further its own growth.
VC limited partnerships	Limited partnerships organized by professional VC firms, which serve as the general partner and organize, invest, and manage the partnership using the limited partners' funds; the professional VCs ultimately liquidate the partnership and distribute the proceeds to all partners.

Deal Structure and Pricing   Regardless of the development stage, venture capital investments are made under a legal contract that clearly allocates responsibilities and ownership interests between existing owners (founders) and the VC fund or limited partnership. The terms of the agreement will depend on numerous factors related to the founders; the business structure, stage of development, and outlook; and other market and timing issues. The specific financial terms will, of course, depend on the value of the enterprise, the amount of funding, and the perceived risk. To control the VC's risk, various covenants are included in the agreement, and the actual funding may be pegged to the achievement of *measurable milestones*. The VC will negotiate numerous other provisions into the contract, both to ensure the firm's success and to control its risk exposure. The contract will have an explicit exit strategy for the VC that may be tied both to measurable milestones and to time.

The amount of equity to which the VC is entitled will, of course, depend on the value of the firm, the terms of the contract, the exit terms, and the minimum compound annual rate of return required by the VC on its investment. Although each VC investment is unique and no standard contract exists, the transaction will be structured to provide the VC with a high rate of return that is consistent with the typically high risk of such transactions. The exit strategy of most VC investments is to take the firm public through an initial public offering.

Going Public

When a firm wishes to sell its stock in the primary market, it has three alternatives. It can make (1) a *public offering,* in which it offers its shares for sale to the general public; (2) a *rights offering,* in which new shares are sold to existing stockholders; or (3) a *private placement,* in which the firm sells new securities directly to an investor or group of investors. Here we focus on public offerings, particularly the **initial public offering (IPO)**, which is the first public sale of a firm's stock. IPOs are typically made by small, rapidly growing companies that either require additional capital to continue expanding or have met a milestone for going public that was established in a contract signed earlier to obtain VC funding.

initial public offering (IPO)
The first public sale of a firm's stock.

To go public, the firm must first obtain the approval of its current shareholders, the investors who own its privately issued stock. Next, the company's auditors and lawyers must certify that all documents for the company are legitimate. The company then finds an investment bank willing to *underwrite* the offering. This underwriter is responsible for promoting the stock and facilitating the sale of the company's IPO shares. The underwriter often brings in other investment banking firms as participants. We'll discuss the role of the investment banker in more detail in the next section.

The company files a registration statement with the SEC. One portion of the registration statement is called the **prospectus**. It describes the key aspects of the issue, the issuer, and its management and financial position. During the waiting period between the statement's filing and its approval, prospective investors can receive a preliminary prospectus. This preliminary version is called a **red herring** because a notice printed in red on the front cover indicates the tentative nature of the offer. The cover of the preliminary prospectus describing the 2013 stock issue of Regado Biosciences is shown in Figure 7.1. Note the red disclaimer printed across the top of the page.

After the SEC approves the registration statement, the investment community can begin analyzing the company's prospects. However, from the time it files until at least 1 month after the IPO is complete, the company must observe a *quiet period* during which there are restrictions on what company officials may say about the company. The purpose of the quiet period is to make sure that all

prospectus
A portion of a security registration statement that describes the key aspects of the issue, the issuer, and its management and financial position.

red herring
A preliminary prospectus made available to prospective investors during the waiting period between the registration statement's filing with the SEC and its approval.

FIGURE 7.1

Cover of a Preliminary Prospectus for a Stock Issue
Some of the key factors related to the 2013 common stock issue by Regado Biosciences are summarized on the cover of the preliminary prospectus. The disclaimer printed in red across the top of the page is what gives the preliminary prospectus its "red herring" name.

The information in this preliminary prospectus is not complete and may be changed. These securities may not be sold until the registration statement filed with the Securities and Exchange Commission is effective. This preliminary prospectus is not an offer to sell nor does it seek an offer to buy these securities in any state or other jurisdiction where the offer or sale is not permitted.

PROSPECTUS (Subject to Completion)   Dated April 29, 2013

Shares

Regado Biosciences

Common Stock

This is the initial public offering of shares of our common stock. We are offering   shares of our common stock. Prior to this offering, there has been no public market for our common stock. We intend to apply to list our common stock on The NASDAQ Global Market under the symbol "RGDO." We expect that the public offering price will be between $ and $ per share.

We are an "emerging growth company" as that term is used in the Jumpstart Our Business Startups Act of 2012 and, as such, have elected to comply with certain reduced public company reporting requirements for this prospectus and future filings. See "Prospectus Summary – Implications of Being an Emerging Growth Company."

Our business and an investment in our common stock involve significant risks. These risks are described under the caption "Risk Factors" beginning on page **9** of this prospectus.

Neither the Securities and Exchange Commission nor any state securities commission has approved or disapproved of these securities or passed upon the adequacy or accuracy of this prospectus. Any representation to the contrary is a criminal offense.

	Per Share	Total
Public offering price	$	$
Underwriting discount	$	$
Proceeds, before expenses, to us	$	$

The underwriters may also purchase up to an additional   shares from us at the public offering price, less the underwriting discount, within 30 days from the date of this prospectus to cover overallotments, if any.

The underwriters expect to deliver the shares against payment in New York, New York on   , 2013.

Cowen and Company   **BMO Capital Markets**

Canaccord Genuity   Needham & Company   Wedbush PacGrow Life Sciences

, 2013

Source: SEC filing Form S-1, Regado Biosciences, filed April 29, 2013.

potential investors have access to the same information about the company—the information presented in the preliminary prospectus—and not to any unpublished data that might give them an unfair advantage.

The investment bankers and company executives promote the company's stock offering through a *road show,* a series of presentations to potential investors around the country and sometimes overseas. In addition to providing investors with information about the new issue, road show sessions help the investment bankers gauge the demand for the offering and set an expected pricing range. After the underwriter sets terms and prices the issue, the SEC must approve the offering.

The Investment Banker's Role

investment banker
Financial intermediary that specializes in selling new security issues and advising firms with regard to major financial transactions.

Most public offerings are made with the assistance of an **investment banker**. The investment banker is a financial intermediary (such as Morgan Stanley or Goldman Sachs) that specializes in selling new security issues and advising firms with regard to major financial transactions. The main activity of the investment banker is **underwriting**. This process involves purchasing the security issue from the issuing corporation at an agreed-on price and bearing the risk of reselling it to the public at a profit. The investment banker also provides the issuer with advice about pricing and other important aspects of the issue.

underwriting
The role of the *investment banker* in bearing the risk of reselling, at a profit, the securities purchased from an issuing corporation at an agreed-on price.

In the case of very large security issues, the investment banker brings in other bankers as partners to form an **underwriting syndicate**. The syndicate shares the financial risk associated with buying the entire issue from the issuer and reselling the new securities to the public. The originating investment banker and the syndicate members put together a **selling group**, normally made up of themselves and a large number of brokerage firms. Each member of the selling group accepts the responsibility for selling a certain portion of the issue and is paid a commission on the securities it sells. The selling process for a large security issue is depicted in Figure 7.2.

underwriting syndicate
A group of other bankers formed by an investment banker to share the financial risk associated with *underwriting* new securities.

selling group
A large number of brokerage firms that join the originating investment banker(s); each accepts responsibility for selling a certain portion of a new security issue on a commission basis.

Compensation for underwriting and selling services typically comes in the form of a discount on the sale price of the securities. For example, an investment banker may pay the issuing firm $24 per share for stock that will be sold for $26 per share. The investment banker may then sell the shares to members of the selling group for $25.25 per share. In this case, the original investment banker earns $1.25 per share ($25.25 sale price minus $24 purchase price). The members of the selling group earn 75 cents for each share they sell ($26 sale price minus $25.25 purchase price). Although some primary security offerings are directly placed by the issuer, the majority of new issues are sold through public offering via the mechanism just described.

→ REVIEW QUESTIONS

7–2 What risks do common stockholders take that other suppliers of capital do not?

7–3 How does a *rights offering* protect a firm's stockholders against the *dilution of ownership?*

7–4 Explain the relationships among authorized shares, outstanding shares, treasury stock, and issued shares.

7–5 What are the advantages to both U.S.-based and foreign corporations of issuing stock outside their home markets? What are *American depositary receipts (ADRs)?* What are *American depositary shares (ADSs)?*

7–6 What claims do preferred stockholders have with respect to distribution of earnings (dividends) and assets?

FIGURE 7.2

The Selling Process for a Large Security Issue
The investment banker hired by the issuing corporation may form an underwriting syndicate. The underwriting syndicate buys the entire security issue from the issuing corporation at an agreed-on price. The underwriters then have the opportunity (and bear the risk) of reselling the issue to the public at a profit. Both the originating investment banker and the other syndicate members put together a selling group to sell the issue on a commission basis to investors.

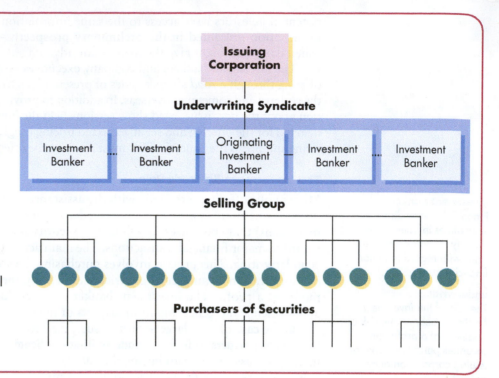

7–7 Explain the *cumulative feature* of preferred stock. What is the purpose of a *call feature* in a preferred stock issue?

7–8 What is the difference between a *venture capitalist (VC)* and an *angel capitalist (angel)*?

7–9 What are the four ways that VCs are most commonly organized? How are their deals structured and priced?

7–10 What general procedures must a private firm follow to go public via an *initial public offering (IPO)*?

7–11 What role does an *investment banker* play in a public offering? Describe an underwriting syndicate.

 LG 4 LG 5   # 7.3 Common Stock Valuation

Common stockholders expect to be rewarded through periodic cash dividends and an increasing share value. Some of these investors decide which stocks to buy and sell based on a plan to maintain a broadly diversified portfolio. Other investors have a more speculative motive for trading. They try to spot companies whose shares are *undervalued,* meaning that the true value of the shares is greater than the current market price. These investors buy shares that they believe to be undervalued and sell shares that they think are *overvalued* (that is, the market price is greater than the true value). Regardless of one's motive for trading, understanding how to value common stocks is an important part of the investment process. Stock valuation is also an important tool for financial managers; how can they work to maximize the stock price without understanding the factors that determine the value of the stock? In this section, we will describe specific stock valuation techniques. First, we will consider the relationship between market efficiency and stock valuation.

MARKET EFFICIENCY

Rational buyers and sellers use their assessment of an asset's risk and return to determine its value. To a buyer, the asset's value represents the maximum purchase price, and to a seller, it represents the minimum sale price. In competitive markets with many active participants, such as a stock exchange, the interactions of many buyers and sellers result in an equilibrium price—the *market value*—for each security. This price reflects the collective actions that buyers and sellers take on the basis of all available information. Buyers and sellers digest new information quickly as it becomes available and, through their purchase and sale activities, create a new market equilibrium price. Because the flow of new information is continual and the content of that information is unpredictable (otherwise, it would not be *new* information), stock prices fluctuate, always moving toward a new equilibrium that reflects the most recent information available. This general concept is known as *market efficiency*.

Matter of fact

The Value of Speed

The University of Michigan produces a monthly survey measuring consumer confidence, and that survey routinely causes stock prices to move when it is released. In June 2013, various news organizations reported that Thomson Reuters had a contract that allowed it to distribute information about the monthly consumer confidence survey to its clients, via a conference call, 5 minutes before the survey results were posted on the university's website. The contract contained another provision that allowed Thomson Reuters to distribute survey results electronically to an elite group of clients at 9:54:58 a.m., 2 seconds prior to the conference call. The 2 seconds of lead time over the rest of the market could allow these clients to trade stocks before most market participants learned about the new information in the survey.

THE EFFICIENT-MARKET HYPOTHESIS

efficient-market hypothesis (EMH)
Theory describing the behavior of an assumed "perfect" market in which (1) securities are in equilibrium, (2) security prices fully reflect all available information and react swiftly to new information, and (3), because stocks are fully and fairly priced, investors need not waste time looking for mispriced securities.

As noted in Chapter 2, active stock markets, such as the NYSE Euronext and the Nasdaq market, are *efficient* in that they are made up of many rational investors who react quickly and objectively to new information. The **efficient-market hypothesis (EMH)**, which is the basic theory describing the behavior of such a market, specifically states that

1. Securities are typically in equilibrium, which means that they are fairly priced and that their expected returns equal their required returns.
2. At any point in time, security prices fully reflect all information available about the firm and its securities, and these prices react swiftly to new information.
3. Because stocks are fully and fairly priced, investors need not waste their time trying to find mispriced (undervalued or overvalued) securities.

Not all market participants are believers in the efficient-market hypothesis. Some believe that it is worthwhile to search for undervalued or overvalued securities and to trade them to profit from market inefficiencies. Others argue that it is mere luck that would allow market participants to anticipate new information correctly and as a result earn *abnormal returns,* that is, actual returns greater than should be expected given the risk of the investment. They believe that it is unlikely that market participants can *over the long run* earn abnormal returns. Contrary to this belief, some well-known investors such as Warren Buffett and Bill Gross *have* over the long run consistently earned abnormal returns on their portfolios. It is unclear whether their success is the result of their superior ability to anticipate new information or of some form of market inefficiency.

The Behavioral Finance Challenge

Although considerable evidence supports the concept of market efficiency, a growing body of academic evidence has begun to cast doubt on the validity of this notion. The research documents various *anomalies*—outcomes that are inconsistent with efficient markets—in stock returns. A number of academics and practitioners have also recognized that emotions and other subjective factors play a role in investment decisions.

behavioral finance
A growing body of research that focuses on investor behavior and its impact on investment decisions and stock prices. Advocates are commonly referred to as "behaviorists."

This focus on investor behavior has resulted in a significant body of research, collectively referred to as **behavioral finance**. Advocates of behavioral finance are commonly referred to as "behaviorists." Daniel Kahneman was awarded the 2002 Nobel Prize in economics for his work in behavioral finance, specifically for integrating insights from psychology and economics. Ongoing research into the psychological factors that can affect investor behavior and the resulting effects on stock prices will likely result in growing acceptance of behavioral finance. The *Focus on Practice* box further explains some of the findings of behavioral finance.

Although challenges to the efficient market hypothesis, such as those presented by advocates of behavioral finance, are interesting and worthy of study, in this text we generally take the position that markets are efficient. We will use the terms *expected return* and *required return* interchangeably because they should be equal in an efficient market. In other words, we will operate under the assumption that a stock's market price at any point in time is the best estimate of its value. We're now ready to look closely at the mechanics of common stock valuation.

BASIC COMMON STOCK VALUATION EQUATION

Like the value of a bond, which we discussed in Chapter 6, *the value of a share of common stock is equal to the present value of all future cash flows (dividends) that it is expected to provide.* Although a stockholder can earn capital gains by selling stock at a price above that originally paid, what the buyer really pays for is the right to all future dividends. What about stocks that do not currently pay dividends? Such stocks have a value attributable to a future dividend stream or to the proceeds from the sale of the company. Therefore, *from a valuation viewpoint, future dividends are relevant.*

The basic valuation model for common stock is given by

$$P_0 = \frac{D_1}{(1 + r_s)^1} + \frac{D_2}{(1 + r_s)^2} + \cdots + \frac{D_\infty}{(1 + r_s)^\infty} \qquad (7.1)$$

focus on PRACTICE

Understanding Human Behavior Helps Us Understand Investor Behavior

in practice Market anomalies are patterns inconsistent with the efficient market hypothesis. Behavioral finance has a number of theories to help explain how human emotions influence people in their investment decision-making processes.

Regret theory deals with the emotional reaction people experience after realizing they have made an error in judgment. When deciding whether to sell a stock, investors become emotionally affected by the price at which they purchased the stock. A sale at a loss would confirm that the investor miscalculated the value of the stock when it was purchased. The correct approach when considering whether to sell a stock is, "Would I buy this stock today if it were already liquidated?" If the answer is "no," it is time to sell. Regret theory also holds true for investors who passed up buying a stock that now is selling at a much higher price. Again, the correct approach is to value the stock today without regard to its prior value.

Herding is another market behavior affecting investor decisions. Some investors rationalize their decision to buy certain stocks with "everyone else is doing it." Investors may feel less embarrassment about losing money on a popular stock than about losing money on an unknown or unpopular stock.

People have a tendency to place particular events into *mental accounts*, and the difference between these compartments sometimes influences behavior more than the events themselves. Researchers have asked people the following question: "Would you purchase a $20 ticket at the local theater if you realize after you get there that you have lost a $20 bill?" Roughly 88 percent of people would do so. Under another scenario, people were asked whether they would buy a second $20 ticket if they arrived at the theater and realized that they had left at home a ticket purchased in advance for $20. Only 40 percent of respondents would buy another. In both scenarios, the person is out $40, but mental accounting leads to a different outcome. In investing, compartmentalization is best illustrated by the hesitation to sell an investment that once had monstrous gains and now has a modest gain. During bull markets, people get accustomed to paper gains. When a market correction deflates investors' net worth, they are hesitant to sell, causing them to wait for the return of that gain.

Other investor behaviors are prospect theory and anchoring. According to *prospect theory*, people express a different degree of emotion toward gains than losses. Individuals are stressed more by prospective losses than they are buoyed by the prospect of equal gains. *Anchoring* is the tendency of investors to place more value on recent information. People tend to give too much credence to recent market opinions and events and mistakenly extrapolate recent trends that differ from historical, long-term averages and probabilities. Anchoring is a partial explanation for the longevity of some bull markets.

Most stock-valuation techniques require that all relevant information be available to properly determine a stock's value and potential for future gain. Behavioral finance may explain the connection between valuation and an investor's actions based on that valuation.

▶ *Theories of behavioral finance can apply to other areas of human behavior in addition to investing. Think of a situation in which you may have demonstrated one of these behaviors. Share your situation with a classmate.*

where

$$P_0 = \text{value today of common stock}$$
$$D_t = \text{per-share dividend } expected \text{ at the end of year } t$$
$$r_s = \text{required return on common stock}$$

The equation can be simplified somewhat by redefining each year's dividend, D_t, in terms of anticipated growth. We will consider three models here: zero growth, constant growth, and variable growth.

Zero-Growth Model

zero-growth model
An approach to dividend valuation that assumes a constant, nongrowing dividend stream.

The simplest approach to dividend valuation, the **zero-growth model**, assumes a constant, nongrowing dividend stream. In terms of the notation already introduced,

$$D_1 = D_2 = \cdots = D_\infty$$

When we let D_1 represent the amount of the annual dividend, Equation 7.1 under zero growth reduces to

$$P_0 = D_1 \times \sum_{t=1}^{\infty} \frac{1}{(1 + r_s)^t} = D_1 \times \frac{1}{r_s} = \frac{D_1}{r_s} \tag{7.2}$$

The equation shows that with zero growth, the value of a share of stock would equal the present value of a perpetuity of D_1 dollars discounted at a rate r_s. (Perpetuities were introduced in Chapter 5; see Equation 5.14 and the related discussion.)

IRF Personal Finance Example 7.2 ▶ Chuck Swimmer estimates that the dividend of Denham Company, an established textile producer, is expected to remain constant at $3 per share indefinitely. If his required return on its stock is 15%, the stock's value is $20 ($3 ÷ 0.15) per share.

MyFinanceLab Solution
Video

Preferred Stock Valuation   Because preferred stock typically provides its holders with a fixed annual dividend and because it never matures, *Equation 7.2 can be used to find the value of preferred stock*. The value of preferred stock can be estimated by substituting the dividend on the preferred stock for D_1 and the required return for r_s in Equation 7.2. For example, a preferred stock paying a $5 annual dividend and having a required return of 13 percent would have a value of $38.46 ($5 ÷ 0.13) per share.

Constant-Growth Model

constant-growth model
A widely cited dividend valuation approach that assumes that dividends will grow at a constant rate, but a rate that is less than the required return.

The most widely cited dividend valuation approach, the **constant-growth model**, assumes that dividends will grow at a constant rate, but a rate that is less than the required return. (The assumption that the constant rate of growth, g, is less than the required return, r_s, is a necessary mathematical condition for deriving this model.[1]) By letting D_0 represent the most recent dividend, we can rewrite Equation 7.1 as

$$P_0 = \frac{D_0 \times (1 + g)^1}{(1 + r_s)^1} + \frac{D_0 \times (1 + g)^2}{(1 + r_s)^2} + \cdots + \frac{D_0 \times (1 + g)^{\infty}}{(1 + r_s)^{\infty}} \tag{7.3}$$

If we simplify Equation 7.3, it can be rewritten as

$$P_0 = \frac{D_1}{r_s - g} \tag{7.4}$$

Gordon growth model
A common name for the *constant-growth model* that is widely cited in dividend valuation.

The constant-growth model in Equation 7.4 is commonly called the **Gordon growth model**. An example will show how it works.

---

1. Another assumption of the constant-growth model as presented is that earnings and dividends grow at the same rate. This assumption is true only in cases in which a firm pays out a fixed percentage of its earnings each year (has a fixed payout ratio). In the case of a declining industry, a negative growth rate ($g < 0\%$) might exist. In such a case, the constant-growth model, as well as the variable-growth model presented in the next section, remains fully applicable to the valuation process.

IRF Example 7.3 ▶

MyFinanceLab Solution
Video

Lamar Company, a small cosmetics company, from 2010 through 2015 paid the following per-share dividends:

Year	Dividend per share
2015	$1.40
2014	1.29
2013	1.20
2012	1.12
2011	1.05
2010	1.00

We assume that the historical annual growth rate of dividends is an accurate estimate of the future constant annual rate of dividend growth, g. To find the historical annual growth rate of dividends, we must solve the following for g:

$$D_{2015} = D_{2010} \times (1 + g)^5$$

$$\frac{D_{2015}}{D_{2010}} = (1 + g)^5$$

$$\frac{\$1.40}{\$1.00} = (1 + g)^5$$

MyFinanceLab Financial
Calculator

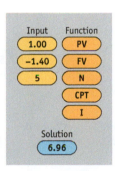

Input	Function
1.00	PV
−1.40	FV
5	N
	CPT
	I

Solution
6.96

Using a financial calculator, we find that the historical annual growth rate of Lamar Company dividends equals approximately 7%. (*Note:* Most calculators require *either* the PV or FV value to be input as a negative number to calculate an unknown interest or growth rate. That approach is used here.) The company estimates that its dividend in 2016, D_1, will equal $1.50 (about 7% more than the last dividend). The required return, r_s, is 15%. By substituting these values into Equation 7.4, we find the value of the stock to be

$$P_0 = \frac{\$1.50}{0.15 - 0.07} = \frac{\$1.50}{0.08} = \underline{\$18.75} \text{ per share}$$

Assuming that the values of D_1, r_s, and g are accurately estimated, Lamar Company's stock value is $18.75 per share.

Variable-Growth Model

variable-growth model
A dividend valuation approach that allows for a change in the dividend growth rate.

The zero- and constant-growth common stock models do not allow for any shift in expected growth rates. Because future growth rates might shift up or down because of changing business conditions, it is useful to consider a **variable-growth model** that allows for a change in the dividend growth rate.[2] We will assume that a single shift in growth rates occurs at the end of year N, and we will use g_1 to represent the initial growth rate and g_2 for the growth rate after the shift. To determine the value of a share of stock in the case of variable growth, we use a four-step procedure:

---

2. More than one change in the growth rate can be incorporated into the model, but to simplify the discussion we will consider only a single growth-rate change. The number of variable-growth valuation models is technically unlimited, but concern over all possible shifts in growth is unlikely to yield much more accuracy than a simpler model.

Step 1 Find the value of the cash dividends at the end of *each year*, D_t, during the initial growth period, years 1 through N. This step may require adjusting the most recent dividend, D_0, using the initial growth rate, g_1, to calculate the dividend amount for each year. Therefore, for the first N years,

$$D_t = D_0 \times (1 + g_1)^t$$

Step 2 Find the present value of the dividends expected during the initial growth period. Using the notation presented earlier, we can give this value as

$$\sum_{t=1}^{N} \frac{D_0 \times (1 + g_1)^t}{(1 + r_s)^t} = \sum_{t=1}^{N} \frac{D_t}{(1 + r_s)^t}$$

Step 3 Find the value of the stock *at the end of the initial growth period*, $P_N = (D_{N+1})/(r_s - g_2)$, which is the present value of all dividends expected from year $N + 1$ to infinity, assuming a constant dividend growth rate, g_2. This value is found by applying the constant-growth model (Equation 7.4) to the dividends expected from year $N + 1$ to infinity. The present value of P_N would represent the value *today* of all dividends that are expected to be received from year $N + 1$ to infinity. This value can be represented by

$$\frac{1}{(1 + r_s)^N} \times \frac{D_{N+1}}{r_s - g_2}$$

Step 4 Add the present value components found in Steps 2 and 3 to find the value of the stock, P_0, given in Equation 7.5:

$$P_0 = \underbrace{\sum_{t=1}^{N} \frac{D_0 \times (1 + g_1)^t}{(1 + r_s)^t}}_{\substack{\text{Present value of} \\ \text{dividends} \\ \text{during initial} \\ \text{growth period}}} + \underbrace{\left[\frac{1}{(1 + r_s)^N} \times \frac{D_{N+1}}{r_s - g_2} \right]}_{\substack{\text{Present value of} \\ \text{price of stock} \\ \text{at end of initial} \\ \text{growth period}}} \tag{7.5}$$

The following example illustrates the application of these steps to a variable-growth situation with only one change in growth rate.

IRF **Personal Finance Example 7.4** ▶   Victoria Robb is considering purchasing the common stock of Warren Industries, a rapidly growing boat manufacturer. She finds that the firm's most recent (2015) annual dividend payment was $1.50 per share. Victoria estimates that these dividends will increase at a 10% annual rate, g_1, over the next 3 years (2016, 2017, and 2018) because of the introduction of a hot new boat. At the end of the 3 years (the end of 2018), she expects the firm's mature product line to result in a slowing of the dividend growth rate to 5% per year, g_2, for the foreseeable future. Victoria's required return, r_s, is 15%. To estimate the current (end-of-2015) value of Warren's common stock, $P_0 = P_{2015}$, she applies the four-step procedure to these data.

TABLE 7.3	Calculation of Present Value of Warren Industries Dividends (2016–2018)				
t	End of year	$D_0 = D_{2015}$ (1)	$(1 + g_1)^t$ (2)	D_t [(1) × (2)] (3)	$(1 + r_s)^t$ (4)	Present value of dividends [(3) ÷ (4)] (5)
1	2013	$1.50	1.100	$1.65	1.150	$1.43
2	2014	1.50	1.210	1.82	1.323	1.37
3	2015	1.50	1.331	2.00	1.521	1.32

$$\text{Sum of present value of dividends} = \sum_{t=1}^{3} \frac{D_0 \times (1 + g_1)^t}{(1 + r_s)^t} = \$4.12$$

Step 1 The value of the cash dividends in each of the next 3 years is calculated in columns 1, 2, and 3 of Table 7.3. The 2016, 2017, and 2018 dividends are $1.65, $1.82, and $2.00, respectively.

Step 2 The present value of the three dividends expected during the 2016–2018 initial growth period is calculated in columns 3, 4, and 5 of Table 7.3. The sum of the present values of the three dividends is $4.12.

Step 3 The value of the stock at the end of the initial growth period (N = 2018) can be found by first calculating $D_{N+1} = D_{2019}$:

$$D_{2019} = D_{2018} \times (1 + 0.05) = \$2.00 \times (1.05) = \$2.10$$

By using D_{2019} = $2.10, a 15% required return, and a 5% dividend growth rate, the value of the stock at the end of 2018 is calculated as

$$P_{2018} = \frac{D_{2019}}{r_s - g_2} = \frac{\$2.10}{0.15 - 0.05} = \frac{\$2.10}{0.10} = \$21.00$$

Finally, in Step 3, the share value of $21 at the end of 2018 must be converted into a present (end-of-2015) value. Using the 15% required return, we get

$$\frac{P_{2018}}{(1 + r_s)^3} = \frac{\$21}{(1 + 0.15)^3} = \$13.81$$

Step 4 Adding the present value of the initial dividend stream (found in Step 2) to the present value of the stock at the end of the initial growth period (found in Step 3) as specified in Equation 7.5, the current (end-of-2015) value of Warren Industries stock is

$$P_{2015} = \$4.12 + \$13.81 = \underline{\$17.93} \text{ per share}$$

Victoria's calculations indicate that the stock is currently worth $17.93 per share.

FREE CASH FLOW VALUATION MODEL

As an alternative to the dividend valuation models presented earlier in this chapter, a firm's value can be estimated by using its projected *free cash flows (FCFs)*. This approach is appealing when one is valuing firms that have no dividend history or are startups or when one is valuing an operating unit or division of a larger public company. Although dividend valuation models are widely used and accepted, in these situations it is preferable to use a more general free cash flow valuation model.

free cash flow valuation model
A model that determines the value of an entire company as the present value of its expected *free cash flows* discounted at the firm's *weighted average cost of capital,* which is its expected average future cost of funds over the long run.

The **free cash flow valuation model** is based on the same basic premise as dividend valuation models: The value of a share of common stock is the present value of all future cash flows it is expected to provide over an infinite time horizon. However, in the free cash flow valuation model, instead of valuing the firm's expected dividends, we value the firm's expected *free cash flows,* defined in Chapter 4 (on page 117, Equation 4.4). They represent the amount of cash flow available to investors—the providers of debt (creditors) and equity (owners)—after all other obligations have been met.

The free cash flow valuation model estimates the value of the entire company by finding the present value of its expected free cash flows discounted at its *weighted average cost of capital,* which is its expected average future cost of funds (we'll say more about this in Chapter 9), as specified in Equation 7.6:

$$V_C = \frac{FCF_1}{(1 + r_a)^1} + \frac{FCF_2}{(1 + r_a)^2} + \cdots + \frac{FCF_\infty}{(1 + r_a)^\infty} \tag{7.6}$$

where

$$V_C = \text{value of the entire company}$$
$$FCF_t = \text{free cash flow } expected \text{ at the end of year } t$$
$$r_a = \text{the firms weighted average cost of capital}$$

Note the similarity between Equations 7.6 and 7.1, the general stock valuation equation.

Because the value of the entire company, V_C, is the market value of the entire enterprise (that is, of all assets), to find common stock value, V_S, we must subtract the market value of all the firm's debt, V_D, and the market value of preferred stock, V_P, from V_C:

$$V_S = V_C - V_D - V_P \tag{7.7}$$

Because it is difficult to forecast a firm's free cash flow, specific annual cash flows are typically forecast for only about 5 years, beyond which a constant growth rate is assumed. Here we assume that the first 5 years of free cash flows are explicitly forecast and that a constant rate of free cash flow growth occurs beyond the end of year 5 to infinity. This model is methodologically similar to the variable-growth model presented earlier in this chapter. Its application is best demonstrated with an example.

IRF Example 7.5 ▶ Dewhurst, Inc., wishes to determine the value of its stock by using the free cash flow valuation model. To apply the model, the firm's CFO developed the data given in Table 7.4. Application of the model can be performed in four steps.

TABLE 7.4	Dewhurst, Inc.'s, Data for the Free Cash Flow Valuation Model	

	Free cash flow	
Year (t)	(FCF_t)	Other data
2016	$400,000	Growth rate of FCF, beyond 2020 to infinity, $g_{FCF} = 3\%$
2017	450,000	Weighted average cost of capital, $r_a = 9\%$
2018	520,000	Market value of all debt, $V_D = \$3,100,000$
2019	560,000	Market value of preferred stock, $V_P = \$800,000$
2020	600,000	Number of shares of common stock outstanding $= 300,000$

Step 1 Calculate the present value of the free cash flow occurring from the end of 2021 to infinity, measured at the beginning of 2021 (that is, at the end of 2020). Because a constant rate of growth in FCF is forecast beyond 2020, we can use the constant-growth dividend valuation model (Equation 7.4) to calculate the value of the free cash flows from the end of 2021 to infinity:

$$\text{Value of } FCF_{2021 \rightarrow \infty} = \frac{FCF_{2021}}{r_a - g_{FCF}}$$

$$= \frac{\$600,000 \times (1 + 0.03)}{0.09 - 0.03}$$

$$= \frac{\$618,000}{0.06} = \$10,300,000$$

Note that to calculate the FCF in 2021, we had to increase the 2020 FCF value of $600,000 by the 3% FCF growth rate, g_{FCF}.

Step 2 Add the present value of the FCF from 2021 to infinity, which is measured at the end of 2020, to the 2020 FCF value to get the total FCF in 2020:

$$\text{Total } FCF_{2020} = \$600,000 + \$10,300,000 = \$10,900,000$$

Step 3 Find the sum of the present values of the FCFs for 2016 through 2020 to determine the value of the entire company, V_C. This calculation is shown in Table 7.5.

TABLE 7.5	Calculation of the Value of the Entire Company for Dewhurst, Inc.		

			Present value of FCF_t
	FCF_t	$(1 + r_a)^t$	$[(1) \times (2)]$
Year (t)	(1)	(2)	(3)
2016	$ 400,000	1.090	$ 366,972
2017	450,000	1.188	378,788
2018	520,000	1.295	401,544
2019	560,000	1.412	396,601
2020	10,900,000[a]	1.539	7,082,521
		Value of entire company, $V_C = $	$8,626,426[b]

[a]This amount is the sum of the FCF_{2020} of $600,000 from Table 7.4 and the $10,300,000 value of the $FCF_{2021 \rightarrow \infty}$ calculated in Step 1.

[b]This value of the entire company is based on the rounded values that appear in the table. The precise value found without rounding is $8,628,234.

Step 4   Calculate the value of the common stock using Equation 7.7. Substituting into Equation 7.7 the value of the entire company, V_C, calculated in Step 3, and the market values of debt, V_D, and preferred stock, V_P, given in Table 7.4, yields the value of the common stock, V_S:

$$V_S = \$8,626,426 - \$3,100,000 - \$800,000 = \underline{\$4,726,426}$$

The value of Dewhurst's common stock is therefore estimated to be $4,726,426. By dividing this total by the 300,000 shares of common stock that the firm has outstanding, we get a common stock value of *$15.75 per share* ($4,726,426 ÷ 300,000).

It should now be clear that the free cash flow valuation model is consistent with the dividend valuation models presented earlier. The appeal of this approach is its focus on the free cash flow estimates rather than on forecasted dividends, which are far more difficult to estimate given that they are paid at the discretion of the firm's board. The more general nature of the free cash flow model is responsible for its growing popularity, particularly with CFOs and other financial managers.

OTHER APPROACHES TO COMMON STOCK VALUATION

Many other approaches to common stock valuation exist. The more popular approaches include book value, liquidation value, and some type of price/earnings multiple.

book value per share
The amount per share of common stock that would be received if all of the firm's assets were *sold for their exact book (accounting) value* and the proceeds remaining after paying all liabilities (including preferred stock) were divided among the common stockholders.

Book Value

Book value per share is simply the amount per share of common stock that would be received if all the firm's assets were *sold for their exact book (accounting) value* and the proceeds remaining after paying all liabilities (including preferred stock) were divided among the common stockholders. This method lacks sophistication and can be criticized on the basis of its reliance on historical balance sheet data. It ignores the firm's expected earnings potential and generally lacks any true relationship to the firm's value in the marketplace. Let us look at an example.

Example 7.6 ▶   At year-end 2015, Lamar Company's balance sheet shows total assets of $6 million, total liabilities and preferred stock of $4.5 million, and 100,000 shares of common stock outstanding. Its book value per share would therefore be

$$\frac{\$6,000,000 - \$4,500,000}{100,000 \text{ shares}} = \underline{\$15} \text{ per share}$$

Because this value assumes that assets could be sold for their book value, it may not represent the minimum price at which shares are valued in the marketplace. As a matter of fact, although most stocks sell above book value, it is not unusual to find stocks selling below book value when investors believe either that assets are overvalued or that the firm's liabilities are understated.

liquidation value per share
The *actual amount* per share of common stock that would be received if all of the firm's assets were *sold for their market value*, liabilities (including preferred stock) were paid, and any remaining money were divided among the common stockholders.

Liquidation Value

Liquidation value per share is the *actual amount* per share of common stock that would be received if all the firm's assets were *sold for their market value*, liabilities and preferred stock were paid, and any remaining money were divided among the common stockholders. This measure is more realistic than book value—because it is based on the current market value of the firm's assets—but it still fails to consider the earning power of those assets. An example will illustrate.

Example 7.7 ▶	Lamar Company found on investigation that it could obtain only $5.25 million if it sold its assets today. The firm's liquidation value per share would therefore be

$$\frac{\$5,250,000 - \$4,500,000}{100,000 \text{ shares}} = \underline{\$7.50} \text{ per share}$$

Ignoring liquidation expenses, this amount would be the firm's minimum value.

Price/Earnings (P/E) Multiples

price/earnings multiple approach
A popular technique used to estimate the firm's share value; calculated by multiplying the firm's expected earnings per share (EPS) by the average price/earnings (P/E) ratio for the industry.

The *price/earnings (P/E) ratio,* introduced in Chapter 3, reflects the amount investors are willing to pay for each dollar of earnings. The average P/E ratio in a particular industry can be used as a guide to a firm's value, if it is assumed that investors value the earnings of that firm in the same way they do the "average" firm in the industry. The **price/earnings multiple approach** is a popular technique used to estimate the firm's share value; it is calculated by multiplying the firm's expected earnings per share (EPS) by the average price/earnings (P/E) ratio for the industry. The average P/E ratio for the industry can be obtained from a source such as *Standard & Poor's Industrial Ratios.*

The P/E ratio valuation technique is a simple method of determining a stock's value and can be quickly calculated after firms make earnings announcements, which accounts for its popularity. Naturally, this use has increased the demand for more frequent announcements or "guidance" regarding future earnings. Some firms believe that pre-earnings guidance creates additional costs and can lead to ethical issues.

The use of P/E multiples is especially helpful in valuing firms that are not publicly traded, but analysts use this approach for public companies too. In any case, the price/earnings multiple approach is considered superior to the use of book or liquidation values because it considers *expected* earnings. An example will demonstrate the use of price/earnings multiples.

Personal Finance Example 7.8 ▶	
MyFinanceLab Solution Video	Ann Perrier plans to use the price/earnings multiple approach to estimate the value of Lamar Company's stock, which she currently holds in her retirement account. She estimates that Lamar Company will earn $2.60 per share next year (2016). This expectation is based on an analysis of the firm's historical earnings trend and of expected economic and industry conditions. She finds the price/earnings (P/E) ratio for firms in the same industry to average 7. Multiplying Lamar's expected earnings per share (EPS) of $2.60 by this ratio gives her a value for the firm's shares of $18.20, assuming that investors will continue to value the average firm at 7 times its earnings.

So how much is Lamar Company's stock really worth? That's a trick question because there's no one right answer. It is important to recognize that the answer depends on the assumptions made and the techniques used. Professional securities analysts typically use a variety of models and techniques to value stocks. For example, an analyst might use the constant-growth model, liquidation value, and a price/earnings (P/E) multiple to estimate the worth of a given stock. If the analyst feels comfortable with his or her estimates, the stock would be valued at no more than the largest estimate. Of course, should the firm's estimated liquidation value per share exceed its "going concern" value per share, estimated by using one of the valuation models (zero-, constant-, or variable-growth or free cash flow) or the P/E multiple approach, the firm would be viewed as being "worth more dead than alive." In such an event, the firm would lack sufficient earning power to justify its existence and should probably be liquidated.

Matter of fact

Problems with P/E Valuation

The P/E multiple approach is a fast and easy way to estimate a stock's value. However, P/E ratios vary widely over time. In 1980, the average stock had a P/E ratio below 9, but by the year 2000, the ratio had risen above 40. Therefore, analysts using the P/E approach in the 1980s would have come up with much lower estimates of value than analysts using the model 20 years later. By 2012, the average stock had a P/E ratio of about 20, which is close to the long-run average. When using this approach to estimate stock values, the estimate will depend more on whether stock market valuations generally are high or low rather than on whether the particular company is doing well or not.

→ **REVIEW QUESTIONS**

7–12 Describe the events that occur in an *efficient market* in response to new information that causes the expected return to exceed the required return. What happens to the market value?

7–13 What does the *efficient-market hypothesis (EMH)* say about (**a**) securities prices, (**b**) their reaction to new information, and (**c**) investor opportunities to profit? What is the *behavioral finance* challenge to this hypothesis?

7–14 Describe, compare, and contrast the following common stock dividend valuation models: (**a**) zero-growth, (**b**) constant-growth, and (**c**) variable-growth.

7–15 Describe the *free cash flow valuation model*, and explain how it differs from the dividend valuation models. What is the appeal of this model?

7–16 Explain each of the three other approaches to common stock valuation: (**a**) book value, (**b**) liquidation value, and (**c**) price/earnings (P/E) multiples. Which of them is considered the best?

LG 6   ## 7.4 Decision Making and Common Stock Value

Valuation equations measure the stock value at a point in time based on expected return and risk. Any decisions of the financial manager that affect these variables can cause the value of the firm to change. Figure 7.3 depicts the relationship among financial decisions, return, risk, and stock value.

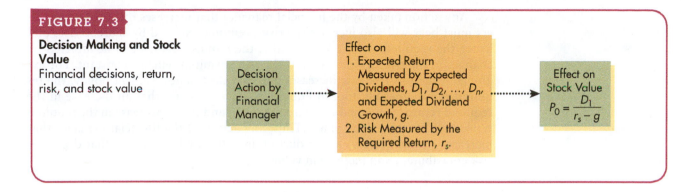

FIGURE 7.3

Decision Making and Stock Value
Financial decisions, return, risk, and stock value

Decision Action by Financial Manager

Effect on
1. Expected Return Measured by Expected Dividends, $D_1, D_2, ..., D_n$, and Expected Dividend Growth, g.
2. Risk Measured by the Required Return, r_s.

Effect on Stock Value
$$P_0 = \frac{D_1}{r_s - g}$$

CHANGES IN EXPECTED DIVIDENDS

Assuming that economic conditions remain stable, any management action that would cause current and prospective stockholders to raise their dividend expectations should increase the firm's value. In Equation 7.4, we can see that P_0 will increase for any increase in D_1 or g. Any action of the financial manager that will increase the level of expected dividends without changing risk (the required return) should be undertaken because it will positively affect owners' wealth.

Example 7.9 ▶ Using the constant-growth model given earlier in Example 7.3, we found Lamar Company to have a share value of $18.75. On the following day, the firm announced a major technological breakthrough that would revolutionize its industry. Current and prospective stockholders would not be expected to adjust their required return of 15%, but they would expect that future dividends will increase. Specifically, they expect that although the dividend next year, D_1, will remain at $1.50, the expected rate of growth thereafter will increase from 7% to 9%. If we substitute $D_1 = \$1.50$, $r_s = 0.15$, and $g = 0.09$ into Equation 7.4, the resulting share value is $25 [$1.50 ÷ (0.15 − 0.09)]. The increased value therefore resulted from the higher expected future dividends reflected in the increase in the growth rate.

CHANGES IN RISK

Although the required return, r_s, is the focus of Chapters 8 and 9, at this point we can consider its fundamental components. Any measure of required return consists of two components, a risk-free rate and a risk premium. We expressed this relationship as Equation 6.1 in Chapter 6, which we repeat here in terms of r_s:

$$r_s = \underbrace{r^* + IP}_{\substack{\text{risk-free} \\ \text{rate, } R_F}} + \underbrace{RP_s}_{\substack{\text{risk} \\ \text{premium}}}$$

In Chapter 8, you will learn that the real challenge in finding the required return is determining the appropriate risk premium. In Chapters 8 and 9, we will discuss how investors and managers can estimate the risk premium for any particular asset. For now, recognize that r_s represents the minimum return that the firm's stock must provide to shareholders to compensate them for bearing the risk of holding the firm's equity.

Any action taken by the financial manager that increases the risk shareholders must bear will also increase the risk premium required by shareholders and hence the required return. Additionally, the required return can be affected by changes in the risk free rate, even if the risk premium remains constant. For example, if the risk-free rate increases due to a shift in government policy, the required return goes up, too. In Equation 7.1, we can see that an increase in the required return, r_s, will reduce share value, P_0, and that a decrease in the required return will increase share value. Thus, any action of the financial manager that increases risk contributes to a reduction in value, and any action that decreases risk contributes to an increase in value.

Example 7.10 ▶ Assume that Lamar Company's 15% required return resulted from a risk-free rate of 9% and a risk premium of 6%. With this return, the firm's share value was calculated in Example 7.3 to be $18.75.

Now imagine that the financial manager makes a decision that, without changing expected dividends, causes the firm's risk premium to increase to 7%. Assuming that *the risk-free rate remains at 9%, the new required return on Lamar stock will be 16% (9% + 7%),* and substituting $D_1 = \$1.50$, $r_s = 0.16$, and $g = 0.07$ into the valuation equation (Equation 7.3) results in a new share value of $16.67 [$1.50 ÷ (0.16 − 0.07)]. As expected, raising the required return, without any corresponding increase in expected dividends, causes the firm's stock value to decline. Clearly, the financial manager's action was not in the owners' best interest.

COMBINED EFFECT

A financial decision rarely affects dividends and risk independently; most decisions affect both factors often in the same direction. As firms take on more risk, their shareholders expect to see higher dividends. The net effect on value depends on the relative size of the changes in these two variables.

Example 7.11 ▶ If we assume that the two changes illustrated for Lamar Company in the preceding examples occur simultaneously, the key variable values would be $D_1 = \$1.50$, $r_s = 0.16$, and $g = 0.09$. Substituting into the valuation model, we obtain a share price of $21.43 [$1.50 ÷ (0.16 − 0.09)]. The net result of the decision, which increased dividend growth (g, from 7% to 9%) as well as required return (r_s, from 15% to 16%), is positive. The share price increased from $18.75 to $21.43. Even with the combined effects, the decision appears to be in the best interest of the firm's owners because it increases their wealth.

→ **REVIEW QUESTIONS**

7–17 Explain the linkages among financial decisions, return, risk, and stock value.

7–18 Assuming that all other variables remain unchanged, what effect would *each* of the following have on stock price? (a) The firm's risk premium increases. (b) The firm's required return decreases. (c) The dividend expected next year decreases. (d) The rate of growth in dividends is expected to increase.

Summary

FOCUS ON VALUE

The price of each share of a firm's common stock is the value of each ownership interest. Although common stockholders typically have voting rights, which indirectly give them a say in management, their most significant right is their claim on the residual cash flows of the firm. This claim is subordinate to those of vendors, employees, customers, lenders, the government (for taxes), and preferred stockholders. The value of the common stockholders' claim is embodied in the future cash flows they are entitled to receive. The present value of those expected cash flows is the firm's share value.

To determine this present value, forecast cash flows are discounted at a rate that reflects their risk. Riskier cash flows are discounted at higher rates, resulting in lower present values than less risky expected cash flows, which are discounted at lower rates. The value of the firm's common stock is therefore driven by its expected cash flows (returns) and risk (certainty of the expected cash flows).

In pursuing the firm's goal of **maximizing the stock price,** the financial manager must carefully consider the balance of return and risk associated with each proposal and must undertake only those actions that create value for owners. By focusing on value creation and by managing and monitoring the firm's cash flows and risk, the financial manager should be able to achieve the firm's goal of share price maximization.

REVIEW OF LEARNING GOALS

LG 1 **Differentiate between debt and equity.** Holders of equity capital (common and preferred stock) are owners of the firm. Typically, only common stockholders have a voice in management. Equityholders' claims on income and assets are secondary to creditors' claims, there is no maturity date, and dividends paid to stockholders are not tax deductible.

LG 2 **Discuss the features of both common and preferred stock.** The common stock of a firm can be privately owned, closely owned, or publicly owned. It can be sold with or without a par value. Preemptive rights allow common stockholders to avoid dilution of ownership when new shares are issued. Not all shares authorized in the corporate charter are outstanding. If a firm has treasury stock, it will have issued more shares than are outstanding. Some firms have two or more classes of common stock that differ mainly in having unequal voting rights. Proxies transfer voting rights from one party to another. The decision to pay dividends to common stockholders is made by the firm's board of directors. Firms can issue stock in foreign markets. The stock of many foreign corporations is traded in U.S. markets in the form of American depositary receipts (ADRs), which are backed by American depositary shares (ADSs).

Preferred stockholders have preference over common stockholders with respect to the distribution of earnings and assets. They do not normally have voting privileges. Preferred stock issues may have certain restrictive covenants, cumulative dividends, a call feature, and a conversion feature.

LG 3 **Describe the process of issuing common stock, including venture capital, going public, and the investment banker.** The initial nonfounder financing for business startups with attractive growth prospects typically comes from private equity investors. These investors can be either angel capitalists or venture capitalists (VCs). VCs usually invest in both early-stage and later-stage companies that they hope to take public so as to cash out their investments.

The first public issue of a firm's stock is called an initial public offering (IPO). The company selects an investment banker to advise it and to sell the securities. The lead investment banker may form a selling syndicate with other investment bankers. The IPO process includes getting SEC approval, promoting the offering to investors, and pricing the issue.

LG 4 **Understand the concept of market efficiency and basic stock valuation using zero-growth, constant-growth, and variable-growth models.** Market efficiency assumes that the quick reactions of rational investors to new information cause the market value of common stock to adjust upward or downward quickly. The efficient-market hypothesis (EMH) suggests that securities are fairly priced, that they reflect fully all publicly available information, and that investors should therefore not waste time trying to find and capitalize on mispriced securities. Behavioral finance advocates challenge this hypothesis by arguing that emotion and other factors play a role in investment decisions.

The value of a share of stock is the present value of all future dividends it is expected to provide over an infinite time horizon. Three dividend growth models—zero-growth, constant-growth, and variable-growth—can be considered in common stock valuation. The most widely cited model is the constant-growth model.

LG 5 **Discuss the free cash flow valuation model and the book value, liquidation value, and price/earnings (P/E) multiple approaches.** The free cash flow valuation model values firms that have no dividend history, startups, or an operating unit or division of a larger public company. The model finds the value of the entire company by discounting the firm's expected free cash flow at its weighted average cost of capital. The common stock value is found by subtracting the market values of the firm's debt and preferred stock from the value of the entire company.

Book value per share is the amount per share of common stock that would be received if all the firm's assets were *sold for their exact book (accounting) value* and the proceeds remaining after paying all liabilities (including preferred stock) were divided among the common stockholders. Liquidation value per share is the *actual amount* per share of common stock that would be received if all the firm's assets were *sold for their market value*, liabilities (including preferred stock) were paid, and the remaining money were divided among the common stockholders. The price/earnings (P/E) multiple approach estimates stock value by multiplying the firm's expected earnings per share (EPS) by the average price/earnings (P/E) ratio for the industry.

LG 6 **Explain the relationships among financial decisions, return, risk, and the firm's value.** In a stable economy, any action of the financial manager that increases the level of expected dividends without changing risk should increase share value; any action that reduces the level of expected dividends without changing risk should reduce share value. Similarly, any action that increases risk (required return) will reduce share value; any action that reduces risk will increase share value. An assessment of the combined effect of return and risk on stock value must be part of the financial decision-making process.

Self-Test Problems (Solutions in Appendix)

 ST7–1 **Common stock valuation** Perry Motors' common stock just paid its annual dividend of $1.80 per share. The required return on the common stock is 12%. Estimate the value of the common stock under each of the following assumptions about the dividend:

IRF

a. Dividends are expected to grow at an annual rate of 0% to infinity.
b. Dividends are expected to grow at a constant annual rate of 5% to infinity.
c. Dividends are expected to grow at an annual rate of 5% for each of the next 3 years, followed by a constant annual growth rate of 4% in years 4 to infinity.

 ST7–2 **Free cash flow valuation** Erwin Footwear wishes to assess the value of its Active Shoe Division. This division has debt with a market value of $12,500,000 and no preferred stock. Its weighted average cost of capital is 10%. The Active Shoe Division's estimated free cash flow each year from 2016 through 2019 is given in the following table. Beyond 2019 to infinity, the firm expects its free cash flow to grow at 4% annually.

IRF

Year (t)	Free cash flow (FCF_t)
2016	$ 800,000
2017	1,200,000
2018	1,400,000
2019	1,500,000

a. Use the *free cash flow valuation model* to estimate the value of Erwin's entire Active Shoe Division.
b. Use your finding in part **a** along with the data provided to find this division's common stock value.
c. If the Active Shoe Division as a public company will have 500,000 shares outstanding, use your finding in part **b** to calculate its value per share.

Warm-Up Exercises All problems are available in MyFinanceLab.

 E7–1 A balance sheet balances assets with their sources of debt and equity financing. If a corporation has assets equal to $5.2 million and a debt ratio of 75.0%, how much debt does the corporation have on its books?

 E7–2 Angina, Inc., has 5 million shares outstanding. The firm is considering issuing an additional 1 million shares. After selling these shares at their $20 per share offering price and netting 95% of the sale proceeds, the firm is obligated by an earlier agreement to sell an additional 250,000 shares at 90% of the offering price. In total, how much cash will the firm net from these stock sales?

LG 2   **E7–3**   Figurate Industries has 750,000 shares of cumulative preferred stock outstanding. It has passed the last three quarterly dividends of $2.50 per share and now (at the end of the current quarter) wishes to distribute a total of $12 million to its shareholders. If Figurate has 3 million shares of common stock outstanding, how large a per-share common stock dividend will it be able to pay?

LG 3   **E7–4**   Today the common stock of Gresham Technology closed at $24.60 per share, down $0.35 from yesterday. If the company has 4.6 million shares outstanding and annual earnings of $11.2 million, what is its P/E ratio today? What was its P/E ratio yesterday?

LG 4   **E7–5**   Stacker Weight Loss currently pays an annual year-end dividend of $1.20 per share. It plans to increase this dividend by 5% next year and maintain it at the new level for the foreseeable future. If the required return on this firm's stock is 8%, what is the value of Stacker's stock?

LG 6   **E7–6**   Brash Corporation initiated a new corporate strategy that fixes its annual dividend at $2.25 per share forever. If the risk-free rate is 4.5% and the risk premium on Brash's stock is 10.8%, what is the value of Brash's stock?

Problems   All problems are available in MyFinanceLab.

LG 2   **P7–1**   **Authorized and available shares** Aspin Corporation's charter authorizes issuance of 2,000,000 shares of common stock. Currently, 1,400,000 shares are outstanding, and 100,000 shares are being held as treasury stock. The firm wishes to raise $48,000,000 for a plant expansion. Discussions with its investment bankers indicate that the sale of new common stock will net the firm $60 per share.
a. What is the maximum number of new shares of common stock that the firm can sell without receiving further authorization from shareholders?
b. Judging on the basis of the data given and your finding in part **a**, will the firm be able to raise the needed funds without receiving further authorization?
c. What must the firm do to obtain authorization to issue more than the number of shares found in part **a**?

LG 2   **P7–2**   **Preferred dividends** Slater Lamp Manufacturing has an outstanding issue of preferred stock with an $80 par value and an 11% annual dividend.
a. What is the annual dollar dividend? If it is paid quarterly, how much will be paid each quarter?
b. If the preferred stock is *noncumulative* and the board of directors has passed the preferred dividend for the last three quarters, how much must be paid to preferred stockholders in the current quarter before dividends are paid to common stockholders?
c. If the preferred stock is *cumulative* and the board of directors has passed the preferred dividend for the last three quarters, how much must be paid to preferred stockholders in the current quarter before dividends are paid to common stockholders?

LG 2   **P7–3**   **Preferred dividends** In each case in the following table, how many dollars of preferred dividends per share must be paid to preferred stockholders in the current period before common stock dividends are paid?

Case	Type	Par value	Dividend per share per period	Periods of dividends passed
A	Cumulative	$ 80	$ 4	3
B	Noncumulative	110	2%	2
C	Noncumulative	100	$3	1
D	Cumulative	60	1.5%	4
E	Cumulative	70	3%	0

LG 2 **P7–4** **Convertible preferred stock** Valerian Corp. convertible preferred stock has a fixed conversion ratio of 5 common shares per 1 share of preferred stock. The preferred stock pays a dividend of $10.00 per share per year. The common stock currently sells for $20.00 per share and pays a dividend of $1.00 per share per year.

a. Judging on the basis of the conversion ratio and the price of the common shares, what is the current conversion value of each preferred share?

b. If the preferred shares are selling at $96.00 each, should an investor convert the preferred shares to common shares?

c. What factors might cause an investor not to convert from preferred to common stock?

LG 4 **P7–5** **Preferred stock valuation** TXS Manufacturing has an outstanding preferred stock issue with a par value of $65 per share. The preferred shares pay dividends annually at a rate of 10%.

a. What is the annual dividend on TXS preferred stock?

b. If investors require a return of 8% on this stock and the next dividend is payable 1 year from now, what is the price of TXS preferred stock?

c. Suppose that TXS has not paid dividends on its preferred shares in the last 2 years, but investors believe that it will start paying dividends again in 1 year. What is the value of TXS preferred stock if it is cumulative and if investors require an 8% rate of return?

Personal Finance Problem

LG 4 **P7–6** **Common stock value: Zero growth** Kelsey Drums, Inc., is a well-established supplier of fine percussion instruments to orchestras all over the United States. The company's class A common stock has paid a dividend of $5.00 per share per year for the last 15 years. Management expects to continue to pay at that amount for the foreseeable future. Sally Talbot purchased 100 shares of Kelsey class A common 10 years ago at a time when the required rate of return for the stock was 16%. She wants to sell her shares today. The current required rate of return for the stock is 12%. How much capital gain or loss will Sally have on her shares?

LG 4 **P7–7** **Preferred stock valuation** Jones Design wishes to estimate the value of its outstanding preferred stock. The preferred issue has an $80 par value and pays an annual dividend of $6.40 per share. Similar-risk preferred stocks are currently earning a 9.3% annual rate of return.

a. What is the market value of the outstanding preferred stock?

b. If an investor purchases the preferred stock at the value calculated in part a, how much does she gain or lose per share if she sells the stock when the required return on similar-risk preferred stocks has risen to 10.5%? Explain.

P7–8   **Common stock value: Constant growth**   Use the constant-growth model (Gordon growth model) to find the value of each firm shown in the following table.

Firm	Dividend expected next year	Dividend growth rate	Required return
A	$1.20	8%	13%
B	4.00	5	15
C	0.65	10	14
D	6.00	8	9
E	2.25	8	20

 P7–9   **Common stock value: Constant growth**   McCracken Roofing, Inc., common stock paid a dividend of $1.20 per share last year. The company expects earnings and dividends to grow at a rate of 5% per year for the foreseeable future.
a. What required rate of return for this stock would result in a price per share of $28?
b. If McCracken expects both earnings and dividends to grow at an annual rate of 10%, what required rate of return would result in a price per share of $28?

 P7–10   **Common stock value: Constant growth**   The common stock of Denis and Denis Research, Inc., trades for $60 per share. Investors expect the company to pay a $3.90 dividend next year, and they expect that dividend to grow at a constant rate forever. If investors require a 10% return on this stock, what is the dividend growth rate that they are anticipating?

Personal Finance Problem

 P7–11   **Common stock value: Constant growth**   Elk County Telephone has paid the dividends shown in the following table over the past 6 years.

Year	Dividend per share
2015	$2.87
2014	2.76
2013	2.60
2012	2.46
2011	2.37
2010	2.25

The firm's dividend per share next year is expected to be $3.02.
a. If you can earn 13% on similar-risk investments, what is the most you would be willing to pay per share?
b. If you can earn only 10% on similar-risk investments, what is the most you would be willing to pay per share?
c. Compare and contrast your findings in parts **a** and **b,** and discuss the impact of changing risk on share value.

 P7–12   **Common stock value: Variable growth**   Newman Manufacturing is considering a cash purchase of the stock of Grips Tool. During the year just completed, Grips earned $4.25 per share and paid cash dividends of $2.55 per share ($D_0 = 2.55$). Grips' earnings and dividends are expected to grow at 25% per year for the next 3 years, after which they are expected to grow at 10% per year to infinity. What is the maximum price per share that Newman should pay for Grips if it has a required return of 15% on investments with risk characteristics similar to those of Grips?

Personal Finance Problem

 P7–13 **Common stock value: Variable growth** Home Place Hotels, Inc., is entering into a 3-year remodeling and expansion project. The construction will have a limiting effect on earnings during that time, but when it is complete, it should allow the company to enjoy much improved growth in earnings and dividends. Last year, the company paid a dividend of $3.40. It expects zero growth in the next year. In years 2 and 3, 5% growth is expected, and in year 4, 15% growth. In year 5 and thereafter, growth should be a constant 10% per year. What is the maximum price per share that an investor who requires a return of 14% should pay for Home Place Hotels common stock?

 P7–14 **Common stock value: Variable growth** Lawrence Industries' most recent annual dividend was $1.80 per share ($D_0 = \$1.80$), and the firm's required return is 11%. Find the market value of Lawrence's shares when:
a. Dividends are expected to grow at 8% annually for 3 years, followed by a 5% constant annual growth rate in years 4 to infinity.
b. Dividends are expected to grow at 8% annually for 3 years, followed by a 0% constant annual growth rate in years 4 to infinity.
c. Dividends are expected to grow at 8% annually for 3 years, followed by a 10% constant annual growth rate in years 4 to infinity.

Personal Finance Problem

 P7–15 **Common stock value: All growth models** You are evaluating the potential purchase of a small business currently generating $42,500 of after-tax cash flow ($D_0 = \$42,500$). On the basis of a review of similar-risk investment opportunities, you must earn an 18% rate of return on the proposed purchase. Because you are relatively uncertain about future cash flows, you decide to estimate the firm's value using several possible assumptions about the growth rate of cash flows.
a. What is the firm's value if cash flows are expected to grow at an annual rate of 0% from now to infinity?
b. What is the firm's value if cash flows are expected to grow at a constant annual rate of 7% from now to infinity?
c. What is the firm's value if cash flows are expected to grow at an annual rate of 12% for the first 2 years, followed by a constant annual rate of 7% from year 3 to infinity?

 P7–16 **Free cash flow valuation** Nabor Industries is considering going public but is unsure of a fair offering price for the company. Before hiring an investment banker to assist in making the public offering, managers at Nabor have decided to make their own estimate of the firm's common stock value. The firm's CFO has gathered data for performing the valuation using the free cash flow valuation model.

The firm's weighted average cost of capital is 11%, and it has $1,500,000 of debt at market value and $400,000 of preferred stock at its assumed market value. The estimated free cash flows over the next 5 years, 2016 through 2020, are given below. Beyond 2020 to infinity, the firm expects its free cash flow to grow by 3% annually.

Year (t)	Free cash flow (FCF_t)
2016	$200,000
2017	250,000
2018	310,000
2019	350,000
2020	390,000

a. Estimate the value of Nabor Industries' entire company by using the *free cash flow valuation model*.
b. Use your finding in part **a**, along with the data provided above, to find Nabor Industries' common stock value.
c. If the firm plans to issue 200,000 shares of common stock, what is its estimated value per share?

Personal Finance Problem

 P7–17 Using the free cash flow valuation model to price an IPO Assume that you have an opportunity to buy the stock of CoolTech, Inc., an IPO being offered for $12.50 per share. Although you are very much interested in owning the company, you are concerned about whether it is fairly priced. To determine the value of the shares, you have decided to apply the free cash flow valuation model to the firm's financial data that you've developed from a variety of data sources. The key values you have compiled are summarized in the following table.

Free cash flow		Other data
Year (t)	**FCF_t**	
2016	$ 700,000	Growth rate of FCF, beyond 2019 to infinity = 2%
2017	800,000	Weighted average cost of capital = 8%
2018	950,000	Market value of all debt = $2,700,000
2019	1,100,000	Market value of preferred stock = $1,000,000
		Number of shares of common stock outstanding = 1,100,000

a. Use the *free cash flow valuation model* to estimate CoolTech's common stock value per share.
b. Judging on the basis of your finding in part **a** and the stock's offering price, should you buy the stock?
c. On further analysis, you find that the growth rate in FCF beyond 2019 will be 3% rather than 2%. What effect would this finding have on your responses in parts **a** and **b**?

P7–18 **Book and liquidation value** The balance sheet for Gallinas Industries is as follows.

Gallinas Industries Balance Sheet December 31			
Assets		**Liabilities and stockholders' equity**	
Cash	$ 40,000	Accounts payable	$100,000
Marketable securities	60,000	Notes payable	30,000
Accounts receivable	120,000	Accrued wages	30,000
Inventories	160,000	Total current liabilities	$160,000
Total current assets	$380,000	Long-term debt	$180,000
Land and buildings (net)	$150,000	Preferred stock	$ 80,000
Machinery and equipment	250,000	Common stock (10,000 shares)	260,000
Total fixed assets (net)	$400,000	Retained earnings	100,000
Total assets	$780,000	Total liabilities and stockholders' equity	$780,000

Additional information with respect to the firm is available:
(1) Preferred stock can be liquidated at book value.
(2) Accounts receivable and inventories can be liquidated at 90% of book value.
(3) The firm has 10,000 shares of common stock outstanding.
(4) All interest and dividends are currently paid up.
(5) Land and buildings can be liquidated at 130% of book value.
(6) Machinery and equipment can be liquidated at 70% of book value.
(7) Cash and marketable securities can be liquidated at book value.

Given this information, answer the following:
a. What is Gallinas Industries' *book value per share?*
b. What is its *liquidation value per share?*
c. Compare, contrast, and discuss the values found in parts a and b.

LG 5   **P7–19**   **Valuation with price/earnings multiples** For each of the firms shown in the following table, use the data given to estimate its common stock value employing price/ earnings (P/E) multiples.

Firm	Expected EPS	Price/earnings multiple
A	$3.00	6.2
B	4.50	10.0
C	1.80	12.6
D	2.40	8.9
E	5.10	15.0

LG 6   **P7–20**   **Management action and stock value** REH Corporation's most recent dividend was $3 per share, its expected annual rate of dividend growth is 5%, and the required return is now 15%. A variety of proposals are being considered by management to redirect the firm's activities. Determine the impact on share price for each of the following proposed actions, and indicate the best alternative.
a. Do nothing, which will leave the key financial variables unchanged.
b. Invest in a new machine that will increase the dividend growth rate to 6% and lower the required return to 14%.

    c. Eliminate an unprofitable product line, which will increase the dividend growth rate to 7% and raise the required return to 17%.

    d. Merge with another firm, which will reduce the growth rate to 4% and raise the required return to 16%.

    e. Acquire a subsidiary operation from another manufacturer. The acquisition should increase the dividend growth rate to 8% and increase the required return to 17%.

LG 4 LG 6   P7–21   Integrative: Risk and valuation Given the following information for the stock of Foster Company, calculate the risk premium on its common stock.

Current price per share of common	$50.00
Expected dividend per share next year	$ 3.00
Constant annual dividend growth rate	9%
Risk-free rate of return	7%

LG 4 LG 6   P7–22   Integrative: Risk and valuation Giant Enterprises' stock has a required return of 14.8%. The company, which plans to pay a dividend of $2.60 per share in the coming year, anticipates that its future dividends will increase at an annual rate consistent with that experienced over the 2009–2015 period, when the following dividends were paid.

Year	Dividend per share
2015	$2.45
2014	2.28
2013	2.10
2012	1.95
2011	1.82
2010	1.80
2009	1.73

    a. If the risk-free rate is 10%, what is the risk premium on Giant's stock?

    b. Using the constant-growth model, estimate the value of Giant's stock.

    c. Explain what effect, if any, a decrease in the risk premium would have on the value of Giant's stock.

LG 4 LG 6   P7–23   Integrative: Risk and valuation Hamlin Steel Company wishes to determine the value of Craft Foundry, a firm that it is considering acquiring for cash. Hamlin wishes to determine the applicable discount rate to use as an input to the constant-growth valuation model. Craft's stock is not publicly traded. After studying the required returns of firms similar to Craft that are publicly traded, Hamlin believes that an appropriate risk premium on Craft stock is about 5%. The risk-free rate is currently 9%. Craft's dividend per share for each of the past 6 years is shown in the following table.

Year	Dividend per share
2015	$3.44
2014	3.28
2013	3.15
2012	2.90
2011	2.75
2010	2.45

a. Given that Craft is expected to pay a dividend of $3.68 next year, determine the maximum cash price that Hamlin should pay for each share of Craft.
b. Describe the effect on the resulting value of Craft of
  (1) A decrease in its dividend growth rate of 2% from that exhibited over the 2010–2015 period.
  (2) A decrease in its risk premium to 4%.

 P7–24 **ETHICS PROBLEM** Melissa is trying to value Generic Utility, Inc.'s, stock, which is clearly not growing at all. Generic declared and paid a $5 dividend last year. The required rate of return for utility stocks is 11%, but Melissa is unsure about the financial reporting integrity of Generic's finance team. She decides to add an extra 1% "credibility" risk premium to the required return as part of her valuation analysis.
a. What is the value of Generic's stock, assuming that the financials are trustworthy?
b. What is the value of Generic's stock, assuming that Melissa includes the extra 1% "credibility" risk premium?
c. What is the difference between the values found in parts **a** and **b**, and how might one interpret that difference?

Spreadsheet Exercise

You are interested in purchasing the common stock of Azure Corporation. The firm recently paid a dividend of $3 per share. It expects its earnings—and hence its dividends—to grow at a rate of 7% for the foreseeable future. Currently, similar-risk stocks have required returns of 10%.

TO DO

a. Given the data above, calculate the present value of this security. Use the constant-growth model (Equation 7.4) to find the stock value.
b. One year later, your broker offers to sell you additional shares of Azure at $73. The most recent dividend paid was $3.21, and the expected growth rate for earnings remains at 7%. If you determine that the appropriate risk premium is 6.74% and you observe that the risk-free rate, R_F, is currently 5.25%, what is the firm's current required return, r_{Azure}?
c. Applying Equation 7.4, determine the value of the stock using the new dividend and required return from part **b**.
d. Given your calculation in part **c**, would you buy the additional shares from your broker at $73 per share? Explain.
e. Given your calculation in part **c**, would you sell your old shares for $73? Explain.

MyFinanceLab Visit www.myfinancelab.com for **Chapter Case: Assessing the Impact of Suarez Manufacturing's Proposed Risky Investment on Its Stock Value,** Group Exercises, and numerous online resources.

Part 4 ▶ Risk and the Required Rate of Return

Most people intuitively understand the principle that risk and return are linked. After all, as the old saying goes, "Nothing ventured, nothing gained." In the next two chapters, we'll explore how investors and financial managers quantify the notion of risk and how they determine how much additional return is appropriate compensation for taking extra risk.

Chapter 8 lays the groundwork, defining the terms *risk* and *return* and explaining why investors think about risk in different ways depending on whether they want to understand the risk of a specific investment or the risk of a broad portfolio of investments. Perhaps the most famous and widely applied theory in all finance, the Capital Asset Pricing Model (or CAPM), is introduced here. The CAPM tells investors and managers alike what return they should expect given the risk of the asset they want to invest in.

Chapter 9 applies these lessons in a managerial finance setting. Firms raise money from two broad sources, owners and lenders. Owners provide equity financing and lenders provide debt. To maximize the value of the firm, managers have to satisfy both groups, and doing so means earning returns high enough to meet investors' expectations. The focus in Chapter 9 is on the cost of capital or, more precisely, the weighted average cost of capital (WACC). The WACC tells managers exactly what kind of return their investments in plant and equipment, advertising, and human resources have to earn if the firm is to satisfy its investors. Essentially, the WACC is a hurdle rate, the minimum acceptable return that a firm should earn on any investment it makes.

8 Risk and Return

Learning Goals

LG 1 Understand the meaning and fundamentals of risk, return, and risk preferences.

LG 2 Describe procedures for assessing and measuring the risk of a single asset.

LG 3 Discuss the measurement of return and standard deviation for a portfolio and the concept of correlation.

LG 4 Understand the risk and return characteristics of a portfolio in terms of correlation and diversification and the impact of international assets on a portfolio.

LG 5 Review the two types of risk and the derivation and role of beta in measuring the relevant risk of both a security and a portfolio.

LG 6 Explain the capital asset pricing model (CAPM), its relationship to the security market line (SML), and the major forces causing shifts in the SML.

Why This Chapter Matters to You

In your *professional* life

ACCOUNTING You need to understand the relationship between risk and return because of the effect that riskier projects will have on the firm's financial statements.

INFORMATION SYSTEMS You need to understand how to do scenario and correlation analyses to build decision packages that help management analyze the risk and return of various business opportunities.

MANAGEMENT You need to understand the relationship between risk and return and how to measure that relationship to evaluate data that come from finance personnel and translate those data into decisions that increase the value of the firm.

OPERATIONS You need to understand why investments in plant, equipment, and systems need to be evaluated in light of their impact on the firm's risk and return, which together will affect the firm's value.

In your *personal* life

The trade-off between risk and return enters into numerous personal financial decisions. You will use risk and return concepts when you invest your savings, buy real estate, finance major purchases, purchase insurance, invest in securities, and implement retirement plans. Although risk and return are difficult to measure precisely, you can get a feel for them and make decisions based on the trade-offs between risk and return in light of your personal disposition toward risk.

LG 1   **8.1** **Risk and Return Fundamentals**

In most important business decisions there are two key financial considerations: risk and return. Each financial decision presents certain risk and return characteristics, and the combination of these characteristics can increase or decrease a firm's share price. Analysts use different methods to quantify risk, depending on whether they are looking at a single asset or a **portfolio**— a collection or group of assets. We will look at both, beginning with the risk of a single asset. First, though, it is important to introduce some fundamental ideas about risk, return, and risk preferences.

portfolio
A collection or group of assets.

RISK DEFINED

risk
A measure of the uncertainty surrounding the return that an investment will earn or, more formally, the *variability of returns associated with a given asset.*

In the most basic sense, **risk** is a measure of the uncertainty surrounding the return that an investment will earn. Investments whose returns are more uncertain are generally riskier. More formally, the term *risk* is used interchangeably with *uncertainty* to refer to the *variability of returns associated with a given asset.* A $1,000 government bond that guarantees its holder $5 interest after 30 days has no risk because there is no variability associated with the return. A $1,000 investment in a firm's common stock is very risky because the value of that stock may move up or down substantially over the same 30 days.

---

focus on ETHICS

If It Seems Too Good to Be True, It Probably Is

 in practice For many years, investors around the world clamored to invest with Bernard Madoff. Those fortunate enough to invest with "Bernie" might not have understood his secret trading system, but they were happy with the double-digit returns that they earned. Madoff was well connected, having been the chairman of the board of directors of the NASDAQ Stock Market and a founding member of the International Securities Clearing Corporation. His credentials seemed to be impeccable.

However, as the old saying goes, if something sounds too good to be true, it probably is. Madoff's investors learned this lesson the hard way when, on December 11, 2008, the U.S. Securities and Exchange Commission (SEC) charged Madoff with securities fraud. Madoff's hedge fund, Ascot Partners, turned out to be a giant Ponzi scheme.

Over the years, suspicions were raised about Madoff. He generated high returns year after year, seemingly with very little risk. Madoff credited his complex trading strategy for his investment performance, but other investors employed similar strategies with much different results than Madoff reported. Harry Markopolos went as far as to submit a report to the SEC 3 years prior to Madoff's arrest, titled "The World's Largest Hedge Fund Is a Fraud," that detailed his concerns.

On June 29, 2009, after a lengthy trial and eventual conviction, Madoff was sentenced to 150 years in prison. Madoff's investors are still working to recover what they can. Fraudulent account statements sent just prior to Madoff's arrest indicated that investors' accounts contained more than $64 billion, in aggregate. Many investors pursued claims based on the balance

reported in these statements. However, a court ruling only permits claims up to the difference between the amount an investor deposited with Madoff and the amount the investor withdrew. The judge also ruled that investors who managed to withdraw at least their initial investment before the fraud was uncovered are not eligible to recover additional funds.

Total out-of-pocket cash losses as a result of Madoff's fraud were estimated to be $17.5 billion. In early 2013, the Securities Investor Protection Corporation reported that more than 53 percent of the funds had either been returned or were in the process of being returned to Madoff's defrauded customers.

▶ *What are some hazards of allowing investors to pursue claims based on their most recent account statements?*

[a] www.sec.gov/news/studies/2009/oig-509/exhibit-0293.pdf

RETURN DEFINED

total rate of return
The total gain or loss experienced on an investment over a given period of time; calculated by dividing the asset's cash distributions during the period, plus change in value, by its beginning-of-period investment value.

Obviously, if we are going to assess risk on the basis of variability of return, we need to be certain we know what *return* is and how to measure it. The **total rate of return** is the total gain or loss experienced on an investment over a given period. Mathematically, an investment's total return is the sum of any cash distributions (for example, dividends or interest payments) plus the change in the investment's value, divided by the beginning-of-period value. The expression for calculating the total rate of return earned on any asset over period t, r_t, is commonly defined as

$$r_t = \frac{C_t + P_t - P_{t-1}}{P_{t-1}} \tag{8.1}$$

where

r_t = actual, expected, or required rate of return during period t
C_t = cash (flow) received from the asset investment in the time period $t - 1$ to t
P_t = price (value) of asset at time t
P_{t-1} = price (value) of asset at time $t - 1$

The return, r_t, reflects the combined effect of cash flow, C_t, and changes in value, $P_t - P_{t-1}$, over the period.[1]

Equation 8.1 is used to determine the rate of return over a time period as short as 1 day or as long as 10 years or more. However, in most cases, t is 1 year, and r therefore represents an annual rate of return.

Example 8.1 ▶

MyFinanceLab Solution
Video

Robin wishes to determine the return on two stocks that she owned during 2012, Apple Inc., and Wal-Mart. At the beginning of the year, Apple stock traded for $411.23 per share, and Wal-Mart was valued at $60.33. During the year, Apple paid $5.30 in dividends, and Wal-Mart shareholders received dividends of $1.59 per share. At the end of the year, Apple stock was worth $532.17, and Wal-Mart sold for $68.23. Substituting into Equation 8.1, we can calculate the annual rate of return, r, for each stock:

Apple: ($5.30 + $532.17 − $411.23) ÷ $411.23 = 30.7%
Wal-Mart: ($1.59 + $68.23 − $60.33) ÷ $60.33 = 15.7%

Robin made money on both stocks in 2012, and her return was higher on Apple both in dollars and on a percentage basis.

Investment returns vary both over time and between different types of investments. By averaging historical returns over a long period of time, we can focus on the differences in returns that different kinds of investments tend to generate.

---

1. This expression does not imply that an investor necessarily buys the asset at time $t - 1$ and sells it at time t. Rather, it represents the increase (or decrease) in wealth that the investor has experienced during the period by holding a particular investment. If the investor sells the asset at time t, we say that the investor has *realized* the return on the investment. If the investor continues to hold the investment, we say that the return is *unrealized*.

TABLE 8.1	Historical Returns on Selected Investments (1900–2011)	
Investment	Average nominal return	Average real return
Treasury bills	3.9%	0.9%
Treasury bonds	5.0	2.0
Common stocks	9.3	6.2

Source: Elroy Dimson, Paul Marsh, Mike Staunton, Paul McGinnie, and Jonathan Wilmot, *Credit Suisse Global Investment Returns Yearbook 2012.*

Table 8.1 shows both the nominal and real average annual rates of return from 1900 to 2011 for three different types of investments: Treasury bills, Treasury bonds, and common stocks. Although bills and bonds are both issued by the U.S. government and are therefore viewed as relatively safe investments, bills have maturities of 1 year or less, whereas bonds have maturities ranging up to 30 years. Consequently, the interest rate risk associated with Treasury bonds is much higher than with bills. Over the last 112 years, bills earned the lowest returns, just 3.9 percent per year on average in nominal returns and only 0.9 percent annually in real terms. The latter number means that average Treasury bill returns barely exceeded the average rate of inflation. Bond returns were higher, 5.0 percent in nominal terms and 2.0 percent in real terms. Clearly, though, stocks outshined the other types of investments, earning average annual nominal returns of 9.3 percent and average real returns of 6.2 percent.

In light of these statistics, you might wonder, "Why would anyone invest in bonds or bills if the returns on stocks are so much higher?" The answer, as you will soon see, is that stocks are much riskier than either bonds or bills and that risk leads some investors to prefer the safer, albeit lower, returns on Treasury securities.

RISK PREFERENCES

risk averse
The attitude toward risk in which investors require an increased return as compensation for an increase in risk.

risk neutral
The attitude toward risk in which investors choose the investment with the higher return regardless of its risk.

risk seeking
The attitude toward risk in which investors prefer investments with greater risk even if they have lower pected returns.

Different people react to risk in different ways. Economists use three categories to describe how investors respond to risk. The first category, *and the one that describes the behavior of most people most of the time,* is called risk aversion. An investor who is **risk averse** prefers less risky over more risky investments, holding the rate of return fixed. A risk-averse investor who believes that two different investments have the same expected return will choose the investment whose returns are more certain. Stated another way, when choosing between two investments, *a risk-averse investor will not make the riskier investment unless it offers a higher expected return to compensate the investor for bearing the additional risk.*

A second attitude toward risk is called risk neutrality. An investor who is **risk neutral** chooses investments based solely on their expected returns, disregarding the risks. When choosing between two investments, *a risk-neutral investor will always choose the investment with the higher expected return regardless of its risk.*

Finally, an investor who is **risk seeking** prefers investments with higher risk and may even sacrifice some expected return when choosing a riskier investment. By design, the average person who buys a lottery ticket or gambles in a casino loses money. After all, state governments and casinos make money off of these endeavors, which implies that the expected return on these activities is negative, and individuals lose on average. People nonetheless buy lottery tickets and visit casinos, and in doing so they exhibit risk-seeking behavior.

→ **REVIEW QUESTIONS**

    8-1 What is *risk* in the context of financial decision making?

    8-2 Define *return,* and describe how to find the rate of return on an investment.

    8-3 Compare the following risk preferences: (**a**) risk averse, (**b**) risk neutral, and (**c**) risk seeking. Which risk preference is most common among financial managers?

LG② **8.2** Risk of a Single Asset

In this section, we refine our understanding of risk. Surprisingly, the concept of risk changes when the focus shifts from the risk of a single asset held in isolation to the risk of a portfolio of assets. Here, we examine different statistical methods to quantify risk; later, we apply those methods to portfolios.

RISK ASSESSMENT

The notion that risk is somehow connected to uncertainty is intuitive. The more uncertain you are about how an investment will perform, the riskier that investment seems. Scenario analysis provides a simple way to quantify that intuition, and probability distributions offer an even more sophisticated way to analyze the risk of an investment.

scenario analysis
An approach for assessing risk that uses several possible alternative outcomes (scenarios) to obtain a sense of the variability among returns.

range
A measure of an asset's risk, which is found by subtracting the return associated with the pessimistic (worst) outcome from the return associated with the optimistic (best) outcome.

Scenario Analysis

Scenario analysis uses several possible alternative outcomes (scenarios) to obtain a sense of the variability of returns.[2] One common method involves considering pessimistic (worst), most likely (expected), and optimistic (best) outcomes and the returns associated with them for a given asset. In this one measure of an investment's risk is the range of possible outcomes. The **range** is found by subtracting the return associated with the pessimistic outcome from the return associated with the optimistic outcome. The greater the range, the more variability, or risk, the asset is said to have.

| Example 8.2 ▶ | Norman Company, a manufacturer of custom golf equipment, wants to choose the better of two investments, A and B. Each requires an initial outlay of $10,000, and each has a *most likely* annual rate of return of 15%. Management has estimated returns associated with each investment's *pessimistic* and *optimistic* |

---

2. The term *scenario analysis* is intentionally used in a general rather than a technically correct fashion here to simplify this discussion. A more technical and precise definition and discussion of this technique and of *sensitivity analysis* are presented in Chapter 11.

TABLE 8.2	Assets A and B	
	Asset A	**Asset B**
Initial investment	$10,000	$10,000
Annual rate of return		
Pessimistic	13%	7%
Most likely	15%	15%
Optimistic	17%	23%
Range	4%	16%

outcomes. The three estimates for each asset, along with its range, are given in Table 8.2. Asset A appears to be less risky than asset B; its range of 4% (17% minus 13%) is less than the range of 16% (23% minus 7%) for asset B. The risk-averse decision maker would prefer asset A over asset B, because A offers the same most likely return as B (15%) with lower risk (smaller range).

It's not unusual for financial managers to think about the best and worst possible outcomes when they are in the early stages of analyzing a new investment project. No matter how great the intuitive appeal of this approach, looking at the range of outcomes that an investment might produce is a very unsophisticated way of measuring its risk. More sophisticated methods require some basic statistical tools.

Probability Distributions

probability
The *chance* that a given outcome will occur.

Probability distributions provide a more quantitative insight into an asset's risk. The **probability** of a given outcome is its *chance* of occurring. An outcome with an 80 percent probability of occurrence would be expected to occur 8 out of 10 times. An outcome with a probability of 100 percent is certain to occur. Outcomes with a probability of zero will never occur.

Matter of fact

Beware of the Black Swan

Is it ever possible to know for sure that a particular outcome can never happen, that the chance of it occurring is 0 percent? In the 2007 best seller *The Black Swan: The Impact of the Highly Improbable*, Nassim Nicholas Taleb argues that seemingly improbable or even impossible events are more likely to occur than most people believe, especially in the area of finance. The book's title refers to a long-held belief that all swans were white, a belief held by many people until a black variety was discovered in Australia. Taleb reportedly earned a large fortune during the 2007–2008 financial crisis by betting that financial markets would plummet.

Example 8.3 ▶ Norman Company's past estimates indicate that the probabilities of the pessimistic, most likely, and optimistic outcomes are 25%, 50%, and 25%, respectively. Note that the sum of these probabilities must equal 100%; that is, they must be based on all the alternatives considered.

FIGURE 8.1

Bar Charts
Bar charts for asset A's
and asset B's returns

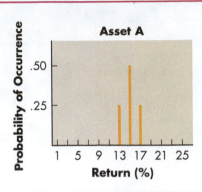

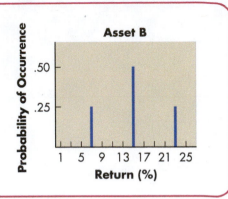

probability distribution
A model that relates
probabilities to the associated
outcomes.

bar chart
The simplest type of probability
distribution; shows only a
limited number of outcomes
and associated probabilities
for a given event.

**continuous probability
distribution**
A probability distribution
showing all the possible
outcomes and associated
probabilities for a given event.

A **probability distribution** is a model that relates probabilities to the associated outcomes. The simplest type of probability distribution is the **bar chart**. The bar charts for Norman Company's assets A and B are shown in Figure 8.1. Although both assets have the same average return, the range of return is much greater, or more dispersed, for asset B than for asset A: 16 percent versus 4 percent.

Most investments have more than two or three possible outcomes. In fact, the number of possible outcomes in most cases is practically infinite. If we knew all the possible outcomes and associated probabilities, we could develop a **continuous probability distribution**. This type of distribution can be thought of as a bar chart for a very large number of outcomes. Figure 8.2 presents continuous probability distributions for assets C and D. Note that although the two assets have the same average return (15 percent), the distribution of returns for asset D has much greater *dispersion* than the distribution for asset C. Apparently, asset D is more risky than asset C.

RISK MEASUREMENT

In addition to considering the *range* of returns that an investment might produce, the risk of an asset can be measured quantitatively by using statistics. The most common statistical measure used to describe an investment's risk is its standard deviation.

FIGURE 8.2

**Continuous Probability
Distributions**
Continuous probability
distributions for asset C's
and asset D's returns

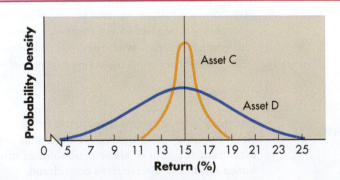

Standard Deviation

standard deviation (σ_r)
The most common statistical indicator of an asset's risk; it measures the dispersion around the *expected value*.

The **standard deviation**, σ_r, measures the dispersion of an investment's return around the *expected return*. The **expected value of a return**, $\bar{r}$, is the average return that an investment is expected to produce over time. For an investment that has j different possible returns, the expected return is calculated as[3]

expected value of a return ($\bar{r}$)
The average return that an investment is expected to produce over time.

$$\bar{r} = \sum_{j=1}^{n} r_j \times Pr_j \tag{8.2}$$

where

$$r_j = \text{return for the } j\text{th outcome}$$
$$Pr_j = \text{probability of occurrence of the } j\text{th outcome}$$
$$n = \text{number of outcomes considered}$$

Example 8.4 ▶ The expected values of returns for Norman Company's assets A and B are presented in Table 8.3. Column 1 gives the Pr_j's, and column 2 gives the r_j's. In each case, n equals 3. The expected value for each asset's return is 15%.

TABLE 8.3	Expected Values of Returns for Assets A and B		
Possible outcomes	Probability (1)	Returns (2)	Weighted value [(1) × (2)] (3)
Asset A			
Pessimistic	0.25	13%	3.25%
Most likely	0.50	15	7.50
Optimistic	0.25	17	4.25
Total	1.00		Expected return 15.00%
Asset B			
Pessimistic	0.25	7%	1.75%
Most likely	0.50	15	7.50
Optimistic	0.25	23	5.75
Total	1.00		Expected return 15.00%

---

3. The formula for finding the expected value of return, $\bar{r}$, when all of the outcomes, r_j, are known and their related probabilities are equal, is a simple arithmetic average:

$$\bar{r} = \frac{\sum_{j=1}^{n} r_j}{n} \tag{8.2a}$$

where n is the number of observations.

The expression for the *standard deviation of returns*, σ_r, is[4]

$$\sigma_r = \sqrt{\sum_{j=1}^{n} (r_j - \bar{r})^2 \times Pr_j} \qquad (8.3)$$

In general, the higher the standard deviation, the greater the risk.

Example 8.5 ▸   Table 8.4 presents the standard deviations for Norman Company's assets A and B, based on the earlier data. The standard deviation for asset A is 1.41%, and the standard deviation for asset B is 5.66%. The higher risk of asset B is clearly reflected in its higher standard deviation.

TABLE 8.4 ▸ **The Calculation of the Standard Deviation of the Returns for Assets A and B**

j	r_j	$\bar{r}$	$r_j - \bar{r}$	$(r_j - \bar{r})^2$	Pr_j	$(r_j - \bar{r})^2 \times Pr_j$
Asset A						
1	13%	15%	−2%	4%	.25	1%
2	15	15	0	0	.50	0
3	17	15	2	4	.25	1

$$\sum_{j=1}^{3} (r_j - \bar{r})^2 \times Pr_j = 2\%$$

$$\sigma_{r_A} = \sqrt{\sum_{j=1}^{3} (r_j - \bar{r})^2 \times Pr_j} = \sqrt{2\%} = \underline{1.41\%}$$

j	r_j	$\bar{r}$	$r_j - \bar{r}$	$(r_j - \bar{r})^2$	Pr_j	$(r_j - \bar{r})^2 \times Pr_j$
Asset A						
1	7%	15%	−8%	64%	.25	16%
2	15	15	0	0	.50	0
3	23	15	8	64	.25	16

$$\sum_{j=1}^{3} (r_j - \bar{r})^2 \times Pr_j = 32\%$$

$$\sigma_{r_B} = \sqrt{\sum_{j=1}^{3} (r_j - \bar{r})^2 \times Pr_j} = \sqrt{32\%} = \underline{5.66\%}$$

Note: Calculations in this table are made in percentage form rather than decimal form, for example, 13% rather than 0.13. As a result, some of the intermediate computations may appear to be inconsistent with those that would result from using decimal form. Regardless, the resulting standard deviations are correct and identical to those that would result from using decimal rather than percentage form.

---

4. In practice, analysts rarely know the full range of possible investment outcomes and their probabilities. In these cases, analysts use historical data to estimate the standard deviation. The formula that applies in this situation is

$$\sigma_r = \sqrt{\frac{\sum_{j=1}^{n} (r_j - \bar{r})^2}{n-1}} \qquad (8.3a)$$

TABLE 8.5	Historical Returns and Standard Deviations on Selected Investments (1900–2011)		
Investment	Average nominal return	Standard deviation	Coefficient of variation
Treasury bills	3.9%	4.7%	1.20
Treasury bonds	5.0	10.3	2.06
Common stocks	9.3	20.2	2.17

Source: Elroy Dimson, Paul Marsh, Mike Staunton, Paul McGinnie, and Jonathan Wilmot, *Credit Suisse Global Investment Returns Yearbook 2012.*

Historical Returns and Risk We can now use the standard deviation as a measure of risk to assess the historical (1900–2011) investment return data in Table 8.1. Table 8.5 repeats the historical nominal average returns in column 1 and shows the standard deviations associated with each of them in column 2. A close relationship can be seen between the investment returns and the standard deviations: Investments with higher returns have higher standard deviations. For example, stocks have the highest average return at 9.3 percent, which is more than double the average return on Treasury bills. At the same time, stocks are much more volatile, with a standard deviation of 20.2 percent, more than four times greater than the standard deviation of Treasury bills. Because higher standard deviations are associated with greater risk, the historical data confirm the existence of a positive relationship between risk and return. That relationship reflects *risk aversion* by market participants, who require higher returns as compensation for greater risk. The historical data in columns 1 and 2 of Table 8.5 clearly show that during the 1900–2011 period, investors were, on average, rewarded with higher returns on higher-risk investments.

Matter of fact

All Stocks Are Not Created Equal

Table 8.5 shows that stocks are riskier than bonds, but are some stocks riskier than others? The answer is emphatically yes. A recent study examined the historical returns of large stocks and small stocks and found that the average annual return on large stocks from 1926 through 2011 was 9.8 percent, while small stocks earned 11.9 percent per year on average. The higher returns on small stocks came with a cost, however. The standard deviation of small stock returns was a whopping 32.8 percent, whereas the standard deviation on large stocks was just 20.5 percent.

normal probability distribution
A symmetrical probability distribution whose shape resembles a "bell-shaped" curve.

Normal Distribution A **normal probability distribution**, depicted in Figure 8.3, resembles a symmetrical "bell-shaped" curve. The symmetry of the curve means that half the probability is associated with the values to the left of the peak and half with the values to the right. As noted on the figure, for normal probability distributions, 68 percent of the possible outcomes will lie between ±1 standard deviation from the expected return, 95 percent of all outcomes will lie between ±2 standard deviations from the expected return, and 99 percent of all outcomes will lie between ±3 standard deviations from the expected return.

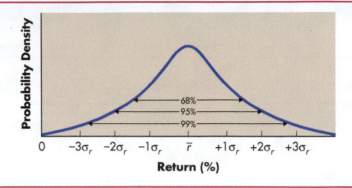

FIGURE 8.3

Bell-Shaped Curve
Normal probability
distribution, with ranges

Example 8.6 ▶ Using the data in Table 8.5 and assuming that the probability distributions of returns for common stocks and bonds are normal, we can surmise that 68% of the possible outcomes would have a return ranging between −10.9% and 29.5% for stocks and between −5.3% and 15.3% for bonds; 95% of the possible return outcomes would range between −31.1% and 49.7% for stocks and between −15.6% and 25.6% for bonds. The greater risk of stocks is clearly reflected in their much wider range of possible returns for each level of confidence (68% or 95%).

Coefficient of Variation: Trading Off Risk and Return

coefficient of variation (CV)
A measure of relative
dispersion that is useful in
comparing the risks of assets
with differing expected returns.

The **coefficient of variation**, *CV*, is a measure of relative dispersion that is useful in comparing the risks of assets with differing expected returns. The expression for the coefficient of variation can be given by

$$CV = \frac{\sigma_r}{\bar{r}} \qquad (8.4)$$

A higher coefficient of variation means that an investment has more volatility relative to its expected return. Because investors prefer higher returns and less risk, one might intuitively expect investors to gravitate towards investments with a low coefficient of variation. However, this logic doesn't always apply for reasons that will emerge in the next section. For now, consider the coefficients of variation in column 3 of Table 8.5. That table reveals that Treasury bills have the lowest coefficient of variation and therefore the lowest risk relative to their return. Does that mean that investors should load up on Treasury bills and divest themselves of stocks? Not necessarily.

Example 8.7 ▶ When the standard deviations (from Table 8.4) and the expected returns (from Table 8.3) for assets A and B are substituted into Equation 8.4, the coefficients of variation for A and B are 0.094 (1.41% ÷ 15%) and 0.377 (5.66% ÷ 15%), respectively. Asset B has the higher coefficient of variation and is therefore more risky than asset A, which we already know from the standard deviation. (Because both assets have the same expected return, the coefficient of variation has not provided any new information.)

Personal Finance Example 8.8 ▶ Marilyn Ansbro is reviewing stocks for inclusion in her investment portfolio. The stock she wishes to analyze is Danhaus Industries, Inc. (DII), a diversified manufacturer of pet products. One of her key concerns is risk; as a rule, she will invest only in stocks with a coefficient of variation below 0.75. She has gathered price and dividend data (shown in the accompanying table) for DII over the past 3 years, 2013–2015, and assumes that each year's return is equally probable.

	Stock Price		
Year	Beginning	End	Dividend paid
2013	$35.00	$36.50	$3.50
2014	36.50	34.50	3.50
2015	34.50	35.00	4.00

Substituting the price and dividend data for each year into Equation 8.1, we get the following information:

Year	Returns
2013	[$3.50 + ($36.50 − $35.00)] ÷ $35.00 = $5.00 ÷ $35.00 = 14.3%
2014	[$3.50 + ($34.50 − $36.50)] ÷ $36.50 = $1.50 ÷ $36.50 = 4.1%
2015	[$4.00 + ($35.00 − $34.50)] ÷ $34.50 = $4.50 ÷ $34.50 = 13.0%

Substituting into Equation 8.2a, given that the returns are equally probable, we get the average return, $\bar{r}_{2013-2015}$:

$$\bar{r}_{2013-2015} = (14.3\% + 4.1\% + 13.0\%) \div 3 = 10.5\%$$

Substituting the average return and annual returns into Equation 8.3a, we get the standard deviation, $\sigma_{r2013-2015}$:

$$\sigma_{r2013-2015} = \sqrt{[(14.3\% - 10.5\%)^2 + (4.1\% - 10.5\%)^2 + (13.0\% - 10.5\%)^2] \div (3 - 1)}$$

$$= \sqrt{(14.44\% + 40.96\% + 6.25\%) \div 2} = \sqrt{30.825\%} = 5.6\%$$

Finally, substituting the standard deviation of returns and the average return into Equation 8.4, we get the coefficient of variation, CV:

$$CV = 5.6\% \div 10.5\% = 0.53$$

Because the coefficient of variation of returns on the DII stock over the 2013–2015 period of 0.53 is well below Marilyn's maximum coefficient of variation of 0.75, she concludes that the DII stock would be an acceptable investment.

→ **REVIEW QUESTIONS**

8–4 Explain how the *range* is used in scenario analysis.

8–5 What does a plot of the *probability distribution* of outcomes show a decision maker about an asset's risk?

8–6 What relationship exists between the size of the *standard deviation* and the degree of asset risk?

8–7 What does the *coefficient of variation* reveal about an investment's risk that the standard deviation does not?

  ## 8.3 Risk of a Portfolio

MyFinanceLab Video

efficient portfolio
A portfolio that maximizes return for a given level of risk.

In real-world situations, the risk of any single investment would not be viewed independently of other assets. New investments must be considered in light of their impact on the risk and return of an investor's *portfolio* of assets. The financial manager's goal is to create an **efficient portfolio,** one that provides the maximum return for a given level of risk. We therefore need a way to measure the return and the standard deviation of a portfolio of assets. As part of that analysis, we will look at the statistical concept of *correlation,* which underlies the process of diversification that is used to develop an efficient portfolio.

PORTFOLIO RETURN AND STANDARD DEVIATION

The *return on a portfolio* is a weighted average of the returns on the individual assets from which it is formed. We can use Equation 8.5 to find the portfolio return, r_p:

$$r_p = (w_1 \times r_1) + (w_2 \times r_2) + \cdots + (w_n \times r_n) = \sum_{j=1}^{n} w_j \times r_j \qquad (8.5)$$

where

w_j = proportion of the portfolio's total dollar value represented by asset j

r_j = return on asset j

Of course, $\sum_{j=1}^{n} w_j = 1$, which means that 100 percent of the portfolio's assets must be included in this computation.

Example 8.9 ▶

MyFinanceLab Solution Video

James purchases 100 shares of Wal-Mart at a price of $55 per share, so his total investment in Wal-Mart is $5,500. He also buys 100 shares of Cisco Systems at $25 per share, so the total investment in Cisco stock is $2,500. Combining these two holdings, James's total portfolio is worth $8,000. Of the total, 68.75% is invested in Wal-Mart ($5,500 ÷ $8,000), and 31.25% is invested in Cisco Systems ($2,500 ÷ $8,000). Thus, $w_1 = 0.6875$, $w_2 = 0.3125$, and $w_1 + w_2 = 1.0$.

The *standard deviation of a portfolio's returns* is found by applying the formula for the standard deviation of a single asset. Specifically, Equation 8.3 is used when the probabilities of the returns are known, and Equation 8.3a (from footnote 4) is applied when analysts use historical data to estimate the standard deviation.

Example 8.10 ▶ Assume that we wish to determine the expected value and standard deviation of returns for portfolio XY, created by combining equal portions (50% each) of assets X and Y. The forecasted returns of assets X and Y for each of the next 5 years (2014–2018) are given in columns 1 and 2, respectively, in part A of Table 8.6. In column 3, the weights of 50% for both assets X and Y along with their respective returns from columns 1 and 2 are substituted into Equation 8.5. Column 4 shows the results of the calculation: an expected portfolio return of 12% for each year, 2014 to 2018.

Furthermore, as shown in part B of Table 8.6, the expected value of these portfolio returns over the 5-year period is also 12% (calculated by using Equation 8.2a, in footnote 3). In part C of Table 8.6, portfolio XY's standard deviation is calculated to be 0% (using Equation 8.3a, in footnote 4). This value should not be surprising because the portfolio return each year is the same: 12%. Portfolio returns do not vary through time.

TABLE 8.6 ▶ Expected Return, Expected Value, and Standard Deviation of Returns for Portfolio XY

A. Expected portfolio returns

Year	Forecasted return Asset X (1)	Forecasted return Asset Y (2)	Portfolio return calculation[a] (3)	Expected portfolio return, r_p (4)
2014	8%	16%	$(0.50 \times 8\%) + (0.50 \times 16\%) =$	12%
2015	10	14	$(0.50 \times 10\%) + (0.50 \times 14\%) =$	12
2016	12	12	$(0.50 \times 12\%) + (0.50 \times 12\%) =$	12
2017	14	10	$(0.50 \times 14\%) + (0.50 \times 10\%) =$	12
2018	16	8	$(0.50 \times 16\%) + (0.50 \times 8\%) =$	12

B. Expected value of portfolio returns, 2014–2018[b]

$$\bar{r}_p = \frac{12\% + 12\% + 12\% + 12\% + 12\%}{5} = \frac{60\%}{5} = \underline{\underline{12\%}}$$

C. Standard deviation of expected portfolio returns[c]

$$\sigma_{r_p} = \sqrt{\frac{(12\% - 12\%)^2 + (12\% - 12\%)^2 + (12\% - 12\%)^2 + (12\% - 12\%)^2 + (12\% - 12\%)^2}{5 - 1}}$$

$$= \sqrt{\frac{0\% + 0\% + 0\% + 0\% + 0\%}{4}}$$

$$= \sqrt{\frac{0\%}{4}} = \underline{\underline{0\%}}$$

[a]Using Equation 8.5.
[b]Using Equation 8.2a, in footnote 3.
[c]Using Equation 8.3a, in footnote 4.

CORRELATION

correlation
A statistical measure of the relationship between any two series of numbers.

positively correlated
Describes two series that move in the same direction.

negatively correlated
Describes two series that move in opposite directions.

correlation coefficient
A measure of the degree of correlation between two series.

perfectly positively correlated
Describes two *positively correlated* series that have a *correlation coefficient* of +1.

perfectly negatively correlated
Describes two *negatively correlated* series that have a *correlation coefficient* of −1.

Correlation is a statistical measure of the relationship between any two series of numbers. The numbers may represent data of any kind, from returns to test scores. If two series tend to vary in the same direction, they are **positively correlated**. If the series vary in opposite directions, they are **negatively correlated**. For example, suppose that we gathered data on the retail price and weight of new cars. It is likely that we would find that larger cars cost more than smaller ones, so we would say that among new cars, weight and price are positively correlated. If we also measured the fuel efficiency of these vehicles (as measured by the number of miles they can travel per gallon of gasoline), we would find that lighter cars are more fuel efficient than heavier cars. In that case, we would say that fuel economy and vehicle weight are negatively correlated.[5]

The degree of correlation is measured by the **correlation coefficient**, which ranges from +1 for **perfectly positively correlated** series to −1 for **perfectly negatively correlated** series. These two extremes are depicted for series M and N in Figure 8.4. The perfectly positively correlated series move exactly together without exception; the perfectly negatively correlated series move in exactly opposite directions.

DIVERSIFICATION

The concept of correlation is essential to developing an efficient portfolio. To reduce overall risk, it is best to *diversify* by combining, or adding to the portfolio, assets that have the lowest possible correlation. Combining assets that have a low correlation with each other can reduce the overall variability of a portfolio's returns. Figure 8.5 shows the returns that two assets, F and G, earn over time. Both assets earn the same average or expected return, $\bar{r}$, but note that when F's return is above average, the return on G is below average and vice versa. In other words, returns on F and G are negatively correlated, and when these two assets are combined in a portfolio, the risk of that portfolio falls without reducing the average return (that is, the portfolio's average return is also $\bar{r}$). For risk-averse investors, that is very good news. They get rid

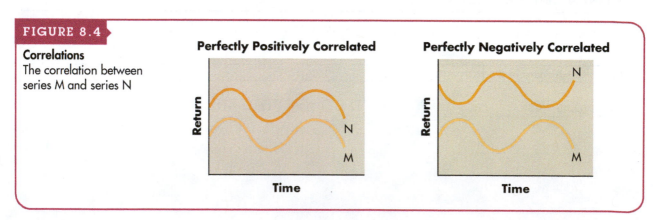

FIGURE 8.4

Correlations
The correlation between series M and series N

5. Note here that we are talking about general tendencies. For instance, a large hybrid SUV might have better fuel economy than a smaller sedan powered by a conventional gasoline engine, but that does not change the general tendency that lighter cars achieve better fuel economy.

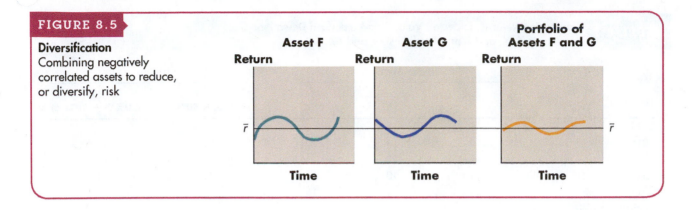

FIGURE 8.5

Diversification
Combining negatively correlated assets to reduce, or diversify, risk

of something they don't like (risk) without having to sacrifice what they do like (return). Even if assets are positively correlated, the lower the correlation between them, the greater the risk reduction that can be achieved through diversification.

Some assets are **uncorrelated**; that is, there is no interaction between their returns. Combining uncorrelated assets can reduce risk, not as effectively as combining negatively correlated assets but more effectively than combining positively correlated assets. The *correlation coefficient for uncorrelated assets is close to zero* and acts as the midpoint between perfectly positive and perfectly negative correlation.

The creation of a portfolio that combines two assets with perfectly positively correlated returns results in overall portfolio risk that at minimum equals that of the least risky asset and at maximum equals that of the most risky asset. However, a portfolio combining two assets with less than perfectly positive correlation *can* reduce total risk to a level below that of either of the components. For example, assume that you buy stock in a company that manufactures machine tools. The business is very *cyclical,* so the stock will do well when the economy is expanding, and it will do poorly during a recession. If you bought shares in another machine-tool company, with sales positively correlated with those of your firm, the combined portfolio would still be cyclical, and risk would not be reduced a great deal. Alternatively, however, you could buy stock in a discount retailer, whose sales are *countercyclical.* It typically performs worse during economic expansions than it does during recessions (when consumers are trying to save money on every purchase). A portfolio that contained both of these stocks might be less volatile than either stock on its own.

uncorrelated
Describes two series that lack any interaction and therefore have a *correlation coefficient* close to zero.

Example 8.11 ▶

Table 8.7 presents the forecasted returns from three different assets—X, Y, and Z—over the next 5 years, along with their expected values and standard deviations. Each of the assets has an expected return of 12% and a standard deviation of 3.16%. The assets therefore have equal return and equal risk. The return patterns of assets X and Y are perfectly negatively correlated. When X enjoys its highest return, Y experiences its lowest return and vice versa. The returns of assets X and Z are perfectly positively correlated. They move in precisely the same direction, so when the return on X is high, so is the return on Z. (*Note:* The

| TABLE 8.7 | Forecasted Returns, Expected Values, and Standard Deviations for Assets X, Y, and Z and Portfolios XY and XZ |

	Assets			Portfolios	
Year	X	Y	Z	XY[a] (50% X + 50% Y)	XZ[b] (50% X + 50% Z)
2014	8%	16%	8%	12%	8%
2015	10	14	10	12	10
2016	12	12	12	12	12
2017	14	10	14	12	14
2018	16	8	16	12	16
Statistics:[c]					
Expected value	12%	12%	12%	12%	12%
Standard deviation[d]	3.16%	3.16%	3.16%	0%	3.16%

[a]Portfolio XY, which consists of 50 percent of asset X and 50 percent of asset Y, illustrates *perfect negative correlation* because these two return streams behave in completely opposite fashion over the 5-year period. Its return values shown here were calculated in part A of Table 8.6.

[b]Portfolio XZ, which consists of 50 percent of asset X and 50 percent of asset Z, illustrates *perfect positive correlation* because these two return streams behave identically over the 5-year period. Its return values were calculated by using the same method demonstrated for portfolio XY in part A of Table 8.6.

[c]Because the probabilities associated with the returns are not given, the general equations, Equation 8.2a in footnote 3 and Equation 8.3a in footnote 4, were used to calculate expected values and standard deviations, respectively. Calculation of the expected value and standard deviation for portfolio XY is demonstrated in parts B and C, respectively, of Table 8.6.

[d]The portfolio standard deviations can be directly calculated from the standard deviations of the component assets with the formula

$$\sigma_{r_p} = \sqrt{w_1^2 \sigma_1^2 + w_2^2 \sigma_2^2 + 2w_1 w_2 c_{1,2} \sigma_1 \sigma_2}$$

where w_1 and w_2 are the proportions of component assets 1 and 2, σ_1 and σ_2 are the standard deviations of component assets 1 and 2, and $c_{1,2}$ is the correlation coefficient between the returns of component assets 1 and 2.

returns for X and Z are identical.)[6] Now let's consider what happens when we combine these assets in different ways to form portfolios.

Portfolio XY Portfolio XY (shown in Table 8.7) is created by combining equal portions of assets X and Y, the perfectly negatively correlated assets. (Calculation of portfolio XY's annual returns, the expected portfolio return, and the standard deviation of returns was demonstrated in Table 8.6 on page 307.) The risk in this portfolio, as reflected by its standard deviation, is reduced to 0%, whereas the expected return remains at 12%. Thus, the combination results in the complete elimination of risk because in each and every year the portfolio earns a 12% return.[7] *Whenever assets are perfectly negatively correlated, some combination of the two assets exists such that the resulting portfolio's returns are risk free.*

Portfolio XZ Portfolio XZ (shown in Table 8.7) is created by combining equal portions of assets X and Z, the perfectly positively correlated assets. Individually, assets X and Z have the same standard deviation, 3.16%, and because they always move together, combining them in a portfolio does nothing to reduce risk; the

---

6. Identical return streams are used in this example to permit clear illustration of the concepts, but it is *not* necessary for return streams to be identical for them to be perfectly positively correlated. Any return streams that move exactly together—regardless of the relative magnitude of the returns—are perfectly positively correlated.

7. Perfect negative correlation means that the ups and downs experienced by one asset are exactly offset by movements in the other asset. Therefore, the portfolio return does not vary over time.

portfolio standard deviation is also 3.16%. As was the case with portfolio XY, the expected return of portfolio XZ is 12%. Because both of these portfolios provide the same expected return, but portfolio XY achieves that expected return with no risk, portfolio XY is clearly preferred by risk-averse investors over portfolio XZ.

CORRELATION, DIVERSIFICATION, RISK, AND RETURN

In general, the lower the correlation between asset returns, the greater the risk reduction that investors can achieve by diversifying. The following example illustrates how correlation influences the risk of a portfolio but not the portfolio's expected return.

Example 8.12 ▶

MyFinanceLab Solution Video

Consider two assets—Lo and Hi—with the characteristics described in the following table.

Asset	Expected return, $\bar{r}$	Risk (standard deviation), σ
Lo	6%	3%
Hi	8	8

Clearly, asset Lo offers a lower return than Hi does, but Lo is also less risky than Hi. It is natural to think that a portfolio combining Lo and Hi would offer a return that is between 6% and 8% and that the portfolio's risk would also fall between the risk of Lo and Hi (between 3% and 8%). That intuition is only partly correct.

The performance of a portfolio consisting of assets Lo and Hi depends not only on the expected return and standard deviation of each asset (given above), but also on how the returns on the two assets are correlated. We will illustrate the results of three specific scenarios: (1) returns on Lo and Hi are perfectly positively correlated, (2) returns on Lo and Hi are uncorrelated, and (3) returns on Lo and Hi are perfectly negatively correlated.

The results of the analysis appear in Figure 8.6. Whether the correlation between Lo and Hi is +1, 0, or −1, a portfolio of those two assets must have an expected return between 6% and 8%. That is why the line segments at left in Figure 8.6 all range between 6% and 8%. However, the standard deviation of a portfolio depends critically on the correlation between Lo and Hi. Only when Lo and Hi are perfectly positively correlated can it be said that the portfolio standard deviation must fall between 3% (Lo's standard deviation) and 8% (Hi's standard deviation). As the correlation between Lo and Hi becomes weaker (that is, as the correlation coefficient falls), investors may find that they can form portfolios of Lo and Hi with standard deviations that are even less than 3% (that is, portfolios that are less risky than holding asset Lo by itself). That is why the line segments at right in Figure 8.6 vary. In the special case when Lo and Hi are perfectly negatively correlated, it is possible to diversify away all the risk and form a portfolio that is risk free.

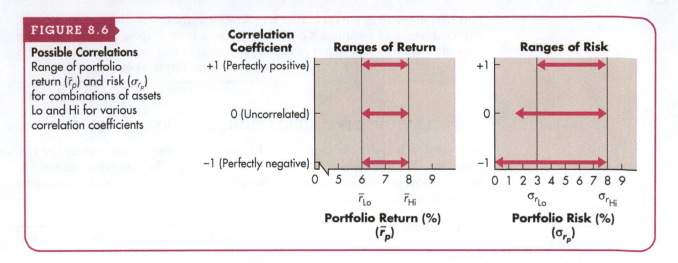

FIGURE 8.6

Possible Correlations
Range of portfolio return ($\bar{r}_p$) and risk (σ_{r_p}) for combinations of assets Lo and Hi for various correlation coefficients

INTERNATIONAL DIVERSIFICATION

One excellent practical example of portfolio diversification involves including foreign assets in a portfolio. The inclusion of assets from countries with business cycles that are not highly correlated with the U.S. business cycle reduces the portfolio's responsiveness to market movements. The ups and the downs different markets around the world offset one another, at least to some extent, and the result is a portfolio that is less risky than one invested entirely in the U.S. market.

Returns from International Diversification

Over long periods, internationally diversified portfolios tend to perform better (meaning that they earn higher returns relative to the risks taken) than purely domestic portfolios. However, over shorter periods such as 1 or 2 years, internationally diversified portfolios may perform better or worse than domestic portfolios. For example, consider what happens when the U.S. economy is performing relatively poorly and the dollar is depreciating in value against most foreign currencies. At such times, the dollar returns to U.S. investors on a portfolio of foreign assets can be very attractive. However, international diversification can yield subpar returns, particularly when the dollar is appreciating in value relative to other currencies. When the U.S. currency appreciates, the dollar value of a foreign-currency-denominated portfolio of assets declines. Even if this portfolio yields a satisfactory return in foreign currency, the return to U.S. investors will be reduced when foreign profits are translated into dollars. Subpar local currency portfolio returns, coupled with an appreciating dollar, can yield truly dismal dollar returns to U.S. investors.

Overall, though, the logic of international portfolio diversification assumes that these fluctuations in currency values and relative performance will average out over long periods. Compared to similar, purely domestic portfolios, an internationally diversified portfolio will tend to yield a comparable return at a lower level of risk.

Risks of International Diversification

political risk
Risk that arises from the possibility that a host government will take actions harmful to foreign investors or that political turmoil will endanger investments.

In addition to the risk induced by currency fluctuations, several other financial risks are unique to international investing. Most important is **political risk**, which arises from the possibility that a host government will take actions harmful to foreign investors or that political turmoil will endanger investments. Political risks are particularly acute in developing countries, where unstable or ideologically motivated governments may attempt to block return of profits by foreign investors or even seize (nationalize) their assets in the host country. For example, reflecting President Hugo Chavez's desire to broaden the country's socialist revolution, Venezuela maintained a list of priority goods for import that excluded a large percentage of the necessary inputs to the automobile production process. As a result, Toyota halted auto production in Venezuela, and three other auto manufacturers temporarily closed or deeply cut their production there. Chavez also forced most foreign energy firms to reduce their stakes and give up control of oil projects in Venezuela.

→ **REVIEW QUESTIONS**

8–8 What is an *efficient portfolio?* How can the return and standard deviation of a portfolio be determined?

8–9 Why is the *correlation* between asset returns important? How does diversification allow risky assets to be combined so that the risk of the portfolio is less than the risk of the individual assets in it?

8–10 How does international diversification enhance risk reduction? When might international diversification result in subpar returns? What are *political risks*, and how do they affect international diversification?

  ## 8.4 Risk and Return: The Capital Asset Pricing Model (CAPM)

Thus far, we have observed a tendency for riskier investments to earn higher returns, and we have learned that investors can reduce risk through diversification. Now we want to quantify the relationship between risk and return. In other words, we want to measure how much additional return an investor should expect from taking a little extra risk. The classic theory that links risk and return for all assets is the **capital asset pricing model (CAPM)**. We will use the CAPM to understand the basic risk–return trade-offs involved in all types of financial decisions.

capital asset pricing model (CAPM)
The basic theory that links risk and return for all assets.

TYPES OF RISK

In the last section, we saw that the standard deviation of a portfolio is often less than the standard deviation of the individual assets in the portfolio. That's the power of diversification. To see this concept more clearly, consider what happens to the risk of a portfolio consisting of a single security (asset) to which we add securities randomly selected from, say, the population of all actively traded securities. Using the standard deviation of return, $\sigma_r p$, to measure the total portfolio risk,

Figure 8.7 depicts the behavior of the total portfolio risk (*y* axis) as more securities are added (*x* axis). With the addition of securities, the total portfolio risk declines, as a result of diversification, and tends to approach a lower limit.

The **total risk** of a security can be viewed as consisting of two parts:

total risk
The combination of a security's *nondiversifiable risk* and *diversifiable risk*.

$$\text{Total security risk} = \text{Nondiversifiable risk} + \text{Diversifiable risk} \qquad (8.6)$$

diversifiable risk
The portion of an asset's risk that is attributable to firm-specific, random causes; can be eliminated through diversification. Also called *unsystematic risk.*

Diversifiable risk (sometimes called *unsystematic risk*) represents the portion of an asset's risk that is associated with random causes that can be eliminated through diversification. It is attributable to firm-specific events, such as strikes, lawsuits, regulatory actions, or the loss of key accounts. Figure 8.7 shows that diversifiable risk gradually disappears as the number of stocks in the portfolio increases. **Nondiversifiable risk** (also called *systematic risk*) is attributable to market factors that affect all firms; it cannot be eliminated through diversification. Factors such as war, inflation, the overall state of the economy, international incidents, and political events account for nondiversifiable risk. In Figure 8.7, nondiversifiable risk is represented by the horizontal black line below which the blue curve can never go, no matter how diversified the portfolio becomes.

nondiversifiable risk
The relevant portion of an asset's risk attributable to market factors that affect all firms; cannot be eliminated through diversification. Also called *systematic risk.*

Because any investor can easily create a portfolio of assets that will eliminate virtually all diversifiable risk, *the only relevant risk is nondiversifiable risk.* Any investor or firm therefore must be concerned solely with nondiversifiable risk. The measurement of nondiversifiable risk is thus of primary importance in selecting assets with the most desired risk–return characteristics.

THE MODEL: CAPM

The capital asset pricing model (CAPM) links nondiversifiable risk to expected returns. We will discuss the model in five sections. The first section deals with the beta coefficient, which is a measure of nondiversifiable risk. The second section presents an equation of the model itself, and the third section graphically describes the relationship between risk and return. The fourth section discusses the effects of changes in inflationary expectations and risk aversion on the relationship between risk and return. The fifth section offers some comments on the CAPM.

FIGURE 8.7

Risk Reduction
Portfolio risk and diversification

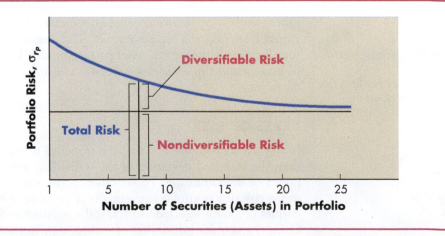

beta coefficient (β)
A relative measure of nondiversifiable risk. An *index* of the degree of movement of an asset's return in response to a change in the *market return.*

market return
The return on the market portfolio of all traded securities.

Beta Coefficient

The **beta coefficient, β,** is a relative measure of nondiversifiable risk. It is an *index* of the degree of movement of an asset's return in response to a change in the *market return.* An asset's historical returns are used in finding the asset's beta coefficient. The **market return** is the return on the market portfolio of all traded securities. The *Standard & Poor's 500 Stock Composite Index* or some similar stock index is commonly used as the market return. Betas for actively traded stocks can be obtained from a variety of sources, but you should understand how they are derived and interpreted and how they are applied to portfolios.

Deriving Beta from Return Data An asset's historical returns are used in finding the asset's beta coefficient. Figure 8.8 plots the relationship between the returns of two assets—R and S—and the market return. Note that the horizontal (x) axis measures the historical market returns and that the vertical (y) axis measures the individual asset's historical returns. The first step in deriving beta involves plotting the coordinates for the market return and asset returns from various points in time. Such annual "market return–asset return" coordinates are shown *for asset S only* for the years 2008 through 2015. For example, in 2015, asset S's return was 20 percent when the market return was 10 percent. By use of statistical techniques, the "characteristic line" that best explains the relationship between the asset return and the market return coordinates is fit to the data points.[8] The slope of this line is *beta.* The beta for asset R is about

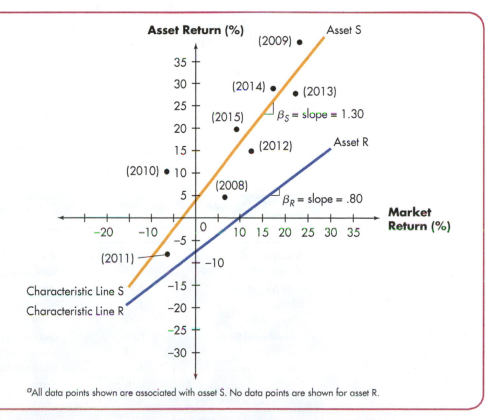

FIGURE 8.8

Beta Derivation[a]
Graphical derivation of beta for assets R and S

[a]All data points shown are associated with asset S. No data points are shown for asset R.

---

8. The empirical measurement of beta is approached by using *least-squares regression analysis.*

TABLE 8.8 > **Selected Beta Coefficients and Their Interpretations**

Beta	Comment	Interpretation
2.0 ⎫ ⎬	Move in same	⎧ Twice as responsive as the market
1.0 ⎬	direction as market	⎨ Same response as the market
0.5 ⎭		⎩ Only half as responsive as the market
0		Unaffected by market movement
−0.5 ⎫	Move in opposite	⎧ Only half as responsive as the market
−1.0 ⎬	direction to	⎨ Same response as the market
−2.0 ⎭	market	⎩ Twice as responsive as the market

0.80, and that for asset S is about 1.30. Asset S's higher beta (steeper characteristic line slope) indicates that its return is more responsive to changing market returns. *Therefore, asset S is more risky than asset R.*

Interpreting Betas   The beta coefficient for the entire market equals 1.0. All other betas are viewed in relation to this value. Asset betas may be positive or negative, but positive betas are the norm. The majority of beta coefficients fall between 0.5 and 2.0. The return of a stock that is half as responsive as the market ($\beta = 0.5$) should change by 0.5 percent for each 1 percent change in the return of the market portfolio. A stock that is twice as responsive as the market ($\beta = 2.0$) should experience a 2 percent change in its return for each 1 percent change in the return of the market portfolio. Table 8.8 provides various beta values and their interpretations. Beta coefficients for actively traded stocks can be obtained from published sources such as *Value Line Investment Survey*, via the Internet, or through brokerage firms. Betas for some selected stocks are given in Table 8.9.

Portfolio Betas   The beta of a portfolio can be easily estimated by using the betas of the individual assets it includes. Letting w_j represent

TABLE 8.9 > **Beta Coefficients for Selected Stocks (May 20, 2013)**

Stock	Beta	Stock	Beta
Amazon.com	0.82	JP Morgan Chase & Co.	1.64
Anheuser-Busch	0.86	Bank of America	1.78
Ford Motor	1.56	Microsoft	1.18
Disney	1.09	Nike, Inc.	0.78
eBay	0.87	PepsiCo, Inc.	0.35
ExxonMobil Corp.	0.86	Qualcomm	1.16
Gap (The), Inc.	1.25	Sempra Energy	0.38
General Electric	1.40	Wal-Mart Stores	0.42
Intel	0.99	Xerox	1.86
Int'l Business Machines	0.65	Yahoo! Inc.	0.89

Source: www.finance.yahoo.com.

the proportion of the portfolio's total dollar value represented by asset j and letting β_j equal the beta of asset j, we can use Equation 8.7 to find the portfolio beta, β_p:

$$\beta_p = (w_1 \times \beta_1) + (w_2 \times \beta_2) + \cdots + (w_n \times \beta_n) = \sum_{j=1}^{n} w_j \times \beta_j \qquad (8.7)$$

Of course, $\sum_{j=1}^{n} w_j = 1$, which means that 100 percent of the portfolio's assets must be included in this computation.

Portfolio betas are interpreted in the same way as the betas of individual assets. They indicate the degree of responsiveness of the *portfolio's* return to changes in the market return. For example, when the market return increases by 10 percent, a portfolio with a beta of 0.75 will experience a 7.5 percent increase in its return ($0.75 \times 10\%$); a portfolio with a beta of 1.25 will experience a 12.5 percent increase in its return ($1.25 \times 10\%$). Clearly, a portfolio containing mostly low-beta assets will have a low beta, and one containing mostly high-beta assets will have a high beta.

Personal Finance Example 8.13 ▶ Mario Austino, an individual investor, wishes to assess the risk of two small portfolios he is considering, V and W. Both portfolios contain five assets, with the proportions and betas shown in Table 8.10. The betas for the two portfolios, β_V and β_W, can be calculated by substituting data from the table into Equation 8.7:

$$\beta_V = (0.10 \times 1.65) + (0.30 \times 1.00) + (0.20 \times 1.30) + (0.20 \times 1.10) + (0.20 \times 1.25)$$
$$= 0.165 + 0.300 + 0.260 + 0.220 + 0.250 = \underline{1.20}$$

$$\beta_W = (0.10 \times 0.80) + (0.10 \times 1.00) + (0.20 \times 0.65) + (0.10 \times 0.75) + (0.50 \times 1.05)$$
$$= 0.080 + 0.100 + 0.130 + 0.075 + 0.525 = \underline{0.91}$$

Portfolio V's beta is about 1.20, and portfolio W's is 0.91. These values make sense because portfolio V contains relatively high-beta assets, and portfolio W contains relatively low-beta assets. Mario's calculations show that portfolio V's returns are more responsive to changes in market returns and are therefore more

	Portfolio V		Portfolio W	
Asset	Proportion	Beta	Proportion	Beta
1	0.10	1.65	0.10	0.80
2	0.30	1.00	0.10	1.00
3	0.20	1.30	0.20	0.65
4	0.20	1.10	0.10	0.75
5	0.20	1.25	0.50	1.05
Totals	1.00		1.00	

TABLE 8.10 Mario Austino's Portfolios V and W

risky than portfolio W's. He must now decide which, if either, portfolio he feels comfortable adding to his existing investments.

The Equation

Using the beta coefficient to measure nondiversifiable risk, the *capital asset pricing model (CAPM)* is given by

$$r_j = R_F + [\beta_j \times (r_m - R_F)] \tag{8.8}$$

where

$$r_j = \text{required return on asset } j$$
$$R_F = \text{risk-free rate of return, commonly measured by the return}$$
$$\text{on a U.S. Treasury bill}$$
$$\beta_j = \text{beta coefficient or index of nondiversifiable risk for asset } j$$
$$r_m = \text{market return; return on the market portfolio of assets}$$

risk-free rate of return (R_F)
The required return on a *risk-free asset,* typically a 3-month U.S. Treasury bill.

U.S. Treasury bills (T-bills)
Short-term IOUs issued by the U.S. Treasury; considered the *risk-free asset.*

The CAPM can be divided into two parts: (1) the **risk-free rate of return,** R_F, which is the required return on a *risk-free asset,* typically a 3-month **U.S. Treasury bill (T-bill)**, a short-term IOU issued by the U.S. Treasury; and (2) the *risk premium.* These parts are, respectively, the two elements on either side of the plus sign in Equation 8.8. The ($r_m - R_F$) portion of the risk premium is called the *market risk premium* because it represents the premium that the investor must receive for taking the average amount of risk associated with holding the market portfolio of assets.

Historical Risk Premiums   Using the historical return data for stocks, bonds, and Treasury bills for the 1900–2011 period shown in Table 8.2, we can calculate the risk premiums for each investment category. The calculation (consistent with Equation 8.8) involves merely subtracting the historical U.S. Treasury bill's average return from the historical average return for a given investment:

Investment	Risk premium[a]
Stocks	9.3% − 3.9% = 5.4%
Treasury bonds	5.0 − 3.9 = 1.1

[a]Return values obtained from Table 8.1.

Reviewing the risk premiums calculated above, we can see that the risk premium is higher for stocks than for bonds. This outcome makes sense intuitively because stocks are riskier than bonds (equity is riskier than debt).

Example 8.14 ▶   Benjamin Corporation, a growing computer software developer, wishes to determine the required return on an asset Z, which has a beta of 1.5. The risk-free rate of return is 7%; the return on the market portfolio of assets is 11%. Substituting

$\beta_Z = 1.5$, $R_F = 7\%$, and $r_m = 11\%$ into the capital asset pricing model given in Equation 8.8 yields a required return of

$$r_Z = 7\% + [1.5 \times (11\% - 7\%)] = 7\% + 6\% = 13\%$$

The market risk premium of 4% (11% − 7%), when adjusted for the asset's index of risk (beta) of 1.5, results in a risk premium of 6% (1.5 × 4%). That risk premium, when added to the 7% risk-free rate, results in a 13% required return.

Other things being equal, *the higher the beta, the higher the required return, and the lower the beta, the lower the required return.*

The Graph: The Security Market Line (SML)

security market line (SML)
The depiction of the *capital asset pricing model (CAPM)* as a graph that reflects the required return in the marketplace for each level of nondiversifiable risk (beta).

When the capital asset pricing model (Equation 8.8) is depicted graphically, it is called the **security market line (SML)**. The SML will, in fact, be a straight line. It reflects the required return in the marketplace for each level of nondiversifiable risk (beta). In the graph, risk as measured by beta, β, is plotted on the *x* axis, and required returns, *r*, are plotted on the *y* axis. The risk–return trade-off is clearly represented by the SML.

Example 8.15 ▶ In the preceding example for Benjamin Corporation, the risk-free rate, R_F, was 7%, and the market return, r_m, was 11%. The SML can be plotted by using the two sets of coordinates for the betas associated with R_F and r_m, β_{R_F} and β_m (that is, $\beta_{R_F} = 0$,[9] $R_F = 7\%$; and $\beta_m = 1.0$, $r_m = 11\%$). Figure 8.9 presents the

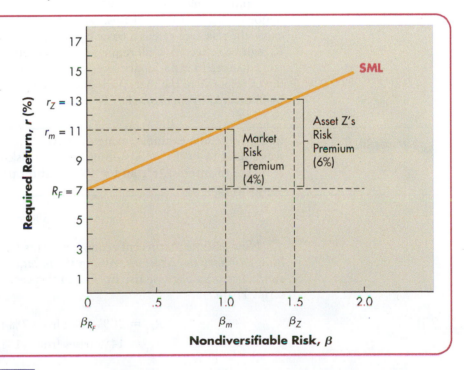

FIGURE 8.9

Security Market Line
Security market line (SML) with Benjamin Corporation's asset Z data shown

9. Because R_F is the rate of return on a risk-free asset, the beta associated with the risk-free asset, β_{R_F}, would equal 0. The zero beta on the risk-free asset reflects not only its absence of risk but also that the asset's return is unaffected by movements in the market return.

resulting security market line. As traditionally shown, the security market line in Figure 8.9 presents the required return associated with all positive betas. The market risk premium of 4% (r_m of 11% − R_F of 7%) has been highlighted. For a beta for asset Z, β_Z, of 1.5, its corresponding required return, r_Z, is 13%. Also shown in the figure is asset Z's risk premium of 6% (r_Z of 13% − R_F of 7%). It should be clear that for assets with betas greater than 1, the risk premium is greater than that for the market; for assets with betas less than 1, the risk premium is less than that for the market.

Shifts in the Security Market Line

The security market line is not stable over time, and shifts in the security market line can result in a change in required return. The position and slope of the SML are affected by two major forces—inflationary expectations and risk aversion—which are analyzed next.[10]

Changes in Inflationary Expectations   Changes in inflationary expectations affect the risk-free rate of return, R_F. The equation for the risk-free rate of return is

$$R_F = r^* + IP \tag{8.9}$$

This equation shows that, assuming a constant real rate of interest, r^*, changes in inflationary expectations, reflected in an inflation premium, IP, will result in corresponding changes in the risk-free rate. Therefore, a change in inflationary expectations that results from events such as international trade embargoes or major changes in Federal Reserve policy will result in a shift in the SML. Because the risk-free rate is a basic component of all rates of return, any change in R_F will be reflected in *all* required rates of return.

Changes in inflationary expectations result in parallel shifts in the SML in direct response to the magnitude and direction of the change. This effect can best be illustrated by an example.

Example 8.16 ▶   In the preceding example, using the CAPM, the required return for asset Z, r_Z, was found to be 13%. Assuming that the risk-free rate of 7% includes a 2% real rate of interest, r^*, and a 5% inflation premium, IP, then Equation 8.9 confirms that

$$R_F = 2\% + 5\% = 7\%$$

Now assume that recent economic events have resulted in an *increase of 3% in inflationary expectations, raising the inflation premium* to 8% (IP_1). As a result, all returns likewise rise by 3%. In this case, the new returns (noted by subscript 1) are

$$R_{F_1} = 10\% \text{ (rises from 7\% to 10\%)}$$
$$r_{m_1} = 14\% \text{ (rises from 11\% to 14\%)}$$

---

10. A firm's beta can change over time as a result of changes in the firm's asset mix, in its financing mix, or in external factors not within management's control, such as earthquakes and toxic spills.

Substituting these values, along with asset Z's beta (β_Z) of 1.5, into the CAPM (Equation 8.8), we find that asset Z's new required return (r_{Z_1}) can be calculated:

$$r_{Z_1} = 10\% + [1.5 \times (14\% - 10\%)] = 10\% + 6\% = \underline{16\%}$$

Comparing r_{Z_1} of 16% to r_Z of 13%, we see that the change of 3% in asset Z's required return exactly equals the change in the inflation premium. The same 3% increase results for all assets.

Figure 8.10 depicts the situation just described. It shows that the 3% increase in inflationary expectations results in a parallel shift upward of 3% in the SML. Clearly, the required returns on all assets rise by 3%. Note that the rise in the inflation premium from 5% to 8% (IP to IP_1) causes the risk-free rate to rise from 7% to 10% (R_F to R_{F_1}) and the market return to increase from 11% to 14% (r_m to r_{m_1}). The security market line therefore shifts upward by 3% (SML to SML$_1$), causing the required return on all risky assets, such as asset Z, to rise by 3%. The important lesson here is that *a given change in inflationary expectations will be fully reflected in a corresponding change in the returns of all assets, as reflected graphically in a parallel shift of the SML.*

Changes in Risk Aversion   The slope of the security market line reflects the general risk preferences of investors in the marketplace. As discussed earlier, most investors are *risk averse*; that is, they require increased returns for increased risk. This positive relationship between risk and return is graphically represented by the SML, which depicts the relationship between nondiversifiable risk as measured by beta (*x* axis) and the required return (*y* axis). The slope of the SML reflects the degree of risk aversion: *the steeper its slope, the greater the degree of risk aversion* because a higher level of return will be required for each level of risk as

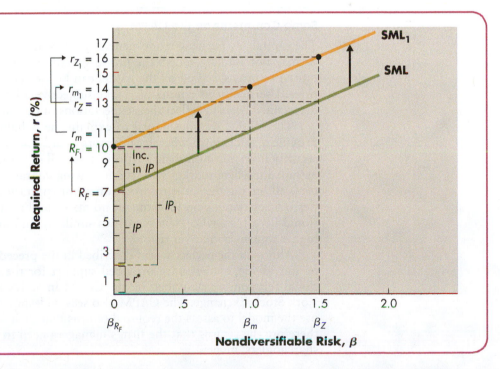

FIGURE 8.10

Inflation Shifts SML
Impact of increased inflationary expectations on the SML

measured by beta. In other words, *risk premiums increase with increasing risk avoidance.*

Changes in risk aversion, and therefore shifts in the SML, result from changing preferences of investors, which generally result from economic, political, or social events. Examples of events that *increase* risk aversion include a stock market crash, assassination of a key political leader, and the outbreak of war. In general, widely shared expectations of hard times ahead tend to cause investors to become more risk averse, requiring higher returns as compensation for accepting a given level of risk. The impact of increased risk aversion on the SML can best be demonstrated by an example.

Example 8.17 ▶   In the preceding examples, the SML in Figure 8.9 reflected a risk-free rate (R_F) of 7%, a market return (r_m) of 11%, a market risk premium ($r_m - R_F$) of 4%, and a required return on asset Z (r_Z) of 13% with a beta (β_Z) of 1.5. Assume that recent economic events have made investors more risk averse, causing a new higher market return (r_{m_1}) of 14%. Graphically, this change would cause the SML to pivot upward as shown in Figure 8.11, causing a new market risk premium ($r_{m_1} - R_F$) of 7%. As a result, the required return on all risky assets will increase. For asset Z, with a beta of 1.5, the new required return (r_{Z_1}) can be calculated by using the CAPM (Equation 8.8):

$$r_{Z_1} = 7\% + [1.5 \times (14\% - 7\%)] = 7\% + 10.5\% = \underline{17.5\%}$$

This value can be seen on the new security market line (SML₁) in Figure 8.11. Note that although asset Z's risk, as measured by beta, did not change, its required return has increased because of the increased risk aversion reflected in th market risk premium. To summarize, *greater risk aversion results in higher re quired returns for each level of risk. Similarly, a reduction in risk aversion causes the required return for each level of risk to decline.*

Some Comments on the CAPM

The capital asset pricing model generally relies on historical data. The betas may or may not actually reflect the *future* variability of returns. Therefore, the required returns specified by the model can be viewed only as rough approximations. Users of betas commonly make subjective adjustments to the historically determined betas to reflect their expectations of the future.

The CAPM was developed to explain the behavior of security prices and provide a mechanism whereby investors could assess the impact of a proposed security investment on their portfolio's overall risk and return. It is based on an assumed efficient market with the following characteristics: many small investors, all having the same information and expectations with respect to securities; no restrictions on investment, no taxes, and no transaction costs; and rational investors, who view securities similarly and are risk averse, preferring higher returns and lower risk.

Although the perfect world described in the preceding paragraph appears to be unrealistic, studies have provided support for the existence of the expectational relationship described by the CAPM in active markets such as the New York Stock Exchange. The CAPM also sees widespread use in corporations that use the model to assess the required returns that their shareholders demand (and therefore the returns that the firm's managers need to achieve when they invest shareholders' money).

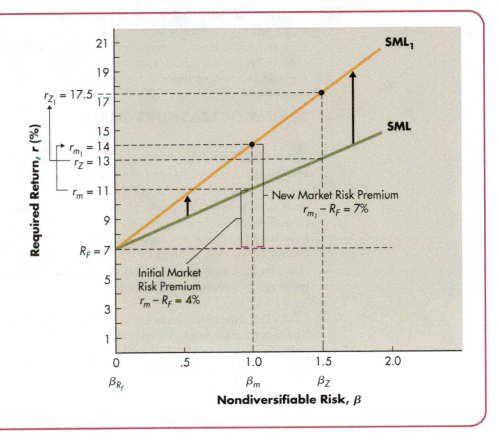

FIGURE 8.11

Risk Aversion Shifts SML
Impact of increased risk
aversion on the SML

→ **REVIEW QUESTIONS**

8–11 How are total risk, nondiversifiable risk, and diversifiable risk related?
Why is nondiversifiable risk the *only relevant risk?*

8–12 What risk does *beta* measure? How can you find the beta of a portfolio?

8–13 Explain the meaning of each variable in the *capital asset pricing model
(CAPM)* equation. What is the *security market line (SML)?*

8–14 What impact would the following changes have on the security market
line and therefore on the required return for a given level of risk? (**a**)
An *increase* in inflationary expectations. (**b**) Investors become *less* risk-
averse.

Summary

FOCUS ON VALUE

A firm's risk and expected return directly affect its share price. Risk and return are
the two key determinants of the firm's value. It is therefore the financial manager's
responsibility to assess carefully the risk and return of all major decisions to ensure that the expected returns justify the level of risk being introduced.

The financial manager can expect to achieve **the firm's goal of increasing its share price** (and thereby benefiting its owners) by taking only those actions that earn returns at least commensurate with their risk. Clearly, financial managers need to recognize, measure, and evaluate risk–return trade-offs to ensure that their decisions contribute to the creation of value for owners.

REVIEW OF LEARNING GOALS

LG 1 **Understand the meaning and fundamentals of risk, return, and risk preferences.** Risk is a measure of the uncertainty surrounding the return that an investment will produce. The total rate of return is the sum of cash distributions, such as interest or dividends, plus the change in the asset's value over a given period, divided by the investment's beginning-of-period value. Investment returns vary both over time and between different types of investments. Investors may be risk averse, risk neutral, or risk seeking. Most financial decision makers are risk averse. A risk-averse decision maker requires a higher expected return on a more risky investment alternative.

LG 2 **Describe procedures for assessing and measuring the risk of a single asset.** The risk of a single asset is measured in much the same way as the risk of a portfolio of assets. Scenario analysis and probability distributions can be used to assess risk. The range, the standard deviation, and the coefficient of variation can be used to measure risk quantitatively.

LG 3 **Discuss the measurement of return and standard deviation for a portfolio and the concept of correlation.** The return of a portfolio is calculated as the weighted average of returns on the individual assets from which it is formed. The portfolio standard deviation is found by using the formula for the standard deviation of a single asset.

Correlation—the statistical relationship between any two series of numbers—can be positively correlated, negatively correlated, or uncorrelated. At the extremes, the series can be perfectly positively correlated or perfectly negatively correlated.

LG 4 **Understand the risk and return characteristics of a portfolio in terms of correlation and diversification and the impact of international assets on a portfolio.** Diversification involves combining assets with low correlation to reduce the risk of the portfolio. The range of risk in a two-asset portfolio depends on the correlation between the two assets. If they are perfectly positively correlated, the portfolio's risk will be between the individual assets' risks. If they are perfectly negatively correlated, the portfolio's risk will be between the risk of the more risky asset and zero.

International diversification can further reduce a portfolio's risk. Foreign assets have the risk of currency fluctuation and political risks.

LG 5 **Review the two types of risk and the derivation and role of beta in measuring the relevant risk of both a security and a portfolio.** The total risk of a security consists of nondiversifiable and diversifiable risk. Diversifiable risk can be eliminated through diversification. Nondiversifiable risk is the only relevant risk.

Nondiversifiable risk is measured by the beta coefficient, which is a relative measure of the relationship between an asset's return and the market return. Beta is derived by finding the slope of the "characteristic line" that best explains the historical relationship between the asset's return and the market return. The beta of a portfolio is a weighted average of the betas of the individual assets that it includes.

LG 6 Explain the capital asset pricing model (CAPM), its relationship to the security market line (SML), and the major forces causing shifts in the SML. The CAPM uses beta to relate an asset's risk relative to the market to the asset's required return. The graphical depiction of the CAPM is SML, which shifts over time in response to changing inflationary expectations and/or changes in investor risk aversion. Changes in inflationary expectations result in parallel shifts in the SML. Increasing risk aversion results in a steepening in the slope of the SML. Decreasing risk aversion reduces the slope of the SML. Although it has some shortcomings, the CAPM provides a useful conceptual framework for evaluating and linking risk and return.

Self-Test Problems (Solutions in Appendix)

LG 3 **LG 4** **ST8–1** **Portfolio analysis** You have been asked for your advice in selecting a portfolio of assets and have been given the following data:

		Expected return	
Year	Asset A	Asset B	Asset C
2016	12%	16%	12%
2017	14	14	14
2018	16	12	16

You have been told that you can create two portfolios—one consisting of assets A and B and the other consisting of assets A and C—by investing equal proportions (50%) in each of the two component assets.
a. What is the expected return for each asset over the 3-year period?
b. What is the standard deviation for each asset's return?
c. What is the expected return for each of the two portfolios?
d. How would you characterize the correlations of returns of the two assets making up each of the two portfolios identified in part **c**?
e. What is the standard deviation for each portfolio?
f. Which portfolio do you recommend? Why?

LG 5 **LG 6** **ST8–2** **Beta and CAPM** Currently under consideration is an investment with a beta, β, of 1.50. At this time, the risk-free rate of return, R_F, is 7%, and the return on the market portfolio of assets, r_m, is 10%. You believe that this investment will earn an annual rate of return of 11%.
a. If the return on the market portfolio were to increase by 10%, what would you expect to happen to the investment's return? What if the market return were to decline by 10%?

b. Use the capital asset pricing model (CAPM) to find the *required return* on this investment.

c. On the basis of your calculation in part **b**, would you recommend this investment? Why or why not?

d. Assume that as a result of investors becoming less risk averse, the market return drops by 1% to 9%. What effect would this change have on your responses in parts **b** and **c**?

Warm-Up Exercises   All problems are available in MyFinanceLab.

LG 1 **E8–1** An analyst predicted last year that the stock of Logistics, Inc., would offer a total return of at least 10% in the coming year. At the beginning of the year, the firm had a stock market value of $10 million. At the end of the year, it had a market value of $12 million even though it experienced a loss, or negative net income, of $2.5 million. Did the analyst's prediction prove correct? Explain using the values for total annual return.

LG 2 **E8–2** Four analysts cover the stock of Fluorine Chemical. One forecasts a 5% return for the coming year. The second expects the return to be negative 5%. The third predicts a 10% return. The fourth expects a 3% return in the coming year. You are relatively confident that the return will be positive but not large, so you arbitrarily assign probabilities of being correct of 35%, 5%, 20%, and 40%, respectively, to the analysts' forecasts. Given these probabilities, what is Fluorine Chemical's *expected return* for the coming year?

LG 2 **E8–3** The expected annual returns are 15% for investment 1 and 12% for investment 2. The standard deviation of the first investment's return is 10%; the second investment's return has a standard deviation of 5%. Which investment is less risky based solely on *standard deviation?* Which investment is less risky based on *coefficient of variation?* Which is a better measure given that the expected returns of the two investments are not the same?

LG 3 **E8–4** Your portfolio has three asset classes. U.S. government T-bills account for 45% of the portfolio, large-company stocks constitute another 40%, and small-company stocks make up the remaining 15%. If the expected returns are 3.8% for the T-bills, 12.3% for the large-company stocks, and 17.4% for the small-company stocks, what is the expected return of the portfolio?

LG 5 **E8–5** You wish to calculate the risk level of your portfolio based on its beta. The five stocks in the portfolio with their respective weights and betas are shown in the accompanying table. Calculate the beta of your portfolio.

Stock	Portfolio weight	Beta
Alpha	20%	1.15
Centauri	10	0.85
Zen	15	1.60
Wren	20	1.35
Yukos	35	1.85

E8-6 **a.** Calculate the required rate of return for an asset that has a beta of 1.8, given a risk-free rate of 5% and a market return of 10%.

b. If investors have become more risk-averse due to recent geopolitical events and the market return rises to 13%, what is the required rate of return for the same asset?

c. Use your findings in part **a** to graph the initial *security market line (SML),* and then use your findings in part **b** to graph (on the same set of axes) the shift in the SML.

Problems All problems are available in MyFinanceLab.

LG 1 **P8-1** **Rate of return** Douglas Keel, a financial analyst for Orange Industries, wishes to estimate the rate of return for two similar-risk investments, X and Y. Douglas's research indicates that the immediate past returns will serve as reasonable estimates of future returns. A year earlier, investment X had a market value of $20,000, and investment Y had a market value of $55,000. During the year, investment X generated cash flow of $1,500, and investment Y generated cash flow of $6,800. The current market values of investments X and Y are $21,000 and $55,000, respectively.

a. Calculate the expected rate of return on investments X and Y using the most recent year's data.

b. Assuming that the two investments are equally risky, which one should Douglas recommend? Why?

LG 1 **P8-2** **Return calculations** For each of the investments shown in the following table, calculate the rate of return earned over the unspecified time period.

Investment	Cash flow during period	Beginning-of-period value	End-of-period value
A	−$ 800	$ 1,100	$ 100
B	15,000	120,000	118,000
C	7,000	45,000	48,000
D	80	600	500
E	1,500	12,500	12,400

LG 1 **P8-3** **Risk preferences** Sharon Smith, the financial manager for Barnett Corporation, wishes to evaluate three prospective investments: X, Y, and Z. Sharon will evaluate each of these investments to decide whether they are superior to investments that her company already has in place, which have an expected return of 12% and a standard deviation of 6%. The expected returns and standard deviations of the investments are as follows:

Investment	Expected return	Standard deviation
X	14%	7%
Y	12	8
Z	10	9

a. If Sharon were *risk neutral,* which investments would she select? Explain why.
b. If she were *risk averse,* which investments would she select? Why?
c. If she were *risk seeking,* which investments would she select? Why?
d. Given the traditional risk preference behavior exhibited by financial managers, which investment would be preferred? Why?

LG 2 **P8-4** **Risk analysis** Solar Designs is considering an investment in an expanded product line. Two possible types of expansion are being considered. After investigating the possible outcomes, the company made the estimates shown in the following table.

	Expansion A	Expansion B
Initial investment	$12,000	$12,000
Annual rate of return		
Pessimistic	16%	10%
Most likely	20%	20%
Optimistic	24%	30%

a. Determine the *range* of the rates of return for each of the two projects.
b. Which project is less risky? Why?
c. If you were making the investment decision, which one would you choose? Why? What does this decision imply about your feelings toward risk?
d. Assume that expansion B's most likely outcome is 21% per year and that all other facts remain the same. Does your answer to part **c** now change? Why?

LG 2 **P8-5** **Risk and probability** Micro-Pub, Inc., is considering the purchase of one of two microfilm cameras, R and S. Both should provide benefits over a 10-year period, and each requires an initial investment of $4,000. Management has constructed the accompanying table of estimates of rates of return and probabilities for pessimistic, most likely, and optimistic results.
a. Determine the *range* for the rate of return for each of the two cameras.
b. Determine the *expected value* of return for each camera.
c. Purchase of which camera is riskier? Why?

	Camera R		Camera S	
	Amount	Probability	Amount	Probability
Initial investment	$4,000	1.00	$4,000	1.00
Annual rate of return				
Pessimistic	20%	0.25	15%	0.20
Most likely	25%	0.50	25%	0.55
Optimistic	30%	0.25	35%	0.25

LG 2 **P8-6** **Bar charts and risk** Swan's Sportswear is considering bringing out a line of designer jeans. Currently, it is negotiating with two different well-known designers. Because of the highly competitive nature of the industry, the two lines of jeans have been

given code names. After market research, the firm has established the expectations shown in the following table about the annual rates of return.

Market acceptance	Probability	Annual rate of return Line J	Line K
Very poor	0.05	0.0075	0.010
Poor	0.15	0.0125	0.025
Average	0.60	0.0850	0.080
Good	0.15	0.1475	0.135
Excellent	0.05	0.1625	0.150

Use the table to:
a. Construct a bar chart for each line's annual rate of return.
b. Calculate the *expected value* of return for each line.
c. Evaluate the relative riskiness for each jean line's rate of return using the bar charts.

 P8–7 **Coefficient of variation** Metal Manufacturing has isolated four alternatives for meeting its need for increased production capacity. The following table summarizes data gathered relative to each of these alternatives.

Alternative	Expected return	Standard deviation of return
A	20%	7.0%
B	22	9.5
C	19	6.0
D	16	5.5

a. Calculate the *coefficient of variation* for each alternative.
b. If the firm wishes to minimize risk, which alternative do you recommend? Why?

 P8–8 **Standard deviation versus coefficient of variation as measures of risk** Greengage, Inc., a successful nursery, is considering several expansion projects. All the alternatives promise to produce an acceptable return. Data on four possible projects follow.

Project	Expected return	Range	Standard deviation
A	12.0%	4.0%	2.9%
B	12.5	5.0	3.2
C	13.0	6.0	3.5
D	12.8	4.5	3.0

a. Which project is least risky, judging on the basis of *range?*
b. Which project has the lowest *standard deviation?* Explain why standard deviation may not be an entirely appropriate measure of risk for purposes of this comparison.
c. Calculate the *coefficient of variation* for each project. Which project do you think Greengage's owners should choose? Explain why.

Personal Finance Problem

P8–9   **Rate of return, standard deviation, and coefficient of variation** Mike is searching for a stock to include in his current stock portfolio. He is interested in Hi-Tech, Inc.; he has been impressed with the company's computer products and believes that Hi-Tech is an innovative market player. However, Mike realizes that any time you consider a technology stock, risk is a major concern. The rule he follows is to include only securities with a coefficient of variation of returns below 0.90.

Mike has obtained the following price information for the period 2012 through 2015. Hi-Tech stock, being growth-oriented, did not pay any dividends during these 4 years.

	Stock price	
Year	Beginning	End
2012	$14.36	$21.55
2013	21.55	64.78
2014	64.78	72.38
2015	72.38	91.80

a. Calculate the *rate of return* for each year, 2012 through 2015, for Hi-Tech stock.
b. Assume that each year's return is equally probable, and calculate the *average return* over this time period.
c. Calculate the *standard deviation* of returns over the past 4 years. (*Hint:* Treat these data as a sample.)
d. Based on **b** and **c**, determine the *coefficient of variation* of returns for the security.
e. Given the calculation in **d**, what should be Mike's decision regarding the inclusion of Hi-Tech stock in his portfolio?

P8–10   **Assessing return and risk** Swift Manufacturing must choose between two asset purchases. The annual rate of return and the related probabilities given in the following table summarize the firm's analysis to this point.

Project 257		Project 432	
Rate of return	Probability	Rate of return	Probability
−10%	0.01	10%	0.05
10	0.04	15	0.10
20	0.05	20	0.10
30	0.10	25	0.15
40	0.15	30	0.20
45	0.30	35	0.15
50	0.15	40	0.10
60	0.10	45	0.10
70	0.05	50	0.05
80	0.04		
100	0.01		

a. For each project, compute:
(1) The range of possible rates of return.
(2) The expected return.

(3) The standard deviation of the returns.

(4) The coefficient of variation of the returns.

b. Construct a bar chart of each distribution of rates of return.

c. Which project would you consider less risky? Why?

LG 2   **P8–11**   **Integrative: Expected return, standard deviation, and coefficient of variation**   Three assets—F, G, and H—are currently being considered by Perth Industries. The probability distributions of expected returns for these assets are shown in the following table.

	Asset F		Asset G		Asset H	
j	Pr_j	Return, r_j	Pr_j	Return, r_j	Pr_j	Return, r_j
1	0.10	40%	0.40	35%	0.10	40%
2	0.20	10	0.30	10	0.20	20
3	0.40	0	0.30	−20	0.40	10
4	0.20	−5			0.20	0
5	0.10	−10			0.10	−20

a. Calculate the expected value of return, $\bar{r}$, for each of the three assets. Which provides the largest expected return?

b. Calculate the standard deviation, σ_r, for each of the three assets' returns. Which appears to have the greatest risk?

c. Calculate the coefficient of variation, CV, for each of the three assets' returns. Which appears to have the greatest *relative* risk?

LG 2   **P8–12**   **Normal probability distribution**   Assuming that the rates of return associated with a given asset investment are normally distributed; that the expected return, $\bar{r}$, is 18.9%; and that the coefficient of variation, CV, is 0.75; answer the following questions.

a. Find the standard deviation of returns, σ_r.

b. Calculate the range of expected return outcomes associated with the following probabilities of occurrence: (1) 68%, (2) 95%, (3) 99%.

c. Draw the probability distribution associated with your findings in parts **a** and **b**.

Personal Finance Problem

LG 3   **P8–13**   **Portfolio return and standard deviation**   Jamie Wong is considering building an investment portfolio containing two stocks, L and M. Stock L will represent 40% of the dollar value of the portfolio, and stock M will account for the other 60%. The expected returns over the next 6 years, 2015–2020, for each of these stocks are shown in the following table.

	Expected return	
Year	Stock L	Stock M
2015	14%	20%
2016	14	18
2017	16	16
2018	17	14
2019	17	12
2020	19	10

a. Calculate the expected portfolio return, r_p, for *each* of the 6 years.
b. Calculate the expected value of portfolio returns, $\bar{r}_p$, over the 6-year period.
c. Calculate the standard deviation of expected portfolio returns, σ_{r_p}, over the 6-year period.
d. How would you characterize the correlation of returns of the two stocks L and M?
e. Discuss any benefits of diversification achieved by Jamie through creation of the portfolio.

LG 3   **P8–14**   **Portfolio analysis** You have been given the expected return data shown in the first table on three assets—F, G, and H—over the period 2016–2019.

		Expected return	
Year	Asset F	Asset G	Asset H
2016	16%	17%	14%
2017	17	16	15
2018	18	15	16
2019	19	14	17

Using these assets, you have isolated the three investment alternatives shown in the following table.

Alternative	Investment
1	100% of asset F
2	50% of asset F and 50% of asset G
3	50% of asset F and 50% of asset H

a. Calculate the expected return over the 4-year period for each of the three alternatives.
b. Calculate the standard deviation of returns over the 4-year period for each of the three alternatives.
c. Use your findings in parts **a** and **b** to calculate the coefficient of variation for each of the three alternatives.
d. On the basis of your findings, which of the three investment alternatives do you recommend? Why?

LG 4   **P8–15**   **Correlation, risk, and return** Matt Peters wishes to evaluate the risk and return behaviors associated with various combinations of assets V and W under three assumed degrees of correlation: perfectly positive, uncorrelated, and perfectly negative. The expected returns and standard deviations calculated for each of the assets are shown in the following table.

Asset	Expected return, $\bar{r}$	Risk (standard deviation), σ_r
V	8%	5%
W	13	10

a. If the returns of assets V and W are *perfectly positively correlated* (correlation coefficient = +1), describe the *range* of (1) expected return and (2) risk associated with all possible portfolio combinations.
b. If the returns of assets V and W are *uncorrelated* (correlation coefficient = 0), describe the *approximate range* of (1) expected return and (2) risk associated with all possible portfolio combinations.
c. If the returns of assets V and W are *perfectly negatively correlated* (correlation coefficient = −1), describe the *range* of (1) expected return and (2) risk associated with all possible portfolio combinations.

Personal Finance Problem

  P8–16 **International investment returns** Joe Martinez, a U.S. citizen living in Brownsville, Texas, invested in the common stock of Telmex, a Mexican corporation. He purchased 1,000 shares at 20.50 pesos per share. Twelve months later, he sold them at 24.75 pesos per share. He received no dividends during that time.
a. What was Joe's investment return (in percentage terms) for the year, on the basis of the peso value of the shares?
b. The exchange rate for pesos was 9.21 pesos per US$1.00 at the time of the purchase. At the time of the sale, the exchange rate was 9.85 pesos per US$1.00. Translate the purchase and sale prices into US$.
c. Calculate Joe's investment return on the basis of the US$ value of the shares.
d. Explain why the two returns are different. Which one is more important to Joe? Why?

P8–17 **Total, nondiversifiable, and diversifiable risk** David Talbot randomly selected securities from all those listed on the New York Stock Exchange for his portfolio. He began with a single security and added securities one by one until a total of 20 securities were held in the portfolio. After each security was added, David calculated the portfolio standard deviation, σ_{r_p}. The calculated values are shown in the following table.

Number of securities	Portfolio risk, σ_{r_p}	Number of securities	Portfolio risk, σ_{r_p}
1	14.50%	11	7.00%
2	13.30	12	6.80
3	12.20	13	6.70
4	11.20	14	6.65
5	10.30	15	6.60
6	9.50	16	6.56
7	8.80	17	6.52
8	8.20	18	6.50
9	7.70	19	6.48
10	7.30	20	6.47

a. Plot the data from the table above on a graph that has the number of securities on the *x*-axis and the portfolio standard deviation on the *y*-axis.
b. Divide the total portfolio risk in the graph into its *nondiversifiable* and *diversifiable* risk components, and label each of these on the graph.
c. Describe which of the two risk components is the *relevant risk,* and explain why it is relevant. How much of this risk exists in David Talbot's portfolio?

P8–18 **Graphical derivation of beta** A firm wishes to estimate graphically the betas for two assets, A and B. It has gathered the return data shown in the following table for the market portfolio and for both assets over the last 10 years, 2006–2015.

| | Actual return | | |
Year	Market portfolio	Asset A	Asset B
2006	6%	11%	16%
2007	2	8	11
2008	−13	−4	−10
2009	−4	3	3
2010	−8	0	−3
2011	16	19	30
2012	10	14	22
2013	15	18	29
2014	8	12	19
2015	13	17	26

a. On a set of "market return (x axis)–asset return (y axis)" axes, use the data given to draw the characteristic line for asset A and for asset B.

b. Use the characteristic lines from part **a** to estimate the betas for assets A and B.

c. Use the betas found in part **b** to comment on the relative risks of assets A and B.

 P8–19 **Graphical derivation and interpreting beta** You are analyzing the performance of two stocks. The first, shown in Panel A, is Cyclical Industries Incorporated. Cyclical Industries makes machine tools and other heavy equipment, the demand for which

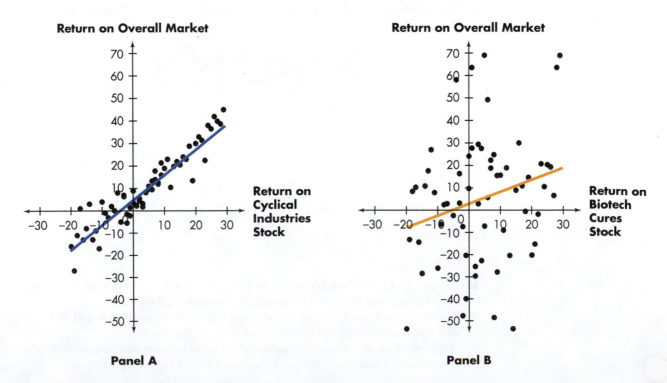

Panel A   **Panel B**

rises and falls closely with the overall state of the economy. The second stock, shown in Panel B, is Biotech Cures Corporation. Biotech Cures uses biotechnology to develop new pharmaceutical compounds to treat incurable diseases. Biotech's fortunes are driven largely by the success or failure of its scientists to discover new and effective drugs. Each data point on the graph shows the monthly return on the stock of interest and the monthly return on the overall stock market. The lines drawn through the data points represent the characteristic lines for each security.

a. Which stock do you think has a higher standard deviation? Why?

b. Which stock do you think has a higher beta? Why?

c. Which stock do you think is riskier? What does the answer to this question depend on?

 P8–20 **Interpreting beta** A firm wishes to assess the impact of changes in the market return on an asset that has a beta of 1.20.

a. If the market return increased by 15%, what impact would this change be expected to have on the asset's return?

b. If the market return decreased by 8%, what impact would this change be expected to have on the asset's return?

c. If the market return did not change, what impact, if any, would be expected on the asset's return?

d. Would this asset be considered more or less risky than the market? Explain.

 P8–21 **Betas** Answer the questions below for assets A to D shown in the table.

Asset	Beta
A	0.50
B	1.60
C	−0.20
D	0.90

a. What impact would a *10% increase* in the market return be expected to have on each asset's return?

b. What impact would a *10% decrease* in the market return be expected to have on each asset's return?

c. If you believed that the market return would *increase* in the near future, which asset would you prefer? Why?

d. If you believed that the market return would *decrease* in the near future, which asset would you prefer? Why?

Personal Finance Problem

 P8–22 **Betas and risk rankings** You are considering three stocks—A, B, and C—for possible inclusion in your investment portfolio. Stock A has a beta of 0.80, stock B has a beta of 1.40, and stock C has a beta of −0.30.

a. Rank these stocks from the most risky to the least risky.

b. If the return on the market portfolio increased by 12%, what change would you expect in the return for each of the stocks?

c. If the return on the market portfolio decreased by 5%, what change would you expect in the return for each of the stocks?

d. If you believed that the stock market was getting ready to experience a significant decline, which stock would you probably add to your portfolio? Why?

e. If you anticipated a major stock market rally, which stock would you add to your portfolio? Why?

Personal Finance Problem

LG 5   **P8–23**   **Portfolio betas**   Rose Berry is attempting to evaluate two possible portfolios, which consist of the same five assets held in different proportions. She is particularly interested in using beta to compare the risks of the portfolios, so she has gathered the data shown in the following table.

		Portfolio weights	
Asset	Asset beta	Portfolio A	Portfolio B
1	1.30	10%	30%
2	0.70	30	10
3	1.25	10	20
4	1.10	10	20
5	0.90	40	20
Totals		100%	100%

a. Calculate the betas for portfolios A and B.

b. Compare the risks of these portfolios to the market as well as to each other. Which portfolio is more risky?

LG 6   **P8–24**   **Capital asset pricing model (CAPM)**   For each of the cases shown in the following table, use the capital asset pricing model to find the required return.

Case	Risk-free rate, R_F	Market return, r_m	Beta, β
A	5%	8%	1.30
B	8	13	0.90
C	9	12	−0.20
D	10	15	1.00
E	6	10	0.60

Personal Finance Problem

   P8–25   **Beta coefficients and the capital asset pricing model**   Katherine Wilson is wondering how much risk she must undertake to generate an acceptable return on her portfolio. The risk-free return currently is 5%. The return on the overall stock market is 16%. Use the CAPM to calculate how high the beta coefficient of Katherine's portfolio would have to be to achieve each of the following expected portfolio returns.

a. 10%

b. 15%

c. 18%

d. 20%

e. Katherine is risk averse. What is the highest return she can expect if she is unwilling to take more than an average risk?

P8–26 **Manipulating CAPM** Use the basic equation for the capital asset pricing model (CAPM) to work each of the following problems.

a. Find the *required return* for an asset with a beta of 0.90 when the risk-free rate and market return are 8% and 12%, respectively.

b. Find the *risk-free rate* for a firm with a required return of 15% and a beta of 1.25 when the market return is 14%.

c. Find the *market return* for an asset with a required return of 16% and a beta of 1.10 when the risk-free rate is 9%.

d. Find the *beta* for an asset with a required return of 15% when the risk-free rate and market return are 10% and 12.5%, respectively.

Personal Finance Problem

  P8–27 **Portfolio return and beta** Jamie Peters invested $100,000 to set up the following portfolio 1 year ago.

Asset	Cost	Beta at purchase	Yearly income	Value today
A	$20,000	0.80	$1,600	$20,000
B	35,000	0.95	1,400	36,000
C	30,000	1.50	—	34,500
D	15,000	1.25	375	16,500

a. Calculate the portfolio beta on the basis of the original cost figures.

b. Calculate the percentage return of each asset in the portfolio for the year.

c. Calculate the percentage return of the portfolio on the basis of original cost, using income and gains during the year.

d. At the time Jamie made his investments, investors were estimating that the market return for the coming year would be 10%. The estimate of the risk-free rate of return averaged 4% for the coming year. Calculate an expected rate of return for each stock on the basis of its beta and the expectations of market and risk-free returns.

e. On the basis of the actual results, explain how each stock in the portfolio performed relative to those CAPM-generated expectations of performance. What factors could explain these differences?

 P8–28 **Security market line (SML)** Assume that the risk-free rate, R_F, is currently 9% and that the market return, r_m, is currently 13%.

a. Draw the security market line (SML) on a set of "nondiversifiable risk (*x* axis)– required return (*y* axis)" axes.

b. Calculate and label the *market risk premium* on the axes in part **a**.

c. Given the previous data, calculate the required return on asset A having a beta of 0.80 and asset B having a beta of 1.30.

d. Draw in the betas and required returns from part **c** for assets A and B on the axes in part **a**. Label the *risk premium* associated with each of these assets, and discuss them.

 P8–29 **Shifts in the security market line** Assume that the risk-free rate, R_F, is currently 8%; the market return, r_m, is 12%; and asset A has a beta, β_A, of 1.10.

a. Draw the security market line (SML) on a set of "nondiversifiable risk (*x* axis)– required return (*y* axis)" axes.

b. Use the CAPM to calculate the required return, r_A, on asset A, and depict asset A's beta and required return on the SML drawn in part **a.**

c. Assume that as a result of recent economic events, inflationary expectations have declined by 2%, lowering R_F and r_m to 6% and 10%, respectively. Draw the new SML on the axes in part **a,** and calculate and show the new required return for asset A.

d. Assume that as a result of recent events, investors have become more risk averse, causing the market return to rise by 1%, to 13%. Ignoring the shift in part **c,** draw the new SML on the same set of axes that you used before, and calculate and show the new required return for asset A.

e. From the previous changes, what conclusions can be drawn about the impact of (1) decreased inflationary expectations and (2) increased risk aversion on the required returns of risky assets?

LG 6 **P8–30** **Integrative: Risk, return, and CAPM** Wolff Enterprises must consider several investment projects, A through E, using the capital asset pricing model (CAPM) and its graphical representation, the security market line (SML). Relevant information is presented in the following table.

Item	Rate of return	Beta, β
Risk-free asset	9%	0.00
Market portfolio	14	1.00
Project A	—	1.50
Project B	—	0.75
Project C	—	2.00
Project D	—	0.00
Project E	—	−0.50

a. Calculate (1) the required rate of return and (2) the risk premium for each project, given its level of nondiversifiable risk.

b. Use your findings in part **a** to draw the security market line (required return relative to nondiversifiable risk).

c. Discuss the relative nondiversifiable risk of projects A through E.

d. Assume that recent economic events have caused investors to become less risk-averse, causing the market return to decline by 2%, to 12%. Calculate the new required returns for assets A through E, and draw the new security market line on the same set of axes that you used in part **b.**

e. Compare your findings in parts **a** and **b** with those in part **d.** What conclusion can you draw about the impact of a decline in investor risk aversion on the required returns of risky assets?

LG 1 **P8–31** **ETHICS PROBLEM** Risk is a major concern of almost all investors. When shareholders invest their money in a firm, they expect managers to take risks with those funds. What do you think are the ethical limits that managers should observe when taking risks with other people's money?

Spreadsheet Exercise

Jane is considering investing in three different stocks or creating three distinct two-stock portfolios. Jane considers herself to be a rather conservative investor. She is able to obtain forecasted returns for the three securities for the years 2015 through 2021. The data are given in the following table.

Year	Stock A	Stock B	Stock C
2015	10%	10%	12%
2016	13	11	14
2017	15	8	10
2018	14	12	11
2019	16	10	9
2020	14	15	9
2021	12	15	10

In any of the possible two-stock portfolios, the weight of each stock in the portfolio will be 50%. The three possible portfolio combinations are AB, AC, and BC.

TO DO

Create a spreadsheet similar to Tables 8.6 and 8.7 to answer the following:

a. Calculate the expected return for each individual stock.
b. Calculate the standard deviation for each individual stock.
c. Calculate the expected returns for portfolios AB, AC, and BC.
d. Calculate the standard deviations for portfolios AB, AC, and BC.
e. Would you recommend that Jane invest in the single stock A or the portfolio consisting of stocks A and B? Explain your answer from a risk–return viewpoint.
f. Would you recommend that Jane invest in the single stock B or the portfolio consisting of stocks B and C? Explain your answer from a risk–return viewpoint.

MyFinanceLab Visit www.myfinancelab.com for **Chapter Case: *Analyzing Risk and Return on Chargers Products' Investments,*** Group Exercises, and numerous online resources.

9 The Cost of Capital

Learning Goals

LG 1 Understand the basic concept and sources of capital associated with the cost of capital.

LG 2 Explain what is meant by the marginal cost of capital.

LG 3 Determine the cost of long-term debt, and explain why the after-tax cost of debt is the relevant cost of debt.

LG 4 Determine the cost of preferred stock.

LG 5 Calculate the cost of common stock equity, and convert it into the cost of retained earnings and the cost of new issues of common stock.

LG 6 Calculate the weighted average cost of capital (WACC), and discuss alternative weighting schemes.

Why This Chapter Matters to You

In your *professional* life

ACCOUNTING You need to understand the various sources of capital and how their costs are calculated to provide the data necessary to determine the firm's overall cost of capital.

INFORMATION SYSTEMS You need to understand the various sources of capital and how their costs are calculated to develop systems that will estimate the costs of those sources of capital as well as the overall cost of capital.

MANAGEMENT You need to understand the cost of capital to select long-term investments after assessing their acceptability and relative rankings.

MARKETING You need to understand the firm's cost of capital because proposed projects must earn returns in excess of it to be acceptable.

OPERATIONS You need to understand the firm's cost of capital to assess the economic viability of investments in plant and equipment needed to improve or grow the firm's capacity.

In your *personal* life

Knowing your *personal cost of capital* will allow you to make informed decisions about your personal consuming, borrowing, and investing. Managing your personal wealth is a lot like managing the wealth of a business in that you need to understand the trade-offs between consuming wealth and growing wealth and how growing wealth can be accomplished by investing your own monies or borrowed monies. Understanding the cost of capital concepts will allow you to make better long-term decisions and maximize the value of your personal wealth.

9.1 Overview of the Cost of Capital

MyFinanceLab Video

cost of capital
Represents the firm's cost of financing and is the minimum rate of return that a project must earn to increase firm value.

Chapter 1 established that the goal of the firm is to maximize shareholder wealth. To do so, managers must make investments that are worth more than they cost. In this chapter, you will learn about the cost of capital, which is the rate of return that financial managers use to evaluate all possible investment opportunities to determine which ones add value to the firm. The **cost of capital** represents the firm's cost of financing and is the minimum rate of return that a project must earn to increase firm value. In particular, the cost of capital refers to the cost of the next dollar of financing necessary to finance a new investment opportunity. Investments with a rate of return above the cost of capital will increase the value of the firm, because these investments are worth more than they cost. In contrast, projects with a rate of return below the cost of capital will decrease firm value.

The cost of capital is an extremely important financial concept. It acts as a major link between the firm's long-term investment decisions and the wealth of the firm's owners as determined by the market value of their shares. Financial managers are ethically bound to invest only in projects that they expect to exceed the cost of capital.

THE BASIC CONCEPT

A firm's cost of capital reflects the *expected average future cost of funds over the long run,* and it reflects the entirety of the firm's financing activities. For example, a firm may raise the money it needs to build a new manufacturing facility by borrowing money (debt), by selling common stock (equity), or by doing both. Managers must take into account respective costs of both forms of capital when they estimate a firm's cost of capital. In fact, most firms do finance their activities with a blend of equity and debt. In Chapter 12, we will explore the factors that determine what mix of debt and equity is optimal for any particular firm. For now, we will simply say that most firms have a desired mix of financing, and the cost of capital must reflect the cost of each type of financing that a firm uses. To capture all the relevant financing costs, assuming some desired mix of financing, we need to look at the *overall cost of capital* rather than just the cost of any single source of financing.

Example 9.1 ▸

MyFinanceLab Solution Video

A firm is currently considering two investment opportunities. Two financial analysts, working independently of each other, are evaluating these opportunities. Assume the following information about investments A and B.

Investment A

$$\text{Cost} = \$100{,}000$$
$$\text{Life} = 20 \text{ years}$$
$$\text{Expected Return} = 7\%$$

The analyst studying this investment recalls that the company recently issued bonds paying a 6% rate of return. He reasons that because the investment project earns 7% while the firm can issue debt at 6%, the project must be worth doing, so he recommends that the company undertake this investment.

Investment B

$$\text{Cost} = \$100,000$$
$$\text{Life} = 20 \text{ years}$$
$$\text{Expected Return} = 12\%$$

Least costly financing source available

$$\text{Equity} = 14\%$$

The analyst assigned to this project knows that the firm has common stock outstanding and that investors who hold the company's stock expect a 14% return on their investment. The analyst decides that the firm should not undertake this investment because it only produces a 12% return while the company's shareholders expect a 14% return.

In this example, each analyst is making a mistake by focusing on one source of financing rather than on the overall financing mix. What if instead the analysts used a *combined* cost of financing? By weighting the cost of each source of financing by its relative *proportion* in the firm's target capital structure, the firm can obtain a *weighted average cost of capital*. Assuming that this firm desires a 50–50 mix of debt and equity, the weighted average cost here would be 10%[(0.50 × 6% debt) + (0.50 × 14% equity)]. With this average cost of financing, the firm should reject the first opportunity (7% expected return < 10% weighted average cost) and accept the second (12% expected return > 10% weighted average cost).

SOURCES OF LONG-TERM CAPITAL

In this chapter, our concern is only with the *long-term* sources of capital available to a firm because they are the sources that supply the financing necessary to support the firm's *capital budgeting* activities. Capital budgeting is the process of evaluating and selecting long-term investments. This process is intended to achieve the firm's goal of maximizing shareholders' wealth. Although the entire capital budgeting process is discussed throughout Part 5, at this point it is sufficient to say that capital budgeting activities are chief among the responsibilities of financial managers and that they cannot be carried out without knowing the appropriate cost of capital with which to judge the firm's investment opportunities.

There are four basic sources of long-term capital for firms: long-term debt, preferred stock, common stock, and retained earnings. All entries on the right-hand side of the balance sheet, other than current liabilities, represent these sources:

Balance Sheet	
	Current liabilities
	Long-term debt
Assets	Stockholders' equity
	Preferred stock
	Common stock equity
	Common stock
	Retained earnings

Sources of long-term capital

Not every firm will use all of these sources of financing. In particular, preferred stock is relatively uncommon. Even so, most firms will have some mix of funds from these sources in their capital structures. Although a firm's existing mix of financing sources may reflect its target capital structure, it is ultimately the marginal cost of capital necessary to raise the next marginal dollar of financing that is relevant for evaluating the firm's future investment opportunities.

→ REVIEW QUESTIONS

9–1 What is the *cost of capital*?

9–2 What role does the cost of capital play in the firm's long-term investment decisions? How does it relate to the firm's ability to maximize shareholder wealth?

9–3 What does the firm's capital structure represent?

9–4 What are the typical sources of long-term capital available to the firm?

9.2 Cost of Long-Term Debt

cost of long-term debt
The financing cost associated with new funds raised through long-term borrowing.

The **cost of long-term debt** is the financing cost associated with new funds raised through long-term borrowing. Typically, the funds are raised through the sale of corporate bonds.

NET PROCEEDS

net proceeds
Funds actually received by the firm from the sale of a security.

flotation costs
The total costs of issuing and selling a security.

The **net proceeds** from the sale of a bond, or any security, are the funds that the firm receives from the sale. The total proceeds are reduced by the **flotation costs**, which represent the total costs of issuing and selling securities. These costs apply to all public offerings of securities: debt, preferred stock, and common stock. They include two components: (1) *underwriting costs*, or compensation earned by investment bankers for selling the security; and (2) *administrative costs*, or issuer expenses such as legal and accounting costs.

Example 9.2 ▶

Duchess Corporation, a major hardware manufacturer, is contemplating selling $10 million worth of 20-year, 9% coupon (stated *annual* interest rate) bonds, each with a par value of $1,000. Because bonds with similar risk earn returns greater than 9%, the firm must sell the bonds for $980 to compensate for the lower coupon interest rate. The flotation costs are 2% of the par value of the bond ($0.02 \times \$1,000$), or $20. The *net proceeds* to the firm from the sale of each bond are therefore $960 ($980 minus $20).

BEFORE-TAX COST OF DEBT

The before-tax cost of debt, r_d, is simply the rate of return the firm must pay on new borrowing. A firm's before-tax cost of debt for bonds can be found in any of three ways: quotation, calculation, or approximation.

Using Market Quotations

A relatively quick method for finding the before-tax cost of debt is to observe the *yield to maturity (YTM)* on the firm's existing bonds or bonds of similar risk issued by other companies. The YTM of existing bonds reflects the rate of return required by the market. For example, if the market requires a YTM of 9.7 percent for a similar-risk bond, this value can be used as the before-tax cost of debt, r_d, for new bonds. Bond yields are widely reported by sources such as the *Wall Street Journal*.

Calculating the Cost

This approach finds the before-tax cost of debt by calculating the YTM generated by the bond's cash flows, given the net proceeds that the firm receives when it issues the bonds. From the issuer's point of view, this value is the *cost to maturity* of the cash flows associated with the debt. The YTM can be calculated by using a financial calculator or an electronic spreadsheet. It represents the annual before-tax percentage cost of the debt.

Example 9.3 ▶   In the preceding example, $960 were the net proceeds of a 20-year bond with a $1,000 par value and 9% coupon interest rate. The calculation of the annual cost is quite simple. The cash flow pattern associated with this bond's sales consists of an initial inflow (the net proceeds) followed by a series of annual outlays (the interest payments). In the final year, when the debt is retired, an outlay representing the repayment of the principal also occurs. The cash flows associated with Duchess Corporation's bond issue are as follows:

End of year(s)	Cash flow
0	$ 960
1–20	−$ 90
20	−$1,000

The initial $960 inflow is followed by annual interest outflows of $90 (9% coupon interest rate × $1,000 par value) over the 20-year life of the bond. In year 20, an outflow of $1,000 (the repayment of the principal) occurs. We can determine the cost of debt by finding the YTM, which is the discount rate that equates the present value of the bond outflows to the initial inflow.

MyFinanceLab Financial Calculator

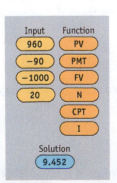

Calculator use (*Note:* Most calculators require either the present value [net proceeds] or the future value [annual interest payments and repayment of principal] to be input as negative numbers when we calculate yield to maturity. That approach is used here.) Using the calculator and the inputs shown at the left, you should find the before-tax cost of debt (yield to maturity) to be 9.452%.

Spreadsheet use The before-tax cost of debt on the Duchess Corporation bond can be calculated using an Excel spreadsheet. The following Excel spreadsheet shows that by referencing the cells containing the bond's net proceeds, coupon payment, years to maturity, and par value as part of Excel's RATE function, you can quickly determine that the appropriate before-tax cost of debt for Duchess Corporation's bond is 9.452%.

	A	B
1	FINDING THE BEFORE-TAX COST OF DEBT	
2	Par value	−$1,000
3	Coupon interest rate	9.0%
4	Interest payments per year	1
5	Interest payment	−$90.00
6	Number of years to maturity	20
7	Net proceeds from sale of bond	$960.00
8	Before-tax cost of debt	9.452%

Entry in Cell B8 =RATE(B6*B4,B5,B7,B2,0).
The minus sign appears before the $1,000.00 in B2 and the $90
in B5 because these values are cash outflows for the corporation.

Although you may not recognize it, both the calculator and the Excel function are using trial-and-error to find the bond's YTM, they just do it faster than you can.

Approximating the Cost

Although not as precise as using a calculator, there is a method for quickly approximating the before-tax cost of debt. The before-tax cost of debt, r_d, for a bond with a $1,000 par value can be approximated by

$$r_d = \frac{I + \dfrac{\$1,000 - N_d}{n}}{\dfrac{N_d + \$1,000}{2}} \tag{9.1}$$

where

$$
\begin{aligned}
I &= \text{annual interest in dollars} \\
N_d &= \text{net proceeds from the sale of debt (bond)} \\
n &= \text{number of years to the bond's maturity}
\end{aligned}
$$

Example 9.4 ▶ Substituting the appropriate values from the Duchess Corporation example into the approximation formula given in Equation 9.1, we get

$$r_d = \frac{\$90 + \dfrac{\$1,000 - \$960}{20}}{\dfrac{\$960 + \$1,000}{2}} = \frac{\$90 + \$2}{\$980}$$

$$= \frac{\$92}{\$980} = 0.09388 \text{ or } \underline{9.388\%}$$

This approximate value of before-tax cost of debt is close to the 9.452%, but it lacks the precision of the value derived using the calculator or spreadsheet.

AFTER-TAX COST OF DEBT

Unlike the dividends paid to equityholders, the interest payments paid to bond-holders are tax deductible for the firm, so the interest expense on debt reduces the firm's taxable income and, therefore, the firm's tax liability. To find the firm's *net* cost of debt, we must account for the tax savings created by debt and solve for the cost of long-term debt on an after-tax basis. The after-tax cost of debt, r_i, can be found by multiplying the before-tax cost, r_d, by 1 minus the tax rate, T:

$$r_i = r_d \times (1 - T) \tag{9.2}$$

Example 9.5 ▶

MyFinanceLab Solution
Video

Duchess Corporation has a 40% tax rate. Using the 9.452% before-tax debt cost calculated above and applying Equation 9.2, we find an after-tax cost of debt of 5.67% [9.452% × (1 − 0.40)]. Typically, the cost of long-term debt for a given firm is less than the cost of preferred or common stock, partly because of the tax deductibility of interest.

Personal Finance Example 9.6 ▶

MyFinanceLab Solution
Video

Kait and Kasim Sullivan, a married couple in the 28% federal income-tax bracket, wish to borrow $60,000 to pay for a new luxury car. To finance the purchase, they can either borrow the $60,000 through the auto dealer at an annual interest rate of 6.0%, or they can take a $60,000 second mortgage on their home. The best annual rate they can get on the second mortgage is 7.2%. They already have qualified for both of the loans being considered.

If they borrow from the auto dealer, the interest on this "consumer loan' will not be deductible for federal tax purposes. However, the interest on the second mortgage would be tax deductible because the tax law allows individuals to deduct interest paid on a home mortgage. To choose the least-cost financing, the Sullivans calculated the after-tax cost of both sources of long-term debt. Because interest on the auto loan is *not* tax deductible, its after-tax cost equals its stated cost of 6.0%. Because the interest on the second mortgage *is* tax deductible, its after-tax cost can be found using Equation 9.2:

After-tax cost of debt = Before-tax cost of debt × (1 − Tax rate)
7.2% × (1 − 0.28) = 7.2% × 0.72 = <u>5.2%</u>

Because the 5.2% after-tax cost of the second mortgage is less than the 6.0% cost of the auto loan, the Sullivans may decide to use the second mortgage to finance the auto purchase.

→ REVIEW QUESTIONS

9-5 What are the *net proceeds* from the sale of a bond? What are *flotation costs,* and how do they affect a bond's net proceeds?

9-6 What methods can be used to find the before-tax cost of debt?

9-7 How is the before-tax cost of debt converted into the after-tax cost?

→ EXCEL REVIEW QUESTION   MyFinanceLab

9-8 The interest expense on debt provides a tax deduction for the issuer so any calculation of a firm's net cost of debt should reflect this benefit

Based on the information provided at MFL, compute a firm's after-tax cost of debt using a spreadsheet model.

LG 4   ## 9.3 Cost of Preferred Stock

Preferred stock represents a special type of ownership interest in the firm. It gives preferred stockholders the right to receive their *stated* dividends before the firm can distribute any earnings to common stockholders. The key characteristics of preferred stock were described in Chapter 7. However, the one aspect of preferred stock that requires review is dividends.

PREFERRED STOCK DIVIDENDS

When dividends are stated as "preferred stock dividends," the stock is often referred to as "*x*-dollar preferred stock." Thus, a "$4 preferred stock" is expected to pay preferred stockholders $4 in dividends each year on each share of preferred stock owned.

Sometimes preferred stock dividends are stated as an *annual percentage rate*. This rate represents the percentage of the stock's par, or face, value that equals the annual dividend. For instance, an 8 percent preferred stock with a $50 par value would be expected to pay an annual dividend of $4 per share (0.08 × $50 par = $4). Before the cost of preferred stock is calculated, any dividends stated as percentages should be converted to annual dollar dividends.

CALCULATING THE COST OF PREFERRED STOCK

cost of preferred stock, r_p
The ratio of the preferred stock dividend to the firm's net proceeds from the sale of preferred stock.

The **cost of preferred stock, r_p**, is the ratio of the preferred stock dividend to the firm's net proceeds from the sale of the preferred stock. The net proceeds represent the amount of money to be received minus any flotation costs. The following equation gives the cost of preferred stock, r_p, in terms of the annual dollar dividend, D_p, and the net proceeds from the sale of the stock, N_p:

$$r_p = \frac{D_p}{N_p} \tag{9.3}$$

Example 9.7 ▶   Duchess Corporation is contemplating issuance of a 10% preferred stock that they expect to sell for $87 per share. The cost of issuing and selling the stock will be $5 per share. The first step in finding the cost of the stock is to calculate the dollar amount of the annual preferred dividend, which is $8.70 (0.10 × $87). The net proceeds per share from the proposed sale of stock equals the sale price minus the flotation costs ($87 − $5 = $82). Substituting the annual dividend, D_p, of $8.70 and the net proceeds, N_p, of $82 into Equation 9.3 gives the cost of preferred stock, 10.6% ($8.70 ÷ $82).

The cost of Duchess's preferred stock (10.6%) is much greater than the cost of its long-term debt (5.67%). This difference exists both because the cost of long-term debt (the interest) is tax deductible and because preferred stock is riskier than long-term debt.

→ **REVIEW QUESTION**

9-9 How would you calculate the cost of preferred stock?

LG 5   ## 9.4 Cost of Common Stock

The *cost of common stock* is the return required on the stock by investors in the marketplace. There are two forms of common stock financing: (1) retained earnings and (2) new issues of common stock. As a first step in finding each of these costs, we must estimate the cost of common stock equity.

FINDING THE COST OF COMMON STOCK EQUITY

cost of common stock equity, r_s
The rate at which investors discount the expected dividends of the firm to determine its share value.

The **cost of common stock equity**, r_s, is the rate at which investors discount the expected common stock dividends of the firm to determine its share value. Two techniques are used to measure the cost of common stock equity. One relies on the constant-growth valuation model, the other on the capital asset pricing model (CAPM).

Using the Constant-Growth Valuation (Gordon Growth) Model

constant-growth valuation (Gordon growth) model
Assumes that the value of a share of stock equals the present value of all future dividends (assumed to grow at a constant rate) that it is expected to provide over an infinite time horizon.

In Chapter 7, we found the value of a share of stock to be equal to the present value of all future dividends, which in one model are assumed to grow at a constant annual rate over an infinite time horizon. This model, the **constant-growth valuation model**, is also known as the **Gordon growth model**. The key expression derived for this model, first presented as Equation 7.4, is

$$P_0 = \frac{D_1}{r_s - g} \qquad (9.4)$$

where

P_0 = value of common stock
D_1 = per-share dividend *expected* at the end of year 1
r_s = required return on common stock
g = constant rate of growth in dividends

Solving Equation 9.4 for r_s results in the following expression for the *cost of common stock equity:*

$$r_s = \frac{D_1}{P_0} + g \qquad (9.5)$$

Equation 9.5 indicates that the cost of common stock equity can be found by dividing the dividend expected at the end of year 1 by the current market price of the stock (the "dividend yield") and adding the expected growth rate (the "capital gains yield").

Example 9.8 ▶   Duchess Corporation wishes to determine its cost of common stock equity, r_s. The market price, P_0, of its common stock is $50 per share. The firm expects to pay a dividend, D_1, of $4 at the end of the coming year, 2016. The dividends paid on the outstanding stock over the past 6 years (2010 through 2015) were as follows:

Year	Dividend
2015	$3.80
2014	3.62
2013	3.47
2012	3.33
2011	3.12
2010	2.97

Using a financial calculator or electronic spreadsheet, in conjunction with the technique described for finding growth rates in Chapter 5, we can calculate the annual rate at which dividends have grown, g, from 2010 to 2015. It turns out to be approximately 5% (more precisely, it is 5.05%). Substituting $D_1 = \$4$, $P_0 = \$50$, and $g = 5\%$ into Equation 9.5 yields the cost of common stock equity:

$$r_s = \frac{\$4}{\$50} + 0.05 = 0.08 + 0.05 = 0.130 \quad \text{or} \quad \underline{13.0\%}$$

The 13.0% cost of common stock equity represents the return required by *existing* shareholders on their investment. If the actual return is less than that, shareholders are likely to begin selling their stock.

Using the Capital Asset Pricing Model (CAPM)

capital asset pricing model (CAPM)
Describes the relationship between the required return, r_s, and the nondiversifiable risk of the firm as measured by the beta coefficient, β.

Recall from Chapter 8 that the **capital asset pricing model (CAPM)** describes the relationship between the required return, r_s, and the nondiversifiable risk of the firm as measured by the beta coefficient, β. The basic CAPM is

$$r_s = R_F + [\beta \times (r_m - R_F)] \tag{9.6}$$

where

R_F = risk-free rate of return
r_m = market return; return on the market portfolio of assets

Using the CAPM indicates that the cost of common stock equity is the return required by investors as compensation for the firm's nondiversifiable risk, measured by beta.

Example 9.9 ▶ Duchess Corporation now wishes to calculate its cost of common stock equity, r_s, by using the CAPM. The firm's investment advisors and its own analysts indicate that the risk-free rate, R_F, equals 7%; the firm's beta, β, equals 1.5; and the market return, r_m, equals 11%. Substituting these values into Equation 9.6, the company estimates the cost of common stock equity, r_s, to be

$$r_s = 7.0\% + [1.5 \times (11.0\% - 7.0\%)] = 7.0\% + 6.0\% = \underline{13.0\%}$$

The 13.0% cost of common stock equity represents the required return of investors in Duchess Corporation common stock. It is the same as that found by using the constant-growth valuation model.

Comparing Constant-Growth and CAPM Techniques

The CAPM technique differs from the constant-growth valuation model in that it directly considers the firm's risk, as reflected by beta, in determining the *required* return or cost of common stock equity. The constant-growth model does not look at risk; it uses the market price, P_0, as a reflection of the *expected* risk–return preference of investors in the marketplace. The constant-growth valuation and CAPM techniques for finding r_s are theoretically equivalent, although in practice estimates from the two methods do not always agree. The two methods can produce different estimates because they require (as inputs) estimates of other quantities, such as the expected dividend growth rate or the firm's beta.

Another difference is that when the constant-growth valuation model is used to find the cost of common stock equity, it can easily be adjusted for flotation costs to find the cost of new common stock; the CAPM does not provide a simple adjustment mechanism. The difficulty in adjusting the cost of common stock equity calculated by using the CAPM occurs because in its common form the model does not include the market price, P_0, a variable needed to make such an adjustment. Although the CAPM has a stronger theoretical foundation, the computational appeal of the traditional constant-growth valuation model justifies its use throughout this text to measure financing costs of common stock. As a practical matter, analysts might want to estimate the cost of equity using both approaches and then take an average of the results to arrive at a final estimate of the cost of equity.

COST OF RETAINED EARNINGS

As you know, dividends are paid out of a firm's earnings. Their payment, made in cash to common stockholders, reduces the firm's retained earnings. Suppose that a firm needs common stock equity financing of a certain amount. It has two choices relative to retained earnings: It can issue additional common stock in that amount and still pay dividends to stockholders out of retained earnings, or it can increase common stock equity by retaining the earnings (not paying the cash dividends) in the needed amount. In a strict accounting sense, the retention of earnings increases common stock equity in the same way that the sale of additional shares of common stock does. Thus, the **cost of retained earnings, r_r,** to the firm is the same as the cost of an *equivalent fully subscribed issue of additional common stock*. Stockholders find the firm's retention of earnings acceptable only if they expect that it will earn at least their required return on the reinvested funds.

cost of retained earnings, r_r
The same as the cost of an *equivalent fully subscribed issue of additional common stock,* which is equal to the cost of common stock equity, r_s.

Viewing retained earnings as a fully subscribed issue of additional common stock, we can set the firm's cost of retained earnings, r_r, equal to the cost of common stock equity as given by Equations 9.5 and 9.6.

$$r_r = r_s \qquad\qquad (9.7)$$

Thus, it is not necessary to adjust the cost of retained earnings for flotation costs because by retaining earnings the firm "raises" equity capital without incurring these costs.

Example 9.10 ▶   The cost of retained earnings for Duchess Corporation was actually calculated in the preceding examples: It is equal to the cost of common stock equity. Thus, r_r equals 13.0%. As we will show in the next section, the cost of retained earnings is always lower than the cost of a new issue of common stock because it entails no flotation costs

COST OF NEW ISSUES OF COMMON STOCK

cost of a new issue of common stock, r_n
The cost of common stock, net of underpricing and associated flotation costs.

underpriced
Stock sold at a price below its current market price, P_0.

Our purpose in finding the firm's overall cost of capital is to determine the after-tax cost of *new* funds required for financing projects. The **cost of a new issue of common stock, r_n,** is determined by calculating the cost of common stock, net of underpricing and associated flotation costs. Normally, when new shares are issued, they are **underpriced,** meaning that they are sold at a discount relative to the current market price, P_0. Underpricing is the difference between the market price and the issue price, which is the price paid by the primary market investors discussed in Chapter 2.

We can use the constant-growth valuation model expression for the cost of existing common stock, r_s, as a starting point. If we let N_n represent the net proceeds from the sale of new common stock after subtracting underpricing and flotation costs, the cost of the new issue, r_n, can be expressed as[2]

$$r_n = \frac{D_1}{N_n} + g \tag{9.8}$$

The net proceeds from sale of new common stock, N_n, will be less than the current market price, P_0. Therefore, the cost of new issues, r_n, will always be greater than the cost of existing issues, r_s, which is equal to the cost of retained earnings, r_r. *The cost of new common stock is normally greater than any other long-term financing cost.*

Example 9.11 ▶ In the constant-growth valuation example, we found Duchess Corporation's cost of common stock equity, r_s, to be 13%, using the following values: an expected dividend, D_1, of \$4; a current market price, P_0, of \$50; and an expected growth rate of dividends, g, of 5%.

To determine its cost of *new* common stock, r_n, Duchess Corporation has estimated that on average, new shares can be sold for \$47. The \$3-per-share underpricing is due to the competitive nature of the market. A second cost associated with a new issue is flotation costs of \$2.50 per share that would be paid to issue and sell the new shares. The total underpricing and flotation costs per share are therefore \$5.50.

Subtracting the \$5.50-per-share underpricing and flotation cost from the current \$50 share price results in expected net proceeds of \$44.50 per share (\$50.00 minus

---

1. *Business in China Survey 2013*, China Europe International Business School.
2. An alternative, but computationally less straightforward, form of this equation is

$$r_n = \frac{D_1}{P_0 \times (1 - f)} + g \tag{9.8a}$$

where f represents the *percentage* reduction in current market price expected as a result of underpricing and flotation costs. Simply stated, N_n in Equation 9.8 is equivalent to $P_0 \times (1 - f)$ in Equation 9.8a. For convenience, Equation 9.8 is used to define the cost of a new issue of common stock, r_n.

$5.50). Substituting $D_1 = \$4$, $N_n = \$44.50$, and $g = 5\%$ into Equation 9.8 results in a cost of new common stock, r_n:

$$r_n = \frac{\$4.00}{\$44.50} + 0.05 = 0.09 + 0.05 = 0.140 \text{ or } \underline{14.0\%}$$

Duchess Corporation's cost of new common stock is therefore 14.0%. That is the value to be used in subsequent calculations of the firm's overall cost of capital.

→ REVIEW QUESTIONS

9–10 What premise about share value underlies the constant-growth valuation (Gordon growth) model that is used to measure the cost of common stock equity, r_s?

9–11 How do the constant-growth valuation model and capital asset pricing model methods for finding the cost of common stock differ?

9–12 Why is the cost of financing a project with retained earnings less than the cost of financing it with a new issue of common stock?

LG 6   9.5 Weighted Average Cost of Capital

weighted average cost of capital (WACC), r_a
Reflects the expected average future cost of capital over the long run; found by weighting the cost of each specific type of capital by its proportion in the firm's capital structure.

As noted earlier, the **weighted average cost of capital** (WACC), r_a, reflects the expected average future cost of capital over the long run. It is found by weighting the cost of each specific type of capital by its proportion in the firm's capital structure.

CALCULATING WEIGHTED AVERAGE COST OF CAPITAL (WACC)

Calculating the weighted average cost of capital (WACC) is straightforward: Multiply the individual cost of each form of financing by its proportion in the firm's capital structure and sum the weighted values. As an equation, the weighted average cost of capital, r_a, can be specified as

$$r_a = (w_i \times r_i) + (w_p \times r_p) + (w_s \times r_{r \text{ or } n}) \qquad (9.9)$$

where

w_i = proportion of long-term debt in capital structure
w_p = proportion of preferred stock in capital structure
w_s = proportion of common stock equity in capital structure
$w_i + w_p + w_s = 1.0$

Three important points should be noted in Equation 9.9:

1. For computational convenience, it is best to convert the weights into decimal form and leave the individual costs in percentage terms.
2. *The weights must be nonnegative and sum to 1.0.* Simply stated, WACC must account for all financing costs within the firm's capital structure.
3. The firm's common stock equity weight, w_s, is multiplied by either the cost of retained earnings, r_r, or the cost of new common stock, r_n. Which cost is used depends on whether the firm's common stock equity will be financed using retained earnings, r_r, or new common stock, r_n.

Example 9.12 ▶ In earlier examples, we found the costs of the various types of capital for Duchess Corporation to be as follows:

$$\text{Cost of debt, } r_i = 5.6\%$$
$$\text{Cost of preferred stock, } r_p = 10.6\%$$
$$\text{Cost of retained earnings, } r_r = 13.0\%$$
$$\text{Cost of new common stock, } r_n = 14.0\%$$

The company uses the following weights in calculating its weighted average cost of capital:

Source of capital	Weight
Long-term debt	40%
Preferred stock	10
Common stock equity	50
Total	100%

Because the firm expects to have a sizable amount of retained earnings available ($300,000), it plans to use its cost of retained earnings, r_r, as the cost of common stock equity. Duchess Corporation's weighted average cost of capital is calculated in Table 9.1. The resulting weighted average cost of capital for Duchess is 9.8%. Assuming an unchanged risk level, the firm should accept all projects that will earn a return greater than 9.8%.

WEIGHTING SCHEMES

Firms can calculate weights on the basis of either *book value* or *market value* using either *historical* or *target* proportions.

Book Value versus Market Value

book value weights
Weights that use accounting values to measure the proportion of each type of capital in the firm's financial structure.

market value weights
Weights that use market values to measure the proportion of each type of capital in the firm's financial structure.

Book value weights use accounting values to measure the proportion of each type of capital in the firm's financial structure. **Market value weights** measure the proportion of each type of capital at its market value. Market value weights are appealing because the market values of securities closely approximate the actual dollars to be received from their sale. Moreover, because firms calculate the costs of the various types of capital by using prevailing market prices, it seems reasonable to use market value weights. In addition, the long-term investment cash flows to which the cost of

TABLE 9.1 Calculation of the Weighted Average Cost of Capital for Duchess Corporation

Source of capital	Weight (1)	Cost (2)	Weighted cost [(1) × (2)] (3)
Long-term debt	0.40	5.6%	2.2%
Preferred stock	0.10	10.6	1.1
Common stock equity	0.50	13.0	6.5
Totals	1.00		WACC = 9.8%

focus on PRACTICE

Uncertain Times Make for an Uncertain Weighted Average Cost of Capital

in practice As U.S. financial markets experienced and recovered from the 2008 financial crisis and 2009 "great recession," firms struggled to keep track of their weighted average cost of capital. The individual component costs were moving rapidly in response to the financial market turmoil. Volatile financial markets can make otherwise manageable cost-of-capital calculations exceedingly complex and inherently error prone, possibly wreaking havoc with investment decisions. If a firm underestimates its cost of capital, it risks making investments that are not economically justified, and if a firm overestimates its financing costs, it risks foregoing value-maximizing investments.

Although the WACC computation does not change when markets become unstable, the uncertainty surrounding the components that comprise the WACC increases dramatically. The financial crisis pushed credit costs to a point where

long-term debt was largely inaccessible, and the great recession saw Treasury bond yields fall to historic lows, making cost of equity projections appear unreasonably low. With these key components in flux, it is exceedingly difficult, if not impossible, for firms to get a handle on a cost of long-term capital.

According to *CFO Magazine,* at least one firm resorted to a two-pronged approach for determining its cost of capital during the uncertain times. Ron Domanico is the chief financial officer (CFO) at Caraustar Industries, Inc., and he reported that his company dealt with the cost-of-capital uncertainty by abandoning the conventional one-size-fits-all approach. "In the past, we had one cost of capital that we applied to all our investment decisions … today that's not the case. We have a short-term cost of capital we apply to short-term opportunities, and a longer-term cost of capital we apply to longer-term opportunities … and

the reality is that the longer-term cost is so high that it has forced us to focus only on those projects that have immediate returns," Mr. Domanico is quoted saying.[a]

Part of Caraustar's motivation for implementing this two-pronged approach was to account for the excessively large spread between short- and long-term debt rates that emerged during the financial market crisis. Mr. Domanico reported that during the crisis Caraustar could borrow short-term funds at the lower of Prime plus 4 percent or LIBOR plus 5 percent, where either rate was reasonable for making short-term investment decisions. Alternatively, long-term investment decisions were being required to clear Caraustar's long-term cost-of-capital calculation accounting for borrowing rates in excess of 12 percent.

▶ *Why don't firms generally use both short- and long-run weighted average costs of capital?*

[a]Randy Myers, "A Losing Formula" (May 2009), www.cfo.com/article.cfm/13522582/c_13526469.

capital is applied are estimated in terms of current as well as future market values. *Market value weights are clearly preferred over book value weights.*

Historical versus Target Weights

historical weights
Either book or market value weights based on *actual* capital structure proportions.

Historical weights can be either book or market value weights based on *actual* capital structure proportions. For example, past or current book value proportions would constitute a form of historical weighting, as would past or current market value proportions. Such a weighting scheme would therefore be based on real—rather than desired—proportions.

target weights
Either book or market value weights based on *desired* capital structure proportions.

Target weights, which can also be based on either book or market values, reflect the firm's *desired* capital structure proportions. Firms using target weights establish such proportions on the basis of the "optimal" capital structure they wish to achieve. (The development of these proportions and the optimal structure are discussed in detail in Chapter 12.)

When one considers the somewhat approximate nature of the calculation of weighted average cost of capital, the choice of weights may not be critical. However, from a strictly theoretical point of view, the *preferred weighting scheme is target market value proportions,* and we assume this scheme throughout this chapter.

| Personal Finance Example 9.13 ▶ | Chuck Solis currently has three loans outstanding, all of which mature in exactly 6 years and can be repaid without penalty |

Chuck Solis currently has three loans outstanding, all of which mature in exactly 6 years and can be repaid without penalty any time prior to maturity. The outstanding balances and annual interest rates on these loans are as follows:

Loan	Outstanding balance	Annual interest rate
1	$26,000	9.6%
2	9,000	10.6
3	45,000	7.4

After a thorough search, Chuck found a lender who would loan him $80,000 for 6 years at an annual interest rate of 9.2% on the condition that the loan proceeds be used to fully repay the three outstanding loans, which combined have an outstanding balance of $80,000 ($26,000 + $9,000 + $45,000).

Chuck wishes to choose the least costly alternative: (1) to do nothing or (2) to borrow the $80,000 and pay off all three loans. He calculates the weighted average cost of his current debt by weighting each debt's annual interest cost by the proportion of the $80,000 total it represents and then summing the three weighted values as follows:

$$
\begin{aligned}
\text{Weighted average} \\
\text{cost of current debt} &= [(\$26,000 \div \$80,000) \times 9.6\%] + [(\$9,000 \div \$80,000) \\
&\quad \times 10.6\%] + [(\$45,000 \div \$80,000) \times 7.4\%] \\
&= (.3250 \times 9.6\%) + (.1125 \times 10.6\%) + (.5625 \times 7.4\%) \\
&= 3.12\% + 1.19\% + 4.16\% = 8.47\% \approx \underline{8.5\%}
\end{aligned}
$$

Given that the weighted average cost of the $80,000 of current debt of 8.5% is below the 9.2% cost of the new $80,000 loan, Chuck should do nothing and just continue to pay off the three loans as originally scheduled.

→ **REVIEW QUESTIONS**

9-13 What is the *weighted average cost of capital (WACC)*, and how is it calculated?

9-14 What is the relationship between the firm's target capital structure and the *weighted average cost of capital (WACC)?*

9-15 Describe the logic underlying the use of *target weights* to calculate the WACC, and compare and contrast this approach with the use of *historical weights*. What is the preferred weighting scheme?

Summary

FOCUS ON VALUE

The cost of capital is an extremely important rate of return, particularly in capital budgeting decisions. It is the expected average future cost to the firm of funds over the long run. Because the cost of capital is the pivotal rate of return used in the investment decision process, its accuracy can significantly affect the quality of these decisions.

Underestimation of the cost of capital can make poor projects look attractive; overestimation can make good projects look unattractive. By applying the techniques presented in this chapter to estimate the firm's cost of capital, the financial manager will improve the likelihood that the firm's long-term decisions will be consistent with the firm's overall goal of **maximizing stock price (owner wealth)**.

REVIEW OF LEARNING GOALS

LG 1 **Understand the basic concept and sources of capital associated with the cost of capital.** The cost of capital is the minimum rate of return that a firm must earn on its investments to grow firm value. A weighted average cost of capital should be used to find the expected average future cost of funds over the long run. The individual costs of the basic sources of capital (long-term debt, preferred stock, retained earnings, and common stock) can be calculated separately.

LG 2 **Explain what is meant by the marginal cost of capital.** The relevant cost of capital for a firm is the marginal cost of capital necessary to raise the next marginal dollar of financing to fund the firm's future investment opportunities. A firm's future investment opportunities in expectation will be required to exceed the firm's cost of capital.

LG 3 **Determine the cost of long-term debt, and explain why the after-tax cost of debt is the relevant cost of debt.** The before-tax cost of long-term debt can be found by using cost quotations, calculations (either by calculator or spreadsheet), or an approximation. The after-tax cost of debt is calculated by multiplying the before-tax cost of debt by 1 minus the tax rate. The after-tax cost of debt is the relevant cost of debt because it is the lowest possible cost of debt for the firm due to the deductibility of interest expenses.

LG 4 **Determine the cost of preferred stock.** The cost of preferred stock is the ratio of the preferred stock dividend to the firm's net proceeds from the sale of preferred stock.

LG 5 **Calculate the cost of common stock equity, and convert it into the cost of retained earnings and the cost of new issues of common stock.** The cost of common stock equity can be calculated by using the constant-growth valuation (Gordon growth) model or the CAPM. The cost of retained earnings is equal to the cost of common stock equity. An adjustment in the cost of common stock equity to reflect underpricing and flotation costs is necessary to find the cost of new issues of common stock.

LG 6 **Calculate the weighted average cost of capital (WACC), and discuss alternative weighting schemes.** The firm's WACC reflects the expected average future cost of funds over the long run. It combines the costs of specific types of capital after weighting each of them by its proportion. The theoretically preferred approach uses target weights based on market values.

Self-Test Problem (Solutions in Appendix)

ST9–1 **Individual costs and WACC** Humble Manufacturing is interested in measuring its overall cost of capital. The firm is in the 40% tax bracket. Current investigation has gathered the following data:

Debt The firm can raise debt by selling $1,000-par-value, 10% coupon interest rate, 10-year bonds on which *annual interest* payments will be made. To sell the issue, an average discount of $30 per bond must be given. The firm must also pay flotation costs of $20 per bond.

Preferred stock The firm can sell 11% (annual dividend) preferred stock at its $100-per-share par value. The cost of issuing and selling the preferred stock is expected to be $4 per share.

Common stock The firm's common stock is currently selling for $80 per share. The firm expects to pay cash dividends of $6 per share next year. The firm's dividends have been growing at an annual rate of 6%, and this rate is expected to continue in the future. The stock will have to be underpriced by $4 per share, and flotation costs are expected to amount to $4 per share.

Retained earnings The firm expects to have $225,000 of retained earnings available in the coming year. Once these retained earnings are exhausted, the firm will use new common stock as the form of common stock equity financing.

a. Calculate the individual cost of each source of financing. (Round to the nearest 0.1%.)
b. Calculate the firm's weighted average cost of capital using the weights shown in the following table, which are based on the firm's target capital structure proportions. (Round to the nearest 0.1%.)

Source of capital	Weight
Long-term debt	40%
Preferred stock	15
Common stock equity	45
Total	100%

c. In which, if any, of the investments shown in the following table do you recommend that the firm invest? Explain your answer. How much new financing is required?

Investment opportunity	Expected rate of return	Initial investment
A	11.2%	$100,000
B	9.7	500,000
C	12.9	150,000
D	16.5	200,000
E	11.8	450,000
F	10.1	600,000
G	10.5	300,000

Warm-Up Exercises   All problems are available in MyFinanceLab.

LG3   **E9–1**   A firm raises capital by selling $20,000 worth of debt with flotation costs equal to 2% of its par value. If the debt matures in 10 years and has a coupon interest rate of 8%, what is the bond's YTM?

LG4   **E9–2**   Your firm, People's Consulting Group, has been asked to consult on a potential preferred stock offering by Brave New World. This 15% preferred stock issue would be sold at its par value of $35 per share. Flotation costs would total $3 per share. Calculate the cost of this preferred stock.

LG5   **E9–3**   Duke Energy has been paying dividends steadily for 20 years. During that time, dividends have grown at a compound annual rate of 7%. If Duke Energy's current stock price is $78 and the firm plans to pay a dividend of $6.50 next year, what is Duke's *cost of common stock equity?*

LG6   **E9–4**   Weekend Warriors, Inc., has 35% debt and 65% equity in its capital structure. The firm's estimated after-tax cost of debt is 8% and its estimated cost of equity is 13%. Determine the firm's *weighted average cost of capital (WACC).*

LG6   **E9–5**   Oxy Corporation uses debt, preferred stock, and common stock to raise capital. The firm's capital structure targets the following proportions: debt, 55%; preferred stock, 10%; and common stock, 35%. If the cost of debt is 6.7%, preferred stock costs 9.2%, and common stock costs 10.6%, what is Oxy's *weighted average cost of capital (WACC)?*

Problems   All problems are available in MyFinanceLab.

LG1   **P9–1**   **Concept of cost of capital** Mace Manufacturing is in the process of analyzing its investment decision-making procedures. Two projects evaluated by the firm recently involved building new facilities in different regions, North and South. The basic variables surrounding each project analysis and the resulting decision actions are summarized in the following table.

Basic variables	North	South
Cost	$6 million	$5 million
Life	15 years	15 years
Expected return	8%	15%
Least-cost financing		
Source	Debt	Equity
Cost (after-tax)	7%	16%
Decision		
Action	Invest	Don't invest
Reason	8% > 7% cost	15% < 16% cost

a. An analyst evaluating the North facility expects that the project will be financed by debt that costs the firm 7%. What recommendation do you think this analyst will make regarding the investment opportunity?
b. Another analyst assigned to study the South facility believes that funding for that project will come from the firm's retained earnings at a cost of 16%. What recommendation do you expect this analyst to make regarding the investment?
c. Explain why the decisions in parts **a** and **b** may not be in the best interests of the firm's investors.
d. If the firm maintains a capital structure containing 40% debt and 60% equity, find its *weighted average cost* using the data in the table.
e. If both analysts had used the weighted average cost calculated in part **d**, what recommendations would they have made regarding the North and South facilities?
f. Compare and contrast the analyst's initial recommendations with your findings in part **e**. Which decision method seems more appropriate? Explain why.

LG 3 **P9–2** **Cost of debt using both methods** Currently, Warren Industries can sell 15-year, $1,000-par-value bonds paying *annual interest* at a 12% coupon rate. As a result of current interest rates, the bonds can be sold for $1,010 each; flotation costs of $30 per bond will be incurred in this process. The firm is in the 40% tax bracket.
a. Find the net proceeds from sale of the bond, N_d.
b. Show the cash flows from the firm's point of view over the maturity of the bond.
c. Calculate the before-tax and after-tax costs of debt.
d. Use the *approximation formula* to estimate the before-tax and after-tax costs of debt.
e. Compare and contrast the costs of debt calculated in parts **c** and **d**. Which approach do you prefer? Why?

Personal Finance Problem

LG 3 **P9–3** **Before-tax cost of debt and after-tax cost of debt** David Abbot is interested in purchasing a bond issued by Sony. He has obtained the following information on the security.

Sony bond			
Par value	$1,000	Coupon interest rate 6%	Corporate tax rate 20%
Cost	$ 930	Years to maturity 10	

a. Calculate the *before-tax cost* of the Sony bond.
b. Calculate the *after-tax cost* of the Sony bond given the corporate tax rate.

LG 3 **P9–4** **Cost of debt using the approximation formula** For each of the following $1,000-par-value bonds, assuming *annual interest* payment and a 40% tax rate, calculate the *after-tax* cost to maturity using the *approximation formula*.

Bond	Life (years)	Underwriting fee	Discount (−) or premium (+)	Coupon interest rate
A	20	$25	−$20	9%
B	16	40	+10	10
C	15	30	−15	12
D	25	15	Par	9
E	22	20	−60	11

P9–5 **The cost of debt** Gronseth Drywall Systems, Inc., is in discussions with its investment bankers regarding the issuance of new bonds. The investment banker has informed the firm that different maturities will carry different coupon rates and sell at different prices. The firm must choose among several alternatives. In each case, the bonds will have a $1,000 par value and flotation costs will be $30 per bond. The company is taxed at a rate of 40%. Calculate the *after-tax cost of financing* with each of the following alternatives.

Alternative	Coupon rate	Time to maturity (years)	Premium or discount
A	9%	16	$250
B	7	5	50
C	6	7	par
D	5	10	− 75

Personal Finance Problem

P9–6 **After-tax cost of debt** Bella Wans is interested in buying a new motorcycle. She has decided to borrow money to pay the $25,000 purchase price of the bike. She is in the 25% federal income tax bracket. She can either borrow the money at an interest rate of 5% from the motorcycle dealer, or she could take out a second mortgage on her home. That mortgage would come with an interest rate of 6%. Interest payments on the mortgage would be tax deductible for Bella, but interest payments on the loan from the motorcycle dealer could not be deducted on Bella's federal tax return.

a. Calculate the *after-tax cost* of borrowing from the motorcycle dealership.
b. Calculate the *after-tax cost* of borrowing through a second mortgage on Bella's home.
c. Which source of borrowing is less costly for Bella?
d. Is there any other consideration that Bella ought to think about when deciding which loan to take out to pay for the motorcycle?

P9–7 **Cost of preferred stock** Taylor Systems has just issued preferred stock. The stock has a 12% annual dividend and a $100 par value and was sold at $97.50 per share. In addition, flotation costs of $2.50 per share must be paid.

a. Calculate the *cost of the preferred stock.*
b. If the firm sells the preferred stock with a 10% annual dividend and nets $90.00 after flotation costs, what is its cost?

P9–8 **Cost of preferred stock** Determine the cost for each of the following preferred stocks.

Preferred stock	Par value	Sale price	Flotation cost	Annual dividend
A	$100	$101	$9.00	11%
B	40	38	$3.50	8%
C	35	37	$4.00	$5.00
D	30	26	5% of par	$3.00
E	20	20	$2.50	9%

P9–9 **Cost of common stock equity: CAPM** J&M Corporation common stock has a beta, β, of 1.2. The risk-free rate is 6%, and the market return is 11%.
a. Determine the risk premium on J&M common stock.
b. Determine the required return that J&M common stock should provide.
c. Determine J&M's *cost of common stock equity* using the CAPM.

P9–10 **Cost of common stock equity** Ross Textiles wishes to measure its cost of common stock equity. The firm's stock is currently selling for $57.50. The firm expects to pay a $3.40 dividend at the end of the year (2016). The dividends for the past 5 years are shown in the following table.

Year	Dividend
2015	$3.10
2014	2.92
2013	2.60
2012	2.30
2011	2.12

After underpricing and flotation costs, the firm expects to net $52 per share on a new issue.
a. Determine the growth rate of dividends from 2011 to 2015.
b. Determine the net proceeds, N_n, that the firm will actually receive.
c. Using the constant-growth valuation model, determine the *cost of retained earnings, r_r.*
d. Using the constant-growth valuation model, determine the *cost of new common stock, r_n.*

P9–11 **Retained earnings versus new common stock** Using the data for each firm shown in the following table, calculate the *cost of retained earnings* and the *cost of new common stock* using the constant-growth valuation model.

Firm	Current market price per share	Dividend growth rate	Projected dividend per share next year	Underpricing per share	Flotation cost per share
A	$50.00	8%	$2.25	$2.00	$1.00
B	20.00	4	1.00	0.50	1.50
C	42.50	6	2.00	1.00	2.00
D	19.00	2	2.10	1.30	1.70

   P9–12 **The effect of tax rate on WACC** K. Bell Jewelers wishes to explore the effect on its cost of capital of the rate at which the company pays taxes. The firm wishes to maintain a capital structure of 40% debt, 10% preferred stock, and 50% common stock. The cost of financing with retained earnings is 10%, the cost of preferred stock financing is 8%, and the before-tax cost of debt financing is 6%. Calculate the weighted average cost of capital (WACC) given the tax rate assumptions in parts a to c.
a. Tax rate = 40%
b. Tax rate = 35%
c. Tax rate = 25%
d. Describe the relationship between changes in the rate of taxation and the weighted average cost of capital.

LG 6   **P9–13**   **WACC: Book weights** Ridge Tool has on its books the amounts and specific (after-tax) costs shown in the following table for each source of capital.

Source of capital	Book value	Individual cost
Long-term debt	$700,000	5.3%
Preferred stock	50,000	12.0
Common stock equity	650,000	16.0

a. Calculate the firm's *weighted average cost of capital using book value weights*.
b. Explain how the firm can use this cost in the investment decision-making process.

LG 6   **P9–14**   **WACC: Book weights and market weights** Webster Company has compiled the information shown in the following table.

Source of capital	Book value	Market value	After-tax cost
Long-term debt	$4,000,000	$3,840,000	6.0%
Preferred stock	40,000	60,000	13.0
Common stock equity	1,060,000	3,000,000	17.0
Totals	$5,100,000	$6,900,000	

a. Calculate the weighted average cost of capital using *book value weights*.
b. Calculate the weighted average cost of capital using *market value weights*.
c. Compare the answers obtained in parts **a** and **b**. Explain the differences.

LG 6   **P9–15**   **WACC and target weights** After careful analysis, Dexter Brothers has determined that its optimal capital structure is composed of the sources and target market value weights shown in the following table.

Source of capital	Target market value weight
Long-term debt	30%
Preferred stock	15
Common stock equity	55
Total	100%

The cost of debt is estimated to be 7.2%, the cost of preferred stock is estimated to be 13.5%, the cost of retained earnings is estimated to be 16.0%, and the cost of new common stock is estimated to be 18.0%. All are after-tax rates. The company's debt represents 25%, the preferred stock represents 10%, and the common stock equity represents 65% of total capital on the basis of the market values of the three components. The company expects to have a significant amount of retained earnings available and does not expect to sell any new common stock.

a. Calculate the weighted average cost of capital on the basis of *historical market value weights*.
b. Calculate the weighted average cost of capital on the basis of *target market value weights*.
c. Compare the answers obtained in parts **a** and **b**. Explain the differences.

LG 3 LG 4   **P9–16**   **Cost of capital**   Edna Recording Studios, Inc., reported earnings available to com-
LG 5 LG 6   mon stock of $4,200,000 last year. From those earnings, the company paid a divi-
dend of $1.26 on each of its 1,000,000 common shares outstanding. The capital
structure of the company includes 40% debt, 10% preferred stock, and 50% common stock. It is taxed at a rate of 40%.

a. If the market price of the common stock is $40 and dividends are expected to
grow at a rate of 6% per year for the foreseeable future, what is the company's
cost of retained earnings financing?
b. If underpricing and flotation costs on new shares of common stock amount to
$7.00 per share, what is the company's *cost of new common stock* financing?
c. The company can issue $2.00 dividend preferred stock for a market price of
$25.00 per share. Flotation costs would amount to $3.00 per share. What is the
cost of preferred stock financing?
d. The company can issue $1,000-par-value, 10% coupon, 5-year bonds that can be
sold for $1,200 each. Flotation costs would amount to $25.00 per bond. Use the
estimation formula to figure the approximate *cost of debt* financing.
e. What is the *WACC?*

LG 3 LG 4   **P9–17**   **Calculation of individual costs and WACC**   Dillon Labs has asked its financial man-
LG 5 LG 6   ager to measure the cost of each specific type of capital as well as the weighted average
cost of capital. The weighted average cost is to be measured by using the following
weights: 40% long-term debt, 10% preferred stock, and 50% common stock equity
(retained earnings, new common stock, or both). The firm's tax rate is 40%.

Debt   The firm can sell for $980 a 10-year, $1,000-par-value bond paying *annual
interest* at a 10% coupon rate. A flotation cost of 3% of the par value is required
in addition to the discount of $20 per bond.

Preferred stock   Eight percent (annual dividend) preferred stock having a par
value of $100 can be sold for $65. An additional fee of $2 per share must be paid
to the underwriters.

Common stock   The firm's common stock is currently selling for $50 per share.
The dividend expected to be paid at the end of the coming year (2016) is $4. Its
dividend payments, which have been approximately 60% of earnings per share in
each of the past 5 years, were as shown in the following table.

Year	Dividend
2015	$3.75
2014	3.50
2013	3.30
2012	3.15
2011	2.85

It is expected that to attract buyers, new common stock must be underpriced $5 per share, and the firm must also pay $3 per share in flotation costs. Dividend payments are expected to continue at 60% of earnings. (Assume that $r_r = r_s$.)

a. Calculate the after-tax cost of debt.
b. Calculate the cost of preferred stock.
c. Calculate the cost of common stock.
d. Calculate the WACC for Dillon Labs.

Personal Finance Problem

 P9–18 **Weighted average cost of capital** John Dough has just been awarded his degree in business. He has three education loans outstanding. They all mature in 5 years and can be repaid without penalty any time before maturity. The amounts owed on each loan and the annual interest rate associated with each loan are given in the following table.

Loan	Balance due	Annual interest rate
1	$20,000	6%
2	12,000	9
3	32,000	5

John can also combine the total of his three debts (that is, $64,000) and create a consolidated loan from his bank. His bank will charge a 7.2% annual interest rate for a period of 5 years.

Should John do nothing (leave the three individual loans as is) or create a consolidated loan (the $64,000 question)?

LG 3 **LG 4** **P9–19** **Calculation of individual costs and WACC** Lang Enterprises is interested in measuring its overall cost of capital. Current investigation has gathered the following data. **LG 5** **LG 6** The firm is in the 40% tax bracket.

Debt The firm can raise debt by selling $1,000-par-value, 8% coupon interest rate, 20-year bonds on which *annual interest* payments will be made. To sell the issue, an average discount of $30 per bond would have to be given. The firm also must pay flotation costs of $30 per bond.

Preferred stock The firm can sell 8% preferred stock at its $95-per-share par value. The cost of issuing and selling the preferred stock is expected to be $5 per share. Preferred stock can be sold under these terms.

Common stock The firm's common stock is currently selling for $90 per share. The firm expects to pay cash dividends of $7 per share next year. The firm's dividends have been growing at an annual rate of 6%, and this growth is expected to continue into the future. The stock must be underpriced by $7 per share, and flotation costs are expected to amount to $5 per share. The firm can sell new common stock under these terms.

Retained earnings When measuring this cost, the firm does not concern itself with the tax bracket or brokerage fees of owners. It expects to have available

$100,000 of retained earnings in the coming year; once these retained earnings are exhausted, the firm will use new common stock as the form of common stock equity financing.

a. Calculate the after-tax cost of debt.
b. Calculate the cost of preferred stock.
c. Calculate the cost of common stock.
d. Calculate the firm's weighted average cost of capital using the capital structure weights shown in the following table. (Round answer to the nearest 0.1%.)

Source of capital	Weight
Long-term debt	30%
Preferred stock	20
Common stock equity	50
Total	100%

 P9–20 **Weighted average cost of capital** American Exploration, Inc., a natural gas producer, is trying to decide whether to revise its target capital structure. Currently, it targets a 50–50 mix of debt and equity, but it is considering a target capital structure with 70% debt. American Exploration currently has 6% after-tax cost of debt and a 12% cost of common stock. The company does not have any preferred stock outstanding.

a. What is American Exploration's current WACC?
b. Assuming that its cost of debt and equity remain unchanged, what will be American Exploration's WACC under the revised target capital structure?
c. Do you think that shareholders are affected by the increase in debt to 70%? If so, how are they affected? Are their common stock claims riskier now?
d. Suppose that in response to the increase in debt, American Exploration's shareholders increase their required return so that cost of common equity is 16%. What will its new WACC be in this case?
e. What does your answer in part **b** suggest about the trade-off between financing with debt versus equity?

 P9–21 **ETHICS PROBLEM** During the 1990s, General Electric put together a long string of consecutive quarters in which the firm managed to meet or beat the earnings forecasts of Wall Street stock analysts. Some skeptics wondered if GE "managed" earnings to meet Wall Street's expectations, meaning that GE used accounting gimmicks to conceal the true volatility in its business. How do you think GE's long run of meeting or beating earnings forecasts affected its cost of capital? If investors learn that GE's performance was achieved largely through accounting gimmicks, how do you think they would respond?

Spreadsheet Exercise

Nova Corporation is interested in measuring the cost of each specific type of capital as well as the weighted average cost of capital. Historically, the firm has raised capital in the following manner:

Source of capital	Weight
Long-term debt	35%
Preferred stock	12
Common stock equity	53

The tax rate of the firm is currently 40%. The needed financial information and data are as follows:

Debt Nova can raise debt by selling $1,000-par-value, 6.5% coupon interest rate, 10-year bonds on which *annual interest payments* will be made. To sell the issue, an average discount of $20 per bond needs to be given. There is an associated flotation cost of 2% of par value.

Preferred stock Preferred stock can be sold under the following terms: The security has a par value of $100 per share, the annual dividend rate is 6% of the par value, and the flotation cost is expected to be $4 per share. The preferred stock is expected to sell for $102 before cost considerations.

Common stock The current price of Nova's common stock is $35 per share. The cash dividend is expected to be $3.25 per share next year. The firm's dividends have grown at an annual rate of 5%, and it is expected that the dividend will continue at this rate for the foreseeable future. The flotation costs are expected to be approximately $2 per share. Nova can sell new common stock under these terms.

Retained earnings The firm expects to have available $100,000 of retained earnings in the coming year. Once these retained earnings are exhausted, the firm will use new common stock as the form of common stock equity financing. (*Note:* When measuring this cost, the firm does not concern itself with the tax bracket or brokerage fees of owners.)

TO DO

Create a spreadsheet to answer the following questions:

a. Calculate the after-tax cost of debt.
b. Calculate the cost of preferred stock.
c. Calculate the cost of retained earnings.
d. Calculate the cost of new common stock.
e. Calculate the firm's weighted average cost of capital using retained earnings and the capital structure weights shown in the table above.
f. Calculate the firm's weighted average cost of capital using new common stock and the capital structure weights shown in the table above.

Part 5 > Long-Term Investment Decisions

Probably nothing that financial managers do is more important to the long-term success of a company than making good investment decisions. The term *capital budgeting* describes the process for evaluating and selecting investment projects. Often, capital expenditures can be very large, such as building a new plant or launching a new product line. These endeavors can create enormous value for shareholders, but they can also bankrupt the company. In this part, you'll learn how financial managers decide which investment opportunities to pursue.

Chapter 10 covers the capital budgeting tools that financial managers and analysts use to evaluate the merits of an investment. Some of these techniques are quite intuitive and simple to use, such as payback analysis. Other techniques are a little more complex, such as the net present value and internal rate of return approaches. In general, the more complex techniques provide more comprehensive evaluations, but the simpler approaches often lead to the same value-maximizing decisions.

Chapter 11 illustrates how to develop the capital budgeting cash flows that the techniques covered in Chapter 10 require. After studying this chapter, you will understand the inputs that are necessary to build the relevant cash flows that are required to determine whether a particular investment is likely to create or destroy value for shareholders.

10 Capital Budgeting Techniques

Learning Goals

LG 1 Understand the key elements of the capital budgeting process.

LG 2 Calculate, interpret, and evaluate the payback period.

LG 3 Calculate, interpret, and evaluate the net present value (NPV) and economic value added (EVA).

LG 4 Calculate, interpret, and evaluate the internal rate of return (IRR).

LG 5 Use net present value profiles to compare NPV and IRR techniques.

LG 6 Discuss NPV and IRR in terms of conflicting rankings and the theoretical and practical strengths of each approach.

Why This Chapter Matters to You

In your *professional* life

ACCOUNTING You need to understand capital budgeting techniques to help determine the relevant cash flows associated with proposed capital expenditures.

INFORMATION SYSTEMS You need to understand capital budgeting techniques to design decision modules that help reduce the amount of work required to analyze proposed capital expenditures.

MANAGEMENT You need to understand capital budgeting techniques to correctly analyze the relevant cash flows of proposed projects and decide whether to accept or reject them.

MARKETING You need to understand capital budgeting techniques to grasp how proposals for new marketing programs, for new products, and for the expansion of existing product lines will be evaluated by the firm's decision makers.

OPERATIONS You need to understand capital budgeting techniques to know how proposals for the acquisition of new equipment and plants will be evaluated by the firm's decision makers.

In your *personal* life
You can use the capital budgeting techniques used by financial managers to measure either the value of a given asset purchase or its compound rate of return. The IRR technique is widely applied in personal finance to measure both actual and forecast rate of returns on investment securities, real estate, credit card debt, consumer loans, and leases.

LG① **10.1 Overview of Capital Budgeting**

MyFinanceLab Video

capital budgeting
The process of evaluating and selecting long-term investments that are consistent with the firm's goal of maximizing owners' wealth.

Long-term investments represent sizable outlays of funds that commit a firm to some course of action. Consequently, the firm needs procedures to analyze and select its long-term investments. **Capital budgeting** is the process of evaluating and selecting long-term investments that are consistent with the firm's goal of maximizing owners' wealth. Firms typically make a variety of long-term investments, but the most common is in *fixed assets,* which include property (land), plant, and equipment. These assets, often referred to as *earning assets,* generally provide the basis for the firm's earning power and value.

Because firms treat capital budgeting (investment) and financing decisions *separately,* Chapters 10 through 11 concentrate on fixed-asset acquisition without regard to the specific method of financing used. We begin by discussing the motives for capital expenditure.

MOTIVES FOR CAPITAL EXPENDITURE

capital expenditure
An outlay of funds by the firm that is expected to produce benefits over a period of time *greater than* 1 year.

operating expenditure
An outlay of funds by the firm resulting in benefits received *within* 1 year.

A **capital expenditure** is an outlay of funds by the firm that is expected to produce benefits over a period of time *greater than* 1 year. An **operating expenditure** is an outlay resulting in benefits received *within* 1 year. Fixed-asset outlays are capital expenditures, but not all capital expenditures are classified as fixed assets. A $60,000 outlay for a new machine with a usable life of 15 years is a capital expenditure that would appear as a fixed asset on the firm's balance sheet. A $60,000 outlay for an advertising campaign that is expected to produce benefits over a long period is also a capital expenditure, but it would rarely be shown as a fixed asset.

Companies make capital expenditures for many reasons. The primary motives for capital expenditures are to expand operations, to replace or renew fixed assets, and to obtain some other, less tangible benefit over a long period.

STEPS IN THE PROCESS

capital budgeting process
Five distinct but interrelated steps: *proposal generation, review and analysis, decision making, implementation,* and *follow-up.*

The **capital budgeting process** consists of five distinct but interrelated steps:

1. *Proposal generation.* Proposals for new investment projects are made at all levels within a business organization and are reviewed by finance personnel. Proposals that require large outlays are more carefully scrutinized than less costly ones.
2. *Review and analysis.* Financial managers perform formal review and analysis to assess the merits of investment proposals.
3. *Decision making.* Firms typically delegate capital expenditure decision making on the basis of dollar limits. Generally, the board of directors must authorize expenditures beyond a certain amount. Often, plant managers are given authority to make decisions necessary to keep the production line moving.
4. *Implementation.* Following approval, expenditures are made and projects implemented. Expenditures for a large project often occur in phases.
5. *Follow-up.* Results are monitored, and actual costs and benefits are compared with those that were expected. Action may be required if actual outcomes differ from projected ones.

Each step in the process is important. Review and analysis and decision making (Steps 2 and 3) consume the majority of time and effort, however. Follow-up (Step 5) is an important but often ignored step aimed at allowing the firm to improve the accuracy of its cash flow estimates continuously. Because of their fundamental importance, this and the following chapters give primary consideration to review and analysis and to decision making.

BASIC TERMINOLOGY

Before we develop the concepts, techniques, and practices related to the capital budgeting process, we need to explain some basic terminology. In addition, we will present some key assumptions that are used to simplify the discussion in the remainder of this chapter and in Chapter 11.

Independent versus Mutually Exclusive Projects

independent projects
Projects whose cash flows are unrelated to (or independent of) one another; the acceptance of one *does not eliminate* the others from further consideration.

Most investments can be placed into one of two categories: (1) independent projects or (2) mutually exclusive projects. **Independent projects** are those with cash flows that are unrelated to (or independent of) one another; the acceptance of one project *does not eliminate* the others from further consideration. **Mutually exclusive projects** are those that have the same function and therefore compete with one another. The acceptance of one *eliminates* from further consideration all other projects that serve a similar function. For example, a firm in need of increased production capacity could obtain it by (1) expanding its plant, (2) acquiring another company, or (3) contracting with another company for production. Clearly accepting any one option eliminates the immediate need for either of the others.

mutually exclusive projects
Projects that compete with one another so that the acceptance of one *eliminates* from further consideration all other projects that serve a similar function.

Unlimited Funds versus Capital Rationing

unlimited funds
The financial situation in which a firm is able to accept all independent projects that provide an acceptable return.

The availability of funds for capital expenditures affects the firm's decisions. If a firm has **unlimited funds** for investment (or if it can raise as much money as it needs by borrowing or issuing stock), making capital budgeting decisions is quite simple: All independent projects that will provide an acceptable return can be accepted. Often, though, firms operate under **capital rationing** instead, which means that they have a fixed budget available for capital expenditures and that numerous projects will compete for these dollars. Procedures for dealing with capital rationing are presented in Chapter 11. The discussions here and in Chapter 11 assume unlimited funds.

capital rationing
The financial situation in which a firm has only a fixed number of dollars available for capital expenditures and numerous projects compete for these dollars.

Accept–Reject versus Ranking Approaches

accept–reject approach
The evaluation of capital expenditure proposals to determine whether they meet the firm's minimum acceptance criterion.

Two standard approaches to capital budgeting decisions are available. The **accept–reject approach** involves evaluating capital expenditure proposals to determine whether they meet the firm's minimum acceptance criterion. This approach can be used when the firm has unlimited funds, as a preliminary step when evaluating mutually exclusive projects, or in a situation in which capital must be rationed. In these cases, only acceptable projects should be considered.

ranking approach
The ranking of capital expenditure projects on the basis of some predetermined measure, such as the rate of return.

The second method, the **ranking approach**, involves ranking projects on the basis of some predetermined measure, such as the rate of return. The project with the highest return is ranked first, and the project with the lowest return is ranked last. Only acceptable projects should be ranked. Ranking is useful in selecting the "best" of a group of mutually exclusive projects and in evaluating projects with a view of capital rationing.

CAPITAL BUDGETING TECHNIQUES

Large firms evaluate dozens, perhaps even hundreds, of different ideas for new investments each year. To ensure that the investment projects selected have the best chance of increasing the value of the firm, financial managers need tools to help them evaluate the merits of individual projects and to rank competing investments. A number of techniques are available for performing such analyses. The preferred approaches integrate time value procedures, risk and return considerations, and valuation concepts to select capital expenditures that are consistent with the firm's goal of maximizing owners' wealth. This chapter focuses on the use of these techniques in an environment of certainty.

Bennett Company's Relevant Cash Flows

We will use one basic problem to illustrate all the techniques described in this chapter. The problem concerns Bennett Company, a medium-sized metal fabricator that is currently contemplating two projects with conventional cash flow patterns:[1] Project A requires an initial investment of $42,000, and project B requires an initial investment of $45,000. The projected relevant cash flows for the two projects are presented in Table 10.1 and depicted on the time lines in Figure 10.1. Both projects involve one initial cash outlay followed by annual cash inflows, a fairly typical pattern for new investments. We begin with a look at the three most popular capital budgeting techniques: payback period, net present value, and internal rate of return.

→ REVIEW QUESTION

10–1 What is the financial manager's goal in selecting investment projects for the firm? Define the capital budgeting process, and explain how it helps managers achieve their goal.

 LG 2 | **10.2 Payback Period**

payback period
The amount of time required for a firm to recover its initial investment in a project as calculated from *cash inflows.*

Small and medium-sized firms often use the payback period approach to evaluate proposed investments. The **payback period** is the time it takes the firm to recover its initial investment in a project, as calculated from *cash inflows.* In the case of an *annuity* (such as the Bennett Company's project A), the payback period can be found by dividing the initial investment by the annual cash inflow. For a *mixed*

TABLE 10.1	Capital Expenditure Data for Bennett Company	
	Project A	Project B
Initial investment	$42,000	$45,000
Year	Operating cash inflows	
1	$14,000	$28,000
2	14,000	12,000
3	14,000	10,000
4	14,000	10,000
5	14,000	10,000

1. A conventional cash flow pattern is one in which the up-front cash flow is negative and all subsequent cash flows are positive. A nonconventional pattern occurs if the up-front cash flow is positive and subsequent cash flows are negative (for example, when a firm sells extended warranties and pays benefits later) or when the cash flows oscillate between positive and negative (as might occur when firms have to reinvest in a project to extend its life).

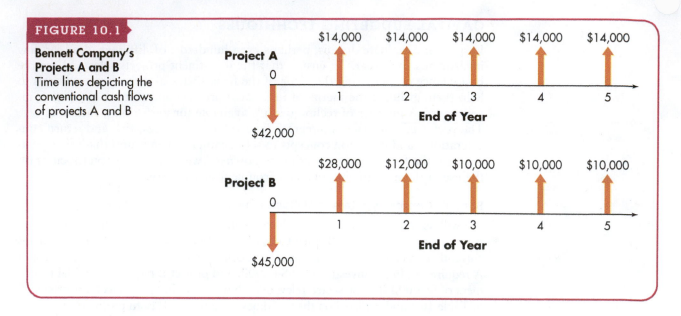

FIGURE 10.1

Bennett Company's Projects A and B
Time lines depicting the conventional cash flows of projects A and B

Project A

$14,000 $14,000 $14,000 $14,000 $14,000

0 — 1 — 2 — 3 — 4 — 5

End of Year

$42,000

Project B

$28,000 $12,000 $10,000 $10,000 $10,000

0 — 1 — 2 — 3 — 4 — 5

End of Year

$45,000

stream of cash inflows (such as project B), the yearly cash inflows must be accumulated until the initial investment is recovered. Although popular, the payback period is generally viewed as an *unsophisticated capital budgeting technique* because it does not *explicitly* consider the time value of money.

DECISION CRITERIA

When the payback period is used to make accept–reject decisions, the following decision criteria apply:

- If the payback period is *less than* the maximum acceptable payback period, *accept* the project.
- If the payback period is *greater than* the maximum acceptable payback period, *reject* the project.

The length of the maximum acceptable payback period is determined by management. This value is set *subjectively* on the basis of a number of factors, including the type of project (expansion, replacement or renewal, other), the product life cycle, the perceived risk of the project, and the perceived relationship between the payback period and the share value. It is simply a value that management feels, on average, will result in value-creating investment decisions.

Example 10.1 ▶ We can calculate the payback period for Bennett Company's projects A and B using the data in Table 10.1. *For project A, which is an annuity, the payback period is 3.0 years ($42,000 initial investment ÷ $14,000 annual cash inflow).* Because project B generates a mixed stream of cash inflows, the calculation of its payback period is not as clear-cut. In year 1, the firm will recover $28,000 of its $45,000 initial investment. By the end of year 2, $40,000 ($28,000 from year 1 + $12,000 from year 2) will have been recovered. At the end of year 3, $50,000 will have been recovered. Only 50% of the year-3 cash inflow of $10,000 is needed to complete the payback of the initial $45,000. *The payback period for project B is therefore 2.5 years (2 years + 50% of year 3).*

If Bennett's maximum acceptable payback period were 2.75 years, project A would be rejected and project B would be accepted. If the maximum acceptable payback period were 2.25 years, both projects would be rejected. If the projects were being ranked, B would be preferred over A because it has a shorter payback period.

PROS AND CONS OF PAYBACK ANALYSIS

Large firms sometimes use the payback approach to evaluate small projects, and small firms use it to evaluate most projects. Its popularity results from its computational simplicity and intuitive appeal. By measuring how quickly the firm recovers its initial investment, the payback period also gives *implicit* consideration to the timing of cash flows and therefore to the time value of money. Because it can be viewed as a measure of *risk exposure,* many firms use the payback period as a decision criterion or as a supplement to other decision techniques. The longer the firm must wait to recover its invested funds, the greater the possibility of a calamity. Hence, the shorter the payback period, the lower the firm's risk exposure.

The major weakness of the payback period is that the appropriate payback period is merely a subjectively determined number. It cannot be specified in light of the wealth maximization goal because it is not based on discounting cash flows to determine whether they add to the firm's value. Instead, the appropriate payback period is simply the maximum acceptable period of time over which management decides that a project's cash flows must break even (that is, just equal to the initial investment).

Personal Finance Example 10.2 ▶ Seema Mehdi is considering investing $20,000 to obtain a 5% interest in a rental property. Her good friend and real estate agent, Akbar Ahmed, put the deal together and he conservatively estimates that Seema should receive between $4,000 and $6,000 per year in cash from her 5% interest in the property. The deal is structured in a way that forces all investors to maintain their investment in the property for at least 10 years. Seema expects to remain in the 25% income-tax bracket for quite a while. To be acceptable, Seema requires the investment to pay itself back in terms of after-tax cash flows in less than 7 years.

Seema's calculation of the payback period on this deal begins with calculation of the range of annual after-tax cash flow:

$$\text{After-tax cash flow} = (1 - \text{tax rate}) \times \text{Pre-tax cash flow}$$
$$= (1 - 0.25) \times \$4,000 = \$3,000$$
$$= (1 - 0.25) \times \$6,000 = \$4,500$$

The after-tax cash flow ranges from $3,000 to $4,500. Dividing the $20,000 initial investment by each of the estimated after-tax cash flows, we get the payback period:

$$\text{Payback period} = \text{Initial investment} \div \text{After-tax cash flow}$$
$$= \$20,000 \div \$3,000 = 6.67 \text{ years}$$
$$= \$20,000 \div \$4,500 = 4.44 \text{ years}$$

Because Seema's proposed rental property investment will pay itself back between 4.44 and 6.67 years, which is a range below her maximum payback of 7 years, the investment is acceptable.

TABLE 10.2	Relevant Cash Flows and Payback Periods for DeYarman Enterprises' Projects	
	Project gold	Project silver
Initial investment	$50,000	$50,000
Year	Operating cash inflows	
1	$ 5,000	$40,000
2	5,000	2,000
3	40,000	8,000
4	10,000	10,000
5	10,000	10,000
Payback period	3 years	3 years

A second weakness is that this approach fails to take *fully* into account the time factor in the value of money.[2] This weakness can be illustrated by an example.

Example 10.3 ▶ DeYarman Enterprises, a small medical appliance manufacturer, is considering two mutually exclusive projects named Gold and Silver. The firm uses only the payback period to choose projects. The cash flows and payback period for each project are given in Table 10.2. Both projects have 3-year payback periods, which would suggest that they are equally desirable. But comparison of the pattern c cash inflows over the first 3 years shows that more of the $50,000 initial invest ment in project Silver is recovered sooner than is recovered for project Gold. For example, in year 1, $40,000 of the $50,000 invested in project Silver is recovered, whereas only $5,000 of the $50,000 investment in project Gold is recovered. Given the time value of money, project Silver would clearly be preferred over project Gold, even though both have identical 3-year payback periods. The payback approach does not fully account for the time value of money, which, if recognized, would cause project Silver to be preferred over project Gold.

A third weakness of payback is its failure to recognize cash flows that occur *after* the payback period.

Example 10.4 ▶ Rashid Company, a software developer, has two investment opportunities, X and Y. Data for X and Y are given in Table 10.3. The payback period for project X is 2 years; for project Y, it is 3 years. Strict adherence to the payback approach suggests that project X is preferable to project Y. However, if we look beyond the payback period, we see that project X returns only an additional $1,200 ($1,000 in year 3 + $100 in year 4 + $100 in year 5), whereas project Y returns an additional $7,000 ($4,000 in year 4 + $3,000 in year 5). On the basis of this

2. To consider differences in timing explicitly in applying the payback method, the *discounted payback period* is sometimes used. It is found by first calculating the present value of the cash inflows at the appropriate discount rate and then finding the payback period by using the present value of the cash inflows.

TABLE 10.3	Calculation of the Payback Period for Rashid Company's Two Alternative Investment Projects	
	Project X	**Project Y**
Initial investment	$10,000	$10,000
Year	Operating cash inflows	
1	$5,000	$3,000
2	5,000	4,000
3	1,000	3,000
4	100	4,000
5	100	3,000
Payback period	2 years	3 years

information, project Y appears preferable to X. The payback approach ignored the cash inflows occurring after the end of the payback period.

→ **REVIEW QUESTIONS**

10–2 What is the *payback period*? How is it calculated?

10–3 What weaknesses are commonly associated with the use of the payback period to evaluate a proposed investment?

 3 **10.3** Net Present Value (NPV)

The method used by most large companies to evaluate investment projects is called *net present value (NPV)*. The intuition behind the NPV method is simple. When firms make investments, they are spending money that they obtained, in one form or another, from investors. Investors expect a return on the money that they give to firms, so a firm should undertake an investment only if the present value of the cash flow that the investment generates is greater than the cost of making the investment in the first place. Because the NPV method takes into account the time value of investors' money, it is a more *sophisticated capital budgeting technique* than the payback rule. The NPV method discounts the firm's cash flows at the firm's cost of capital. This rate—as discussed in Chapter 9—represents the firm's cost of financing and is the minimum return that must be earned on a project to satisfy the firm's investors. Projects with lower returns fail to meet investors' expectations and therefore decrease firm value, and projects with higher returns increase firm value.

net present value (NPV)
A sophisticated capital budgeting technique; found by subtracting a project's initial investment from the present value of its cash inflows discounted at a rate equal to the firm's cost of capital.

The **net present value (NPV)** is found by subtracting a project's initial investment (CF_0) from the present value of its cash inflows (CF_t) discounted at a rate equal to the firm's cost of capital (r):

NPV = Present value of cash inflows − Initial investment

$$NPV = \sum_{t=1}^{n} \frac{CF_t}{(1 + r)^t} - CF_0 \qquad (10.1)$$

When NPV is used, both inflows and outflows are measured in terms of present dollars. For a project that has cash outflows beyond the initial investment, the net present value of a project would be found by subtracting the present value of outflows from the present value of inflows.

DECISION CRITERIA

When NPV is used to make accept–reject decisions, the decision criteria are as follows:

- If the NPV is *greater than* $0, *accept* the project.
- If the NPV is *less than* $0, *reject* the project.

If the NPV is greater than $0, the firm will earn a return greater than its cost of capital. Such action should increase the market value of the firm, and therefore the wealth of its owners, by an amount equal to the NPV.

Example 10.5 ▶

MyFinanceLab Solution
Video

We can illustrate the net present value (NPV) approach by using the Bennett Company data presented in Table 10.1. If the firm has a 10% cost of capital, the net present values for projects A (an annuity) and B (a mixed stream) can be calculated as shown on the time lines in Figure 10.2. These calculations result in net present values for projects A and B of $11,071 and $10,924, respectively. Both

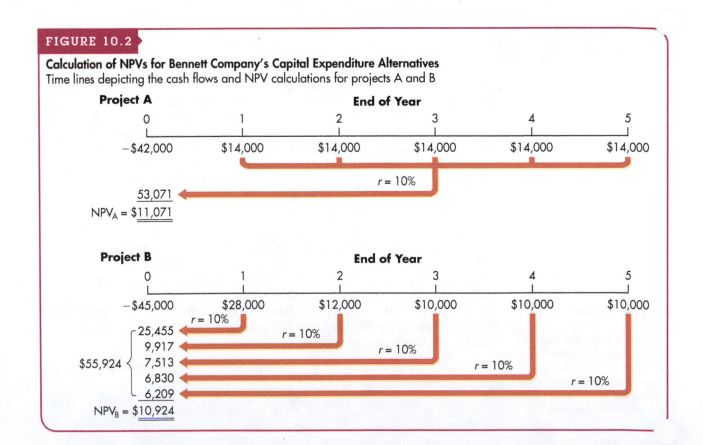

FIGURE 10.2

Calculation of NPVs for Bennett Company's Capital Expenditure Alternatives
Time lines depicting the cash flows and NPV calculations for projects A and B

projects are acceptable because the net present value of each is greater than $0. If the projects were being ranked, however, project A would be considered superior to B because it has a higher net present value than that of B ($11,071 versus $10,924).

Calculator use The preprogrammed NPV function in a financial calculator can be used to simplify the NPV calculation. The keystrokes for project A—the annuity—typically are as shown at left. Note that because project A is an annuity, only its first cash inflow, $CF_1 = 14000$, is input, followed by its frequency, $N = 5$.

The keystrokes for project B—the mixed stream—are as also shown. Because the last three cash inflows for project B are the same ($CF_3 = CF_4 = CF_5 = 10,000$), after inputting the first of these cash inflows, CF_3, we merely input its frequency, $N = 3$.

The calculated NPVs for projects A and B of $11,071 and $10,924, respectively, agree with the NPVs already cited.

Spreadsheet use The NPVs can be calculated as shown on the following Excel spreadsheet.

MyFinanceLab Financial Calculator

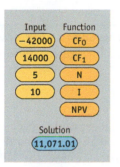

Input	Function
−42000	CF₀
14000	CF₁
5	N
10	I
	NPV

Solution
11,071.01

Project A

MyFinanceLab Financial Calculator

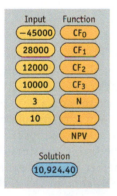

Input	Function
−45000	CF₀
28000	CF₁
12000	CF₂
10000	CF₃
3	N
10	I
	NPV

Solution
10,924.40

Project B

	A	B	C
1	DETERMINING THE NET PRESENT VALUE		
2	Firm's cost of capital		10%
3		Year-End Cash Flow	
4	Year	Project A	Project B
5	0	$ −42,000	$ −45,000
6	1	$ 14,000	$ 28,000
7	2	$ 14,000	$ 12,000
8	3	$ 14,000	$ 10,000
9	4	$ 14,000	$ 10,000
10	5	$ 14,000	$ 10,000
11	NPV	$ 11,071	$ 10,924
12	Choice of project		Project A

Entry in Cell B11 is
=NPV(C2,B6:B10)+B5
Copy the entry in Cell B11 to Cell C11.
Entry in Cell C12 is =IF(B11>C11,B4,C4).

NPV AND THE PROFITABILITY INDEX

A variation of the NPV rule is called the profitability index (PI). For a project that has an initial cash outflow followed by cash inflows, the profitability index (PI) is simply equal to the present value of cash inflows divided by the initial cash outflow:[3]

$$PI = \frac{\sum_{t=1}^{n} \frac{CF_t}{(1 + r)^t}}{CF_0} \qquad (10.2)$$

3. To be a bit more precise, the denominator in Equation 10.2 should be a positive number, so we are taking the absolute value of the initial cash outflow.

When companies evaluate investment opportunities using the PI, the decision rule they follow is to invest in the project when the index is greater than 1.0. A PI greater than 1.0 implies that the present value of cash inflows is greater than the (absolute value of the) initial cash outflow, so a profitability index greater than 1.0 corresponds to a net present value greater than 0. In other words, the NPV and PI methods will always come to the same conclusion regarding whether a particular investment is worth doing or not.

Example 10.6 ▶

We can refer back to Figure 10.2, which shows the present value of cash inflows for projects A and B, to calculate the PI for each of Bennett's investment options:

$$PI_A = \$53,071 \div \$42,000 = 1.26$$
$$PI_B = \$55,924 \div \$45,000 = 1.24$$

According to the profitability index, both projects are acceptable (because PI > 1.0 for both), which shouldn't be surprising because we already know that both projects have positive NPVs. Furthermore, in this particular case, the NPV rule and the PI both indicate that project A is preferred over project B. It is not always true that the NPV and PI methods will rank projects in exactly the same order. Different rankings can occur when alternative projects require initial outlays that have very different magnitudes.

NPV AND ECONOMIC VALUE ADDED

Economic Value Added (EVA), a registered trademark of the consulting firm Stern Stewart & Co., is another close cousin of the NPV method. Whereas the NPV approach calculates the value of an investment over its entire life, the EVA approach is typically used to measure an investment's performance on a year-by-year basis. The EVA method begins the same way that NPV does: by calculating a project's net cash flows. However, the EVA approach subtracts from those cash flows a charge that is designed to capture the return that the firm's investors demand on the project. That is, the EVA calculation asks whether a project generates positive cash flows *above and beyond what investors demand*. If so, the project is worth undertaking.

pure economic profit
A profit above and beyond the normal competitive rate of return in a line of business.

The EVA method determines whether a project earns a *pure economic profit*. When accountants say that a firm has earned a profit, they mean that revenues are greater than expenses. But the term **pure economic profit** refers to a profit that is higher than expected given the competitive rate of return on a particular line of business. A firm that shows a positive profit on its income statement may or may not earn a pure economic profit, depending on how large the profit is relative to the capital invested in the business. For instance, in the four quarters ending on March 30, 2013, Alcoa Inc., the aluminum producing giant, reported that it had earned a net profit of $264 million. Does that seem like a large profit? Perhaps it doesn't when you consider that Alcoa's balance sheet showed total assets of more than $40 billion. In other words, Alcoa's profit represented a return of 0.6% on the firm's assets. That return was not far from the rate offered on risk-free government securities in 2013, so it clearly fell below the expectations of Alcoa's investors (who would have expected a higher return as compensation for the risks they were taking). Thus, the compan earned a *pure economic loss* over those four quarters. Stated differently, Alcoa's EVA during that period was negative.

Example 10.7 ▶	Suppose that a certain project costs $1,000,000 up front, but after that it will generate net cash inflows each year (in perpetuity) of $120,000. To calculate the NPV of this project, we would simply discount the cash flows and add them up. If the firm's cost of capital is 10%, the project's NPV is:[4]

$$\text{NPV} = -\$1,000,000 + (\$120,000 \div 0.10) = \$200,000$$

To calculate the investment's economic value added in any particular year, we start with the annual $120,000 cash flow. Next, we assign a charge that accounts for the return that investors demand on the capital that the firm has invested in the project. In this case, the firm invested $1,000,000, and investors expect a 10% return. That means that the project's annual capital charge is $100,000 ($1,000,000 × 10%), and its EVA is $20,000 per year:

$$\text{EVA} = \text{project cash flow} - [(\text{cost of capital}) \times (\text{invested capital})]$$
$$= \$120,000 - \$100,000 = \$20,000$$

In other words, this project earns more than its cost of capital each year, so the project is clearly worth doing. To calculate the EVA for the project over its entire life, we would simply discount the annual EVA figures using the firm's cost of capital. In this case, the project produces an annual EVA of $20,000 in perpetuity. Discounting at 10% gives a project EVA of $200,000 ($20,000 ÷ 0.10), identical to the NPV. In this example, both the NPV and EVA methods reach the same conclusion, namely that the project creates $200,000 in value for shareholders. If the cash flows in our example had fluctuated through time rather than remaining fixed at $120,000 per year, an analyst would calculate the investment's EVA every year and then discount those figures to the present using the firm's cost of capital. If the resulting figure is positive, the project generates a positive EVA and is worth doing.

→ REVIEW QUESTIONS

10–4 How is the *net present value (NPV)* calculated for a project with a *conventional cash flow pattern?*

10–5 What are the acceptance criteria for NPV? How are they related to the firm's market value?

10–6 Explain the similarities and differences between NPV, PI, and EVA.

→ EXCEL REVIEW QUESTION MyFinanceLab

10–7 Almost all firms have to deal with limited financial resources and therefore cannot undertake all positive NPV projects. Based on the information provided at MFL, use a spreadsheet to rank various projects based on their NPVs.

---

4. We are using Equation 5.7 to calculate the present value of the perpetual stream of $120,000 cash flows.

internal rate of return (IRR)
The discount rate that equates the NPV of an investment opportunity with $0 (because the present value of cash inflows equals the initial investment); it is the rate of return that the firm will earn if it invests in the project and receives the given cash inflows.

The **internal rate of return (IRR)** is the discount rate that equates the NPV of an investment opportunity with $0 (because the present value of cash inflows equals the initial investment). It is the rate of return that the firm will earn if it invests in the project and receives the given cash inflows. Mathematically, the IRR is the value of r in Equation 10.1 that causes NPV to equal $0, or

$$\$0 = \sum_{t=1}^{n} \frac{CF_t}{(1 + IRR)^t} - CF_0 \qquad (10.3)$$

$$\sum_{t=1}^{n} \frac{CF_t}{(1 + IRR)^t} = CF_0 \qquad (10.3a)$$

DECISION CRITERIA

When IRR is used to make accept–reject decisions, the decision criteria are as follows:

- If the IRR is *greater than* the cost of capital, *accept* the project.
- If the IRR is *less than* the cost of capital, *reject* the project.

These criteria guarantee that the firm will earn at least its required return. Such an outcome should increase the market value of the firm and therefore the wealth of its owners.

CALCULATING THE IRR

With these calculators, you merely punch in all cash flows just as if to calculate NPV and then depress IRR to find the internal rate of return. Computer software, including spreadsheets, is also available for simplifying these calculations. All NPV and IRR values presented in this and subsequent chapters are obtained by using these functions on a financial calculator.

Example 10.8 ▶

MyFinanceLab Solution Video

We can demonstrate the internal rate of return (IRR) approach by using the Bennett Company data presented in Table 10.1. Figure 10.3 uses time lines to depict the framework for finding the IRRs for Bennett's projects A and B. We can see in the figure that the IRR is the unknown discount rate that causes the NPV to equal $0.

Calculator use To find the IRR using the preprogrammed function in a financial calculator, the keystrokes for each project are the same as those shown on page 377 for the NPV calculation, except that the last two NPV keystrokes (punching **I** and then **NPV**) are replaced by a single **IRR** keystroke.

Comparing the IRRs of projects A and B given in Figure 10.3 to Bennett Company's 10% cost of capital, we can see that both projects are acceptable because

$$IRR_A = 19.9\% > 10.0\% \text{ cost of capital}$$
$$IRR_B = 21.7\% > 10.0\% \text{ cost of capital}$$

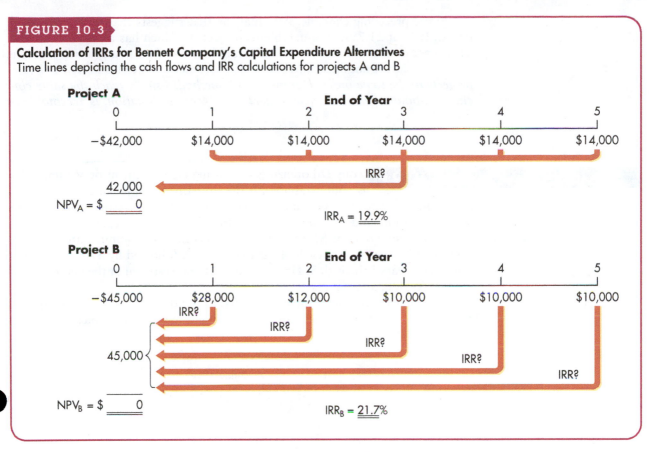

FIGURE 10.3

Calculation of IRRs for Bennett Company's Capital Expenditure Alternatives
Time lines depicting the cash flows and IRR calculations for projects A and B

Comparing the two projects' IRRs, we prefer project B over project A because project B delivers a higher IRR ($IRR_B = 21.7\% > IRR_A = 19.9\%$). If these projects are mutually exclusive, meaning that we can choose one project or the other but not both, the IRR decision technique would recommend project B.

Spreadsheet use The internal rate of return also can be calculated as shown on the following Excel spreadsheet.

	A	B	C
1	DETERMINING THE INTERNAL RATE OF RETURN		
2		Year-End Cash Flow	
3	Year	Project A	Project B
4	0	$ −42,000	$ −45,000
5	1	$ 14,000	$ 28,000
6	2	$ 14,000	$ 12,000
7	3	$ 14,000	$ 10,000
8	4	$ 14,000	$ 10,000
9	5	$ 14,000	$ 10,000
10	IRR	19.9%	21.7%
11	Choice of project		Project B

Entry in Cell B10 is =IRR(B4:B9).
Copy the entry in Cell B10 to Cell C10.
Entry in Cell C11 is =IF(B10>C10,B3,C3).

In the preceding example, note that the IRR suggests that project B, which has an IRR of 21.7%, is preferable to project A, which has an IRR of 19.9%. This suggestion conflicts with the NPV rankings obtained in an earlier example. Such conflicts are not unusual. *There is no guarantee that NPV and IRR will rank projects in the same order. However, both methods usually reach the same conclusion about whether a single project, considered in isolation, is acceptable or not.*

Personal Finance Example 10.9 ▸ Tony DiLorenzo is evaluating an investment opportunity. He is comfortable with the investment's level of risk. Based on competing investment opportunities, he believes that this investment must earn a minimum compound annual after-tax return of 9% to be acceptable. Tony's initial investment would be $7,500, and he expects to receive annual after-tax cash flows of $500 per year in each of the first 4 years, followed by $700 per year at the end of years 5 through 8. He plans to sell the investment at the end of year 8 and net $9,000, after taxes.

To calculate the investment's IRR (compound annual return), Tony first summarizes the after-tax cash flows as shown in the following table:

Year	Cash flow (− or +)
0	−$7,500 (Initial investment)
1	500
2	500
3	500
4	500
5	700
6	700
7	700
8	9,700 ($700 + $9,000)

Substituting the after-tax cash flows for years 0 through 8 into a financial calculator or spreadsheet, he finds the investment's IRR of 9.54%. Given that the expected IRR of 9.54% exceeds Tony's required minimum IRR of 9%, the investment is acceptable.

→ REVIEW QUESTIONS

10–8 What is the *internal rate of return (IRR)* on an investment? How is it determined?

10–9 What are the acceptance criteria for IRR? How are they related to the firm's market value?

10–10 Do the net present value (NPV) and internal rate of return (IRR) always agree with respect to accept–reject decisions? With respect to ranking decisions? Explain.

→ **EXCEL REVIEW QUESTION** MyFinanceLab

10–11 In addition to using NPV to evaluate projects, most firms also use IRR. Based on the information provided at MFL, use a spreadsheet to rank various projects based on their IRRs.

LG 5 **LG 6** # 10.5 Comparing NPV and IRR Techniques

To understand the differences between the NPV and IRR techniques and decision makers' preferences in their use, we need to look at net present value profiles, conflicting rankings, and the question of which approach is better.

NET PRESENT VALUE PROFILES

net present value profile
Graph that depicts a project's NPVs for various discount rates.

Projects can be compared graphically by constructing **net present value profiles** that depict the project's NPVs for various discount rates. These profiles are useful in evaluating and comparing projects, especially when conflicting rankings exist. They are best demonstrated via an example.

Example 10.10 ►

To prepare net present value profiles for Bennett Company's two projects, A and B, the first step is to develop a number of "discount rate–net present value" coordinates. Three coordinates can be easily obtained for each project; they are at a discount rate of 0%, at a discount rate of 10% (the cost of capital, r), and the IRR. The net present value at a 0% discount rate is found by merely adding all the cash inflows and subtracting the initial investment. Using the data in Table 10.1 and Figure 10.1, we get

For project A:

$$(\$14,000 + \$14,000 + \$14,000 + \$14,000 + \$14,000) - \$42,000 = \$28,000$$

For project B:

$$(\$28,000 + \$12,000 + \$10,000 + \$10,000 + \$10,000) - \$45,000 = \$25,000$$

The net present values for projects A and B at the 10% cost of capital are $11,071 and $10,924, respectively (from Figure 10.2). Because the IRR is the discount rate for which net present value equals zero, the IRRs (from Figure 10.3) of 19.9% for project A and 21.7% for project B result in $0 NPVs. The three sets of coordinates for each of the projects are summarized in Table 10.4.

TABLE 10.4	**Discount Rate–NPV Coordinates for Projects A and B**	
	Net present value	
Discount rate	Project A	Project B
0%	$28,000	$25,000
10	11,071	10,924
19.9	0	—
21.7	—	0

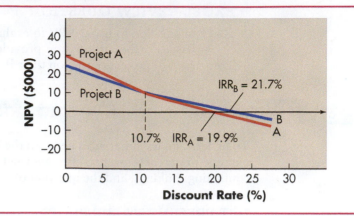

FIGURE 10.4

NPV Profiles
Net present value profiles for Bennett Company's projects A and B

Plotting the data from Table 10.4 results in the net present value profiles for projects A and B shown in Figure 10.4. The figure reveals three important facts:

1. The IRR of project B is greater than the IRR of project A, so managers using the IRR method to rank projects will always choose B over A if both projects are acceptable.
2. The NPV of project A is sometimes higher and sometimes lower than the NPV of project B; thus, the NPV method will not consistently rank A above B or vice versa. The NPV ranking will depend on the firm's cost of capital.
3. When the cost of capital is approximately 10.7%, projects A and B have identical NPVs.

The cost of capital for Bennett Company is 10%; at that rate, project A has a higher NPV than project B (the red line is above the blue line in Figure 10.4 when the discount rate is 10%). Therefore, the NPV and IRR methods rank the two projects differently. If Bennett's cost of capital were a little higher, say 12%, the NPV method would rank project B over project A and there would be no conflict in the rankings provided by the NPV and IRR approaches.

CONFLICTING RANKINGS

Ranking different investment opportunities is an important consideration when projects are mutually exclusive or when capital rationing is necessary. When projects are mutually exclusive, ranking enables the firm to determine which project is best from a financial standpoint. When capital rationing is necessary, ranking projects will provide a logical starting point for determining which group of projects to accept. As we'll see, **conflicting rankings** using NPV and IRR result from *differences in the reinvestment rate assumption, the timing of each project's cash flows, and the magnitude of the initial investment.*

conflicting rankings
Conflicts in the ranking given a project by NPV and IRR, resulting from *differences in the magnitude and timing of cash flows.*

intermediate cash inflows
Cash inflows received prior to the termination of a project.

Reinvestment Assumption

One underlying cause of conflicting rankings is different implicit assumptions about the *reinvestment* of **intermediate cash inflows**, cash inflows received prior to the termination of a project. NPV assumes that intermediate cash inflows are reinvested at the cost of capital, whereas IRR assumes that intermediate cash inflows are reinvested at a rate equal to the project's IRR.[5] These differing assumptions can be demonstrated with an example.

Example 10.11 ▶

A project requiring a $170,000 initial investment is expected to provide operating cash inflows of $52,000, $78,000, and $100,000 at the end of each of the next 3 years. The NPV of the project (at the firm's 10% cost of capital) is $16,867, and its IRR is 15%. Clearly, the project is acceptable (NPV = $16,867 > $0 and IRR = 15% > 10% cost of capital). Table 10.5 demonstrates calculation of the project's future value at the end of its 3-year life, assuming both a 10% (its cost of capital) and a 15% (its IRR) rate of return. A future value of $248,720 results from reinvestment at the 10% cost of capital, and a future value of $258,470 results from reinvestment at the 15% IRR.

If the future value in each case in Table 10.5 were viewed as the return received 3 years from today from the $170,000 initial investment, the cash flows would be those given in Table 10.6. The NPVs and IRRs in each case are shown below the cash flows in Table 10.6. You can see that at the 10% reinvestment rate, the NPV remains at $16,867; reinvestment at the 15% IRR produces an NPV of $24,192.

From this result, it should be clear that the NPV technique assumes reinvestment at the cost of capital (10% in this example). (Note that with reinvestment at 10%, the IRR would be 13.5%.) On the other hand, the IRR technique assumes an ability to reinvest intermediate cash inflows at the IRR. If reinvestment does not occur at this rate, the IRR will differ from 15%. Reinvestment at a rate lower than the IRR would result in an IRR lower than that calculated (at 13.5%, for

			Reinvestment rate	
	Operating cash inflows	Number of years earnings interest (*t*)	10%	15%
Year			Future value	Future value
1	$ 52,000	2	$ 62,920	$ 68,770
2	78,000	1	85,800	89,700
3	100,000	0	100,000	100,000
		Future value end of year 3	$248,720	$258,470

TABLE 10.5 ▷ Reinvestment Rate Comparisons for a Project

NPV @ 10% = $16,867

IRR = 15%

Note: Initial investment in this project is $170,000.

---

5. To eliminate the reinvestment rate assumption of the IRR, some practitioners calculate the *modified internal rate of return (MIRR).* The MIRR is found by converting each operating cash inflow to its future value measured at the end of the project's life and then summing the future values of all inflows to get the project's *terminal value.* Each future value is found by using the cost of capital, thereby eliminating the reinvestment rate criticism of the traditional IRR. The MIRR represents the discount rate that causes the terminal value just to equal the initial investment. Because it uses the cost of capital as the reinvestment rate, the MIRR is generally viewed as a better measure of a project's true profitability than the IRR. Although this technique is frequently used in commercial real estate valuation and is a preprogrammed function on some financial calculators, its failure to resolve the issue of conflicting rankings and its theoretical inferiority to NPV have resulted in the MIRR receiving only limited attention and acceptance in the financial literature.

TABLE 10.6	Project Cash Flows after Reinvestment	
	Reinvestment rate	
	10%	15%
Initial investment	$170,000	
Year	**Operating cash inflows**	
1	$ 0	$ 0
2	0	0
3	248,720	258,470
NPV @ 10%	$ 16,867	$ 24,192
IRR	13.5%	15.0%

example, if the reinvestment rate were only 10%). Reinvestment at a rate higher than the IRR would result in an IRR higher than that calculated.

Timing of the Cash Flow

Another reason the IRR and NPV methods may provide different rankings for investment options has to do with differences in the timing of cash flows. Go back to the timelines for investments A and B in Figure 10.1 on page 372. Th up-front investment required by each investment is similar, but after that, the timing of each project's cash flows is quite different. Project B has a large cash inflow almost immediately (in year 1), whereas Project A provides cash flows that are distributed evenly across time. Because so much of Project B's cash flows arrive early in its life (especially compared to the timing for Project A), the NPV of Project B will not be particularly sensitive to changes in the discount rate. Project A's NPV, on the other hand, will fluctuate more as the discount rate changes. In essence, Project B is somewhat akin to a short-term bond, whose price doesn't change much when interest rates move, and Project A is more like a long-term bond whose price fluctuates a great deal when rates change.

You can see this pattern if you review the NPV profiles for projects A and B in Figure 10.4 on page 384. The red line representing project A is considerably steeper than the blue line representing project B. At very low discount rates, project A has a higher NPV, but as the discount rate increases, the NPV of project A declines rapidly. When the discount rate is high enough, the NPV of project B overtakes that of project A.

We can summarize this discussion as follows. Because project A's cash flows arrive later than project B's cash flows do, when the firm's cost of capital is relatively low (to be specific, below about 10.7 percent), the NPV method will rank project A ahead of project B. At a higher cost of capital, the early arrival of project B's cash flows becomes more advantageous, and the NPV method will rank project B over project A. The differences in the timing of cash flows between the two projects does not affect the ranking provided by the IRR method, which always puts project B ahead of project A. Table 10.7 illustrates how the conflict i

TABLE 10.7	Ranking Projects A and B Using IRR and NPV Methods	
Method	Project A	Project B
IRR		✓
NPV		
if $r < 10.7\%$	✓	
if $r > 10.7\%$		✓

rankings between the NPV and IRR approaches depends on the firm's cost of capital.

Magnitude of the Initial Investment

Suppose that someone offered you the following two investment options. You could invest $2 today and receive $3 tomorrow, or you could invest $1,000 today and receive $1,100 tomorrow. The first investment provides a return (an IRR) of 50 percent in just 1 day, a return that surely would surpass any reasonable hurdle rate. But after making this investment, you're only better off by $1. On the other hand, the second choice offers a return of 10 percent in a single day. That's far less than the first opportunity, but earning 10 percent in a single day is still a very high return. In addition, if you accept this investment, you will be $100 better off tomorrow than you were today.

Most people would choose the second option presented above, even though the rate of return on that option (10 percent) is far less than the rate offered by the first option (50 percent). They reason (correctly) that it is sometimes better to accept a lower return on a larger investment than to accept a very high return on a small investment. Said differently, most people know that they are better off taking the investment that pays them a $100 profit in just 1 day rather than the investment that generates just a $1 profit.[6]

The preceding example illustrates what is known as the scale (or magnitude) problem. The scale problem occurs when two projects are very different in terms of how much money is required to invest in each project. In these cases, the IRR and NPV methods may rank projects differently. The IRR approach (and the PI method) may favor small projects with high returns (like the $2 loan that turns into $3), whereas the NPV approach favors the investment that makes the investor the most money (like the $1,000 investment that yields $1,100 in 1 day). In the case of the Bennett Company's projects, the scale problem is not likely to be the cause of the conflict in project rankings because the initial investment required to fund each project is quite similar.

To summarize, it is important for financial managers to keep an eye out for conflicts in project rankings provided by the NPV and IRR methods, but differences in the magnitude and timing of cash inflows do not guarantee conflicts in ranking. In general, the greater the difference between the magnitude and timing

---

6. Note that the profitability index also provides an incorrect ranking in this example. The first option has a PI of 1.5 ($3 ÷ $2), and the second option's PI equals 1.1 ($1,100 ÷ $1,000). Just like the IRR, the PI suggests that the first option is better, but we know that the second option makes more money.

of cash inflows, the greater the likelihood of conflicting rankings. Conflicts based on NPV and IRR can be reconciled computationally; to do so, one creates and analyzes an incremental project reflecting the difference in cash flows between the two mutually exclusive projects.

WHICH APPROACH IS BETTER?

Many companies use both the NPV and IRR techniques because current technology makes them easy to calculate. But it is difficult to choose one approach over the other because the theoretical and practical strengths of the approaches differ. Clearly, it is wise to evaluate NPV and IRR techniques from both theoretical and practical points of view.

Theoretical View

On a purely theoretical basis, NPV is the better approach to capital budgeting as a result of several factors. Most important, the NPV measures how much wealth a project creates (or destroys if the NPV is negative) for shareholders. Given that the financial manager's objective is to maximize shareholder wealth, the NPV approach has the clearest link to this objective and therefore is the "gold standard" for evaluating investment opportunities.

multiple IRRs
More than one IRR resulting from a capital budgeting project with a *nonconventional cash flow pattern;* the maximum number of IRRs for a project is equal to the number of sign changes in its cash flows.

In addition, certain mathematical properties may cause a project with a *nonconventional cash flow pattern* to have **multiple IRRs,** or more than one IRR. Mathematically, the maximum number of *real* roots to an equation is equal to its number of sign changes. Take an equation like $x^2 - 5x + 6 = 0$, which has two sign changes in its coefficients—from positive ($+x^2$) to negative ($-5x$) and then from negative ($-5x$) to positive ($+6$). If we factor the equation (remember factoring from high school math?), we get $(x - 2) \times (x - 3)$, which means that x can equal either 2 or 3; there are two correct values for x. Substitute them back into the equation, and you'll see that both values work.

This same outcome can occur when finding the IRR for projects with nonconventional cash flows because they have more than one sign change in the stream of cash flows. Clearly, when multiple IRRs occur for nonconventional cash flows, the analyst faces the time-consuming need to interpret their meanings so as to evaluate the project. That such a challenge does not exist when using NPV enhances its theoretical superiority.

Practical View

Evidence suggests that despite the theoretical superiority of NPV, *financial managers use the IRR approach just as often as the NPV method.* The appeal of the IRR technique is due to the general disposition of business people to think in terms of *rates of return* rather than actual *dollar returns.* Because interest rates, profitability, and so on are most often expressed as annual rates of return, the use of IRR makes sense to financial decision makers. They tend to find NPV less intuitive because it does not measure benefits *relative to the amount invested.* Because a variety of techniques are available for avoiding the pitfalls of the IRR, its widespread use does not imply a lack of sophistication on the part of financial decision makers. Clearly, corporate financial analysts are responsible for identifying and resolving problems with the IRR before the decision makers use it as a decision technique.

Matter of fact

Which Methods Do Companies Actually Use?

Researchers surveyed chief financial officers (CFOs) about what methods the CFOs used to evaluate capital investment projects. One interesting finding was that many companies use more than one of the approaches we've covered in this chapter. The most popular approaches by far were IRR and NPV, used by 76 percent and 75 percent (respectively) of the CFOs responding to the survey. These techniques enjoy wider use in larger firms, with the payback approach being more common in smaller firms.[7]

In addition, decision makers should keep in mind that nonfinancial considerations may be important elements in project selection, as discussed in the *Focus on Ethics* box.

focus on **ETHICS**

Nonfinancial Considerations in Project Selection

in practice Corporate ethics codes are often faulted for being "window dressing," for having little or no effect on actual behavior. Financial ethics expert John Dobson says day-to-day behavior in the workplace "acculturates" employees, teaching them that the behavior they see is rational and acceptable in that environment. The good news is that professional ethics codes, such as those developed for chartered financial analysts, corporate treasury professionals, and certified financial planners, actually provide sound guidelines for behavior. These codes, notes Dobson, are based on economically rational concepts such as integrity and trustworthiness, which guide the decision maker in attempting to increase shareholder wealth. Financial executives insist that there should be no separation between an individual's personal ethics and his or her business ethics. "It's a jungle out there" and "Business is business" should not be excuses for engaging in unethical behavior.

How do ethics codes apply to project selection and capital budgeting? For most companies, ethical considerations are primarily concerned with the reduction of potential risks associated with a project. For example, Gateway Computers clearly outlines in its corporate code of ethics the increased regulatory and procurement laws with which an employee must be familiar so as to sell to the government. The company points out that knowingly submitting a false claim or statement to a governmental agency could subject Gateway and its employees to significant monetary civil damages, penalties, and even criminal sanctions.

Another way to incorporate nonfinancial considerations into capital project evaluation is to take into account the likely effect of decisions on nonshareholder parties or stakeholders: employees, customers, the local community, and suppliers. Chipotle Mexican Grill's "Food with Integrity" mission is one example. Chipotle's philosophy is that the company "can always do better in terms of the food we buy. And when

we say better, we mean better in every sense of the word—better tasting, coming from better sources, better for the environment, better for the animals, and better for the farmers who raise the animals and grow the produce."[a]

In support of their mission, Chipotle sources meat from animals that are raised humanely, fed a vegetarian diet, and never given antibiotics or hormones. The company favors locally grown produce, organically grown beans, and dairy products made from milk from cows raised in pastures and free of growth hormones. Chipotle's efforts have been rewarded, as sales increased by nearly 50 percent from 2007 to 2009 and by nearly 80 percent from 2009 to 2012. Investors have also profited, as shares that sold for $44 at the company's 2006 initial public offering were priced at over $400 in mid-2013.

▶ *What are the potential risks to a company of unethical behaviors by employees? What are potential risks to the public and to stakeholders?*

[a]www.chipotle.com/html/fwi.aspx.

7. John R. Graham and Campbell R. Harvey, "The Theory and Practice of Corporate Finance: Evidence from the Field," *Journal of Financial Economics* 60 (2001), pp. 187–243.

→ **REVIEW QUESTIONS**

10–12 How is a *net present value profile* used to compare projects? What causes conflicts in the ranking of projects via net present value and internal rate of return?

10–13 Does the assumption concerning the reinvestment of intermediate cash inflow tend to favor NPV or IRR? In practice, which technique is preferred and why?

Summary

FOCUS ON VALUE

The financial manager must apply appropriate decision techniques to assess whether proposed investment projects create value. Net present value (NPV) and internal rate of return (IRR) are the generally preferred capital budgeting techniques. Both use the cost of capital as the required return. The appeal of NPV and IRR stems from both indicating whether a proposed investment creates or destroys shareholder value.

NPV clearly indicates the expected dollar amount of wealth creation from a proposed project, whereas IRR only provides the same accept-or-reject decision as NPV. As a consequence of some fundamental differences, NPV and IRR do not necessarily rank projects in the same way. NPV is the theoretically preferred approach. In practice, however, IRR enjoys widespread use because of its intuitive appeal. Regardless, the application of NPV and IRR to good estimates of relevant cash flows should enable the financial manager to recommend projects that are consistent with the firm's goal of **maximizing shareholder wealth.**

REVIEW OF LEARNING GOALS

LG① **Understand the key elements of the capital budgeting process.** Capital budgeting techniques are the tools used to assess project acceptability and ranking. Applied to each project's relevant cash flows, they indicate which capital expenditures are consistent with the firm's goal of maximizing owners' wealth.

LG② **Calculate, interpret, and evaluate the payback period.** The payback period is the amount of time required for the firm to recover its initial investment, as calculated from cash inflows. Shorter payback periods are preferred. The payback period is relatively easy to calculate, has simple intuitive appeal, considers cash flows, and measures risk exposure. Its weaknesses include lack of linkage to the wealth maximization goal, failure to consider time value explicitly, and that it ignores cash flows that occur after the payback period.

LG③ **Calculate, interpret, and evaluate the net present value (NPV) and economic value added (EVA).** Because it gives explicit consideration to the time value of money, NPV is considered a sophisticated capital budgeting technique.

NPV measures the amount of value created by a given project; only positive NPV projects are acceptable. The rate at which cash flows are discounted in calculating NPV is called the discount rate, required return, cost of capital, or opportunity cost. By whatever name, this rate represents the minimum return that must be earned on a project to leave the firm's market value unchanged. The EVA method begins the same way that NPV does: by calculating a project's net cash flows. However, the EVA approach subtracts from those cash flows a charge that is designed to capture the return that the firm's investors demand on the project. That is, the EVA calculation asks whether a project generates positive cash flows above and beyond what investors demand. If so, the project is worth undertaking.

LG 4 **Calculate, interpret, and evaluate the internal rate of return (IRR).** Like NPV, IRR is a sophisticated capital budgeting technique. IRR is the compound annual rate of return that the firm will earn by investing in a project and receiving the given cash inflows. By accepting only those projects with IRRs in excess of the firm's cost of capital, the firm should enhance its market value and the wealth of its owners. Both NPV and IRR yield the same accept–reject decisions, but they often provide conflicting rankings.

LG 5 **Use net present value profiles to compare NPV and IRR techniques.** A net present value profile is a graph that depicts projects' NPVs for various discount rates. The NPV profile is prepared by developing a number of "discount rate–net present value" coordinates (including discount rates of 0 percent, the cost of capital, and the IRR for each project) and then plotting them on the same set of discount rate–NPV axes.

LG 6 **Discuss NPV and IRR in terms of conflicting rankings and the theoretical and practical strengths of each approach.** Conflicting rankings of projects frequently emerge from NPV and IRR as a result of differences in the reinvestment rate assumption as well as the magnitude and timing of cash flows. NPV assumes reinvestment of intermediate cash inflows at the more conservative cost of capital; IRR assumes reinvestment at the project's IRR. On a purely theoretical basis, NPV is preferred over IRR because NPV assumes the more conservative reinvestment rate and does not exhibit the mathematical problem of multiple IRRs that often occurs when IRRs are calculated for nonconventional cash flows. In practice, the IRR is more commonly used because it is consistent with the general preference of business professionals for rates of return, and corporate financial analysts can identify and resolve problems with the IRR before decision makers use it.

Self-Test Problem (Solutions in Appendix)

  ST10–1 **All techniques with NPV profile: Mutually exclusive projects** Fitch Industries is in the process of choosing the better of two equal-risk, mutually exclusive capital expenditure projects, M and N. The relevant cash flows for each project are shown in the following table. The firm's cost of capital is 14%.

IRF

	Project M	Project N
Initial investment (CF_0)	$28,500	$27,000
Year (t)	Cash inflows (CF_t)	
1	$10,000	$11,000
2	10,000	10,000
3	10,000	9,000
4	10,000	8,000

a. Calculate each project's *payback period*.
b. Calculate the *net present value (NPV)* for each project.
c. Calculate the *internal rate of return (IRR)* for each project.
d. Summarize the preferences dictated by each measure you calculated, and indicate which project you would recommend. Explain why.
e. Draw the *net present value profiles* for these projects on the same set of axes, and explain the circumstances under which a conflict in rankings might exist.

Warm-Up Exercises All problems are available in MyFinanceLab.

LG 2 **E10–1** Elysian Fields, Inc., uses a maximum payback period of 6 years and currently must choose between two mutually exclusive projects. Project Hydrogen requires an initial outlay of $25,000; project Helium requires an initial outlay of $35,000. Using the expected cash inflows given for each project in the following table, calculate each project's *payback period*. Which project meets Elysian's standards?

	Expected cash inflows	
Year	Hydrogen	Helium
1	$6,000	$7,000
2	6,000	7,000
3	8,000	8,000
4	4,000	5,000
5	3,500	5,000
6	2,000	4,000

LG 3 **E10–2** Herky Foods is considering acquisition of a new wrapping machine. The initial investment is estimated at $1.25 million, and the machine will have a 5-year life with no salvage value. Using a 6% discount rate, determine the *net present value (NPV)* of the machine given its expected operating cash inflows shown in the following table. Based on the project's NPV, should Herky make this investment?

Year	Cash inflow
1	$400,000
2	375,000
3	300,000
4	350,000
5	200,000

LG 3 **E10–3** Axis Corp. is considering investment in the best of two mutually exclusive projects. Project Kelvin involves an overhaul of the existing system; it will cost $45,000 and generate cash inflows of $20,000 per year for the next 3 years. Project Thompson involves replacement of the existing system; it will cost $275,000 and generate cash inflows of $60,000 per year for 6 years. Using an 8% cost of capital, calculate each project's NPV, and make a recommendation based on your findings.

LG 4 **E10–4** Billabong Tech uses the *internal rate of return (IRR)* to select projects. Calculate the IRR for each of the following projects and recommend the best project based on this measure. Project T-Shirt requires an initial investment of $15,000 and generates cash inflows of $8,000 per year for 4 years. Project Board Shorts requires an initial investment of $25,000 and produces cash inflows of $12,000 per year for 5 years.

LG 4 **LG 5** **E10–5** Cooper Electronics uses *NPV profiles* to visually evaluate competing projects. Key data for the two projects under consideration are given in the following table. Using these data, graph, on the same set of axes, the NPV profiles for each project using discount rates of 0%, 8%, and the IRR.

	Terra	Firma
Initial investment	$30,000	$25,000
Year	Operating cash inflows	
1	$ 7,000	$6,000
2	10,000	9,000
3	12,000	9,000
4	10,000	8,000

Problems

All problems are available in MyFinanceLab.

LG 2 **P10–1** **Payback period** Jordan Enterprises is considering a capital expenditure that requires an initial investment of $42,000 and returns after-tax cash inflows of $7,000 per year for 10 years. The firm has a maximum acceptable payback period of 8 years.

a. Determine the *payback period* for this project.

b. Should the company accept the project? Why or why not?

LG 2 **P10–2** **Payback comparisons** Nova Products has a 5-year maximum acceptable payback period. The firm is considering the purchase of a new machine and must choose between two alternative ones. The first machine requires an initial investment of $14,000 and generates annual after-tax cash inflows of $3,000 for each of the next 7 years. The second machine requires an initial investment of $21,000 and provides an annual cash inflow after taxes of $4,000 for 20 years.

a. Determine the *payback period* for each machine.
b. Comment on the acceptability of the machines, assuming that they are independent projects.
c. Which machine should the firm accept? Why?
d. Do the machines in this problem illustrate any of the weaknesses of using payback? Discuss.

LG 2 **P10–3** **Choosing between two projects with acceptable payback periods** Shell Camping Gear, Inc., is considering two mutually exclusive projects. Each requires an initial investment of $100,000. John Shell, president of the company, has set a maximum payback period of 4 years. The after-tax cash inflows associated with each project are shown in the following table.

	Cash inflows (CF_t)	
Year	Project A	Project B
1	$10,000	$40,000
2	20,000	30,000
3	30,000	20,000
4	40,000	10,000
5	20,000	20,000

a. Determine the *payback period* of each project.
b. Because they are mutually exclusive, Shell must choose one. Which should the company invest in?
c. Explain why one of the projects is a better choice than the other.

Personal Finance Problem

LG 2 **P10–4** **Long-term investment decision, payback method** Bill Williams has the opportunity to invest in project A that costs $9,000 today and promises to pay annual end-of-year payments of $2,200, $2,500, $2,500, $2,000, and $1,800 over the next 5 years. Or, Bill can invest $9,000 in project B that promises to pay annual end-of-year payments of $1,500, $1,500, $1,500, $3,500, and $4,000 over the next 5 years.

a. How long will it take for Bill to recoup his initial investment in project A?
b. How long will it take for Bill to recoup his initial investment in project B?
c. Using the *payback period*, which project should Bill choose?
d. Do you see any problems with his choice?

LG 3 **P10–5** **NPV** Calculate the *net present value (NPV)* for the following 15-year projects. Comment on the acceptability of each. Assume that the firm has a cost of capital of 9%.

a. Initial investment is $1,000,000; cash inflows are $150,000 per year.
b. Initial investment is $2,500,000; cash inflows are $320,000 per year.
c. Initial investment is $3,000,000; cash inflows are $365,000 per year.

LG 3 **P10–6** **NPV for varying costs of capital** Dane Cosmetics is evaluating a new fragrance-mixing machine. The machine requires an initial investment of $24,000 and will generate after-tax cash inflows of $5,000 per year for 8 years. For each of the costs of capital listed, (1) calculate the *net present value (NPV)*, (2) indicate whether to accept or reject the machine, and (3) explain your decision.
a. The cost of capital is 10%.
b. The cost of capital is 12%.
c. The cost of capital is 14%.

LG 3 **P10–7** **Net present value: Independent projects** Using a 14% cost of capital, calculate the *net present value* for each of the independent projects shown in the following table, and indicate whether each is acceptable.

	Project A	Project B	Project C	Project D	Project E
Initial investment (CF_0)	$26,000	$500,000	$170,000	$950,000	$80,000
Year (*t*)			Cash inflows (CF_t)		
1	$4,000	$100,000	$20,000	$230,000	$ 0
2	4,000	120,000	19,000	230,000	0
3	4,000	140,000	18,000	230,000	0
4	4,000	160,000	17,000	230,000	20,000
5	4,000	180,000	16,000	230,000	30,000
6	4,000	200,000	15,000	230,000	0
7	4,000		14,000	230,000	50,000
8	4,000		13,000	230,000	60,000
9	4,000		12,000		70,000
10	4,000		11,000		

LG 3 **P10–8** **NPV** Simes Innovations, Inc., is negotiating to purchase exclusive rights to manufacture and market a solar-powered toy car. The car's inventor has offered Simes the choice of either a one-time payment of $1,500,000 today or a series of five year-end payments of $385,000.
a. If Simes has a cost of capital of 9%, which form of payment should it choose?
b. What yearly payment would make the two offers identical in value at a cost of capital of 9%?
c. Would your answer to part **a** of this problem be different if the yearly payments were made at the beginning of each year? Show what difference, if any, that change in timing would make to the present value calculation.
d. The after-tax cash inflows associated with this purchase are projected to amount to $250,000 per year for 15 years. Will this factor change the firm's decision about how to fund the initial investment?

LG 3 **P10–9** **NPV and maximum return** A firm can purchase new equipment for a $150,000 initial investment. The equipment generates an annual after-tax cash inflow of $44,400 for 4 years.
a. Determine the *net present value (NPV)* of the equipment, assuming that the firm has a 10% cost of capital. Is the project acceptable?
b. If the firm's cost of capital is lower than 10%, does the investment in equipment become more or less desirable? What is the highest cost of capital (closest whole-percentage rate) that the firm can have and still find that purchasing the equipment is worthwhile? Discuss this finding in light of your response in part **a**.

LG 3   **P10–10**   **NPV: Mutually exclusive projects** Hook Industries is considering the replacement of one of its old drill presses. Three alternative replacement presses are under consideration. The relevant cash flows associated with each are shown in the following table. The firm's cost of capital is 15%.

	Press A	Press B	Press C
Initial investment (CF_0)	$85,000	$60,000	$130,000
Year (t)		Cash inflows (CF_t)	
1	$18,000	$12,000	$50,000
2	18,000	14,000	30,000
3	18,000	16,000	20,000
4	18,000	18,000	20,000
5	18,000	20,000	20,000
6	18,000	25,000	30,000
7	18,000	—	40,000
8	18,000	—	50,000

a. Calculate the *net present value (NPV)* of each press.
b. Using NPV, evaluate the acceptability of each press.
c. Rank the presses from best to worst using NPV.
d. Calculate the *profitability index (PI)* for each press.
e. Rank the presses from best to worst using *PI*.

Personal Finance Problem

LG 3   **P10–11**   **Long-term investment decision, NPV method** Jenny Jenks has researched the financial pros and cons of entering into a 1-year MBA program at her state university. The tuition and books for the master's program will have an up-front cost of $50,000. If she enrolls in an MBA program, Jenny will quit her current job, which pays $50,000 per year after taxes (for simplicity, treat any lost earnings as part of the up-front cost). On average, a person with an MBA degree earns an extra $20,000 per year (after taxes) over a business career of 40 years. Jenny believes that her opportunity cost of capital is 6%. Given her estimates, find the *net present value (NPV)* of entering this MBA program. Are the benefits of further education worth the associated costs?

LG 2 **LG 3**   **P10–12**   **Payback and NPV** Neil Corporation has three projects under consideration. The cash flows for each project are shown in the following table. The firm has a 16% cost of capital.

	Project A	Project B	Project C
Initial investment (CF_0)	$40,000	$40,000	$40,000
Year (t)		Cash inflows (CF_t)	
1	$13,000	$ 7,000	$19,000
2	13,000	10,000	16,000
3	13,000	13,000	13,000
4	13,000	16,000	10,000
5	13,000	19,000	7,000

a. Calculate each project's *payback period*. Which project is preferred according to this method?

b. Calculate each project's *net present value (NPV)*. Which project is preferred according to this method?

c. Comment on your findings in parts **a** and **b,** and recommend the best project. Explain your recommendation.

LG 3 **P10–13** **NPV and EVA** A project costs $2,500,000 up front and will generate cash flows in perpetuity of $240,000. The firm's cost of capital is 9%.

a. Calculate the project's NPV.

b. Calculate the annual EVA in a typical year.

c. Calculate the overall project EVA and compare to your answer in part **a.**

LG 4 **P10–14** **Internal rate of return** For each of the projects shown in the following table, calculate the *internal rate of return (IRR).* Then indicate, for each project, the maximum cost of capital that the firm could have and still find the IRR acceptable.

	Project A	Project B	Project C	Project D
Initial investment (CF_0)	$90,000	$490,000	$20,000	$240,000
Year (t)	Cash inflows (CF_t)			
1	$20,000	$150,000	$7,500	$120,000
2	25,000	150,000	7,500	100,000
3	30,000	150,000	7,500	80,000
4	35,000	150,000	7,500	60,000
5	40,000	—	7,500	—

LG 4 **P10–15** **Internal rate of return** Peace of Mind, Inc. (PMI), sells extended warranties for durable consumer goods such as washing machines and refrigerators. When PMI sells an extended warranty, it receives cash up front from the customer, but later PMI must cover any repair costs that arise. An analyst working for PMI is considering a warranty for a new line of big-screen TVs. A consumer who purchases the 2-year warranty will pay PMI $200. On average, the repair costs that PMI must cover will average $106 for each of the warranty's 2 years. If PMI has a cost of capital of 7%, should it offer this warranty for sale?

LG 4 **P10–16** **IRR: Mutually exclusive projects** Bell Manufacturing is attempting to choose the better of two mutually exclusive projects for expanding the firm's warehouse capacity. The relevant cash flows for the projects are shown in the following table. The firm's cost of capital is 15%.

	Project X	Project Y
Initial investment (CF_0)	$500,000	$325,000
Year (t)	Cash inflows (CF_t)	
1	$100,000	$140,000
2	120,000	120,000
3	150,000	95,000
4	190,000	70,000
5	250,000	50,000

a. Calculate the *IRR* to the nearest whole percent for each of the projects.
b. Assess the acceptability of each project on the basis of the IRRs found in part **a.**
c. Which project, on this basis, is preferred?

Personal Finance Problem

LG 4   **P10–17**   **Long-term investment decision, IRR method** Billy and Mandy Jones have $25,000 to invest. On average, they do not make any investment that will not return at least 7.5% per year. They have been approached with an investment opportunity that requires $25,000 up front and has a payout of $6,000 at the end of each of the next 5 years. Using the *internal rate of return (IRR)* method and their requirements, determine whether Billy and Mandy should undertake the investment.

LG 4   **P10–18**   **IRR, investment life, and cash inflows** Oak Enterprises accepts projects earning more than the firm's 15% cost of capital. Oak is currently considering a 10-year project that provides annual cash inflows of $10,000 and requires an initial investment of $61,450. (*Note:* All amounts are after taxes.)
a. Determine the *IRR* of this project. Is it acceptable?
b. Assuming that the cash inflows continue to be $10,000 per year, how many *additional years* would the flows have to continue to make the project acceptable (that is, to make it have an IRR of 15%)?
c. With the given life, initial investment, and cost of capital, what is the minimum annual cash inflow that the firm should accept?

LG 3 **LG 4**   **P10–19**   **NPV and IRR** Benson Designs has prepared the following estimates for a long-term project it is considering. The initial investment is $18,250, and the project is expected to yield after-tax cash inflows of $4,000 per year for 7 years. The firm has a 10% cost of capital.
a. Determine the *net present value (NPV)* for the project.
b. Determine the *internal rate of return (IRR)* for the project.
c. Would you recommend that the firm accept or reject the project? Explain your answer.

LG 3 **LG 4**   **P10–20**   **NPV, with rankings** Botany Bay, Inc., a maker of casual clothing, is considering four projects. Because of past financial difficulties, the company has a high cost of capital at 15%.

	Project A	Project B	Project C	Project D
Initial investment (CF_0)	$50,000	$100,000	$80,000	$180,000
Year (t)	Cash inflows (CF_t)			
1	$20,000	$35,000	$20,000	$100,000
2	20,000	50,000	40,000	80,000
3	20,000	50,000	60,000	60,000

a. Calculate the *NPV* of each project, using a cost of capital of 15%.
b. Rank acceptable projects by NPV.
c. Calculate the *IRR* of each project, and use it to determine the highest cost of capital at which all the projects would be acceptable.

P10–21 **All techniques, conflicting rankings** Nicholson Roofing Materials, Inc., is considering two mutually exclusive projects, each with an initial investment of $150,000. The company's board of directors has set a maximum 4-year payback requirement and has set its cost of capital at 9%. The cash inflows associated with the two projects are shown in the following table.

	Cash inflows (CF_t)	
Year	Project A	Project B
1	$45,000	$75,000
2	45,000	60,000
3	45,000	30,000
4	45,000	30,000
5	45,000	30,000
6	45,000	30,000

a. Calculate the *payback period* for each project.
b. Calculate the *NPV* of each project at 0%.
c. Calculate the *NPV* of each project at 9%.
d. Derive the *IRR* of each project.
e. Rank the projects by each of the techniques used. Make and justify a recommendation.
f. Go back one more time and calculate the NPV of each project using a cost of capital of 12%. Does the ranking of the two projects change compared to your answer in part **e**? Why?

P10–22 **Payback, NPV, and IRR** Rieger International is attempting to evaluate the feasibility of investing $95,000 in a piece of equipment that has a 5-year life. The firm has estimated the *cash inflows* associated with the proposal as shown in the following table. The firm has a 12% cost of capital.

Year (t)	Cash inflows (CF_t)
1	$20,000
2	25,000
3	30,000
4	35,000
5	40,000

a. Calculate the *payback period* for the proposed investment.
b. Calculate the *net present value (NPV)* for the proposed investment.
c. Calculate the *internal rate of return (IRR)*, rounded to the nearest whole percent, for the proposed investment.
d. Evaluate the acceptability of the proposed investment using NPV and IRR. What recommendation would you make relative to implementation of the project? Why?

P10–23 **NPV, IRR, and NPV profiles** Thomas Company is considering two mutually exclusive projects. The firm, which has a 12% cost of capital, has estimated its cash flows as shown in the following table.

	Project A	Project B
Initial investment (CF_0)	$130,000	$85,000
Year (t)	Cash inflows (CF_t)	
1	$25,000	$40,000
2	35,000	35,000
3	45,000	30,000
4	50,000	10,000
5	55,000	5,000

a. Calculate the *NPV* of each project, and assess its acceptability.
b. Calculate the *IRR* for each project, and assess its acceptability.
c. Draw the *NPV profiles* for both projects on the same set of axes.
d. Evaluate and discuss the rankings of the two projects on the basis of your findings in parts **a**, **b**, and **c**.
e. Explain your findings in part **d** in light of the pattern of cash inflows associated with each project.

   P10–24   **All techniques: Decision among mutually exclusive investments**   Pound Industries is attempting to select the best of three mutually exclusive projects. The initial investment and after-tax cash inflows associated with these projects are shown in the following table.

Cash flows	Project A	Project B	Project C
Initial investment (CF_0)	$60,000	$100,000	$110,000
Cash inflows (CF_t), $t = 1$ to 5	20,000	31,500	32,500

a. Calculate the *payback period* for each project.
b. Calculate the *net present value (NPV)* of each project, assuming that the firm has a cost of capital equal to 13%.
c. Calculate the *internal rate of return (IRR)* for each project.
d. Draw the *net present value profiles* for both projects on the same set of axes, and discuss any conflict in ranking that may exist between NPV and IRR.
e. Summarize the preferences dictated by each measure, and indicate which project you would recommend. Explain why.

     P10–25   **All techniques with NPV profile: Mutually exclusive projects**   Projects A and B, of equal risk, are alternatives for expanding Rosa Company's capacity. The firm's cost of capital is 13%. The cash flows for each project are shown in the following table.
a. Calculate each project's *payback period*.
b. Calculate the *net present value (NPV)* for each project.
c. Calculate the *internal rate of return (IRR)* for each project.
d. Draw the *net present value profiles* for both projects on the same set of axes, and discuss any conflict in ranking that may exist between NPV and IRR.
e. Summarize the preferences dictated by each measure, and indicate which project you would recommend. Explain why.

	Project A	Project B
Initial investment (CF_0)	$80,000	$50,000
Year (t)	Cash inflows (CF_t)	
1	$15,000	$15,000
2	20,000	15,000
3	25,000	15,000
4	30,000	15,000
5	35,000	15,000

 P10–26 **Integrative: Multiple IRRs** Froogle Enterprises is evaluating an unusual investment project. What makes the project unusual is the stream of cash inflows and outflows shown in the following table.

Year	Cash flow
0	$ 200,000
1	−920,000
2	1,582,000
3	−1,205,200
4	343,200

a. Why is it difficult to calculate the *payback period* for this project?
b. Calculate the investment's net present value at each of the following discount rates: 0%, 5%, 10%, 15%, 20%, 25%, 30%, 35%.
c. What does your answer to part **b** tell you about this project's *IRR?*
d. Should Froogle invest in this project if its cost of capital is 5%? What if the cost of capital is 15%?
e. In general, when faced with a project like this one, how should a firm decide whether to invest in the project or reject it?

LG 3 **LG 4** **P10–27** **Integrative: Conflicting Rankings** The High-Flying Growth Company (HFGC) has
LG 5 been growing very rapidly in recent years, making its shareholders rich in the process. The average annual rate of return on the stock in the last few years has been 20%, and HFGC managers believe that 20% is a reasonable figure for the firm's cost of capital. To sustain a high growth rate, HFGC's CEO argues that the company must continue to invest in projects that offer the highest rate of return possible. Two projects are currently under review. The first is an expansion of the firm's production capacity, and the second involves introducing one of the firm's existing products into a new market. Cash flows from each project appear in the following table.
a. Calculate the NPV, IRR, and PI for both projects.
b. Rank the projects based on their NPVs, IRRs, and PIs.
c. Do the rankings in part **b** agree or not? If not, why not?
d. The firm can only afford to undertake one of these investments, and the CEO favors the product introduction because it offers a higher rate of return (that is, a higher IRR) than the plant expansion. What do you think the firm should do? Why?

Year	Plant expansion	Product introduction
0	−$3,500,000	−$500,000
1	1,500,000	250,000
2	2,000,000	350,000
3	2,500,000	375,000
4	2,750,000	425,000

   P10–28 **ETHICS PROBLEM** Diane Dennison is a financial analyst working for a large chain of discount retail stores. Her company is looking at the possibility of replacing the existing fluorescent lights in all of its stores with LED lights. The main advantage of making this switch is that the LED lights are much more efficient and will cost less to operate. In addition, the LED lights last much longer and will have to be replaced after ten years, whereas the existing lights have to be replaced after five years. Of course, making this change will require a large investment to purchase new LED lights and to pay for the labor of switching out tens of thousands of bulbs. Diane plans to use a 10-year horizon to analyze this proposal, figuring that changes to lighting technology will eventually make this investment obsolete.

Diane's friend and coworker, David, has analyzed another energy-saving investment opportunity that involves replacing outdoor lighting with solar-powered fixtures in a few of the company's stores. David also used a 10-year horizon to conduct his analysis. Cash flow forecasts for each project appear below. The company uses a 10% discount rate to analyze capital budgeting proposals.

Year	LED project	Solar project
0	−$4,200,000	−$500,000
1	700,000	60,000
2	700,000	60,000
3	700,000	60,000
4	700,000	60,000
5	1,000,000	60,000
6	700,000	60,000
7	700,000	60,000
8	700,000	60,000
9	700,000	60,000
10	700,000	60,000

a. What is the NPV of each investment? Which investment (if either) should the company undertake?

b. David approaches Diane for a favor. David says that the solar lighting project is a pet project of his boss, and David really wants to get the project approved to curry favor with his boss. He suggests to Diane that they roll their two projects into a single proposal. The cash flows for this combined project would simply equal the sum of the two individual projects. Calculate the NPV of the combined project. Does it appear to be worth doing? Would you recommend investing in the combined project?

c. What is the ethical issue that Diane faces? Is any harm done if she does the favor for David as he asks?

Spreadsheet Exercise

The Drillago Company is involved in searching for locations in which to drill for oil. The firm's current project requires an initial investment of $15 million and has an estimated life of 10 years. The expected future cash inflows for the project are as shown in the following table.

Year	Cash inflows
1	$ 600,000
2	1,000,000
3	1,000,000
4	2,000,000
5	3,000,000
6	3,500,000
7	4,000,000
8	6,000,000
9	8,000,000
10	12,000,000

The firm's current cost of capital is 13%.

TO DO

Create a spreadsheet to answer the following questions.

a. Calculate the project's *net present value (NPV)*. Is the project acceptable under the NPV technique? Explain.
b. Calculate the project's *internal rate of return (IRR)*. Is the project acceptable under the IRR technique? Explain.
c. In this case, did the two methods produce the same results? Generally, is there a preference between the NPV and IRR techniques? Explain.
d. Calculate the *payback period* for the project. If the firm usually accepts projects that have payback periods between 1 and 7 years, is this project acceptable?

MyFinanceLab Visit **www.myfinancelab.com** for **Chapter Case: *Making Norwich Tool's Lathe Investment Decision,*** Group Exercises, and numerous online resources.

11

Capital Budgeting Cash Flows and Risk Refinements

Learning Goals

Why This Chapter Matters to You

In your *professional* life

ACCOUNTING You need to understand capital budgeting cash flows to provide revenue, cost, depreciation, and tax data for use in developing and monitoring project cash flows, and you also need to understand the risk caused by the variability of cash flows.

INFORMATION SYSTEMS You need to understand capital budgeting cash flows to maintain and facilitate the retrieval of cash flow data for projects and also understand how risk is incorporated into capital budgeting techniques so as to design decision modules for use in analyzing proposed capital projects.

MANAGEMENT You need to understand capital budgeting cash flows and behavioral approaches for dealing with risk so that you will understand which cash flows are relevant in making decisions about proposals for acquiring additional production facilities, for new marketing programs, for new products, and for the expansion of existing product lines.

MARKETING You need to understand capital budgeting cash flows and how the risk of proposed projects is measured in capital budgeting so that you can make revenue and cost estimates for proposals for new marketing programs, for new products, and for the expansion of existing product lines.

OPERATIONS You need to understand capital budgeting so that you can make revenue and cost estimates for proposals for the acquisition of new equipment and production facilities. You need to understand that capital budgeting cash flows associated with proposals for the acquisition of new equipment and plants will be evaluated by the firm's decision makers, especially projects that are risky, have unequal lives, may need to be abandoned or slowed, or have limited capital.

In your *personal* life
You are not mandated to provide financial statements prepared using GAAP, so you naturally focus on cash flows. When considering a major outflow of funds (for example, purchase of a house, funding of a college education), you can project the associated cash flows and use these estimates to assess the value and affordability of the assets and any associated future outlays. You should also consider risk in the decision-making process. Failing to incorporate risk into your financial decision-making process will likely result in poor decisions and reduced personal wealth.

11.1 Relevant Cash Flows

relevant cash flows
The *incremental cash outflow (investment) and resulting subsequent inflows* associated with a proposed capital expenditure.

incremental cash flows
The *additional* cash flows—outflows or inflows—expected to result from a proposed capital expenditure.

Chapter 10 introduced the capital budgeting process and the techniques financial managers use for evaluating and selecting long-term investments. To evaluate investment opportunities, financial managers must determine the **relevant cash flows** associated with the project: the *incremental cash outflows (investment) and inflows (return)*. The **incremental cash flows** represent the *additional* cash flows—outflows or inflows—expected to result from a proposed capital expenditure. As noted in Chapter 4, we focus on cash flows rather than accounting figures because cash flows directly affect the firm's ability to pay bills and purchase assets. The *Focus on Ethics* box discusses the accuracy of cash flow estimates and cites one reason even well-estimated deals may not work out as planned.

The remainder of this chapter is devoted to the procedures for measuring the relevant cash flows associated with proposed capital expenditures.

focus on ETHICS

A Question of Accuracy

in practice The process of capital budgeting based on projected cash flows has been a part of the investment decision process for many years. This procedure for evaluating investment opportunities works well when cash flows can be estimated with certainty, but in real-world corporate practice, many investment decisions involve a high degree of uncertainty. The decision is even more complicated when the project under consideration is the acquisition of another company or part of another company.

Because estimates of the cash flows from an investment project involve making assumptions about the future, they may be subject to considerable error. The problem becomes more complicated as the period of time under consideration becomes longer as well as when the project is unique and there are no historical precedents to use in forming cash flow forecasts. Other complications may arise involving accounting for additional (extraordinary) cash flows, such as the cost of litigation,

compliance with tougher environmental standards, or the costs of disposal or recycling of an asset at the completion of the project.

For managers of a firm, undertaking a new, major investment can be exhilarating. All too often, however, the initial champagne celebration gives way once the final cost of a deal is tallied. A large body of research suggests that, on average, mergers and acquisitions do not create much value for the acquiring firms, and, in fact, these deals may harm acquiring shareholders more often than not. Although the financial data necessary to generate discounted cash flow estimates are ever more readily available, more attention is being paid to the accuracy of the numbers. Inspired in part by increased scrutiny from government and the threat of shareholder lawsuits, board members have been pushing corporate managers to make a stronger case for the deals they propose. Says Glenn Gurtcheff, managing director and cohead of middle market M&A for Piper Jaffray & Co., "They're

not just taking the company's audited and unaudited financial statements at face value; they are really diving into the numbers and trying to understand not just their accuracy, but what they mean in terms of trends."

If valuation has improved so much, why do analyses show that the shareholders of acquiring companies often do not benefit from mergers and acquisitions? The answer may be found in the CEO's office. Improvements in valuation techniques can be negated when the process deteriorates into a game of tweaking the numbers to justify a deal the CEO wants to do, regardless of price. This "make it work" form of capital budgeting may result in building the empire under the CEO's control at the expense of the firm's shareholders.

▶ *What would your options be when faced with the demands of an assertive CEO who expects you to "make it work"? Brainstorm several options.*

MAJOR CASH FLOW COMPONENTS

initial investment
The relevant cash outflow for a proposed project at time zero.

operating cash inflows
The incremental after-tax cash inflows resulting from implementation of a project during its life.

terminal cash flow
The after-tax nonoperating cash flow occurring in the final year of a project. It is usually attributable to liquidation of the project.

The cash flows of any project may include three basic components: (1) an initial investment, (2) operating cash flows (which may be inflows or outflows), and (3) terminal cash flow. All projects—whether for expansion, replacement or renewal, or some other purpose—have the first two components. Some, however, lack the final component, terminal cash flow.

Figure 11.1 depicts on a time line the cash flows for a project. The **initial investment** for the proposed project is $50,000, the relevant cash outflow at time zero. The **operating cash flows,** which are the net incremental after-tax cash inflows and outflows resulting from implementation of the project during its life, gradually increase from $4,000 in its first year to $10,000 in its tenth and final year. For the project depicted in Figure 11.1, the net operating cash flows are all positive, but that is not necessarily the case for every investment opportunity. The **terminal cash flow** is the after-tax nonoperating cash flow occurring in the final year of the project. It is usually attributable to liquidation of the project. In this case, it is $25,000, received at the end of the project's 10-year life. Note that the terminal cash flow does *not* include the $10,000 operating cash inflow for year 10.

EXPANSION VERSUS REPLACEMENT DECISIONS

Developing relevant cash flow estimates is most straightforward in the case of *expansion decisions*. In this case, the initial investment, operating cash flows, and terminal cash flow are merely the after-tax cash outflow and inflows associate with the proposed capital expenditure.

Identifying relevant cash flows for *replacement decisions* is more complicated because the firm must identify the *incremental* cash outflows and inflows that would result from the proposed replacement. The initial investment in the case of replacement is the difference between the initial investment needed to acquire the new asset and any after-tax cash inflows or outflows expected from liquidation of the old asset. The operating cash flows are the difference between the operating cash flows from the new asset and those from the old asset. The terminal cash flow is the difference between the after-tax cash flows expected upon termination of the new and the old assets. These relationships are shown in Figure 11.2.

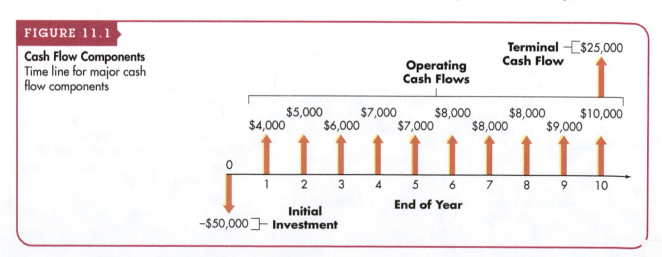

FIGURE 11.1

Cash Flow Components
Time line for major cash flow components

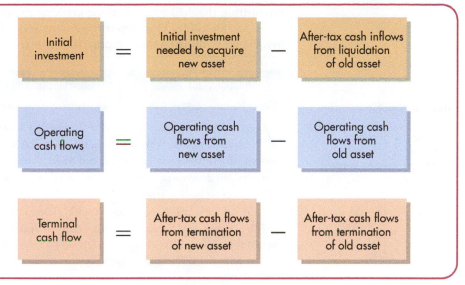

FIGURE 11.2

Relevant Cash Flows for Replacement Decisions Calculation of the three components of relevant cash flows for a replacement decision

Actually, all capital budgeting decisions can be viewed as replacement decisions. *Expansion decisions are merely replacement decisions in which all cash flows from the old asset are zero.* In light of this fact, this chapter focuses primarily on replacement decisions.

SUNK COSTS AND OPPORTUNITY COSTS

sunk costs
Cash outlays that have already been made (past outlays) and therefore have no effect on the cash flows relevant to a current decision.

opportunity costs
Cash flows that could be realized from the best alternative use of an owned asset.

When estimating the relevant cash flows associated with a proposed capital expenditure, the firm must recognize any sunk costs and opportunity costs. These costs are easy to mishandle or ignore, particularly when determining a project's incremental cash flows. **Sunk costs** are cash outlays that have already been made (past outlays) and cannot be recovered. Sunk costs have no effect on the cash flows relevant to the current decision. As a result, *sunk costs should not be included in a project's incremental cash flows.*

Opportunity costs are cash flows that could be realized from the best alternative use of an asset that is already in place. They therefore represent cash flows that *will not be realized* as a result of employing that asset in the proposed project. Thus, any *opportunity costs should be included as cash outflows when one is determining a project's incremental cash flows.*

Example 11.1 ▶

MyFinanceLab Solution
Video

Jankow Equipment is considering renewing its drill press X12, which it purchased 3 years earlier for $237,000, by retrofitting it with the computerized control system from an obsolete piece of equipment it owns. The obsolete equipment could be sold today for $42,000, but without its computerized control system, it would be worth nothing. Jankow is in the process of estimating the labor and materials costs of retrofitting the system to drill press X12 and the benefits expected from the retrofit. The $237,000 cost of drill press X12 is a *sunk cost* because it represents an earlier cash outlay. It *would not be included* as a cash outflow when determining the cash flows relevant to the retrofit decision. On the other hand, if Jankow uses the computerized control system of the obsolete machine, there is an *opportunity cost* of $42,000, which is the cash that Jankow could have received by selling the obsolete equipment in its current condition. By retrofitting the drill press, Jankow gives up the opportunity to sell the old equipment for $42,000. This opportunity cost *would be included* as a cash outflow associated with using the computerized control system.

foreign direct investment (FDI)
The transfer of capital, managerial, and technical assets to a foreign country.

Matter of fact

Who Receives the Most Foreign Direct Investment (FDI)?

According to the U.S. Department of Commerce's Bureau of Economic Analysis (BEA), FDI plays an important role in the U.S. economy. BEA divides FDI into two categories: (1) Greenfield Investment and (2) Mergers and Acquisitions. Greenfield Investments creates new enterprises and develops or expands production facilities. Mergers and Acquisitions involves the purchase of an existing enterprise.

In 2012, the United States was the world's largest recipient of FDI, receiving $174.7 billion in FDI. However, that figure represented a decrease from the record $234 billion in FDI received in 2011. Perhaps not surprisingly, China is not far behind the United States. In fact, for the first half of 2012, more FDI flowed into China than into any other country.

→ **REVIEW QUESTIONS**

11–1 Why is it important to evaluate capital budgeting projects on the basis of *incremental cash flows*?

11–2 What three components of cash flow may exist for a given project? How can expansion decisions be treated as replacement decisions? Explain.

11–3 What effect do *sunk costs* and *opportunity costs* have on a project's i cremental cash flows?

11–4 How can *currency risk* and *political risk* be minimized when one is making *foreign direct investment*?

LG 3 **11.2** Finding the Initial Investment

The term *initial investment* as used here refers to the relevant cash outflows to be considered when evaluating a prospective capital expenditure. Our discussion of capital budgeting will focus on projects with initial investments that occur at *time zero,* the time at which the expenditure is made. The initial investment is calculated by subtracting all cash inflows occurring at time zero from all cash outflows occurring at time zero.

The basic format for determining the initial investment is given in Table 11.1. The cash flows that must be considered when determining the initial investment associated with a capital expenditure are the installed cost of the new asset, the after-tax proceeds (if any) from the sale of an old asset, and the change (if any) in net working capital. Note that if there are no installation costs and the firm is not replacing an existing asset, the cost (purchase price) of the new asset, adjusted for any change in net working capital, is equal to the initial investment.

INSTALLED COST OF NEW ASSET

cost of new asset
The net outflow necessary to acquire a new asset.

As shown in Table 11.1, the installed cost of the new asset is found by adding the cost of the new asset to its installation costs. The **cost of new asset** is the net outflow that its acquisition requires. Usually, we are concerned with the acquisiti

TABLE 11.1	The Basic Format for Determining Initial Investment

(1) Installed cost of new asset =
   Cost of new asset + Installation costs

(2) After-tax proceeds from sale of old asset =
   Proceeds from sale of old asset
   ∓ Tax on sale of old asset

(3) Change in net working capital
   ───────────────────────────────────────
   Initial investment cash flow = (1) − (2) +/− (3)

installation costs
Any added costs that are necessary to place an asset into operation.

installed cost of new asset
The *cost of new asset* plus its *installation costs;* equals the asset's depreciable value.

after-tax proceeds from sale of old asset
The difference between the old asset's sale proceeds and any applicable taxes or tax refunds related to its sale.

proceeds from sale of old asset
The cash inflows, net of any *removal* or *cleanup costs,* resulting from the sale of an existing asset.

tax on sale of old asset
Tax that depends on the relationship between the old asset's sale price and *book value* and on existing government tax rules.

book value
The strict accounting value of an asset, calculated by subtracting its accumulated depreciation from its installed cost.

of a fixed asset for which a definite purchase price is paid. **Installation costs** are any added costs that are necessary to place an asset into operation. The Internal Revenue Service requires the firm to add installation costs to the purchase price of an asset to determine its depreciable value, which is expensed over a period of years. The **installed cost of new asset,** calculated by adding the *cost of new asset* to its *installation costs,* equals its depreciable value.

AFTER-TAX PROCEEDS FROM SALE OF OLD ASSET

Table 11.1 shows that the **after-tax proceeds from sale of old asset** decrease the firm's initial investment in the new asset. These proceeds are the difference between the old asset's sale proceeds and any applicable taxes or tax refunds related to its sale. The **proceeds from sale of old asset** are the net cash inflows it provides. This amount is net of any costs incurred in the process of removing the asset. Included in these *removal costs* are *cleanup costs,* such as those related to removal and disposal of chemical and nuclear wastes. These costs may not be trivial, and in some cases they may outweigh any sale proceeds received from the old asset. In other words, the net proceeds from selling or disposing of the old asset may be positive or negative.

The proceeds from the sale of an old asset are normally subject to some type of tax.[1] This **tax on sale of old asset** depends on the relationship between its sale price and *book value* and on existing government tax rules.

Book Value

The **book value** of an asset is its strict accounting value. It can be calculated by the equation

$$\text{Book value} = \text{Installed cost of asset} - \text{Accumulated depreciation} \qquad (11.1)$$

---

1. A brief discussion of the tax treatment of ordinary and capital gains income was presented in Chapter 2. Because corporate capital gains and ordinary income are taxed at the same rate, for convenience we do not differentiate between them in the following discussions.

Example 11.2 ▶

Hudson Industries, a small electronics company, acquired a machine tool 2 years ago with an installed cost of $100,000. The asset was being depreciated under MACRS using a 5-year recovery period. Table 4.2 (on page 120) shows that under MACRS for a 5-year recovery period, 20% and 32% of the installed cost would be depreciated in years 1 and 2, respectively. In other words, 52% (20% + 32%) of the $100,000 cost, or $52,000 (0.52 × $100,000), would represent the accumulated depreciation at the end of year 2. Substituting into Equation 11.1, we get

$$\text{Book value} = \$100,000 - 52,000 = \underline{\$48,000}$$

The book value of Hudson's asset at the end of year 2 is therefore $48,000.

Basic Tax Rules

Three potential tax situations can occur when a firm sells an asset. These situations depend on the relationship between the asset's sale price and its book value. The two key forms of taxable income and their associated tax treatments are defined and summarized in Table 11.2. The assumed tax rates used throughout this text are noted in the final column. There are three possible tax situations: The asset may be sold (1) for more than its book value, (2) for its book value, or (3) for less than its book value. An example will illustrate.

Example 11.3 ▶

MyFinanceLab Solution Video

The old asset purchased 2 years ago for $100,000 by Hudson Industries has a current book value of $48,000. What will happen if the firm now decides to sell the asset and replace it? The tax consequences depend on the sale price. Figure 11.3 depicts the taxable income resulting from four possible sale prices in light of the asset's initial purchase price of $100,000 and its current book value of $48,000. The taxable consequences of each of these sale prices are described in the following paragraphs.

recaptured depreciation
The portion of an asset's sale price that is above its book value and below its initial purchase price.

The sale of the asset for more than its book value   If Hudson sells the old asset for $110,000, it realizes a gain of $62,000 ($110,000 − $48,000). Technically, this gain is made up of two parts: a capital gain and **recaptured depreciation**, which is the portion of the sale price that is above book value and below the initial purchase price. For Hudson, the capital gain is $10,000 ($110,000 sale price − $100,000 initial purchase price); recaptured depreciation is $52,000 (the $100,000 initial purchase price − $48,000 book value).

TABLE 11.2	Tax Treatment on Sales of Assets		
Form of taxable income	**Definition**	**Tax treatment**	**Assumed tax rate**
Gain on sale of asset	Portion of the sale price that is *greater than* book value.	All gains above book value are taxed as ordinary income.	40%
Loss on sale of asset	Amount by which sale price is *less than* book value.	If the asset is depreciable and used in business, loss is deducted from ordinary income.	40% of loss is a tax savings
		If the asset is *not* depreciable or is *not* used in business, loss is deductible only against capital gains.	40% of loss is a tax savings

FIGURE 11.3

Taxable Income from Sale of Asset
Taxable income from sale of asset at
various sale prices for Hudson Industries

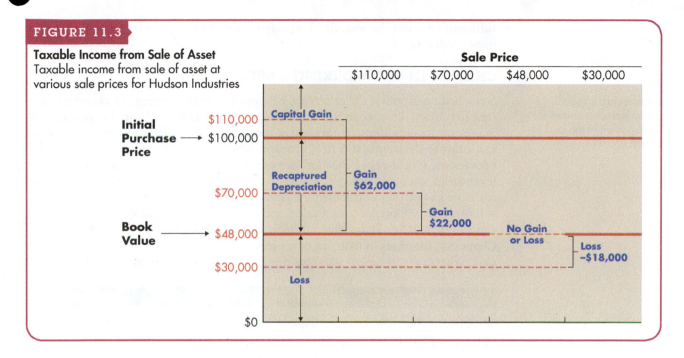

Both the $10,000 capital gain and the $52,000 recaptured depreciation are shown under the $110,000 sale price in Figure 11.3. The total gain above book value of $62,000 is taxed as ordinary income at the 40% rate, resulting in taxes of $24,800 (0.40 × $62,000). These taxes should be used in calculating the initial investment in the new asset, using the format in Table 11.1. In effect, the taxes raise the amount of the firm's initial investment in the new asset by reducing the proceeds from the sale of the old asset.

If Hudson instead sells the old asset for $70,000, it experiences a gain above book value (in the form of *recaptured depreciation*) of $22,000 ($70,000 − $48,000), as shown under the $70,000 sale price in Figure 11.3. This gain is taxed as ordinary income. Because the firm is in the 40% tax bracket, the taxes on the $22,000 gain are $8,800 (0.40 × $22,000). This amount in taxes should be used in calculating the initial investment in the new asset.

The sale of the asset for its book value   If the asset is sold for $48,000, its book value, the firm breaks even. There is no gain or loss, as shown under the $48,000 sale price in Figure 11.3. Because *no tax results from selling an asset for its book value*, there is no tax effect on the initial investment in the new asset.

The sale of the asset for less than its book value   If Hudson sells the asset for $30,000, it experiences a loss of $18,000 ($48,000 − $30,000), as shown under the $30,000 sale price in Figure 11.3. The firm may use the loss to offset ordinary operating income if the asset is a depreciable asset used in the business. If the asset is *not* depreciable or is *not* used in the business, the firm can use the loss only to offset capital gains. In either case, the loss will save the firm $7,200 (0.40 × $18,000) in taxes. And, if current operating earnings or capital gains are not sufficient to offset the loss, the firm may be able to apply these losses to prior or future years' taxes.

CHANGE IN NET WORKING CAPITAL

net working capital
The difference between the firm's current assets and its current liabilities.

Net working capital is the difference between the firm's current assets and its current liabilities. This topic is treated in depth in Chapter 14; at this point, it is important to note that changes in net working capital often accompany capital expenditure decisions. If a firm acquires new machinery to expand its level of operations, it will experience an increase in levels of cash, accounts receivable, inventories, accounts payable, and accruals. These increases result from the need for more cash to support expanded operations, more accounts receivable and inventories to support increased sales, and more accounts payable and accruals to support increased outlays made to meet expanded product demand. As noted in Chapter 4, increases in cash, accounts receivable, and inventories are *outflows of cash*, whereas increases in accounts payable and accruals are *inflows of cash*.

Matter of fact

Europeans Squeeze Working Capital

Because, from a firm's perspective, an increase in working capital is a cash outflow, companies around the world work hard to economize on their working capital requirements. A PWC study of European companies found that working capital was at an all-time low in 2011.[2] According to the study, the companies that were most efficient in their use of working capital had a strong focus on process optimization and worked hard to instill a cash-based culture among their employees. In addition, these companies tended to be early adopters of new technologies, which facilitated reduced working capital needs.

change in net working capital
The difference between a change in current assets and a change in current liabilities.

The difference between the change in current assets and the change in current liabilities is the **change in net working capital.** Generally, when a company makes a major new investment, current assets increase by more than current liabilities, resulting in an increased investment in net working capital. This increased investment in working capital is treated as an initial outflow.[3] If the change in net working capital were negative, it would be shown as an initial inflow. The change in net working capital—regardless of whether it is an increase or a decrease—*is not taxable* because it merely involves a net buildup or net reduction of current accounts.

Example 11.4 ▸

Danson Company, a metal products manufacturer, is contemplating expanding its operations. Financial analysts expect that the changes in current accounts summarized in Table 11.3 will occur and will be maintained over the life of the expansion. Current assets are expected to increase by $22,000, and current liabilities are expected to increase by $9,000, resulting in a $13,000 increase in net working capital. In this case, the change will represent an increased net working capital investment and will be treated as a cash outflow in calculating the initial investment.

---

2. "PWC European Working Capital Annual Review" 2012.
3. When changes in net working capital apply to the initial investment associated with a proposed capital expenditure, they are for convenience assumed to be instantaneous and thereby occurring at time zero. In practice, the change in net working capital will frequently occur over a period of months as the capital expenditure is implemented.

TABLE 11.3	Calculation of Change in Net Working Capital for Danson Company

Current account	Change in balance	
Cash	+ $ 4,000	
Accounts receivable	+ 10,000	
Inventories	+ 8,000	
(1) Current assets		+$22,000
Accounts payable	+ $ 7,000	
Accruals	+ 2,000	
(2) Current liabilities		+ 9,000
Change in net working capital [(1) − (2)]		+$13,000

CALCULATING THE INITIAL INVESTMENT

A variety of tax and other considerations enter into the initial investment calculation. The following example illustrates calculation of the initial investment according to the format in Table 11.1.[4]

Example 11.5 ▶ Powell Corporation, a large, diversified manufacturer of aircraft components, is trying to determine the initial investment required to replace an old machine with a new, more sophisticated model. The proposed machine's purchase price is $380,000, and an additional $20,000 will be necessary to install it. It will be depreciated under MACRS using a 5-year recovery period. The present (old) machine was purchased 3 years ago at a cost of $240,000 and was being depreciated under MACRS using a 5-year recovery period. The firm has found a buyer willing to pay $280,000 for the present machine and to remove it at the buyer's expense. The firm expects that a $35,000 increase in current assets and an $18,000 increase in current liabilities will accompany the replacement; these changes will result in a $17,000 ($35,000 − $18,000) *increase* in net working capital. The firm pays taxes at a rate of 40%.

The only component of the initial investment calculation that is difficult to obtain is taxes. The book value of the present machine can be found by using the depreciation percentages from Table 4.2 (on page 120) of 20%, 32%, and 19% for years 1, 2, and 3, respectively. The resulting *book value* is $240,000 − [(0.20 + 0.32 + 0.19) × $240,000], or $69,600. A *gain* of $210,400 ($280,000 − $69,600) is realized on the sale. The total taxes on the gain are $84,160 (0.40 × $210,400). These taxes must be subtracted from the $280,000 sale price of the present machine to calculate the after-tax proceeds from its sale.

Substituting the relevant amounts into the format in Table 11.1 results in an initial investment of $221,160, which represents the net cash outflow required at time zero.

[4.] Throughout the discussions of capital budgeting, all assets evaluated as candidates for replacement are assumed to be depreciable assets that are directly used in the business, so any losses on the sale of these assets can be applied against ordinary operating income. The decisions are also structured to ensure that the usable life remaining on the old asset is just equal to the life of the new asset; this assumption enables us to avoid the problem of unequal lives at this stage.

Installed cost of proposed machine

Cost of proposed machine	$380,000	
+ Installation costs	20,000	
Total installed cost—proposed (depreciable value)		$400,000
− After-tax proceeds from sale of present machine		
Proceeds from sale of present machine	$280,000	
− Tax on sale of present machine	84,160	
Total after-tax proceeds		195,840
+ Change in net working capital		17,000
Initial investment		$221,160

→ **REVIEW QUESTIONS**

11–5 Explain how each of the following inputs is used to calculate the *initial investment*: (**a**) cost of new asset, (**b**) installation costs, (**c**) proceeds from sale of old asset, (**d**) tax on sale of old asset, and (**e**) change in net working capital.

11–6 How is the *book value* of an asset calculated? What are the two key forms of taxable income?

11–7 What three tax situations may result from the sale of an asset that is being replaced?

11–8 Referring to the basic format for calculating initial investment, explain how a firm would determine the *depreciable value* of the new asset.

LG 3   11.3 Finding the Operating Cash Flows

As the name implies, operating cash flows are the incremental, after-tax cash flows that occur after a new investment is made. In this section, we use the income statement format to clarify what we mean by incremental, after-tax cash flows.

INTERPRETING THE TERM *AFTER-TAX*

Benefits that result from capital expenditures must be measured on an *after-tax basis* because the firm will not have the use of any benefits until it has satisfied the government's tax claims. These claims depend on the firm's taxable income, so deducting taxes *before* making comparisons between proposed investments is necessary for consistency when evaluating capital expenditure alternatives.

INTERPRETING THE TERM *CASH FLOWS*

All costs and benefits expected from a proposed project must be measured on a *cash flow basis*. Cash outflows respresent costs incurred by the firm, and cash inflows represent dollars that can be spent by the firm. Cash flows generally are not equal to accounting profits. One of the main reasons that accounting profits do not equal cash flows is because accounting does not allow firms to fully deduct or expense the cost of fixed assets at the time of purchase. Instead, firms expense a portion of the cost of fixed assets through depreciation deductions over the useful life of the fixed asset. As a result, when a firm pays cash for a fixed asset, the firm's profits will not fully reflect the cost of the asset in the year of purchase. In subsequent years, firms reduce their profits by taking depreciation expenses, even though there are no cash outlays tied to those depreciation charges.

There is a simple technique for converting after-tax net profits into operating cash flows. The calculation requires adding depreciation and any other *noncash charges* (amortization and depletion) deducted as expenses on the firm's income statement back to net profits after taxes. Recognize that depreciation expenses are not actually cash inflows themselves. Adding depreciation to profit simply recognizes that the profit calculation requires firms to deduct an expense that is not tied to a specific cash outlay. In a sense, adding depreciation to profit "corrects" this issue and provides a number that better matches the actual cash inflows and outflows.

Example 11.6 ▸   Powell Corporation's estimates of its revenue and expenses (excluding depreciation and interest), with and without the proposed new machine described in Example 11.5, are given in Table 11.4. Note that both the expected usable life of the proposed machine and the remaining usable life of the present machine are 5 years. The amount to be depreciated with the proposed machine is calculated by summing the purchase price of $380,000 and the installation costs of $20,000. The proposed machine is to be depreciated under MACRS using a 5-year recovery period.[5] The resulting depreciation on this machine for each of the 6 years, as well as the remaining 3 years of depreciation (years 4, 5, and 6) on the present machine, are calculated in Table 11.5.[6]

The *operating cash flows* each year can be calculated by using the income statement format shown in Table 11.6. Note that we exclude interest because we are focusing purely on the "investment decision." The interest is relevant to the "financing decision," which is separately considered. Because we exclude interest expense, "earnings before interest and taxes" (EBIT) is equivalent to "net profits before taxes," and the calculation of "operating cash flow" (OCF) in Table 11.6

TABLE 11.4	Powell Corporation's Revenue and Expenses (Excluding Depreciation and Interest) for Proposed and Present Machines					
	With proposed machine			With present machine		
Year	Revenue (1)	Expenses (excl. depr. and int.) (2)	Year	Revenue (1)	Expenses (excl. depr. and int.) (2)	
1	$2,520,000	$2,300,000	1	$2,200,000	$1,990,000	
2	2,520,000	2,300,000	2	2,300,000	2,110,000	
3	2,520,000	2,300,000	3	2,400,000	2,230,000	
4	2,520,000	2,300,000	4	2,400,000	2,250,000	
5	2,520,000	2,300,000	5	2,250,000	2,120,000	

---

5. As noted in Chapter 4, it takes $n + 1$ years to depreciate an n-year class asset under current tax law. Therefore, MACRS percentages are given for each of 6 years for use in depreciating an asset with a 5-year recovery period.
6. It is important to recognize that although both machines will provide 5 years of use, the proposed new machine will be depreciated over the 6-year period, whereas the present machine, as noted in the preceding example, has been depreciated over 3 years and therefore has remaining only its final 3 years (years 4, 5, and 6) of depreciation (12%, 12%, and 5%, respectively, under MACRS).

TABLE 11.5	Depreciation Expense for Proposed and Present Machines for Powell Corporation		
Year	Cost (1)	Applicable MACRS depreciation percentages (from Table 4.2) (2)	Depreciation [(1) × (2)] (3)
With proposed machine			
1	$400,000	20%	$ 80,000
2	400,000	32	128,000
3	400,000	19	76,000
4	400,000	12	48,000
5	400,000	12	48,000
6	400,000	5	20,000
Totals		100%	$400,000
With present machine			
1	$240,000	12% (year-4 depreciation)	$28,800
2	240,000	12 (year-5 depreciation)	28,800
3	240,000	5 (year-6 depreciation)	12,000
4		Because the present machine is at the end of the third year	0
5		of its cost recovery at the time the analysis is performed, it	0
6		has only the final 3 years of depreciation (as noted above)	0
Total		still applicable.	$69,600[a]

[a]The total $69,600 represents the book value of the present machine at the end of the third year, as calculated in Example 11.5.

is identical to the definition that we provided in Chapter 4 (defined in Equation 4.3, on page 117). Simply stated, the income statement format calculates the OCF.

Substituting the data from Tables 11.4 and 11.5 into this format and assuming a 40% tax rate, we get Table 11.7, which demonstrates the calculation of operating cash flows for each year for both the proposed and the present machine. Because the proposed machine is depreciated over 6 years, the analysis must be performed over the 6-year period to capture fully the tax effect of its year-6 depreciation. The resulting operating cash flows appear in the final row of

TABLE 11.6	Calculation of Operating Cash Flows Using the Income Statement Format

Revenue

$-$ Expenses (excluding depreciation and interest)

Earnings before depreciation, interest, and taxes (EBDIT)

$-$ Depreciation

Earnings before interest and taxes (EBIT)

$-$ Taxes (rate $= T$)

Net operating profit after taxes (NOPAT) $=$ EBIT $\times (1 - T)$

$+$ Depreciation

Operating cash flows (OCF) (same as OCF in Equation 4.3)

TABLE 11.7	Calculation of Operating Cash Flows for Powell Corporation's Proposed and Present Machines					
	Year 1	Year 2	Year 3	Year 4	Year 5	Year 6
With proposed machine						
Revenue[a]	$2,520,000	$2,520,000	$2,520,000	$2,520,000	$2,520,000	$ 0
− Expenses (excluding depreciation and interest)[b]	2,300,000	2,300,000	2,300,000	2,300,000	2,300,000	0
Earnings before depreciation, interest, and taxes	$ 220,000	$ 220,000	$ 220,000	$ 220,000	$ 220,000	$ 0
− Depreciation[c]	80,000	128,000	76,000	48,000	48,000	20,000
Earnings before interest and taxes	$ 140,000	$ 92,000	$ 144,000	$ 172,000	$ 172,000	−$20,000
− Taxes (rate, $T = 40\%$)	56,000	36,800	57,600	68,800	68,800	− 8,000
Net operating profit after taxes	$ 84,000	$ 55,200	$ 86,400	$ 103,200	$ 103,200	−$12,000
+ Depreciation[c]	80,000	128,000	76,000	48,000	48,000	20,000
Operating cash flows	$ 164,000	$ 183,200	$ 162,400	$ 151,200	$ 151,200	$ 8,000
With present machine						
Revenue[a]	$2,200,000	$2,300,000	$2,400,000	$2,400,000	$2,250,000	$ 0
− Expenses (excluding depreciation and interest)[b]	1,990,000	2,110,000	2,230,000	2,250,000	2,120,000	0
Earnings before depreciation, interest, and taxes	$ 210,000	$ 190,000	$ 170,000	$ 150,000	$ 130,000	$ 0
− Depreciation[c]	28,800	28,800	12,000	0	0	0
Earnings before interest and taxes	$ 181,200	$ 161,200	$ 158,000	$ 150,000	$ 130,000	$ 0
− Taxes (rate, $T = 40\%$)	72,480	64,480	63,200	60,000	52,000	0
Net operating profit after taxes	$ 108,720	$ 96,720	$ 94,800	$ 90,000	$ 78,000	$ 0
+ Depreciation[c]	28,800	28,800	12,000	0	0	0
Operating cash flows	$ 137,520	$ 125,520	$ 106,800	$ 90,000	$ 78,000	$ 0

[a]From column 1 of Table 11.4.

[b]From column 2 of Table 11.4.

[c]From column 3 of Table 11.5.

Table 11.7 for each machine. The $8,000 year-6 operating cash inflow for the proposed machine results solely from the tax benefit of its year-6 depreciation deduction.[7]

INTERPRETING THE TERM *INCREMENTAL*

The final step in estimating the operating cash flows for a proposed replacement project is to calculate the *incremental (relevant)* cash flows. Incremental operating cash flows are needed because our concern is *only* with the change in operating cash flows that result from the proposed project. Clearly, if it were an expansion project, the project's cash flows would be the incremental cash flows.

7. Although here we have calculated the year-6 operating cash flow for the proposed machine, this cash flow will later be eliminated as a result of the assumed sale of the machine at the end of year 5.

TABLE 11.8	Incremental (Relevant) Operating Cash Flows for Powell Corporation		

	Operating cash flows		
Year	Proposed machine[a] (1)	Present machine[a] (2)	Incremental (relevant) [(1) − (2)] (3)
1	$164,000	$137,520	$26,480
2	183,200	125,520	57,680
3	162,400	106,800	55,600
4	151,200	90,000	61,200
5	151,200	78,000	73,200
6	8,000	0	8,000

[a]From final row for respective machine in Table 11.7.

Example 11.7 ▶

Table 11.8 demonstrates the calculation of Powell Corporation's *incremental (relevant) operating cash flows* for each year. The estimates of operating cash flows developed in Table 11.7 appear in columns 1 and 2. Column 2 values represent the amount of operating cash flows that Powell Corporation will receive if it does not replace the present machine. If the proposed machine replaces the present machine, the firm's operating cash flows for each year will be those shown in column 1. Subtracting the present machine's operating cash flows from the proposed machine's operating cash flows, we get the incremental operating cash flows for each year, shown in column 3. These cash flows represent the amounts by which each respective year's cash flows will increase as a result of the replacement. For example, in year 1, Powell Corporation's cash flows would increase by $26,480 if the proposed project were undertaken. Clearly, these are the relevant inflows to be considered when evaluating the benefits of making a capital expenditure for the proposed machine.[8]

---

8. The following equation can be used to calculate more directly the incremental cash flow in year t, ICI_t:

$$ICI_t = [\Delta EBDIT_t \times (1 - T)] + (\Delta D_t \times T)$$

where

$\Delta EBDIT_t$ = change in earnings before depreciation, interest, and taxes [revenues − expenses (excl. depr. and int.)] in year t

T = firm's marginal tax rate

ΔD_t = change in depreciation expense in year t

Applying this formula to the Powell Corporation data given in Tables 11.4 and 11.5 for year 3, we get the following values of variables:

$$\Delta EBDIT_3 = (\$2,520,000 - \$2,300,000) - (\$2,400,000 - \$2,230,000)$$
$$= \$220,000 - \$170,000 = \$50,000$$
$$\Delta D_3 = \$76,000 - \$12,000 = \$64,000$$
$$T = 0.40$$

Substituting into the equation yields

$$ICI_3 = [\$50,000 \times (1 - 0.40)] + (\$64,000 \times 0.40)$$
$$= \$30,000 + \$25,600 = \underline{\$55,600}$$

The $55,600 of incremental cash inflow for year 3 is the same value as that calculated for year 3 in column 3 of Table 11.8.

→ **REVIEW QUESTIONS**

11–9 How does depreciation enter into the calculation of operating cash flows? How does the income statement format in Table 11.6 relate to Equation 4.3 (on page 117) for finding operating cash flow (OCF)?

11–10 How are the *incremental (relevant) operating cash flows* that are associated with a replacement decision calculated?

11.4 Finding the Terminal Cash Flow

Terminal cash flow is the cash flow resulting from termination and liquidation of a project at the end of its economic life. It represents the after-tax cash flow, exclusive of operating cash flows, that occurs in the final year of the project. When it applies, this flow can significantly affect the capital expenditure decision. Terminal cash flow can be calculated for replacement projects by using the basic format presented in Table 11.9.

PROCEEDS FROM SALE OF ASSETS

The proceeds from sale of the new and the old asset, often called "salvage value," represent the amount *net of any removal or cleanup costs* expected on termination of the project. For replacement projects, proceeds from both the new asset and the old asset must be considered. For expansion and renewal types of capital expenditures, the proceeds from the old asset are zero. Of course, it is not unusual for the value of an asset to be zero at the termination of a project.

TAXES ON SALE OF ASSETS

When the investment being analyzed involves replacing an old asset with a new one, there are two key elements in finding the terminal cash flow. First, at the end of the project's life, the firm will dispose of the new asset, possibly by selling it, so the after-tax proceeds from selling the new asset represent a cash inflow. However, remember that if the firm had not replaced the old asset, the firm would have received proceeds from sale of the old asset at the end of the project (rather than counting those proceeds up front as part of the initial investment). Therefore, we must count as a cash outflow the after-tax proceeds that the firm would

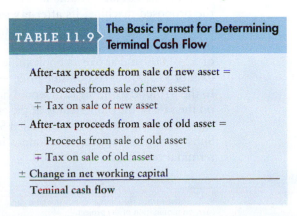

TABLE 11.9	The Basic Format for Determining Terminal Cash Flow

After-tax proceeds from sale of new asset =
   Proceeds from sale of new asset
 ∓ Tax on sale of new asset
− After-tax proceeds from sale of old asset =
   Proceeds from sale of old asset
 ∓ Tax on sale of old asset
± Change in net working capital
  Terminal cash flow

have received from disposal of the old asset. Taxes come into play whenever an asset is sold for a value different from its book value. If the net proceeds from the sale are expected to exceed book value, a tax payment shown as an *outflow* (deduction from sale proceeds) will occur. When the net proceeds from the sale are less than book value, a tax benefit shown as a cash *inflow* (addition to sale proceeds) will result. For assets sold to net exactly book value, no taxes will be due.

CHANGE IN NET WORKING CAPITAL

When we calculated the initial investment, we took into account any change in net working capital that is attributable to the new asset. Now, when we calculate the terminal cash flow, the change in net working capital represents the reversion of any initial net working capital investment. Most often, this will show up as a cash inflow due to the reduction in net working capital; with termination of the project, the need for the increased net working capital investment is assumed to end.[9] Because the net working capital investment is in no way consumed, the amount recovered at termination will equal the amount shown in the calculation of the initial investment. Tax considerations are not involved.

Calculating the terminal cash flow involves the same procedures as those used to find the initial investment. In the following example, the terminal cash flow is calculated for a replacement decision.

Example 11.8 ▶

Continuing with the Powell Corporation example, assume that the firm expects to be able to liquidate the new machine at the end of its 5-year usable life to net $50,000 after paying removal and cleanup costs. Had it not been replaced by th new machine, the old machine would have been liquidated at the end of the 5 years to net $10,000. The firm expects to recover its $17,000 net working capital investment upon termination of the project. The firm pays taxes at a rate of 40%.

From the analysis of the operating cash flows presented earlier, we can see that the proposed (new) machine will have a book value of $20,000 (equal to the year-6 depreciation) at the end of 5 years. The present (old) machine would have been fully depreciated and therefore would have a book value of zero at the end of the 5 years. Because the sale price of $50,000 for the proposed (new) machine is below its initial installed cost of $400,000 but greater than its book value of $20,000, taxes will have to be paid only on the recaptured depreciation of $30,000 ($50,000 sale proceeds − $20,000 book value). Applying the ordinary tax rate of 40% to this $30,000 results in a tax of $12,000 (0.40 × $30,000) on the sale of the proposed machine. Its after-tax sale proceeds would therefore equal $38,000 ($50,000 sale proceeds − $12,000 taxes). Because the old machine would have been sold for $10,000 at termination, which is less than its original purchase price of $240,000 and above its book value of zero, it would have experienced a taxable gain of $10,000 ($10,000 sale price − $0 book value). Applying the 40% tax rate to the $10,000 gain, the firm would have owed a tax of $4,000 (0.40 × $10,000) on the sale of the old machine at the end of year 5. Its after-tax sale proceeds from the old machine would have equaled $6,000 ($10,000 sale price − $4,000 taxes). Substituting the appropriate values into the format in Table 11.9 results in the terminal cash inflow of $49,000.

---

9. As noted earlier, the change in net working capital is for convenience assumed to occur instantaneously, in th case, on termination of the project.

After-tax proceeds from sale of proposed machine

Proceeds from sale of proposed machine	$50,000	
− Tax on sale of proposed machine	12,000	
Total after-tax proceeds: Proposed		$38,000
− **After-tax proceeds from sale of present machine**		
Proceeds from sale of present machine	$10,000	
− Tax on sale of present machine	4,000	
Total after-tax proceeds: Present		6,000
+ **Change in net working capital**		17,000
Terminal cash flow		$49,000

→ **REVIEW QUESTION**

11–11 Explain how the *terminal cash flow* is calculated for replacement projects.

11.5 Risk in Capital Budgeting (Behavioral Approaches)

In our discussion of capital budgeting thus far, we have assumed that a firm's investment projects all have the same risk, which implies that the acceptance of any project would not change the firm's overall risk. In actuality, these assumptions often do not hold: Projects are not equally risky, and the acceptance of a project can increase or decrease the firm's overall risk. We begin this chapter by relaxing these assumptions and focusing on how managers evaluate the risks of different projects. Naturally, we will use many of the risk concepts developed in Chapter 8.

We continue the Bennett Company example from Chapter 10. The relevant cash flows and NPVs for Bennett Company's two mutually exclusive projects—A and B—appear in Table 11.10.

TABLE 11.10	Relevant Cash Flows and NPVs for Bennett Company's Projects	
	Project A	**Project B**
A. Relevant cash flows		
Initial investment	−$42,000	−$45,000
Year	Operating cash inflows	
1	$14,000	$28,000
2	14,000	12,000
3	14,000	10,000
4	14,000	10,000
5	14,000	10,000
B. Decision technique		
NPV @ 10% cost of capital[a]	$11,071	$10,924

[a]From Figure 10.2 on page 376; calculated using a financial calculator.

Managers use *behavioral approaches* for dealing with risk to get a "feel" for a project's risk, whereas other approaches try to quantify and measure that risk. A few widespread behavioral approaches for dealing with risk in capital budgeting include breakeven analysis, scenario analysis, and simulation.

BREAKEVEN ANALYSIS

risk (in capital budgeting)
The uncertainty surrounding the cash flows that a project will generate or, more formally, the degree of variability of cash flows.

In the context of capital budgeting, the term **risk** refers to the uncertainty surrounding the cash flows that a project will generate. More formally, risk in capital budgeting is the degree of variability of cash flows. Projects with a broad range of possible cash flows are more risky than projects that have a narrow range of possible cash flows.

In many projects, risk stems almost entirely from the *cash flows* that a project will generate several years in the future because the initial investment is generally known with relative certainty. The subsequent cash flows, of course, derive from a number of variables related to revenues, expenditures, and taxes. Examples include the level of sales, the cost of raw materials, labor rates, utility costs, and tax rates. We will concentrate on the risk in the cash flows, but remember that this risk actually results from the interaction of these underlying variables. Therefore, to assess the risk of a proposed capital expenditure, the analyst needs to evaluate the probability that the cash inflows will be large enough to produce a positive NPV.

Example 11.9 ▶   Treadwell Tire Company, a tire retailer with a 10% cost of capital, is considerin investing in either of two mutually exclusive projects, A and B. Each requires $10,000 initial investment, and both are expected to provide constant annual cash inflows over their 15-year lives. For either project to be acceptable, its NPV must be greater than zero. In other words, the present value of the annuity (that is, the project's cash inflows) must be greater than the initial cash outflow. If we let CF equal the annual cash inflow and CF_0 equal the initial investment, the following condition must be met for projects with annuity cash inflows, such as A and B, to be acceptable:[10]

breakeven cash inflow
The minimum level of cash inflow necessary for a project to be acceptable, that is, NPV > $0.

$$\text{NPV} = \left(\frac{CF}{r}\right) \times \left[1 - \frac{1}{(1 + r)^n}\right] - CF_0 > \$0 \qquad (11.2)$$

By substituting $r = 10\%$, $n = 15$ years, and $CF_0 = \$10,000$, we can find the **breakeven cash inflow,** the minimum level of cash inflow necessary for Treadwell's projects to be acceptable.

MyFinanceLab Financial Calculator

Calculator use Recognizing that the initial investment (CF_0) is the present value (PV), we can use the calculator inputs shown at the left to find the breakeven cash inflow (CF), which is an ordinary annuity (PMT).

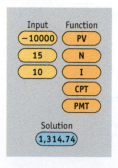

Spreadsheet use The breakeven cash inflow also can be calculated as shown on the following Excel spreadsheet.

_____

10. This equation makes use of the algebraic shortcut for the present value of an annuity.

	A	B
1	BREAKEVEN CASH INFLOW	
2	Cost of capital	10%
3	Number of years	15
4	Initial investment	−$10,000
5	Breakeven cash inflow	$1,314.74

Entry in Cell B5 is =PMT(B2,B3,B4,0,0).
The minus sign appears before the initial
investment in B4 because it is a cash outflow.

The calculator and spreadsheet values indicate that, for the projects to be acceptable, they must have annual cash inflows of at least $1,315. Given this breakeven level of cash inflows, the risk of each project can be assessed by determining the probability that the project's cash inflows will equal or exceed this breakeven level. The various statistical techniques that would determine that probability are covered in more advanced courses.[11] For now, we can simply assume that such a statistical analysis results in the following:

$$\text{Probability of } CF_A > \$1,315 \rightarrow 100\%$$

$$\text{Probability of } CF_B > \$1,315 \rightarrow 65\%$$

Because project A is certain (100% probability) to have a positive net present value, whereas there is only a 65% chance that project B will have a positive NPV, project A seems less risky than project B. Of course, the expected level of annual cash inflow and NPV associated with each project must be evaluated in view of the firm's risk preference before the preferred project is selected.

The example clearly identifies risk as it is related to the chance that a project is acceptable, but it does not address the issue of cash flow variability. Even though project B has a greater chance of loss than project A, it might result in higher potential NPVs. Recall that it is the *combination* of risk and return that determines value. Similarly, the benefit of a capital expenditure and its impact on the firm's value must be viewed in light of both risk and return. The analyst must therefore consider the *variability* of cash inflows and NPVs to assess project risk and return fully.

SCENARIO ANALYSIS

Scenario analysis can be used to deal with project risk to capture the variability of cash inflows and NPVs. *Scenario analysis* is a behavioral approach that uses several possible alternative outcomes (scenarios) to obtain a sense of the variability of returns, measured here by NPV. This technique is often useful in getting a feel for the variability of return in response to changes in a key outcome. In capital budgeting, one of the most common scenario approaches is to estimate the NPVs associated with pessimistic (worst), most likely (expected), and optimistic (best)

---

11. Normal distributions are commonly used to develop the concept of the *probability of success*, that is, of a project having a positive NPV. The reader interested in learning more about this technique should see any second- or MBA-level managerial finance text.

estimates of cash inflow. The *range* can be determined by subtracting the pessimistic-outcome NPV from the optimistic-outcome NPV.

Example 11.10 ▶   Continuing with Treadwell Tire Company, assume that the financial manager created three scenarios for each project: pessimistic, most likely, and optimistic. The cash inflows and resulting NPVs in each case are summarized in Table 11.11. Comparing the ranges of cash inflows ($1,000 for project A and $4,000 for B) and, more important, the ranges of NPVs ($7,606 for project A and $30,424 for B) makes it clear that project A is less risky than project B. Given that both projects have the same most likely NPV of $5,212, the assumed risk-averse decision maker will take project A because it has less risk (smaller NPV range) and no possibility of loss (all NPVs > $0).

TABLE 11.11	Scenario Analysis of Treadwell's Projects A and B	
	Project A	**Project B**
Initial investment	−$10,000	−$10,000
	Annual cash inflows	
Outcome		
Pessimistic	$1,500	$ 0
Most likely	2,000	2,000
Optimistic	2,500	4,000
Range	1,000	4,000
	Net present values[a]	
Outcome		
Pessimistic	$1,409	$10,000
Most likely	5,212	5,212
Optimistic	9,015	20,424
Range	7,606	30,424

[a]These values were calculated by using the corresponding annual cash inflows. A 10% cost of capital and a 15-year life for the annual cash inflows were used.

The widespread availability of computers and spreadsheets has greatly enhanced the use of scenario analysis because technology allows analysts to create a wide range of different scenarios quickly.

SIMULATION

simulation
A statistics-based behavioral approach that applies predetermined probability distributions and random numbers to estimate risky outcomes.

Simulation is a statistics-based behavioral approach that applies predetermined probability distributions to estimate risky outcomes. By tying the various cash flow components together in a mathematical model and then randomly sampling from the range of values that these components might take, the financial manager can develop a probability distribution of project returns.

Figure 11.4 presents a flowchart of the simulation of a project's net present value. Using the probability distributions to randomly generate possible cash inflows and outflows enables the financial manager to calculate one possibl

FIGURE 11.4

NPV Simulation
Flowchart of a net present value simulation

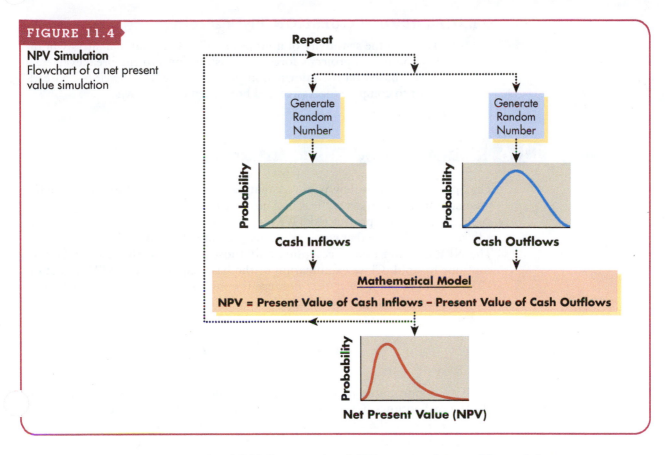

project NPV. By repeating this process perhaps a thousand times, managers can calculate a thousand different NPVs (each one tied to a different combination of cash inflows and outflows). The analyst can then plot a distribution of these NPVs to see not only the range of possible outcomes but also the likelihood of particular outcomes.

Simulations allow analysts to specify probability distributions not just for a project's overall cash inflows and outflow but also for the underlying components that drive these cash flows, such as sales volume, raw materials costs, and wages. Technology allows managers to build highly complex simulations and to obtain results from those simulations very rapidly. The output of simulation provides an excellent basis for decision making because it enables the decision maker to view a continuum of risk–return trade-offs rather than a single-point estimate.

→ **REVIEW QUESTIONS**

11–12 Are most mutually exclusive capital budgeting projects equally risky? If you think about a firm as a portfolio of many different kinds of investments, how can the acceptance of a project change a firm's overall risk?

11–13 Define *risk* in terms of the cash flows from a capital budgeting project. How can determination of the *breakeven cash inflow* be used to gauge project risk?

11–14 Describe how each of the following behavioral approaches can be used to deal with project risk: (**a**) scenario analysis and (**b**) simulation.

→ **EXCEL REVIEW QUESTION** MyFinanceLab

11–15 To judge the sensitivity of a project's NPV, financial managers will often compare a project's forecasted cash inflows to the breakeven cash flows. Based on the information provided at MFL, develop a spreadsheet to compare forecasted and breakeven cash inflows.

LG 5 — 11.6 Risk-Adjusted Discount Rates

The approaches for dealing with risk that have been presented so far enable the financial manager to get a "feel" for project risk. Unfortunately, they do not explicitly recognize project risk. We will now illustrate the most popular risk-adjustment technique that employs the net present value (NPV) decision method. The NPV decision rule of accepting only those projects with NPVs > $0 will continue to hold. Close examination of the basic equation for NPV, Equation 10.1, should make it clear that because the initial investment (CF_0) is known with certainty, a project's risk is embodied in the present value of its cash inflows:

$$NPV = \sum_{t=1}^{n} \frac{CF_t}{(1 + r)^t} - CF_0$$

Two opportunities to adjust the present value of cash inflows for risk exist (1) The cash inflows (CF_t) can be adjusted, or (2) the discount rate (r) can be adjusted. Adjusting the cash inflows is highly subjective, so here we describe the more popular process of adjusting the discount rate. In addition, we consider the portfolio effects of project analysis as well as the practical aspects of the risk-adjusted discount rate.

DETERMINING RISK-ADJUSTED DISCOUNT RATES (RADRS)

A popular approach for risk adjustment involves the use of risk-adjusted discount rates (RADRs). This approach uses Equation 10.1 but employs a risk-adjusted discount rate, as noted in the expression:[12]

$$NPV = \sum_{t=1}^{n} \frac{CF_t}{(1 + RADR)^t} - CF_0 \tag{11.3}$$

risk-adjusted discount rate (RADR)
The rate of return that must be earned on a given project to compensate the firm's owners adequately, that is, to maintain or improve the firm's share price.

The **risk-adjusted discount rate (RADR)** is the rate of return that must be earned on a given project to compensate the firm's owners adequately (that is, to maintain or improve the firm's share price). The higher the risk of a project, the higher the RADR and therefore the lower the net present value for a given stream of cash inflows.

12. The risk-adjusted discount rate approach can be applied in using the internal rate of return as well as the net present value. When the IRR is used, the risk-adjusted discount rate becomes the cutoff rate that must be exceeded by the IRR for the project to be accepted. When NPV is used, the projected cash inflows are merely discounted at the risk-adjusted discount rate.

Personal Finance Example 11.11 ▶ Talor Namtig is considering investing $1,000 in either of two stocks, A or B. She plans to hold the stock for exactly 5 years and expects both stocks to pay $80 in annual end-of-year cash dividends. At the end of year 5, she estimates that stock A can be sold to net $1,200 and stock B can be sold to net $1,500. Talor has carefully researched the two stocks and believes that although stock A has average risk, stock B is considerably riskier. Her research indicates that she should earn an annual return on an average-risk stock of 11%. Because stock B is considerably riskier, she will require a 14% return from it. Talor makes the following calculations to find the risk-adjusted net present values (NPVs) for the two stocks:

$$\text{NPV}_\text{A} = \frac{\$80}{(1 + 0.11)^1} + \frac{\$80}{(1 + 0.11)^2} + \frac{\$80}{(1 + 0.11)^3} + \frac{\$80}{(1 + 0.11)^4}$$
$$+ \frac{\$80}{(1 + 0.11)^5} + \frac{\$1,200}{(1 + 0.11)^5} - \$1,000 = \$7.81$$

$$\text{NPV}_\text{B} = \frac{\$80}{(1 + 0.14)^1} + \frac{\$80}{(1 + 0.14)^2} + \frac{\$80}{(1 + 0.14)^3} + \frac{\$80}{(1 + 0.14)^4}$$
$$+ \frac{\$80}{(1 + 0.14)^5} + \frac{\$1,500}{(1 + 0.14)^5} - \$1,000 = \$53.70$$

Although Talor's calculations indicate that both stock investments are acceptable (NPVs > $0) on a risk-adjusted basis, she should invest in stock B because it has a higher NPV.

Because the logic underlying the use of RADRs is closely linked to the capital asset pricing model (CAPM) developed in Chapter 8, here we review that model and discuss its use in finding RADRs.

Review of CAPM

In Chapter 8, we used the *capital asset pricing model (CAPM)* to link the *relevant* risk and return for all assets traded in *efficient markets*. In the development of the CAPM, the *total risk* of an asset was defined as

Total risk = Nondiversifiable risk + Diversifiable risk   (11.4)

For assets traded in an efficient market, the *diversifiable risk*, which results from uncontrollable or random events, can be eliminated through diversification. The relevant risk is therefore the *nondiversifiable risk*, the risk for which owners of these assets are rewarded. Nondiversifiable risk for securities is commonly measured by using *beta*, which is an index of the degree of movement of an asset's return in response to a change in the market return.

Using beta, β_j, to measure the relevant risk of any asset j, the CAPM is

$$r_j = R_F + [\beta_j \times (r_m - R_F)] \tag{11.5}$$

where

r_j = required return on asset j
R_F = risk-free rate of return
β_j = beta coefficient for asset j
r_m = return on the market portfolio of asset

In Chapter 8, we demonstrated that the required return on any asset could be determined by substituting values of R_F, β_j, and r_m into the CAPM (Equation 11.5). Any security that is expected to earn in excess of its required return would be acceptable, and those that are expected to earn an inferior return would be rejected.

Using CAPM to Find RADRs

If we assume for a moment that real corporate assets such as computers, machine tools, and special-purpose machinery are traded in efficient markets, the CAPM can be redefined as

$$r_{\text{project } j} = R_F + [\beta_{\text{project } j} \times (r_m - R_F)] \tag{11.6}$$

The *security market line* (SML)—the graphical depiction of the CAPM—is shown for Equation 11.6 in Figure 11.5. Any project having an IRR above the SML would be acceptable because its IRR would exceed the required return, r_{project}; any project with an IRR below r_{project} would be rejected. In terms of NPV, any project falling above the SML would have a positive NPV, and any project falling below the SML would have a negative NPV.[13]

FIGURE 11.5

CAPM and SML
CAPM and SML in capital budgeting decision making

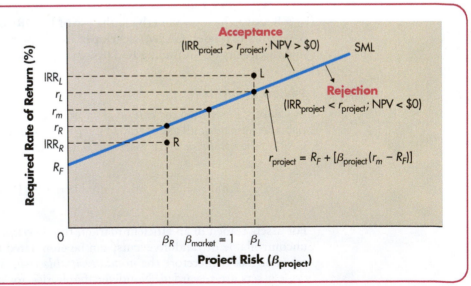

13. Whenever the IRR is above the cost of capital or required return (IRR > r), the NPV is positive, and whenever the IRR is below the cost of capital or required return (IRR < r), the NPV is negative. Because by definition the IRR is the discount rate that causes NPV to equal zero and the IRR and NPV always agree on accept–reject decisions, the relationship noted in Figure 11.5 logically follows.

Example 11.12 ▶

Figure 11.5 shows two projects, L and R. Project L has a beta, b_L, and generates an internal rate of return, IRR_L. The required return for a project with risk b_L is r_L. Because project L generates a return greater than that required ($IRR_L > r_L$), this project is acceptable. Project L will have a positive NPV when its cash inflows are discounted at its required return, r_L. Project R, on the other hand, generates an IRR below that required for its risk, b_R ($IRR_R < r_R$). This project will have a negative NPV when its cash inflows are discounted at its required return, r_R. Project R should be rejected.

APPLYING RADRS

Because the CAPM is based on an assumed efficient market, which does *not* always exist for real corporate (nonfinancial) assets such as plant and equipment, managers sometimes argue that the CAPM is not directly applicable in calculating RADRs. Instead, financial managers sometimes assess the *total risk* of a project and use it to determine the risk-adjusted discount rate (RADR), which can be used in Equation 11.3 to find the NPV.

If a firm fails to incorporate all relevant risks in its decision-making process, it may discount a risky project's cash inflows at too low a rate and accept the project. The firm's market price may drop later as investors recognize that the firm itself has become more risky. Conversely, if the firm discounts a project's cash inflows at too high a rate, it will reject acceptable projects. Eventually, the firm's market price may drop because investors who believe that the firm is being overly conservative will sell their stock, putting downward pressure on the firm's market value.

Unfortunately, there is no formal mechanism for linking *total project risk* to the level of required return. As a result, most firms subjectively determine the RADR by adjusting their existing required return. They adjust it up or down depending on whether the proposed project is more or less risky, respectively, than the average risk of the firm. This CAPM-type of approach provides a "rough estimate" of the project risk and required return because both the project risk measure and the linkage between risk and required return are estimates.

Example 11.13 ▶

Bennett Company wishes to use the risk-adjusted discount rate approach to determine, according to NPV, whether to implement project A or project B. In addition to the data presented in part A of Table 11.10, Bennett's management after much analysis subjectively assigned "risk indexes" of 1.6 to project A and 1.0 to project B. The risk index is merely a numerical scale used to classify project risk: Higher index values are assigned to higher-risk projects and vice versa. The CAPM-type relationship used by the firm to link risk (measured by the risk index) and the required return (RADR) is shown in the following table. Management developed this relationship after analyzing CAPM and the risk–return relationships of the projects that they considered and implemented during the past few years.

Because project A is riskier than project B, its RADR of 14% is greater than project B's 11%. The net present value of each project, calculated using its RADR, is found as shown on the time lines in Figure 11.6 on page 431. The results clearly show that project B is preferable because its risk-adjusted NPV of $9,798 is greater than the $6,063 risk-adjusted NPV for project A. As reflected

	Risk index	Required return (RADR)
	0.0	6% (risk-free rate, RF)
	0.2	7
	0.4	8
	0.6	9
	0.8	10
Project B →	1.0	11
	1.2	12
	1.4	13
Project A →	1.6	14
	1.8	16
	2.0	18

by the NPVs in part B of Table 11.10, if the discount rates were not adjusted for risk, project A would be preferred to project B.

Calculator use We can again use the preprogrammed NPV function in a financial calculator to simplify the NPV calculation. The keystrokes for project A—the annuity—typically are as shown at the left. The keystrokes for project B—the mixed stream—are also shown at the left. The calculated NPVs for projects A and B of $6,063 and $9,798, respectively, agree with those shown in Figure 11.6.

Spreadsheet use Analysis of projects using risk-adjusted discount rates (RADRs) also can be performed as shown on the following Excel spreadsheet.

MyFinanceLab Financial Calculator

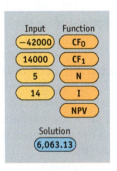

Project A

Project B

	A	B	C	D
1	\multicolumn{4}{c}{ANALYSIS OF PROJECTS USING RISK-ADJUSTED DISCOUNT RATES}
2	Year(s)	Cash Inflow	Present Value	Formulas for Calculated Values in Column C
3		Project A		
4	5	$14,000	$48,063	=−PV(C7,A4,B4,0,0)
5	Initial Investment		−$42,000	
6	Net Present Value		$6,063	=SUM(C4:C5)
7	Required Return (RADR)		14%	
8		Project B		
9	1	$28,000	$25,225	=−PV(C17,A9,0,B9,0)
10	2	$12,000	$9,739	=−PV(C17,A10,0,B10,0)
11	3	$10,000	$7,312	=−PV(C17,A11,0,B11,0)
12	4	$10,000	$6,587	=−PV(C17,A12,0,B12,0)
13	5	$10,000	$5,935	=−PV(C17,A13,0,B13,0)
14	Initial Investment		−$45,000	
15	Net Present Value		$9,798	=SUM(C9:C14)
16	Required Return (RADR)		11%	
17	Choice of project		B	=IF(C6>=C16,"A","B")

The minus signs appear before the entries in Cells C4 and C9:C13 to convert the results to positive values.

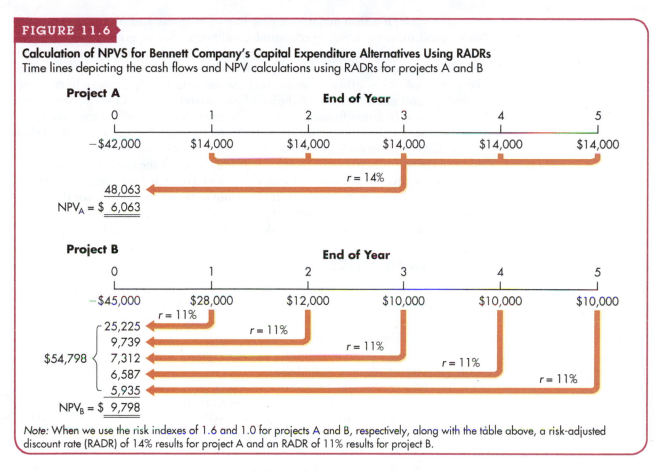

FIGURE 11.6

Calculation of NPVS for Bennett Company's Capital Expenditure Alternatives Using RADRs
Time lines depicting the cash flows and NPV calculations using RADRs for projects A and B

Note: When we use the risk indexes of 1.6 and 1.0 for projects A and B, respectively, along with the table above, a risk-adjusted discount rate (RADR) of 14% results for project A and an RADR of 11% results for project B.

The usefulness of risk-adjusted discount rates should now be clear. The real difficulty lies in estimating project risk and linking it to the required return (RADR).

PORTFOLIO EFFECTS

As noted in Chapter 8, because investors are not rewarded for taking diversifiable risk, they should hold a diversified portfolio of securities to eliminate that risk. Because a business firm can be viewed as a portfolio of assets, is it similarly important that the firm maintain a diversified portfolio of assets?

It seems logical that the firm could reduce the variability of its cash flows by holding a diversified portfolio. By combining two projects with negatively correlated cash inflows, the firm could reduce the combined cash inflow variability and therefore the risk.

Are firms rewarded for diversifying risk in this fashion? If they are, the value of the firm could be enhanced through diversification into other lines of business. Surprisingly, the value of the stock of firms whose shares are traded publicly in an efficient marketplace is generally *not* affected by diversification. In other words, diversification is not normally rewarded and therefore is generally not necessary.

Why are firms not rewarded for diversification? It is because investors themselves can diversify by holding securities in a variety of firms; they do not need the firm to do it for them. And investors can diversify more readily. They can make transactions more easily and at a lower cost because of the greater availability of information and trading mechanisms.

Of course, if a firm acquires a new line of business and its cash flows tend to respond more to changing economic conditions (that is, greater nondiversifiable risk), greater returns would be expected. If, for the additional risk, the firm earned a return in excess of that required (IRR > r), the value of the firm could be enhanced. Also, other benefits, such as increased cash, greater borrowing capacity, and guaranteed availability of raw materials, could result from and therefore justify diversification, despite any immediate impact on cash flow.

Although a strict theoretical view supports the use of a technique that relies on the CAPM framework, the presence of market imperfections causes the market for real corporate assets to be inefficient at least some of the time. The relative inefficiency of this market, coupled with difficulties associated with measurement of nondiversifiable project risk and its relationship to return, tends to favor the use of total risk to evaluate capital budgeting projects. Therefore, the use of *total risk* as an approximation for the relevant risk does have widespread practical appeal.

RADRS IN PRACTICE

Despite the appeal of total risk, *RADRs are often used in practice.* Their popularity stems from two facts: (1) They are consistent with the general disposition of financial decision makers toward rates of return, and (2) they are easily estimated and applied. The first reason is clearly a matter of personal preference, but the second is based on the computational convenience and well-developed procedures involved in the use of RADRs.

In practice, firms often establish a number of *risk classes,* with an RADR assigned to each. Like the CAPM-type risk–return relationship described earlier, management develops the risk classes and RADRs based on both CAPM and the risk–return behaviors of past projects. Each new project is then subjectively placed in the appropriate risk class, and the corresponding RADR is used to evaluate it. This evaluation is sometimes done on a division-by-division basis, in which case each division has its own set of risk classes and associated RADRs, similar to those for Bennett Company in Table 11.12. The use of *divisional costs of capital* and associated risk classes enables a large multidivisional firm to incorporate

TABLE 11.12	Bennett Company's Risk Classes and RADRs	
Risk class	Description	Risk-adjusted discount rate, RADR
I	*Below-average risk:* Projects with low risk. Typically involve routine replacement without renewal of existing activities.	8%
II	*Average risk:* Projects similar to those currently implemented. Typically involve replacement or renewal of existing activities.	10%[a]
III	*Above-average risk:* Projects with higher than normal, but not excessive, risk. Typically involve expansion of existing or similar activities.	14%
IV	*Highest risk:* Projects with very high risk. Typically involve expansion into new or unfamiliar activities.	20%

[a]This RADR is actually the firm's cost of capital, which is discussed in detail in Chapter 9. It represents the firm's required return on its existing portfolio of projects, which is assumed to be unchanged with acceptance of the "average-risk" project.

differing levels of divisional risk into the capital budgeting process and still recognize differences in the levels of individual project risk.

Example 11.14 ▶ Assume that the management of Bennett Company decided to use risk classes to analyze projects and so placed each project in one of four risk classes according to its perceived risk. The classes ranged from I for the lowest-risk projects to IV for the highest-risk projects. Associated with each class was an RADR appropriate to the level of risk of projects in the class as given in Table 11.12. Bennett classified as lower-risk those projects that tend to involve routine replacement or renewal activities; higher-risk projects involve expansion, often into new or unfamiliar activities.

The financial manager of Bennett has assigned project A to class III and project B to class II. The cash flows for project A would be evaluated using a 14% RADR, and project B's would be evaluated using a 10% RADR.[14] The NPV of project A at 14% was calculated in Figure 11.6 to be $6,063, and the NPV for project B at a 10% RADR was shown in Table 11.10 to be $10,924. Clearly, with RADRs based on the use of risk classes, project B is preferred over project A. As noted earlier, this result is contrary to the preferences shown in Table 11.10, where differing risks of projects A and B were not taken into account. ■

→ REVIEW QUESTIONS

11–16 Describe the basic procedures involved in using *risk-adjusted discount rates (RADRs)*. How is this approach related to the *capital asset pricing model (CAPM)*?

11–17 Explain why a firm whose stock is actively traded in the securities markets need not concern itself with diversification. Despite this reason, how is the risk of capital budgeting projects frequently measured? Why?

11–18 How are *risk classes* often used to apply RADRs?

LG 6 | 11.7 Capital Budgeting Refinements

Refinements must often be made in the analysis of capital budgeting projects to accommodate special circumstances. These adjustments permit the relaxation of certain simplifying assumptions presented earlier. Three areas in which special forms of analysis are frequently needed are (1) comparison of mutually exclusive projects having unequal lives, (2) recognition of real options, and (3) capital rationing caused by a binding budget constraint.

COMPARING PROJECTS WITH UNEQUAL LIVES

The financial manager must often select the best of a group of unequal-lived projects. If the projects are independent, the length of the project lives is not critical. But when unequal-lived projects are mutually exclusive, the impact of differing lives must be considered because the projects do not provide service over comparable time periods. This step is especially important when continuing service is needed from the project under consideration. The discussions that follow assume

---

14. Note that the 10 percent RADR for project B using the risk classes in Table 11.12 differs from the 11 percent RADR used in the preceding example for project B. This difference is attributable to the less precise nature of the use of risk classes.

that the unequal-lived, mutually exclusive projects being compared *are ongoing*. If they were not, the project with the highest NPV would be selected.

The Problem

A simple example will demonstrate the general problem of noncomparability caused by the need to select the best of a group of mutually exclusive projects with differing usable lives.

Example 11.15 ▶

The AT Company, a regional cable television company, is evaluating two projects, X and Y. The relevant cash flows for each project are given in the following table. The applicable cost of capital for use in evaluating these equally risky projects is 10%.

	Project X	Project Y
Initial investment	−$70,000	−$85,000
Year	Annual cash inflows	
1	$28,000	$35,000
2	33,000	30,000
3	38,000	25,000
4	—	20,000
5	—	15,000
6	—	10,000

MyFinanceLab Financial Calculator

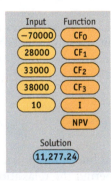

Input	Function
−70000	CF₀
28000	CF₁
33000	CF₂
38000	CF₃
10	I
	NPV

Solution
11,277.24

Project X

Input	Function
−85000	CF₀
35000	CF₁
30000	CF₂
25000	CF₃
20000	CF₄
15000	CF₅
10000	CF₆
10	I
	NPV

Solution
19,013.27

Project Y

Calculator use Employing the preprogrammed NPV function in a financial calculator, we use the keystrokes shown at the left for project X and for project Y to find their respective NPVs of $11,277.24 and $19,013.27.

Spreadsheet use The net present values of two projects with unequal lives also can be compared as shown on the following Excel spreadsheet.

	A	B	C
1	COMPARISON OF NET PRESENT VALUES OF TWO PROJECTS WITH UNEQUAL LIVES		
2		Cost of Capital	10%
3		Year-End Cash Flows	
4	Year	Project X	Project Y
5	0	−$70,000	−$85,000
6	1	$28,000	$35,000
7	2	$33,000	$30,000
8	3	$38,000	$25,000
9	4		$20,000
10	5		$15,000
11	6		$10,000
12	NPV	$11,277.24	$19,013.27
13	Choice of project		Project Y

Entry in Cell B12 is =NPV(C2,B6:B11)+B5.
Copy the entry in Cell B12 to Cell C12.
Entry in Cell C13 is
=IF(B12>C12,B4,IF(C12>B12,C4,"Indifferent")).

Ignoring the differences in project lives, we can see that both projects are acceptable (both NPVs are greater than zero) and that project Y is preferred over project X. If the projects were independent and only one could be accepted, project Y—with the larger NPV—would be preferred. If the projects were mutually exclusive, their differing lives would have to be considered. Project Y provides 3 more years of service than project X.

The analysis in the preceding example is incomplete if the projects are mutually exclusive (which will be our assumption throughout the remaining discussions). To compare these unequal-lived, mutually exclusive projects correctly, we must consider the differing lives in the analysis; an incorrect decision could result from simply using NPV to select the better project. Although a number of approaches are available for dealing with unequal lives, here we present the most efficient technique: the *annualized net present value (ANPV) approach*.

Annualized Net Present Value (ANPV) Approach

annualized net present value (ANPV) approach
An approach to evaluating unequal-lived projects that converts the net present value of unequal-lived, mutually exclusive projects into an equivalent annual amount (in NPV terms).

The **annualized net present value (ANPV) approach**[15] converts the net present value of unequal-lived, mutually exclusive projects into an equivalent annual amount (in NPV terms) that can be used to select the best project.[16] This net present value based approach can be applied to unequal-lived, mutually exclusive projects by using the following steps:

Step 1   Calculate the net present value of each project j, NPV_j, over its life, n_j, using the appropriate cost of capital, r.

Step 2   Convert the NPV_j into an annuity having life n_j. That is, find an annuity that has the same life and the same NPV as the project.

Step 3   Select the project that has the highest ANPV.

Example 11.16 ▶

MyFinanceLab Solution Video

By using the AT Company data presented earlier for projects X and Y, we can apply the three-step ANPV approach as follows:

Step 1   The net present values of projects X and Y discounted at 10%—as calculated in the preceding example for a single purchase of each asset—are

$$NPV_X = \$11,277.24$$
$$NPV_Y = \$19,013.27$$

Step 2   In this step, we want to convert the NPVs from Step 1 into annuities. For project X, we are trying to find the answer to the question, what 3-year annuity (equal to the life of project X) has a present value of $11,277.24 (the NPV of project X)? Likewise, for project Y we want to know what 6-year annuity has a present value of $19,013.27. Once we have these values, we can determine which project, X or Y, delivers a higher annual cash flow on a present value basis.

---

15. This approach is also called the "equivalent annual annuity (EAA)" or the "equivalent annual cost." The term *annualized net present value (ANPV)* is used here due to its descriptive clarity.
16. The theory underlying this as well as other approaches for comparing projects with unequal lives assumes that each project can be replaced in the future for the same initial investment and that each will provide the same expected future cash inflows. Although changing technology and inflation will affect the initial investment and expected cash inflows, the lack of specific attention to them does not detract from the usefulness of this technique.

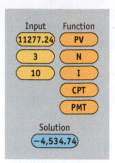

Project X

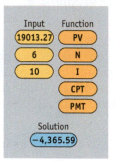

Project Y

Calculator use The keystrokes required to find the ANPV on a financial calculator are identical to those demonstrated in Chapter 5 for finding the annual payments on an installment loan. These keystrokes are shown at the left for project X and for project Y. The resulting ANPVs for projects X and Y are $4,534.74 and $4,365.59, respectively. (Note that the calculator solutions are shown as negative values because the PV inputs were entered as positive values.)

Spreadsheet use The annualized net present values of two projects with unequal lives also can be compared as shown on the following Excel spreadsheet.

	A	B	C
1	COMPARISON OF ANNUALIZED NET PRESENT VALUES OF TWO PROJECTS WITH UNEQUAL LIVES		
2		Cost of Capital	10%
3		Year-End Cash Flows	
4	Year	Project X	Project Y
5	0	−$70,000	−$85,000
6	1	$28,000	$35,000
7	2	$33,000	$30,000
8	3	$38,000	$25,000
9	4		$20,000
10	5		$15,000
11	6		$10,000
12	NPV	$11,277.24	$19,013.27
13	ANPV	$4,534.74	$4,365.59
14	Choice of project		Project X

Entry in Cell B12 is =NPV(C2,B6:B11)+B5.
Copy the entry in Cell B12 to Cell C12.
Entry in Cell B13 is =−PMT(C2,A8,B12,0,0).
Entry in Cell C13 is =−PMT(C2,A11,C12,0,0).
Entry in Cell C14 is
=IF(B13>C13,B4,IF(C13>B13,C4,"Indifferent")).

Step 3 Reviewing the ANPVs calculated in Step 2, we can see that project X would be preferred over project Y. Given that projects X and Y are mutually exclusive, project X would be the recommended project because it provides the higher annualized net present value.

RECOGNIZING REAL OPTIONS

The procedures described in Chapter 10 and thus far in this chapter suggest that to make capital budgeting decisions, we must (1) estimate relevant cash flows, (2) apply an appropriate decision technique such as NPV or IRR to those cash flows, and (3) recognize and adjust the decision technique for project risk. Although this traditional procedure is believed to yield good decisions, a more *strategic approach* to these decisions has emerged in recent years. This more modern view considers any **real options**, opportunities that are embedded in capital projects ("real," rather than financial, asset investments) that enable managers to alter their cash flows and risk in a way that affects project acceptability (NPV). Because these opportunities are more likely to exist in, and be more important to, large "strategic" capital budgeting projects, they are sometimes called *strategic options*.

real options
Opportunities that are embedded in capital projects that enable managers to alter their cash flows and risk in a way that affects project acceptability (NPV). Also called *strategic options*.

TABLE 11.13	Major Types of Real Options
Option type	**Description**
Abandonment option	The option to abandon or terminate a project prior to the end of its planned life. This option allows management to avoid or minimize losses on projects that turn bad. Explicitly recognizing the abandonment option when evaluating a project often increases its NPV.
Flexibility option	The option to incorporate flexibility into the firm's operations, particularly production. It generally includes the opportunity to design the production process to accept multiple inputs, to use flexible production technology to create a variety of outputs by reconfiguring the same plant and equipment, and to purchase and retain excess capacity in capital-intensive industries subject to wide swings in output demand and long lead time in building new capacity from scratch. Recognition of this option embedded in a capital expenditure should increase the NPV of the project.
Growth option	The option to develop follow-on projects, expand markets, expand or retool plants, and so on that would not be possible without implementation of the project that is being evaluated. If a project being considered has the measurable potential to open new doors if successful, recognition of the cash flows from such opportunities should be included in the initial decision process. Growth opportunities embedded in a project often increase the NPV of the project in which they are embedded.
Timing option	The option to determine when various actions with respect to a given project are taken. This option recognizes the firm's opportunity to delay acceptance of a project for one or more periods, to accelerate or slow the process of implementing a project in response to new information, or to shut down a project temporarily in response to changing product market conditions or competition. As in the case of the other types of options, the explicit recognition of timing opportunities can improve the NPV of a project that fails to recognize this option in an investment decision.

Table 11.13 briefly describes some of the more common types of real options—abandonment, flexibility, growth, and timing. It should be clear from their descriptions that each of these types of options could be embedded in a capital budgeting decision and that explicit recognition of them would probably alter the cash flow and risk of a project and change its NPV.

By explicitly recognizing these options when making capital budgeting decisions, managers can make improved, more strategic decisions that consider in advance the economic impact of certain contingent actions on project cash flow and risk. The explicit recognition of real options embedded in capital budgeting projects will cause the project's *strategic NPV* to differ from its *traditional NPV*, as indicated by Equation 11.7.

$$\text{NPV}_{\text{strategic}} = \text{NPV}_{\text{traditional}} + \text{Value of real options} \qquad (11.7)$$

Application of this relationship is illustrated in the following example.

Example 11.17 ▶ Assume that a strategic analysis of Bennett Company's projects A and B (see cash flows and NPVs in Table 11.10) finds no real options embedded in project A and two real options embedded in project B. The two real options in project B are as follows: (1) The project would have, during the first 2 years, some downtime that would result in unused production capacity that could be used to perform contract manufacturing for another firm; and (2) the project's computerized control system could, with some modification, control two other machines, thereby reducing labor cost, without affecting operation of the new project.

Bennett's management estimated the NPV of the contract manufacturing over the 2 years following implementation of project B to be $1,500 and the NPV of the computer control sharing to be $2,000. Management believed that there was a 60% chance that the contract manufacturing option would be exercised and only a 30% chance that the computer control sharing option would be exercised. The combined value of these two real options would be the sum of their expected values:

$$\text{Value of real options for project B} = (0.60 \times \$1,500) + (0.30 \times \$2,000)$$
$$= \$900 + \$600 = \$1,500$$

Substituting the $1,500 real options value along with the traditional NPV of $10,924 for project B (from Table 11.10) into Equation 11.7, we get the strategic NPV for project B:

$$\text{NPV}_{\text{strategic}} = \$10,924 + \$1,500 = \underline{\$12,424}$$

Bennett Company's project B therefore has a strategic NPV of $12,424, which is above its traditional NPV and now exceeds project A's NPV of $11,071. Clearly, recognition of project B's real options improved its NPV (from $10,924 to $12,424) and causes it to be preferred over project A (NPV of $12,424 for B > NPV of $11,071 for A), which has no real options embedded in it.

It is important to realize that the recognition of attractive real options when determining NPV could cause an otherwise unacceptable project ($\text{NPV}_{\text{tradition}} < \$0$) to become acceptable ($\text{NPV}_{\text{strategic}} > \$0$). The failure to recognize the value of real options could therefore cause management to reject projects that are acceptable. Although doing so requires more strategic thinking and analysis, it is important for the financial manager to identify and incorporate real options in the NPV process. The procedures for doing so efficiently are emerging, and the use of the strategic NPV that incorporates real options is expected to become more commonplace in the future.

CAPITAL RATIONING

Firms commonly operate under *capital rationing* in that they have more acceptable independent projects than they can fund. In theory, capital rationing should not exist. Firms should accept all projects that have positive NPVs (or IRRs > the cost of capital). However, in practice, most firms operate under capital rationing. Generally, firms attempt to isolate and select the best acceptable projects subject to a capital expenditure budget set by management. Research has found that management internally imposes capital expenditure constraints to avoid what it deems to be "excessive" levels of new financing, particularly debt. Although failing to fund all acceptable independent projects is theoretically inconsistent with the goal of maximizing owner wealth, here we will discuss capital rationing procedures because they are widely used in practice.

The objective of *capital rationing* is to select the group of projects that provides the *highest overall net present value* and does not require more dollars tha

internal rate of return approach
An approach to capital rationing that involves graphing project IRRs in descending order against the total dollar investment to determine the group of acceptable projects.

investment opportunities schedule (IOS)
The graph that plots project IRRs in descending order against the total dollar investment.

are budgeted. As a prerequisite to capital rationing, the best of any mutually exclusive projects must be chosen and placed in the group of independent projects. Two basic approaches to project selection under capital rationing are discussed here.

Internal Rate of Return Approach

The **internal rate of return approach** involves graphing project IRRs in descending order against the total dollar investment. This graph is called the **investment opportunities schedule (IOS)**. By drawing the cost-of-capital line and then imposing a budget constraint, the financial manager can determine the group of acceptable projects. The problem with this technique is that it does not guarantee the maximum dollar return to the firm. It merely provides an intuitively appealing solution to capital-rationing problems.

Example 11.18 ▸

MyFinanceLab Solution
Video

Tate Company, a fast-growing plastics company, is confronted with six projects competing for its fixed budget of $250,000. The initial investment and IRR for each project are as follows:

Project	Initial investment	IRR
A	− $ 80,000	12%
B	−70,000	20
C	−100,000	16
D	−40,000	8
E	−60,000	15
F	−110,000	11

The firm has a cost of capital of 10%. Figure 11.7 presents the IOS that results from ranking the six projects in descending order on the basis of their IRRs. According to the schedule, only projects B, C, and E should be accepted. Together

FIGURE 11.7

Investment Opportunities Schedule
Investment opportunities schedule (IOS) for Tate Company projects

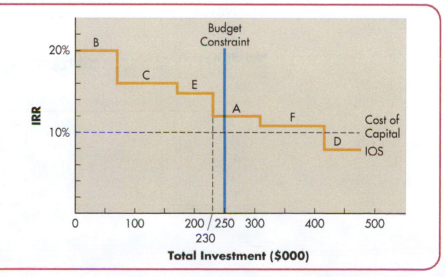

they will absorb $230,000 of the $250,000 budget. Projects A and F are acceptable but cannot be chosen because of the budget constraint. Project D is not worthy of consideration; its IRR is less than the firm's 10% cost of capital.

The drawback of this approach is that there is no guarantee that the acceptance of projects B, C, and E will maximize *total dollar returns* and therefore owners' wealth.

Net Present Value Approach

net present value approach
An approach to capital rationing that is based on the use of present values to determine the group of projects that will maximize owners' wealth.

The **net present value approach** is based on the use of present values to determine the group of projects that will maximize owners' wealth. It is implemented by ranking projects on the basis of IRRs and then evaluating the present value of the benefits from each potential project to determine *the combination of projects with the highest overall present value.* This method is the same as maximizing net present value because the entire budget is viewed as the total initial investment. Any portion of the firm's budget that is not used does not increase the firm's value. At best, the unused money can be invested in marketable securities or returned to the owners in the form of cash dividends. In either case, the wealth of the owners is not likely to be enhanced.

Example 11.19 ►

The projects described in the preceding example are ranked in Table 11.14 on the basis of IRRs. The present value of the cash inflows associated with the projects is also included in the table. Projects B, C, and E, which together require $230,000, yield a present value of $336,000. However, if projects B, C, and A were implemented, the total budget of $250,000 would be used, and the present value of the cash inflows would be $357,000, which is greater than the return expected from selecting the projects on the basis of the highest IRRs. Implementing B, C, and A is preferable because they maximize the present value for the given budget. *The firm's objective is to use its budget to generate the highest present value of inflows.* Assuming that any unused portion of the budget does not gain or lose money, the total NPV for projects B, C, and E would be $106,000 ($336,000 − $230,000), whereas the total NPV for projects B, C, and A would be $107,000 ($357,000 − $250,000). Selection of projects B, C, and A will therefore maximize NPV.

TABLE 11.14	**Rankings for Tate Company Projects**		
Project	Initial investment	IRR	Present value of inflows at 10%
B	−$ 70,000	20%	$112,000
C	−100,000	16	145,000
E	−60,000	15	79,000
A	−80,000	12	100,000
F	−110,000	11	126,500
D	−40,000	8	36,000

Cutoff point (IRR < 10%)

→ **REVIEW QUESTIONS**

11–19 Explain why a mere comparison of the NPVs of unequal-lived, ongoing, mutually exclusive projects is inappropriate. Describe the *annualized net present value (ANPV) approach* for comparing unequal-lived, mutually exclusive projects.

11–20 What are *real options*? What are some major types of real options?

11–21 What is the difference between the *strategic NPV* and the *traditional NPV*? Do they always result in the same accept–reject decisions?

11–22 What is *capital rationing*? In theory, should capital rationing exist? Why does it frequently occur in practice?

11–23 Compare and contrast the *internal rate of return approach* and the *net present value approach* to capital rationing. Which is better? Why?

→ **EXCEL REVIEW QUESTION**   MyFinanceLab

11–24 Comparing projects with unequal lives is often done by comparing the projects' annualized net present value. Based on the information provided at MFL, use a spreadsheet to compare projects based on their ANPV.

Summary

FOCUS ON VALUE

A key responsibility of financial managers is to review and analyze proposed investment decisions to make sure that the firm undertakes only those that contribute positively to the value of the firm. Using a variety of tools and techniques, financial managers estimate the cash flows that a proposed investment will generate and then apply decision techniques to assess the investment's impact on the firm's value. The most difficult and important aspects of the capital budgeting process are developing good estimates of the relevant cash flows and properly refining the process to account for risk.

The relevant cash flows are the incremental after-tax cash flows resulting from a proposed investment. These estimates represent the cash flow benefits that are likely to accrue to the firm as a result of implementing the investment. When evaluating investment cash flows, it is important to remember that not all capital budgeting projects have the same risk as the firm's existing projects. The financial manager must adjust projects for differences in risk when evaluating their acceptability. Without such adjustments, management could mistakenly accept projects that destroy shareholder value or could reject projects that create shareholder value.

Risk-adjusted discount rates (RADRs) provide a mechanism for adjusting the discount rate so that it is consistent with the risk–return preferences of market participants. Procedures for comparing projects with unequal lives, for explicitly recognizing real options embedded in capital projects, and for selecting projects under capital rationing enable the financial manager to refine the capital budgeting process further. These procedures, along with risk-adjustment techniques, should enable the financial manager to make capital budgeting decisions that are consistent with the firm's goal of **maximizing stock price.**

REVIEW OF LEARNING GOALS

LG 1 **Discuss relevant cash flows and the three major cash flow components.** The relevant cash flows for capital budgeting decisions are the incremental cash outflow (investment) and resulting subsequent inflows associated with a proposed capital expenditure. The three major cash flow components of any project can include (1) an initial investment, (2) operating cash inflows, and (3) terminal cash flow. The initial investment occurs at time zero, the operating cash inflows occur during the project life, and the terminal cash flow occurs at the end of the project.

LG 2 **Discuss expansion versus replacement decisions, sunk costs, and opportunity costs.** For replacement decisions, the relevant cash flows are the difference between the cash flows of the new asset and the old asset. Expansion decisions are viewed as replacement decisions in which all cash flows from the old asset are zero. When estimating relevant cash flows, ignore sunk costs and include opportunity costs as cash outflows.

LG 3 **Calculate the initial investment, operating cash inflows, and terminal cash flow associated with a proposed capital expenditure.** The initial investment is the initial outflow required, taking into account the installed cost of the new asset, the after-tax proceeds from the sale of the old asset, and any change in net working capital. The operating cash flows are the incremental after-tax cash flows expected to result from a project. The relevant (incremental) cash flows for a replacement project are the difference between the operating cash flows of the proposed project and those of the present project. The terminal cash flow represents the after-tax cash flow (exclusive of operating cash flows) that is expected from liquidation of a project. It is calculated for replacement projects by finding the difference between the after-tax proceeds from sales of the new and the old asset at termination and adjusting this difference for any change in net working capital.

LG 4 **Understand the importance of recognizing risk in the analysis of capital budgeting projects, and discuss risk and cash flows, scenario analysis, and simulation as behavioral approaches for dealing with risk.** The cash flows associated with capital budgeting projects typically have different levels of risk, and the acceptance of a project generally affects the firm's overall risk. Risk in capital budgeting is the degree of variability of cash flows, which for conventional capital budgeting projects stems almost entirely from net cash flows. Finding the breakeven cash inflow and estimating the probability that it will be realized make up one behavioral approach for assessing capital budgeting risk. Scenario analysis is another behavioral approach for capturing the variability of cash inflows and NPVs. Simulation is a statistically based approach that results in a probability distribution of project returns.

LG 5 **Describe the determination and use of risk-adjusted discount rates (RADRs), portfolio effects, and the practical aspects of RADRs.** The risk of a project whose initial investment is known with certainty is embodied in the present value of its cash inflows, using NPV. There are two opportunities to adjust the present value of cash inflows for risk: (1) adjust the cash inflows or (2) adjust the discount rate. Because adjusting the cash inflows is highly subjective, adjusting discount rates is more popular. RADRs use a market-based adjustment of the discount rate to calculate NPV. The RADR is closely linked to CAPM, but because real corporate assets are generally not traded in an efficient market, the CAPM cannot be applied directly to capital budgeting. Instead, firms develop some CAPM-type relationship to link a project's risk to its required return, which is used as the discount rate. Often, for convenience, firms will rely on total risk as an approximation for relevant risk when estimating required project returns. RADRs are commonly used in practice because decision makers find rates of return easy to estimate and apply.

LG 6 Select the best of a group of unequal-lived, mutually exclusive projects using annualized net present values (ANPVs), and explain the role of real options and the objective and procedures for selecting projects under capital rationing. The ANPV approach is the most efficient method of comparing ongoing, mutually exclusive projects that have unequal usable lives. It converts the NPV of each unequal-lived project into an equivalent annual amount, its ANPV. Real options are opportunities that are embedded in capital projects and that allow managers to alter their cash flow and risk in a way that affects project acceptability (NPV). By explicitly recognizing real options, the financial manager can find a project's strategic NPV. Capital rationing exists when firms have more acceptable independent projects than they can fund. Capital rationing commonly occurs in practice. Its objective is to select from all acceptable projects the group that provides the highest overall net present value and does not require more dollars than are budgeted. The two basic approaches for choosing projects under capital rationing are the internal rate of return approach and the net present value approach.

Self-Test Problems (Solutions in Appendix)

LG 3 **ST11–1** **Determining relevant cash flows** A machine currently in use was originally purchased 2 years ago for $40,000. The machine is being depreciated under MACRS using a 5-year recovery period; it has 3 years of usable life remaining. The current machine can be sold today to net $42,000 after removal and cleanup costs. A new machine, using a 3-year MACRS recovery period, can be purchased at a price of $140,000. It requires $10,000 to install and has a 3-year usable life. If the new machine is acquired, the investment in accounts receivable will be expected to rise by $10,000, the inventory investment will increase by $25,000, and accounts payable will increase by $15,000. *Earnings before depreciation, interest, and taxes* are expected to be $70,000 for each of the next 3 years with the old machine and to be $120,000 in the first year and $130,000 in the second and third years with the new machine. At the end of 3 years, the market value of the old machine will equal zero, but the new machine could be sold to net $35,000 before taxes. The firm is subject to a 40% tax rate. (Table 4.2 on page 112 contains the applicable MACRS depreciation percentages.)

a. Determine the *initial investment* associated with the proposed replacement decision.

b. Calculate the *incremental operating cash flows* for years 1 to 4 associated with the proposed replacement. (*Note:* Only depreciation cash flows must be considered in year 4.)

c. Calculate the *terminal cash flow* associated with the proposed replacement decision. (*Note:* This decision is made at the end of year 3.)

d. Depict on a time line the relevant cash flows found in parts **a, b,** and **c** that are associated with the proposed replacement decision, assuming that it is terminated at the end of year 3.

 ST11–2 Risk-adjusted discount rates CBA Company is considering two mutually exclusive projects, A and B. The following table shows the CAPM-type relationship between a risk index and the required return (RADR) applicable to CBA Company.

Risk index	Required return (RADR)
0.0	7.0% (risk-free rate, R_F)
0.2	8.0
0.4	9.0
0.6	10.0
0.8	11.0
1.0	12.0
1.2	13.0
1.4	14.0
1.6	15.0
1.8	16.0
2.0	17.0

Project data are as follows:

	Project A	Project B
Initial investment (CF_0)	−$15,000	−$20,000
Project life	3 years	3 years
Annual cash inflow (CF)	$7,000	$10,000
Risk index	0.4	1.8

a. Ignoring any differences in risk and assuming that the firm's cost of capital is 10%, calculate the *net present value (NPV)* of each project.

b. Use NPV to evaluate the projects, using *risk-adjusted discount rates (RADRs)* to account for risk.

c. Compare, contrast, and explain your findings in parts **a** and **b.**

Warm-Up Exercises
All problems are available in MyFinanceLab.

 E11–1 Iridium Corp. has spent $3.5 billion over the past decade developing a satellite-based telecommunication system. It is currently trying to decide whether to spend an additional $350 million on the project. The firm expects that this outlay will finish the project and will generate cash flow of $15 million per year over the next 5 years. A competitor has offered $450 million for the satellites already in orbit. Classify the firm's outlays as *sunk costs* or *opportunity costs*, and specify the *relevant cash flows.*

LG 3   **E11–2**   Canvas Reproductions, Inc., has spent $4,500 dollars researching a new project. The project requires $20,000 worth of new machinery, which would cost $3,000 to install. The company would realize $4,500 in after-tax proceeds from the sale of old machinery. If Canvas's working capital is unaffected by this project, what is the initial investment amount for this project?

LG 3   **E11–3**   A few years ago, Largo Industries implemented an inventory auditing system at an installed cost of $175,000. Since then, it has taken depreciation deductions totaling $124,250. What is the system's current *book value*? If Largo sold the system for $110,000, how much *recaptured depreciation* would result?

LG 4   **E11–4**   Birkenstock is considering an investment in a nylon-knitting machine. The machine requires an initial investment of $25,000, has a 5-year life, and has no residual value at the end of the 5 years. The company's cost of capital is 12%. Known with less certainty are the actual after-tax cash inflows for each of the 5 years. The company has estimated expected cash inflows for three scenarios: pessimistic, most likely, and optimistic. These expected cash inflows are listed in the following table. Calculate the range for the NPV given each scenario.

	Expected cash inflows		
Year	Pessimistic	Most likely	Optimistic
1	$5,500	$ 8,000	$10,500
2	6,000	9,000	12,000
3	7,500	10,500	14,500
4	6,500	9,500	11,500
5	4,500	6,500	7,500

LG 5   **E11–5**   Like most firms in its industry, Yeastime Bakeries uses a subjective risk assessment tool of its own design. The tool is a simple index by which projects are ranked by level of perceived risk on a scale of 0 to 10. The scale is recreated in the following table.

Risk index	Required return
0	4.0% (current risk-free rate)
1	4.5
2	5.0
3	5.5
4	6.0
5	6.5 (current IRR)
6	7.0
7	7.5
8	8.0
9	8.5
10	9.0

The firm is analyzing two projects based on their RADRs. Project Sourdough requires an initial investment of $12,500 and is assigned a risk index of 6. Project Greek Salad requires an initial investment of $7,500 and is assigned a risk index of 8. The two projects have 7-year lives. Sourdough is projected to generate cash inflows of $5,500 per year. Greek Salad is projected to generate cash inflows of $4,000 per year. Use each project's RADR to select the better project.

   E11–6   Outcast, Inc., has hired you to advise the firm on a capital budgeting issue involving two unequal-lived, mutually exclusive projects, M and N. The cash flows for each project are presented in the following table. Calculate the NPV and the *annualized net present value (ANPV)* for each project using the firm's cost of capital of 8%. Which project would you recommend?

	Project M	Project N
Initial investment	−$35,000	−$55,000
Year	Cash inflows	
1	$12,000	$18,000
2	25,000	15,000
3	30,000	25,000
4	—	10,000
5	—	8,000
6	—	5,000
7	—	5,000

Problems   All problems are available in MyFinanceLab.

P11–1   **Relevant cash flow and timeline depiction**   For each of the following projects, determine the *relevant cash flows,* and depict the cash flows on a time line.
a. A project that requires an initial investment of $120,000 and will generate annual operating cash inflows of $25,000 for the next 18 years. In each of the 18 years, maintenance of the project will require a $5,000 cash outflow.
b. A new machine with an installed cost of $85,000. Sale of the old machine will yield $30,000 after taxes. Operating cash inflows generated by the replacement will exceed the operating cash inflows of the old machine by $20,000 in each year of a 6-year period. At the end of year 6, liquidation of the new machine will yield $20,000 after taxes, which is $10,000 greater than the after-tax proceeds expected from the old machine had it been retained and liquidated at the end of year 6.
c. An asset that requires an initial investment of $2 million and will yield annual operating cash inflows of $300,000 for each of the next 10 years. Operating cash outlays will be $20,000 for each year except year 6, when an overhaul requiring an additional cash outlay of $500,000 will be required. The asset's liquidation value at the end of year 10 is expected to be zero.

P11–2   **Expansion versus replacement cash flows**   Edison Systems has estimated the cash flows over the 5-year lives for two projects, A and B. These cash flows are summarized in the table below.

	Project A	Project B
Initial investment	$40,000	$12,000[a]
Year	Operating cash inflows	
1	$10,000	$ 6,000
2	12,000	6,000
3	14,000	6,000
4	16,000	6,000
5	10,000	6,000

[a]After-tax cash inflow expected from liquidation.

   a. If project A were actually a *replacement* for project B and the $12,000 initial investment shown for project B were the after-tax cash inflow expected from liquidating it, what would be the *relevant cash flows* for this replacement decision?
   b. How can an *expansion decision* such as project A be viewed as a special form of a replacement decision? Explain.

 P11–3   **Sunk costs and opportunity costs**   Masters Golf Products, Inc., spent 3 years and $1,000,000 to develop its new line of club heads to replace a line that is becoming obsolete. To begin manufacturing them, the company will have to invest $1,800,000 in new equipment. The new clubs are expected to generate an increase in operating cash inflows of $750,000 per year for the next 10 years. The company has determined that the existing line could be sold to a competitor for $250,000.
   a. How should the $1,000,000 in development costs be classified?
   b. How should the $250,000 sale price for the existing line be classified?
   c. Depict all the known relevant cash flows on a time line.

 P11–4   **Sunk costs and opportunity costs**   Covol Industries is developing the relevant cash flows associated with the proposed replacement of an existing machine tool with a new, technologically advanced one. Given the following costs related to the proposed project, explain whether each would be treated as a *sunk cost* or an *opportunity cost* in developing the relevant cash flows associated with the proposed replacement decision.
   a. Covol would be able to use the same tooling, which had a book value of $40,000, on the new machine tool as it had used on the old one.
   b. Covol would be able to use its existing computer system to develop programs for operating the new machine tool. The old machine tool did not require these programs. Although the firm's computer has excess capacity available, the capacity could be leased to another firm for an annual fee of $17,000.
   c. Covol would have to obtain additional floor space to accommodate the larger new machine tool. The space that would be used is currently being leased to another company for $10,000 per year.
   d. Covol would use a small storage facility to store the increased output of the new machine tool. The storage facility was built by Covol 3 years earlier at a cost of $120,000. Because of its unique configuration and location, it is currently of no use to either Covol or any other firm.

e. Covol would retain an existing overhead crane, which it had planned to sell for its $180,000 market value. Although the crane was not needed with the old machine tool, it would be used to position raw materials on the new machine tool.

Personal Finance Problem

LG 2   **P11–5**   **Sunk and opportunity cash flows**   Dave and Ann Stone have been living at their present home for the past 6 years. During that time, they have replaced the water heater for $375, have replaced the dishwasher for $599, and have had to make miscellaneous repair and maintenance expenditures of approximately $1,500. They have decided to move out and rent the house for $975 per month. Newspaper advertising will cost $75. Dave and Ann intend to paint the interior of the home and power-wash the exterior. They estimate that that will run about $900.

The house should be ready to rent after that. In reviewing the financial situation, Dave views all the expenditures as being relevant, so he plans to net out the estimated expenditures discussed above from the rental income.

a. Do Dave and Ann understand the difference between *sunk costs* and *opportunity costs*? Explain the two concepts to them.

b. Which of the expenditures should be classified as sunk cash flows, and which should be viewed as opportunity cash flows?

LG 3   **P11–6**   **Book value**   Find the book value for each of the assets shown in the accompanying table, assuming that MACRS depreciation is being used. See Table 4.2 on page 112 for the applicable depreciation percentages.

Asset	Installed cost	Recovery period (years)	Elapsed time since purchase (years)
A	$ 950,000	5	3
B	40,000	3	1
C	96,000	5	4
D	350,000	5	1
E	1,500,000	7	5

LG 4   **P11–7**   **Change in net working capital calculation**   Samuels Manufacturing is considering the purchase of a new machine to replace one it believes is obsolete. The firm has total current assets of $920,000 and total current liabilities of $640,000. As a result of the proposed replacement, the following *changes* are anticipated in the levels of the current asset and current liability accounts noted.

Account	Change
Accruals	+$ 40,000
Marketable securities	0
Inventories	− 10,000
Accounts payable	+ 90,000
Notes payable	0
Accounts receivable	+ 150,000
Cash	+ 15,000

a. Using the information given, calculate any *change in net working capital* that is expected to result from the proposed replacement action.

b. Explain why a change in these current accounts would be relevant in determining the *initial investment* for the proposed capital expenditure.

c. Would the change in net working capital enter into any of the other cash flow components that make up the relevant cash flows? Explain.

LG 3   **P11–8**   **Calculating initial investment** Vastine Medical, Inc., is considering replacing its existing computer system, which was purchased 2 years ago at a cost of $325,000. The system can be sold today for $200,000. It is being depreciated using MACRS and a 5-year recovery period (see Table 4.2, page 112). A new computer system will cost $500,000 to purchase and install. Replacement of the computer system would not involve any change in net working capital. Assume a 40% tax rate.

a. Calculate the *book value* of the existing computer system.

b. Calculate the after-tax proceeds of its sale for $200,000.

c. Calculate the *initial investment* associated with the replacement project.

LG 3   **P11–9**   **Initial investment at various sale prices** Edwards Manufacturing Company (EMC) is considering replacing one machine with another. The old machine was purchased 3 years ago for an installed cost of $10,000. The firm is depreciating the machine under MACRS, using a 5-year recovery period. (See Table 4.2 on page 112 for the applicable depreciation percentages.) The new machine costs $24,000 and requires $2,000 in installation costs. The firm is subject to a 40% tax rate. In each of the following cases, calculate the *initial investment* for the replacement.

a. EMC sells the old machine for $11,000.

b. EMC sells the old machine for $7,000.

c. EMC sells the old machine for $2,900.

d. EMC sells the old machine for $1,500.

LG 3   **P11–10**   **Calculating initial investment** DuPree Coffee Roasters, Inc., wishes to expand and modernize its facilities. The installed cost of a proposed computer-controlled automatic-feed roaster will be $130,000. The firm has a chance to sell its 4-year-old roaster for $35,000. The existing roaster originally cost $60,000 and was being depreciated using MACRS and a 7-year recovery period. (See Table 4.2 on page 112 for the applicable depreciation percentages.) DuPree is subject to a 40% tax rate.

a. What is the *book value* of the existing roaster?

b. Calculate the after-tax proceeds of the sale of the existing roaster.

c. Calculate the *change in net working capital* using the figures given in the following table.

Anticipated Changes in Current Assets and Current Liabilities	
Accruals	−$20,000
Inventory	+ 50,000
Accounts payable	+ 40,000
Accounts receivable	+ 70,000
Cash	0
Notes payable	+ 15,000

d. Calculate the *initial investment* associated with the proposed new roaster.

LG 3 **P11–11** **Incremental operating cash inflows** A firm is considering renewing its equipment to meet increased demand for its product. The cost of equipment modifications is $1.9 million plus $100,000 in installation costs. The firm will depreciate the equipment modifications under MACRS, using a 5-year recovery period. (See Table 4.2 on page 112 for the applicable depreciation percentages.) Additional sales revenue from the renewal should amount to $1,200,000 per year, and additional operating expenses and other costs (excluding depreciation and interest) will amount to 40% of the additional sales. The firm is subject to a tax rate of 40%. (*Note:* Answer the following questions for each of the next 6 *years.*)

a. What incremental earnings before depreciation, interest, and taxes will result from the renewal?
b. What incremental net operating profits after taxes will result from the renewal?
c. What *incremental operating cash flows* will result from the renewal?

Personal Finance Problem

LG 3 **P11–12** **Incremental operating cash flows** Richard and Linda Thomson operate a local lawn maintenance service for commercial and residential property. They have been using a John Deere riding mower for the past several years and believe that it is time to buy a new one. They would like to know the incremental (relevant) cash flows associated with the replacement of the old riding mower. The following data are available:

There are 5 years of remaining useful life on the old mower.

The old mower has a zero book value.

The new mower is expected to last 5 years.

The Thomsons will follow a 5-year MACRS recovery period for the new mower.

Depreciable value of the new mower is $1,800.

They are subject to a 40% tax rate.

The new mower is expected to be more fuel efficient, maneuverable, and durable than previous models and can result in reduced operating expenses of $500 per year.

The Thomsons will buy a maintenance contract that calls for annual payments of $120.

Create an *incremental operating cash flow* statement for the replacement of Richard and Linda's John Deere riding mower. Show the incremental operating cash flow for the next 6 years.

LG 3 **P11–13** **Incremental operating cash flows** Strong Tool Company has been considering purchasing a new lathe to replace a fully depreciated lathe that will last 5 more years. The new lathe is expected to have a 5-year life and depreciation charges of $2,000 in year 1; $3,200 in year 2; $1,900 in year 3; $1,200 in both year 4 and year 5; and $500 in year 6. The firm estimates the revenues and expenses (excluding depreciation and interest) for the new and the old lathes to be as shown in the table at the top of next page. The firm is subject to a 40% tax rate.

a. Calculate the *operating cash flows* associated with each lathe. (*Note:* Be sure to consider the depreciation in year 6.)
b. Calculate the *incremental (relevant) operating cash flows* resulting from the proposed lathe replacement.
c. Depict on a time line the incremental operating cash flows calculated in part **b.**

	New lathe		Old lathe	
Year	Revenue	Expenses (excluding depreciation and interest)	Revenue	Expenses (excluding depreciation and interest)
1	$40,000	$30,000	$35,000	$25,000
2	41,000	30,000	35,000	25,000
3	42,000	30,000	35,000	25,000
4	43,000	30,000	35,000	25,000
5	44,000	30,000	35,000	25,000

LG 3   **P11–14**   **Terminal cash flow: Various lives and sale prices** Looner Industries is currently analyzing the purchase of a new machine that costs $160,000 and requires $20,000 in installation costs. Purchase of this machine is expected to result in an increase in net working capital of $30,000 to support the expanded level of operations. The firm plans to depreciate the machine under MACRS using a 5-year recovery period (see Table 4.2 on page 112 for the applicable depreciation percentages) and expects to sell the machine to net $10,000 before taxes at the end of its usable life. The firm is subject to a 40% tax rate.

    a. Calculate the *terminal cash flow* for a usable life of (1) 3 years, (2) 5 years, and (3) 7 years.

    b. Discuss the effect of usable life on terminal cash flows using your findings in part **a.**

    c. Assuming a 5-year usable life, calculate the terminal cash flow if the machine were sold to net (1) $9,000 or (2) $170,000 (before taxes) at the end of 5 years.

    d. Discuss the effect of sale price on terminal cash flow using your findings in part **c.**

LG 3   **P11–15**   **Terminal cash flow: Replacement decision** Russell Industries is considering replacing a fully depreciated machine that has a remaining useful life of 10 years with a newer, more sophisticated machine. The new machine will cost $200,000 and will require $30,000 in installation costs. It will be depreciated under MACRS using a 5-year recovery period (see Table 4.2 on page 112 for the applicable depreciation percentages). A $25,000 increase in net working capital will be required to support the new machine. The firm's managers plan to evaluate the potential replacement over a 4-year period. They estimate that the old machine could be sold at the end of 4 years to net $15,000 before taxes; the new machine at the end of 4 years will be worth $75,000 before taxes. Calculate the *terminal cash flow* at the end of year 4 that is relevant to the proposed purchase of the new machine. The firm is subject to a 40% tax rate.

LG 3   **P11–16**   **Relevant cash flows: No terminal value** Central Laundry and Cleaners is considering replacing an existing piece of machinery with a more sophisticated machine. The old machine was purchased 3 years ago at a cost of $50,000, and this amount was being depreciated under MACRS using a 5-year recovery period. The machine has 5 years of usable life remaining. The new machine that is being considered costs $76,000 and requires $4,000 in installation costs. The new machine would be depreciated under MACRS using a 5-year recovery period. The firm can currently sell the old machine for $55,000 without incurring any removal or cleanup costs. The firm is subject to a tax rate of 40%. The revenues and expenses (excluding depreciation and interest) associated with the new and the old machines for the next 5 years are given in the table below. (See Table 4.2 on page 112 for the applicable depreciation percentages.)

	New machine		Old machine	
Year	Revenue	Expenses (excl. depr. and int.)	Revenue	Expenses (excl. depr. and int.)
1	$750,000	$720,000	$674,000	$660,000
2	750,000	720,000	676,000	660,000
3	750,000	720,000	680,000	660,000
4	750,000	720,000	678,000	660,000
5	750,000	720,000	674,000	660,000

a. Calculate the *initial investment* associated with replacement of the old machine by the new one.
b. Determine the *incremental operating cash flows* associated with the proposed replacement. (*Note:* Be sure to consider the depreciation in year 6.)
c. Depict on a time line the *relevant cash flows* found in parts a and b associated with the proposed replacement decision.

LG 3   **P11–17** **Integrative: Determining relevant cash flows** Lombard Company is contemplating the purchase of a new high-speed widget grinder to replace the existing grinder. The existing grinder was purchased 2 years ago at an installed cost of $60,000; it was being depreciated under MACRS using a 5-year recovery period. The existing grinder is expected to have a usable life of 5 more years. The new grinder costs $105,000 and requires $5,000 in installation costs; it has a 5-year usable life and would be depreciated under MACRS using a 5-year recovery period. Lombard can currently sell the existing grinder for $70,000 without incurring any removal or cleanup costs. To support the increased business resulting from purchase of the new grinder, accounts receivable would increase by $40,000, inventories by $30,000, and accounts payable by $58,000. At the end of 5 years, the existing grinder would have a market value of zero; the new grinder would be sold to net $29,000 after removal and cleanup costs and before taxes. The firm is subject to a 40% tax rate. The estimated *earnings before depreciation, interest, and taxes* over the 5 years for both the new and the existing grinder are shown in the following table. (See Table 4.2 on page 112 for the applicable depreciation percentages.)

	Earnings before depreciation, interest, and taxes	
Year	New grinder	Existing grinder
1	$43,000	$26,000
2	43,000	24,000
3	43,000	22,000
4	43,000	20,000
5	43,000	18,000

a. Calculate the *initial investment* associated with the replacement of the existing grinder by the new one.

b. Determine the *incremental operating cash flows* associated with the proposed grinder replacement. (*Note:* Be sure to consider the depreciation in year 6.)

c. Determine the *terminal cash flow* expected at the end of year 5 from the proposed grinder replacement.

d. Depict on a time line the *relevant cash flows* associated with the proposed grinder replacement decision.

 P11–18 **Recognizing risk** Caradine Corp., a media services firm with net earnings of $3,200,000 in the last year, is considering the following projects.

Project	Initial investment	Details
A	−$ 35,000	Replace existing office furnishings.
B	−500,000	Purchase digital video editing equipment for use with several existing accounts.
C	−450,000	Develop proposal to bid for a $2,000,000 per year 10-year contract with the U.S. Navy, not now an account.
D	−685,000	Purchase the exclusive rights to market a quality educational television program in syndication to local markets in the European Union, a part of the firm's existing business activities.

The media services business is cyclical and highly competitive. The board of directors has asked you, as chief financial officer, to do the following:

a. Evaluate the risk of each proposed project and rank it "low," "medium," or "high."

b. Comment on why you chose each ranking.

 P11–19 **Breakeven cash inflows and risk** Blair Gasses and Chemicals is a supplier of highly purified gases to semiconductor manufacturers. A large chip producer has asked Blair to build a new gas production facility close to an existing semiconductor plant. Once the new gas plant is in place, Blair will be the exclusive supplier for that semiconductor fabrication plant for the subsequent 5 years. Blair is considering one of two plant designs. The first is Blair's "standard" plant, which will cost $30 million to build. The second is for a "custom" plant, which will cost $40 million to build. The custom plant will allow Blair to produce the highly specialized gases that are required for an emerging semiconductor manufacturing process. Blair estimates that its client will order $10 million of product per year if the traditional plant is constructed, but if the customized design is put in place, Blair expects to sell $15 million worth of product annually to its client. Blair has enough money to build either type of plant, and, in the absence of risk differences, accepts the project with the highest NPV. The cost of capital is 12%.

a. Find the NPV for each project. Are the projects acceptable?

b. Find the *breakeven cash inflow* for each project.

c. The firm has estimated the probabilities of achieving various ranges of cash inflows for the two projects as shown in the table at the top of the next page. What is the probability that each project will achieve at least the breakeven cash inflow found in part **b?**

Range of cash inflow ($ millions)	Probability of achieving cash inflow in given range	
	Standard plant	Custom plant
$0 to $5	0%	5%
$5 to $8	10	10
$8 to $11	60	15
$11 to $14	25	25
$14 to $17	5	20
$17 to $20	0	15
Above $20	0	10

d. Which project is more risky? Which project has the potentially higher NPV? Discuss the risk–return trade-offs of the two projects.

e. If the firm wished to minimize losses (that is, NPV < $0), which project would you recommend? Which would you recommend if the goal were to achieve a higher NPV?

  P11–20 **Basic scenario analysis** Murdock Paints is in the process of evaluating two mutually exclusive additions to its processing capacity. The firm's financial analysts have developed pessimistic, most likely, and optimistic estimates of the annual cash inflows associated with each project. These estimates are shown in the following table.

	Project A	Project B
Initial investment (CF₀)	−$8,000	−$8,000
Outcome	Annual cash inflows (CF)	
Pessimistic	$ 200	$ 900
Most likely	1,000	1,000
Optimistic	1,800	1,100

a. Determine the *range* of annual cash inflows for each of the two projects.

b. Assume that the firm's cost of capital is 10% and that both projects have 20-year lives. Construct a table similar to this one for the NPVs for each project. Include the *range* of NPVs for each project.

c. Do parts **a** and **b** provide consistent views of the two projects? Explain.

d. Which project do you recommend? Why?

  P11–21 **Scenario analysis** Automated Food Distribution Corp. (AFDC) produces vending machines and places them in public buildings. The company has obtained permission to place one of its machines in a local library. The company makes two types of machines. One distributes soft drinks, and the other distributes snack foods. AFDC expects both machines to provide benefits over a 10-year period, and each has a required investment of $3,000. The firm uses a 10% cost of capital. Management has constructed the table of estimates of annual cash inflows for pessimistic, most likely, and optimistic results shown at the top of the next page.

	Soft drinks	Snack foods
Initial investment (CF_0)	−$3,000	−$3,000
Outcome	Annual cash inflows (CF)	
Pessimistic	$ 500	$ 400
Most likely	750	750
Optimistic	1,000	1,200

a. Determine the *range* of annual cash inflows for each of the two vending machines.
b. Construct a table similar to this one for the NPVs associated with each outcome for both machines.
c. Find the *range* of NPVs, and subjectively compare the risks associated with these machines.

Personal Finance Problem

LG 4 **P11–22** **Impact of inflation on investments** You are interested in an investment project that costs $40,000 initially. The investment has a 5-year horizon and promises future end-of-year cash inflows of $12,000, $12,500, $11,500, $9,000, and $8,500, respectively. Your current opportunity cost is 6.5% per year. However, the Fed has stated that inflation may rise by 1.5% or may fall by the same amount over the next 5 years.

Assume a direct positive impact of inflation on the prevailing rates (Fisher effect) and answer the following questions. (Assume that inflation has an impact on the opportunity cost, but that the cash flows are contractually fixed and are not affected by inflation).

a. What is the *net present value (NPV)* of the investment under the current required rate of return?
b. What is the *net present value (NPV)* of the investment under a period of rising inflation?
c. What is the *net present value (NPV)* of the investment under a period of falling inflation?
d. From your answers in **a, b,** and **c,** what relationship do you see emerge between changes in inflation and asset valuation?

LG 4 **P11–23** **Simulation** Ogden Corporation has compiled the following information on a capital expenditure proposal:

1. The projected cash *inflows* are normally distributed with a mean of $36,000 and a standard deviation of $9,000.
2. The projected cash *outflows* are normally distributed with a mean of $30,000 and a standard deviation of $6,000.
3. The firm has an 11% cost of capital.
4. The probability distributions of cash inflows and cash outflows are not expected to change over the project's 10-year life.

   a. Describe how the foregoing data can be used to develop a simulation model for finding the net present value of the project.
   b. Discuss the advantages of using a simulation to evaluate the proposed project.

LG 5 **P11–24** **Risk-adjusted discount rates: Basic** Country Wallpapers is considering investing in one of three mutually exclusive projects, E, F, and G. The firm's cost of capital, *r*, is 15%, and the risk-free rate, R_F, is 10%. The firm has gathered the basic cash flow and risk index data for each project as shown in the table at the top of the next page.

	Project (j)		
	E	F	G
Initial investment (CF_0)	−$15,000	−$11,000	−$19,000
Year (t)	Cash inflows (CF_t)		
1	$6,000	$6,000	$ 4,000
2	6,000	4,000	6,000
3	6,000	5,000	8,000
4	6,000	2,000	12,000
Risk index (RI_j)	1.80	1.00	0.60

a. Find the *net present value (NPV)* of each project using the firm's cost of capital. Which project is preferred in this situation?

b. The firm uses the following equation to determine the risk-adjusted discount rate, $RADR_j$, for each project j:

$$RADR_j = R_F + [RI_j \times (r - R_F)]$$

where

$$R_F = \text{risk-free rate of return}$$
$$RI_j = \text{risk index for project } j$$
$$r = \text{cost of capital}$$

Substitute each project's risk index into this equation to determine its RADR.

c. Use the RADR for each project to determine its *risk-adjusted NPV*. Which project is preferable in this situation?

d. Compare and discuss your findings in parts **a** and **c**. Which project do you recommend that the firm accept?

 P11–25 **Risk-adjusted discount rates: Tabular** After a careful evaluation of investment alternatives and opportunities, Masters School Supplies has developed a CAPM-type relationship linking a risk index to the required return (RADR) as shown in the following table.

Risk index	Required return (RADR)
0.0	7.0% (risk-free rate, R_F)
0.2	8.0
0.4	9.0
0.6	10.0
0.8	11.0
1.0	12.0
1.2	13.0
1.4	14.0
1.6	15.0
1.8	16.0
2.0	17.0

The firm is considering two mutually exclusive projects, A and B. Following are the data that the firm has been able to gather about the projects.

	Project A	Project B
Initial investment (CF_0)	−$20,000	−$30,000
Project life	5 years	5 years
Annual cash inflow (CF)	$7,000	$10,000
Risk index	0.2	1.4

All the firm's cash inflows have already been adjusted for taxes.
a. Evaluate the projects using *risk-adjusted discount rates*.
b. Discuss your findings in part **a**, and recommend the preferred project.

Personal Finance Problem

LG 5 **P11–26** **Mutually exclusive investments and risk** Lara Fredericks is interested in two mutually exclusive investments. Both investments cover the same time horizon of 6 years. The cost of the first investment is $10,000, and Lara expects equal and consecutive year-end payments of $3,000. The second investment promises equal and consecutive payments of $3,800 with an initial outlay of $12,000 required. The current required return on the first investment is 8.5%, and the second carries a required return of 10.5%.
a. What is the *net present value* of the first investment?
b. What is the *net present value* of the second investment?
c. Being mutually exclusive, which investment should Lara choose? Explain.
d. Which investment was relatively more risky? Explain.

LG 5 **P11–27** **Risk-adjusted rates of return using CAPM** Centennial Catering, Inc., is considering two mutually exclusive investments. The company wishes to use a CAPM-type risk-adjusted discount rate (RADR) in its analysis. Centennial's managers believe that the appropriate market rate of return is 12%, and they observe that the current risk-free rate of return is 7%. Cash flows associated with the two projects are shown in the following table.

	Project X	Project Y
Initial investment (CF_0)	−$70,000	−$78,000
Year (t)	Cash inflows (CF_t)	
1	$30,000	$22,000
2	30,000	32,000
3	30,000	38,000
4	30,000	46,000

a. Use a *risk-adjusted discount rate* approach to calculate the net present value of each project, given that project X has an RADR factor of 1.20 and project Y has an RADR factor of 1.40. The RADR factors are similar to project betas. (Use Equation 11.5 to calculate the required project return for each.)
b. Discuss your findings in part **a**, and recommend the preferred project.

P11–28   **Risk classes and RADR** Moses Manufacturing is attempting to select the best of three mutually exclusive projects, X, Y, and Z. Although all the projects have 5-year lives, they possess differing degrees of risk. Project X is in class V, the highest-risk class; project Y is in class II, the below-average-risk class; and project Z is in class III, the average-risk class. The basic cash flow data for each project and the risk classes and risk-adjusted discount rates (RADRs) used by the firm are shown in the following tables.

	Project X	Project Y	Project Z
Initial investment (CF_0)	−$180,000	−$235,000	−$310,000
Year (t)		Cash inflows (CF_t)	
1	$80,000	$50,000	$90,000
2	70,000	60,000	90,000
3	60,000	70,000	90,000
4	60,000	80,000	90,000
5	60,000	90,000	90,000

Risk Classes and RADRs		
Risk class	Description	Risk-adjusted discount rate (RADR)
I	Lowest risk	10%
II	Below-average risk	13
III	Average risk	15
IV	Above-average risk	19
V	Highest risk	22

a. Find the *risk-adjusted* NPV for each project.
b. Which project, if any, would you recommend that the firm undertake?

P11–29   **Unequal lives: ANPV approach** Evans Industries wishes to select the best of three possible machines, each of which is expected to satisfy the firm's ongoing need for additional aluminum-extrusion capacity. The three machines—A, B, and C—are equally risky. The firm plans to use a 12% cost of capital to evaluate each of them. The initial investment and annual cash inflows over the life of each machine are shown in the following table.

	Machine A	Machine B	Machine C
Initial investment (CF_0)	−$92,000	−$65,000	−$100,500
Year (t)		Cash inflows (CF_t)	
1	$12,000	$10,000	$30,000
2	12,000	20,000	30,000
3	12,000	30,000	30,000
4	12,000	40,000	30,000
5	12,000	—	30,000
6	12,000	—	—

a. Calculate the *NPV* for each machine over its life. Rank the machines in descending order on the basis of NPV.
b. Use the *annualized net present value (ANPV)* approach to evaluate and rank the machines in descending order on the basis of ANPV.
c. Compare and contrast your findings in parts **a** and **b**. Which machine would you recommend that the firm acquire? Why?

P11–30   **Unequal lives: ANPV approach**   JBL Co. has designed a new conveyor system. Management must choose among three alternative courses of action: (1) The firm can sell the design outright to another corporation with payment over 2 years; (2) it can license the design to another manufacturer for a period of 5 years, its likely product life; or (3) it can manufacture and market the system itself, an alternative that will result in 6 years of cash inflows. The company has a cost of capital of 12%. Cash flows associated with each alternative are as shown in the following table.

Alternative	Sell	License	Manufacture
Initial investment (CF_0)	−$200,000	−$200,000	−$450,000
Year (t)		Cash inflows (CF_t)	
1	$200,000	$250,000	$200,000
2	250,000	100,000	250,000
3	—	80,000	200,000
4	—	60,000	200,000
5	—	40,000	200,000
6	—	—	200,000

a. Calculate the *net present value* of each alternative and rank the alternatives on the basis of NPV.
b. Calculate the *annualized net present value (ANPV)* of each alternative, and rank them accordingly.
c. Why is ANPV preferred over NPV when ranking projects with unequal lives?

Personal Finance Problem

P11–31   **NPV and ANPV decisions**   Richard and Linda Butler decide that it is time to purchase a high-definition (HD) television because the technology has improved and prices have fallen over the past 3 years. From their research, they narrow their choices to two sets, the Samsung 64-inch plasma with 1080p capability and the Sony 64-inch plasma with 1080p features. The price of the Samsung is $2,350, and the Sony will cost $2,700. They expect to keep the Samsung for 3 years; if they buy the more expensive Sony unit, they will keep the Sony for 4 years. They expect to be able to sell the Samsung for $400 by the end of 3 years; they expect they could sell the Sony for $350 at the end of year 4. Richard and Linda estimate the end-of-year entertainment benefits (that is, not going to movies or events and watching at home) from the Samsung to be $900 and for the Sony to be $1,000. Both sets can be viewed as quality units and are equally risky purchases. They estimate their opportunity cost to be 9%.

The Butlers wish to choose the better alternative from a purely financial perspective. To perform this analysis they wish to do the following:
a. Determine the *NPV* of the Samsung HD plasma TV.
b. Determine the *ANPV* of the Samsung HD plasma TV.

    c. Determine the *NPV* of the Sony HD plasma TV.

    d. Determine the *ANPV* of the Sony HD plasma TV.

    e. Which set should the Butlers purchase? Why?

LG 6 **P11–32** **Real options and the strategic NPV** Jenny Rene, the CFO of Asor Products, Inc., has just completed an evaluation of a proposed capital expenditure for equipment that would expand the firm's manufacturing capacity. Using the traditional NPV methodology, she found the project unacceptable because

$$\text{NPV}_{\text{traditional}} = -\$1,700 < \$0$$

Before recommending rejection of the proposed project, she has decided to assess whether there might be real options embedded in the firm's cash flows. Her evaluation uncovered three options:

> *Option 1: Abandonment.* The project could be abandoned at the end of 3 years, resulting in an addition to NPV of $1,200.

> *Option 2: Growth.* If the projected outcomes occurred, an opportunity to expand the firm's product offerings further would become available at the end of 4 years. Exercise of this option is estimated to add $3,000 to the project's NPV.

> *Option 3: Timing.* Certain phases of the proposed project could be delayed if market and competitive conditions caused the firm's forecast revenues to develop more slowly than planned. Such a delay in implementation at that point has an NPV of $10,000.

    Jenny estimated that there was a 25% chance that the abandonment option would need to be exercised, a 30% chance that the growth option would be exercised, and only a 10% chance that the implementation of certain phases of the project would affect timing.

    a. Use the information provided to calculate the *strategic NPV*, $\text{NPV}_{\text{strategic}}$, for Asor Products' proposed equipment expenditure.

    b. Judging on the basis of your findings in part **a,** what action should Jenny recommend to management with regard to the proposed equipment expenditure?

    c. In general, how does this problem demonstrate the importance of considering real options when making capital budgeting decisions?

LG 6 **P11–33** **Capital rationing: IRR and NPV approaches** Valley Corporation is attempting to select the best of a group of independent projects competing for the firm's fixed capital budget of $4.5 million. The firm recognizes that any unused portion of this budget will earn less than its 15% cost of capital, thereby resulting in a present value of inflows that is less than the initial investment. The firm has summarized, in the following table, the key data to be used in selecting the best group of projects.

    a. Use the *internal rate of return (IRR) approach* to select the best group of projects.

    b. Use the *net present value (NPV) approach* to select the best group of projects.

    c. Compare, contrast, and discuss your findings in parts **a** and **b.**

    d. Which projects should the firm implement? Why?

Project	Initial investment	IRR	Present value of inflows at 15%
A	−$5,000,000	17%	$5,400,000
B	−800,000	18	1,100,000
C	−2,000,000	19	2,300,000
D	−1,500,000	16	1,600,000
E	−800,000	22	900,000
F	−2,500,000	23	3,000,000
G	−1,200,000	20	1,300,000

LG 6   **P11–34** **Capital rationing: NPV approach** A firm with a 13% cost of capital must select the optimal group of projects from those shown in the following table, given its capital budget of $1 million.

Project	Initial investment	NPV at 13% cost of capital
A	−$300,000	$ 84,000
B	−200,000	10,000
C	−100,000	25,000
D	−900,000	90,000
E	−500,000	70,000
F	−100,000	50,000
G	−800,000	160,000

a. Calculate the *present value of cash inflows* associated with each project.
b. Select the optimal group of projects, keeping in mind that unused funds are costly.

LG 5   **P11–35** **ETHICS PROBLEM** The Environmental Protection Agency sometimes imposes penalties on firms that pollute the environment (see the *Focus on Ethics* box on page 000). But did you know that there is a legal market for pollution? A mechanism that has been developed to limit excessive air pollution is to use carbon credits. Carbon credits are a tradable permit scheme that allows businesses that cannot meet their greenhouse-gas-emissions limits to purchase carbon credits from businesses that are below their quota. By allowing credits to be bought and sold, a business for which reducing its emissions would be expensive or prohibitive can pay another business to make the reduction for it. Do you agree with this arrangement? How would you feel as an investor in a company that uses carbon credits to legally exceed its pollution limits?

Spreadsheet Exercise

Isis Corporation has two projects that it would like to undertake. However, due to capital restraints, the two projects—Alpha and Beta—must be treated as mutually exclusive. Both projects are equally risky, and the firm plans to use a 10% cost of capital to evaluate each. Project Alpha has an estimated life of 12 years, and project Beta has an estimated life of 9 years. The cash flow data have been prepared as shown in the following table.

	Cash flows	
	Project alpha	**Project beta**
CF_0	−$5,500,000	−$6,500,000
CF_1	300,000	400,000
CF_2	500,000	600,000
CF_3	500,000	800,000
CF_4	550,000	1,100,000
CF_5	700,000	1,400,000
CF_6	800,000	2,000,000
CF_7	950,000	2,500,000
CF_8	1,000,000	2,000,000
CF_9	1,250,000	1,000,000
CF_{10}	1,500,000	
CF_{11}	2,000,000	
CF_{12}	2,500,000	

TO DO

Create a spreadsheet to answer the following questions.

a. Calculate the *NPV* for each project over its respective life. Rank the projects in descending order on the basis of NPV. Which one would you choose?

b. Use the *annualized net present value (ANPV) approach* to evaluate and rank the projects in descending order on the basis of ANPV. Which one would you choose?

c. Compare and contrast your findings in parts **a** and **b.** Which project would you recommend that the firm choose? Explain.

MyFinanceLab Visit **www.myfinancelab.com** for **Chapter Case: *Evaluating Cherone Equipment's Risky Plans for Increasing Its Production Capacity,*** Group Exercises, and numerous online resources.

Part 6 ▷ Long-Term Financial Decisions

Chapters 10 through 11 focused on how firms should invest money, but those chapters were silent on where firms obtained the money to invest in the first place. In Chapters 12 and 13, we examine firms' long-term financial decisions. Broadly speaking, these chapters focus on the trade-offs associated with different sources of investment capital.

Chapter 12 looks at the firm's most basic long-term financial decision: whether to raise money by selling stock (equity) or by borrowing money (debt). A firm's mix of debt and equity financing is called its capital structure. Some firms choose a capital structure that contains no debt at all, whereas other firms rely more heavily on debt financing than on equity. The capital structure choice is extremely important because how much debt a firm uses influences the returns that a firm can provide to its investors as well as the risks associated with those returns. More debt generally means higher returns but also higher risks. Chapter 12 illustrates how firms balance that trade-off.

Chapter 13 focuses on payout policy. Payout policy refers to the decisions that firms make about whether and how to distribute cash to shareholders via dividends and share repurchases. We can make a similar observation about payout policy that we made about capital structure. Some firms choose to distribute no cash at all, preferring instead to reinvest cash in the business or to build up large cash reserves that might be used for strategic investments like acquisitions. Other firms pay billions in dividends and stock buybacks each year. Chapter 13 explains the factors that firms consider when forming their payout policies.

12 Leverage and Capital Structure

Learning Goals

LG 1 Discuss leverage, capital structure, breakeven analysis, the operating breakeven point, and the effect of changing costs on the breakeven point.

LG 2 Understand operating, financial, and total leverage and the relationships among them.

LG 3 Describe the types of capital, external assessment of capital structure, the capital structure of non–U.S. firms, and capital structure theory.

LG 4 Explain the optimal capital structure using a graphical view of the firm's cost-of-capital functions and a zero-growth valuation model.

LG 5 Discuss the EBIT–EPS approach to capital structure.

LG 6 Review the return and risk of alternative capital structures, their linkage to market value, and other important considerations related to capital structure.

Why This Chapter Matters to You

In your *professional* life

ACCOUNTING You need to understand how to calculate and analyze operating and financial leverage and to be familiar with the tax and earnings effects of various capital structures.

INFORMATION SYSTEMS You need to understand the types of capital and what capital structure is because you will provide much of the information needed in management's determination of the best capital structure for the firm.

MANAGEMENT You need to understand leverage so that you can control risk and magnify returns for the firm's owners and to understand capital structure theory so that you can make decisions about the firm's optimal capital structure.

MARKETING You need to understand breakeven analysis, which you will use in pricing and product feasibility decisions.

OPERATIONS You need to understand the impact of fixed and variable operating costs on the firm's breakeven point and its operating leverage because these costs will have a major effect on the firm's risk and return.

In your *personal* life

Like corporations, you routinely incur debt, using both credit cards for short-term needs and negotiated long-term loans. When you borrow over the long term, you experience the benefits and consequences of leverage. Also, the level of your outstanding debt relative to net worth is conceptually the same as a firm's capital structure. It reflects your financial risk and affects the availability and cost of borrowing.

12.1 Leverage

leverage
Refers to the effects that fixed costs have on the returns that shareholders earn; higher leverage generally results in higher but more volatile returns.

Leverage refers to the effects that fixed costs have on the returns that shareholders earn. By "fixed costs," we mean costs that do not rise and fall with changes in a firm's sales. Firms have to pay these fixed costs whether business conditions are good or bad. These fixed costs may be operating costs, such as the costs incurred by purchasing and operating plant and equipment, or they may be financial costs, such as the fixed costs of making debt payments. We say that a firm with higher fixed costs has greater leverage. Generally, leverage magnifies both returns and risks. A firm with more leverage may earn higher returns on average than a firm with less leverage, but the returns on the more leveraged firm will also be more volatile.

Many business risks are out of the control of managers, but not the risks associated with leverage. Managers can either increase or decrease leverage by adopting strategies that rely more heavily on fixed or variable costs. For example, a choice that many firms confront is whether to make their own products or to outsource manufacturing to another firm. A company that does its own manufacturing may invest billions in factories around the world. These factories generate costs whether they are running or not so a firm that does its own manufacturing will tend to have higher leverage. In contrast, a company that outsources production can quickly reduce its costs when demand is low simply by not placing orders. Therefore, such a firm will generally have lower leverage compared to a firm that manufactures its own goods.

capital structure
The mix of long-term debt and equity maintained by the firm.

Managers also influence leverage by choosing a specific **capital structure**, which is the mix of long-term debt and equity maintained by a firm. The more debt a firm issues, the higher are its debt repayment costs, and those costs must be paid regardless of how the firm's products are selling. Because leverage can have such a large impact on a firm, the financial manager must understand how to measure and evaluate leverage, particularly when making capital structure decisions.

Table 12.1 uses an income statement to highlight where different sources of leverage come from.

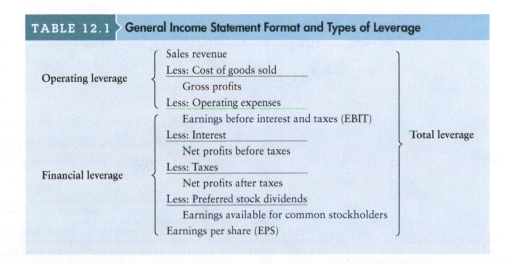

TABLE 12.1 General Income Statement Format and Types of Leverage

Operating leverage:
Sales revenue
Less: Cost of goods sold
Gross profits
Less: Operating expenses

Financial leverage:
Earnings before interest and taxes (EBIT)
Less: Interest
Net profits before taxes
Less: Taxes
Net profits after taxes
Less: Preferred stock dividends
Earnings available for common stockholders
Earnings per share (EPS)

Total leverage

- *Operating leverage* is concerned with the relationship between the firm's sales revenue and its earnings before interest and taxes (EBIT) or *operating profits*. When costs of operations (such as cost of goods sold and operating expenses) are largely fixed, small changes in revenue will lead to much larger changes in EBIT.

- *Financial leverage* is concerned with the relationship between the firm's EBIT and its common stock earnings per share (EPS). On the income statement, you can see that the deductions taken from EBIT to get to EPS include interest, taxes, and preferred dividends. Taxes are clearly variable, rising and falling with the firm's profits, but interest expense and preferred dividends are usually fixed. When these fixed items are large (that is, when the firm has a lot of financial leverage), small changes in EBIT produce larger changes in EPS.

- *Total leverage* is the combined effect of operating and financial leverage. It is concerned with the relationship between the firm's sales revenue and EPS.

We will examine the three types of leverage concepts in detail. First, though, we will look at breakeven analysis, which lays the foundation for leverage concepts by demonstrating the effects of fixed costs on the firm's operations.

BREAKEVEN ANALYSIS

breakeven analysis
Used to indicate the level of operations necessary to cover all costs and to evaluate the profitability associated with various levels of sales; also called *cost-volume-profit analysis.*

Firms use **breakeven analysis,** also called *cost-volume-profit analysis,* (1) to determine the level of operations necessary to cover all costs and (2) to evaluate the profitability associated with various levels of sales. The firm's **operating breakeven point** is the level of sales necessary to cover all *operating costs*. At that point, earnings before interest and taxes (EBIT) equals \$0.[1]

operating breakeven point
The level of sales necessary to cover all *operating costs;* the point at which EBIT = \$0.

The first step in finding the operating breakeven point is to divide the cost of goods sold and operating expenses into fixed and variable operating costs. *Fixed costs* are costs that the firm must pay in a given period regardless of the sales volume achieved during that period. These costs are typically contractual; rent, for example, is a fixed cost. Because fixed costs do not vary with sales, we typically measure them relative to time. For example, we would typically measure rent as the amount due *per month*. *Variable costs* vary directly with sales volume. Shipping costs, for example, are a variable cost.[2] We typically measure variable costs in dollars per unit sold.

Algebraic Approach

Using the following variables, we can recast the operating portion of the firm's income statement given in Table 12.1 into the algebraic representation shown in Table 12.2, where

$$P = \text{sale price per unit}$$
$$Q = \text{sales quantity in units}$$
$$FC = \text{fixed } operating \text{ cost per period}$$
$$VC = \text{variable } operating \text{ cost per unit}$$

---

1. Quite often, the breakeven point is calculated so that it represents the point at which *all costs—both operating and financial*—are covered. For now, we focus on the operating breakeven point as a way to introduce the concept of operating leverage. We will discuss financial leverage later.
2. Some costs, commonly called *semifixed* or *semivariable,* are partly fixed and partly variable. An example is sales commissions that are fixed for a certain volume of sales and then increase to higher levels for higher volumes. For convenience and clarity, we assume that all costs can be classified as either fixed or variable.

TABLE 12.2	Operating Leverage, Costs, and Breakeven Analysis	
	Item	Algebraic representation
Operating leverage {	Sales revenue	$(P \times Q)$
	Less: Fixed operating costs	$- \quad FC$
	Less: Variable operating costs	$-(VC \times Q)$
	Earnings before interest and taxes	EBIT

Rewriting the algebraic calculations in Table 12.2 as a formula for earnings before interest and taxes yields Equation 12.1:

$$EBIT = (P \times Q) - FC - (VC \times Q) \tag{12.1}$$

Simplifying Equation 12.1 yields

$$EBIT = Q \times (P - VC) - FC \tag{12.2}$$

As noted above, the operating breakeven point is the level of sales at which all fixed and variable *operating costs* are covered, that is, the level at which EBIT equals $0. Setting EBIT equal to $0 and solving Equation 12.2 for Q yields

$$Q = \frac{FC}{P - VC} \tag{12.3}$$

where Q is the firm's operating breakeven point.[3]

Example 12.1 ▶

MyFinanceLab Solution Video

Assume that Cheryl's Posters, a small poster retailer, has fixed operating costs of $2,500. Its sale price is $10 per poster, and its variable operating cost is $5 per poster. Applying Equation 12.3 to these data yields

$$Q = \frac{\$2,500}{\$10 - \$5} = \frac{\$2,500}{\$5} = 500 \text{ units}$$

At sales of 500 units, the firm's EBIT should just equal $0. The firm will have positive EBIT for sales greater than 500 units and negative EBIT, or a loss, for sales less than 500 units. We can confirm this conclusion by substituting values above and below 500 units, along with the other values given, into Equation 12.1.

---

3. Because the firm is assumed to be a single-product firm, its operating breakeven point is found in terms of unit sales, Q. For multiproduct firms, the operating breakeven point is generally found in terms of dollar sales, S. We can find S by substituting the contribution margin, which is 100 percent minus total variable operating costs as a percentage of total sales, denoted $VC\%$, into the denominator of Equation 12.3. The result is Equation 12.3a:

$$S = \frac{FC}{1 - VC\%} \tag{12.3a}$$

This multiproduct-firm breakeven point assumes that the firm's product mix remains the same at all levels of sales.

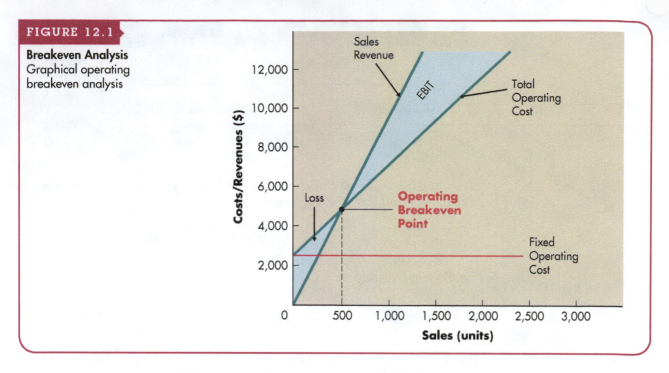

FIGURE 12.1

Breakeven Analysis
Graphical operating breakeven analysis

Graphical Approach

Figure 12.1 presents in graphical form the breakeven analysis of the data in the preceding example. The firm's operating breakeven point is the point at which it *total operating cost*—the sum of its fixed and variable operating costs—equals sales revenue. At this point, EBIT equals $0. The figure shows that for sales *below* 500 units, total operating cost exceeds sales revenue, and EBIT is less than $0 (a loss). For sales *above* the breakeven point of 500 units, sales revenue exceeds total operating cost, and EBIT is greater than $0.

Changing Costs and the Operating Breakeven Point

A firm's operating breakeven point is sensitive to a number of variables: the fixed operating cost (FC), the sale price per unit (P), and the variable operating cost per unit (VC). Refer to Equation 12.3 to see how increases or decreases in these variables affect the breakeven point. The sensitivity of the breakeven sales volume (Q) to an *increase* in each of these variables is summarized in Table 12.3. As

TABLE 12.3	Sensitivity of Operating Breakeven Point to Increases in Key Breakeven Variables
Increase in variable	Effect on operating breakeven point
Fixed operating cost (FC)	Increase
Sale price per unit (P)	Decrease
Variable operating cost per unit (VC)	Increase

Note: Decreases in each of the variables shown would have the opposite effect on the operating breakeven point.

might be expected, an increase in cost (*FC* or *VC*) tends to increase the operating breakeven point, whereas an increase in the sale price per unit (*P*) decreases the operating breakeven point.

Example 12.2 ▶

Assume that Cheryl's Posters wishes to evaluate the impact of several options: (1) increasing fixed operating costs to $3,000, (2) increasing the sale price per unit to $12.50, (3) increasing the variable operating cost per unit to $7.50, and (4) simultaneously implementing all three of these changes. Substituting the appropriate data into Equation 12.3 yields

$$(1) \text{ Operating breakeven point} = \frac{\$3,000}{\$10 - \$5} = 600 \text{ units}$$

$$(2) \text{ Operating breakeven point} = \frac{\$2,500}{\$12.50 - \$5} = 333\tfrac{1}{3} \text{ units}$$

$$(3) \text{ Operating breakeven point} = \frac{\$2,500}{\$10 - \$7.50} = 1,000 \text{ units}$$

$$(4) \text{ Operating breakeven point} = \frac{\$3,000}{\$12.50 - \$7.50} = 600 \text{ units}$$

Comparing the resulting operating breakeven points to the initial value of 500 units, we can see that the cost increases (actions 1 and 3) raise the breakeven point, whereas the revenue increase (action 2) lowers the breakeven point. The combined effect of increasing all three variables (action 4) also results in an increased operating breakeven point.

Personal Finance Example 12.3 ▶

Rick Polo is considering having a new fuel-saving device installed in his car. The installed cost of the device is $240 paid up front plus a monthly fee of $15. He can terminate use of the device any time without penalty. Rick estimates that the device will reduce his average monthly gas consumption by 20%, which, assuming no change in his monthly mileage, translates into a savings of about $28 per month. He is planning to keep the car for 2 more years and wishes to determine whether he should have the device installed in his car.

To assess the financial feasibility of purchasing the device, Rick calculates the number of months it will take for him to break even. Letting the installed cost of $240 represent the fixed cost (*FC*), the monthly savings of $28 represent the benefit (*P*), and the monthly fee of $15 represent the variable cost (*VC*), and substituting these values into the breakeven point equation, Equation 12.3, we get

$$\text{Breakeven point (in months)} = \$240 \div (\$28 - \$15) = \$240 \div \$13$$
$$= \underline{18.5 \text{ months}}$$

Because the fuel-saving device pays itself back in 18.5 months, which is less than the 24 months that Rick is planning to continue owning the car, he should have the fuel-saving device installed in his car.

FIGURE 12.2

Operating Leverage
Breakeven analysis and operating leverage

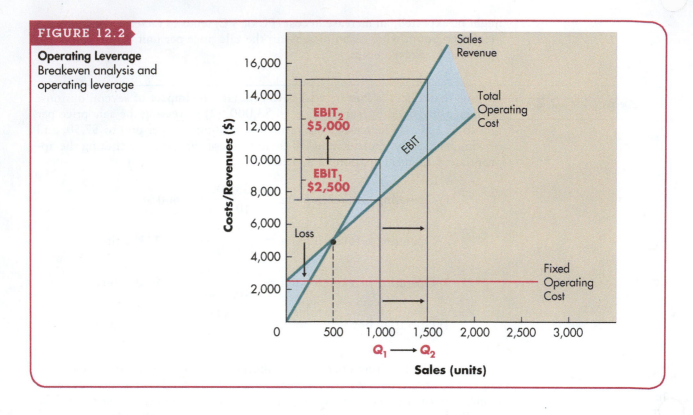

OPERATING LEVERAGE

operating leverage
The use of *fixed operating costs* to magnify the effects of changes in sales on the firm's earnings before interest and taxes.

Operating leverage results from the existence of *fixed costs* that the firm must pay to operate. Using the structure presented in Table 12.2, we can define **operating leverage** as the use of *fixed operating costs* to magnify the effects of changes in sales on the firm's earnings before interest and taxes.

Example 12.4 ▶

Using the data for Cheryl's Posters (sale price, $P = \$10$ per unit; variable operating cost, $VC = \$5$ per unit; fixed operating cost, $FC = \$2,500$), Figure 12.2 presents the operating breakeven graph originally shown in Figure 12.1. The additional notations on the graph indicate that as the firm's sales increase from 1,000 to 1,500 units (Q_1 to Q_2), its EBIT increases from $2,500 to $5,000 (EBIT$_1$ to EBIT$_2$). In other words, a 50% increase in sales (1,000 to 1,500 units) results in a 100% increase in EBIT ($2,500 to $5,000). Table 12.4 includes the data for Figure 12.2 as well as relevant data for a 500-unit sales level. We can illustrate two cases using the 1,000-unit sales level as a reference point:

Case 1 A 50% *increase* in sales (from 1,000 to 1,500 units) results in a 100% *increase* in earnings before interest and taxes (from $2,500 to $5,000).

Case 2 A 50% *decrease* in sales (from 1,000 to 500 units) results in a 100% *decrease* in earnings before interest and taxes (from $2,500 to $0).

From the preceding example, we see that operating leverage works in *both directions*. When a firm has fixed operating costs, operating leverage is presen

TABLE 12.4	The EBIT for Various Sales Levels		
		Case 2	Case 1
		−50%	+50%
Sales (in units)	500	1,000	1,500
Sales revenue[a]	$5,000	$10,000	$15,000
Less: Variable operating costs[b]	2,500	5,000	7,500
Less: Fixed operating costs	2,500	2,500	2,500
Earnings before interest and taxes (EBIT)	$ 0	$ 2,500	$ 5,000
		−100%	+100%

[a]Sales revenue = $10/unit × sales in units.
[b]Variable operating costs = $5/unit × sales in units.

An increase in sales results in a more-than-proportional increase in EBIT; a decrease in sales results in a more-than-proportional decrease in EBIT.

Measuring the Degree of Operating Leverage (DOL)

degree of operating leverage (DOL)
The numerical measure of the firm's operating leverage.

The **degree of operating leverage (DOL)** is a numerical measure of the firm's operating leverage. It can be derived using the equation[4]

$$DOL = \frac{\text{Percentage change in EBIT}}{\text{Percentage change in sales}} \quad (12.4)$$

Whenever the percentage change in EBIT resulting from a given percentage change in sales is greater than the percentage change in sales, operating leverage exists. In other words, as long as DOL is greater than 1, there is operating leverage.

Example 12.5 ▶

MyFinanceLab Solution Video

Applying Equation 12.4 to cases 1 and 2 in Table 12.4 yields the following results:

Case 1 $\quad \dfrac{+100\%}{+50\%} = 2.0$

Case 2 $\quad \dfrac{-100\%}{-50\%} = 2.0$

These calculations show that Cheryl's Posters' EBIT changes twice as much (on a percentage basis) as its sales. For a given base level of sales, the higher the value resulting from applying Equation 12.4, the greater the degree of operating leverage.

---

4. The degree of operating leverage also depends on the base level of sales used as a point of reference. The closer the base sales level used is to the operating breakeven point, the greater the operating leverage. *Comparison of the degree of operating leverage of two firms is valid only when the same base level of sales is used for both firms.*

A more direct formula for calculating the degree of operating leverage at a base sales level, Q, is[5]

$$\text{DOL at base sales level } Q = \frac{Q \times (P - VC)}{Q \times (P - VC) - FC} \quad (12.5)$$

Example 12.6 ▶

Substituting $Q = 1,000$, $P = \$10$, $VC = \$5$, and $FC = \$2,500$ into Equation 12.5 gives us

$$\text{DOL at 1,000 units} = \frac{1,000 \times (\$10 - \$5)}{1,000 \times (\$10 - \$5) - \$2,500} = \frac{\$5,000}{\$2,500} = 2.0$$

As before, the DOL value of 2.0 means that at Cheryl's Posters a change in sales volume results in an EBIT change that is twice as large in percentage terms.[6]

See the *Focus on Practice* box for a discussion of operating leverage at software maker Adobe.

---

focus on PRACTICE

Adobe's Leverage

in practice Adobe Systems, one of the largest PC software companies in the United States, dominates the graphic design, imaging, dynamic media, and authoring-tool software markets. Website designers favor its Photoshop and Illustrator software applications, and Adobe's Acrobat software has become a standard for sharing documents online.

Adobe's ability to manage discretionary expenses helps keep its bottom line strong. Adobe has an additional advantage: *operating leverage*, the use of fixed operating costs to magnify the effect of changes in sales on earnings before interest and taxes (EBIT). Adobe and its peers in the software industry incur the bulk of their costs early in a product's life cycle, in the research and development

and initial marketing stages. The up-front development costs are fixed, and subsequent production costs are practically zero. The economies of scale are huge: Once a company sells enough copies to cover its fixed costs, incremental dollars go primarily to profit.

As demonstrated in the following table, operating leverage magnified Adobe's *increase* in EBIT in 2007, 2010, and 2012 while magnifying the

decrease in EBIT in 2009. A 22.6 percent increase in 2007 sales resulted in EBIT growth of 39.7 percent, but in 2009 as the economy endured a severe recession, Adobe revenues plunged 17.7 percent. The effect of operating leverage was that EBIT declined even faster, posting a 35.3 percent drop.

▶ Summarize the pros and cons of operating leverage.

Item	FY2007	FY2008	FY2009	FY2010	FY2011	FY2012
Sales revenue (millions)	$3,158	$3,580	$2,946	$3,800	$4,216	$4,404
EBIT (millions)	$947	$1,089	$705	$1,000	$1,102	$1,186
(1) Percent change in sales	22.6%	13.4%	−17.7%	29.0%	11.0%	4.4%
(2) Percent change in EBIT	39.7%	15.0%	−35.3%	41.9%	10.2%	7.6%
DOL [(2) ÷ (1)]	1.8	1.1	2.0	1.4	0.9	1.7

Source: Adobe Systems Inc., "2009 and 2012 Annual Reports," http://www.adobe.com/investor-relations/financial-documents.html.

---

5. Technically, the formula for DOL given in Equation 12.5 should include absolute value signs because it is possible to get a negative DOL when the EBIT for the base sales level is negative. Because we assume that the EBIT for the base level of sales is positive, we do not use the absolute value signs.

6. When total revenue in dollars from sales—instead of unit sales—is available, the following equation, in which TR = total revenue in dollars at a base level of sales and TVC = total variable operating costs in dollars, can be used:

$$\text{DOL at base dollar sales } TR = \frac{TR - TVC}{TR - TVC - FC}$$

This formula is especially useful for finding the DOL for multiproduct firms. It should be clear that because in the case of a single-product firm, $TR = Q \times P$ and $TVC = Q \times VC$, substitution of these values into Equation 12.5 results in the equation given here.

Fixed Costs and Operating Leverage

Changes in fixed operating costs affect operating leverage significantly. Firms sometimes can alter the mix of fixed and variable costs in their operations. For example, a firm could make fixed-dollar lease payments rather than payments equal to a specified percentage of sales. or it could compensate sales representatives with a fixed salary and bonus rather than on a pure percent-of-sales commission basis. The effects of changes in fixed operating costs on operating leverage can best be illustrated by continuing our example.

Example 12.7 ▶
Assume that Cheryl's Posters eliminates sales commissions and increases salaries. This exchange results in a reduction in the variable cost per unit from $5 to $4.50 and an increase in the fixed costs from $2,500 to $3,000. Table 12.5 presents an analysis like that in Table 12.4, but using the new costs. Although the EBIT of $2,500 at the 1,000-unit sales level is the same as before the shift in cost structure, Table 12.5 shows that the firm has increased its operating leverage by increasing fixed costs and lowering variable costs.

With the substitution of the appropriate values into Equation 12.5, the degree of operating leverage at the 1,000-unit base level of sales becomes

$$\text{DOL at 1,000 units} = \frac{1,000 \times (\$10 - \$4.50)}{1,000 \times (\$10 - \$4.50) - \$3,000} = \frac{\$5,500}{\$2,500} = 2.2$$

Comparing this value to the DOL of 2.0 before the shift to more fixed costs makes it clear that the higher the firm's fixed operating costs relative to variable operating costs, the greater the degree of operating leverage. Under the new cost structure, a 50% change in sales would lead to a 110% (50% × 2.2) change in EBIT.

FINANCIAL LEVERAGE

financial leverage
The use of *fixed financial costs* to magnify the effects of changes in earnings before interest and taxes on the firm's earnings per share.

Financial leverage results from the presence of *fixed financial costs* that the firm must pay. Using the framework in Table 12.1, we can define **financial leverage** as the use of *fixed financial costs* to magnify the effects of changes in earnings

TABLE 12.5 ▷ Operating Leverage and Increased Fixed Costs

	Case 2		Case 1
	−50%		+50%
Sales (in units)	500	1,000	1,500
Sales revenue[a]	$5,000	$10,000	$15,000
Less: Variable operating costs[b]	2,250	4,500	6,750
Less: Fixed operating costs	3,000	3,000	3,000
Earnings before interest and taxes (EBIT)	−$ 250	$ 2,500	$ 5,250
	−110%		+110%

[a]Sales revenue was calculated as indicated in Table 12.4.
[b]Variable operating costs = $4.50/unit × sales in units.

before interest and taxes on the firm's earnings per share. The two most common fixed financial costs are (1) interest on debt and (2) preferred stock dividends. These charges must be paid regardless of the amount of EBIT available to pay them.[7]

Example 12.8 ▶

Chen Foods, a small Asian food company, expects EBIT of $10,000 in the current year. It has a $20,000 bond with a 10% (annual) coupon rate of interest and an issue of 600 shares of $4 (annual dividend per share) preferred stock outstanding. It also has 1,000 shares of common stock outstanding. The annual interest on the bond issue is $2,000 (0.10 × $20,000). The annual dividends on the preferred stock are $2,400 ($4.00/share × 600 shares). Table 12.6 presents the earnings per share (EPS) corresponding to levels of EBIT of $6,000, $10,000, and $14,000, assuming that the firm is in the 40% tax bracket. The table illustrates two situations:

Case 1 A 40% *increase* in EBIT (from $10,000 to $14,000) results in a 100% *increase* in earnings per share (from $2.40 to $4.80).

Case 2 A 40% *decrease* in EBIT (from $10,000 to $6,000) results in a 100% *decrease* in earnings per share (from $2.40 to $0).

TABLE 12.6	The EPS for Various EBIT Levels[a]				
		Case 2		**Case 1**	
		−40%		+40%	
EBIT		$6,000	$10,000		$14,000
Less: Interest (*I*)		2,000	2,000		2,000
Net profits before taxes		$4,000	$ 8,000		$12,000
Less: Taxes (*T* = 0.40)		1,600	3,200		4,800
Net profits after taxes		$2,400	$ 4,800		$ 7,200
Less: Preferred stock dividends (*PD*)		2,400	2,400		2,400
Earnings available for common (EAC)		$ 0	$ 2,400		$ 4,800
Earnings per share (EPS)		$\frac{\$0}{1,000} = \$0$	$\frac{\$2,400}{1,000} = \$2.40$		$\frac{\$4,800}{1,000} = \$4.80$
		−100%		+100%	

[a]As noted in Chapter 2, for accounting and tax purposes, interest is a *tax-deductible expense,* whereas dividends must be paid from after-tax cash flows.

The effect of financial leverage is such that an increase in the firm's EBIT results in a more-than-proportional increase in the firm's earnings per share, whereas a decrease in the firm's EBIT results in a more-than-proportional decrease in EPS.

7. Although a firm's board of directors can elect to stop paying preferred stock dividends, the firm typically cannot pay dividends on common stock until the preferred shareholders receive all the dividends that they are owed. Although failure to pay preferred dividends cannot force the firm into bankruptcy, it increases the common stockholders' risk because they cannot receive dividends until the claims of preferred stockholders are satisfied.

Measuring the Degree of Financial Leverage (DFL)

degree of financial leverage (DFL)
The numerical measure of the firm's financial leverage.

The **degree of financial leverage (DFL)** is a numerical measure of the firm's financial leverage. Computing it is much like computing the degree of operating leverage. One approach for obtaining the DFL is[8]

$$\text{DFL} = \frac{\text{Percentage change in EPS}}{\text{Percentage change in EBIT}} \quad (12.6)$$

Whenever the percentage change in EPS resulting from a given percentage change in EBIT is greater than the percentage change in EBIT, financial leverage exists. In other words, whenever DFL is greater than 1, there is financial leverage.

Example 12.9 ▶

Applying Equation 12.6 to cases 1 and 2 in Table 12.6 yields the following two cases:

Case 1 $\quad \dfrac{+100\%}{+40\%} = 2.5$

Case 2 $\quad \dfrac{-100\%}{-40\%} = 2.5$

These calculations show that when Chen Foods' EBIT changes, its EPS changes 2.5 times as fast on a percentage basis due to the firm's financial leverage. The higher this value is, the greater the degree of financial leverage.

Personal Finance Example 12.10 ▶

Shanta and Ravi Shandra wish to assess the impact effect of additional long-term borrowing on their degree of financial leverage (DFL). The Shandras currently have $4,200 available after meeting all their monthly living (operating) expenses, *before* making monthly loan payments. They currently have monthly loan payment obligations of $1,700 and are considering the purchase of a new car, which would result in a $500 per month increase (to $2,200) in their total monthly loan payments. Because a large portion of Ravi's monthly income represents commissions, the Shandras believe that the $4,200 per month currently available for making loan payments could vary by 20% above or below that amount.

To assess the potential impact of the additional borrowing on their financial leverage, the Shandras calculate their DFL for both their current ($1,700) and proposed ($2,200) loan payments as shown on the next page using the currently available $4,200 as a base and a 20% change.

Based on their calculations, the amount the Shandras will have available after loan payments with their current debt changes by 1.68% for every 1% change in the amount they will have available for making the loan payments.

---

8. This approach is valid only when the same base level of EBIT is used to calculate and compare these values. In other words, *the base level of EBIT must be held constant to compare the financial leverage associated with different levels of fixed financial costs.*

	Current DFL			Proposed DFL		
Available for making loan payments	$4,200	(+20%)	$5,040	$4,200	(+20%)	$5,040
Less: Loan payments	1,700		1,700	2,200		2,200
Available after loan payments	$2,500	(+33.6%)	$3,340	$2,000	(+42%)	$2,840

$$\text{DFL} = \frac{+33.6\%}{+20\%} = \underline{1.68}$$ $$\text{DFL} = \frac{+42\%}{+20\%} = \underline{2.10}$$

This change is considerably less responsive—and therefore less risky—than the 2.10% change in the amount available after loan payments for each 1% change in the amount available for making loan payments with the proposed additional $500 in monthly debt payments. Although it appears that the Shandras can afford the additional loan payments, they must decide if, given the variability of Ravi's income, they are comfortable with the increased financial leverage and risk.

A more direct formula for calculating the degree of financial leverage at a base level of EBIT is given by Equation 12.7, where the notation from Table 12.6 is used.[9] Note that in the denominator the term $1/(1 - T)$ converts the after-tax preferred stock dividend to a before-tax amount for consistency with the other terms in the equation.

$$\text{DFL at base level EBIT} = \frac{\text{EBIT}}{\text{EBIT} - I - \left(PD \times \dfrac{1}{1 - T}\right)} \tag{12.7}$$

Example 12.11 ▶

Entering EBIT = $10,000, I = $2,000, PD = $2,400, and the tax rate (T = 0.40) from Table 12.6 into Equation 12.7 yields

$$\text{DFL at \$10,000 EBIT} = \frac{\$10,000}{\$10,000 - \$2,000 - \left(\$2,400 \times \dfrac{1}{1 - 0.40}\right)}$$

$$= \frac{\$10,000}{\$4,000} = 2.5$$

Note that the formula given in Equation 12.7 provides a more direct method for calculating the degree of financial leverage than the approach illustrated using Table 12.6 and Equation 12.6.

---

9. By using the formula for DFL in Equation 12.7, it is possible to get a negative value for the DFL if the EPS for the base level of EBIT is negative. Rather than show absolute value signs in the equation, we instead assume that the base-level EPS is positive.

TOTAL LEVERAGE

total leverage
The use of *fixed costs, both operating and financial,* to magnify the effects of changes in sales on the firm's earnings per share.

We also can assess the combined effect of operating and financial leverage on the firm's risk by using a framework similar to that used to develop the individual concepts of leverage. This combined effect, or **total leverage,** can be defined as the use of *fixed costs, both operating and financial,* to magnify the effects of changes in sales on the firm's earnings per share. Total leverage can therefore be viewed as the *total impact of the fixed costs* in the firm's operating and financial structure.

Example 12.12 ▶

Cables, Inc., a computer cable manufacturer, expects sales of 20,000 units at $5 per unit in the coming year and must meet the following obligations: variable operating costs of $2 per unit, fixed operating costs of $10,000, interest of $20,000, and preferred stock dividends of $12,000. The firm is in the 40% tax bracket and has 5,000 shares of common stock outstanding. Table 12.7 presents the levels of earnings per share associated with the expected sales of 20,000 units and with sales of 30,000 units.

Table 12.7 illustrates that as a result of a 50% increase in sales (from 20,000 to 30,000 units), the firm would experience a 300% increase in earnings per share (from $1.20 to $4.80). Although it is not shown in the table, a 50% decrease in sales would, conversely, result in a 300% decrease in earnings per share. The linear nature of the leverage relationship accounts for the fact that sales changes of equal magnitude in opposite directions result in EPS changes of equal magnitude in the corresponding direction. At this point, it should be clear that whenever a firm has fixed costs—operating or financial—in its structure, total leverage will exist.

TABLE 12.7 ▶ The Total Leverage Effect

	+50%	
Sales (in units)	20,000	30,000
Sales revenue[a]	$100,000	$150,000
Less: Variable operating costs[b]	40,000	60,000
Less: Fixed operating costs	10,000	10,000
Earnings before interest and taxes (EBIT)	$ 50,000	$ 80,000
	+60%	
Less: Interest	20,000	20,000
Net profits before taxes	$ 30,000	$ 60,000
Less: Taxes ($T = 0.40$)	12,000	24,000
Net profits after taxes	$ 18,000	$ 36,000
Less: Preferred stock dividends	12,000	12,000
Earnings available for common stockholders	$ 6,000	$ 24,000
Earnings per share (EPS)	$\frac{\$6,000}{5,000} = \$1.20$	$\frac{\$24,000}{5,000} = \$4.80$
	+300%	

$$DOL = \frac{+60\%}{+50\%} = 1.2$$

$$DFL = \frac{+300\%}{+60\%} = 5.0$$

$$DTL = \frac{+300\%}{+50\%} = 6.0$$

[a]Sales revenue = $5/unit × sales in units.
[b]Variable operating costs = $2/unit × sales in units.

Measuring the Degree of Total Leverage (DTL)

degree of total leverage (DTL)
The numerical measure of the firm's total leverage.

The **degree of total leverage (DTL)** is a numerical measure of the firm's total leverage. It can be computed much like operating and financial leverage are computed. One approach for measuring DTL is[10]

$$DTL = \frac{\text{Percentage change in EPS}}{\text{Percentage change in sales}} \qquad (12.8)$$

Whenever the percentage change in EPS resulting from a given percentage change in sales is greater than the percentage change in sales, total leverage exists. In other words, as long as the DTL is greater than 1, there is total leverage.

Example 12.13 ▶

Applying Equation 12.8 to the data in Table 12.7 yields

$$DTL = \frac{+300\%}{+50\%} = 6.0$$

Because this result is greater than 1, total leverage exists. The higher the value is, the greater the degree of total leverage.

A more direct formula for calculating the degree of total leverage at a given base level of sales, Q, is given by the following equation,[11] which uses the same notation that was presented earlier:

$$DTL \text{ at base sales level } Q = \frac{Q \times (P - VC)}{Q \times (P - VC) - FC - I - \left(PD \times \dfrac{1}{1 - T}\right)} \qquad (12.9)$$

Example 12.14 ▶

Substituting $Q = 20{,}000$, $P = \$5$, $VC = \$2$, $FC = \$10{,}000$, $I = \$20{,}000$, $PD = \$12{,}000$, and the tax rate ($T = 0.40$) into Equation 12.9 yields

DTL at 20,000 units

$$= \frac{20{,}000 \times (\$5 - \$2)}{20{,}000 \times (\$5 - \$2) - \$10{,}000 - \$20{,}000 - \left(\$12{,}000 \times \dfrac{1}{1 - 0.40}\right)}$$

$$= \frac{\$60{,}000}{\$10{,}000} = 6.0$$

Clearly, the formula used in Equation 12.9 provides a more direct method for calculating the degree of total leverage than the approach illustrated using Table 12.7 and Equation 12.8.

---

10. This approach is valid only when the same base level of sales is used to calculate and compare these values. In other words, *the base level of sales must be held constant if we are to compare the total leverage associated with different levels of fixed costs.*

11. By using the formula for DTL in Equation 12.9, it is possible to get a negative value for the DTL if the EPS for the base level of sales is negative. For our purposes, rather than show absolute value signs in the equation, we instead assume that the base-level EPS is positive.

Relationship of Operating, Financial, and Total Leverage

Total leverage reflects the *combined impact* of operating and financial leverage on the firm. High operating leverage and high financial leverage will cause total leverage to be high. The opposite will also be true. The relationship between operating leverage and financial leverage is *multiplicative* rather than *additive*. The relationship between the degree of total leverage (DTL) and the degrees of operating leverage (DOL) and financial leverage (DFL) is given by

$$\text{DTL} = \text{DOL} \times \text{DFL} \qquad (12.10)$$

Example 12.15 ▶ Substituting the values calculated for DOL and DFL, shown on the right-hand side of Table 12.7, into Equation 12.10 yields

$$\text{DTL} = 1.2 \times 5.0 = 6.0$$

The resulting degree of total leverage is the same value that we calculated directly in the preceding examples.

→ REVIEW QUESTIONS

12–1 What is meant by the term *leverage*? How are operating leverage, financial leverage, and total leverage related to the income statement?

12–2 What is the *operating breakeven point*? How do changes in fixed operating costs, the sale price per unit, and the variable operating cost per unit affect it?

12–3 What is *operating leverage*? What causes it? How is the *degree of operating leverage (DOL)* measured?

12–4 What is *financial leverage*? What causes it? How is the *degree of financial leverage (DFL)* measured?

12–5 What is the general relationship among operating leverage, financial leverage, and the total leverage of the firm? Do these types of leverage complement one another? Why or why not?

  ## 12.2 The Firm's Capital Structure

MyFinanceLab Video

Capital structure is one of the most complex areas of financial decision making because of its interrelationship with other financial decision variables. Poor capital structure decisions can result in a high cost of capital, thereby lowering the NPVs of projects and making more of them unacceptable. Effective capital structure decisions can lower the cost of capital, resulting in higher NPVs and more acceptable projects and thereby increasing the value of the firm.

TYPES OF CAPITAL

All the items on the right-hand side of the firm's balance sheet, excluding current liabilities, are sources of capital. The following simplified balance sheet illustrates the basic breakdown of total capital into its two components, *debt capital* and *equity capital*:

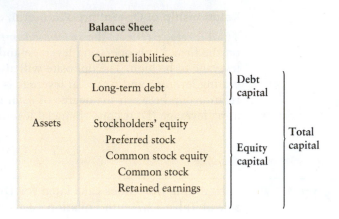

The cost of debt is lower than the cost of other forms of financing. Lenders demand relatively lower returns because they take the least risk of any contributors of long-term capital. Lenders have a higher priority of claim against any earnings or assets available for payment, and they can exert far greater legal pressure against the company to make payment than can owners of preferred or common stock. The tax deductibility of interest payments also lowers the debt cost to the firm substantially.

Unlike debt capital, which the firm must eventually repay, *equity capital* remains invested in the firm indefinitely; it has no maturity date. The two main sources of equity capital are (1) preferred stock and (2) common stock equity, which includes common stock and retained earnings. Common stock is typically the most expensive form of equity, followed by retained earnings and then preferred stock. Our concern here is the relationship between debt and equity capital. In general, the more debt a firm uses, the greater will be the firm's financial leverage. That leverage makes the claims of common stockholders even more risky. In addition, a firm that increases its use of leverage significantly can see its cost of debt rise as lenders begin to worry about the firm's ability to repay its debts. Whether the firm borrows very little or a great deal, it is always true that the claims of common stockholders are riskier than those of lenders, so the cost of equity always exceeds the cost of debt.

EXTERNAL ASSESSMENT OF CAPITAL STRUCTURE

We saw earlier that *financial leverage* results from the use of fixed-cost financing, such as debt and preferred stock, to magnify return and risk. The amount of leverage in the firm's capital structure can affect its value by affecting return and risk. Those outside the firm can make a rough assessment of capital structure by using measures found in the firm's financial statements. Some of these important debt ratios were presented in Chapter 3. For example, a direct measure of the degree of indebtedness is the *debt ratio* (total liabilities ÷ total assets). The higher this ratio is, the greater the relative amount of debt (or financial leverage) in the firm's capital structure. Measures of the firm's ability to meet contractual payments associated with debt include the *times interest earned ratio* (EBIT ÷ interest) and the *fixed-payment coverage ratio* (see page 74). These ratios provide indirect information on financial leverage. Generally, the smaller these ratios, the greater the firm's financial leverage and the less able it is to meet payments as they come due.

The level of debt (financial leverage) that is acceptable for one industry or line of business can be highly risky in another, because different industries and

TABLE 12.8 Median Debt Ratios for Selected Industries (Fiscal Year 2011)		
NAICS Industry	Debt ratio	Times interest earned ratio
Agriculture, forestry, fishing, and hunting	41.0%	2.6
Mining, quarrying, and oil and gas extraction	44.8	1.8
Utilities	69.2	3.1
Construction	57.7	1.2
Manufacturing	47.8	3.8
Wholesale trade	58.7	5.5
Retail trade	56.4	5.2
Transportation and warehousing	61.2	2.8
Information	52.6	2.3
Finance and insurance	88.3	3.9
Real estate and rental and leasing	56.4	1.3
Professional, scientific, and technical services	46.9	3.9
Administrative and support and waste management and remediation services	54.9	3.7
Educational services	38.8	21.5
Health care and social assistance	62.0	3.1
Arts, entertainment, and recreation	54.7	2.2
Accommodation and food services	59.3	2.8
Other services (except public administration)	76.2	3.0

Source: Author-generated values. Industries are 2012 NAICS industry sectors.

lines of business have different operating characteristics. Table 12.8 presents the debt and times interest earned ratios for selected industries and lines of business. Significant industry differences can be seen in these data. Differences in debt positions are also likely to exist *within* an industry or line of business.

Personal Finance Example 12.16 ▶ Those who lend to individuals, like lenders to corporations, typically use ratios to assess the applicant's ability to meet the contractual payments associated with the requested debt. The lender, after obtaining information from a loan application and other sources, calculates ratios and compares them to predetermined allowable values. Typically, if the applicant's ratio values are within the acceptable range, the lender will make the requested loan.

The best example of this process is a real estate mortgage loan application. The mortgage lender usually invokes the following two requirements:

1. Monthly mortgage payments < 25% to 30% of monthly gross (before-tax) income
2. Total monthly installment payments (including the mortgage payment) < 33% to 38% of monthly gross (before-tax) income

Assume that the Loo family is applying for a mortgage loan. The family's monthly gross (before-tax) income is $5,380, and they currently have monthly installment loan obligations that total $560. The $200,000 mortgage loan they are applying for will require monthly payments of $1,400. The lender requires

(1) the monthly mortgage payment to be less than 28% of monthly gross income and (2) total monthly installment payments (including the mortgage payment) to be less than 37% of monthly gross income. The lender calculates and evaluates these ratios for the Loos, as shown below.

1. Mort. pay. ÷ Gross income = $1,400 ÷ $5,380
$$= 26\% < 28\% \text{ maximum, therefore } \mathbf{OK}$$

2. Tot. instal. pay. ÷ Gross income = ($560 + $1,400) ÷ $5,380
$$= \$1,960 \div \$5,380$$
$$= 36.4\% < 37\% \text{ maximum, therefore } \mathbf{OK}$$

The Loos' ratios meet the lender's standards. So, assuming that they have adequate funds for the down payment and meet other lender requirements, the Loos will be granted the loan.

CAPITAL STRUCTURE OF NON–U.S. FIRMS

In general, non–U.S. companies have much higher degrees of indebtedness than their U.S. counterparts. Most of the reasons are because U.S. capital markets are more developed than those elsewhere and have played a greater role in corporate financing than has been the case in other countries. In most European countries, and especially in Japan and other Pacific Rim nations, large commercial banks are more actively involved in the financing of corporate activity than has been true in the United States. Furthermore, in many of these countries, banks are allowed to make large equity investments in nonfinancial corporations, a practice prohibited for U.S. banks. Finally, share ownership tends to be more tightly controlled among founding-family, institutional, and even public investors in Europe and Asia than it is for most large U.S. corporations. Tight ownership enables owners to understand the firm's financial condition better, resulting in their willingness to tolerate a higher degree of indebtedness.

> ### Matter of fact
>
> **Leverage around the World**
>
> A study of the use of long-term debt in 42 countries found that firms in Argentina used more long-term debt than firms in any other country. Relative to their assets, firms in Argentina used almost 60 percent more long-term debt than did U.S. companies. Indian firms were heavy users of long-term debt as well. At the other end of the spectrum, companies from Italy, Greece, and Poland used very little long-term debt. In those countries, firms used only about 40 percent as much long-term debt as did their U.S. counterparts.

On the other hand, similarities do exist between U.S. corporations and corporations in other countries. First, the same industry patterns of capital structure tend to be found all around the world. For example, in nearly all countries, pharmaceutical and other high-growth industrial firms tend to have lower debt ratios than do steel companies, airlines, and electric utility companies. In part, it has to do with the nature of assets held by these firms. High-growth firms whose main assets are intangibles (such as patents and rights to intellectual property) tend to borrow less tha-firms that have tangible assets that can be pledged as collateral for loans. Second, the capital structures of the largest U.S.–based multinational companies, which have access to capital markets around the world, typically resemble the capital structures of multinational companies from other countries more than they resemble those of smaller U.S. companies. In other words, in most countries there is a tendency for larger firms to borrow more than smaller firms do. Third, companies that are riskier and have more volatile income streams tend to borrow less, as do firms that are highly profitable. Finally, the worldwide trend is away from reliance on banks for financing and toward greater reliance on security issuance. Over time, the differences in the capital structures of U.S. and non–U.S. firms will probably lessen.

CAPITAL STRUCTURE THEORY

Research suggests that there is an optimal capital structure range. *It is not yet possible to provide financial managers with a precise methodology for determining a firm's optimal capital structure.* Nevertheless, financial theory does offer help in understanding how a firm's capital structure affects the firm's value.

In 1958, Franco Modigliani and Merton H. Miller[12] (commonly known as "M and M") demonstrated mathematically that, assuming perfect markets,[13] the capital structure that a firm chooses does not affect its value. Many researchers, including M and M, have examined whether capital structure may in fact affect firm value in imperfect, real-world markets. The result is a theoretical *optimal* capital structure based on balancing the benefits and costs of debt financing. The major benefit of debt financing is the *tax shield,* which allows interest payments to be deducted in calculating taxable income. The cost of debt financing results from (1) the increased probability of bankruptcy caused by debt obligations, (2) the *agency costs* of the lender's constraining the firm's actions, and (3) the costs associated with managers having more information about the firm's prospects than do investors.

Tax Benefits

Allowing firms to deduct interest payments on debt when calculating taxable income reduces the amount of the firm's earnings paid in taxes, thereby making more earnings available for bondholders and stockholders. The deductibility of interest means the cost of debt, r_i, to the firm is subsidized by the government. Letting r_d equal the before-tax cost of debt and letting T equal the tax rate, from Chapter 9 (Equation 9.2), we have $r_i = r_d \times (1 - T)$.

Probability of Bankruptcy

The chance that a firm will become bankrupt because of an inability to meet its obligations as they come due depends largely on its levels of both business risk and financial risk.

Business Risk   We define *business risk* as the risk to the firm of being unable to cover its operating costs. In general, the greater the firm's *operating*

12. Franco Modigliani and Merton H. Miller, "The Cost of Capital, Corporation Finance, and the Theory of Investment," *American Economic Review* (June 1958), pp. 261–297.
13. Perfect-market assumptions include (1) no taxes, (2) no brokerage or flotation costs for securities, (3) symmetrical information (that is, investors and managers have the same information about the firm's investment prospects), and (4) investor ability to borrow at the same rate as corporations.

leverage—the use of fixed operating costs—the higher its business risk. Although operating leverage is an important factor affecting business risk, two other factors—revenue stability and cost stability—also affect it. *Revenue stability* reflects the relative variability of the firm's sales revenues. Firms with stable levels of demand and product prices tend to have stable revenues. The result is low levels of business risk. Firms with highly volatile product demand and prices have unstable revenues that result in high levels of business risk. *Cost stability* reflects the relative predictability of input prices such as those for labor and materials. The more predictable and stable these input prices are, the lower the business risk; the less predictable and stable they are, the higher the business risk.

Business risk varies among firms, regardless of their lines of business, and is not affected by capital structure decisions. The level of business risk must be taken as a "given." The higher a firm's business risk, the more cautious the firm must be in establishing its capital structure. Firms with high business risk therefore tend toward less highly leveraged capital structures, and firms with low business risk tend toward more highly leveraged capital structures. We will hold business risk constant throughout the discussions that follow.

Example 12.17 ▶   Cooke Company, a soft drink manufacturer, is preparing to make a capital structure decision. It has obtained estimates of sales and the associated levels of earnings before interest and taxes (EBIT) from its forecasting group: There is a 25% chance that sales will total $400,000, a 50% chance that sales will total $600,000, and a 25% chance that sales will total $800,000. Fixed operating costs total $200,000, and variable operating costs equal 50% of sales. These data are summarized, and the resulting EBIT calculated, in Table 12.9.

Table 12.9 shows that there is a 25% chance that the EBIT will be $0, a 50% chance that it will be $100,000, and a 25% chance that it will be $200,000. When developing the firm's capital structure, the financial manager must accept as given these levels of EBIT and their associated probabilities. These EBIT data effectively reflect a certain level of business risk that captures the firm's operating leverage, sales revenue variability, and cost predictability.

TABLE 12.9 Sales and Associated EBIT Calculations for Cooke Company ($000)			
Probability of sales	0.25	0.50	0.25
Sales revenue	$400	$600	$800
Less: Fixed operating costs	200	200	200
Less: Variable operating costs (50% of sales)	200	300	400
Earnings before interest and taxes (EBIT)	$ 0	$100	$200

The penalty for not meeting financial obligations is bankruptcy. The more fixed-cost financing—debt (including financial leases) and preferred stock—a firm has in its capital structure, the greater its financial leverage and risk. Financial risk depends on the capital structure decision made by the management, and that decision is affected by the business risk the firm faces.

Total Risk   The *total risk* of a firm—business and financial risk combined—determines its probability of bankruptcy. Financial risk, its relationship to business risk, and their combined impact can be demonstrated by continuing the Cooke Company example.

Example 12.18 ▶   Cooke Company's current capital structure is as follows:

Current capital structure	
Long-term debt	$ 0
Common stock equity (25,000 shares at $20)	500,000
Total capital (assets)	$ 500,000

Let us assume that the firm is considering seven alternative capital structures. If we measure these structures using the debt ratio, they are associated with ratios of 0%, 10%, 20%, 30%, 40%, 50%, and 60%. Assuming that (1) the firm has no current liabilities, (2) its capital structure currently contains all equity as shown, and (3) the total amount of capital remains constant[14] at $500,000, the mix of debt and equity associated with the seven debt ratios would be as shown in Table 12.10. Also shown in the table is the number of shares of common stock outstanding under each alternative.

Associated with each of the debt levels in column 3 of Table 12.10 would be an interest rate that would be expected to increase with increases in financial

TABLE 12.10	Capital Structures Associated with Alternative Debt Ratios for Cooke Company

| | Capital structure ($000) | | | Shares of common stock outstanding (000) |
Debt ratio (1)	Total assets[a] (2)	Debt [(1) × (2)] (3)	Equity [(2) − (3)] (4)	[(4) ÷ $20][b] (5)
0%	$500	$ 0	$500	25.00
10	500	50	450	22.50
20	500	100	400	20.00
30	500	150	350	17.50
40	500	200	300	15.00
50	500	250	250	12.50
60	500	300	200	10.00

[a]Because the firm, for convenience, is assumed to have no current liabilities, its total assets equal its total capital of $500,000.

[b]The $20 value represents the book value per share of common stock equity noted earlier.

14. This assumption is needed so that we can assess alternative capital structures without having to consider the returns associated with the investment of additional funds raised. Attention here is given only to the *mix* of capital, not to its investment.

TABLE 12.11	Level of Debt, Interest Rate, and Dollar Amount of Annual Interest Associated with Cooke Company's Alternative Capital Structures

Capital structure debt ratio	Debt ($000) (1)	Interest rate on *all* debt (2)	Interest ($000) [(1) × (2)] (3)
0%	$ 0	0.0%	$ 0.00
10	50	9.0	4.50
20	100	9.5	9.50
30	150	10.0	15.00
40	200	11.0	22.00
50	250	13.5	33.75
60	300	16.5	49.50

leverage. The level of debt, the associated interest rate (assumed to apply to *all* debt), and the dollar amount of annual interest associated with each of the alternative capital structures are summarized in Table 12.11. Because both the level of debt and the interest rate increase with increasing financial leverage (debt ratios), the annual interest increases as well.

Table 12.12 uses the levels of EBIT and associated probabilities developed in Table 12.9, the number of shares of common stock found in column 5 of Table 12.10, and the annual interest values calculated in column 3 of Table 12.11 to calculate the earnings per share (EPS) for debt ratios of 0%, 30%, and 60% A 40% tax rate is assumed. Also shown are the resulting expected EPS, the standard deviation of EPS, and the coefficient of variation of EPS associated with each debt ratio.[15]

Table 12.13 summarizes the pertinent data for the seven alternative capital structures. The values shown for 0%, 30%, and 60% debt ratios were developed in Table 12.12; calculations of similar values for the other debt ratios (10%, 20%, 40%, and 50%) are not shown. Because the coefficient of variation measures the risk relative to the expected EPS, it is the preferred risk measure for use in comparing capital structures. As the firm's financial leverage increases, so does its coefficient of variation of EPS. As expected, an increasing level of risk is associated with increased levels of financial leverage.

The relative risks of the two extremes of the capital structures evaluated in Table 12.12 (debt ratios = 0% and 60%) can be illustrated by showing the probability distribution of EPS associated with each of them. Figure 12.3 shows these two distributions. The expected level of EPS increases with increasing financial leverage, and so does risk as reflected by the difference in dispersion between the distributions. Clearly, the uncertainty of the expected EPS, as well as the chance of experiencing negative EPS, is greater when higher degrees of financial leverage are employed.

Further, the nature of the risk–return trade-off associated with the seven capital structures under consideration can be clearly observed by plotting the

---

15. For explanatory convenience, the *coefficient of variation of EPS,* which measures total (nondiversifiable and diversifiable) risk, is used throughout this chapter as a proxy for beta, which measures the relevant nondiversifiable risk.

TABLE 12.12	Calculation of EPS for Selected Debt Ratios ($000) for Cooke Company		
Probability of EBIT	0.25	0.50	0.25
Debt ratio = 0%			
EBIT (Table 12.9)	$ 0.00	$100.00	$200.00
Less: Interest (Table 12.11)	0.00	0.00	0.00
Net profits before taxes	$ 0.00	$100.00	$200.00
Less: Taxes ($T = 0.40$)	0.00	40.00	80.00
Net profits after taxes	$0.00	$ 60.00	$120.00
EPS (25.0 shares, Table 12.10)	$ 0.00	$ 2.40	$ 4.80
Expected EPS[a]	$2.40		
Standard deviation of EPS[a]	$1.70		
Coefficient of variation of EPS[a]	0.71		
Debt ratio = 30%			
EBIT (Table 12.9)	$ 0.00	$100.00	$200.00
Less: Interest (Table 12.11)	15.00	15.00	15.00
Net profits before taxes	($15.00)	$ 85.00	$185.00
Less: Taxes ($T = 0.40$)	(6.00)[b]	34.00	74.00
Net profits after taxes	($ 9.00)	$ 51.00	$111.00
EPS (17.50 shares, Table 12.10)	(0.51)	$ 2.91	$ 6.34
Expected EPS[a]	$2.91		
Standard deviation of EPS[a]	$2.42		
Coefficient of variation of EPS[a]	0.83		
Debt ratio = 60%			
EBIT (Table 12.9)	$ 0.00	$100.00	$200.00
Less: Interest (Table 12.11)	49.50	49.50	49.50
Net profits before taxes	($49.50)	$ 50.50	$150.50
Less: Taxes ($T = 0.40$)	(19.80)[b]	20.20	60.20
Net profits after taxes	($29.70)	$ 30.30	$ 90.30
EPS (10.00 shares, Table 12.10)	($ 2.97)	$ 3.03	$ 9.03
Expected EPS[a]	$3.03		
Standard deviation of EPS[a]	$4.24		
Coefficient of variation of EPS[a]	1.40		

[a]The procedures used to calculate the expected value, standard deviation, and coefficient of variation were presented in Chapter 8.

[b]It is assumed that the firm receives the tax benefit from its loss in the current period as a result of applying the *tax loss carryback* procedures specified in the tax law but not discussed in this text.

expected EPS and coefficient of variation relative to the debt ratio. Plotting the data from Table 12.13 results in Figure 12.4. The figure shows that as debt is substituted for equity (as the debt ratio increases), the level of EPS rises and then begins to fall (graph a). The graph demonstrates that the peak of earnings per

TABLE 12.13	Expected EPS, Standard Deviation, and Coefficient of Variation for Alternative Capital Structures for Cooke Company		
Capital structure debt ratio	Expected EPS (1)	Standard deviation of EPS (2)	Coefficient of variation of EPS [(2) ÷ (1)] (3)
0%	$2.40	$1.70	0.71
10	2.55	1.88	0.74
20	2.72	2.13	0.78
30	2.91	2.42	0.83
40	3.12	2.83	0.91
50	3.18	3.39	1.07
60	3.03	4.24	1.40

share occurs at a debt ratio of 50%. The decline in earnings per share beyond that ratio results from the fact that the significant increases in interest are not fully offset by the reduction in the number of shares of common stock outstanding.

If we look at the risk behavior as measured by the coefficient of variation (graph **b**), we can see that risk increases with increasing leverage. A portion of th~ risk can be attributed to business risk, but the portion that changes in response increasing financial leverage would be attributed to financial risk.

FIGURE 12.3

Probability Distributions
Probability distributions of EPS for debt ratios of 0 percent and 60 percent for Cooke Company

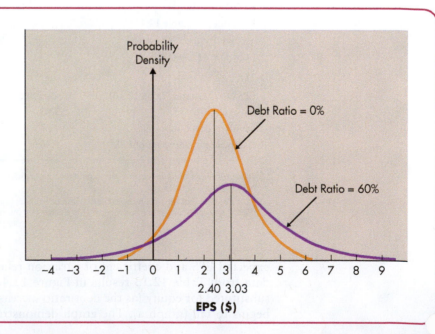

FIGURE 12.4

Expected EPS and Coefficient of Variation of EPS
Expected EPS and coefficient of variation of EPS for alternative capital structures for Cooke Company

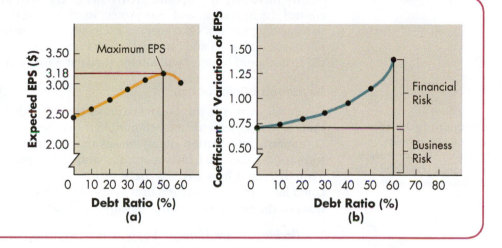

Clearly, a risk–return trade-off exists relative to the use of financial leverage. Later in the chapter, we will address how to combine these risk–return factors into a valuation framework. The key point to recognize here is that as a firm introduces more leverage into its capital structure, it will typically experience increases in both the expected level of return and the associated risk.

Agency Costs Imposed by Lenders

As noted in Chapter 1, the managers of firms typically act as *agents* of the owners (stockholders). The owners give the managers the authority to manage the firm for the owners' benefit. The *agency problem* created by this relationship extends not only to the relationship between owners and managers but also to the relationship between owners and lenders.

When a lender provides funds to a firm, the interest rate charged is based on the lender's assessment of the firm's risk. The lender–borrower relationship therefore depends on the lender's expectations for the firm's subsequent behavior. The borrowing rates are, in effect, locked in when the loans are negotiated. After obtaining a loan at a certain rate, the firm could increase its risk by investing in risky projects or by incurring additional debt. Such action could weaken the lender's position in terms of its claim on the cash flow of the firm. From another point of view, if these risky investment strategies paid off, the stockholders would benefit. Because payment obligations to the lender remain unchanged, the excess cash flows generated by a positive outcome from the riskier action would enhance the value of the firm to its owners. In other words, if the risky investments pay off, the owners receive all the benefits; if the risky investments do not pay off, the lenders share in the costs.

Clearly, an incentive exists for the managers acting on behalf of the stockholders to "take advantage" of lenders. To avoid this situation, lenders impose certain monitoring techniques on borrowers, who as a result incur *agency costs*. The most obvious strategy is to deny subsequent loan requests or to increase the cost of future loans to the firm. But this strategy is an after-the-fact approach. Therefore, lenders typically protect themselves by including in the loan agreement provisions that limit the firm's ability to alter its business and financial risk. These loan provisions tend to center on issues such as the minimum level of liquidity, asset acquisitions, executive salaries, and dividend payments.

By including appropriate provisions in the loan agreement, the lender can control the firm's risk and thus protect itself against the adverse consequences of this agency problem. Of course, in exchange for incurring agency costs by agreeing to the operating and financial constraints placed on it by the loan provisions, the firm should benefit by obtaining funds at a lower cost.

Asymmetric Information

asymmetric information
The situation in which managers of a firm have more information about operations and future prospects than do investors.

When two parties in an economic transaction have different information, we say that there is **asymmetric information**. In the context of capital structure decisions, asymmetric information simply means that managers of the firm have more information about the firm's operations and future prospects than investors have. To understand how asymmetric information between managers and investors could have implications for a firm's capital structure, consider the following illustrations of the *pecking order* and *signaling theories*.

Pecking Order Theory   Suppose that managers of a firm have a highly profitable investment opportunity that requires financing. Managers would like to tell investors about this great investment opportunity, but investors are skeptical. After all, managers always have incentives to claim that their investment decisions will lead to fabulous profits, but investors have no way to verify these claims. If managers try to sell stock to finance the investments, investors are only willing to pay a price that reflects the verifiable information that they have, which means that managers have to sell stock at a discount (relative to the price that they could get if there were no asymmetric information). This situation makes raising new equity very costly, and sometimes managers may decide to pass up positive NPV investments to avoid having to sell equity to investors at a discount.

One solution to this problem is for managers to maintain financial slack, cash reserves from retained earnings that they can use to finance new investments. When firms do not have enough financial slack to finance their profitable investment opportunities, managers will prefer to raise external financing by issuing debt rather than equity. Providers of debt financing receive a fixed return, so when the new investment begins to generate high returns for the firm, those cash flows will largely go to the firm's existing stockholders.

pecking order theory
A hierarchy of financing that begins with retained earnings, which is followed by debt financing and finally external equity financing.

The consequence is that there is a financial **pecking order**, meaning a hierarchy of financing that begins with retained earnings, followed by debt, and finally new stock issues. When managers want to finance a new project, they will first do so using retained earnings. If internally generated cash is insufficient to fund new investments, managers will raise external financing through the debt markets. Issuing new equity is their last resort.

This pecking order theory is consistent with several facts about firms' financing decisions. First, the vast majority of new investments are funded through retained earnings, with firms raising external financing infrequently. Second, firms do raise debt with greater frequency than equity as the pecking order theory predicts. Third, as we have already noted, there is a general tendency for profitable companies (who have plenty of financial slack) to borrow less than unprofitable firms.

Signaling Theory   There is an old saying that goes, "Put your money where your mouth is." The idea is that anyone can brag, but only those who are willing to put real dollars at stake behind their claims ought to be believed. How does this aphorism relate to capital structure decisions? Suppose, for example, that management has information that the prospects for the firm's future are very good

Managers could issue a press release trying to convince investors that the firm's future is bright, but investors will want tangible evidence for the claims. Furthermore, providing that evidence has to be costly to the firm; otherwise, other firms with less rosy prospects will just mimic the actions of the firm with truly excellent prospects. One thing that managers might do is to borrow a lot of money by issuing debt. In so doing, they are demonstrating to the market that they have faith that the firm will generate sufficient cash flows in the future to retire the outstanding debt. Firms whose prospects are not as good will hesitate to issue a lot of debt because they may have difficulty repaying the debt and may even go bankrupt. In other words, issuing debt is a credible **signal** that managers believe the firm's performance will be very good in the future. Debt financing is a *positive signal* suggesting that management believes that the stock is "undervalued" and therefore a bargain.

By the same token, when firms decide to issue stock, investors worry that this move could be a *negative signal,* indicating that managers believe that the firm's future profitability may be rather poor and that the stock price is currently overvalued. Therefore, investors often interpret the announcement of a stock issue as bad news, and the stock price declines.

Most research casts doubt on the importance of signaling as a primary determinant of firms' capital structure choices. For instance, we have already seen that the most profitable firms tend to borrow less, whereas the signaling theory says that profitable firms should borrow more as a way to convince investors of just how high the firm's future profits will be. Furthermore, in surveys that ask managers to describe how they choose between debt and equity financing, managers rarely say that they choose debt as a way to convey information to investors. Still, the signaling theory predicts that a firm's stock price should rise when it issues debt and fall when it issues equity, and that is exactly what happens in the real world much of the time.

signaling theory
A financing action by management that is believed to reflect its view of the firm's stock value; generally, debt financing is viewed as a *positive signal* that management believes the stock is "undervalued," and a stock issue is viewed as a *negative signal* that management believes the stock is "overvalued."

OPTIMAL CAPITAL STRUCTURE

What, then, *is* the optimal capital structure, even if it exists (so far) only in theory? To provide some insight into an answer, we will examine some basic financial relationships. Because the value of a firm equals the present value of its future cash flows, it follows that *the value of the firm is maximized when the cost of capital is minimized.* In other words, the present value of future cash flows is at its highest when the discount rate (the cost of capital) is at its lowest. By using a modification of the simple zero-growth valuation model (see Equation 7.2 in Chapter 7), we can define the value of the firm, V, as

$$V = \frac{\text{EBIT} \times (1 - T)}{r_a} = \frac{\text{NOPAT}}{r_a} \qquad (12.11)$$

where

$$\begin{aligned}
\text{EBIT} &= \text{earnings before interest and taxes} \\
T &= \text{tax rate} \\
\text{NOPAT} &= \text{net operating profits after taxes, which is the after-} \\
&\quad \text{tax operating earnings available to the debt and} \\
&\quad \text{equity holders, EBIT} \times (1 - T) \\
r_a &= \text{weighted average cost of capital}
\end{aligned}$$

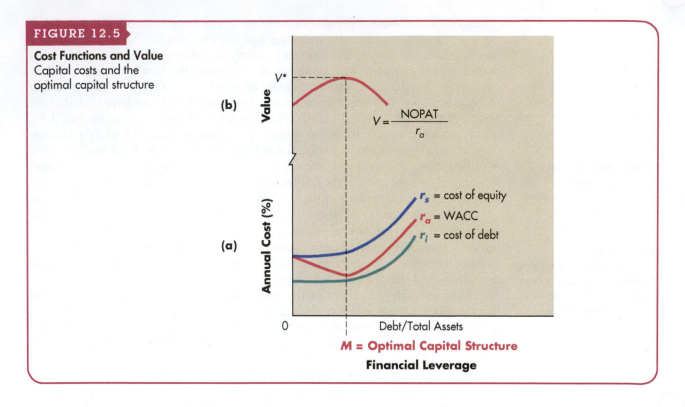

FIGURE 12.5

Cost Functions and Value
Capital costs and the optimal capital structure

Clearly, if we assume that NOPAT (and therefore EBIT) is constant, the value of the firm, V, is maximized by minimizing the weighted average cost of capital, r_a.

Cost Functions

Figure 12.5(*a*) plots three cost functions—the cost of debt, the cost of equity, and the weighted average cost of capital (WACC)—as a function of financial leverage measured by the debt ratio (debt to total assets). The *cost of debt, r_i,* remains low because of the tax shield, but it slowly increases as leverage increases, to compensate lenders for increasing risk. The *cost of equity, r_s,* is above the cost of debt. It increases as financial leverage increases, but it generally increases more rapidly than the cost of debt. The cost of equity rises because the stockholders require a higher return as leverage increases to compensate for the higher degree of financial risk.

The *weighted average cost of capital, r_a,* results from a weighted average of the firm's debt and equity capital costs. At a debt ratio of zero, the firm is 100 percent equity financed. As debt is substituted for equity and as the debt ratio increases, the WACC declines because the after-tax debt cost is less than the equity cost ($r_i < r_s$). In this range, the tax benefits of additional debt outweigh the costs of borrowing more. However, as the debt ratio continues to increase, the increased debt and equity costs eventually cause the WACC to rise, as can be seen after point M in Figure 12.5(*a*). In other words, the bankruptcy costs, agency costs, and other costs associated with higher debt levels eventually outweigh the additional tax benefits that the firm could generate by borrowing even more. This behavior results in a U-shaped, or saucer-shaped, weighted average cost-of-capital function, r_a.

Graphical View of Optimal Structure

optimal capital structure
The capital structure at which the weighted average cost of capital is minimized, thereby maximizing the firm's value.

Because the maximization of value, V, is achieved when the overall cost of capital, r_a, is at a minimum (see Equation 12.11), the **optimal capital structure** is that at which the weighted average cost of capital, r_a, is minimized. In Figure 12.5(a), point M represents the *minimum weighted average cost of capital,* the point of optimal financial leverage and hence of optimal capital structure for the firm. Figure 12.5(b) is a graph of the value of the firm that results from substitution of r_a in Figure 12.5(a) for various levels of financial leverage into the zero-growth valuation model in Equation 12.11. As shown in Figure 12.5(b), at the optimal capital structure, point M, the value of the firm is maximized at V^*.

Simply stated, minimizing the weighted average cost of capital allows management to undertake a larger number of profitable projects, thereby further increasing the value of the firm. However, as a practical matter, there is no way to calculate the optimal capital structure implied by Figure 12.5. Because it is impossible either to know or to remain at the precise optimal capital structure, firms generally try to operate in a *range* that places them near what they believe to be the optimal capital structure. In other words, firms usually manage toward a *target capital structure.*

→ REVIEW QUESTIONS

12–6 What is a firm's *capital structure*? What ratios assess the degree of financial leverage in a firm's capital structure?

12–7 In what ways are the capital structures of U.S. and non–U.S. firms different? How are they similar?

12–8 What is the major benefit of debt financing? How does it affect the firm's cost of debt?

12–9 What are *business risk* and *financial risk*? How does each of them influence the firm's capital structure decisions?

12–10 Briefly describe the *agency problem* that exists between owners and lenders. How do lenders cause firms to incur *agency costs* to resolve this problem?

12–11 How does *asymmetric information* affect the firm's capital structure decisions? How do the firm's financing actions give investors *signals* that reflect management's view of stock value?

12–12 How do the cost of debt, the cost of equity, and the weighted average cost of capital (WACC) behave as the firm's financial leverage increases from zero? Where is the *optimal capital structure*? What is its relationship to the firm's value at that point?

LG 5 | 12.3 | EBIT–EPS Approach to Capital Structure

It should be clear from earlier chapters that the goal of the financial manager is to maximize owner wealth, that is, the firm's stock price. One of the widely followed variables affecting the firm's stock price is its earnings, which represents the returns earned on behalf of owners. Even though focusing on earnings ignores risk (the other key variable affecting the firm's stock price), earnings per share (EPS) can be conveniently used to analyze alternative capital structures. The **EBIT–EPS approach** to capital structure involves selecting the capital structure that maximizes EPS over the expected range of earnings before interest and taxes (EBIT).

EBIT–EPS approach
An approach for selecting the capital structure that maximizes earnings per share (EPS) over the expected range of earnings before interest and taxes (EBIT).

PRESENTING A FINANCING PLAN GRAPHICALLY

To analyze the effects of a firm's capital structure on the owners' returns, we consider the relationship between earnings before interest and taxes (EBIT) and earnings per share (EPS). In other words, we want to see how changes in EBIT lead to changes in EPS under different capital structures. In all our examples, we will assume that business risk remains constant. That is, the firm's basic operational risks remain constant, and only financial risk varies as capital structures change. EPS is used to measure the owners' returns, which are expected to be closely related to share price.[16]

Data Required

To draw a graph illustrating how changes in EBIT lead to changes in EPS, we simply need to find two coordinates and plot a straight line between them. On our graph, we will plot EBIT on the horizontal axis and EPS on the vertical axis. The following example illustrates the approach for constructing the graph.

Example 12.19 ▶ We can plot coordinates on the EBIT–EPS graph by assuming specific EBIT values and calculating the EPS associated with them.[17] Such calculations for three capital structures—debt ratios of 0%, 30%, and 60%—for Cooke Company were presented in Table 12.12. For EBIT values of $100,000 and $200,000, the associated EPS values calculated there are summarized in the table below the graph in Figure 12.6.

Plotting the Data

The Cooke Company data can be plotted on a set of EBIT–EPS axes as shown in Figure 12.6. The figure shows the level of EPS expected for each level of EBIT. For levels of EBIT below the x-axis intercept, a loss (negative EPS) results. Each

---

16. The relationship that is expected to exist between EPS and owner wealth is not one of cause and effect. As indicated in Chapter 1, the maximization of profits does not necessarily ensure that owners' wealth is also maximized. Nevertheless, it is expected that the movement of earnings per share will have some effect on owners' wealth because EPS data constitute one of the few pieces of information investors receive, and they often bid the firm's share price up or down in response to the level of these earnings.

17. A convenient method for finding one EBIT–EPS coordinate is to calculate the *financial breakeven point,* the level of EBIT for which the firm's EPS just equals $0. It is the level of EBIT needed just to cover all fixed financial costs: annual interest (I) and preferred stock dividends (PD). The equation for the financial breakeven point is

$$\text{Financial breakeven point} = I + \frac{PD}{1 - T}$$

where T is the tax rate. It can be seen that when $PD = \$0$, the financial breakeven point is equal to I, the annual interest payment.

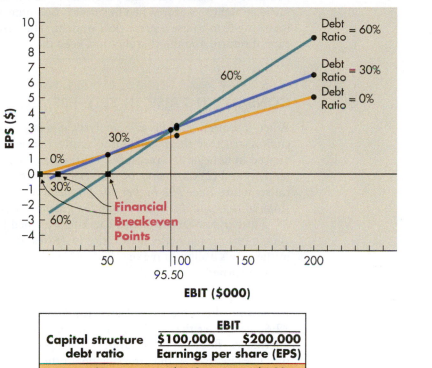

FIGURE 12.6

EBIT–EPS Approach
A comparison of selected capital structures for Cooke Company (data from Table 12.12)

Capital structure debt ratio	EBIT	
	$100,000	**$200,000**
	Earnings per share (EPS)	
0%	$2.40	$4.80
30	2.91	6.34
60	3.03	9.03

financial breakeven point
The level of EBIT necessary to just cover all *fixed financial costs;* the level of EBIT for which EPS = $0.

of the *x*-axis intercepts is a **financial breakeven point,** the level of EBIT necessary to just cover all *fixed financial costs* (EPS = $0).

COMPARING ALTERNATIVE CAPITAL STRUCTURES

We can compare alternative capital structures by graphing financing plans as shown in Figure 12.6.

Example 12.20 ▶ Cooke Company's capital structure alternatives were plotted on the EBIT–EPS axes in Figure 12.6. This figure shows that each capital structure is superior to the others in terms of maximizing EPS over certain ranges of EBIT. Having no debt at all (debt ratio = 0%) is best for levels of EBIT between $0 and $50,000. That conclusion makes sense because when business conditions are relatively weak, Cooke would have difficulty meeting its financial obligations if it had any debt. Between $50,000 and $95,500 of EBIT, the capital structure associated with a debt ratio of 30% produces higher EPS than either of the other two capital structures. And when EBIT exceeds $95,500, the 60% debt ratio capital structure provides the highest earnings per share.[18] Again, the intuition behind this result is fairly straightforward. When business is booming, the best thing for shareholders is for the firm to use a great deal of debt. The firm pays lenders a relatively low rate of return, and the shareholders keep the rest.

CONSIDERING RISK IN EBIT–EPS ANALYSIS

When interpreting EBIT–EPS analysis, it is important to consider the risk of each capital structure alternative. Graphically, the risk of each capital structure can be viewed in light of two measures: (1) the *financial breakeven point* (EBIT-axis intercept) and (2) the *degree of financial leverage* reflected in the slope of the capital structure line: *The higher the financial breakeven point and the steeper the slope of the capital structure line, the greater the financial risk.*[19]

Further assessment of risk can be performed by using ratios. As financial leverage (measured by the debt ratio) increases, we expect a corresponding decline in the firm's ability to make scheduled interest payments (measured by the times interest earned ratio).

Example 12.21 ▶   Reviewing the three capital structures plotted for Cooke Company in Figure 12.6, we can see that as the debt ratio increases, so does the financial risk of each alternative. Both the financial breakeven point and the slope of the capital structure lines increase with increasing debt ratios. If we use the $100,000 EBIT value, for example, the times interest earned ratio (EBIT ÷ interest) for the zero-leverage capital structure is infinity ($100,000 ÷ $0); for the 30% debt case, it is 6.67 ($100,000 ÷ $15,000); and for the 60% debt case, it is 2.02 ($100,000 ÷ $49,500). Because lower times interest earned ratios reflect higher risk, these ratios support the conclusion that the risk of the capital structures increases with

---

18. An algebraic technique can be used to find the *indifference points* between the capital structure alternatives. This technique involves expressing each capital structure as an equation stated in terms of earnings per share, setting the equations for two capital structures equal to each other, and solving for the level of EBIT that causes the equations to be equal. When we use the notation from footnote 17 and let n equal the number of shares of common stock outstanding, the general equation for the earnings per share from a financing plan is

$$EPS = \frac{(1 - T) \times (EBIT - I) - PD}{n}$$

Comparing Cooke Company's 0% and 30% capital structures, we get

$$\frac{(1 - 0.40) \times (EBIT - \$0) - \$0}{25.00} = \frac{(1 - 0.40) \times (EBIT - \$15.00) - \$0}{17.50}$$

$$\frac{0.60 \times EBIT}{25.00} = \frac{0.60 \times EBIT - \$9.00}{17.50}$$

$$10.50 \times EBIT = 15.00 \times EBIT - \$225.00$$

$$\$225.00 = 4.50 \times EBIT$$

$$EBIT = \$50$$

The calculated value of the indifference point between the 0% and 30% capital structures is therefore $50,000, as can be seen in Figure 12.6.

19. The degree of financial leverage (DFL) is reflected in the slope of the EBIT–EPS function. The steeper the slope, the greater the degree of financial leverage, because the change in EPS (y axis) that results from a given change in EBIT (x axis) increases with increasing slope and decreases with decreasing slope.

increasing financial leverage. The capital structure for a debt ratio of 60% is riskier than that for a debt ratio of 30%, which in turn is riskier than the capital structure for a debt ratio of 0%.

BASIC SHORTCOMING OF EBIT–EPS ANALYSIS

The most important point to recognize when using EBIT–EPS analysis is that this technique tends to concentrate on *maximizing earnings* rather than maximizing owner wealth as reflected in the firm's stock price. The use of an EPS-maximizing approach generally ignores risk. If investors did not require risk premiums (additional returns) as the firm increased the proportion of debt in its capital structure, a strategy involving maximizing EPS would also maximize stock price. But because risk premiums increase with increases in financial leverage, the maximization of EPS *does not* ensure owner wealth maximization. To select the best capital structure, firms must integrate both return (EPS) and risk (via the required return, r_s) into a valuation framework consistent with the capital structure theory presented earlier.

→ REVIEW QUESTION

12–13 Explain the *EBIT–EPS approach* to capital structure. Include in your explanation a graph indicating the *financial breakeven point;* label the axes. Is this approach consistent with maximization of the owners' wealth?

LG 6   12.4 Choosing the Optimal Capital Structure

This section describes the procedures for linking to market value the return and risk associated with alternative capital structures.

LINKAGE

To determine the firm's value under alternative capital structures, the firm must find the level of return that it must earn to compensate owners for the risk being incurred. This approach is consistent with the overall valuation framework developed in Chapters 6 and 7 and applied to capital budgeting decisions in Chapters 10 and 11.

The required return associated with a given level of financial risk can be estimated in a number of ways. Theoretically, the preferred approach would be first to estimate the beta associated with each alternative capital structure and then to use the CAPM framework presented in Equation 8.8 to calculate the required return, r_s. A more operational approach involves linking the financial risk associated with each capital structure alternative directly to the required return. Such an approach is similar to the CAPM-type approach demonstrated in Chapter 11 for linking project risk and required return (RADR). Here it involves estimating the required return associated with each level of financial risk as measured by a statistic such as the coefficient of variation of EPS. Regardless

TABLE 12.14	Required Returns for Cooke Company's Alternative Capital Structures	
Capital structure debt ratio	Coefficient of variation of EPS (from column 3 of Table 12.13) (1)	Estimated required return, r_s (2)
0%	0.71	11.5%
10	0.74	11.7
20	0.78	12.1
30	0.83	12.5
40	0.91	14.0
50	1.07	16.5
60	1.40	19.0

of the approach used, one would expect the required return to increase as the financial risk increases.

Example 12.22 ▶ Cooke Company, using as risk measures the coefficients of variation of EPS associated with each of the seven alternative capital structures, estimated the associated required returns, which are shown in Table 12.14. As expected, the estimated required return of owners, r_s, increases with increasing risk, as measured by the coefficient of variation of EPS.

ESTIMATING VALUE

The value of the firm associated with alternative capital structures can be estimated using one of the standard valuation models. If, for simplicity, we assume that all earnings are paid out as dividends, we can use a standard zero-growth valuation model such as that developed in Chapter 7. The model, originally stated in Equation 7.2, is restated here with EPS substituted for dividends (because in each year the dividends would equal EPS):

$$P_0 = \frac{\text{EPS}}{r_s} \tag{12.12}$$

By substituting the expected level of EPS and the associated required return, r_s, into Equation 12.12, we can estimate the per-share value of the firm, P_0.

Example 12.23 ▶ We can now estimate the value of Cooke Company's stock under each of the alternative capital structures. Substituting the expected EPS (column 1 of Table 12.13) and the required returns, r_s (column 2 of Table 12.14 in decimal form), into Equation 12.12 for each of the capital structures, we obtain the share values given in column 3 of Table 12.15. Plotting the resulting share values against the associated debt ratios, as shown in Figure 12.7, clearly illustrates that the maximum share value occurs at the capital structure associated with a debt ratio of 30%.

| TABLE 12.15 | Calculation of Share Value Estimates Associated with Alternative Capital Structures for Cooke Company |

Capital structure debt ratio	Expected EPS (from column 1 of Table 12.13) (1)	Estimated required return, r_s (from column 2 of Table 12.14) (2)	Estimated share value [(1) ÷ (2)] (3)
0%	$2.40	0.115	$20.87
10	2.55	0.117	21.79
20	2.72	0.121	22.48
30	2.91	0.125	23.28
40	3.12	0.140	22.29
50	3.18	0.165	19.27
60	3.03	0.190	15.95

MAXIMIZING VALUE VERSUS MAXIMIZING EPS

Throughout this text, we have specified the goal of the financial manager as maximizing owner wealth, not profit. Although some relationship exists between expected profit and value, there is no reason to believe that

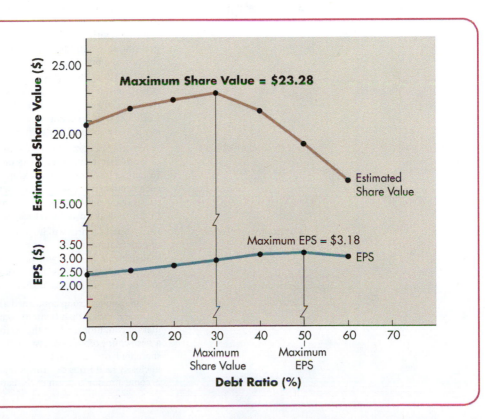

FIGURE 12.7

Estimating Value
Estimated share value and EPS for alternative capital structures for Cooke Company

profit-maximizing strategies necessarily result in wealth maximization. It is therefore the wealth of the owners as reflected in the estimated share value that should serve as the criterion for selecting the best capital structure. A final look at Cooke Company will highlight this point.

Example 12.24 ▸   Further analysis of Figure 12.7 clearly shows that although the firm's profits (EPS) are maximized at a debt ratio of 50%, share value is maximized at a 30% debt ratio. Therefore, the preferred capital structure would be the 30% debt ratio. The two approaches provide different conclusions because EPS maximization does not consider risk.

SOME OTHER IMPORTANT CONSIDERATIONS

Because there is really no practical way to calculate the optimal capital structure, any quantitative analysis of capital structure must be tempered with other important considerations. Table 12.16 summarizes some of the more important additional factors involved in capital structure decisions.

TABLE 12.16	**Important Factors to Consider in Making Capital Structure Decisions**	
Concern	Factor	Description
Business risk	Revenue stability	Firms that have stable and predictable revenues can more safely undertake highly leveraged capital structures than can firms with volatile patterns of sales revenue. Firms with growing sales tend to benefit from added debt; they can reap the positive benefits of financial leverage, which magnifies the effect of these increases.
	Cash flow	When considering a new capital structure, the firm must focus on its ability to generate the cash flows necessary to meet obligations. Cash forecasts reflecting an ability to service debts (and preferred stock) must support any shift in capital structure.
Agency costs	Contractual obligations	A firm may be contractually constrained with respect to the type of funds that it can raise. For example, a firm might be prohibited from selling additional debt except when the claims of holders of such debt are made subordinate to the existing debt. Contractual constraints on the sale of additional stock, as well as on the ability to distribute dividends on stock, might also exist.
	Management preferences	Occasionally, a firm will impose an internal constraint on the use of debt to limit its risk exposure to a level deemed acceptable to management. In other words, because of risk aversion, the firm's management constrains the firm's capital structure at a level that may or may not be the true optimum.
	Control	A management group concerned about control may prefer to issue debt rather than (voting) common stock. Under favorable market conditions, a firm that wanted to sell equity could make a *preemptive offering* or issue *nonvoting shares*, allowing each shareholder to maintain proportionate ownership. Generally, only in closely held firms or firms threatened by takeover does control become a major concern in the capital structure decision.

(continued)

TABLE 12.16 ⟩ **Important Factors to Consider in Making Capital Structure Decisions** *(continued)*		
Asymmetric information	External risk assessment	The firm's ability to raise funds quickly and at favorable rates depends on the external risk assessments of lenders and bond raters. The firm must consider the impact of capital structure decisions both on share value and on published financial statements from which lenders and raters assess the firm's risk.
	Timing	At times when interest rates are low, debt financing might be more attractive; when interest rates are high, the sale of stock may be more appealing. Sometimes both debt and equity capital become unavailable at reasonable terms. General economic conditions—especially those of the capital market—can thus significantly affect capital structure decisions.

→ **REVIEW QUESTIONS**

12–14 Why do *maximizing EPS* and *maximizing value* not necessarily lead to the same conclusion about the optimal capital structure?

12–15 What important factors in addition to quantitative factors should a firm consider when it is making a capital structure decision?

Summary

FOCUS ON VALUE

The amount of leverage (fixed-cost assets or funds) employed by a firm directly affects its risk, return, and share value. Generally, higher leverage raises risk and return, and lower leverage reduces risk and return. Operating leverage concerns the level of fixed operating costs; financial leverage focuses on fixed financial costs, particularly interest on debt and any preferred stock dividends. The firm's capital structure determines its financial leverage. Because of its fixed interest payments, the more debt a firm employs relative to its equity, the greater its financial leverage.

The value of the firm is clearly affected by its degree of operating leverage and by the composition of its capital structure. The financial manager must therefore carefully consider the types of operating and financial costs the firm will incur, recognizing that higher risk comes with greater fixed costs. Major decisions with regard to both operating cost structure and capital structure must therefore focus on their impact on the firm's value. The firm should implement only those leverage and capital structure decisions that are consistent with its goal of **maximizing its stock price**.

REVIEW OF LEARNING GOALS

LG 1 Discuss leverage, capital structure, breakeven analysis, the operating breakeven point, and the effect of changing costs on the breakeven point. Leverage results from the use of fixed costs to magnify returns to a firm's owners. Capital structure, the firm's mix of long-term debt and equity, affects leverage and therefore the firm's value. Breakeven analysis measures the level of sales necessary to cover total operating costs. The operating breakeven point may be calculated algebraically by dividing fixed operating costs by the difference between the sale price per unit and variable operating cost per unit, or it may be determined graphically. The operating breakeven point increases with increased fixed and variable operating costs and decreases with an increase in sale price, and vice versa.

LG 2 **Understand operating, financial, and total leverage and the relationships among them.** Operating leverage is the use of fixed operating costs by the firm to magnify the effects of changes in sales on EBIT. The higher the fixed operating costs, the greater the operating leverage. Financial leverage is the use of fixed financial costs by the firm to magnify the effects of changes in EBIT on EPS. The higher the fixed financial costs, the greater the financial leverage. The total leverage of the firm is the use of fixed costs—both operating and financial—to magnify the effects of changes in sales on EPS.

LG 3 **Describe the types of capital, external assessment of capital structure, the capital structure of non–U.S. firms, and capital structure theory.** Debt capital and equity capital make up a firm's capital structure. Capital structure can be externally assessed by using financial ratios: debt ratio, times interest earned ratio, and fixed-payment coverage ratio. Non–U.S. companies tend to have much higher degrees of indebtedness than do their U.S. counterparts, primarily because U.S. capital markets are more developed.

Research suggests that there is an optimal capital structure that balances the firm's benefits and costs of debt financing. The major benefit of debt financing is the tax shield. The costs of debt financing include the probability of bankruptcy, agency costs imposed by lenders, and asymmetric information, which typically causes firms to raise funds in a pecking order so as to send positive signals to the market and thereby enhance shareholder wealth.

LG 4 **Explain the optimal capital structure using a graphical view of the firm's cost-of-capital functions and a zero-growth valuation model.** The zero-growth valuation model defines the firm's value as its net operating profits after taxes (NOPAT), or after-tax EBIT, divided by its weighted average cost of capital. Assuming that NOPAT is constant, the value of the firm is maximized by minimizing its weighted average cost of capital (WACC). The optimal capital structure minimizes the WACC. Graphically, the firm's WACC exhibits a U-shape curve whose minimum value defines the optimal capital structure that maximizes owner wealth.

LG 5 **Discuss the EBIT–EPS approach to capital structure.** The EBIT–EPS approach evaluates capital structures in light of the returns they provide the firm's owners and their degree of financial risk. Under the EBIT–EPS approach, the preferred capital structure is the one that is expected to provide maximum EPS over the firm's expected range of EBIT. Graphically, this approach reflects risk in terms of the financial breakeven point and the slope of the capital structure line. The major shortcoming of EBIT–EPS analysis is that it concentrates on maximizing earnings (returns) rather than owners' wealth, which considers risk as well as return.

LG 6 **Review the return and risk of alternative capital structures, their linkage to market value, and other important considerations related to capital structure.** The best capital structure can be selected by using a valuation model to link return and risk factors. The preferred capital structure is the one that results in the highest estimated share value, not the highest EPS. Other important nonquantitative factors must also be considered when making capital structure decisions.

Self-Test Problems (Solutions in Appendix)

  ST12–1 **Breakeven point and all forms of leverage** TOR most recently sold 100,000 units at $7.50 each; its variable operating costs are $3.00 per unit, and its fixed operating costs are $250,000. Annual interest charges total $80,000, and the firm has 8,000 shares of $5 (annual dividend) preferred stock outstanding. It currently has 20,000 shares of common stock outstanding. Assume that the firm is subject to a 40% tax rate.

a. At what level of sales (in units) would the firm break even on operations (that is, EBIT = $0)?

b. Calculate the firm's *earnings per share (EPS)* in tabular form at (1) the current level of sales and (2) a 120,000-unit sales level.

c. Using the current *$750,000 level of sales as a base,* calculate the firm's degree of operating leverage (DOL).

d. Using the EBIT *associated with the $750,000 level of sales as a base,* calculate the firm's degree of financial leverage (DFL).

e. Use the degree of total leverage (DTL) concept to determine the effect (in percentage terms) of a 50% increase in TOR's sales *from the $750,000 base level* on its earnings per share.

 ST12–2 **EBIT–EPS analysis** Newlin Electronics is considering additional financing of $10,000. It currently has $50,000 of 12% (annual interest) bonds and 10,000 shares of common stock outstanding. The firm can obtain the financing through a 12% (annual interest) bond issue or through the sale of 1,000 shares of common stock. The firm has a 40% tax rate.

a. Calculate two EBIT–EPS coordinates for each plan by selecting any two EBIT values and finding their associated EPS values.

b. Plot the two financing plans on a set of EBIT–EPS axes.

c. On the basis of your graph in part **b**, at what level of EBIT does the bond plan become superior to the stock plan?

  ST12–3 **Optimal capital structure** Hawaiian Macadamia Nut Company has collected the data in the following table with respect to its capital structure, expected earnings per share, and required return.

Capital structure debt ratio	Expected earnings per share	Required return, r_s
0%	$3.12	13%
10	3.90	15
20	4.80	16
30	5.44	17
40	5.51	19
50	5.00	20
60	4.40	22

a. Compute the *estimated share value* associated with each of the capital structures, using the simplified method described in this chapter (see Equation 12.12).
b. Determine the optimal capital structure on the basis of (1) maximization of expected earnings per share and (2) maximization of share value.
c. Which capital structure do you recommend? Why?

Warm-Up Exercises   All problems are available in MyFinanceLab.

LG①   **E12–1**   Canvas Reproductions has fixed operating costs of $12,500 and variable operating costs of $10 per unit and sells its paintings for $25 each. At what level of unit sales will the company break even in terms of EBIT?

LG①   **E12–2**   The Great Fish Taco Corporation currently has fixed operating costs of $15,000, sells its premade tacos for $6 per box, and incurs variable operating costs of $2.50 per box. If the firm has a potential investment that would simultaneously raise its fixed costs to $16,500 and allow it to charge a per-box sale price of $6.50 due to better-textured tacos, what will the impact be on its operating breakeven point in boxes?

LG②   **E12–3**   Chico's has sales of 15,000 units at a price of $20 per unit. The firm incurs fixed operating costs of $30,000 and variable operating costs of $12 per unit. What is Chico's *degree of operating leverage (DOL)* at a base level of sales of 15,000 units?

LG②   **E12–4**   Parker Investments has EBIT of $20,000, interest expense of $3,000, and preferred dividends of $4,000. If it pays taxes at a rate of 38%, what is Parker's *degree of financial leverage (DFL)* at a base level of EBIT of $20,000?

LG④   **E12–5**   Cobalt Industries had sales of 150,000 units at a price of $10 per unit. It faced fixed operating costs of $250,000 and variable operating costs of $5 per unit. The company is subject to a tax rate of 38% and has a weighted average cost of capital of 8.5%. Calculate Cobalt's *net operating profits after taxes (NOPAT),* and use it to estimate the value of the firm.

Problems   All problems are available in MyFinanceLab.

LG①   **P12–1**   **Breakeven point: Algebraic** Kate Rowland wishes to estimate the number of flower arrangements she must sell at $24.95 to break even. She has estimated fixed operating costs of $12,350 per year and variable operating costs of $15.45 per arrangement. How many flower arrangements must Kate sell to break even on operating costs?

LG①   **P12–2**   **Breakeven comparisons: Algebraic** Given the price and cost data shown in the accompanying table for each of the three firms, F, G, and H, answer the questions that follow.

Firm	F	G	H
Sale price per unit	$ 18.00	$ 21.00	$ 30.00
Variable operating cost per unit	6.75	13.50	12.00
Fixed operating cost	45,000	30,000	90,000

a. What is the *operating breakeven point* in units for each firm?

b. How would you rank these firms in terms of their risk?

LG 1 **P12–3** **Breakeven point: Algebraic and graphical** Fine Leather Enterprises sells its single product for $129.00 per unit. The firm's fixed operating costs are $473,000 annually, and its variable operating costs are $86.00 per unit.

a. Find the firm's *operating breakeven point* in units.

b. Label the *x* axis "Sales (units)" and the *y* axis "Costs/Revenues ($)," and then graph the firm's sales revenue, total operating cost, and fixed operating cost functions on these axes. In addition, label the operating breakeven point and the areas of loss and profit (EBIT).

LG 1 **P12–4** **Breakeven analysis** Barry Carter is considering opening a video store. He wants to estimate the number of DVDs he must sell to break even. The DVDs will be sold for $13.98 each, variable operating costs are $10.48 per DVD, and annual fixed operating costs are $73,500.

a. Find the *operating breakeven point* in number of DVDs.

b. Calculate the total operating costs at the breakeven volume found in part **a.**

c. If Barry estimates that at a minimum he can sell 2,000 CDs *per month,* should he go into the video business?

d. How much EBIT will Barry realize if he sells the minimum 2,000 DVDs per month noted in part **c?**

Personal Finance Problem

LG 1 **P12–5** **Breakeven analysis** Paul Scott has a 2008 Cadillac that he wants to update with a GPS system so that he will have access to up-to-date road maps and directions. Aftermarket equipment can be fitted for a flat fee of $500, and the service provider requires monthly charges of $20. In his line of work as a traveling salesperson, he estimates that this device can save him time and money, about $35 per month (as the price of gas keeps increasing). He plans to keep the car for another 3 years.

a. Calculate the *breakeven point* for the device in months.

b. Based on **a,** should Paul have the GPS system installed in his car?

LG 1 **P12–6** **Breakeven point: Changing costs/revenues** JWG Company publishes *Creative Crosswords.* Last year, the book of puzzles sold for $10, with a variable operating cost of $8 per book and a fixed operating cost of $40,000.

a. How many books must JWG sell this year to achieve the *breakeven point* for the stated operating costs if all figures remain the same as for last year?

b. How many books must JWG sell this year to achieve the *breakeven point* for the stated operating costs if fixed operating costs increase to $44,000 and all other figures remain the same?

c. How many books must JWG sell this year to achieve the *breakeven point* for the stated operating costs if the selling price increases to $10.50 and all costs remain the same as for last year?

d. How many books must JWG sell this year to achieve the *breakeven point* for the stated operating costs if the variable operating cost per book increases to $8.50 and all other figures remain the same?

e. What conclusions about the operating breakeven point can be drawn from your answers?

P12–7   **Breakeven analysis** Molly Jasper and her sister, Caitlin Peters, got into the novelties business almost by accident. Molly, a talented sculptor, often made little figurines as gifts for friends. Occasionally, she and Caitlin would set up a booth at a crafts fair and sell a few of the figurines along with jewelry that Caitlin made. Little by little, demand for the figurines, now called Mollycaits, grew, and the sisters began to reproduce some of the favorites in resin, using molds of the originals. The day came when a buyer for a major department store offered them a contract to produce 1,500 figurines of various designs for $10,000. Molly and Caitlin realized that it was time to get down to business. To make bookkeeping simpler, Molly had priced all the figurines at $8.00 each. Variable operating costs amounted to an average of $6.00 per unit. To produce the order, Molly and Caitlin would have to rent industrial facilities for a month, which would cost them $4,000.

a. Calculate Mollycaits' *operating breakeven point*.

b. Calculate Mollycaits' EBIT on the department store order.

c. If Molly renegotiates the contract at a price of $10.00 per figurine, what will the EBIT be?

d. If the store refuses to pay more than $8.00 per unit but is willing to negotiate quantity, what quantity of figurines will result in an EBIT of $4,000?

e. At this time, Mollycaits come in 15 different varieties. Whereas the average variable cost per unit is $6.00, the actual cost varies from unit to unit. What recommendation would you have for Molly and Caitlin with regard to pricing and the numbers and types of units that they offer for sale?

 P12–8   **EBIT sensitivity** Stewart Industries sells its finished product for $9 per unit. Its fixed operating costs are $20,000, and the variable operating cost per unit is $5.

a. Calculate the firm's earnings before interest and taxes (EBIT) for sales of 10,000 units.

b. Calculate the firm's EBIT for sales of 8,000 and 12,000 units, respectively.

c. Calculate the percentage changes in sales (from the 10,000-unit base level) and associated percentage changes in EBIT for the shifts in sales indicated in part **b.**

d. On the basis of your findings in part **c,** comment on the sensitivity of changes in EBIT in response to changes in sales.

LG 2 **P12–9**   **Degree of operating leverage** Grey Products has fixed operating costs of $380,000, variable operating costs of $16 per unit, and a selling price of $63.50 per unit.

a. Calculate the *operating breakeven point* in units.

b. Calculate the firm's EBIT at 9,000, 10,000, and 11,000 units, respectively.

c. With 10,000 units as a base, what are the percentage changes in units sold and EBIT as sales move from the base to the other sales levels used in part **b?**

d. Use the percentages computed in part **c** to determine the *degree of operating leverage (DOL).*

e. Use the formula for degree of operating leverage to determine the DOL at 10,000 units.

LG 2 **P12–10** **Degree of operating leverage: Graphical** Levin Corporation has fixed operating costs of $72,000, variable operating costs of $6.75 per unit, and a selling price of $9.75 per unit.

a. Calculate the *operating breakeven point* in units.

b. Compute the *degree of operating leverage (DOL)* using the following unit sales levels as a base: 25,000, 30,000, 40,000. Use the formula given in the text.

c. Graph the DOL figures that you computed in part **b** (on the *y* axis) against base sales levels (on the *x* axis).

d. Compute the degree of operating leverage at 24,000 units; add this point to your graph.

e. What principle do your graph and figures illustrate?

LG 2 **P12–11** **EPS calculations** Southland Industries has $60,000 of 16% (annual interest) bonds outstanding, 1,500 shares of preferred stock paying an annual dividend of $5 per share, and 4,000 shares of common stock outstanding. Assuming that the firm has a 40% tax rate, compute *earnings per share (EPS)* for the following levels of EBIT:

a. $24,600

b. $30,600

c. $35,000

LG 2 **P12–12** **Degree of financial leverage** Northwestern Savings and Loan has a current capital structure consisting of $250,000 of 16% (annual interest) debt and 2,000 shares of common stock. The firm pays taxes at the rate of 40%.

a. Using EBIT values of $80,000 and $120,000, determine the associated *earnings per share (EPS)*.

b. Using $80,000 of EBIT as a base, calculate the *degree of financial leverage (DFL)*.

c. Rework parts **a** and **b** assuming that the firm has $100,000 of 16% (annual interest) debt and 3,000 shares of common stock.

Personal Finance Problem

LG 2 **P12–13** **Financial leverage** Max Small has outstanding school loans that require a monthly payment of $1,000. He needs to buy a new car for work and estimates that this purchase will add $350 per month to his existing monthly obligations. Max will have $3,000 available after meeting all his monthly living (operating) expenses. This amount could vary by plus or minus 10%.

a. To assess the potential impact of the additional borrowing on his financial leverage, calculate the *DFL* in tabular form for both the current and proposed loan payments using Max's available $3,000 as a base and a 10% change.

b. Can Max afford the additional loan payment?

c. Should Max take on the additional loan payment?

LG 2 **LG 5** **P12–14** **DFL and graphical display of financing plans** Wells and Associates has an EBIT of $67,500. Interest costs are $22,500, and the firm has 15,000 shares of common stock outstanding. Assume a 40% tax rate.

a. Use the degree of financial leverage (DFL) formula to calculate the *DFL* for the firm.

b. Using a set of EBIT–EPS axes, plot Wells and Associates' financing plan.

c. If the firm also has 1,000 shares of preferred stock paying a $6.00 annual dividend per share, what is the DFL?

d. Plot the financing plan, including the 1,000 shares of $6.00 preferred stock, on the axes used in part **b**.

e. Briefly discuss the graph of the two financing plans.

P12–15 **Integrative: Multiple leverage measures** Play-More Toys produces inflatable beach balls, selling 400,000 balls per year. Each ball produced has a variable operating cost of $0.84 and sells for $1.00. Fixed operating costs are $28,000. The firm has annual interest charges of $6,000, preferred dividends of $2,000, and a 40% tax rate.

a. Calculate the *operating breakeven point* in units.
b. Use the degree of operating leverage (DOL) formula to calculate *DOL*.
c. Use the degree of financial leverage (DFL) formula to calculate *DFL*.
d. Use the degree of total leverage (DTL) formula to calculate *DTL*. Compare this answer with the product of DOL and DFL calculated in parts **b** and **c**.

P12–16 **Integrative: Leverage and risk** Firm R has sales of 100,000 units at $2.00 per unit, variable operating costs of $1.70 per unit, and fixed operating costs of $6,000. Interest is $10,000 per year. Firm W has sales of 100,000 units at $2.50 per unit, variable operating costs of $1.00 per unit, and fixed operating costs of $62,500. Interest is $17,500 per year. Assume that both firms are in the 40% tax bracket.

a. Compute the degree of operating, financial, and total leverage for firm R.
b. Compute the degree of operating, financial, and total leverage for firm W.
c. Compare the relative risks of the two firms.
d. Discuss the principles of leverage that your answers illustrate.

P12–17 **Integrative: Multiple leverage measures and prediction** Carolina Fastener, Inc., makes a patented marine bulkhead latch that wholesales for $6.00. Each latch has variable operating costs of $3.50. Fixed operating costs are $50,000 per year. The firm pays $13,000 interest and preferred dividends of $7,000 per year. At this point, the firm is selling 30,000 latches per year and is taxed at a rate of 40%.

a. Calculate Carolina Fastener's *operating breakeven point*.
b. On the basis of the firm's current sales of 30,000 units per year and its interest and preferred dividend costs, calculate its EBIT and earnings available for common.
c. Calculate the firm's *degree of operating leverage (DOL)*.
d. Calculate the firm's *degree of financial leverage (DFL)*.
e. Calculate the firm's *degree of total leverage (DTL)*.
f. Carolina Fastener has entered into a contract to produce and sell an additional 15,000 latches in the coming year. Use the DOL, DFL, and DTL to predict and calculate the changes in EBIT and earnings available for common. Check your work by a simple calculation of Carolina Fastener's EBIT and earnings available for common, using the basic information given.

Personal Finance Problem

P12–18 **Capital structure** Kirsten Neal is interested in purchasing a new house given that mortgage rates are low. Her bank has specific rules regarding an applicant's ability to meet the contractual payments associated with the requested debt. Kirsten must submit personal financial data for her income, expenses, and existing installment loan payments. The bank then calculates and compares certain ratios to predetermined allowable values to determine if it will make the requested loan. The requirements are as follows:

(1) Monthly mortgage payments < 28% of monthly gross (before-tax) income.

(2) Total monthly installment payments (including the mortgage payments) < 37% of monthly gross (before-tax) income.

Kirsten submits the following personal financial data:

Monthly gross (before-tax) income	$ 4,500
Monthly installment loan obligations	375
Requested mortgage	150,000
Monthly mortgage payments	1,100

a. Calculate the ratio for requirement 1.

b. Calculate the ratio for requirement 2.

c. Assuming that Kirsten has adequate funds for the down payment and meets other lender requirements, will Kirsten be granted the loan?

LG 3   **P12–19**   **Various capital structures**   Charter Enterprises currently has $1 million in total assets and is totally equity financed. It is contemplating a change in its capital structure. Compute the amount of debt and equity that would be outstanding if the firm were to shift to each of the following debt ratios: 10%, 20%, 30%, 40%, 50%, 60%, and 90%. (*Note:* The amount of total assets would not change.) Is there a limit to the debt ratio's value?

LG 3   **P12–20**   **Debt and financial risk**   Tower Interiors has made the forecast of sales shown in the following table. Also given is the probability of each level of sales.

Sales	Probability
$200,000	0.20
300,000	0.60
400,000	0.20

The firm has fixed operating costs of $75,000 and variable operating costs equal to 70% of the sales level. The company pays $12,000 in interest per period. The tax rate is 40%.

a. Compute the earnings before interest and taxes (EBIT) for each level of sales.

b. Compute the earnings per share (EPS) for each level of sales, the expected EPS, the standard deviation of the EPS, and the coefficient of variation of EPS, assuming that there are 10,000 shares of common stock outstanding.

c. Tower has the opportunity to reduce its leverage to zero and pay no interest. This change will require that the number of shares outstanding be increased to 15,000. Repeat part **b** under this assumption.

d. Compare your findings in parts **b** and **c**, and comment on the effect of the reduction of debt to zero on the firm's financial risk.

P12–21   **EPS and optimal debt ratio** Williams Glassware has estimated, at various debt ratios, the expected earnings per share and the standard deviation of the earnings per share as shown in the following table.

Debt ratio	Earnings per share (EPS)	Standard deviation of EPS
0%	$2.30	$1.15
20	3.00	1.80
40	3.50	2.80
60	3.95	3.95
80	3.80	5.53

a. Estimate the *optimal debt ratio* on the basis of the relationship between earnings per share and the debt ratio. You will probably find it helpful to graph the relationship.
b. Graph the relationship between the *coefficient of variation* and the debt ratio. Label the areas associated with business risk and financial risk.

 P12–22   **EBIT–EPS and capital structure** Data-Check is considering two capital structures. The key information is shown in the following table. Assume a 40% tax rate.

Source of capital	Structure A	Structure B
Long-term debt	$100,000 at 16% coupon rate	$200,000 at 17% coupon rate
Common stock	4,000 shares	2,000 shares

a. Calculate two *EBIT–EPS coordinates* for each of the structures by selecting any two EBIT values and finding their associated EPS values.
b. Plot the two capital structures on a set of EBIT–EPS axes.
c. Indicate over what EBIT range, if any, each structure is preferred.
d. Discuss the leverage and risk aspects of each structure.
e. If the firm is fairly certain that its EBIT will exceed $75,000, which structure would you recommend? Why?

 P12–23   **EBIT–EPS and preferred stock** Litho-Print is considering two possible capital structures, A and B, shown in the following table. Assume a 40% tax rate.

Source of capital	Structure A	Structure B
Long-term debt	$75,000 at 16% coupon rate	$50,000 at 15% coupon rate
Preferred stock	$10,000 with an 18% annual dividend	$15,000 with an 18% annual dividend
Common stock	8,000 shares	10,000 shares

a. Calculate two *EBIT–EPS coordinates* for each of the structures by selecting any two EBIT values and finding their associated EPS values.
b. Graph the two capital structures on the same set of EBIT–EPS axes.

c. Discuss the leverage and risk associated with each of the structures.
d. Over what range of EBIT is each structure preferred?
e. Which structure do you recommend if the firm expects its EBIT to be $35,000? Explain.

LG 3 **LG 4** **P12–24** **Integrative: Optimal capital structure** Medallion Cooling Systems, Inc., has total as-
LG 6 sets of $10,000,000, EBIT of $2,000,000, and preferred dividends of $200,000 and is taxed at a rate of 40%. In an effort to determine the optimal capital structure, the firm has assembled data on the cost of debt, the number of shares of common stock for various levels of indebtedness, and the overall required return on investment:

Capital structure debt ratio	Cost of debt, r_d	Number of common stock shares	Required return, r_s
0%	0%	200,000	12%
15	8	170,000	13
30	9	140,000	14
45	12	110,000	16
60	15	80,000	20

a. Calculate *earnings per share* for each level of indebtedness.
b. Use Equation 12.12 and the earnings per share calculated in part **a** to calculate a *price per share* for each level of indebtedness.
c. Choose the optimal capital structure. Justify your choice.

LG 3 **LG 4** **P12–25** **Integrative: Optimal capital structure** Nelson Corporation has made the following
LG 6 forecast of sales, with the associated probabilities of occurrence noted.

Sales	Probability
$200,000	0.20
300,000	0.60
400,000	0.20

The company has fixed operating costs of $100,000 per year, and variable operating costs represent 40% of sales. The existing capital structure consists of 25,000 shares of common stock that have a $10 per share book value. No other capital items are outstanding. The marketplace has assigned the following required returns to risky earnings per share.

Coefficient of variation of EPS	Estimated required return, r_s
0.43	15%
0.47	16
0.51	17
0.56	18
0.60	22
0.64	24

The company is contemplating *shifting its capital structure* by substituting debt in the capital structure for common stock. The three different debt ratios under consideration are shown in the following table, along with an estimate, for each ratio, of the corresponding required interest rate on *all* debt.

Debt ratio	Interest rate on *all* debt
20%	10%
40	12
60	14

The tax rate is 40%. The market value of the equity for a leveraged firm can be found by using the simplified method (see Equation 12.12).

a. Calculate the expected earnings per share (EPS), the standard deviation of EPS, and the coefficient of variation of EPS for the three proposed capital structures.

b. Determine the *optimal capital structure,* assuming (1) maximization of earnings per share and (2) maximization of share value.

c. Construct a graph (similar to Figure 12.7) showing the relationships in part **b.** (*Note:* You will probably have to sketch the lines because you have only three data points.)

LG 3 LG 4   **P12–26**   **Integrative: Optimal capital structure** The board of directors of Morales Publishing, Inc., has commissioned a capital structure study. The company has total assets of $40,000,000. It has earnings before interest and taxes of $8,000,000 and is taxed at

LG 5 LG 6   a rate of 40%.

a. Create a spreadsheet like the one in Table 12.10 showing values of debt and equity as well as the total number of shares, assuming a book value of $25 per share.

% Debt	Total assets	$ Debt	$ Equity	Number of shares @ $25
0%	$40,000,000	$_____	$_____	_____
10	40,000,000	_____	_____	_____
20	40,000,000	_____	_____	_____
30	40,000,000	_____	_____	_____
40	40,000,000	_____	_____	_____
50	40,000,000	_____	_____	_____
60	40,000,000	_____	_____	_____

b. Given the before-tax cost of debt at various levels of indebtedness, calculate the yearly interest expenses.

% Debt	$ Total debt	Before-tax cost of debt, r_d	$ Interest expense
0%	$_____	0.0%	$_____
10	_____	7.5	_____
20	_____	8.0	_____
30	_____	9.0	_____
40	_____	11.0	_____
50	_____	12.5	_____
60	_____	15.5	_____

c. Using EBIT of $8,000,000, a 40% tax rate, and the information developed in parts **a** and **b,** calculate the most likely earnings per share for the firm at various levels of indebtedness. Mark the level of indebtedness that maximizes EPS.

% Debt	EBIT	Interest expense	EBT	Taxes	Net income	Number of shares	EPS
0%	$8,000,000	$_____	$_____	$_____	$_____	_____	$_____
10	8,000,000	_____	_____	_____	_____	_____	_____
20	8,000,000	_____	_____	_____	_____	_____	_____
30	8,000,000	_____	_____	_____	_____	_____	_____
40	8,000,000	_____	_____	_____	_____	_____	_____
50	8,000,000	_____	_____	_____	_____	_____	_____
60	8,000,000	_____	_____	_____	_____	_____	_____

d. Using the EPS developed in part **c,** the estimates of required return, r_s, and Equation 12.12, estimate the value per share at various levels of indebtedness. Mark the level of indebtedness in the following table that results in the maximum price per share, P_0.

Debt	EPS	r_s	P_0
0%	$_____	10.0%	$_____
10	_____	10.3	_____
20	_____	10.9	_____
30	_____	11.4	_____
40	_____	12.6	_____
50	_____	14.8	_____
60	_____	17.5	_____

e. Prepare a recommendation to the board of directors of Morales Publishing that specifies the degree of indebtedness that will accomplish the firm's goal of optimizing shareholder wealth. Use your findings in parts **a** through **d** to justify your recommendation.

P12–27 **Integrative: Optimal capital structure** Country Textiles, which has fixed operating costs of $300,000 and variable operating costs equal to 40% of sales, has made the following three sales estimates, with their probabilities noted.

Sales	Probability
$ 600,000	0.30
900,000	0.40
1,200,000	0.30

The firm wishes to analyze five possible capital structures: 0%, 15%, 30%, 45%, and 60% debt ratios. The firm's total assets of $1 million are assumed to be constant. Its common stock has a book value of $25 per share, and the firm is in the 40% tax bracket. The following additional data have been gathered for use in analyzing the five capital structures under consideration.

Capital structure debt ratio	Before-tax cost of debt, r_d	Required return, r_s
0%	0.0%	10.0%
15	8.0	10.5
30	10.0	11.6
45	13.0	14.0
60	17.0	20.0

a. Calculate the level of EBIT associated with each of the three levels of sales.
b. Calculate the amount of debt, the amount of equity, and the number of shares of common stock outstanding for each of the five capital structures being considered.
c. Calculate the annual interest on the debt under each of the five capital structures being considered. (*Note:* The before-tax cost of debt, r_d, is the interest rate applicable to *all* debt associated with the corresponding debt ratio.)
d. Calculate the EPS associated with each of the three levels of EBIT calculated in part **a** for each of the five capital structures being considered.
e. Calculate (1) the expected EPS, (2) the standard deviation of EPS, and (3) the coefficient of variation of EPS for each of the five capital structures, using your findings in part **d**.
f. Plot the expected EPS and coefficient of variation of EPS against the capital structures (*x* axis) on separate sets of axes, and comment on the return and risk relative to capital structure.
g. Using the EBIT–EPS data developed in part **d**, plot the 0%, 30%, and 60% capital structures on the same set of EBIT–EPS axes, and discuss the ranges over which each is preferred. What is the major problem with the use of this approach?
h. Using the valuation model given in Equation 12.12 and your findings in part **e**, estimate the share value for each of the capital structures being considered.
i. Compare and contrast your findings in parts **f** and **h**. Which structure is preferred if the goal is to *maximize EPS?* Which structure is preferred if the goal is to *maximize share value?* Which capital structure do you recommend? Explain.

LG 3   P12–28   ETHICS PROBLEM "Information asymmetry lies at the heart of the ethical dilemma that managers, stockholders, and bondholders confront when companies initiate management buyouts or swap debt for equity." Comment on this statement. What steps might a board of directors take to ensure that the company's actions are ethical with regard to all parties?

Spreadsheet Exercise

Starstruck Company would like to determine its optimal capital structure. Several of its managers believe that the best method is to rely on the estimated earnings per share (EPS) of the firm because they believe that profits and stock price are closely related. The financial managers have suggested another method that uses estimated required returns to estimate the share value of the firm. The following financial data are available.

Capital structure debt ratio	Estimated EPS	Estimated required return
0%	$1.75	11.40%
10	1.90	11.80
20	2.25	12.50
30	2.55	13.25
40	3.18	18.00
50	3.06	19.00
60	3.10	25.00

TO DO

a. Based on the given financial data, create a spreadsheet to calculate the estimated share values associated with the seven alternative capital structures. Refer to Table 12.15.

b. Use Excel to graph the relationship between capital structure and the estimated EPS of the firm. What is the optimal debt ratio? Refer to Figure 12.7.

c. Use Excel to graph the relationship between capital structure and the estimated share value of the firm. What is the optimal debt ratio? Refer to Figure 12.7.

d. Do both methods lead to the same *optimal capital structure?* Which method do you favor? Explain.

e. What is the major difference between the EPS and share value methods?

MyFinanceLab Visit **www.myfinancelab.com** for **Chapter Case: *Evaluating Tampa Manufacturing's Capital Structure,*** Group Exercises, and numerous online resources.

13 Payout Policy

Learning Goals

LG 1 Understand cash payout procedures, their tax treatment, and the role of dividend reinvestment plans.

LG 2 Describe the residual theory of dividends and the key arguments with regard to dividend irrelevance and relevance.

LG 3 Discuss the key factors involved in establishing a dividend policy.

LG 4 Review and evaluate the three basic types of dividend policies.

LG 5 Evaluate stock dividends from accounting, shareholder, and company points of view.

LG 6 Explain stock splits and the firm's motivation for undertaking them.

Why This Chapter Matters to You

In your *professional* life

ACCOUNTING You need to understand the types of dividends and payment procedures for them because you will need to record and report the declaration and payment of dividends; you also will provide the financial data that management must have to make dividend decisions.

INFORMATION SYSTEMS You need to understand types of dividends, payment procedures, and the financial data that the firm must have to make and implement dividend decisions.

MANAGEMENT To make appropriate dividend decisions for the firm, you need to understand types of dividends, arguments about the relevance of dividends, the factors that affect dividend policy, and types of dividend policies.

MARKETING You need to understand factors affecting dividend policy because you may want to argue that the firm would be better off retaining funds for use in new marketing programs or products, rather than paying them out as dividends.

OPERATIONS You need to understand factors affecting dividend policy because you may find that the firm's dividend policy imposes limitations on planned expansion, replacement, or renewal projects.

In your *personal* life

Many individual investors buy common stock for the anticipated cash dividends. From a personal finance perspective, you should understand why and how firms pay dividends and the informational and financial implications of receiving them. Such understanding will help you select common stocks that have dividend-paying patterns consistent with your long-term financial goals.

13.1 The Basics of Payout Policy

payout policy
Decisions that a firm makes regarding whether to distribute cash to shareholders, how much cash to distribute, and the means by which cash should be distributed.

The term **payout policy** refers to the decisions that firms make about whether to distribute cash to shareholders, how much cash to distribute, and by what means the cash should be distributed. Although these decisions are probably less important than the investment decisions covered in Chapters 10 and 11 and the financing choices discussed in Chapter 12, they are nonetheless decisions that managers and boards of directors face routinely. Investors monitor firms' payout policies carefully, and unexpected changes in those policies can have significant effects on firms' stock prices. The recent history of Whirlpool Corporation demonstrates many of the important dimensions of payout policy.

ELEMENTS OF PAYOUT POLICY

Dividends are not the only means by which firms can distribute cash to shareholders. Firms can also conduct share repurchases, in which they typically buy back some of their outstanding common stock through purchases in the open market. Whirlpool Corporation, like many other companies, uses both methods to put cash in the hands of their stockholders. In addition to increasing its dividend payout, Whirlpool also resumed its share repurchase program in 2013, which had been halted during the economic recession. At the time of resuming the share repurchase program, the company's free cash flow was between $600 million and $650 million and expected to increase to between $650 million and $700 million. Whirlpool's chief executive officer, Jeff Fettig, stated that "sales increased in every region of the world" as the company continued to expand its margins and that as the company continued to execute its "long-term growth strategy . . . [it would] continue to drive actions to further create value for . . . shareholders."

If we generalize the lessons about payout policy, we may expect the following to be true:

1. Rapidly growing firms generally do not pay out cash to shareholders.
2. Slowing growth, positive cash flow generation, and favorable tax conditions can prompt firms to initiate cash payouts to investors. The ownership base of the company can also be an important factor in the decision to distribute cash.
3. Cash payouts can be made through dividends or share repurchases. Many companies use both methods. In some years, more cash is paid out via dividends, but sometimes share repurchases are larger than dividend payments.
4. When business conditions are weak, firms are more willing to reduce share buybacks than to cut dividends.

TRENDS IN EARNINGS AND DIVIDENDS

Figure 13.1 illustrates both long-term trends and cyclical movements in earnings and dividends paid by large U.S. firms that are part of the Standard & Poor's 500 Stock Composite Index. The figure plots monthly earnings and dividend payments from 1950 through the first quarter of 2013. The top line represents the earnings per share of the S&P 500 index, and the lower line represents dividends

FIGURE 13.1

Per Share Earnings and Dividends of the S&P 500 Index
Monthly U.S. dollar amount of earnings and dividends per share of the S&P 500 index from 1950 through the first quarter of 2013 (the figure uses a logarithmic vertical scale)

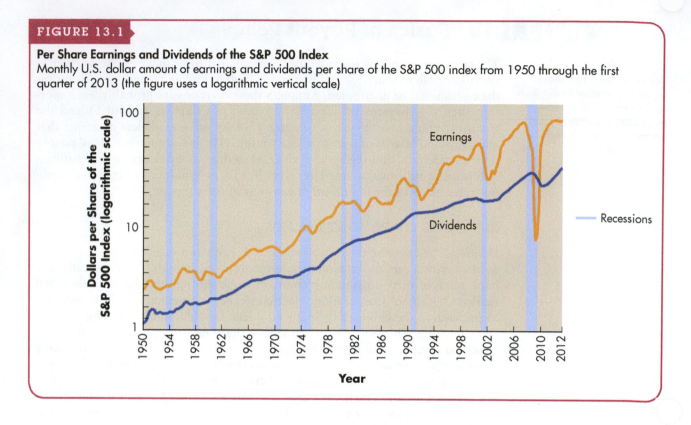

per share. The vertical bars highlight ten periods during which the U.S. economy was in recession. Several important lessons can be gleaned from the figure. First, observe that over the long term the earnings and dividends lines tend to move together. Figure 13.1 uses a logarithmic scale, so the slope of each line represents the growth rate of earnings or dividends. Over the 60 years shown in the figure, the two lines tend to have about the same slope, meaning that earnings and dividends grow at about the same rate when you take a long-term perspective. It makes perfect sense: Firms pay dividends out of earnings, so for dividends to grow over the long-term, earnings must grow too.

Second, the earnings series is much more volatile than the dividends series. That is, the line plotting earnings per share is quite bumpy, but the dividend line is much smoother, which suggests that firms do not adjust their dividend payments each time earnings move up or down. Instead, firms tend to smooth dividends, increasing them slowly when earnings are growing rapidly and maintaining dividend payments, rather than cutting them, when earnings decline.

To see this second point more clearly, look closely at the vertical bars in Figure 13.1. It is apparent that during recessions corporate earnings usually decline, but dividends either do not decline at all or do not decline as sharply as earnings. In six of the last ten recessions, dividends were actually higher when the recession ended than just before it began, although the last two recessions are notable exceptions to this pattern. Note also that, just after the end of a recession, earnings typically increase quite rapidly. Dividends increase, too, but not as fast.

A third lesson from Figure 13.1 is that the effect of the recent recession on both corporate earnings and dividends was large by historical standards. A

P&G's Dividend History

Few companies have replicated the dividend achievements of the consumer products giant Procter & Gamble (P&G). P&G has paid dividends every year for more than a century, and it increased its dividend in every year from 1956 through 2012.

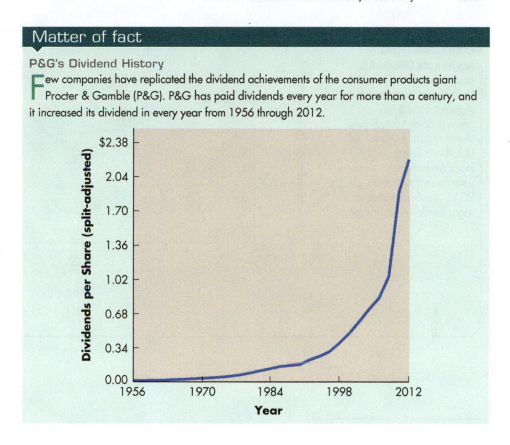

enormous earnings decline occurred from 2007 to 2009. This decline forced firms to cut dividends more drastically than they had in years; nonetheless, the drop in dividends was slight compared with the earnings decrease.

TRENDS IN DIVIDENDS AND SHARE REPURCHASES

When firms want to distribute cash to shareholders, they can either pay dividends or repurchase outstanding shares. Figure 13.2 plots aggregate dividends and share repurchases from 1971 through 2011 for all U.S. firms listed on U.S. stock exchanges (again, the figure uses a logarithmic vertical scale). A quick glance at the figure reveals that share repurchases played a relatively minor role in firms' payout practices in the 1970s. In 1971, for example, aggregate dividends totaled $21 billion, but share repurchases that year were just $1.1 billion. In the 1980s, share repurchases began to grow rapidly and then slowed again in the early 1990s. The value of aggregate share repurchases first eclipsed total dividend payments in 1998. That year, firms paid $175 billion in dividends, but they repurchased $185 billion worth of stock. Share repurchases continued to outpace dividends for all but three of the next 13 years, peaking at $677 billion in 2007.

Whereas aggregate dividends rise smoothly over time, Figure 13.2 shows that share repurchases display much more volatility. The largest drops in repurchase activity occurred in 1974–1975, 1981, 1986, 1989–1991, 2000–2002, and 2008–2010. All these drops correspond to periods when the U.S. economy was

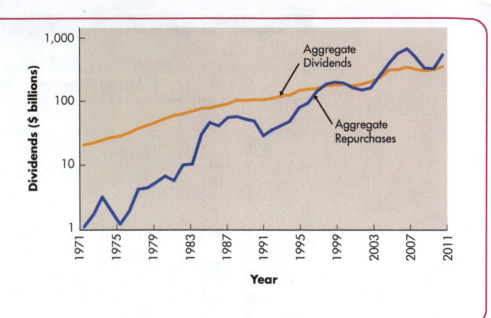

FIGURE 13.2

Aggregate Dividends and Repurchases for All U.S.–Listed Companies
Aggregate U.S. dollar amount of dividends and share repurchases for all U.S. firms listed on U.S. stock exchanges in each year from 1971 through 2011 (the figure uses a logarithmic vertical scale)

focus on ETHICS

Are Buybacks Really a Bargain?

in practice When CBS announced in March 2007 that it would buy back $1.4 billion worth of stock, its sagging share price saw the biggest spike since the media giant parted ways with Viacom in 2005. The 4.5 percent jump may have been an omen of good fortune—at the very least, it showed how much shareholders like buybacks.

Companies have been gobbling up their own shares faster than ever in a world of inexpensive capital and swollen balance sheets. Since 2003, the market for buybacks has boomed, with repurchases nearly on a par with capital expenditures. Some, however, have questioned the moves and motives that lead to a big buyback.

In addition to simply returning cash to shareholders, many companies also repurchase stock because they believe

that their stock is undervalued. New research, however, shows that companies often use creative financial reporting to push earnings downward before buybacks, making the stock seem undervalued and causing its price to bounce higher after the buyback. That pleases investors who then amplify the effect by pushing the price even higher.

"Managers who are acting opportunistically can use their reporting discretion to reduce the repurchase price by temporarily deflating earnings," argue Guojin Gong, Henock Louis, and Amy Sun at Penn State University's Smeal College of Business. Observing data from 1,720 companies, the authors say companies can easily create an apparent slump by speeding up or slowing down expense recognition, changing inventory accounting, or revising estimates of bad debt, all of which are

classic methods of making the numbers look worse without actually breaking accounting rules.

The penalty for being caught deliberately managing earnings in advance of a buyback could be severe. With the variety of accounting scandals that popped up regularly in the early 2000s, executives would no doubt be wary of deflating earnings just to get a boost from a buyback. Still, that's what Louis believes some are doing. "I don't think what they're doing is illegal," he says. "But it's misleading their investors."

▶ *Do you agree that corporate managers would manipulate their stock's value prior to a buyback, or do you believe that corporations are more likely to initiate a buyback to enhance shareholder value?*

mired in or just emerging from a recession. During most of these periods, dividends continued to grow modestly. Only during the recent, severe recession did both share repurchases and dividends fall.

Combining the lessons from Figures 13.1 and 13.2, we can draw three broad conclusions about firms' payout policies. First, firms exhibit a strong desire to maintain modest, steady growth in dividends that is roughly consistent with the long-run growth in earnings. Second, share repurchases have accounted for a growing fraction of total cash payouts over time. Third, when earnings fluctuate, firms adjust their short-term payouts primarily by adjusting share repurchases (rather than dividends), cutting buybacks during recessions, and increasing them rapidly during economic expansions.

Matter of fact

Share Repurchases Gain Worldwide Popularity

The growing importance of share repurchases in corporate payout policy is not confined to the United States. In most of the world's largest economies, repurchases have been on the rise in recent years, eclipsing dividend payments at least some of the time in countries as diverse as Belgium, Denmark, Finland, Hungary, Ireland, Japan, Netherlands, South Korea, and Switzerland. A study of payout policy at firms from 25 different countries found that share repurchases rose at an annual rate of 19 percent from 1999 through 2008.

→ REVIEW QUESTIONS

13–1 What are the two ways that firms can distribute cash to shareholders?

13–2 Why do rapidly growing firms generally pay no dividends?

13–3 The dividend payout ratio equals dividends paid divided by earnings. How would you expect this ratio to behave during a recession? What about during an economic boom?

 ## 13.2 The Mechanics of Payout Policy

At quarterly or semiannual meetings, a firm's board of directors decides whether and in what amount to pay cash dividends. If the firm has already established a precedent of paying dividends, the decision facing the board is usually whether to maintain or increase the dividend, and that decision is based primarily on the firm's recent performance and its ability to generate cash flow in the future. Boards rarely cut dividends unless they believe that the firm's ability to generate cash is in serious jeopardy. Figure 13.3 plots the number of U.S. public industrial firms that increased, decreased, or maintained their dividend payment in each year from 1981 through 2011. Clearly, the number of firms increasing their dividends is far greater than the number of companies cutting dividends in most years. When the economy is strong, as it was from 2003 to 2006, the ratio of industrial firms increasing dividends to those cutting dividends may be 10 to 1 or higher. However, a sign of the severity of the most recent recession was that in 2009 this ratio was just 1.5 to 1. That year, 401 U.S. public industrial firms increased their dividend, whereas 266 firms cut dividends.

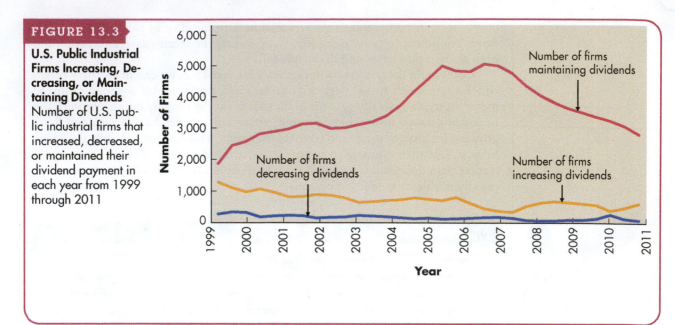

FIGURE 13.3

U.S. Public Industrial Firms Increasing, Decreasing, or Maintaining Dividends
Number of U.S. public industrial firms that increased, decreased, or maintained their dividend payment in each year from 1999 through 2011

Figure 13.3 clearly shows that firms prefer to increase rather than decrease dividends, but what is most evident is that firms prefer to maintain their established dividend levels. In the average year, 79 percent of U.S. industrial firms elec to maintain their previous year's dividend payout, and 96 percent avoid decreasing their dividend. Although some firms will choose to grow their dividend payout, the main goal of nearly all firms is to do whatever is necessary to avoid cutting dividends.

CASH DIVIDEND PAYMENT PROCEDURES

When a firm's directors declare a dividend, they issue a statement indicating the dividend amount and setting three important dates: the *date of record,* the *ex-dividend date,* and the *payment date.* All persons whose names are recorded as stockholders on the **date of record** receive the dividend. These stockholders are often referred to as *holders of record.*

Because of the time needed to make bookkeeping entries when a stock is traded, the stock begins selling **ex dividend** 2 *business days* prior to the date of record. Purchasers of a stock selling ex dividend do not receive the current dividend. A simple way to determine the first day on which the stock sells ex dividend is to subtract 2 business days from the date of record.

The **payment date** is the actual date on which the firm mails the dividend payment to the holders of record. It is generally a few weeks after the record date. An example will clarify the various dates and the accounting effects.

date of record (dividends)
Set by the firm's directors, the date on which all persons whose names are recorded as stockholders receive a declared dividend at a specified future time.

ex dividend
A period beginning 2 *business days* prior to the date of record, during which a stock is sold without the right to receive the current dividend.

payment date
Set by the firm's directors, the actual date on which the firm mails the dividend payment to the holders of record.

Example 13.1 ▶   On August 21, 2013, the board of directors of Best Buy announced that the firm's next quarterly cash dividend would be $0.17 per share, payable on October 1, 2013, to shareholders of record on Tuesday, September 10, 2013. Best Buy shares would begin trading ex dividend on the previous Friday, September 6. At the tim

FIGURE 13.4

Dividend Payment Time Line

Time line for the announcement and payment of a cash dividend for Best Buy

Declaration Date

Wednesday, August 21

Board of directors declares $0.17 per share dividend, payable to holders of record on Tuesday, September 10, payable on Tuesday, October 1.

Ex Dividend Date

Friday, September 6

Date of Record

Tuesday, September 10

Stock begins to sell ex dividend on Friday, September 6, which is 2 business days before the Tuesday, September 10, date of record.

Payment Date

Tuesday, October 1

Checks of $0.17 per share are mailed on Tuesday, October 1, to all holders of record on Tuesday, September 10.

Time ⟶

of the announcement, Best Buy had 340,967,179 shares of common stock outstanding, so the total dividend payment would be $57,964,420. Figure 13.4 shows a time line depicting the key dates relative to the Best Buy dividend. Before the dividend was declared, the key accounts of the firm were as follows (dollar values quoted in thousands):[1]

Cash	$680,000	Dividends payable	$ 0
		Retained earnings	3,395,000

When the dividend was announced by the directors, almost $58 million of the retained earnings ($0.17 per share × 341 million shares) was transferred to the dividends payable account. The key accounts thus became

Cash	$680,000	Dividends payable	$ 57,964
		Retained earnings	3,337,036

When Best Buy actually paid the dividend on October 26, this produced the following balances in the key accounts of the firm:

Cash	$622,036	Dividends payable	$ 0
		Retained earnings	3,337,036

The net effect of declaring and paying the dividend was to reduce the firm's total assets (and stockholders' equity) by almost $58 million.

SHARE REPURCHASE PROCEDURES

open-market share repurchase
A share repurchase program in which firms simply buy back some of their outstanding shares on the open market.

The mechanics of cash dividend payments are virtually the same for every dividend paid by every public company. With share repurchases, firms can use at least two different methods to get cash into the hands of shareholders. The most common method of executing a share repurchase program is called an open-market share repurchase. In an **open-market share repurchase,** as the name suggests,

---

1. The accounting transactions described here reflect only the effects of the dividend. Best Buy's actual financial statements during this period obviously reflect many other transactions.

firms simply buy back some of their outstanding shares on the open market. Firms have a great deal of latitude regarding when and how they execute these open-market purchases. Some firms make purchases in fixed amounts at regular intervals, whereas other firms try to behave more opportunistically, buying back more shares when they think that the share price is relatively low and fewer shares when they think that the price is high.

In contrast, firms sometimes repurchase shares through a *self-tender offer* or simply a *tender offer*. In a **tender offer share repurchase**, a firm announces the price it is willing to pay to buy back shares and the quantity of shares it wishes to repurchase. The tender offer price is usually set at a significant premium above the current market price. Shareholders who want to participate let the firm know how many shares they would like to sell back to the firm at the stated price. If shareholders do not offer to sell back as many shares as the firm wants to repurchase, the firm may either cancel or extend the offer. If the offer is oversubscribed, meaning that shareholders want to sell more shares than the firms wants to repurchase, the firm typically repurchases shares on a pro rata basis. For example, if the firm wants to buy back 10 million shares, but 20 million shares are tendered by investors, the firm would repurchase exactly half of the shares tendered by each shareholder.

A third method of buying back shares is called a **Dutch auction share repurchase**. In a Dutch auction, the firm specifies a range of prices at which it is willing to repurchase shares and the quantity of shares that it desires. Investors can tender their shares to the firm at any price in the specified range, which allows the firm to trace out a demand curve for their stock. That is, the demand curve specifies how many shares investors will sell back to the firm at each price in the offer range. This analysis allows the firm to determine the minimum price required to repurchase the desired quantity of shares, and every shareholder receives that price.

tender offer share repurchase
A repurchase program in which a firm offers to repurchase a fixed number of shares, usually at a premium relative to the market value, and shareholders decide whether or not they want to sell back their shares at that price.

Dutch auction share repurchase
A repurchase method in which the firm specifies how many shares it wants to buy back and a range of prices at which it is willing to repurchase shares. Investors specify how many shares they will sell at each price in the range, and the firm determines the minimum price required to repurchase its target number of shares. All investors who tender receive the same price.

Example 13.2 ▸

In July 2013, Fidelity National Information Services announced a Dutch auction repurchase for 86 million common shares at prices ranging from $29 to $31.50 per share. Fidelity shareholders were instructed to contact the company to indicate how many shares they would be willing to sell at different prices in this range. Suppose that after accumulating this information from investors, Fidelity constructed the following demand schedule:

Offer price	Shares tendered	Cumulative total
$29	5,000,000	5,000,000
29.25	10,000,000	15,000,000
29.50	15,000,000	30,000,000
29.75	18,000,000	48,000,000
30	18,500,000	66,500,000
31.25	19,500,000	86,000,000
31.50	20,000,000	106,000,000

At a price of $31.25, shareholders are willing to tender a total of 86 million shares, exactly the amount that Fidelity wants to repurchase. Each shareholder who expressed a willingness to tender their shares at a price of $31.25 *or less* receives $31.25 and Fidelity repurchases all 86 million shares at a cost of roughly $2.7 billion.

TAX TREATMENT OF DIVIDENDS AND REPURCHASES

For many years, dividends and share repurchases had very different tax consequences. The dividends that investors received were generally taxed at ordinary income tax rates. Therefore, if a firm paid $10 million in dividends, that payout would trigger significant tax liabilities for the firm's shareholders (at least those subject to personal income taxes). On the other hand, when firms repurchased shares, the taxes triggered by that type of payout were generally much lower. There were several reasons for this difference. Only those shareholders who sold their shares as part of the repurchase program had any immediate tax liability. Shareholders who did not participate did not owe any taxes. Furthermore, some shareholders who did participate in the repurchase program might not owe any taxes on the funds they received if they were tax-exempt institutions or if they sold their shares at a loss. Finally, even those shareholders who participated in the repurchase program and sold their shares for a profit paid taxes only at the (usually lower) capital gains tax rate (assuming the shares were held for at least one year), and even that tax only applied to the gain, not to the entire value of the shares repurchased. Consequently, investors could generally expect to pay far less in taxes on money that a firm distributed through a share repurchase compared to money paid out as dividends. That differential tax treatment in part explains the growing popularity of share repurchase programs in the 1980s and 1990s.

The *Jobs and Growth Tax Relief Reconciliation Act of 2003* significantly changed the tax treatment of corporate dividends for most taxpayers. Prior to passage of the 2003 law, dividends received by investors were taxed as ordinary income at rates as high as 35 percent. The 2003 act reduced the tax rate on corporate dividends for most taxpayers to the tax rate applicable to capital gains, which is a maximum rate of 5 percent to 15 percent, depending on the taxpayer's tax bracket. This change significantly diminishes the degree of "double taxation" of dividends, which results when the corporation is first taxed on its income and then shareholders pay taxes on the dividends that they receive. After-tax cash flow to dividend recipients is much greater at the lower applicable tax rate; the result is noticeably higher dividend payouts by corporations today than prior to passage of the 2003 legislation.

In early 2012, Congress passed the American Taxpayer Relief Act of 2012. For eveyone except those individuals in the newly established highest tax bracket, dividends and capital gains continue to be taxed at 15 percent.

> **Personal Finance Example 13.3** ▶

MyFinanceLab Solution
Video

The board of directors of Espinoza Industries, Inc., on October 4 of the current year, declared a quarterly dividend of $0.46 per share payable to all holders of record on Friday, October 30, with a payment date of November 19. Rob and Kate Heckman, who purchased 500 shares of Espinoza's common stock on Thursday, October 15, wish to determine whether they will receive the recently declared dividend and, if so, when and how much they would net after taxes from the dividend given that the dividends would be subject to a 15% federal income tax.

Given the Friday, October 30, date of record, the stock would begin selling *ex dividend* 2 business days earlier on Wednesday, October 28. Purchasers of the stock on or before Tuesday, October 27, would receive the right to the dividend. Because the Heckmans purchased the stock on October 15, they would be eligible to receive the dividend of $0.46 per share. Thus, the Heckmans will receive $230 in dividends ($0.46 per share × 500 shares), which will be mailed to them on the November 19 payment date. Because they are subject to a 15% federal income tax on the dividends, the Heckmans will net $195.50 [$(1 - 0.15) \times \$230$] after taxes from the Espinoza Industries dividend.

DIVIDEND REINVESTMENT PLANS

Today, many firms offer **dividend reinvestment plans (DRIPs)**, which enable stockholders to use dividends received on the firm's stock to acquire additional shares—even fractional shares—at little or no transaction cost. Some companies even allow investors to make their *initial purchases* of the firm's stock directly from the company without going through a broker. With DRIPs, plan participants typically can acquire shares at about 5 percent below the prevailing market price. From its point of view, the firm can issue new shares to participants more economically, avoiding the underpricing and flotation costs that would accompany the public sale of new shares. Clearly, the existence of a DRIP may enhance the market appeal of a firm's shares.

STOCK PRICE REACTIONS TO CORPORATE PAYOUTS

What happens to the stock price when a firm pays a dividend or repurchases shares? In theory, the answers to those questions are straightforward. Take a dividend payment for example. Suppose that a firm has $1 billion in assets, financed entirely by 10 million shares of common stock. Each share should be worth $100 ($1 billion ÷ 10,000,000 shares). Now suppose that the firm pays a $1 per share cash dividend, for a total dividend payout of $10 million. The assets of the firm fall to $990 million. Because shares outstanding remain at 10 million, each share should be worth $99. In other words, the stock price should fall by $1, exactly the amount of the dividend. The reduced share price simply reflects that cash formerly held by the firm is now in the hands of investors. To be precise, this reduction in share price should occur not when the dividend checks are mailed but rather when the stock begins trading ex dividend.

For share repurchases, the intuition is that "you get what you pay for." In other words, if the firm buys back shares at the going market price, the reduction in cash is exactly offset by the reduction in the number of shares outstanding, so the market price of the stock should remain the same. Once again, consider the firm with $1 billion in assets and 10 million shares outstanding worth $100 each. Let's say that the firm decides to distribute $10 million in cash by repurchasing 100,000 shares of stock. After the repurchase is completed, the firm's assets will fall by $10 million to $990 million, but the shares outstanding will fall by 100,000 to 9,900,000. The new share price is therefore $990,000,000 ÷ 9,900,000, or $100, as before.

In practice, taxes and a variety of other market imperfections may cause the actual change in share price in response to a dividend payment or share repurchase to deviate from what we expect in theory. Furthermore, the stock price reaction to a cash payout may be different than the reaction to an announcement about an upcoming payout. For example, when a firm announces that it will increase its dividend, the share price usually rises on that news, even though the share price will fall when the dividend is actually paid. The next section discusses the impact of payout policy on the value of the firm in greater depth.

→ REVIEW QUESTIONS

13–4 Who are *holders of record*? When does a stock sell *ex dividend*?

13–5 What effect did the *Jobs and Growth Tax Relief Reconciliation Act of 2003* have on the taxation of corporate dividends? On corporate dividend payouts?

13–6 What benefit is available to participants in a *dividend reinvestment plan*? How might the firm benefit?

LG 2 ## 13.3 Relevance of Payout Policy

The financial literature has reported numerous theories and empirical findings concerning payout policy. Although this research provides some interesting insights about payout policy, capital budgeting and capital structure decisions are generally considered far more important than payout decisions. In other words, firms should not sacrifice good investment and financing decisions for a payout policy of questionable importance.

The most important question about payout policy is this one: Does payout policy have a significant effect on the value of a firm? A number of theoretical and empirical answers to this question have been proposed, but as yet there is no widely accepted rule to help a firm find its "optimal" payout policy. Most of the theories that have been proposed to explain the consequences of payout policy have focused on dividends. From here on, we will use the terms *dividend policy* and *payout policy* interchangeably, meaning that we make no distinction between dividend payouts and share repurchases in terms of the theories that try to explain whether these policies have an effect on firm value.

RESIDUAL THEORY OF DIVIDENDS

residual theory of dividends
A school of thought that suggests that the dividend paid by a firm should be viewed as a *residual,* the amount left over after all acceptable investment opportunities have been undertaken.

The **residual theory of dividends** is a school of thought that suggests that the dividend paid by a firm should be viewed as a *residual,* that is, the amount left over after all acceptable investment opportunities have been undertaken. Using this approach, the firm would treat the dividend decision in three steps as follows:

Step 1 Determine its optimal level of capital expenditures, which would be the level that exploits all a firm's positive NPV projects.

Step 2 Using the optimal capital structure proportions (see Chapter 12), estimate the total amount of equity financing needed to support the expenditures generated in Step 1.

Step 3 Because the cost of retained earnings, r_r, is less than the cost of new common stock, r_n, use retained earnings to meet the equity requirement determined in Step 2. If retained earnings are inadequate to meet this need, sell new common stock. If the available retained earnings are in excess of this need, distribute the surplus amount—the residual—as dividends.

According to this approach, as long as the firm's equity need exceeds the amount of retained earnings, no cash dividend is paid. The argument for this approach is that it is sound management to be certain that the company has the money it needs to compete effectively. This view of dividends suggests that the required return of investors, r_s, is *not* influenced by the firm's dividend policy, a premise that in turn implies that dividend policy is irrelevant in the sense that it does not affect firm value.

THE DIVIDEND IRRELEVANCE THEORY

dividend irrelevance theory
Miller and Modigliani's theory that, in a perfect world, the firm's value is determined solely by the earning power and risk of its assets (investments) and that the manner in which it splits its earnings stream between dividends and internally retained (and reinvested) funds does not affect this value.

The residual theory of dividends implies that if the firm cannot invest its earnings to earn a return that exceeds the cost of capital, it should distribute the earnings by paying dividends to stockholders. This approach suggests that dividends represent an earnings residual rather than an active decision variable that affects the firm's value. Such a view is consistent with the **dividend irrelevance theory** put forth by Merton H. Miller and Franco Modigliani (M and M).[2] They argue that the firm's value is determined solely by the earning power and risk of its assets (investments) and that the manner in which it splits its earnings stream between dividends and internally retained (and reinvested) funds does not affect this value. M and M's theory suggests that in a perfect world (certainty, no taxes, no transactions costs, and no other market imperfections), the value of the firm is unaffected by the distribution of dividends.

Of course, real markets do not satisfy the "perfect markets" assumptions of Modigliani and Miller's original theory. One market imperfection that may be important is taxation. Historically, dividends have usually been taxed at higher rates than capital gains. A firm that pays out its earnings as dividends may trigger higher tax liabilities for its investors than a firm that retains earnings. As a firm retains earnings, its share price should rise, and investors enjoy capital gains. Investors can defer paying taxes on these gains indefinitely simply by not selling their shares. Even if they do sell their shares, they may pay a relatively low tax rate on the capital gains. In contrast, when a firm pays dividends, investors receive cash immediately and pay taxes at the rates dictated by then-current tax laws.

clientele effect
The argument that different payout policies attract different types of investors but still do not change the value of the firm.

Even though this discussion makes it seem that retaining profits rather than paying them out as dividends may be better for shareholders on an after-tax basis, Modigliani and Miller argue that this assumption may not be the case. They observe that not all investors are subject to income taxation. Some institutional investors, such as pension funds, do not pay taxes on the dividends and capital gains that they earn. For these investors, the payout policies of different firms have no impact on the taxes that investors have to pay. Therefore, Modigliani and Miller argue, there can be a **clientele effect** in which different types of investors are attracted to firms with different payout policies due to tax effects. Tax-exempt investors may invest more heavily in firms that pay dividends because they are not affected by the typically higher tax rates on dividends. Investors who would have to pay higher taxes on dividends may prefer to invest in firms that retain more earnings rather than paying dividends. If a firm changes its payout policy, the value of the firm will not change; instead, what will change is the type of investor who holds the firm's shares. According to this argument, tax clienteles mean that payout policies cannot affect firm value, but they can affect the ownership base of the company.

In summary, M and M and other proponents of dividend irrelevance argue that, all else being equal, an investor's required return—and therefore the value of the firm—is unaffected by dividend policy. In other words, there is no "optimal" dividend policy for a particular firm.

ARGUMENTS FOR DIVIDEND RELEVANCE

Modigliani and Miller's assertion that dividend policy was irrelevant was a radical idea when it was first proposed. The prevailing wisdom at the time was that payout

---

2. Merton H. Miller and Franco Modigliani, "Dividend Policy, Growth and the Valuation of Shares," *Journal of Business* 34 (October 1961), pp. 411–433.

dividend relevance theory
The theory, advanced by Gordon and Lintner, that there is a direct relationship between a firm's dividend policy and its market value.

bird-in-the-hand argument
The belief, in support of *dividend relevance theory*, that investors see current dividends as less risky than future dividends or capital gains.

policy could improve the value of the firm and therefore was relevant. The key argument in support of **dividend relevance theory** is attributed to Myron J. Gordon and John Lintner,[3] who suggest that there is, in fact, a direct relationship between the firm's dividend policy and its market value. Fundamental to this proposition is their **bird-in-the-hand argument,** which suggests that investors see current dividends as less risky than future dividends or capital gains: "A bird in the hand is worth two in the bush." Gordon and Lintner argue that current dividend payments reduce investor uncertainty, causing investors to discount the firm's earnings at a lower rate and, all else being equal, to place a higher value on the firm's stock. Conversely, if dividends are reduced or are not paid, investor uncertainty will increase, raising the required return and lowering the stock's value.

Modigliani and Miller argued that the bird-in-the-hand theory was a fallacy. They said that investors who want immediate cash flow from a firm that did not pay dividends could simply sell off a portion of their shares. Remember that the stock price of a firm that retains earnings should rise over time as cash builds up inside the firm. By selling a few shares every quarter or every year, investors could, according to Modigliani and Miller, replicate the same cash flow stream that they would have received if the firm had paid dividends rather than retaining earnings.

Studies have shown that large changes in dividends do affect share price. Increases in dividends result in increased share price, and decreases in dividends result in decreased share price. One interpretation of this evidence is that it is not the dividends per se that matter but rather the **informational content** of dividends with respect to future earnings. In other words, investors view a change in dividends, up or down, as a *signal* that management expects future earnings to change in the same direction. Investors view an increase in dividends as a *positive signal,* and they bid up the share price. They view a decrease in dividends as a *negative signal* that causes investors to sell their shares, resulting in the share price decreasing.

informational content
The information provided by the dividends of a firm with respect to future earnings, which causes owners to bid up or down the price of the firm's stock.

Another argument in support of the idea that dividends can affect the value of the firm is the *agency cost theory*. Recall that agency costs are costs that arise due to the separation between the firm's owners and its managers. Managers sometimes have different interests than owners. Managers may want to retain earnings simply to increase the size of the firm's asset base. There is greater prestige and perhaps higher compensation associated with running a larger firm. Shareholders are aware of the temptations that managers face, and they worry that retained earnings may not be invested wisely. The *agency cost theory* says that a firm that commits to paying dividends is reassuring shareholders that managers will not waste their money. Given this reassurance, investors will pay higher prices for firms that promise regular dividend payments.

Although many other arguments related to dividend relevance have been put forward, *empirical studies have not provided evidence that conclusively settles the debate about whether and how payout policy affects firm value.* As we have already said, even if dividend policy really matters, it is almost certainly less important than other decisions that financial mangers make, such as the decision to invest in a large new project or the decision about what combination of debt and equity the firm should use to finance its operations. Still, most financial managers today, especially those running large corporations, believe that payout policy can affect the value of the firm.

---

3. Myron J. Gordon, "Optimal Investment and Financing Policy," *Journal of Finance* 18 (May 1963), pp. 264–272; and John Lintner, "Dividends, Earnings, Leverage, Stock Prices, and the Supply of Capital to Corporations," *Review of Economics and Statistics* 44 (August 1962), pp. 243–269.

→ **REVIEW QUESTIONS**

13–7 Does following the *residual theory of dividends* lead to a stable dividend? Is this approach consistent with dividend relevance?

13–8 Contrast the basic arguments about dividend policy advanced by Miller and Modigliani (M and M) and by Gordon and Lintner.

LG 3 ## 13.4 Factors Affecting Dividend Policy

dividend policy
The firm's plan of action to be followed whenever it makes a dividend decision.

The firm's **dividend policy** represents a plan of action to be followed whenever it makes a dividend decision. Firms develop policies consistent with their goals. Before we review some of the popular types of dividend policies, we discuss five factors that firms consider in establishing a dividend policy. They are legal constraints, contractual constraints, the firm's growth prospects, owner considerations, and market considerations.

LEGAL CONSTRAINTS

Most states prohibit corporations from paying out as cash dividends any portion of the firm's "legal capital," which is typically measured by the par value of common stock. Other states define legal capital to include not only the par value of the common stock but also any paid-in capital in excess of par. These *capital impairment restrictions* are generally established to provide a sufficient equity base to protect creditors' claims. An example will clarify the differing definitions of capital.

Example 13.4 ▶

The stockholders' equity account of Miller Flour Company, a large grain processor, is presented in the following table.

Miller Flour Company Stockholders' Equity	
Common stock at par	$100,000
Paid-in capital in excess of par	200,000
Retained earnings	140,000
Total stockholders' equity	$440,000

In states where the firm's legal capital is defined as the par value of its common stock, the firm could pay out $340,000 ($200,000 + $140,000) in cash dividends without impairing its capital. In states where the firm's legal capital includes all paid-in capital, the firm could pay out only $140,000 in cash dividends.

Firms sometimes impose an earnings requirement limiting the amount of dividends. With this restriction, the firm cannot pay more in cash dividends than the sum of its most recent and past retained earnings. However, *the firm is not prohibited from paying more in dividends than its current earnings.*[4]

---

4. A firm that has an operating loss in the current period can still pay cash dividends as long as sufficient retained earnings against which to charge the dividend are available and, of course, as long as it has the cash with which to make the payments.

Example 13.5 ▶	Assume that Miller Flour Company, from the preceding example, in the year just ended has $30,000 in earnings available for common stock dividends. As the table in Example 13.4 indicates, the firm has past retained earnings of $140,000. Thus, it can legally pay dividends of up to $170,000.

excess earnings accumulation tax
The tax the IRS levies on retained earnings above $250,000 for most businesses when it determines that the firm has accumulated an excess of earnings to allow owners to delay paying ordinary income taxes on dividends received.

If a firm has overdue liabilities or is legally insolvent or bankrupt, most states prohibit its payment of cash dividends. In addition, the Internal Revenue Service prohibits firms from accumulating earnings to reduce the owners' taxes. If the IRS can determine that a firm has accumulated an excess of earnings to allow owners to delay paying ordinary income taxes on dividends received, it may levy an **excess earnings accumulation tax** on any retained earnings above $250,000 for most businesses.

During the recent financial crisis, a number of financial institutions received federal financial assistance. Those firms had to agree to restrictions on dividend payments to shareholders until they repaid the money that they received from the government. Bank of America, for example, had more than 30 years of consecutive dividend increases before accepting federal bailout money. As part of its bailout, Bank of America had to cut dividends to $0.01 per share.

CONTRACTUAL CONSTRAINTS

Often, the firm's ability to pay cash dividends is constrained by restrictive provisions in a loan agreement. Generally, these constraints prohibit the payment of cash dividends until the firm achieves a certain level of earnings, or they may limit dividends to a certain dollar amount or percentage of earnings. Constraints on dividends help to protect creditors from losses due to the firm's insolvency.

GROWTH PROSPECTS

The firm's financial requirements are directly related to how much it expects to grow and what assets it will need to acquire. It must evaluate its profitability and risk to develop insight into its ability to raise capital externally. In addition, the firm must determine the cost and speed with which it can obtain financing. Generally, a large, mature firm has adequate access to new capital, whereas a rapidly growing firm may not have sufficient funds available to support its acceptable projects. A growth firm is likely to have to depend heavily on internal financing through retained earnings, so it is likely to pay out only a very small percentage of its earnings as dividends. A more established firm is in a better position to pay out a large proportion of its earnings, particularly if it has ready sources of financing.

OWNER CONSIDERATIONS

The firm must establish a policy that has a favorable effect on the wealth of the *majority* of owners. One consideration is the *tax status of a firm's owners*. If a firm has a large percentage of wealthy stockholders who have sizable incomes, it may decide to pay out a *lower* percentage of its earnings to allow the owners to delay the payment of taxes until they sell the stock. Because cash dividends are taxed at the same rate as capital gains (as a result of the 2003 and 2012 Tax Acts), this strategy benefits owners through the tax deferral rather than as a result of a lower tax rate. Lower-income shareholders, however, who need dividend income, will prefer a *higher* payout of earnings.

A second consideration is the *owners' investment opportunities*. A firm should not retain funds for investment in projects yielding lower returns than the owners could obtain from external investments of equal risk. If it appears that the owners have better opportunities externally, the firm should pay out a higher percentage of its earnings. If the firm's investment opportunities are at least as good as similar-risk external investments, a lower payout is justifiable.

A final consideration is the *potential dilution of ownership*. If a firm pays out a high percentage of earnings, new equity capital will have to be raised with common stock. The result of a new stock issue may be dilution of both control and earnings for the existing owners. By paying out a low percentage of its earnings, the firm can minimize the possibility of such dilution.

MARKET CONSIDERATIONS

catering theory
A theory that says firms cater to the preferences of investors, initiating or increasing dividend payments during periods in which high-dividend stocks are particularly appealing to investors.

One of the more recent theories proposed to explain firms' payout decisions is called the *catering theory*. According to the **catering theory**, investors' demands for dividends fluctuate over time. For example, during an economic boom accompanied by a rising stock market, investors may be more attracted to stocks that offer prospects of large capital gains. When the economy is in recession and the stock market is falling, investors may prefer the security of a dividend. The catering theory suggests that firms are more likely to initiate dividend payments or to increase existing payouts when investors exhibit a strong preference for dividends. Firms *cater to* the preferences of investors.

→ REVIEW QUESTION

13–9 What five factors do firms consider in establishing *dividend policy*? Briefly describe each of them.

LG 4 | 13.5 Types of Dividend Policies

The firm's dividend policy must be formulated with two objectives in mind: providing for sufficient financing and maximizing the wealth of the firm's owners. Three different dividend policies are described in the following sections. A particular firm's cash dividend policy may incorporate elements of each.

CONSTANT-PAYOUT-RATIO DIVIDEND POLICY

dividend payout ratio
Indicates the percentage of each dollar earned that a firm distributes to the owners in the form of cash. It is calculated by dividing the firm's cash dividend per share by its earnings per share.

constant-payout-ratio dividend policy
A dividend policy based on the payment of a certain percentage of earnings to owners in each dividend period.

One type of dividend policy involves use of a constant payout ratio. The **dividend payout ratio** indicates the percentage of each dollar earned that the firm distributes to the owners in the form of cash. It is calculated by dividing the firm's cash dividend per share by its earnings per share. With a **constant-payout-ratio dividend policy,** the firm establishes that a certain percentage of earnings is paid to owners in each dividend period.

The problem with this policy is that if the firm's earnings drop or if a loss occurs in a given period, the dividends may be low or even nonexistent. Because dividends are often considered an indicator of the firm's future condition and status, the firm's stock price may be adversely affected.

Example 13.6 ▶ Peachtree Industries, a miner of potassium, has a policy of paying out 40% of earnings in cash dividends. In periods when a loss occurs, the firm's policy is to pay no cash dividends. Data on Peachtree's earnings, dividends, and average stock prices for the past 6 years follow.

Year	Earnings/share	Dividends/share	Average price/share
2015	−$0.50	$0.00	$42.00
2014	3.00	1.20	52.00
2013	1.75	0.70	48.00
2012	−1.50	0.00	38.00
2011	2.00	0.80	46.00
2010	4.50	1.80	50.00

Dividends increased in 2013 and in 2014 but decreased in the other years. In years of decreasing dividends, the firm's stock price dropped; when dividends increased, the price of the stock increased. Peachtree's sporadic dividend payments appear to make its owners uncertain about the returns they can expect.

REGULAR DIVIDEND POLICY

regular dividend policy
dividend policy based on the payment of a fixed-dollar dividend in each period.

The **regular dividend policy** is based on the payment of a fixed-dollar dividend in each period. Often, firms that use this policy increase the regular dividend once a *sustainable* increase in earnings has occurred. Under this policy, dividends are almost never decreased.

Example 13.7 ▶ The dividend policy of Woodward Laboratories, a producer of a popular artificial sweetener, is to pay annual dividends of $1.00 per share until per-share earnings have exceeded $4.00 for 3 consecutive years. At that point, the annual dividend is raised to $1.50 per share, and a new earnings plateau is established. The firm does not anticipate decreasing its dividend unless its liquidity is in jeopardy. Data for Woodward's earnings, dividends, and average stock prices for the past 12 years follow.

Year	Earnings/share	Dividends/share	Average price/share
2015	$4.50	$1.50	$47.50
2014	3.90	1.50	46.50
2013	4.60	1.50	45.00
2012	4.20	1.00	43.00
2011	5.00	1.00	42.00
2010	2.00	1.00	38.50
2009	6.00	1.00	38.00
2008	3.00	1.00	36.00
2007	0.75	1.00	33.00
2006	0.50	1.00	33.00
2005	2.70	1.00	33.50
2004	2.85	1.00	35.00

Whatever the level of earnings, Woodward Laboratories paid dividends of $1.00 per share through 2012. In 2013, the dividend increased to $1.50 per share because earnings in excess of $4.00 per share had been achieved for 3 years. In 2013, the firm also had to establish a new earnings plateau for further dividend increases. Woodward Laboratories' average price per share exhibited a stable, increasing behavior in spite of a somewhat volatile pattern of earnings.

target dividend-payout ratio
A dividend policy under which the firm attempts to pay out a certain *percentage* of earnings as a stated dollar dividend and adjusts that dividend toward a target payout as proven earnings increases occur.

Often, a regular dividend policy is built around a **target dividend-payout ratio.** Under this policy, the firm attempts to pay out a certain *percentage* of earnings, but rather than let dividends fluctuate, it pays a stated dollar dividend and adjusts that dividend toward the target payout as proven earnings increases occur. For instance, Woodward Laboratories appears to have a target payout ratio of around 35 percent. The payout was about 35 percent ($1.00 ÷ $2.85) when the dividend policy was set in 2004, and when the dividend was raised to $1.50 in 2013, the payout ratio was about 33 percent ($1.50 ÷ $4.60).

LOW-REGULAR-AND-EXTRA DIVIDEND POLICY

low-regular-and-extra dividend policy
A dividend policy based on paying a low regular dividend, supplemented by an additional ("extra") dividend when earnings are higher than normal in a given period.

extra dividend
An additional dividend optionally paid by the firm when earnings are higher than normal in a given period.

Some firms establish a **low-regular-and-extra dividend policy,** paying a low regular dividend, supplemented by an additional ("extra") dividend when earnings are higher than normal in a given period. By calling the additional dividend an **extra dividend,** the firm avoids setting expectations that the dividend increase will be permanent. This policy is especially common among companies that experience cyclical shifts in earnings.

By establishing a low regular dividend that is paid each period, the firm gives investors the stable income necessary to build confidence in the firm, and the extra dividend permits them to share in the earnings from an especially good period. Firms using this policy must raise the level of the regular dividend once proven increases in earnings have been achieved. The extra dividend should not be a regular event; otherwise, it becomes meaningless. The use of a target dividend-payout ratio in establishing the regular dividend level is advisable.

→ REVIEW QUESTION

13–10 Describe a constant-payout-ratio dividend policy, a regular dividend policy, and a low-regular-and-extra dividend policy. What are the effects of these policies?

13.6 Other Forms of Dividends

Two common transactions that bear some resemblance to cash dividends are stock dividends and stock splits. Although the stock dividends and stock splits are closely related to each other, their economic effects are quite different than those of cash dividends or share repurchases.

STOCK DIVIDENDS

stock dividend
The payment, to existing owners, of a dividend in the form of stock.

A **stock dividend** is the payment, to existing owners, of a dividend in the form of stock. Often firms pay stock dividends as a replacement for or a supplement to cash dividends. In a stock dividend, investors simply receive additional shares in proportion to the shares they already own. No cash is distributed, and no real value is transferred from the firm to investors. Instead, because the number of outstanding shares increases, the stock price declines roughly in line with the amount of the stock dividend.

Accounting Aspects

small (ordinary) stock dividend
A stock dividend representing less than 20 percent to 25 percent of the common stock outstanding when the dividend is declared.

In an accounting sense, the payment of a stock dividend is a shifting of funds between stockholders' equity accounts rather than an outflow of funds. When a firm declares a stock dividend, the procedures for announcement and distribution are the same as those described earlier for a cash dividend. The accounting entries associated with the payment of a stock dividend vary depending on its size. A **small (ordinary) stock dividend** is a stock dividend that represents less than 20 percent to 25 percent of the common stock outstanding when the dividend is declared. Small stock dividends are most common.

Example 13.8 ▶

The current stockholders' equity on the balance sheet of Garrison Corporation, a distributor of prefabricated cabinets, is as shown in the following accounts.

Preferred stock	$ 300,000
Common stock (100,000 shares at $4 par)	400,000
Paid-in capital in excess of par	600,000
Retained earnings	700,000
Total stockholders' equity	$2,000,000

Garrison, which has 100,000 shares of common stock outstanding, declares a 10% stock dividend when the market price of its stock is $15 per share. Because 10,000 new shares (10% of 100,000) are issued at the prevailing market price of $15 per share, $150,000 ($15 per share × 10,000 shares) is shifted from retained earnings to the common stock and paid-in capital accounts. A total of $40,000 ($4 par × 10,000 shares) is added to common stock, and the remaining $110,000 [($15 − $4) × 10,000 shares] is added to the paid-in capital in excess of par. The resulting account balances are as follows:

Preferred stock	$ 300,000
Common stock (110,000 shares at $4 par)	440,000
Paid-in capital in excess of par	710,000
Retained earnings	550,000
Total stockholders' equity	$2,000,000

The firm's total stockholders' equity has not changed; funds have merely been *shifted* among stockholders' equity accounts.

Shareholder's Viewpoint

The shareholder receiving a stock dividend typically receives nothing of value. After the dividend is paid, the per-share value of the shareholder's stock decreases in proportion to the dividend in such a way that the market value of his or her total holdings in the firm remains unchanged. Therefore, stock dividends are usually nontaxable. The shareholder's proportion of ownership in the firm also remains the same, and *as long as the firm's earnings remain unchanged,* so does his or her share of total earnings. (However, if the firm's earnings and cash dividends increase when the stock dividend is issued, an increase in share value is likely to result.)

Example 13.9 ▶ Ms. X owned 10,000 shares of Garrison Corporation's stock. The company's most recent earnings were $220,000, and earnings are not expected to change in the near future. Before the stock dividend, Ms. X owned 10% (10,000 shares ÷ 100,000 shares) of the firm's stock, which was selling for $15 per share. Earnings per share were $2.20 ($220,000 ÷ 100,000 shares). Because Ms. X owned 10,000 shares, her earnings were $22,000 ($2.20 per share × 10,000 shares). After receiving the 10% stock dividend, Ms. X has 11,000 shares, which again is 10% of the ownership (11,000 shares ÷ 110,000 shares). The market price of the stock can be expected to drop to $13.64 per share [$15 × (1.00 ÷ 1.10)], which means that the market value of Ms. X's holdings is $150,000 (11,000 shares × $13.64 per share). This is the same as the initial value of her holdings (10,000 shares × $15 per share). The future earnings per share drops to $2 ($220,000 ÷ 110,000 shares) because the same $220,000 in earnings must now be divided among 110,000 shares. Because Ms. X still owns 10% of the stock, her share of total earnings is still $22,000 ($2 per share × 11,000 shares).

In summary, if the firm's earnings remain constant and total cash dividends do not increase, a stock dividend results in a lower per-share market value for the firm's stock.

The Company's Viewpoint

Stock dividends are more costly to issue than cash dividends, but certain advantages may outweigh these costs. Firms find the stock dividend to be a way to give owners something without having to use cash. Generally, when a firm needs to preserve cash to finance rapid growth, it uses a stock dividend. When the stockholders recognize that the firm is reinvesting the cash flow so as to maximize future earnings, the market value of the firm should at least remain unchanged. However, if the stock dividend is paid so as to retain cash to satisfy past-due bills, a decline in market value may result.

STOCK SPLITS

stock split
A method commonly used to lower the market price of a firm's stock by increasing the number of shares belonging to each shareholder.

Although not a type of dividend, *stock splits* have an effect on a firm's share price similar to that of stock dividends. A **stock split** is a method commonly used to lower the market price of a firm's stock by increasing the number of shares belonging to each shareholder. In a 2-for-1 split, for example, two new shares are exchanged for each old share, with each new share being worth half the value of each old share. A stock split has no effect on the firm's capital structure and is usually nontaxable.

Quite often, a firm believes that its stock is priced too high and that lowering the market price will enhance trading activity. Stock splits are often made prior to issuing additional stock to enhance that stock's marketability and stimulate market activity. It is not unusual for a stock split to cause a slight increase in the market value of the stock, attributable to its informational content and because *total* dividends paid commonly increase slightly after a split.[5]

Example 13.10 ▸

MyFinanceLab Solution Video

Delphi Company, a forest products concern, had 200,000 shares of $2-par-value common stock and no preferred stock outstanding. Because the stock is selling at a high market price, the firm has declared a 2-for-1 stock split. The total before- and after-split stockholders' equity is shown in the following table.

Before split		After 2-for-1 split	
Common stock		**Common stock**	
(200,000 shares at $2 par)	$ 400,000	(400,000 shares at $1 par)	$ 400,000
Paid-in capital in excess of par	4,000,000	Paid-in-capital in excess of par	4,000,000
Retained earnings	2,000,000	Retained earnings	2,000,000
Total stockholders' equity	$6,400,000	Total stockholders' equity	$6,400,000

The insignificant effect of the stock split on the firm's books is obvious.

reverse stock split
A method used to raise the market price of a firm's stock by exchanging a certain number of outstanding shares for one new share.

Stock can be split in any way desired. Sometimes a **reverse stock split** is made: The firm exchanges a certain number of outstanding shares for one new share. For example, in a 1-for-3 split, one new share is exchanged for three old shares. In a reverse stock split, the firm's stock price rises due to the reduction in shares outstanding. Firms may conduct a reverse split if their stock price is getting so low that the exchange where the stock trades threatens to delist the stock. For example, the New York Stock Exchange requires that the average closing price of a listed security must be no less than $1 over any consecutive 30-day trading period. In June 2010, the video chain Blockbuster asked shareholders to approve a reverse stock split to prevent the NYSE from delisting Blockbuster's stock. Shareholders didn't approve the measure, and the NYSE delisted Blockbuster stock the following month.

Personal Finance Example 13.11 ▸   Shakira Washington, a single investor in the 25% federal income tax bracket, owns 260 shares of Advanced Technology, Inc., common stock. She originally bought the stock 2 years ago at its initial public offering (IPO) price of $9 per share. The stock of this fast-growing technology company is currently trading for $60 per share, so the current value of her Advanced Technology stock is $15,600 (260 shares × $60 per share). Because the firm's board believes that the stock would trade more actively in the $20 to $30 price range, it just announced a 3-for-1 stock split. Shakira wishes to determine the impact of the stock split on her holdings and taxes.

---

5. Eugene F. Fama, Lawrence Fisher, Michael C. Jensen, and Richard Roll, "The Adjustment of Stock Prices to New Information," *International Economic Review* 10 (February 1969), pp. 1–21, found that the stock price increases before the split announcement and that the increase in stock price is maintained if dividends per share are increased but is lost if dividends per share are *not* increased, following the split.

Because the stock will split 3 for 1, after the split Shakira will own 780 shares (3 × 260 shares). She should expect the market price of the stock to drop to $20 (1/3 × $60) immediately after the split; the value of her after-split holding will be $15,600 (780 shares × $20 per share). Because the $15,600 value of her after-split holdings in Advanced Technology stock exactly equals the before-split value of $15,600, Shakira has experienced neither a gain nor a loss on the stock as a result of the 3-for-1 split. Even if there were a gain or loss attributable to the split, Shakira would not have any tax liability unless she actually sold the stock and realized that (or any other) gain or loss.

→ REVIEW QUESTIONS

13–11 Why do firms issue *stock dividends?* Comment on the following statement: "I have a stock that promises to pay a 20 percent stock dividend every year, and therefore it guarantees that I will break even in 5 years."

13–12 Compare a *stock split* with a *stock dividend.*

Summary

FOCUS ON VALUE

Payout policy refers to the cash flows that a firm distributes to its common stockholders. A share of common stock gives its owner the right to receive all future dividends. The present value of all those future dividends expected over a firm's assumed infinite life determines the firm's stock value.

Corporate payouts not only represent cash flows to shareholders but also contain useful information about the firm's current and future performance. Such information affects the shareholders' perception of the firm's risk. A firm can also pay stock dividends, initiate stock splits, or repurchase stock. All these dividend-related actions can affect the firm's risk, return, and value as a result of their cash flows and informational content.

Although the theory of relevance of dividends is still evolving, the behavior of most firms and stockholders suggests that dividend policy affects share prices. Therefore, financial managers try to develop and implement dividend policy that is consistent with the firm's goal of **maximizing stock price.**

REVIEW OF LEARNING GOALS

LG 1 Understand cash payout procedures, their tax treatment, and the role of dividend reinvestment plans. The board of directors makes the cash payout decision and, for dividends, establishes the record and payment dates. As a result of tax-law changes in 2003 and 2012, most taxpayers pay taxes on corporate dividends at a maximum rate of 5 percent to 15 percent, depending on the taxpayer's tax bracket. Some firms offer dividend reinvestment plans that allow stockholders to acquire shares in lieu of cash dividends.

LG 2 Describe the residual theory of dividends and the key arguments with regard to dividend irrelevance and relevance. The residual theory suggests that dividends should be viewed as the earnings left after all acceptable investment opportunities have been undertaken. Miller and Modigliani argue in favor of dividend irrelevance, using a perfect world in which market imperfections such as transaction costs and taxes do not exist. Gordon and Lintner advance the theory of dividend relevance, basing their argument on the uncertainty-reducing effect of dividends, supported by their bird-in-the-hand argument. Empirical studies fail to provide clear support of dividend relevance. Even so, the actions of financial managers and stockholders tend to support the belief that dividend policy does affect stock value.

LG 3 **Discuss the key factors involved in establishing a dividend policy.** A firm's dividend policy should provide for sufficient financing and maximize stockholders' wealth. Dividend policy is affected by legal and contractual constraints, by growth prospects, and by owner and market considerations. Legal constraints prohibit corporations from paying out as cash dividends any portion of the firm's "legal capital," nor can firms with overdue liabilities and legally insolvent or bankrupt firms pay cash dividends. Contractual constraints result from restrictive provisions in the firm's loan agreements. Growth prospects affect the relative importance of retaining earnings rather than paying them out in dividends. The tax status of owners, the owners' investment opportunities, and the potential dilution of ownership are important owner considerations. Finally, market considerations are related to the stockholders' preference for the continuous payment of fixed or increasing streams of dividends.

LG 4 **Review and evaluate the three basic types of dividend policies.** With a constant-payout-ratio dividend policy, the firm pays a fixed percentage of earnings to the owners each period; dividends move up and down with earnings, and no dividend is paid when a loss occurs. Under a regular dividend policy, the firm pays a fixed-dollar dividend each period; it increases the amount of dividends only after a proven increase in earnings. The low-regular-and-extra dividend policy is similar to the regular dividend policy except that it pays an extra dividend when the firm's earnings are higher than normal.

LG 5 **Evaluate stock dividends from accounting, shareholder, and company points of view.** Firms may pay stock dividends as a replacement for or supplement to cash dividends. The payment of stock dividends involves a shifting of funds between capital accounts rather than an outflow of funds. Stock dividends do not change the market value of stockholders' holdings, proportion of ownership, or share of total earnings. Therefore, stock dividends are usually nontaxable. However, stock dividends may satisfy owners and enable the firm to preserve its market value without having to use cash.

LG 6 **Explain stock splits and the firm's motivation for undertaking them.** Stock splits are used to enhance trading activity of a firm's shares by lowering or raising their market price. A stock split merely involves accounting adjustments; it has no effect on the firm's cash or on its capital structure and is usually nontaxable.

To retire outstanding shares, firms can repurchase stock in lieu of paying a cash dividend. Reducing the number of outstanding shares increases earnings per share and the market price per share. Stock repurchases also defer the tax payments of stockholders.

Self-Test Problem (Solutions in Appendix)

 ST13–1 **Stock repurchase** The Off-Shore Steel Company has earnings available for common stockholders of $2 million and has 500,000 shares of common stock outstanding at $60 per share. The firm is currently contemplating the payment of $2 per share in cash dividends.

  a. Calculate the firm's current *earnings per share (EPS)* and *price/earnings (P/E) ratio*.

  b. If the firm can repurchase stock at $62 per share, how many shares can be purchased in lieu of making the proposed cash dividend payment?

  c. How much will the EPS be after the proposed repurchase? Why?

  d. If the stock sells at the old P/E ratio, what will the market price be after repurchase?

  e. Compare and contrast the earnings per share before and after the proposed repurchase.

  f. Compare and contrast the stockholders' position under the dividend and repurchase alternatives.

Warm-Up Exercises All problems are available in MyFinanceLab.

LG 1 **E13–1** Stephanie's Cafes, Inc., has declared a dividend of $1.30 per share for shareholders of record on Tuesday, May 2. The firm has 200,000 shares outstanding and will pay the dividend on May 24. How much cash will be needed to pay the dividend? When will the stock begin selling *ex dividend*?

LG 2 **E13–2** Chancellor Industries has retained earnings available of $1.2 million. The firm plans to make two investments that require financing of $950,000 and $1.75 million, respectively. Chancellor uses a target capital structure with 60% debt and 40% equity. Apply the *residual theory* to determine what dividends, if any, can be paid out, and calculate the resulting *dividend payout ratio*.

LG 3 **E13–3** Ashkenazi Companies has the following stockholders' equity account:

Common stock (350,000 shares at $3 par)	$1,050,000
Paid-in capital in excess of par	2,500,000
Retained earnings	750,000
Total stockholders' equity	$4,300,000

Assuming that state laws define legal capital solely as the par value of common stock, how much of a *per-share dividend* can Ashkenazi pay? If legal capital were more broadly defined to include all paid-in capital, how much of a *per-share dividend* could Ashkenazi pay?

LG 4 **E13–4** The board of Kopi Industries is considering a new dividend policy that would set dividends at 60% of earnings. The recent past has witnessed earnings per share (EPS) and dividends paid per share as shown in the following table.

Year	EPS	Dividend/share
2012	$1.75	$0.95
2013	1.95	1.20
2014	2.05	1.25
2015	2.25	1.30

Based on Kopi's historical dividend payout ratio, discuss whether a *constant payout ratio* of 60% would benefit shareholders.

 E13–5   The current stockholders' equity account for Hilo Farms is as follows:

Common stock (50,000 shares at $3 par)	$150,000
Paid-in capital in excess of par	250,000
Retained earnings	450,000
Total stockholders' equity	$850,000

Hilo has announced plans to issue an additional 5,000 shares of common stock as part of its stock dividend plan. The current market price of Hilo's common stock is $20 per share. Show how the proposed *stock dividend* would affect the stockholder's equity account.

Problems   All problems are available in MyFinanceLab.

 P13–1   **Dividend payment procedures**   At the quarterly dividend meeting, Wood Shoes declared a cash dividend of $1.10 per share for holders of record on Monday, July 10. The firm has 300,000 shares of common stock outstanding and has set a payment date of July 31. Prior to the dividend declaration, the firm's key accounts were as follows:

Cash	$500,000	Dividends payable	$ 0
		Retained earnings	2,500,000

a. Show the entries after the meeting adjourned.
b. When is the *ex dividend* date?
c. What values would the key accounts have after the July 31 payment date?
d. What effect, if any, will the dividend have on the firm's total assets?
e. Ignoring general market fluctuations, what effect, if any, will the dividend have on the firm's stock price on the ex dividend date?

Personal Finance Problem

P13–2   **Dividend payment**   Kathy Snow wishes to purchase shares of Countdown Computing, Inc. The company's board of directors has declared a cash dividend of $0.80 to be paid to holders of record on Wednesday, May 12.

a. What is the last day that Kathy can purchase the stock (trade date) and still receive the dividend?
b. What day does this stock begin trading ex dividend?

c. What change, if any, would you expect in the price per share when the stock begins trading on the ex dividend day?

d. If Kathy held the stock for less than one quarter and then sold it for $39 per share, would she achieve a higher investment return by (1) buying the stock *prior to* the ex dividend date at $35 per share and collecting the $0.80 dividend or (2) buying it *on* the ex dividend date at $34.20 per share but not receiving the dividend?

LG 2   **P13–3**   **Residual dividend policy** As president of Young's of California, a large clothing chain, you have just received a letter from a major stockholder. The stockholder asks about the company's dividend policy. In fact, the stockholder has asked you to estimate the amount of the dividend that you are likely to pay next year. You have not yet collected all the information about the expected dividend payment, but you do know the following:

(1) The company follows a residual dividend policy.
(2) The total capital budget for next year is likely to be one of three amounts, depending on the results of capital budgeting studies that are currently under way. The capital expenditure amounts are $2 million, $3 million, and $4 million.
(3) The forecasted level of potential retained earnings next year is $2 million.
(4) The target or optimal capital structure is a debt ratio of 40%.

You have decided to respond by sending the stockholder the best information available to you.

a. Describe a *residual dividend policy*.
b. Compute the amount of the dividend (or the amount of new common stock needed) and the dividend payout ratio for each of the three capital expenditure amounts.
c. Compare, contrast, and discuss the amount of dividends (calculated in part **b**) associated with each of the three capital expenditure amounts.

LG 3   **P13–4**   **Dividend constraints** The Howe Company's stockholders' equity account follows:

Common stock (400,000 shares at $4 par)	$1,600,000
Paid-in capital in excess of par	1,000,000
Retained earnings	1,900,000
Total stockholders' equity	$4,500,000

The earnings available for common stockholders from this period's operations are $100,000, which have been included as part of the $1.9 million retained earnings.

a. What is the *maximum dividend per share* that the firm can pay? (Assume that legal capital includes *all* paid-in capital.)
b. If the firm has $160,000 in cash, what is the largest per-share dividend it can pay without borrowing?
c. Indicate the accounts and changes, if any, that will result if the firm pays the dividends indicated in parts **a** and **b**.
d. Indicate the effects of an $80,000 cash dividend on stockholders' equity.

LG 3   **P13–5**   **Dividend constraints** A firm has $800,000 in paid-in capital, retained earnings of $40,000 (including the current year's earnings), and 25,000 shares of common stock outstanding. In the current year, it has $29,000 of earnings available for the common stockholders.

a. What is the most the firm can pay in cash dividends to each common stock-holder? (Assume that legal capital includes *all* paid-in capital.)

b. What effect would a cash dividend of $0.80 per share have on the firm's balance sheet entries?

c. If the firm cannot raise any new funds from external sources, what do you con-sider the key constraint with respect to the magnitude of the firm's dividend pay-ments? Why?

 P13–6 **Low-regular-and-extra dividend policy** Bennett Farm Equipment Sales, Inc., is in a highly cyclic business. Although the firm has a target payout ratio of 25%, its board re-alizes that strict adherence to that ratio would result in a fluctuating dividend and create uncertainty for the firm's stockholders. Therefore, the firm has declared a regular divi-dend of $0.50 per share per year with extra cash dividends to be paid when earnings jus-tify them. Earnings per share for the last several years are shown in the following table.

Year	EPS	Year	EPS
2015	$3.00	2012	$2.80
2014	2.40	2011	2.15
2013	2.20	2010	1.97

a. Calculate the *payout ratio* for each year on the basis of the regular $0.50 divi-dend and the cited EPS.

b. Calculate the difference between the regular $0.50 dividend and a 25% payout for each year.

c. Bennett has established a policy of paying an extra dividend of $0.25 only when the difference between the regular dividend and a 25% payout amounts to $1.00 or more. Show the regular and extra dividends in those years when an extra dividend would be paid. What would be done with the "extra" earnings that are not paid out?

d. The firm expects that future earnings per share will continue to cycle but will re-main above $2.20 per share in most years. What factors should be considered in making a revision to the amount paid as a regular dividend? If the firm revises the regular dividend, what new amount should it pay?

 P13–7 **Alternative dividend policies** Over the last 10 years, a firm has had the earnings per share shown in the following table.

Year	Earnings per share	Year	Earnings per share
2015	$4.00	2010	$2.40
2014	3.80	2009	1.20
2013	3.20	2008	1.80
2012	2.80	2007	−0.50
2011	3.20	2006	0.25

a. If the firm's dividend policy were based on a *constant payout ratio* of 40% for all years with positive earnings and 0% otherwise, what would be the annual divi-dend for each year?

b. If the firm had a dividend payout of $1.00 per share, increasing by $0.10 per share whenever the dividend payout fell below 50% for two consecutive years, what annual dividend would the firm pay each year?

c. If the firm's policy were to pay $0.50 per share each period except when earnings per share exceed $3.00, when an extra dividend equal to 80% of earnings beyond $3.00 would be paid, what annual dividend would the firm pay each year?

d. Discuss the pros and cons of each dividend policy described in parts **a** through **c**.

 P13–8   **Alternative dividend policies**   Given the earnings per share over the period 2008–2015 shown in the following table, determine the annual dividend per share under each of the policies set forth in parts **a** through **d**.

Year	Earnings per share
2015	$1.40
2014	1.56
2013	1.20
2012	−0.85
2011	1.05
2010	0.60
2009	1.00
2008	0.44

a. Pay out 50% of earnings in all years with positive earnings.

b. Pay $0.50 per share and increase to $0.60 per share whenever earnings per share rise above $0.90 per share for two consecutive years.

c. Pay $0.50 per share except when earnings exceed $1.00 per share, in which case pay an extra dividend of 60% of earnings above $1.00 per share.

d. Combine the policies described in parts **b** and **c**. When the dividend is raised (in part **b**), raise the excess dividend base (in part **c**) from $1.00 to $1.10 per share.

e. Compare and contrast each of the dividend policies described in parts **a** through **d**.

 P13–9   **Stock dividend: Firm**   Columbia Paper has the following stockholders' equity account. The firm's common stock has a current market price of $30 per share.

Preferred stock	$100,000
Common stock (10,000 shares at $2 par)	20,000
Paid-in capital in excess of par	280,000
Retained earnings	100,000
Total stockholders' equity	$500,000

a. Show the effects on Columbia of a 5% stock dividend.

b. Show the effects of (1) a 10% and (2) a 20% stock dividend.

c. In light of your answers to parts **a** and **b**, discuss the effects of stock dividends on stockholders' equity.

P13–10   **Cash versus stock dividend**   Milwaukee Tool has the following stockholders' equity account. The firm's common stock currently sells for $4 per share.

Preferred stock	$ 100,000
Common stock (400,000 shares at $1 par)	400,000
Paid-in capital in excess of par	200,000
Retained earnings	320,000
Total stockholders' equity	$1,020,000

a. Show the effects on the firm of a *cash* dividend of $0.01, $0.05, $0.10, and $0.20 per share.

b. Show the effects on the firm of a 1%, 5%, 10%, and 20% *stock* dividend.

c. Compare the effects in parts **a** and **b**. What are the significant differences between the two methods of paying dividends?

Personal Finance Problem

 P13–11 **Stock dividend: Investor** Sarah Warren currently holds 400 shares of Nutri-Foods. The firm has 40,000 shares outstanding. The firm most recently had earnings available for common stockholders of $80,000, and its stock has been selling for $22 per share. The firm intends to retain its earnings and pay a 10% stock dividend.

a. How much does the firm currently earn per share?

b. What proportion of the firm does Sarah currently own?

c. What proportion of the firm will Sarah own after the stock dividend? Explain your answer.

d. At what market price would you expect the stock to sell after the stock dividend?

e. Discuss what effect, if any, the payment of stock dividends will have on Sarah's share of the ownership and earnings of Nutri-Foods.

Personal Finance Problem

 P13–12 **Stock dividend: Investor** Security Data Company has outstanding 50,000 shares of common stock currently selling at $40 per share. The firm most recently had earnings available for common stockholders of $120,000, but it has decided to retain these funds and is considering either a 5% or a 10% stock dividend in lieu of a cash dividend.

a. Determine the firm's current *earnings per share*.

b. If Sam Waller currently owns 500 shares of the firm's stock, determine his proportion of ownership currently and under each of the proposed stock dividend plans. Explain your findings.

c. Calculate and explain the market price per share under each of the stock dividend plans.

d. For each of the proposed stock dividends, calculate the earnings per share after payment of the stock dividend.

e. What is the value of Sam's holdings under each of the plans? Explain.

f. Should Sam have any preference with respect to the proposed stock dividends? Why or why not?

P13–13 **Stock split: Firm** Growth Industries' current stockholders' equity account is as follows:

Preferred stock	$ 400,000
Common stock (600,000 shares at $3 par)	1,800,000
Paid-in capital in excess of par	200,000
Retained earnings	800,000
Total stockholders' equity	$3,200,000

a. Indicate the change, if any, expected if the firm declares a 2-for-1 stock split.
b. Indicate the change, if any, expected if the firm declares a 1-for-1½ *reverse* stock split.
c. Indicate the change, if any, expected if the firm declares a 3-for-1 stock split.
d. Indicate the change, if any, expected if the firm declares a 6-for-1 stock split.
e. Indicate the change, if any, expected if the firm declares a 1-for-4 *reverse* stock split.

Personal Finance Problem

 **P13–14**   **Stock splits**   Nathan Detroit owns 400 shares of the food company General Mills, Inc., which he purchased during the recession in January 2009 for $35 per share. General Mills is regarded as a relatively safe company because it provides a basic product that consumers need in good and bad economic times. Nathan read in the *Wall Street Journal* that the company's board of directors had voted to split the stock 2-for-1. In June 2010, just before the stock split, General Mills shares were trading for $75.14.

     Answer the following questions about the impact of the stock split on his holdings and taxes. Nathan is in the 28% federal income tax bracket.
a. How many shares of General Mills will Nathan own after the stock split?
b. Immediately after the split, what do you expect the value of General Mills to be?
c. Compare the total value of Nathan's stock holdings before and after the split, given that the price of General Mills stock immediately after the split was $37.50. What do you find?
d. Does Nathan experience a gain or loss on the stock as a result of the 2-for-1 split?
e. What is Nathan's tax liability from the event?

P13–15   **Stock split versus stock dividend: Firm**   Mammoth Corporation is considering a 3-for-2 stock split. It currently has the stockholders' equity position shown. The current stock price is $120 per share. The most recent period's earnings available for common stock are included in retained earnings.

Preferred stock	$ 1,000,000
Common stock (100,000 shares at $3 par)	300,000
Paid-in capital in excess of par	1,700,000
Retained earnings	10,000,000
Total stockholders' equity	$13,000,000

a. What effects on Mammoth would result from the *stock split?*
b. What change in stock price would you expect to result from the stock split?
c. What is the maximum cash dividend per share that the firm could pay on common stock before and after the stock split? (Assume that legal capital includes *all* paid-in capital.)
d. Contrast your answers to parts **a** through **c** with the circumstances surrounding a 50% *stock dividend.*
e. Explain the differences between stock splits and stock dividends.

P13–16   **Stock dividend versus stock split: Firm**   The board of Wicker Home Health Care, Inc., is exploring ways to expand the number of shares outstanding in an effort to reduce the market price per share to a level that the firm considers more appealing to investors. The options under consideration are a 20% stock dividend and, alternatively, a 5-for-4 stock split. At the present time, the firm's equity account and other per-share information are as follows:

Preferred stock	$ 0
Common stock (100,000 shares at $1 par)	100,000
Paid-in capital in excess of par	900,000
Retained earnings	700,000
Total stockholders' equity	$1,700,000
Price per share	$30.00
Earnings per share	$3.60
Dividend per share	$1.08

a. Show the effect on the equity accounts and per-share data of a 20% *stock dividend*.
b. Show the effect on the equity accounts and per-share data of a 5-for-4 *stock split*.
c. Which option will accomplish Wicker's goal of reducing the current stock price while maintaining a stable level of retained earnings?
d. What legal constraints might encourage the firm to choose a stock split over a stock dividend?

LG 6 **P13–17** **Stock repurchase** The following financial data on the Bond Recording Company are available:

Earnings available for common stockholders	$800,000
Number of shares of common stock outstanding	400,000
Earnings per share ($800,000 ÷ 400,000)	$2
Market price per share	$20
Price/earnings (P/E) ratio ($20 ÷ $2)	10

The firm is currently considering whether it should use $400,000 of its earnings to pay cash dividends of $1 per share or to repurchase stock at $21 per share.
a. Approximately how many shares of stock can the firm repurchase at the $21-per-share price, using the funds that would have gone to pay the cash dividend?
b. Calculate the *EPS* after the repurchase. Explain your calculations.
c. If the stock still sells at 10 times earnings, what will the *market price* be after the repurchase?
d. Compare the pre- and postrepurchase earnings per share.
e. Compare and contrast the stockholders' positions under the dividend and repurchase alternatives. What are the tax implications under each alternative?

LG 6 **P13–18** **Stock repurchase** Harte Textiles, Inc., a maker of custom upholstery fabrics, is concerned about preserving the wealth of its stockholders during a cyclic downturn in the home furnishings business. The company has maintained a constant dividend payout of $2.00 tied to a target payout ratio of 40%. Management is preparing a share repurchase recommendation to present to the firm's board of directors. The data at the top of the following page have been gathered from the last 2 years.
a. How many shares should the company have outstanding in 2015 if its earnings available for common stockholders in that year are $1,200,000 and it pays a dividend of $2.00, given that its desired payout ratio is 40%?

	2014	2015
Earnings available for common stockholders	$1,260,000	$1,200,000
Number of shares outstanding	300,000	300,000
Earnings per share	$4.20	$4.00
Market price per share	$23.50	$20.00
Price/earnings ratio	5.6	5.0

b. How many shares would Harte have to repurchase to have the level of shares outstanding calculated in part **a**?

 P13–19   **ETHICS PROBLEM**   Assume that you are the CFO of a company contemplating a stock repurchase next quarter. You know that there are several methods of reducing the current quarterly earnings, which may cause the stock price to fall prior to the announcement of the proposed stock repurchase. What course of action would you recommend to your CEO? If your CEO came to you first and recommended reducing the current quarter's earnings, what would be your response?

Spreadsheet Exercise

One way to lower the market price of a firm's stock is via a stock split. Rock-O Corporation finds itself in a different situation: Its stock has been selling at relatively low prices. To increase the market price of the stock, the company chooses to use a *reverse stock split* of 2-for-3.

The company currently has 700,000 common shares outstanding and no preferred stock. The common stock carries a par value of $1. At this time, the paid-in capital in excess of par is $7,000,000, and the firm's retained earnings are $3,500,000.

TO DO

Create a spreadsheet to determine the following:

a. The stockholders' equity section of the balance sheet *before* the reverse stock split.
b. The stockholders' equity section of the balance sheet *after* the reverse stock split.

MyFinanceLab   Visit www.myfinancelab.com for **Chapter Case: Establishing General Access Company's Dividend Policy and Initial Dividend,** Group Exercises, and numerous online resources.

Part 7 ▶ Short-Term Financial Decisions

Short-term financial decisions are guided by the same financial management principles as long-term financial decisions, but the time frame is different: days, weeks, and months rather than years. Working capital management focuses on the management of short-term cash flows by evaluating their timing, risk, and impact on firm value. Although long-term financial decisions ultimately determine the firm's ability to maximize shareholder wealth, there may not be a long term if financial managers fail to make effective short-term financial decisions.

Chapter 14 discusses the techniques and strategies for managing working capital and current assets. The fundamentals of net working capital and the importance of the cash conversion cycle are introduced. Chapter 15 discusses the importance of controlling accounts payable expenses and managing other current liabilities. You will learn how some companies use current liabilities, including accounts payable, accruals, lines of credit, commercial paper, and short-term loans, to finance current assets. Successful adherence to the fundamentals of working capital management will help ensure that the firm can meet its operating obligations and maximize its long-term investments.

14

Working Capital and Current Assets Management

Learning Goals

LG 1 Understand working capital management, net working capital, and the related trade-off between profitability and risk.

LG 2 Describe the cash conversion cycle, its funding requirements, and the key strategies for managing it.

LG 3 Discuss inventory management: differing views, common techniques, and international concerns.

LG 4 Explain the credit selection process and the quantitative procedure for evaluating changes in credit standards.

LG 5 Review the procedures for quantitatively considering cash discount changes, other aspects of credit terms, and credit monitoring.

LG 6 Understand the management of receipts and disbursements, including float, speeding up collections, slowing down payments, cash concentration, zero-balance accounts, and investing in marketable securities.

Why This Chapter Matters to You

In your *professional* life

ACCOUNTING You need to understand the cash conversion cycle and the management of inventory, accounts receivable, and receipts and disbursements of cash.

INFORMATION SYSTEMS You need to understand the cash conversion cycle, inventory, accounts receivable, and receipts and disbursements of cash to design financial information systems that facilitate effective working capital management.

MANAGEMENT You need to understand the management of working capital so that you can efficiently manage current assets and decide whether to finance the firm's funds requirements aggressively or conservatively.

MARKETING You need to understand credit selection and monitoring because sales will be affected by the availability of credit to purchasers; sales will also be affected by inventory management.

OPERATIONS You need to understand the cash conversion cycle because you will be responsible for reducing the cycle through the efficient management of production, inventory, and costs.

In your *personal* life
You often will be faced with short-term purchasing decisions, which tend to focus on consumable items. Many involve trade-offs between quantity and price: Should you buy large quantities so as to pay a lower unit price, hold the items, and use them over time? Or should you buy smaller quantities more frequently and pay a slightly higher unit price? Analyzing these types of short-term purchasing decisions will help you make the most of your money.

14.1 Net Working Capital Fundamentals

MyFinanceLab Video

The balance sheet provides information about the structure of a firm's investments on the one hand and the structure of its financing sources on the other hand. The structures chosen should consistently lead to the maximization of the value of the owners' investment in the firm.

WORKING CAPITAL MANAGEMENT

working capital (or short-term financial) management
Management of current assets and current liabilities.

The importance of efficient working capital management is indisputable given that a firm's viability relies on the financial manager's ability to effectively manage receivables, inventory, and payables. The goal of **working capital (or short-term financial) management** is to manage each of the firm's current assets (inventory, accounts receivable, marketable securities, and cash) and current liabilities (notes payable, accruals, and accounts payable) to achieve a balance between profitability and risk that contributes positively to the firm's value.

Firms are able to reduce financing costs or increase the funds available for expansion by minimizing the amount of funds tied up in working capital. Therefore, it should not be surprising to learn that working capital is one of the financial manager's most important and time-consuming activities. Surveys by *CFO* magazine and Duke University have found that corporate CFOs spend almost 30 hours per month engaged in working capital and cash management, which is more time than they spend on any other single activity. Similar surveys have found that CFOs believe that their efforts to manage working capital effectively add as much value to the firm as any other activity in which they engage.

Matter of fact

CFOs Value Working Capital Management

A survey of CFOs from firms around the world suggests that working capital management is at the top of the list of most valued finance functions. Among 19 different finance functions, CFOs viewed working capital management as equally important as capital structure, debt issuance and management, bank relationships, and tax management. Their satisfaction with the performance of working capital management was quite the opposite, however. CFOs viewed the performance of working capital management as being better only than the performance of pension management. Consistent with their view that working capital management is a high-value but low-satisfaction activity, it was identified as the finance function second most in need of additional resources.[1]

Next, we use *net working capital* to consider the relationship between current assets and current liabilities and then use the *cash conversion cycle* to consider the key aspects of current asset management. In Chapter 15, we consider current liability management.

1. Henri Servaes and Peter Tufano, "CFO Views on the Importance and Execution of the Finance Function," *CFO Views* (January 2006), pp. 1–104.

NET WORKING CAPITAL

working capital
Current assets, which represent the portion of investment that circulates from one form to another in the ordinary conduct of business.

Current assets, commonly called **working capital**, represent the portion of investment that circulates from one form to another in the ordinary conduct of business. This idea embraces the recurring transition from cash to inventories to accounts receivable and back to cash. As cash substitutes, *marketable securities* are also part of working capital.

Current liabilities represent the firm's short-term financing, because they include all debts of the firm that come due in 1 year or less. These debts usually include amounts owed to suppliers (accounts payable), employees and governments (accruals), and banks (notes payable), among others. (You can refer to Chapter 3 for a full discussion of balance sheet items.)

net working capital
The difference between the firm's current assets and its current liabilities.

As noted in Chapter 11, **net working capital** is defined as the difference between the firm's current assets and its current liabilities. When current assets exceed current liabilities, the firm has *positive net working capital*. When current assets are less than current liabilities, the firm has *negative net working capital*.

The conversion of current assets from inventory to accounts receivable to cash provides the cash used to pay current liabilities. The cash outlays for current liabilities are relatively predictable. When an obligation is incurred, the firm generally knows when the corresponding payment will be due. What is difficult to predict are the cash inflows: the conversion of the current assets to more liquid forms. The more predictable its cash inflows, the less net working capital a firm needs. Because most firms are unable to match cash inflows to cash outflows with certainty, they usually need current assets that more than cover outflows for current liabilities. In general, the greater the margin by which a firm's current assets cover current liabilities, the better able it will be to pay its bills as they come due.

TRADE-OFF BETWEEN PROFITABILITY AND RISK

profitability
The relationship between revenues and costs generated by using the firm's assets—both current and fixed—in productive activities.

risk (of insolvency)
The probability that a firm will be unable to pay its bills as they come due.

insolvent
Describes a firm that is unable to pay its bills as they come due.

A trade-off exists between a firm's profitability and its risk. **Profitability**, in this context, is the relationship between revenues and costs generated by using the firm's assets—both current and fixed—in productive activities. A firm can increase its profits by (1) increasing revenues or (2) decreasing costs. **Risk**, in the context of working capital management, is the probability that a firm will be unable to pay its bills as they come due. A firm that cannot pay its bills as they come due is said to be **insolvent**. It is generally assumed that the greater the firm's net working capital, the lower its risk. In other words, the more net working capital, the more liquid the firm and therefore the lower its risk of becoming insolvent. Using these definitions of profitability and risk, we can demonstrate the trade-off between them by considering changes in current assets and current liabilities separately.

Changes in Current Assets

We can demonstrate how changing the level of the firm's current assets affects its profitability–risk trade-off by using the ratio of current assets to total assets. This ratio indicates the *percentage of total assets* that is current. For purposes of illustration, we will assume that the level of total assets remains unchanged. The effects on both profitability and risk of an increase or decrease in this ratio are summarized in the upper portion of Table 14.1. When the ratio increases—that is, when current assets increase—profitability decreases. Why? The answer is because current assets are less profitable than fixed assets. Fixed assets are mo

TABLE 14.1	Effects of Changing Ratios on Profits and Risk		
Ratio	Change in ratio	Effect on profit	Effect on risk
Current assets	Increase	Decrease	Decrease
Total assets	Decrease	Increase	Increase
Current liabilities	Increase	Increase	Increase
Total assets	Decrease	Decrease	Decrease

profitable because they add more value to the product than that provided by current assets.

The risk effect, however, decreases as the ratio of current assets to total assets increases. The increase in current assets increases net working capital, thereby reducing the risk of insolvency. In addition, as you go down the asset side of the balance sheet, the risk associated with the assets increases: Investment in cash and marketable securities is less risky than investment in accounts receivable, inventories, and fixed assets. Accounts receivable investment is less risky than investment in inventories and fixed assets. Investment in inventories is less risky than investment in fixed assets. The nearer an asset is to cash, the less risky it is. The opposite effects on profit and risk result from a decrease in the ratio of current assets to total assets.

In an effort to manage the risk effect, firms have been steadily moving away from riskier current asset components, such as inventory. Figure 14.1 shows that over time current assets consistently account for about 60 percent of total assets in U.S. manufacturing firms, but inventory levels are dropping dramatically. That current assets relative to total assets remains fairly constant while inventory investment is shrinking indicates that U.S. manufacturing firms are substituting less risky current assets for inventory, the riskiest current asset. Indeed, Figure 14.1 shows that cash levels are increasing relative to total assets.

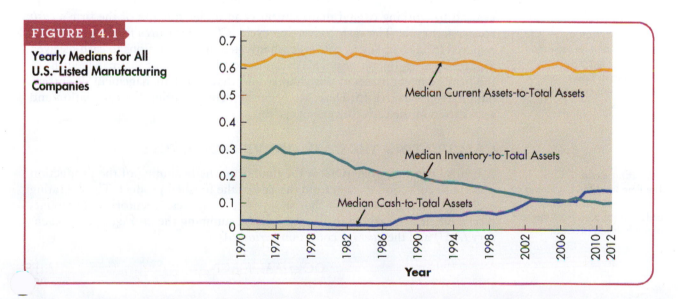

FIGURE 14.1

Yearly Medians for All U.S.–Listed Manufacturing Companies

Changes in Current Liabilities

We also can demonstrate how changing the level of the firm's current liabilities affects its profitability–risk trade-off by using the ratio of current liabilities to total assets. This ratio indicates the percentage of total assets that has been financed with current liabilities. Again, assuming that total assets remain unchanged, the effects on both profitability and risk of an increase or decrease in the ratio are summarized in the lower portion of Table 14.1. When the ratio increases, profitability increases. Why? Here it is because the firm uses more of the less-expensive current liabilities financing and less long-term financing. Current liabilities are less expensive because only notes payable, which represent about 20 percent of the typical manufacturer's current liabilities, have a cost. The other current liabilities are basically debts on which the firm pays no charge or interest. However, when the ratio of current liabilities to total assets increases, the risk of insolvency also increases because the increase in current liabilities in turn decreases net working capital. The opposite effects on profit and risk result from a decrease in the ratio of current liabilities to total assets.

→ **REVIEW QUESTIONS**

14–1 Why is *working capital management* one of the most important and time-consuming activities of the financial manager? What is *net working capital*?

14–2 What is the relationship between the predictability of a firm's cash inflows and its required level of net working capital? How are net working capital, liquidity, and *risk of insolvency* related?

14–3 Why does an increase in the ratio of current assets to total assets decrease both profits and risk as measured by net working capital? How do changes in the ratio of current liabilities to total assets affect profitability and risk?

LG 2 **14.2 Cash Conversion Cycle**

cash conversion cycle (CCC)
The length of time required for a company to convert cash invested in its operations to cash received as a result of its operations.

Central to working capital management is an understanding of the firm's *cash conversion cycle*. The **cash conversion cycle (CCC)** measures the length of time required for a company to convert cash invested in its operations to cash received as a result of its operations. This cycle frames discussion of the management of the firm's current assets in this chapter and that of the management of current liabilities in Chapter 15. Here, we begin by demonstrating the calculation and application of the cash conversion cycle.

CALCULATING THE CASH CONVERSION CYCLE

operating cycle (OC)
The time from the beginning of the production process to collection of cash from the sale of the finished product.

A firm's **operating cycle (OC)** is the time from the beginning of the production process to collection of cash from the sale of the finished product. The operating cycle encompasses two major short-term asset categories, inventory and accounts receivable. It is measured in elapsed time by summing the *average age of inventory (AAI)* and the *average collection period (ACP)*:

$$OC = AAI + ACP \qquad (14.1)$$

However, the process of producing and selling a product also includes the purchase of production inputs (raw materials) on account, which results in accounts payable. Accounts payable reduce the number of days a firm's resources are tied up in the operating cycle. The time it takes to pay the accounts payable, measured in days, is the *average payment period (APP)*. The operating cycle less the average payment period yields the cash conversion cycle. The formula for the cash conversion cycle is

$$CCC = OC - APP \tag{14.2}$$

Substituting the relationship in Equation 14.1 into Equation 14.2, we can see that the cash conversion cycle has three main components—(1) average age of the inventory, (2) average collection period, and (3) average payment period—so

$$CCC = AAI + ACP - APP \tag{14.3}$$

Clearly, if a firm changes any of these time periods, it changes the amount of resources tied up in the day-to-day operation of the firm.

Example 14.1 ▶

MyFinanceLab Solution
Video

In its 2012 annual report, Whirlpool Corporation reported that it had revenues of $18.1 billion, cost of goods sold of $15.2 billion, accounts receivable of 2.0 billion, and inventory of $2.4 billion. From this information (and assuming for simplicity that cost of goods sold equals purchases), we can determine that the company's average age of inventory was 58 days, its average collection period was 40 days, and its average payment period was 89 days. Thus, the cash conversion cycle for Whirlpool was just 9 days (58 + 40 − 89). Figure 14.2 presents Whirlpool's cash conversion cycle as a time line.

The resources Whirlpool had invested in this cash conversion cycle (assuming a 365-day year) were

Inventory	= $15.2 billion × (58 ÷ 365) =	$2.4
+ Accounts receivable	= 18.1 billion × (40 ÷ 365) =	2.0
− Accounts payable	= 15.2 billion × (89 ÷ 365) =	<u>3.7</u>
= Resources invested	=	<u>$0.7</u>

With roughly $700 million committed to working capital, Whirlpool was surely motivated to make improvements. Changes in any of the component cycles will change the resources tied up in Whirlpool's operations. For example, if Whirlpool could reduce its collection period from 40 days to 30 days, holding all else equal, its working capital requirement would fall by more than $500 million. It is clear why companies pay close attention to working capital management.

FUNDING REQUIREMENTS OF THE CASH CONVERSION CYCLE

We can use the cash conversion cycle as a basis for discussing how the firm funds its required investment in operating assets. We first differentiate between permanent and seasonal funding needs and then describe aggressive and conservative seasonal funding strategies.

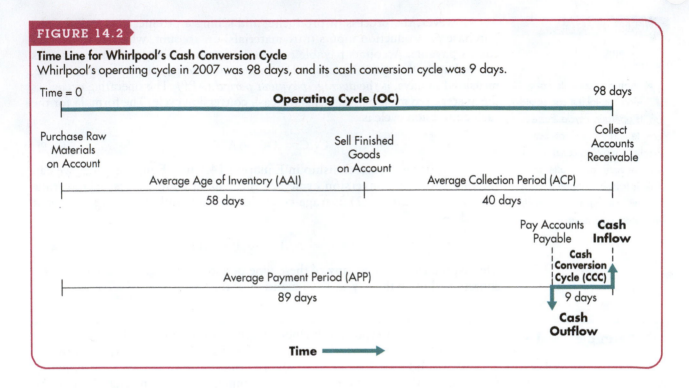

FIGURE 14.2

Time Line for Whirlpool's Cash Conversion Cycle
Whirlpool's operating cycle in 2007 was 98 days, and its cash conversion cycle was 9 days.

Permanent versus Seasonal Funding Needs

permanent funding requirement
A constant investment in operating assets resulting from constant sales over time.

If the firm's sales are constant, its investment in operating assets should also be constant, and the firm will have only a **permanent funding requirement**. If the firm's sales are cyclic, its investment in operating assets will vary over time with its sales cycles, and the firm will have **seasonal funding requirements** in addition to the permanent funding required for its minimum investment in operating assets.

Example 14.2 ▶

MyFinanceLab Solution Video

seasonal funding requirement
An investment in operating assets that varies over time as a result of cyclic sales.

Nicholson Company holds, on average, $50,000 in cash and marketable securities, $1,250,000 in inventory, and $750,000 in accounts receivable. Nicholson's business is very stable over time, so its operating assets can be viewed as permanent. In addition, Nicholson's accounts payable of $425,000 are stable over time. Thus, Nicholson has a permanent investment in operating assets of $1,625,000 ($50,000 + $1,250,0000 + $750,000 − $425,000). That amount would also equal its permanent funding requirement.

In contrast, Semper Pump Company, which produces bicycle pumps, has seasonal funding needs. Semper has seasonal sales, with its peak sales being driven by the summertime purchases of bicycle pumps. Semper holds, at minimum, $25,000 in cash and marketable securities, $100,000 in inventory, and $60,000 in accounts receivable. At peak times, Semper's inventory increases to $750,000, and its accounts receivable increase to $400,000. To capture production efficiencies, Semper produces pumps at a constant rate throughout the year. Thus, accounts payable remain at $50,000 throughout the year. Accordingly, Semper has a permanent funding requirement for its minimum level of operating assets of $135,000 ($25,000 + $100,000 + $60,000 − $50,000) and peak seasonal funding requirements (in excess of its permanent need) o

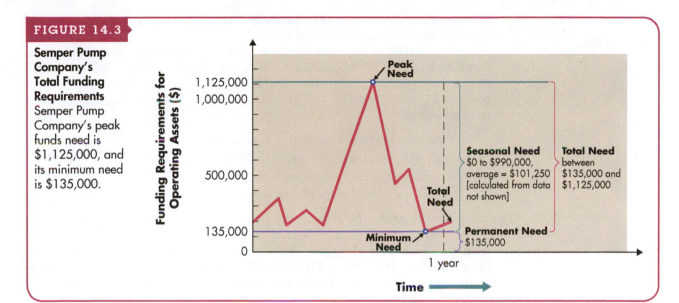

FIGURE 14.3

Semper Pump Company's Total Funding Requirements
Semper Pump Company's peak funds need is $1,125,000, and its minimum need is $135,000.

$990,000 [($25,000 + $750,000 + $400,000 − $50,000) − $135,000]. Semper's total funding requirements for operating assets vary from a minimum of $135,000 (permanent) to a seasonal peak of $1,125,000 ($135,000 + $990,000). Figure 14.3 depicts these needs over time.

Aggressive versus Conservative Seasonal Funding Strategies

aggressive funding strategy
A funding strategy under which the firm funds its seasonal requirements with short-term debt and its permanent requirements with long-term debt.

conservative funding strategy
A funding strategy under which the firm funds both its seasonal and its permanent requirements with long-term debt.

Short-term funds are typically less expensive than long-term funds. That is, interest rates on short-term loans are typically lower than rates on long-term loans because the yield curve is typically upward sloping. However, long-term funds allow the firm to lock in its cost of funds over a period of time and thus avoid the risk of increases in short-term interest rates. Also, long-term funding ensures that the required funds are available to the firm when needed. Short-term funding exposes the firm to the risk that it may not be able to obtain the funds needed to cover its seasonal peaks. Under an **aggressive funding strategy**, the firm funds its seasonal requirements with short-term debt and its permanent requirements with long-term debt. Under a **conservative funding strategy**, the firm funds both its seasonal and its permanent requirements with long-term debt.

Example 14.3 ▶

Semper Pump Company has a permanent funding requirement of $135,000 in operating assets and seasonal funding requirements that vary between $0 and $990,000 and average $101,250 (calculated from data not shown). If Semper can borrow short-term funds at 6.25% and long-term funds at 8%, and if it can earn 5% on the investment of any surplus balances, then the annual cost of an aggressive strategy for seasonal funding will be

Cost of short-term financing	= 0.0625 ×	$101,250	=	$ 6,328.13
+ Cost of long-term financing	= 0.0800 ×	135,000	=	10,800.00
− Earnings on surplus balances	= 0.0500 ×	0	=	0
Total cost of aggressive strategy				$17,128.13

Because under this strategy the amount of financing exactly equals the estimated funding need, no surplus balances exist.

Alternatively, Semper can choose a conservative strategy, under which surplus cash balances are fully invested. (In Figure 14.3, this surplus will be the difference between the peak need of $1,125,000 and the total need, which varies between $135,000 and $1,125,000 during the year.) The cost of the conservative strategy will be

$$
\begin{array}{lllr}
\text{Cost of short-term financing} & = 0.0625 \times \$ & 0 = \$ & 0 \\
+ \text{ Cost of long-term financing} & = 0.0800 \times & 1,125,000 = & 90,000.00 \\
- \text{ Earnings on surplus balances} & = 0.0500 \times & 888,750 = & \underline{44,437.50} \\
& \text{Total cost of conservative strategy} & & \underline{\$45,562.50}
\end{array}
$$

The average surplus balance would be calculated by subtracting the sum of the permanent need ($135,000) and the average seasonal need ($101,250) from the seasonal peak need ($1,125,000) to get $888,750 ($1,125,000 − $135,000 − $101,250). This represents the surplus amount of financing that on average could be invested in short-term assets that earn a 5% annual return.

It is clear from these calculations that for Semper, the aggressive strategy is far less expensive than the conservative strategy. However, it is equally clear that Semper has substantial peak-season operating-asset needs and that it must have adequate funding available to meet the peak needs and ensure ongoing operations.

Clearly, the aggressive strategy's heavy reliance on short-term financing makes it riskier than the conservative strategy because of interest rate swings and possible difficulties in obtaining needed short-term financing quickly when seasonal peaks occur. The conservative strategy avoids these risks through the locked-in interest rate and long-term financing, but it is more costly because of the negative spread between the earnings rate on surplus funds (5 percent in the example) and the cost of the long-term funds that create the surplus (8 percent in the example). Where the firm operates, between the extremes of the aggressive and conservative seasonal funding strategies, depends on management's disposition toward risk and the strength of its banking relationships.

STRATEGIES FOR MANAGING THE CASH CONVERSION CYCLE

Some firms establish a *target* cash conversion cycle and then monitor and manage the *actual* cash conversion cycle toward the targeted value. A positive cash conversion cycle, as was the case for Whirlpool in 2012, means the firm must use negotiated liabilities (such as bank loans) to support its operating assets. Negotiated liabilities carry an explicit cost, so the firm benefits by minimizing their use in supporting operating assets. Simply stated, the goal is to *minimize the length of the cash conversion cycle*, which minimizes negotiated liabilities. This goal can be realized through use of the following strategies:

1. *Turn over inventory as quickly as possible* without stockouts that result in lost sales.
2. *Collect accounts receivable as quickly as possible* without losing sales from high-pressure collection techniques.

3. *Manage mail, processing, and clearing time* to reduce them when collecting from customers and to increase them when paying suppliers.
4. *Pay accounts payable as slowly as possible* without damaging the firm's credit rating or its relationships with suppliers.

Techniques for implementing these four strategies are the focus of the remainder of this chapter and the following chapter.

→ **REVIEW QUESTIONS**

14–4 What is the difference between the firm's *operating cycle* and its *cash conversion cycle?*

14–5 Why is it helpful to divide the funding needs of a seasonal business into its permanent and seasonal funding requirements when developing a funding strategy?

14–6 What are the benefits, costs, and risks of an *aggressive funding strategy* and of a *conservative funding strategy?* Under which strategy is the borrowing often in excess of the actual need?

14–7 Why is it important for a firm to minimize the length of its cash conversion cycle?

LG 3 | **14.3 Inventory Management**

The first component of the cash conversion cycle is the average age of inventory. The objective for managing inventory, as noted earlier, is to turn over inventory as quickly as possible without losing sales from stockouts. The financial manager tends to act as an advisor or "watchdog" in matters concerning inventory. He or she does not have direct control over inventory but does provide input to the inventory management process.

DIFFERING VIEWPOINTS ABOUT INVENTORY LEVEL

Differing viewpoints about appropriate inventory levels commonly exist among a firm's finance, marketing, manufacturing, and purchasing managers. Each views inventory levels in light of his or her own objectives. The *financial manager's* general disposition toward inventory levels is to keep them low, to ensure that the firm's money is not being unwisely invested in excess resources. The *marketing manager,* on the other hand, would like to have large inventories of the firm's finished products. This would ensure that all orders could be filled quickly, eliminating the need for backorders due to stockouts.

The *manufacturing manager's* major responsibility is to implement the production plan so that it results in the desired amount of finished goods of acceptable quality available on time at a low cost. In fulfilling this role, the manufacturing manager would keep raw materials inventories high to avoid production delays. He or she also would favor large production runs for the sake of lower unit production costs, which would result in high finished goods inventories.

The *purchasing manager* is concerned solely with the raw materials inventories. He or she must have on hand, in the correct quantities at the desired times and at a favorable price, whatever raw materials are required by production.

Without proper control, in an effort to get quantity discounts or in anticipation of rising prices or a shortage of certain materials, the purchasing manager may purchase larger quantities of resources than are actually needed at the time.

COMMON TECHNIQUES FOR MANAGING INVENTORY

Numerous techniques are available for effectively managing the firm's inventory. Here we briefly consider four commonly used techniques.

ABC System

ABC inventory system
Inventory management technique that divides inventory into three groups—A, B, and C, in descending order of importance and level of monitoring—on the basis of the dollar investment in each.

A firm using the **ABC inventory system** divides its inventory into three groups: A, B, and C. The A group includes those items with the largest dollar investment. Typically, this group consists of 20 percent of the firm's inventory items but 80 percent of its investment in inventory. The B group consists of items that account for the next largest investment in inventory. The C group consists of a large number of items that require a relatively small investment.

The inventory group of each item determines the item's level of monitoring. The A group items receive the most intense monitoring because of the high dollar investment. Typically, A group items are tracked on a perpetual inventory system that allows daily verification of each item's inventory level. B group items are frequently controlled through periodic, perhaps weekly, checking of their levels. C group items are monitored with unsophisticated techniques, such as the two-bin method. With the **two-bin method**, the item is stored in two bins. As an item is needed, inventory is removed from the first bin. When that bin is empty, an order is placed to refill the first bin while inventory is drawn from the second bin. The second bin is used until empty, and so on.

two-bin method
Unsophisticated inventory-monitoring technique that is typically applied to C group items and involves reordering inventory when one of two bins is empty.

The large dollar investment in A and B group items suggests the need for a better method of inventory management than the ABC system. The EOQ model, discussed next, is an appropriate model for the management of A and B group items.

Economic Order Quantity (EOQ) Model

economic order quantity (EOQ) model
Inventory management technique for determining an item's optimal order size, which is the size that minimizes the total of its *order costs* and *carrying costs*.

One of the most common techniques for determining the optimal order size for inventory items is the **economic order quantity (EOQ) model**. The EOQ model considers various costs of inventory and then determines what order size minimizes total inventory cost.

EOQ assumes that the relevant costs of inventory can be divided into *order costs* and *carrying costs*. (The model excludes the actual cost of the inventory item.) Each of them has certain key components and characteristics. **Order costs** include the fixed clerical costs of placing and receiving orders: the cost of writing a purchase order, of processing the resulting paperwork, and of receiving an order and checking it against the invoice. Order costs are stated in dollars per order. **Carrying costs** are the variable costs per unit of holding an item of inventory for a specific period of time. Carrying costs include storage costs, insurance costs, the costs of deterioration and obsolescence, and the opportunity or financial cost of having funds invested in inventory. These costs are stated in dollars per unit per period.

order costs
The fixed clerical costs of placing and receiving an inventory order.

carrying costs
The variable costs per unit of holding an item in inventory for a specific period of time.

Order costs decrease as the size of the order increases. Carrying costs, however, increase with increases in the order size. The EOQ model analyzes the trade-off between order costs and carrying costs to determine the *order quantity that minimizes the total inventory cost*.

Mathematical Development of EOQ   A formula can be developed for determining the firm's EOQ for a given inventory item, where

$$S = \text{usage in units per period}$$
$$O = \text{order cost per order}$$
$$C = \text{carrying cost per unit per period}$$
$$Q = \text{order quantity in units}$$

The first step is to derive the cost functions for order cost and carrying cost. The order cost can be expressed as the product of the cost per order and the number of orders. Because the number of orders equals the usage during the period divided by the order quantity (S/Q), the order cost can be expressed as follows:

$$\text{Order cost} = O \times (S \div Q) \tag{14.4}$$

The carrying cost is defined as the cost of carrying a unit of inventory per period multiplied by the firm's average inventory. The average inventory is the order quantity divided by 2 ($Q/2$), because inventory is assumed to be depleted at a constant rate. Thus, carrying cost can be expressed as

$$\text{Carrying cost} = C \times (Q \div 2) \tag{14.5}$$

total cost of inventory
The sum of order costs and carrying costs of inventory.

The firm's **total cost of inventory** is found by summing the order cost and the carrying cost. Thus, the total cost function is

$$\text{Total cost} = [\,O \times (S \div Q)\,] + [\,C \times (Q \div 2)\,] \tag{14.6}$$

Because the EOQ is defined as the order quantity that minimizes the total cost function, we must solve the total cost function for the EOQ.[2] The resulting equation is

$$\text{EOQ} = \sqrt{\dfrac{2 \times S \times O}{C}} \tag{14.7}$$

Although the EOQ model has weaknesses, it is certainly better than subjective decision making. Even though the use of the EOQ model is outside the control of the financial manager, the financial manager must be aware of its utility and must provide certain inputs, specifically with respect to inventory carrying costs.

---

2. In this simple model, the EOQ occurs at the point where the order cost $[\,O \times (S \div Q)\,]$ just equals the carrying cost $[\,C \times (Q \div 2)\,]$. To demonstrate, we set the two costs equal and solve for Q:

$$[\,O \times (S \div Q)\,] = [\,C \times (Q \div 2)\,]$$

Then cross-multiplying, we get

$$2 \times O \times S = C \times Q^2$$

Dividing both sides by C, we get

$$Q^2 = (2 \times O \times S) \div C$$

so

$$Q = \sqrt{(2 \times O \times S) \div C}$$

Personal Finance Example 14.4 ▶ Individuals sometimes are confronted with personal finance decisions involving cost trade-offs similar to the trade-off between the fixed order costs and variable carrying costs of inventory that corporations face. Take the case of the von Dammes, who are trying to decide whether a conventional car (uses gas) or a hybrid car (uses gas and electric battery) would be more cost effective.

The von Dammes plan to keep whichever car they choose for 3 years and expect to drive it 12,000 miles in each of those years. They will use the same dollar amount of financing repaid under the same terms for either car, and they expect the cars to have identical repair costs over the 3-year ownership period. They also assume that the trade-in value of the two cars at the end of 3 years will be identical. Both cars use regular unleaded gas, which they estimate will cost, on average, $3.20 per gallon over the 3 years. The key data for each car are as follows:

	Conventional	Hybrid
Total cost	$24,500	$27,300
Average miles per gallon	27	42

We can begin by calculating the total fuel cost for each car over the 3-year ownership period:

Conventional: $[(3 \text{ years} \times 12,000 \text{ miles per year}) \div 27 \text{ miles per gallon}]$

$\times \$3.20 \text{ per gallon}$

$= 1,333.33 \text{ gallons} \times \$3.20 \text{ per gallon} = \$4,267$

Hybrid: $[(3 \text{ years} \times 12,000 \text{ miles per year}) \div 42 \text{ miles per gallon}]$

$\times \$3.20 \text{ per gallon}$

$= 857.14 \text{ gallons} \times \$3.20 \text{ per gallon} = \$2,743$

To buy the hybrid car, the von Dammes will have to pay $2,800 more ($27,300 − $24,500) than the cost of the conventional car, but they will save about $1,524 ($4,267 − $2,743) in fuel costs over the 3-year ownership period. Ignoring differences in timing, on a strict economic basis *they should buy the conventional car because the $2,800 marginal cost of the hybrid results in a marginal fuel cost savings of only $1,524.* Clearly, other factors such as environmental concerns and the reasonableness of the assumptions could affect their decision.

reorder point
The point at which to reorder inventory, expressed as days of lead time × daily usage.

Reorder Point Once the firm has determined its economic order quantity, it must determine when to place an order. The **reorder point** reflects the number of days of lead time the firm needs to place and receive an order and the firm's daily usage of the inventory item. Assuming that inventory is used at a constant rate, the formula for the reorder point is

$$\text{Reorder point} = \text{Days of lead time} \times \text{Daily usage} \qquad (14.8)$$

For example, if a firm knows it takes 3 days to place and receive an order and if it uses 15 units per day of the inventory item, the reorder point is 45 unit of inventory (3 days × 15 units/day). Thus, as soon as the item's inventory level falls to the reorder point (45 units, in this case), an order will be placed at the item's EOQ. If the estimates of lead time and usage are correct, the order will arrive exactly as the inventory level reaches zero. However, lead times and usage rates are not precise, so most firms hold **safety stock** (extra inventory) to prevent stockouts of important items.

safety stock
Extra inventory that is held to prevent stockouts of important items.

Example 14.5 ▶

MAX Company, a producer of dinnerware, has an A group inventory item that is vital to the production process. This item costs $1,500, and MAX uses 1,100 units of the item per year. MAX wants to determine its optimal order strategy for the item. To calculate the EOQ, we need the following inputs:

$$\text{Order cost per order} = \$150$$
$$\text{Carrying cost per unit per year} = \$200$$

Substituting into Equation 14.7, we get

$$EOQ = \sqrt{\frac{2 \times 1,100 \times \$150}{\$200}} \approx \underline{41} \text{ units}$$

The reorder point for MAX depends on the number of days MAX operates per year. Assuming that MAX operates 250 days per year and uses 1,100 units of this item, its daily usage is 4.4 units (1,100 ÷ 250). If its lead time is 2 days and MAX wants to maintain a safety stock of 4 units, the reorder point for this item is $[(2 \times 4.4) + 4]$, or 12.8 units. However, orders are made only in whole units, so the order is placed when the inventory falls to 13 units.

The firm's goal for inventory is to turn it over as quickly as possible without stockouts. Inventory turnover is best calculated by dividing cost of goods sold by average inventory. The EOQ model determines the optimal order size and, indirectly, through the assumption of constant usage, the average inventory. Thus, the EOQ model determines the firm's optimal inventory turnover rate, given the firm's specific costs of inventory.

Just-in-Time (JIT) System

just-in-time (JIT) system
Inventory management technique that minimizes inventory investment by having materials arrive at exactly the time they are needed for production.

The **just-in-time (JIT) system** is used to minimize inventory investment. The philosophy is that materials should arrive at exactly the time they are needed for production. Ideally, the firm would have only work-in-process inventory. Because its objective is to minimize inventory investment, a JIT system uses no (or very little) safety stock. Extensive coordination among the firm's employees, its suppliers, and shipping companies must exist to ensure that material inputs arrive on time. Failure of materials to arrive on time results in a shutdown of the production line until the materials arrive. Likewise, a JIT system requires high-quality parts from suppliers. When quality problems arise, production must be stopped until the problems are resolved.

The goal of the JIT system is manufacturing efficiency. It uses inventory as a tool for attaining efficiency by emphasizing quality of the materials used and their timely delivery. When JIT is working properly, it forces process inefficiencies to surface.

Knowing the level of inventory is, of course, an important part of any inventory management system. As described in the *Focus on Practice* box, radio

focus on PRACTICE

RFID: The Wave of the Future?

in practice Wal-Mart Stores, Inc., the world's number one retailer, operates almost 11,000 retail units under 55 different banners in 27 countries and employs more than two million people around the world. What's more, Wal-Mart came in third place among general merchandisers in *Fortune* magazine's 2013 Most Admired Companies survey. With fiscal 2013 sales of $469 billion, Wal-Mart is able to exert tremendous pressure on its suppliers. When Wal-Mart announced in April 2004 that it was beginning a pilot program to test *radio frequency identification* (RFID) technology to improve its inventory and supply chain management, suppliers and competitors took notice.

One of the first companies to introduce bar codes in the early 1980s, Wal-Mart required its top 100 suppliers to put RFID tags on shipping crates and pallets by January 2005, with the next 200 largest suppliers using the technology by January 2006. Wal-Mart officials believed that RFID tags would allow the company to wring out inefficiencies from its inventory and supply chain operations, thereby lowering

expenses and working capital investments. As of February 2007, Wal-Mart officials said that 600 of its suppliers were RFID-enabled. Nevertheless, Wal-Mart's ultimate goal to have all its 100,000-plus suppliers on board using electronic product codes (EPC) with RFID technology began to stall. The company failed to show dramatic reductions in inventory (in fact, inventories went up, not down, after the RFID program was put in place), and some suppliers resisted the change.

The major issue with RFID tags is per-chip cost. In 2004, when Wal-Mart announced its intent to use RFID tags, the tags sold for 30 to 50 cents each. Wal-Mart requested a price of 5 cents per tag, expecting increased demand and economies of scale to push the price down to make them more competitive with inexpensive barcodes. Increased demand has brought the price of current-generation RFID tags to about 15 cents apiece, but barcodes cost only a fraction of a cent. Barcodes help track inventory and can match a product to a price, but they lack the electronic tags' ability to store more detailed information, such as

the serial number of a product, the location of the factory that made it, when it was made, and when it was sold.

Wal-Mart expects the RFID technology to improve its inventory management, and it remains committed to advancing its use of RFID. During the 2010 National Retail Federation's Big Show convention, Wal-Mart's chief information officer (CIO), Rollin Ford, said, "We're still bullish on RFID." He also indicated that Wal-Mart ran some apparel pilots last year that showed good results and that the retailer plans to "eat what we cook." Wal-Mart manufactures some apparel items and controls its own supply chain, and Ford indicated that Wal-Mart plans to use RFID technology in its apparel supply chain. Wal-Mart will then share the benefits and best practices with its suppliers, which might want to achieve the same benefits from the technology.

▶ *What problem might occur with the full implementation of RFID technology in retail industries? Specifically, consider the amount of data that might be collected.*

Source: "2010 Most Admired Companies," *Fortune* (March 22, 2010); Wal-Mart, *Wal-Mart 2010 Financial Report,* http://cdn.walmartstores.com/sites/AnnualReport/2010/PDF/01_WMT%202010_Financials.pdf; Mark Roberti, "Wal-Mart CIO Still 'Bullish' on RFID." *RFID Journal* retail blog, http://www.rfidjournal.com/article/view/7315.

---

materials requirement planning (MRP) system
Inventory management technique that applies EOQ concepts and a computer to compare production needs to available inventory balances and determine when orders should be placed for various items on a product's *bill of materials.*

frequency identification technology may be the "next new thing" in improving inventory and supply chain management.

Computerized Systems for Resource Control

Today, a number of systems are available for controlling inventory and other resources. One of the most basic is the **materials requirement planning (MRP) system**. It is used to determine what materials to order and when to order them. MRP applies EOQ concepts to determine how much to order. Using a computer, MRP simulates each product's bill of materials, inventory status, and manufacturing process. The *bill of materials* is simply a list of all parts and materials that go into making the finished product. For a given productio plan, the computer simulates material requirements by comparing production needs to available inventory balances. On the basis of the time it takes for a product that is in process to move through the various production stages and the lead time to get materials, the MRP system determines when orders should be placed for various items on the bill of materials. The objective of this system is to lower the firm's inventory investment without impairing production. If the firm's pretax opportunity cost of capital for investments of equal risk is 20 percent, every dollar of investment released from inventory will increase before-tax profits by $0.20.

manufacturing resource planning II (MRP II)
A sophisticated computerized system that integrates data from numerous areas such as finance, accounting, marketing, engineering, and manufacturing and generates production plans as well as numerous financial and management reports.

A popular extension of MRP is **manufacturing resource planning II (MRP II)**, which integrates data from numerous areas such as finance, accounting, marketing, engineering, and manufacturing using a sophisticated computer system. This system generates production plans as well as numerous financial and management reports. In essence, it models the firm's processes so that the effects of changes in one area of operations on other areas can be assessed and monitored. For example, the MRP II system would allow the firm to assess the effect of an increase in labor costs on sales and profits.

enterprise resource planning (ERP)
A computerized system that electronically integrates external information about the firm's suppliers and customers with the firm's departmental data so that information on all available resources—human and material—can be instantly obtained in a fashion that eliminates production delays and controls costs.

Whereas MRP and MRP II tend to focus on internal operations, **enterprise resource planning (ERP)** systems expand the focus to the external environment by including information about suppliers and customers. ERP electronically integrates all a firm's departments so that, for example, production can call up sales information and immediately know how much must be produced to fill customer orders. Because all available resources—human and material—are known, the system can eliminate production delays and control costs. ERP systems automatically note changes, such as a supplier's inability to meet a scheduled delivery date, so that necessary adjustments can be made.

INTERNATIONAL INVENTORY MANAGEMENT

International inventory management is typically much more complicated for exporters in general, and for multinational companies in particular, than for purely domestic firms. The production and manufacturing economies of scale that might be expected from selling products globally may prove elusive if products must be tailored for individual local markets, as frequently happens, or if actual production takes place in factories around the world. When raw materials, intermediate goods, or finished products must be transported over long distances—particularly by ocean shipping—there will be more delays, confusion, damage, and theft than occur in a one-country operation. The international inventory manager therefore puts a premium on flexibility. He or she is usually less concerned about ordering the economically optimal quantity of inventory than about making sure that sufficient quantities of inventory are delivered where they are needed, when they are needed, and in a condition to be used as planned.

→ **REVIEW QUESTIONS**

14–8 What are likely to be the viewpoints of each of the following managers about the levels of the various types of inventory: finance, marketing, manufacturing, and purchasing? Why is inventory an investment?

14–9 Briefly describe the following techniques for managing inventory: (1) ABC system, economic order quantity (EOQ) model, (2) just-in-time (JIT) system, and (3) three computerized systems for resource control, MRP, MRP II, and ERP.

14–10   What factors make managing inventory more difficult for exporters and multinational companies?

  14.4   Accounts Receivable Management

The second component of the cash conversion cycle is the average collection period. This period is the average length of time from a sale on credit until the payment becomes usable funds for the firm. The average collection period has two parts. The first part is the time from the sale until the customer mails the payment. The second part is the time from when the payment is mailed until the firm has the collected funds in its bank account. The first part of the average collection period involves managing the credit available to the firm's customers, and the second part involves collecting and processing payments. This section of the chapter discusses the firm's accounts receivable credit management.

The objective for managing accounts receivable is to collect accounts receivable as quickly as possible without losing sales from high-pressure collection techniques. Accomplishing this goal encompasses three topics: (1) credit selection and standards, (2) credit terms, and (3) credit monitoring.

CREDIT SELECTION AND STANDARDS

credit standards
The firm's minimum requirements for extending credit to a customer.

Credit selection involves application of techniques for determining which customers should receive credit. This process involves evaluating the customer's creditworthiness and comparing it to the firm's **credit standards**, its minimum requirements for extending credit to a customer.

five C's of credit
The five key dimensions—character, capacity, capital, collateral, and conditions—used by credit analysts to provide a framework for in-depth credit analysis.

Five C's of Credit

One popular credit selection technique is the **five C's of credit**, which provides a framework for in-depth credit analysis. Because of the time and expense involved, this credit selection method is used for large-dollar credit requests. The five C's are as follows:

1. *Character:* The applicant's record of meeting past obligations.
2. *Capacity:* The applicant's ability to repay the requested credit, as judged in terms of financial statement analysis focused on cash flows available to repay debt obligations.
3. *Capital:* The applicant's debt relative to equity.
4. *Collateral:* The amount of assets the applicant has available for use in securing the credit. The larger the amount of available assets, the greater the chance that a firm will recover funds if the applicant defaults.
5. *Conditions:* Current general and industry-specific economic conditions and any unique conditions surrounding a specific transaction.

Analysis via the five C's of credit does not yield a specific accept/reject decision, so its use requires an analyst experienced in reviewing and granting credit requests. Application of this framework tends to ensure that the firm's credit customers will pay, without being pressured, within the stated credit terms.

Credit Scoring

credit scoring
A credit selection method commonly used with high-volume/small-dollar credit requests; relies on a credit score determined by applying statistically derived weights to a credit applicant's scores on key financial and credit characteristics.

Credit scoring is a method of credit selection that firms commonly use with high-volume/small-dollar credit requests. **Credit scoring** applies statistically derived weights to a credit applicant's scores on key financial and credit characteristics to predict whether he or she will pay the requested credit in a timely fashion. Simply stated, the procedure results in a score that measures the applicant's overall credit strength, and the score is used to make the accept/reject decision for granting the applicant credit. Credit scoring is most commonly used by large credit card operations, such as those of banks, oil companies, and department stores. The purpose of credit scoring is to make a relatively informed credit decision quickly and inexpensively, recognizing that the cost of a single bad scoring decision is small. However, if bad debts from scoring decisions increase, the scoring system must be reevaluated.

Changing Credit Standards

The firm sometimes will contemplate changing its credit standards in an effort to improve its returns and create greater value for its owners. To demonstrate, consider the following changes and effects on profits expected to result from the *relaxation* of credit standards.

Effects of Relaxation of Credit Standards

Variable	Direction of change	Effect on profits
Sales volume	Increase	Positive
Investment in accounts receivable	Increase	Negative
Bad-debt expenses	Increase	Negative

If credit standards were tightened, the opposite effects would be expected.

Example 14.6 ▶

Dodd Tool, a manufacturer of lathe tools, is currently selling a product for $10 per unit. Sales (all on credit) for last year were 60,000 units. The variable cost per unit is $6. The firm's total fixed costs are $120,000.

The firm is currently contemplating a *relaxation of credit standards* that is expected to result in the following: a 5% increase in unit sales to 63,000 units; an increase in the average collection period from 30 days (the current level) to 45 days; an increase in bad-debt expenses from 1% of sales (the current level) to 2%. The firm determines that its cost of tying up funds in receivables is 15% before taxes.

To determine whether to relax its credit standards, Dodd Tool must calculate its effect on the firm's additional profit contribution from sales, the cost of the marginal investment in accounts receivable, and the cost of marginal bad debts.

Additional Profit Contribution from Sales Because fixed costs are "sunk" and therefore are unaffected by a change in the sales level, the only cost relevant to a change in sales is variable costs. Sales are expected to increase by 5%, or 3,000 units. The profit contribution per unit will equal the difference between the sale price per unit ($10) and the variable cost per unit ($6). The profit contribution per unit therefore will be $4. The total additional profit contribution from sales will be $12,000 (3,000 units × $4 per unit).

Cost of the Marginal Investment in Accounts Receivable To determine the cost of the marginal investment in accounts receivable, Dodd must find the difference between the cost of carrying receivables under the two credit standards. Because its concern is only with the out-of-pocket costs, *the relevant cost is the variable cost.* The average investment in accounts receivable can be calculated by using the formula

$$\frac{\text{Average investment}}{\text{in accounts receivable}} = \frac{\text{Total variable cost of annual sales}}{\text{Turnover of accounts receivable}} \qquad (14.9)$$

where

$$\text{Turnover of accounts receivable} = \frac{365}{\text{Average collection period}}$$

The total variable cost of annual sales under the present and proposed plans can be found as follows, using the variable cost per unit of $6.

Total variable cost of annual sales

Under present plan: ($6 × 60,000 units) = $360,000

Under proposed plan: ($6 × 63,000 units) = $378,000

The turnover of accounts receivable is the number of times each year that the firm's accounts receivable are actually turned into cash. It is found by dividing the average collection period into 365 (the number of days assumed in a year).

Turnover of accounts receivable

$$\text{Under present plan: } \frac{365}{30} = 12.2$$

$$\text{Under proposed plan: } \frac{365}{45} = 8.1$$

By substituting the cost and turnover data just calculated into Equation 14.9 for each case, we get the following average investments in accounts receivable:

Average investment in accounts receivable

$$\text{Under present plan: } \frac{\$360,000}{12.2} = \$29,508$$

$$\text{Under proposed plan: } \frac{\$378,000}{8.1} = \$46,667$$

We calculate the marginal investment in accounts receivable and its cost as follows:

Cost of marginal investment in accounts receivable

Average investment under proposed plan	$46,667
− Average investment under present plan	29,508
Marginal investment in accounts receivable	$17,159
× Cost of funds tied up in receivables	0.15
Cost of marginal investment in A/R	$ 2,574

The resulting value of $2,574 is considered a cost because it represents the maximum amount that could have been earned before taxes on the $17,159 had it been placed in an equally risky investment earning 15% before taxes.

Cost of Marginal Bad Debts We find the cost of marginal bad debts by taking the difference between the levels of bad debts before and after the proposed relaxation of credit standards.

> *Cost of marginal bad debts*
>
> Under proposed plan: (0.02 × $10/unit × 63,000 units) = $12,600
>
> − Under present plan: (0.01 × $10/unit × 60,000 units) = 6,000
>
> Cost of marginal bad debts $ 6,600

Note that the bad-debt costs are calculated by using the sale price per unit ($10) to deduct not just the true loss of variable cost ($6) that results when a customer fails to pay its account but also the profit contribution per unit (in this case, $4) that is included in the "additional profit contribution from sales." Thus, the resulting cost of marginal bad debts is $6,600.

Making the Credit Standard Decision To decide whether to relax its credit standards, the firm must compare the additional profit contribution from sales to the added costs of the marginal investment in accounts receivable and marginal bad debts. If the additional profit contribution is greater than marginal costs, credit standards should be relaxed.

Example 14.7 ▶ The results and key calculations related to Dodd Tool's decision whether to relax its credit standards are summarized in Table 14.2. The net addition to total profits resulting from such an action will be $2,826 per year. Therefore, the firm *should* relax its credit standards as proposed.

The procedure described here for evaluating a proposed change in credit standards is also commonly used to evaluate other changes in the management of accounts receivable. If Dodd Tool had been contemplating tightening its credit standards, for example, the cost would have been a reduction in the profit contribution from sales, and the return would have been from reductions in the cost of the investment in accounts receivable and in the cost of bad debts. Another application of this procedure is demonstrated later in this chapter.

Managing International Credit

Credit management is difficult enough for managers of purely domestic companies, and these tasks become much more complex for companies that operate internationally. It is partly because (as we have seen before) international operations typically expose a firm to *exchange rate risk*. It is also due to the dangers and delays involved in shipping goods long distances and in having to cross international borders.

Exports of finished goods are usually priced in the currency of the importer's local market; most commodities, on the other hand, are priced in dollars. Therefore, a U.S. company that sells a product in Japan, for example, would have to

TABLE 14.2	Effects on Dodd Tool of a Relaxation of Credit Standards	
Additional profit contribution from sales		
$\quad$ [3,000 units × ($10 − $6)]		$12,000
Cost of marginal investment in A/R^a		
$\quad$ Average investment under proposed plan:		
$\quad$ $\dfrac{\$6 \times 63,000}{8.1} = \dfrac{\$378,000}{8.1}$	$46,667	
$\quad$ − Average investment under present plan:		
$\quad$ $\dfrac{\$6 \times 60,000}{12.2} = \dfrac{\$360,000}{12.2}$	$\underline{29,508}$	
$\quad$ Marginal investment in A/R	$17,159	
$\quad\quad$ Cost of marginal investment in A/R (0.15 × $17,159)		(2,574)
Cost of marginal bad debts		
$\quad$ Bad debts under proposed plan (0.02 × $10 × 63,000)	$12,600	
$\quad$ − Bad debts under present plan (0.01 × $10 × 60,000)	$\underline{6,000}$	
$\quad\quad$ Cost of marginal bad debts		($\underline{6,600}$)
Net profit from implementation of proposed plan		$\underline{\$\ \ 2,826}$

^{a}The denominators 8.1 and 12.2 in the calculation of the average investment in accounts receivable under the proposed and present plans are the accounts receivable turnovers for each of these plans (365 ÷ 45 = 8.1 and 365 ÷ 30 = 12.2).

price that product in Japanese yen and extend credit to a Japanese wholesaler in the local currency (yen). If the yen *depreciates* against the dollar before the U.S exporter collects on its account receivable, the U.S. company experiences an exchange rate loss; the yen collected are worth fewer dollars than expected at the time the sale was made. Of course, the yen could just as easily appreciate against the dollar, yielding an exchange rate gain to the U.S. exporter. Most companies fear the loss more than they welcome the gain.

For a major currency such as the Japanese yen, the exporter can *hedge* against this risk by using the currency futures, forward, or options markets, but it is costly to do so, particularly for relatively small amounts. If the exporter is selling to a customer in a developing country, there will probably be no effective instrument available for protecting against exchange rate risk at any price. This risk may be further magnified because credit standards may be much lower (and acceptable collection techniques much different) in developing countries than in the United States. Although it may seem tempting to just "not bother" with exporting, U.S. companies no longer can concede foreign markets to international rivals. These export sales, if carefully monitored and (where possible) effectively hedged against exchange rate risk, often prove to be very profitable.

CREDIT TERMS

credit terms
The terms of sale for customers who have been extended credit by the firm.

cash discount
A percentage deduction from the purchase price; available to the credit customer who pays its account within a specified time.

Credit terms are the terms of sale for customers who have been extended credit by the firm. Terms of *net 30* mean the customer has 30 days from the beginning of the credit period (typically *end of month* or *date of invoice*) to pay the full invoice amount. Some firms offer **cash discounts**, percentage deductions from the purchase price for paying within a specified time. For example, terms of *2/10 net 30* mean the customer can take a 2 percent discount from the invoice amount i the payment is made within 10 days of the beginning of the credit period or can pay the full amount of the invoice within 30 days.

A firm's business strongly influences its regular credit terms. For example, a firm selling perishable items will have very short credit terms because its items have little long-term collateral value; a firm in a seasonal business may tailor its terms to fit the industry cycles. A firm wants its regular credit terms to conform to its industry's standards. If its terms are more restrictive than its competitors', it will lose business; if its terms are less restrictive than its competitors', it will attract poor-quality customers that probably could not pay under the standard industry terms. The bottom line is that a firm should compete on the basis of quality and price of its product and service offerings, not its credit terms. Accordingly, the firm's regular credit terms should match the industry standards, but individual customer terms should reflect the riskiness of the customer.

Cash Discount

Including a cash discount in the credit terms is a popular way to speed up collections without putting pressure on customers. The cash discount provides an incentive for customers to pay sooner. By speeding collections, the discount decreases the firm's investment in accounts receivable, but it also decreases the per-unit profit. Additionally, initiating a cash discount should reduce bad debts because customers will pay sooner, and it should increase sales volume because customers who take the discount pay a lower price for the product. Accordingly, firms that consider offering a cash discount must perform a benefit–cost analysis to determine whether extending a cash discount is profitable.

Example 14.8 ▸ MAX Company has annual sales of $10 million and an average collection period of 40 days (turnover = 365 ÷ 40 = 9.1). In accordance with the firm's credit terms of net 30, this period is divided into 32 days until the customers place their payments in the mail (not everyone pays within 30 days) and 8 days to receive, process, and collect payments once they are mailed. MAX is considering initiating a cash discount by changing its credit terms from net 30 to 2/10 net 30. The firm expects this change to reduce the amount of time until the payments are placed in the mail, resulting in an average collection period of 25 days (turnover = 365 ÷ 25 = 14.6).

As noted earlier in Example 14.5, MAX has a raw material with current annual usage of 1,100 units. Each finished product produced requires one unit of this raw material at a variable cost of $1,500 per unit, incurs another $800 of variable cost in the production process, and sells for $3,000 on terms of net 30. Variable costs therefore total $2,300 ($1,500 + $800). MAX estimates that 80% of its customers will take the 2% discount and that offering the discount will increase sales of the finished product by 50 units (from 1,100 to 1,150 units) per year but will not alter its bad-debt percentage. MAX's opportunity cost of funds invested in accounts receivable is 14%. Should MAX offer the proposed cash discount? An analysis similar to that demonstrated earlier for the credit standard decision, presented in Table 14.3, shows a net loss from the cash discount of $6,640. Thus, *MAX should not initiate the proposed cash discount.* However, other discounts may be advantageous.

TABLE 14.3	Analysis of Initiating a Cash Discount for MAX Company	
Additional profit contribution from sales		
[50 units × ($3,000 − $2,300)]		$35,000
Cost of marginal investment in A/R[a]		
Average investment presently (without discount):		
$\dfrac{\$2,300 \times 1,100 \text{ units}}{9.1} = \dfrac{\$2,530,000}{9.1}$	$278,022	
− Average investment with proposed cash discount:[b]		
$\dfrac{\$2,300 \times 1,150 \text{ units}}{14.6} = \dfrac{\$2,645,000}{14.6}$	181,164	
Reduction in accounts receivable investment	$ 96,858	
Cost savings from reduced investment		
in accounts receivable (0.14 × $96,858)[c]		13,560
Cost of cash discount (0.02 × 0.80 × 1,150 × $3,000)		(55,200)
Net profit from initiation of proposed cash discount		($ 6,640)

[a]In analyzing the investment in accounts receivable, we use the variable cost of the product sold ($1,500 raw materials cost + $800 production cost = $2,300 per unit variable cost) instead of the sale price because the variable cost is a better indicator of the firm's investment.

[b]The average investment in accounts receivable with the proposed cash discount is estimated to be tied up for an average of 25 days instead of the 40 days under the original terms.

[c]MAX's opportunity cost of funds is 14%.

Cash Discount Period

cash discount period
The number of days after the beginning of the credit period during which the cash discount is available.

The financial manager can change the **cash discount period**, the number of days after the beginning of the credit period during which the cash discount is available. The net effect of changes in this period is difficult to analyze because of the nature of the forces involved. For example, if a firm were to increase its cash discount period by 10 days (for example, changing its credit terms from 2/10 net 30 to 2/20 net 30), the following changes would be expected to occur: (1) Sales would increase, positively affecting profit; (2) bad-debt expenses would decrease, positively affecting profit; and (3) the profit per unit would decrease as a result of more people taking the discount, negatively affecting profit.

The difficulty for the financial manager lies in assessing what impact an increase in the cash discount period would have on the firm's investment in accounts receivable. This investment will decrease because of non–discount takers now paying earlier. However, the investment in accounts receivable will increase for two reasons: (1) Discount takers will still get the discount but will pay later, and (2) new customers attracted by the new policy will result in new accounts receivable. If the firm were to decrease the cash discount period, the effects would be the opposite of those just described.

Credit Period

credit period
The number of days after the beginning of the credit period until full payment of the account is due.

Changes in the **credit period**, the number of days after the beginning of the credit period until full payment of the account is due, also affect a firm's profitability. For example, increasing a firm's credit period from net 30 days to net 45 days should increase sales, positively affecting profit. But both the investmen in accounts receivable and bad-debt expenses would also increase, negatively affecting profit. The increased investment in accounts receivable would result from both more sales and generally slower pay, on average, as a result of the longer credit period. The increase in bad-debt expenses is because the longer the credit period, the more time available for a firm to fail, making it unable to pay its accounts payable. A decrease in the length of the credit period is likely to have the opposite effects. Note that the variables affected by an increase in the credit period behave in the same way they would have if the credit standards had been relaxed, as demonstrated earlier in Table 14.2.

CREDIT MONITORING

credit monitoring
The ongoing review of a firm's accounts receivable to determine whether customers are paying according to the stated credit terms.

The final issue a firm should consider in its accounts receivable management is credit monitoring. **Credit monitoring** is an ongoing review of the firm's accounts receivable to determine whether customers are paying according to the stated credit terms. If they are not paying in a timely manner, credit monitoring will alert the firm to the problem. Slow payments are costly to a firm because they lengthen the average collection period and thus increase the firm's investment in accounts receivable. Two frequently used techniques for credit monitoring are average collection period and aging of accounts receivable. In addition, a number of popular collection techniques are used by firms.

Average Collection Period

The *average collection period* is the second component of the cash conversion cycle. As noted in Chapter 3, it is the average number of days that credit sales are outstanding. The average collection period has two components: (1) the time from sale until the customer places the payment in the mail and (2) the time to receive, process, and collect the payment once it has been mailed by the customer. The formula for finding the average collection period is

$$\text{Average collection period} = \frac{\text{Accounts receivable}}{\text{Average sales per day}} \qquad (14.10)$$

Assuming receipt, processing, and collection time is constant, the average collection period tells the firm, on average, when its customers pay their accounts.

Knowing its average collection period enables the firm to determine whether there is a general problem with accounts receivable. For example, a firm that has credit terms of net 30 would expect its average collection period (minus receipt, processing, and collection time) to equal about 30 days. If the actual collection period is significantly greater than 30 days, the firm has reason to review its credit operations. If the firm's average collection period is increasing over time, it has cause for concern about its accounts receivable management. A first step in analyzing an accounts receivable problem is to "age" the accounts receivable. By this process, the firm can determine whether the problem exists in its accounts receivable in general or is attributable to a few specific accounts.

aging schedule
A credit-monitoring technique that breaks down accounts receivable into groups on the basis of their time of origin; it indicates the percentages of the total accounts receivable balance that have been outstanding for specified periods of time.

Aging of Accounts Receivable

An **aging schedule** breaks down accounts receivable into groups on the basis of their time of origin. The breakdown is typically made on a month-by-month basis, going back 3 or 4 months. The resulting schedule indicates the percentages of the total accounts receivable balance that have been outstanding for specified periods of time. The purpose of the aging schedule is to enable the firm to pinpoint problems. A simple example will illustrate the form and evaluation of an aging schedule.

Example 14.9 ▶ The accounts receivable balance on the books of Dodd Tool on December 31, 2015, was $200,000. The firm extends net 30-day credit terms to its customers. To gain insight into the firm's relatively lengthy—51.3-day—average collection period, Dodd prepared the following aging schedule.

Age of account	Balance outstanding	Percentage of total balance outstanding
0–30 days	$ 80,000	40%
31–60 days	36,000	18
61–90 days	52,000	26
91–120 days	26,000	13
Over 120 days	6,000	3
Totals at 12/31/15	$200,000	100%

Because Dodd extends 30-day credit terms to its customers, they have 30 days after the end of the month of sale to remit payment. Therefore, the 40% of the balance outstanding with an age of 0–30 days is *current*. The balances outstanding for 31–60 days, 61–90 days, 91–120 days, and over 120 days are *overdue*.

Reviewing the aging schedule, we see that 40% of the accounts are current (age < 30 days) and the remaining 60% are overdue (age > 30 days). Eighteen percent of the balance outstanding is 1–30 days overdue, 26% is 31–60 days overdue, 13% is 61–90 days overdue, and 3% is more than 90 days overdue. Although the collections seem generally slow, a noticeable irregularity in these data is the high percentage of the balance outstanding that is 31–60 days overdue (ages of 61–90 days). Clearly, a problem must have occurred 61–90 days ago. Investigation may find that the problem can be attributed to the hiring of a new credit manager, the acceptance of a new account that made a large credit purchase but has not yet paid for it, or ineffective collection policy. When this type of discrepancy is found in the aging schedule, the analyst should determine, evaluate, and remedy its cause.

Popular Collection Techniques

A number of collection techniques, ranging from letters to legal action, are employed. As an account becomes more and more overdue, the collection effort becomes more personal and more intense. In Table 14.4, the popular collection techniques are listed and briefly described in the order typically followed in the collection process.

TABLE 14.4	Popular Collection Techniques
Technique[a]	Brief description
Letters	After a certain number of days, the firm sends a polite letter reminding the customer of the overdue account. If the account is not paid within a certain period after this letter has been sent, a second, more demanding letter is sent.
Telephone calls	If letters prove unsuccessful, a telephone call may be made to the customer to request immediate payment. If the customer has a reasonable excuse, arrangements may be made to extend the payment period. A call from the seller's attorney may be used.
Personal visits	This technique is much more common at the consumer credit level, but it may also be effectively employed by industrial suppliers. Sending a local salesperson or a collection person to confront the customer can be very effective. Payment may be made on the spot.
Collection agencies	A firm can turn uncollectible accounts over to a collection agency or an attorney for collection. The fees for this service are typically quite high; the firm may receive less than 50 cents on the dollar from accounts collected in this way.
Legal action	Legal action is the most stringent step, an alternative to the use of a collection agency. Not only is direct legal action expensive, but it may force the debtor into bankruptcy without guaranteeing the ultimate receipt of the overdue amount.

[a]The techniques are listed in the order in which they are typically followed in the collection process.

→ **REVIEW QUESTIONS**

14–11 What is the role of the *five C's of credit* in the credit selection activity?

14–12 Explain why *credit scoring* is typically applied to consumer credit decisions rather than to mercantile credit decisions.

14–13 What are the basic trade-offs in a *tightening* of credit standards?

14–14 Why are the risks involved in international credit management more complex than those associated with purely domestic credit sales?

14–15 Why do a firm's regular credit terms typically conform to those of its industry?

14–16 Why should a firm actively monitor the accounts receivable of its credit customers? How are the *average collection period* and an *aging schedule* used for credit monitoring?

LG 6 14.5 Management of Receipts and Disbursements

The third component of the cash conversion cycle, the average payment period, also has two parts: (1) the time from purchase of goods on account until the firm mails its payment and (2) the receipt, processing, and collection time required by the firm's suppliers. The receipt, processing, and collection time for the firm, both from its customers and to its suppliers, is the focus of receipts and disbursements management.

FLOAT

float
Funds that have been sent by the payer but are not yet usable funds to the payee.

Float refers to funds that have been sent by the payer but are not yet usable funds to the payee. Float is important in the cash conversion cycle because its presence lengthens both the firm's average collection period and its average payment period. However, the goal of the firm should be to shorten its average collection period and lengthen its average payment period. Both can be accomplished by managing float.

Float has three component parts:

mail float
The time delay between when payment is placed in the mail and when it is received.

processing float
The time between receipt of a payment and its deposit into the firm's account.

clearing float
The time between deposit of a payment and when spendable funds become available to the firm.

1. **Mail float** is the time delay between when payment is placed in the mail and when it is received.
2. **Processing float** is the time between receipt of the payment and its deposit into the firm's account.
3. **Clearing float** is the time between deposit of the payment and when spendable funds become available to the firm. This component of float is attributable to the time required for a check to clear the banking system.

Some popular techniques for managing the component parts of float to speed up collections and slow down payments are described here.

SPEEDING UP COLLECTIONS

Speeding up collections reduces customer *collection float* time and thus reduces the firm's average collection period, which reduces the investment the firm must make in its cash conversion cycle. In our earlier examples, MAX Company had annual sales of $10 million and 8 days of total collection float (receipt, processing, and collection time). If MAX can reduce its float time by 3 days, it will reduce its investment in the cash conversion cycle by $82,192 [$10,000,000 $\times$ (3 $\div$ 365)].

lockbox system
A collection procedure in which customers mail payments to a post office box that is emptied regularly by the firm's bank, which processes the payments and deposits them in the firm's account. This system speeds up collection time by reducing processing time as well as mail and clearing time.

A popular technique for speeding up collections is a lockbox system. A **lockbox system** works as follows: Instead of mailing payments to the company, customers mail payments to a post office box. The firm's bank empties the post office box regularly, processes each payment, and deposits the payments in the firm's account. Deposit slips, along with payment enclosures, are sent (or transmitted electronically) to the firm by the bank so that the firm can properly credit customers' accounts. Lockboxes are geographically dispersed to match the locations of the firm's customers. A lockbox system affects all three components of float. Lockboxes reduce mail time and often clearing time by being near the firm's customers. Lockboxes reduce processing time to nearly zero because the bank deposits payments before the firm processes them. Obviously, a lockbox system reduces collection float time, but not without a cost; therefore, a firm must perform an economic analysis to determine whether to implement a lockbox system.

Matter of fact

U.S.P.S. Problems Create Opportunities for Banks

For decades, the United State Postal Service has been struggling financially. In 2012, the USPS announced that to cut costs it would dramatically reduce the number of mail processing facilities that it operated. For companies, this change meant an increase in mail float. For Fifth Third Bank, it was an opportunity. The bank announced a new remote lockbox capture program in which business-to-business payments would be retrieved at local post offices around the country. Next, Fifth Third would make electronic images of those payments, and the images would be processed at the bank's Cincinnati processing hub. Fifth Third promised customers that it would reduce mail float and speed up the collection process for its clients.

Lockbox systems are commonly used by large firms whose customers are geographically dispersed. However, a firm does not have to be large to benefit from a lockbox. Smaller firms can also benefit from a lockbox system. The benefit to small firms often comes primarily from transferring the processing of payments to the bank.

SLOWING DOWN PAYMENTS

controlled disbursing
The strategic use of mailing points and bank accounts to lengthen mail float and clearing float, respectively.

Float is also a component of the firm's average payment period. In this case, the float is in the favor of the firm. The firm may benefit by increasing all three of the components of its *payment float*. One popular technique for increasing payment float is **controlled disbursing**, which involves the strategic use of mailing points and bank accounts to lengthen mail float and clearing float, respectively. Firms must use this approach carefully, though, because longer payment periods may strain supplier relations.

In summary, a reasonable overall policy for float management is (1) to collect payments as quickly as possible because once the payment is in the mail the funds belong to the firm and (2) to delay making payment to suppliers because once the payment is mailed the funds belong to the supplier.

CASH CONCENTRATION

cash concentration
The process used by the firm to bring lockbox and other deposits together into one bank, often called the *concentration bank*.

Cash concentration is the process used by the firm to bring lockbox and other deposits together into one bank, often called the *concentration bank*. Cash concentration has three main advantages. First, it creates a large pool of funds for use in making short-term cash investments. Because there is a fixed-cost component in the transaction cost associated with such investments, investing a single pool of funds reduces the firm's transaction costs. The larger investment pool also allows the firm to choose from a greater variety of short-term investment vehicles. Second, concentrating the firm's cash in one account improves the tracking and internal control of the firm's cash. Third, having one concentration bank enables the firm to implement payment strategies that reduce idle cash balances.

depository transfer check (DTC)
An unsigned check drawn on one of a firm's bank accounts and deposited in another.

There are a variety of mechanisms for transferring cash from the lockbox bank and other collecting banks to the concentration bank. One mechanism is a **depository transfer check** (DTC), which is an unsigned check drawn on one of the firm's bank accounts and deposited in another. For cash concentration, a DTC is drawn on each lockbox or other collecting bank account and deposited in the concentration bank account. Once the DTC has cleared the bank on which it is drawn (which may take several days), the transfer of funds is completed. Most firms currently provide deposit information by telephone to the concentration bank, which then prepares and deposits into its account the DTC drawn on the lockbox or other collecting bank account.

ACH (automated clearinghouse) transfer
Preauthorized electronic withdrawal from the payer's account and deposit into the payee's account via a settlement among banks by the *automated clearinghouse*, or *ACH*.

A second mechanism is an **ACH (automated clearinghouse) transfer**, which is a preauthorized electronic withdrawal from the payer's account. A computerized clearing facility (called the *automated clearinghouse*, or *ACH*) makes a paperless transfer of funds between the payer and payee banks. An ACH settles accounts among participating banks. Individual accounts are settled by respective bank balance adjustments. ACH transfers clear in 1 day. For cash concentration, an ACH transfer is made from each lockbox bank or other collecting bank to the concentration bank. An ACH transfer can be thought of as

wire transfer
An electronic communication that, via bookkeeping entries, removes funds from the payer's bank and deposits them in the payee's bank.

an electronic DTC, but because the ACH transfer clears in 1 day, it provides benefits over a DTC; however, both banks in the ACH transfer must be members of the clearinghouse.

A third cash concentration mechanism is a **wire transfer**. A wire transfer is an electronic communication that, via bookkeeping entries, removes funds from the payer's bank and deposits them in the payee's bank. Wire transfers can eliminate mail and clearing float and may reduce processing float as well. For cash concentration, the firm moves funds using a wire transfer from each lockbox or other collecting account to its concentration account. Wire transfers are a substitute for DTC and ACH transfers, but they are more expensive.

It is clear that the firm must balance the costs and benefits of concentrating cash to determine the type and timing of transfers from its lockbox and other collecting accounts to its concentration account. The transfer mechanism selected should be the one that is most profitable. (The profit per period of any transfer mechanism equals earnings on the increased availability of funds minus the cost of the transfer system.)

ZERO-BALANCE ACCOUNTS

zero-balance account (ZBA)
A disbursement account that always has an end-of-day balance of zero because the firm deposits money to cover checks drawn on the account only as they are presented for payment each day.

Zero-balance accounts (**ZBAs**) are disbursement accounts that always have an end-of-day balance of zero. The purpose is to eliminate nonearning cash balances in corporate checking accounts. A ZBA works well as a disbursement account under a cash concentration system.

ZBAs work as follows: Once all a given day's checks are presented for payment from the firm's ZBA, the bank notifies the firm of the total amount o checks, and the firm transfers funds into the account to cover the amount of tha. day's checks. This transfer leaves an end-of-day balance of $0 (zero dollars). The ZBA enables the firm to keep all its operating cash in an interest-earning account, thereby eliminating idle cash balances. Thus, a firm that used a ZBA in conjunction with a cash concentration system would need two accounts. The firm would concentrate its cash from the lockboxes and other collecting banks into an interest-earning account and would write checks against its ZBA. The firm would cover the exact dollar amount of checks presented against the ZBA with transfers from the interest-earning account, leaving the end-of-day balance in the ZBA at $0.

A ZBA is a disbursement-management tool. As we discussed earlier, the firm would prefer to maximize its payment float. However, some cash managers believe that actively attempting to increase float time on payments is unethical. A ZBA enables the firm to maximize the use of float on each check without altering the float time of payments to its suppliers. Keeping all the firm's cash in an interest-earning account enables the firm to maximize earnings on its cash balances by capturing the full float time on each check it writes.

> **Personal Finance Example 14.10 ▶** Megan Laurie, a 25-year-old nurse, works at a hospital that pays her every 2 weeks by direct deposit into her checking account, which pays no interest and has no minimum balance requirement. She takes home about $1,800 every 2 weeks, or about $3,600 per month. She maintains a checking account balance of around $1,500. Whenever it exceeds that amount, she transfers the excess into her savings account, which currently pays 1.5% annual interest. She currently has a savings account balance of $17,00⁻

and estimates that she transfers about $600 per month from her checking account into her savings account.

Megan pays her bills immediately when she receives them. Her monthly bills average about $1,900, and her monthly cash outlays for food and gas total about $900. An analysis of Megan's bill payments indicates that on average she pays her bills 8 days early. Most marketable securities are currently yielding about 4.2% annual interest. Megan is interested in learning how she might better manage her cash balances.

Megan talks with her sister, who has had a finance course, and they come up with three ways for Megan to better manage her cash balance:

1. **Invest current balances.** Megan can transfer her current savings account balances into a liquid marketable security, thereby increasing the rate of interest earned from 1.5% to about 4.2%. On her current $17,000 balance, she will immediately increase her annual interest earnings by about $460 [(0.042 − 0.015) × $17,000].
2. **Invest monthly surpluses.** Megan can transfer monthly the $600 from her checking account to the liquid marketable security, thereby increasing the annual earnings on each monthly transfer by about $16 [(0.042 − 0.015) × $600], which for the 12 transfers would generate additional annual earnings of about $192 (12 months × $16).
3. **Slow down payments.** Rather than paying her bills immediately on receipt, Megan can pay her bills nearer their due date. By doing so, she can gain 8 days of disbursement float each month, or 96 days per year (8 days per month × 12 months), on an average of $1,900 of bills. Assuming that she can earn 4.2% annual interest on the $1,900, slowing down her payments would save about $21 annually [(96 ÷ 365) × 0.042 × $1,900].

Based on these three recommendations, Megan would increase her annual earnings by a total of about $673 ($460 + $192 + $21). Clearly, Megan can grow her earnings by better managing her cash balances.

INVESTING IN MARKETABLE SECURITIES

Marketable securities are short-term, interest-earning, money market instruments that can easily be converted into cash. Marketable securities are classified as part of the firm's liquid assets. The firm uses them to earn a return on temporarily idle funds. To be truly marketable, a security must have (1) a ready market so as to minimize the amount of time required to convert it into cash and (2) safety of principal, which means that it experiences little or no loss in value over time.

The securities that are most commonly held as part of the firm's marketable-securities portfolio are divided into two groups: (1) government issues, which have relatively low yields as a consequence of their low risk; and (2) nongovernment issues, which have slightly higher yields than government issues with similar maturities because of the slightly higher risk associated with them. Table 14.5 summarizes the key features for popular marketable securities.

→ **REVIEW QUESTIONS**

14–17 What is *float,* and what are its three components?

14–18 What are the firm's objectives with regard to *collection float* and to *payment float?*

TABLE 14.5	Features of Popular Marketable Securities			
Security	Issuer	Description	Initial maturity	Risk and return
Government issues				
Treasury bills	U.S. Treasury	Issued weekly at auction; sold at a discount; strong secondary market	4, 13, and 26 weeks	Lowest, virtually risk-free
Treasury notes	U.S. Treasury	Stated interest rate; interest paid semiannually; strong secondary market	1 to 10 years	Low, but higher than U.S. Treasury bills
Treasury bonds	U.S. Treasury	Stated interest rate; interest paid semiannually; strong secondary market	11 to 30 years	Less than corporate bonds, but higher than U.S. Treasury bills and notes
Federal agency issues	Agencies of federal government	Not an obligation of U.S. Treasury; strong secondary market	9 months to 30 years	Slightly higher than U.S. Treasury issues
Nongovernment issues				
Negotiable certificates of deposit (CDs)	Commercial banks	Represent specific cash deposits in commercial banks; amounts and maturities tailored to investor needs; large denominations; good secondary market	1 month to 3 years	Higher than U.S. Treasury issues and comparable to commercial paper
Commercial paper	Corporation with a high credit standing	Unsecured note of issuer; large denominations	3 to 270 days	Higher than U.S. Treasury issues and comparable to negotiable CDs
Banker's acceptances	Banks	Results from a bank guarantee of a business transaction; sold at discount from maturity value	30 to 180 days	About the same as negotiable CDs and commercial paper but higher than U.S. Treasury issues
Eurodollar deposits	Foreign banks	Deposits of currency not native to the country in which the bank is located; large denominations; active secondary market	1 day to 3 years	High, due to less regulation of depository banks and some foreign exchange risk
Money market mutual funds	Professional portfolio management companies	Professionally managed portfolios of marketable securities; provide instant liquidity	None—depends on wishes of investor	Vary, but generally higher than U.S. Treasury issues and comparable to negotiable CDs and commercial paper
Repurchase agreements	Bank or securities dealer	Bank or securities dealer sells specific securities to firm and agrees to repurchase them at a specific price and time	Customized to purchaser's needs	Generally slightly below that associated with the outright purchase of the security

14–19 What are the three main advantages of *cash concentration*?

14–20 What are three mechanisms of cash concentration? What is the objective of using a *zero-balance account (ZBA)* in a cash concentration system?

14–21 What two characteristics make a security marketable? Why are the yields on nongovernment marketable securities generally higher than the yields on government issues with similar maturities?

Summary

FOCUS ON VALUE

It is important for a firm to maintain a reasonable level of net working capital. To do so, it must balance the high profit and high risk associated with low levels of current assets and high levels of current liabilities against the low profit and low risk that result from high levels of current assets and low levels of current liabilities. A strategy that achieves a reasonable balance between profits and risk should positively contribute to the firm's value.

Similarly, the firm should manage its cash conversion cycle by turning inventory quickly; collecting accounts receivable quickly; managing mail, processing, and clearing time; and paying accounts payable slowly. These strategies should enable the firm to manage its current accounts efficiently and to minimize the amount of resources invested in operating assets.

The financial manager can manage inventory, accounts receivable, and cash receipts to minimize the firm's operating cycle investment, thereby reducing the amount of resources needed to support its business. Employing these strategies, and managing accounts payable and cash disbursements so as to shorten the cash conversion cycle, should minimize the negotiated liabilities needed to support the firm's resource requirements. Active management of the firm's net working capital and current assets should positively contribute to the firm's goal of **maximizing its stock price.**

REVIEW OF LEARNING GOALS

LG 1 Understand working capital management, net working capital, and the related trade-off between profitability and risk. Working capital (or short-term financial) management focuses on managing each of the firm's current assets (inventory, accounts receivable, cash, and marketable securities) and current liabilities (accounts payable, accruals, and notes payable) in a manner that positively contributes to the firm's value. Net working capital is the difference between current assets and current liabilities. Risk, in the context of short-term financial decisions, is the probability that a firm will be unable to pay its bills as they come due. Assuming a constant level of total assets, the higher a firm's ratio of current assets to total assets, the less profitable the firm and the less risky it is. The converse is also true. With constant total assets, the higher a firm's ratio of current liabilities to total assets, the more profitable and the more risky the firm is. The converse of this statement is also true.

LG 2 Describe the cash conversion cycle, its funding requirements, and the key strategies for managing it. The cash conversion cycle has three components: (1) average age of inventory, (2) average collection period, and (3) average payment period. The length of the cash conversion cycle determines the amount of time resources are tied up in the firm's day-to-day operations. The firm's investment in short-term assets often consists of both permanent and seasonal funding requirements. The seasonal requirements can be financed using either an aggressive (low-cost, high-risk) financing strategy or a conservative (high-cost, low-risk) financing strategy. The firm's funding decision for its cash conversion cycle ultimately depends on management's disposition toward risk and the strength of the firm's banking relationships. To minimize its reliance on negotiated liabilities, the financial manager seeks to (1) turn over inventory as quickly as possible; (2) collect accounts receivable as quickly as possible; (3) manage mail, processing, and clearing time; and (4) pay accounts payable as slowly as possible. Use of these strategies should minimize the length of the cash conversion cycle.

LG 3 **Discuss inventory management: differing views, common techniques, and international concerns.** The viewpoints of marketing, manufacturing, and purchasing managers about the appropriate levels of inventory tend to cause higher inventories than those deemed appropriate by the financial manager. Four commonly used techniques for effectively managing inventory to keep its level low are (1) the ABC system, (2) the economic order quantity (EOQ) model, (3) the just-in-time (JIT) system, and (4) computerized systems for resource control: MRP, MRP II, and ERP. International inventory managers place greater emphasis on making sure that sufficient quantities of inventory are delivered where and when needed, and in the right condition, than on ordering the economically optimal quantities.

LG 4 **Explain the credit selection process and the quantitative procedure for evaluating changes in credit standards.** Credit selection techniques determine which customers' creditworthiness is consistent with the firm's credit standards. Two popular credit selection techniques are the five C's of credit and credit scoring. Changes in credit standards can be evaluated mathematically by assessing the effects of a proposed change on profits from sales, the cost of accounts receivable investment, and bad-debt costs.

LG 5 **Review the procedures for quantitatively considering cash discount changes, other aspects of credit terms, and credit monitoring.** Changes in credit terms—the cash discount, the cash discount period, and the credit period—can be quantified similarly to changes in credit standards. Credit monitoring, the ongoing review of accounts receivable, frequently involves use of the average collection period and an aging schedule. Firms use a number of popular collection techniques.

LG 6 **Understand the management of receipts and disbursements, including float, speeding up collections, slowing down payments, cash concentration, zero-balance accounts, and investing in marketable securities.** Float refers to funds that have been sent by the payer but are not yet usable funds to the payee. The components of float are mail time, processing time, and clearing time. Float occurs in both the average collection period and the average payment period. One technique for speeding up collections is a lockbox system. A popular technique for slowing payments is controlled disbursing.

The goal for managing operating cash is to balance the opportunity cost of nonearning balances against the transaction cost of temporary investments. Firms commonly use depository transfer checks (DTCs), ACH transfers, and wire transfers to transfer lockbox receipts to their concentration banks quickly. Zero-balance accounts (ZBAs) can be used to eliminate nonearning cash balances in corporate checking accounts. Marketable securities are short-term, interest-earning, money market instruments used by the firm to earn a return on temporarily idle funds. They may be government or nongovernment issues.

Self-Test Problems (Solutions in Appendix)

LG 2 **ST14–1** **Cash conversion cycle** Hurkin Manufacturing Company pays accounts payable on the tenth day after purchase. The average collection period is 30 days, and the average age of inventory is 40 days. The firm currently has annual sales of about $18 million and purchases of $14 million. The firm is considering a plan that would stretch its accounts payable by 20 days. If the firm pays 12% per year for its resource investment, what annual savings can it realize by this plan? Assume a 360-day year.

LG 3 **ST14–2** **EOQ analysis** Thompson Paint Company uses 60,000 gallons of pigment per year. The cost of ordering pigment is $200 per order, and the cost of carrying the pigment in inventory is $1 per gallon per year. The firm uses pigment at a constant rate every day throughout the year.
a. Calculate the EOQ.
b. Assuming that it takes 20 days to receive an order once it has been placed, determine the reorder point in terms of gallons of pigment. (*Note:* Use a 365-day year.)

LG 4 **ST14–3** **Relaxing credit standards** Regency Rug Repair Company is trying to decide whether it should relax its credit standards. The firm repairs 72,000 rugs per year at an average price of $32 each. Bad-debt expenses are 1% of sales, the average collection period is 40 days, and the variable cost per unit is $28. Regency expects that if it does relax its credit standards, the average collection period will increase to 48 days and that bad debts will increase to $1^{1}/_{2}$% of sales. Sales will increase by 4,000 repairs per year. If the firm has a required rate of return on equal-risk investments of 14%, what recommendation would you give the firm? Use your analysis to justify your answer. (*Note:* Use a 365-day year.)

Warm-Up Exercises All problems are available in MyFinanceLab.

LG 2 **E14–1** Everdeen, Inc., has a 100-day *operating cycle*. If its average age of inventory is 35 days, how long is its average collection period? If its average payment period is 30 days, what is its *cash conversion cycle?* Place all this information on a time line similar to Figure 14.2 on page 556.

LG 2 **E14–2** Icy Treats, Inc., is a seasonal business that sells frozen desserts. At the peak of its summer selling season, the firm has $35,000 in cash, $125,000 in inventory, $70,000 in accounts receivable, and $65,000 in accounts payable. During the slow winter period, the firm holds $10,000 in cash, $55,000 in inventory, $40,000 in accounts receivable, and $35,000 in accounts payable. Calculate Icy Treats' minimum and peak funding requirements.

LG 3 **E14–3** Mama Leone's Frozen Pizzas uses 50,000 pounds of cheese per year. Each pound costs $2.50. The ordering cost for the cheese is $250 per order, and its carrying cost is $0.50 per pound per year. Calculate the firm's *economic order quantity (EOQ)* for the cheese. Mama Leone's operates 250 days per year and maintains a minimum inventory level of 2 days' worth of cheese as a safety stock. Assuming that the lead time to receive orders of cheese is 3 days, calculate the *reorder point*.

LG 4   **E14–4**   Forrester Fashions has annual credit sales of 250,000 units with an average collection period of 70 days. The company has a per-unit variable cost of $20 and a per-unit sale price of $30. Bad debts currently are 5% of sales. The firm estimates that a proposed relaxation of credit standards would not affect its 70-day average collection period but would increase bad debts to 7.5% of sales, which would increase to 300,000 units per year. Forrester requires a 12% return on investments. Show all necessary calculations required to evaluate Forrester's proposed relaxation of credit standards.

LG 5   **E14–5**   Klein's Tools is considering offering a cash discount to speed up the collection of accounts receivable. Currently, the firm has an average collection period of 65 days, annual sales are 35,000 units, the per-unit price is $40, and the per-unit variable cost is $29. A 2% cash discount is being considered. Klein's Tools estimates that 80% of its customers will take the 2% discount. If sales are expected to rise to 37,000 units per year and the firm has a 15% required rate of return, what minimum average collection period is required to approve the cash discount plan?

Problems   All problems are available in MyFinanceLab.

LG 2   **P14–1**   **Cash conversion cycle** American Products is concerned about managing cash efficiently. On the average, inventories have an age of 90 days, and accounts receivable are collected in 60 days. Accounts payable are paid approximately 30 days after they arise. The firm has annual sales of about $30 million. Cost of goods sold are $20 million, and purchases are $15 million.
a. Calculate the firm's *operating cycle*.
b. Calculate the firm's *cash conversion cycle*.
c. Calculate the amount of resources needed to support the firm's cash conversion cycle.
d. Discuss how management might be able to reduce the cash conversion cycle.

LG 2   **P14–2**   **Changing cash conversion cycle** Camp Manufacturing turns over its inventory five times each year, has an average payment period of 35 days, and has an average collection period of 60 days. The firm has annual sales of $3.5 million and cost of goods sold of $2.4 million.
a. Calculate the firm's *operating cycle* and *cash conversion cycle*.
b. What is the dollar value of inventory held by the firm?
c. If the firm could reduce the average age of its inventory from 73 days to 63 days, by how much would it reduce its dollar investment in working capital?

LG 2   **P14–3**   **Multiple changes in cash conversion cycle** Garrett Industries turns over its inventory six times each year; it has an average collection period of 45 days and an average payment period of 30 days. The firm's annual sales are $3 million. Assume that there is no difference in the investment per dollar of sales in inventory, receivables, and payables, and assume a 365-day year.

a. Calculate the firm's *cash conversion cycle,* its daily cash operating expenditure, and the amount of resources needed to support its cash conversion cycle.
b. Find the firm's cash conversion cycle and resource investment requirement if it makes the following changes simultaneously.
   (1) Shortens the average age of inventory by 5 days.
   (2) Speeds the collection of accounts receivable by an average of 10 days.
   (3) Extends the average payment period by 10 days.
c. If the firm pays 13% for its resource investment, by how much, if anything, could it increase its annual profit as a result of the changes in part b?
d. If the annual cost of achieving the profit in part c is $35,000, what action would you recommend to the firm? Why?

LG 2   **P14–4**   **Aggressive versus conservative seasonal funding strategy** Dynabase Tool has forecast its total funds requirements for the coming year as shown in the following table.

Month	Amount	Month	Amount
January	$2,000,000	July	$12,000,000
February	2,000,000	August	14,000,000
March	2,000,000	September	9,000,000
April	4,000,000	October	5,000,000
May	6,000,000	November	4,000,000
June	9,000,000	December	3,000,000

a. Divide the firm's monthly funds requirement into (1) a *permanent* component and (2) a *seasonal* component, and find the monthly average for each of these components.
b. Describe the amount of long-term and short-term financing used to meet the total funds requirement under (1) an *aggressive funding strategy* and (2) a *conservative funding strategy*. Assume that, under the aggressive strategy, long-term funds finance permanent needs and short-term funds are used to finance seasonal needs.
c. Assuming that short-term funds cost 5% annually and that the cost of long-term funds is 10% annually, use the averages found in part a to calculate the total cost of each of the strategies described in part b. Assume that the firm can earn 3% on any excess cash balances.
d. Discuss the profitability–risk trade-offs associated with the aggressive strategy and those associated with the conservative strategy.

LG 3   **P14–5**   **EOQ analysis** Tiger Corporation purchases 1,200,000 units per year of one component. The fixed cost per order is $25. The annual carrying cost of the item is 27% of its $2 cost.
a. Determine the EOQ if (1) the conditions stated above hold, (2) the order cost is zero rather than $25, and (3) the order cost is $25 but the carrying cost is $0.01.
b. What do your answers illustrate about the EOQ model? Explain.

LG 3   **P14–6**   **EOQ, reorder point, and safety stock** Alexis Company uses 800 units of a product per year on a continuous basis. The product has a fixed cost of $50 per order, and its carrying cost is $2 per unit per year. It takes 5 days to receive a shipment after an order is placed, and the firm wishes to hold 10 days' usage in inventory as a safety stock.

a. Calculate the EOQ.

b. Determine the average level of inventory. (*Note:* Use a 365-day year to calculate daily usage.)

c. Determine the *reorder point*.

d. Indicate which of the following variables change if the firm does not hold the safety stock: (1) order cost, (2) carrying cost, (3) total inventory cost, (4) reorder point, (5) economic order quantity. Explain.

Personal Finance Problem

 P14–7 **Marginal costs** Jimmy Johnson is interested in buying a new Jeep SUV. There are two options available, a V-6 model and a V-8 model. Whichever model he chooses, he plans to drive it for a period of 5 years and then sell it. Assume that the trade-in value of the two vehicles at the end of the 5-year ownership period will be identical.

There are definite differences between the two models, and Jimmy needs to make a financial comparison. The manufacturer's suggested retail price (MSRP) of the V-6 and V-8 are $30,260 and $44,320, respectively. Jimmy believes that the difference of $14,060 to be the marginal cost difference between the two vehicles. However, much more data are available, and you suggest to Jimmy that his analysis may be too simple and will lead him to a poor financial decision. Assume that the prevailing discount rate for both vehicles is 5.5% annually. Other pertinent information on this purchase is shown in the following table.

	V-6	V-8
MSRP	$30,260	$44,320
Engine (liters)	3.7	5.7
Cylinders	6	8
Depreciation over 5 years	$17,337	$25,531
Finance charges[a] over entire 5-year period	$5,171	$7,573
Insurance over 5 years	$7,546	$8,081
Taxes and fees over 5 years	$2,179	$2,937
Maintenance/repairs over 5 years	$5,600	$5,600
Average miles per gallon	19	14
Ownership period in years	5	5
Miles driven per year over 5 years	15,000	15,000
Cost per gallon of gas over 5-year ownership	$3.15	$3.15

[a]The finance charges are the difference between the total principal and interest paid over the entire 5-year period less the actual cost of the SUV. Assuming an annual 5.5% discount rate over each of the 5 years and the respective present values of $30,260 for the V-6 and $44,320 for the V-8, the annual annuity payments are $7,086.20 and $10,379.70, respectively. [V-6: (5 × $7,086.20) − $30,260 = $5,171, and V-8: (5 × $10,379.70) − $44,320 = $7,573]

a. Calculate the total "true" cost for each vehicle over the 5-year ownership period.

b. Calculate the total fuel cost for each vehicle over the 5-year ownership period.

c. What is the marginal fuel cost from purchasing the larger V-8 SUV?

d. What is the marginal cost of purchasing the larger and more expensive V-8 SUV

e. What is the total marginal cost associated with purchasing the V-8 SUV? How does this figure compare with the $14,060 that Jimmy calculated?

LG 4 **P14–8** **Accounts receivable changes without bad debts** Tara's Textiles currently has credit sales of $360 million per year and an average collection period of 60 days. Assume that the price of Tara's products is $60 per unit and that the variable costs are $55 per unit. The firm is considering an accounts receivable change that will result in a 20% increase in sales and a 20% increase in the average collection period. No change in bad debts is expected. The firm's equal-risk opportunity cost on its investment in accounts receivable is 14%. (*Note:* Use a 365-day year.)
a. Calculate the *additional profit contribution from sales* that the firm will realize if it makes the proposed change.
b. What *marginal investment in accounts receivable* will result?
c. Calculate the *cost of the marginal investment in accounts receivable*.
d. Should the firm implement the proposed change? What other information would be helpful in your analysis?

LG 4 **P14–9** **Accounts receivable changes with bad debts** A firm is evaluating an accounts receivable change that would increase bad debts from 2% to 4% of sales. Sales are currently 50,000 units, the selling price is $20 per unit, and the variable cost per unit is $15. As a result of the proposed change, sales are forecast to increase to 60,000 units.
a. What are bad debts in dollars currently and under the proposed change?
b. Calculate the *cost of the marginal bad debts* to the firm.
c. Ignoring the additional profit contribution from increased sales, if the proposed change saves $3,500 and causes no change in the average investment in accounts receivable, would you recommend it? Explain.
d. Considering *all* changes in costs and benefits, would you recommend the proposed change? Explain.
e. Compare and discuss your answers in parts c and d.

LG 4 **P14–10** **Relaxation of credit standards** Lewis Enterprises is considering relaxing its credit standards to increase its currently sagging sales. As a result of the proposed relaxation, sales are expected to increase by 10% from 10,000 to 11,000 units during the coming year, the average collection period is expected to increase from 45 to 60 days, and bad debts are expected to increase from 1% to 3% of sales. The sale price per unit is $40, and the variable cost per unit is $31. The firm's required return on equal-risk investments is 25%. Evaluate the proposed relaxation, and make a recommendation to the firm. (*Note:* Assume a 365-day year.)

LG 5 **P14–11** **Initiating a cash discount** Gardner Company currently makes all sales on credit and offers no cash discount. The firm is considering offering a 2% cash discount for payment within 15 days. The firm's current average collection period is 60 days, sales are 40,000 units, selling price is $45 per unit, and variable cost per unit is $36. The firm expects that the change in credit terms will result in an increase in sales to 42,000 units, that 70% of the sales will take the discount, and that the average collection period will fall to 30 days. If the firm's required rate of return on equal-risk investments is 25%, should the proposed discount be offered? (*Note:* Assume a 365-day year.)

LG 5 **P14–12** **Shortening the credit period** A firm is contemplating *shortening* its credit period from 40 to 30 days and believes that, as a result of this change, its average collection period will decline from 45 to 36 days. Bad-debt expenses are expected to decrease from 1.5% to 1% of sales. The firm is currently selling 12,000 units but believes that sales will decline to 10,000 units as a result of the proposed change. The sale price per unit is $56, and the variable cost per unit is $45. The firm has a required return on equal-risk investments of 25%. Evaluate this decision, and make a recommendation to the firm. (*Note:* Assume a 365-day year.)

LG 5   **P14–13**   **Lengthening the credit period** Parker Tool is considering lengthening its credit period from 30 to 60 days. All customers will continue to pay on the net date. The firm currently bills $450,000 for sales and has $345,000 in variable costs. The change in credit terms is expected to increase sales to $510,000. Bad-debt expenses will increase from 1% to 1.5% of sales. The firm has a required rate of return on equal-risk investments of 20%. (*Note:* Assume a 365-day year.)

a. What *additional profit contribution from sales* will be realized from the proposed change?

b. What is the *cost of the marginal investment in accounts receivable*?

c. What is the *cost of the marginal bad debts*?

d. Do you recommend this change in credit terms? Why or why not?

LG 6   **P14–14**   **Float** Simon Corporation has daily cash receipts of $65,000. A recent analysis of its collections indicated that customers' payments were in the mail an average of 2.0 days. Once received, the payments are processed in 2.0 days. After payments are deposited, it takes an average of 2.5 days for these receipts to clear the banking system.

a. How much *collection float (in days)* does the firm currently have?

b. If the firm's opportunity cost is 9%, would it be economically advisable for the firm to pay an annual fee of $16,500 to reduce collection float by 3 days? Explain why or why not.

LG 6   **P14–15**   **Lockbox system** Eagle Industries believes that a lockbox system can shorten its accounts receivable collection period by 3 days. Credit sales are $3,240,000 per year, billed on a continuous basis. The firm has other equally risky investments that earn a return of 15%. The cost of the lockbox system is $9,000 per year. (*Note:* Assume a 365-day year.)

a. What amount of cash will be made available for other uses under the lockbox system?

b. What net benefit (cost) will the firm realize if it adopts the lockbox system? Should it adopt the proposed lockbox system?

LG 6   **P14–16**   **Zero-balance account** Union Company is considering establishment of a zero-balance account. The firm currently maintains an average balance of $420,000 in its disbursement account. As compensation to the bank for maintaining the zero-balance account, the firm will have to pay a monthly fee of $1,000 and maintain a $300,000 non–interest-earning deposit in the bank. The firm currently has no other deposits in the bank. Evaluate the proposed zero-balance account, and make a recommendation to the firm, assuming that it has a 12% opportunity cost.

Personal Finance Problem

LG 6   **P14–17**   **Management of cash balance** Alexis Morris, an assistant manager at a local department store, gets paid every 2 weeks by direct deposit into her checking account. This account pays no interest and has no minimum balance requirement. Her monthly income is $4,200. Alexis has a "target" cash balance of around $1,200, and whenever it exceeds that amount, she transfers the excess into her savings account, which currently pays 2.0% annual interest. Her current savings balance is $15,000, and Alexis estimates that she transfers about $500 per month from her checking account into her savings account. Alexis doesn't waste any time in paying her bills, and her monthly bills average about $2,000. Her monthly cash outlay for food, gas, and other sundry items totals about $850. Reviewing her payment habits indicates that on average she pays her bills 9 days early. At this time, most marketable securities are yielding about 4.75% annual interest.

   Show how Alexis can better manage her cash balance.

a. What can Alexis do regarding the handling of her current balances?
b. What do you suggest that she do with her monthly surpluses?
c. What do you suggest Alexis do about the manner in which she pays her bills?
d. Can Alexis grow her earnings by better managing her cash balances? Show your work.

 P14–18 **ETHICS PROBLEM** A group of angry shareholders has placed a corporate resolution before all shareholders at a company's annual stockholders' meeting. The resolution demands that the company *stretch its accounts payable* because these shareholders have determined that all the company's competitors do so, and the firm operates in a highly competitive industry. How could management at the annual stockholders' meeting defend the firm's practice of paying suppliers on time?

Spreadsheet Exercise

 The current balance in accounts receivable for Eboy Corporation is $443,000. This level was achieved with annual (365 days) credit sales of $3,544,000. The firm offers its customers credit terms of *net 30.* However, in an effort to help its cash flow position and to follow the actions of its rivals, the firm is considering changing its credit terms from net 30 to *2/10 net 30.* The objective is to speed up the receivable collections and thereby improve the firm's cash flows. Eboy would like to increase its accounts receivable turnover to 12.0.

   The firm works with a raw material whose current annual usage is 1,450 units. Each finished product requires one unit of this raw material at a variable cost of $2,600 per unit and sells for $4,200 on terms of net 30. It is estimated that 70% of the firm's customers will take the 2% cash discount and that, with the discount, sales of the finished product will increase by 50 units per year. The firm's opportunity cost of funds invested in accounts receivable is 12.5%.

   In analyzing the investment in accounts receivable, use the variable cost of the product sold instead of the sale price because the variable cost is a better indicator of the firm's investment.

TO DO

Create a spreadsheet similar to Table 14.3 to analyze whether the firm should initiate the proposed cash discount. What is your advice? Make sure that you calculate the following:

a. Additional profit contribution from sales.
b. Average investment in accounts receivable at present (without cash discount).

    c. Average investment in accounts receivable with the proposed cash discount.

    d. Reduction in investment in accounts receivable.

    e. Cost savings from reduced investment in accounts receivable.

    f. Cost of the cash discount.

    g. Net profit (loss) from initiation of proposed cash discount.

MyFinanceLab   Visit www.myfinancelab.com for **Chapter Case: *Assessing Roche Publishing Company's Cash Management Efficiency,*** Group Exercises, and numerous online resources.

15

Current Liabilities Management

Learning Goals

Why This Chapter Matters to You

In your *professional* life

ACCOUNTING You need to understand how to analyze supplier credit terms to decide whether the firm should take or give up cash discounts; you also need to understand the various types of short-term loans, both unsecured and secured, that you will be required to record and report.

INFORMATION SYSTEMS You need to understand what data the firm will need to process accounts payable, track accruals, and meet bank loans and other short-term debt obligations in a timely manner.

MANAGEMENT You need to know the sources of short-term loans so that, if short-term financing is needed, you will understand its availability and cost.

MARKETING You need to understand how accounts receivable and inventory can be used as loan collateral; the procedures used by the firm to secure short-term loans with such collateral could affect customer relationships.

OPERATIONS You need to understand the use of accounts payable as a form of short-term financing and the effect on one's suppliers of stretching payables; you also need to understand the process by which a firm uses inventory as collateral.

In your *personal* life

Management of current liabilities is an important part of your financial strategy. It takes discipline to avoid viewing cash and credit purchases equally. You need to borrow for a purpose, not convenience. You need to repay credit purchases in a timely fashion. Excessive use of short-term credit, particularly with credit cards, can create personal liquidity problems and, at the extreme, personal bankruptcy.

15.1 Spontaneous Liabilities

spontaneous liabilities
Financing that arises from the normal course of business; the two major short-term sources of such liabilities are accounts payable and accruals.

Spontaneous liabilities arise from the normal course of business. For example, when a retailer orders goods for inventory, the manufacturer of those goods usually does not demand immediate payment but instead extends a short-term loan to the retailer that appears on the retailer's balance sheet under accounts payable. The more goods the retailer orders, the greater will be the accounts payable balance. Also in response to increasing sales, the firm's accruals increase as wages and taxes rise because of greater labor requirements and the increased taxes on the firm's increased earnings. There is normally no explicit cost attached to either of these current liabilities, although they do have certain implicit costs. In addition, both are forms of **unsecured short-term financing**, short-term financing obtained without pledging specific assets as collateral. The firm should take advantage of these "interest-free" sources of unsecured short-term financing whenever possible.

unsecured short-term financing
Short-term financing obtained without pledging specific assets as collateral.

ACCOUNTS PAYABLE MANAGEMENT

Accounts payable are the major source of unsecured short-term financing for business firms. They result from transactions in which merchandise is purchased but no formal note is signed to show the purchaser's liability to the seller. The purchaser in effect agrees to pay the supplier the amount required in accordance with credit terms normally stated on the supplier's invoice. The discussion of accounts payable here is presented from the viewpoint of the purchaser.

Role in the Cash Conversion Cycle

The average payment period is the final component of the *cash conversion cycle* introduced in Chapter 14. The average payment period has two parts: (1) the time from the purchase of raw materials until the firm mails the payment and (2) payment float time (the time it takes after the firm mails its payment until the supplier has withdrawn spendable funds from the firm's account). In Chapter 14, we discussed issues related to payment float time. Here we discuss the firm's management of the time that elapses between its purchase of raw materials and its mailing payment to the supplier. This activity is **accounts payable management**.

accounts payable management
Management by the firm of the time that elapses between its purchase of raw materials and its mailing payment to the supplier.

When the seller of goods charges no interest and offers no discount to the buyer for early payment, the buyer's goal is to pay as slowly as possible without damaging its credit rating. In other words, accounts should be paid on the last day possible, given the supplier's stated credit terms. For example, if the terms are net 30, the account should be paid 30 days from the *beginning of the credit period,* which is typically either the *date of invoice* or the *end of the month (EOM)* in which the purchase was made. This timing allows for the maximum use of an interest-free loan from the supplier and will not damage the firm's credit rating (because the account is paid within the stated credit terms). In addition, some firms offer an explicit or implicit "grace period" that extends a few days beyond the stated payment date; if taking advantage of that grace period does no harm to the buyer's relationship with the seller, the buyer will typically take advantage of the grace period.

Example 15.1 ▶

In 2013, Brown-Forman Corporation (BF), manufacturer of alcoholic beverage brands such as Jack Daniels, had annual revenue of $3.8 billion, cost of revenue of $1.8 billion, and accounts payable of $468 million. BF had an average age of inventory (AAI) of 168 days, an average collection period (ACP) of 55 days, and an average payment period (APP) of 136 days (BF's purchases were $1.3 billion). Thus, the cash conversion cycle for BF was 87 days (168 + 55 − 136).

The resources BF had invested in this cash conversion cycle (assuming a 365-day year) were

$$
\begin{array}{lll}
\text{Inventory} & = \$1.8 \text{ billion} \times (168 \div 365) = & \$0.83 \text{ billion} \\
+ \text{ Accounts receivable} & = 3.8 \text{ billion} \times (55 \div 365) = & 0.57 \text{ billion} \\
- \text{ Accounts payable} & = 1.3 \text{ billion} \times (136 \div 365) = & \underline{0.48 \text{ billion}} \\
& = \text{ Resources invested} & = \underline{\underline{\$0.92 \text{ billion}}}
\end{array}
$$

Based on BF's APP and average accounts payable, the daily accounts payable generated by BF is about $3.5 million ($0.48 billion ÷ 136). If BF were to increase its average payment period by 5 days, its accounts payable would increase by about $17.5 million (5 × $3.5 million). As a result, BF's cash conversion cycle would decrease by 5 days, and the firm would reduce its investment in operations by $17.5 million. Clearly, if this action did not damage BF's credit rating, it would be in the company's best interest.

Analyzing Credit Terms

The credit terms that a firm is offered by its suppliers enable it to delay payments for its purchases. Because the supplier's cost of having its money tied up in merchandise after it is sold is probably reflected in the purchase price, the purchaser is already indirectly paying for this benefit. Sometimes a supplier will offer a cash discount for early payment. In that case, the purchaser should carefully analyze credit terms to determine the best time to repay the supplier. The purchaser must weigh the benefits of paying the supplier as late as possible against the costs of passing up the discount for early payment.

Taking the Cash Discount If a firm intends to take a cash discount, it should pay on the last day of the discount period. There is no added benefit from paying earlier than that date.

Example 15.2 ▶

Lawrence Industries, operator of a small chain of video stores, purchased $1,000 worth of merchandise on February 27 from a supplier extending terms of 2/10 net 30 EOM. If the firm takes the cash discount, it must pay $980 [$1,000 − (0.02 × $1,000)] by March 10, thereby saving $20.

cost of giving up a cash discount
The implied rate of interest paid to delay payment of an account payable for an additional number of days.

Giving Up the Cash Discount If the firm chooses to give up the cash discount, it should pay on the final day of the credit period. There is an implicit cost associated with giving up a cash discount. The **cost of giving up a cash discount** is the implied rate of interest paid to delay payment of an account payable for an additional number of days. In other words, when a firm gives up a discount, it pays a

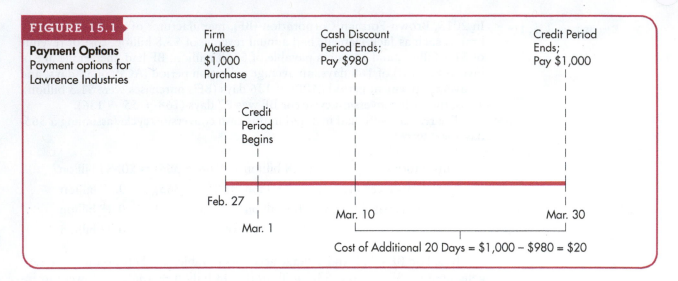

FIGURE 15.1

Payment Options
Payment options for
Lawrence Industries

Firm
Makes
$1,000
Purchase

Credit
Period
Begins

Cash Discount
Period Ends;
Pay $980

Credit Period
Ends;
Pay $1,000

Feb. 27

Mar. 1

Mar. 10

Mar. 30

Cost of Additional 20 Days = $1,000 − $980 = $20

higher cost for the goods that it orders. The higher cost that the firm pays is like interest on a loan, and the length of this loan is the number of additional days that the purchaser can delay payment to the seller. This cost can be illustrated by a simple example. The example assumes that payment will be made on the last possible day (either the final day of the cash discount period or the final day of the credit period).

Example 15.3 ▶

MyFinanceLab Solution
Video

In Example 15.2, we saw that Lawrence Industries could take the cash discoun on its February 27 purchase by paying $980 on March 10. If Lawrence gives up the cash discount, it can pay on March 30. To keep its money for an extra 20 days, the firm must pay an extra $20, or $1,000 rather than $980. In other words, if the firm pays on March 30, it will pay $980 (what it could have paid on March 10) plus $20. The extra $20 is like interest on a loan, and in this case the $980 is like the loan principal. Lawrence Industries owes $980 to its supplier on March 10, but the supplier is willing to accept $980 plus $20 in interest on March 30. Figure 15.1 shows the payment options that are open to the company.

To calculate the implied interest rate associated with giving up the cash discount, we simply treat $980 as the loan principal, $20 as the interest, and 20 days (the time from March 10 to March 30) as the term of the loan. Again, the trade-off that Lawrence faces is that it can pay $980 on March 10 or $980 plus $20 in interest 20 days later on March 30. Therefore, the interest rate that Lawrence is paying by giving up the discount is 2.04% ($20 ÷ $980). Keep in mind that the 2.04% interest rate applies to a 20-day loan. To calculate an annualized interest rate, we multiply the interest rate on this transaction times the number of 20-day periods during a year. The general expression for calculating the annual percentage cost of giving up a cash discount can be expressed as[1]

$$\text{Cost of giving up cash discount} = \frac{CD}{100\% - CD} \times \frac{365}{N} \qquad (15.1)$$

1. Equation 15.1 and the related discussions are based on the assumption that only one discount is offered. In the event that multiple discounts are offered, calculation of the cost of giving up the discount must be made for each alternative.

where

$$CD = \text{stated cash discount in percentage terms}$$

$$N = \text{number of days that payment can} \\ \text{be delayed by giving up the cash discount}$$

Substituting the values for CD (2%) and N (20 days) into Equation 15.1 results in an annualized cost of giving up the cash discount of 37.24% [(2% ÷ 98%) × (365 ÷ 20)].

A simple way to *approximate* the cost of giving up a cash discount is to use the stated cash discount percentage, CD, in place of the first term of Equation 15.1:

$$\text{Approximate cost of giving up cash discount} = CD \times \frac{365}{N} \qquad (15.2)$$

The smaller the cash discount, the closer the approximation to the actual cost of giving it up. Using this approximation, the cost of giving up the cash discount for Lawrence Industries is 36.5% [2% × (365 ÷ 20)].

Using the Cost of Giving Up a Cash Discount in Decision Making   The financial manager must determine whether it is advisable to take a cash discount. A primary consideration influencing this decision is the cost of other short-term sources of funding. When a firm can obtain financing from a bank or other institution at a lower cost than the implicit interest rate offered by its suppliers, the firm is better off borrowing from the bank and taking the discount offered by the supplier.

Example 15.4 ▶   Mason Products, a large building-supply company, has four possible suppliers, each offering different credit terms. Otherwise, their products and services are identical. Table 15.1 presents the credit terms offered by suppliers A, B, C, and D and the cost of giving up the cash discounts in each transaction. The approximation method of calculating the cost of giving up a cash discount (Equation 15.2) has been used. The cost of giving up the cash discount from supplier A is 36.5%; from supplier B, 4.9%; from supplier C, 21.9%; and from supplier D, 29.2%.

If the firm needs short-term funds, which it can borrow from its bank at an interest rate of 6%, and if each of the suppliers is viewed *separately*, which (if any) of the suppliers' cash discounts will the firm give up? In dealing with supplier A, the firm takes the cash discount, because the cost of giving it up is 36.5%, and then borrows the funds it requires from its bank at 6% interest. With

TABLE 15.1	Cash Discounts and Associated Costs for Mason Products	
Supplier	Credit terms	Approximate cost of giving up a cash discount
A	2/10 net 30 EOM	36.5%
B	1/10 net 85 EOM	4.9
C	3/20 net 70 EOM	21.9
D	4/10 net 60 EOM	29.2

supplier B, the firm would do better to give up the cash discount, because the cost of this action is less than the cost of borrowing money from the bank (4.9% versus 6%). With either supplier C or supplier D, the firm should take the cash discount, because in both cases the cost of giving up the discount is greater than the 6% cost of borrowing from the bank.

The example shows that the cost of giving up a cash discount is relevant when one is evaluating a single supplier's credit terms in light of certain *bank borrowing costs*. However, other factors relative to payment strategies may also need to be considered. For example, some firms, particularly small firms and poorly managed firms, routinely give up *all* discounts because they either lack alternative sources of unsecured short-term financing or fail to recognize the implicit costs of their actions.

Effects of Stretching Accounts Payable

stretching accounts payable
Paying bills as late as possible without damaging the firm's credit rating.

A strategy that is often employed by a firm is **stretching accounts payable**, that is, paying bills as late as possible without damaging its credit rating. Such a strategy can reduce the cost of giving up a cash discount.

Example 15.5 ▶ Lawrence Industries was extended credit terms of 2/10 net 30 EOM. The cost of giving up the cash discount, assuming payment on the last day of the credit period, was approximately 36.5% [2% × (365 ÷ 20)]. If the firm were able to stretch its account payable to 70 days without damaging its credit rating, the cost of giving up the cash discount would be only 12.2% [2% × (365 ÷ 60)]. Stretching accounts payable reduces the implicit cost of giving up a cash discount.

Although stretching accounts payable may be financially attractive, it raises an important ethical issue: It may cause the firm to violate the agreement it entered into with its supplier when it purchased merchandise. Clearly, a supplier would not look kindly on a customer who regularly and purposely postponed paying for purchases.

Personal Finance Example 15.6 ▶ Jack and Mary Nobel, a young married couple, are in the process of purchasing a 50-inch HD TV at a cost of $1,900. The electronics dealer currently has a special financing plan that would allow them to either (1) put $200 down and finance the balance of $1,700 at 3% annual interest over 24 months, resulting in payments of $73 per month; or (2) receive an immediate $150 cash rebate, thereby paying only $1,750 cash. The Nobels, who have saved enough to pay cash for the TV, can currently earn 5% annual interest on their savings. They wish to determine whether to borrow or to pay cash to purchase the TV.

The upfront outlay for the financing alternative is the $200 down payment, whereas the Nobels will pay out $1,750 up front under the cash purchase alternative. So, the cash purchase will require an initial outlay that is $1,550 ($1,750 − $200) greater than under the financing alternative. Assuming that they can earn a simple interest rate of 5% on savings, the cash purchase will cause the Nobels to give up an opportunity to earn $155 (2 years × 0.05 × $1,550) over the 2 years.

If they choose the financing alternative, the $1,550 would grow to $1,705 ($1,550 + $155) at the end of 2 years. But under the financing alternative, th

Nobels will pay out a total of $1,752 (24 months $\times$ $73 per month) over the 2-year loan term. The cost of the financing alternative can be viewed as $1,752, and the cost of the cash payment (including forgone interest earnings) would be $1,705. Because it is less expensive, *the Nobels should pay cash for the TV.* The lower cost of the cash alternative is largely the result of the $150 cash rebate.

ACCRUALS

accruals
Liabilities for services received for which payment has yet to be made.

The second spontaneous source of short-term business financing is accruals. **Accruals** are liabilities for services received for which payment has yet to be made. The most common items accrued by a firm are wages and taxes. Because taxes are payments to the government, their accrual cannot be manipulated by the firm. However, the accrual of wages can be manipulated to some extent by delaying payment of wages, thereby receiving an interest-free loan from employees who are paid sometime after they have performed the work. The pay period for employees who earn an hourly rate is often governed by union regulations or by state or federal law. However, in other cases, the frequency of payment is at the discretion of the company's management.

focus on ETHICS

Accruals Management

in practice On June 2, 2010, Diebold, Inc., agreed to pay a $25 million fine to settle accounting fraud charges brought by the U.S. Securities and Exchange Commission (SEC). According to the SEC, the management of the Ohio-based manufacturer of ATMs, bank security systems, and electronic voting machines regularly received reports comparing the company's earnings to analyst forecasts. When earnings were below forecasts, management identified opportunities, some of which amounted to accounting fraud, to close the gap.

"Diebold's financial executives borrowed from many different chapters of the deceptive accounting playbook to fraudulently boost the company's bottom line," SEC Enforcement Director Robert Khuzami said in a statement. "When executives disregard their professional obligations to investors, both they and their companies face significant legal consequences."[a]

A number of the SEC's claims focused on premature revenue recognition. For example, Diebold was charged with improper use of "bill and hold" transactions. Under generally accepted accounting principles, revenue is typically recognized after a product is shipped. However, in some cases, sellers can recognize revenue before shipment for certain bill and hold transactions. The SEC claimed that Diebold improperly used bill and hold accounting to record revenue prematurely.

The SEC also claimed that Diebold manipulated various accounting accruals. Diebold was accused of understating liabilities tied to its Long Term Incentive Plan, commissions to be paid to sales personnel, and incentives to be paid to service personnel. Diebold temporarily reduced a liability account set up for payment of customer rebates. The company was also accused of overstating the value of inventory and improper inventory write-ups.

Each of these activities allowed Diebold to inflate the company's financial performance. According to the SEC's complaint, Diebold's fraudulent activities misstated reported pretax earnings by at least $127 million between 2002 and 2007. Two years prior to the settlement, Diebold restated earnings for the period covered by the charges.

The clawback provision of the 2002 Sarbanes-Oxley antifraud law requires executives to repay compensation they receive while their company misled shareholders. Diebold's former CEO, Walden O'Dell, agreed to return $470,000 in cash, plus stock and options. The SEC is currently pursuing a lawsuit against two other former Diebold executives for their part in the matter.

▶ *Why might financial managers still be tempted to manage earnings when a clawback is a legitimate possibility?*

[a]U.S. Securities and Exchange Commission, "SEC Charges Diebold and Former Executives with Accounting Fraud," press release, June 2, 2010, **www.sec.gov/news/press/2010/2010-93.htm**.

Example 15.7 ▶   Tenney Company, a large janitorial service company, currently pays its employees at the end of each work week. The weekly payroll totals $400,000. If the firm were to extend the pay period so as to pay its employees 1 week later throughout an entire year, the employees would in effect be lending the firm $400,000 for a year. If the firm could earn 10% annually on invested funds, such a strategy would be worth $40,000 per year (0.10 × $400,000).

→ REVIEW QUESTIONS

15–1 What are the two major sources of spontaneous short-term financing for a firm? How do their balances behave relative to the firm's sales?

15–2 Is there a cost associated with *taking a cash discount*? Is there any cost associated with *giving up a cash discount*? How do short-term borrowing costs affect the cash discount decision?

15–3 What is "stretching accounts payable"? What effect does this action have on the cost of giving up a cash discount?

15.2 Unsecured Sources of Short-Term Loans

Businesses obtain unsecured short-term loans from two major sources, banks and sales of commercial paper. Unlike the spontaneous sources of unsecured short-term financing, bank loans and commercial paper are negotiated and result from actions taken by the firm's financial manager. Bank loans are more popular because they are available to firms of all sizes; commercial paper tends to be available only to large firms. In addition, firms can use international loans to finance international transactions.

BANK LOANS

short-term, self-liquidating loan
An unsecured short-term loan in which the use to which the borrowed money is put provides the mechanism through which the loan is repaid.

Banks are a major source of unsecured short-term loans to businesses. The major type of loan made by banks to businesses is the **short-term, self-liquidating loan**. These loans are intended merely to carry the firm through seasonal peaks in financing needs that are due primarily to buildups of inventory and accounts receivable. As the firm converts inventories and receivables into cash, the funds needed to retire these loans are generated. In other words, the use to which the borrowed money is put provides the mechanism through which the loan is repaid, hence the term *self-liquidating*.

Banks lend unsecured, short-term funds in three basic ways: through single-payment notes, through lines of credit, and through revolving credit agreements. Before we look at these types of loans, we consider loan interest rates.

prime rate of interest (prime rate)
The lowest rate of interest charged by leading banks on business loans to their most important business borrowers.

Loan Interest Rates

The interest rate on a bank loan can be a fixed or a floating rate, and the interest rate is often based on the prime rate of interest. The **prime rate of interest (prime rate)** is the lowest rate of interest charged by leading banks on business loans to their most important business borrowers. The prime rate fluctuates wit' changing supply-and-demand relationships for short-term funds. Banks generally determine the rate to be charged to various borrowers by adding a premium to the prime rate to adjust it for the borrower's "riskiness." The premium may amount to 4 percent or more, although many unsecured short-term loans carry premiums of less than 2 percent.

Fixed- and Floating-Rate Loans   Loans can have either fixed or floating interest rates. On a **fixed-rate loan**, the rate of interest is determined at a set increment above the prime rate on the date of the loan and remains unvarying at that fixed rate until maturity. On a **floating-rate loan**, the increment above the prime rate is initially established, and the rate of interest is allowed to "float," or vary, above prime *as the prime rate varies* until maturity. Generally, the increment above the prime rate will be *lower* on a floating-rate loan than on a fixed-rate loan of equivalent risk because the lender bears less risk with a floating-rate loan. *Most short-term business loans are floating-rate loans.*

Method of Computing Interest   Once the *nominal (or stated) annual rate* is established, the method of computing interest is determined. Interest can be paid either when a loan matures or in advance. If interest is paid *at maturity,* the *effective (or true) annual rate*—the actual rate of interest paid—for an assumed 1-year period is equal to

fixed-rate loan
A loan with a rate of interest that is determined at a set increment above the prime rate and remains unvarying until maturity.

floating-rate loan
A loan with a rate of interest initially set at an increment above the prime rate and allowed to "float," or vary, above prime *as the prime rate varies* until maturity.

$$\frac{\text{Interest}}{\text{Amount borrowed}} \tag{15.3}$$

Most bank loans to businesses require the interest payment at maturity.

When interest is paid *in advance,* it is deducted from the loan so that the borrower actually receives less money than is requested (and less than they must repay). Loans on which interest is paid in advance are called **discount loans**. The *effective annual rate for a discount loan,* assuming a 1-year period, is calculated as

discount loan
Loan on which interest is paid in advance by being deducted from the amount borrowed.

$$\frac{\text{Interest}}{\text{Amount borrowed} - \text{Interest}} \tag{15.4}$$

Paying interest in advance raises the effective annual rate above the stated annual rate.

Example 15.8 ▶   Wooster Company, a manufacturer of athletic apparel, wants to borrow $10,000 at a stated annual rate of 10% interest for 1 year. If the interest on the loan is paid at maturity, the firm will pay $1,000 (0.10 × $10,000) for the use of the $10,000 for the year. At the end of the year, Wooster will write a check to the lender for $11,000, consisting of the $1,000 interest as well as the return of the $10,000 principal. Substituting into Equation 15.3 reveals that the effective annual rate is therefore

$$\frac{\$1,000}{\$10,000} = 10.0\%$$

If the money is borrowed at the same *stated* annual rate for 1 year but interest is paid in advance, the firm still pays $1,000 in interest, but it receives only $9,000 ($10,000 − $1,000). The effective annual rate in this case is

$$\frac{\$1,000}{\$10,000 - \$1,000} = \frac{\$1,000}{\$9,000} = 11.1\%$$

In this case, at the end of the year Wooster writes a check to the lender for $10,000, having "paid" the $1,000 in interest up front by borrowing just $9,000. Paying interest in advance thus makes the effective annual rate (11.1%) greater than the stated annual rate (10.0%).

Single-Payment Notes

single-payment note
A short-term, one-time loan made to a borrower who needs funds for a specific purpose for a short period.

A **single-payment note** can be obtained from a commercial bank by a creditworthy business borrower. This type of loan is usually a one-time loan made to a borrower who needs funds for a specific purpose for a short period. The resulting instrument is a *note,* signed by the borrower, that states the terms of the loan, including the length of the loan and the interest rate. This type of short-term note generally has a maturity of 30 days to 9 months or more. The interest charged is usually tied in some way to the prime rate of interest.

Example 15.9 ▶

Gordon Manufacturing, a producer of rotary mower blades, recently borrowed $100,000 from each of two banks, bank A and bank B. The loans were incurred on the same day, when the prime rate of interest was 6%. Each loan involved a 90-day note with interest to be paid at the end of 90 days. The interest rate was set at $1\frac{1}{2}\%$ above the prime rate on bank A's *fixed-rate note.* Over the 90-day period, the rate of interest on this note will remain at $7\frac{1}{2}\%$ (6% prime rate + $1\frac{1}{2}\%$ increment) regardless of fluctuations in the prime rate. The total interest cost on this loan is $1.849 [$100,000 × ($7\frac{1}{2}\%$ × 90 ÷ 365)], which means that the 90-day rate on this loan is 1.85% ($1,849 ÷ $100,000).

Assuming that the loan from bank A is rolled over each 90 days throughout the year under the same terms and circumstances, we can find its effective *annual* interest rate, or *EAR,* by using Equation 5.10. Because the loan costs 1.85% for 90 days, it is necessary to compound (1 + 0.0185) for 4.06 periods in the year (that is, 365 ÷ 90) and then subtract 1:

$$EAR = (1 + 0.0185)^{4.06} - 1$$

$$= 1.0773 - 1 = 0.0773 = \underline{7.73\%}$$

The effective annual rate of interest on the fixed-rate, 90-day note is 7.73%.

Bank B set the interest rate at 1% above the prime rate on its *floating-rate note.* The rate charged over the 90 days will vary directly with the prime rate. Initially, the rate will be 7% (6% + 1%), but when the prime rate changes, so will the rate of interest on the note. For instance, if after 30 days the prime rate rises to 6.5% and after another 30 days it drops to 6.25%, the firm will be paying 0.575% for the first 30 days (7% × 30 ÷ 365), 0.616% for the next 30 days (7.5% × 30 ÷ 365), and 0.596% for the last 30 days (7.25% × 30 ÷ 365). Its total interest cost will be $1,787 [$100,000 × (0.575% + 0.616% + 0.596%)], resulting in a 90-day r̶ of 1.79% ($1,787 ÷ $100,000).

Again, assuming the loan is rolled over each 90 days throughout the year under the same terms and circumstances, its effective *annual* rate is 7.46%:

$$EAR = (1 + 0.01787)^{4.06} - 1$$
$$= 1.0746 - 1 = 0.0746 = \underline{7.46\%}$$

Clearly, in this case the floating-rate loan would have been less expensive than the fixed-rate loan because of its generally lower effective annual rate.

Personal Finance Example 15.10 ▶ Megan Schwartz has been approved by Clinton National Bank for a 180-day loan of $30,000 that will allow her to make the down payment and close the loan on her new condo. She needs the funds to bridge the time until the sale of her current condo, from which she expects to receive $42,000.

Clinton National offered Megan the following two financing options for the $30,000 loan: (1) a *fixed-rate loan* at 2% above the prime rate or (2) a *variable-rate loan* at 1% above the prime rate. Currently, the prime rate of interest is 8%, and the consensus forecast of a group of mortgage economists for changes in the prime rate over the next 180 days is as follows:

60 days from today the prime rate will rise by 1%.

90 days from today the prime rate will rise another $\frac{1}{2}$%.

150 days from today the prime rate will drop by 1%.

Using the forecast prime rate changes, Megan wishes to determine the lowest interest-cost loan for the next 6 months.

Fixed-Rate Loan: Total interest cost over 180 days

$$= \$30,000 \times (0.08 + 0.02) \times (180 \div 365)$$
$$= \$30,000 \times 0.04932 \approx \underline{\$1,480}$$

Variable-Rate Loan: The applicable interest rate would begin at 9% (8% + 1%) and remain there for 60 days. Then the applicable rate would rise to 10% (9% + 1%) for the next 30 days and then to 10.50% (10% + 0.50%) for the next 60 days. Finally, the applicable rate would drop to 9.50% (10.50% − 1%) for the final 30 days.

Total interest cost over 180 days

$$= \$30,000 \times [\,(0.09 \times 60 \div 365) + (0.10 \times 30 \div 365)$$
$$+ (0.105 \times 60 \div 365) + (0.095 \times 30 \div 365)\,]$$
$$= \$30,000 \times (0.01479 + 0.00822 + 0.01726 + 0.00781)$$
$$= \$30,000 \times 0.04808 \approx \underline{\$1,442}$$

Because the estimated total interest cost on the variable-rate loan of $1,442 is less than the total interest cost of $1,480 on the fixed-rate loan, *Megan should take the variable-rate loan.* By doing so, she will save about $38 ($1,480 − $1,442) in interest cost over the 180 days.

---

line of credit
An agreement between a commercial bank and a business specifying the amount of unsecured short-term borrowing the bank will make available to the firm over a given period of time.

Lines of Credit

A **line of credit** is an agreement between a commercial bank and a business, specifying the amount of unsecured short-term borrowing that the bank will make available to the firm over a given period of time. It is similar to the agreement under which issuers of bank credit cards, such as MasterCard, Visa, and Discover, extend preapproved credit to cardholders. A line-of-credit agreement is typically made for a period of 1 year and often places certain constraints on the borrower. It is *not a guaranteed loan;* rather, it indicates that if the bank has sufficient funds available, it will allow the borrower to owe it *up to* a certain amount of money. The amount of a line of credit is the *maximum amount the firm can owe the bank* at any point in time.

When applying for a line of credit, the borrower may be required to submit such documents as its cash budget, pro forma income statement, pro forma balance sheet, and recent financial statements. If the bank finds the customer acceptable, the line of credit will be extended. The major attraction of a line of credit from the bank's point of view is that it eliminates the need to examine the creditworthiness of a customer each time it borrows money within the year.

Interest Rates   The interest rate on a line of credit is normally stated as a floating rate: the *prime rate plus a premium.* If the prime rate changes, the interest rate charged on new *as well as outstanding* borrowing automatically changes. The amount a borrower is charged in excess of the prime rate depends on its creditworthiness. The more creditworthy the borrower, the lower the premium (interest increment) above prime and vice versa.

Operating-Change Restrictions   In a line-of-credit agreement, a bank may impose **operating-change restrictions**, which give it the right to revoke the line if any major changes occur in the firm's financial condition or operations. The firm is usually required to submit up-to-date, and preferably audited, financial statements for periodic review. In addition, the bank typically needs to be informed of shifts in key managerial personnel or in the firm's operations before changes take place. Such changes may affect the future success and debt-paying ability of the firm and thus could alter its credit status. If the bank does not agree with the proposed changes and the firm makes them anyway, the bank has the right to revoke the line of credit.

Compensating Balances   To ensure that the borrower will be a "good customer," many short-term unsecured bank loans—single-payment notes and lines of credit—require the borrower to maintain, in a checking account, a **compensating balance** equal to a certain percentage of the amount borrowed. Banks frequently require compensating balances of 10 to 20 percent. A compensating balance not only forces the borrower to be a good customer of the bank but may also raise the interest cost to the borrower.

operating-change restrictions
Contractual restrictions that a bank may impose on a firm's financial condition or operations as part of a line-of-credit agreement.

compensating balance
A required checking account balance equal to a certain percentage of the amount borrowed from a bank under a line-of-credit or revolving credit agreement.

Example 15.11 ▶

MyFinanceLab Solution Video

Estrada Graphics, a graphic design firm, has borrowed $1 million under a line-of-credit agreement. It must pay a stated interest rate of 10% and maintain, in its checking account, a compensating balance equal to 20% of the amount borrowed, or $200,000. Thus, it actually receives the use of only $800,000. To use that amount for a year, the firm pays interest of $100,000 (0.10 × $1,000,000). The effective annual rate on the funds is therefore 12.5% ($100,000 ÷ $800,000), which is 2.5% more than the stated rate of 10%.

If the firm normally maintains a balance of $200,000 or more in its checking account, the effective annual rate equals the stated annual rate of 10% because none of the $1 million borrowed is needed to satisfy the compensating-balance requirement. If the firm normally maintains a $100,000 balance in its checking account, only an additional $100,000 will have to be tied up, leaving it with $900,000 of usable funds. The effective annual rate in this case would be 11.1% ($100,000 ÷ $900,000). Thus, a compensating balance raises the cost of borrowing *only if* it is larger than the firm's normal cash balance.

Annual Cleanups   To ensure that money lent under a line-of-credit agreement is actually being used to finance seasonal needs, many banks require an **annual cleanup**. In these cases, the borrower must have a loan balance of zero—that is, owe the bank nothing—for a certain number of days during the year. Insisting that the borrower carry a zero loan balance for a certain period ensures that short-term loans do not turn into long-term loans.

All the characteristics of a line-of-credit agreement are negotiable to some extent. Today, banks bid competitively to attract large, well-known firms. A prospective borrower should attempt to negotiate a line of credit with the most favorable interest rate, for an optimal amount of funds, and with a minimum of restrictions. Borrowers today frequently pay fees to lenders instead of maintaining deposit balances as compensation for loans and other services. The lender attempts to get a good return with maximum safety. Negotiations should produce a line of credit that is suitable to both borrower and lender.

annual cleanup
The requirement that for a certain number of days during the year borrowers under a line of credit carry a zero loan balance (that is, owe the bank nothing).

Revolving Credit Agreements

A **revolving credit agreement** is nothing more than a *guaranteed line of credit*. It is guaranteed in the sense that the commercial bank assures the borrower that a specified amount of funds will be made available regardless of the scarcity of money. The interest rate and other requirements are similar to those for a line of credit. It is not uncommon for a revolving credit agreement to be for a period greater than 1 year.[2] Because the bank guarantees the availability of funds, a **commitment fee** is normally charged on a revolving credit agreement. This fee often applies to the average unused balance of the borrower's credit line. It is normally about 0.5 percent of the *average unused portion* of the line.

revolving credit agreement
A line of credit *guaranteed* to a borrower by a commercial bank regardless of the scarcity of money.

commitment fee
The fee that is normally charged on a *revolving credit agreement;* it often applies to the *average unused portion* of the borrower's credit line.

Example 15.12 ▶

REH Company, a major real estate developer, has a $2 million revolving credit agreement with its bank. Its average borrowing under the agreement for the past year was $1.5 million. The bank charges a commitment fee of 0.5% on the average unused balance. Because the average unused portion of the committed funds was $500,000 ($2 million − $1.5 million), the commitment fee for the year was $2,500 (0.005 × $500,000). Of course, REH also had to pay interest on the actual $1.5 million borrowed under the agreement. Assuming that $112,500 interest was paid on the $1.5 million borrowed, the effective cost of the agreement was 7.67% [($112,500 + $2,500) ÷ $1,500,000]. Although more expensive than a line of credit, a revolving credit agreement can be less risky from the borrower's viewpoint because the availability of funds is guaranteed.

---

2. Many authors classify the revolving credit agreement as a form of *intermediate-term financing,* defined as having a maturity of 1 to 7 years, but we do not use the intermediate-term financing classification; only short-term and long-term classifications are made. Because many revolving credit agreements are for more than 1 year, they can be classified as a form of long-term financing; however, they are discussed here because of their similarity to line-of-credit agreements.

COMMERCIAL PAPER

commercial paper
A form of financing consisting of short-term, unsecured promissory notes issued by firms with a high credit standing.

Commercial paper is a form of financing that consists of short-term, unsecured promissory notes issued by firms with a high credit standing. Generally, only large firms of unquestionable financial soundness are able to issue commercial paper. Most commercial paper issues have maturities ranging from 3 to 270 days. Although there is no set denomination, such financing is generally issued in multiples of $100,000 or more. A large portion of the commercial paper today is issued by finance companies; manufacturing firms account for a smaller portion of this type of financing. Businesses often purchase commercial paper, which they hold as marketable securities, to provide an interest-earning reserve of liquidity.

Interest on Commercial Paper

Commercial paper is sold at a discount from its *par*, or *face, value*. The size of the discount and the length of time to maturity determine the interest paid by the issuer of commercial paper. The actual interest earned by the purchaser is determined by certain calculations, illustrated by the following example.

Example 15.13 ▶

MyFinanceLab Solution Video

Bertram Corporation, a large shipbuilder, has just issued $1 million worth of commercial paper that has a 90-day maturity and sells for $990,000. At the end of 90 days, the purchaser of this paper will receive $1 million for its $990,000 investment. The interest paid on the financing is therefore $10,000 on a principal of $990,000. The effective 90-day rate on the paper is 1.01% ($10,000 ÷ $990,000). Assuming that the paper is rolled over each 90 days throughout the year (that is, $365 \div 90 = 4.06$ times per year), the effective annual rate for Bertram's commercial paper, found by using Equation 5.10, is 4.16% $[(1 + 0.0101)^{4.06} - 1]$.

An interesting characteristic of commercial paper is that its interest cost is *normally* 2 percent to 4 percent below the prime rate. In other words, firms are able to raise funds more cheaply by selling commercial paper than by borrowing from a commercial bank. The reason is that many suppliers of short-term funds do not have the option, as banks do, of making low-risk business loans at the prime rate. They can invest safely only in marketable securities such as Treasury bills and commercial paper.

Although the stated interest cost of borrowing through the sale of commercial paper is normally lower than the prime rate, the *overall cost* of commercial paper may not be less than that of a bank loan. Additional costs include various fees and flotation costs. Also, even if it is slightly more expensive to borrow from a commercial bank, it may at times be advisable to do so to establish a good working relationship with a bank. This strategy ensures that when money is tight, funds can be obtained promptly and at a reasonable interest rate.

Matter of fact

Lending Limits

Commercial banks are legally prohibited from lending amounts in excess of 15 percent (plus an additional 10 percent for loans secured by readily marketable collateral) of the bank's unimpaired capital and surplus to any one borrower. This restriction is intended to protect depositors by forcing the commercial bank to spread its risk across a number of borrowers. In addition, smaller commercial banks do not have many opportunities to lend to large, high-quality business borrowers.

INTERNATIONAL LOANS

 In some ways, arranging short-term financing for international trade is no different from financing purely domestic operations. In both cases, producers must finance production and inventory and then continue to finance accounts receivable before collecting any cash payments from sales. In other ways, however, the short-term financing of international sales and purchases is fundamentally different from that of strictly domestic trade.

International Transactions

The important difference between international and domestic transactions is that payments are often made or received in a foreign currency. Not only must a U.S. company pay the costs of doing business in the foreign exchange market, but it also is exposed to *exchange rate risk*. A U.S.-based company that exports goods and has accounts receivable denominated in a foreign currency faces the risk that the U.S. dollar will appreciate in value relative to the foreign currency. The risk to a U.S. importer with foreign-currency-denominated accounts payable is that the dollar will depreciate. Although *exchange rate risk* can often be *hedged* by using currency forward, futures, or options markets, doing so is costly and is not possible for all foreign currencies.

Typical international transactions are large in size and have long maturity dates. Therefore, companies that are involved in international trade generally have to finance larger dollar amounts for longer time periods than companies that operate domestically. Furthermore, because foreign companies are rarely well known in the United States, some financial institutions are reluctant to lend to U.S. exporters or importers, particularly smaller firms.

Financing International Trade

letter of credit
A letter written by a company's bank to the company's foreign supplier, stating that the bank guarantees payment of an invoiced amount if all the underlying agreements are met.

Several specialized techniques have evolved for financing international trade. Perhaps the most important financing vehicle is the **letter of credit**, a letter written by a company's bank to the company's foreign supplier, stating that the bank guarantees payment of an invoiced amount if all the underlying agreements are met. The letter of credit essentially substitutes the bank's reputation and creditworthiness for that of its commercial customer. A U.S. exporter is more willing to sell goods to a foreign buyer if the transaction is covered by a letter of credit issued by a well-known bank in the buyer's home country.

Firms that do business in foreign countries on an ongoing basis often finance their operations, at least in part, in the local market. A company that has an assembly plant in Mexico, for example, might choose to finance its purchases of Mexican goods and services with peso funds borrowed from a Mexican bank. This practice not only minimizes exchange rate risk but also improves the company's business ties to the host community. Multinational companies, however, sometimes finance their international transactions through dollar-denominated loans from international banks. The *Eurocurrency loan markets* allow creditworthy borrowers to obtain financing on attractive terms.

Transactions between Subsidiaries

Much international trade involves transactions between corporate subsidiaries. A U.S. company might, for example, manufacture one part in an Asian plant and another part in the United States, assemble the product in Brazil, and sell it in Europe. The shipment of goods back and forth between subsidiaries creates accounts receivable and accounts payable, but the parent company has considerable discretion about how and when payments are made. In particular, the parent can minimize foreign exchange fees and other transaction costs by "netting" what affiliates owe each other and paying only the net amount due rather than having both subsidiaries pay each other the gross amounts due.

→ **REVIEW QUESTIONS**

15–4 How is the *prime rate of interest* relevant to the cost of short-term bank borrowing? What is a *floating-rate loan*?

15–5 How does the *effective annual rate* differ between a loan requiring interest payments *at maturity* and another, similar loan requiring interest *in advance*?

15–6 What are the basic terms and characteristics of a *single-payment note*? How is the *effective annual rate* on such a note found?

15–7 What is a *line of credit*? Describe each of the following features that are often included in these agreements: (**a**) operating-change restrictions, (**b**) compensating balance, and (**c**) annual cleanup.

15–8 What is a *revolving credit agreement*? How does this arrangement differ from the line-of-credit agreement? What is a *commitment fee*?

15–9 How do firms use *commercial paper* to raise short-term funds? Who can issue commercial paper? Who buys commercial paper?

15–10 What is the important difference between international and domestic transactions? How is a *letter of credit* used in financing international trade transactions? How is "netting" used in transactions between subsidiaries?

  # 15.3 Secured Sources of Short-Term Loans

secured short-term financing
Short-term financing (loan) that has specific assets pledged as collateral.

security agreement
The agreement between the borrower and the lender that specifies the collateral held against a secured loan.

When a firm has exhausted its sources of unsecured short-term financing, it may be able to obtain additional short-term loans on a secured basis. **Secured short-term financing** has specific assets pledged as collateral. The *collateral* commonly takes the form of an asset, such as accounts receivable or inventory. The lender obtains a security interest in the collateral through the execution of a **security agreement** with the borrower that specifies the collateral held against the loan. In addition, the terms of the loan against which the security is held form part of the security agreement. A copy of the security agreement is filed in a public office within the state, usually a county or state court. Filing provides subsequent lenders with information about which assets of a prospective borrower are unavailable for use as collateral. The filing requirement protects the lender by legally establishing the lender's security interest.

CHARACTERISTICS OF SECURED SHORT-TERM LOANS

Although many people believe that holding collateral as security reduces the risk that a loan will default, lenders do not usually view loans in this way. Lenders recognize that holding collateral can reduce losses if the borrower defaults, but *the presence of collateral has no impact on the risk of default*. A lender requires collateral to ensure recovery of some portion of the loan in the event of default

What the lender wants above all, however, is to be repaid as scheduled. In general, lenders prefer to make less risky loans at lower rates of interest than to be in a position in which they must liquidate collateral.

Collateral and Terms

Lenders of secured short-term funds prefer collateral that has a duration closely matched to the term of the loan. Current assets are the most desirable short-term-loan collateral because they can normally be converted into cash much sooner than fixed assets. Thus, the short-term lender of secured funds generally accepts only liquid current assets as collateral.

percentage advance
The percentage of the book value of the collateral that constitutes the principal of a secured loan.

Typically, the lender determines the desirable **percentage advance** to make against the collateral. This percentage advance constitutes the principal of the secured loan and is normally between 30 and 100 percent of the book value of the collateral. It varies according to the type and liquidity of collateral.

The interest rate that is charged on secured short-term loans is typically *higher* than the rate on unsecured short-term loans. Lenders do not normally consider secured loans less risky than unsecured loans. In addition, negotiating and administering secured loans is more troublesome for the lender than negotiating and administering unsecured loans. The lender therefore normally requires added compensation in the form of a service charge, a higher interest rate, or both.

Institutions Extending Secured Short-Term Loans

The primary sources of secured short-term loans to businesses are commercial banks and commercial finance companies. Both institutions deal in short-term loans secured primarily by accounts receivable and inventory. We have already described the operations of commercial banks. **Commercial finance companies** are lending institutions that make *only* secured loans—both short-term and long-term—to businesses. Unlike banks, finance companies are not permitted to hold deposits.

commercial finance companies
Lending institutions that make *only* secured loans—both short-term and long-term—to businesses.

Only when its unsecured and secured short-term borrowing power from the commercial bank is exhausted will a borrower turn to the commercial finance company for additional secured borrowing. Because the finance company generally ends up with higher-risk borrowers, its interest charges on secured short-term loans are usually higher than those of commercial banks. The leading U.S. commercial finance companies include the CIT Group and General Electric Corporate Financial Services.

USE OF ACCOUNTS RECEIVABLE AS COLLATERAL

Two commonly used means of obtaining short-term financing with accounts receivable are *pledging accounts receivable* and *factoring accounts receivable*. Actually, only a pledge of accounts receivable creates a secured short-term loan; factoring really entails the *sale* of accounts receivable at a discount. Although factoring is not actually a form of secured short-term borrowing, it does involve the use of accounts receivable to obtain needed short-term funds.

Pledging Accounts Receivable

pledge of accounts receivable
The use of a firm's accounts receivable as security, or collateral, to obtain a short-term loan.

A **pledge of accounts receivable** is often used to secure a short-term loan. Because accounts receivable are normally quite liquid, they are an attractive form of short-term-loan collateral.

The Pledging Process When a firm requests a loan against accounts receivable, the lender first evaluates the firm's accounts receivable to determine their desirability as collateral. The lender makes a list of the acceptable accounts, along with the billing dates and amounts. If the borrowing firm requests a loan for a fixed amount, the lender needs to select only enough accounts to secure the funds requested. If the borrower wants the maximum loan available, the lender evaluates all the accounts to select the maximum amount of acceptable collateral.

After selecting the acceptable accounts, the lender normally adjusts the dollar value of these accounts for expected returns on sales and other allowances. If a customer whose account has been pledged returns merchandise or receives some type of allowance, such as a cash discount for early payment, the amount of the collateral is automatically reduced. For protection from such occurrences, the lender normally reduces the value of the acceptable collateral by a fixed percentage.

Next, the percentage to be advanced against the collateral must be determined. The lender evaluates the quality of the acceptable receivables and the expected cost of their liquidation. This percentage represents the principal of the loan and typically ranges between 50 and 90 percent of the face value of acceptable accounts receivable. To protect its interest in the collateral, the lender files a **lien**, which is a publicly disclosed legal claim on the collateral.

lien
A publicly disclosed legal claim on loan collateral.

nonnotification basis
The basis on which a borrower, having pledged an account receivable, continues to collect the account payments without notifying the account customer.

Notification Pledges of accounts receivable are normally made on a **nonnotification basis**, meaning that a customer whose account has been pledged as collateral is not notified. Under the nonnotification arrangement, the borrower still collects the pledged account receivable, and the lender trusts the borrower to remit these payments as they are received. If a pledge of accounts receivable is made on a **notification basis**, the customer is notified to remit payment directly to the lender.

notification basis
The basis on which an account customer whose account has been pledged (or factored) is notified to remit payment directly to the lender (or factor).

Matter of fact

Receivables Trading

Founded in 2007, the Receivables Exchange is an online marketplace where organizations such as hedge funds and commercial banks looking for short-term investments can bid on receivables pledged by small, medium-sized, and large companies from a wide range of industries. Companies that need cash put their receivables up for auction on the Receivables Exchange, and investors bid on them. In its first few years of operation, the Receivables Exchange provided funding of more than $1 billion to companies selling their receivables. The Receivables Exchange attracted the attention of the NYSE Euronext, which purchased a minority stake in the company in 2011.

factoring accounts receivable
The outright sale of accounts receivable at a discount to a *factor* or other financial institution.

Pledging Cost The stated cost of a pledge of accounts receivable is normally 2 to 5 percent above the prime rate. In addition to the stated interest rate, a service charge of up to 3 percent may be levied by the lender to cover its administrative costs. Clearly, pledges of accounts receivable are a high-cost source of short-term financing.

Factoring Accounts Receivable

factor
A financial institution that specializes in purchasing accounts receivable from businesses.

Factoring accounts receivable involves selling them outright, at a discount, to a financial institution. A **factor** is a financial institution that specializes in purchasing accounts receivable from businesses. Although it is not the same as obtaining a short-term loan, factoring accounts receivable is similar to borrowing with accounts receivable as collateral.

Factoring Agreement   A factoring agreement normally states the exact conditions and procedures for the purchase of an account. The factor, like a lender against a pledge of accounts receivable, chooses accounts for purchase, selecting only those that appear to be acceptable credit risks. Where factoring is to be on a continuing basis, the factor will actually make the firm's credit decisions because this will guarantee the acceptability of accounts. Factoring is normally done on a *notification basis,* and the factor receives payment of the account directly from the customer. In addition, most sales of accounts receivable to a factor are made on a **nonrecourse basis,** meaning that the factor agrees to accept all credit risks. Thus, if a purchased account turns out to be uncollectible, the factor must absorb the loss.

nonrecourse basis
The basis on which accounts receivable are sold to a factor with the understanding that the factor accepts all credit risks on the purchased accounts.

Matter of fact

Quasi Factoring

The use of credit cards such as MasterCard, Visa, and Discover by consumers has some similarity to factoring because the vendor that accepts the card is reimbursed at a discount for purchases made with the card. The difference between factoring and credit cards is that cards are nothing more than a line of credit extended by the issuer, which charges the vendors a fee for accepting the cards. In factoring, the factor does not analyze credit until after the sale has been made; in many cases (except when factoring is done on a continuing basis), the initial credit decision is the responsibility of the vendor, not the factor that purchases the account.

Typically, the factor is not required to pay the firm until the account is collected or until the last day of the credit period, whichever occurs first. The factor sets up an account similar to a bank deposit account for each customer. As payment is received or as due dates arrive, the factor deposits money into the seller's account, from which the seller is free to make withdrawals as needed.

In many cases, if the firm leaves the money in the account, a *surplus* will exist on which the factor will pay interest. In other instances, the factor may make *advances* to the firm against uncollected accounts that are not yet due. These advances represent a negative balance in the firm's account, on which interest is charged.

Factoring Cost   Factoring costs include commissions, interest levied on advances, and interest earned on surpluses. The factor deposits in the firm's account the book value of the collected or due accounts purchased by the factor, less the commissions. The commissions are typically stated as a 1 to 3 percent discount from the book value of factored accounts receivable. The *interest levied on advances* is generally 2 to 4 percent above the prime rate. It is levied on the actual amount advanced. The *interest paid on surpluses* is generally between 0.2 and 0.5 percent per month.

Although its costs may seem high, factoring has certain advantages that make it attractive to many firms. One is the ability it gives the firm to *turn accounts receivable immediately into cash* without having to worry about repayment. Another advantage is that it ensures a *known pattern of cash flows.* In addition, if factoring is undertaken on a continuing basis, the firm *can eliminate its credit and collection departments.*

USE OF INVENTORY AS COLLATERAL

Inventory is generally second to accounts receivable in desirability as short-term loan collateral. Inventory normally has a market value that is greater than its book value, which is used to establish its value as collateral. A lender whose loan is secured with inventory will probably be able to sell that inventory for at least book value if the borrower defaults on its obligations.

The most important characteristic of inventory being evaluated as loan collateral is *marketability*. A warehouse of *perishable* items, such as fresh peaches, may be quite marketable, but if the cost of storing and selling the peaches is high, they may not be desirable collateral. *Specialized items,* such as moon-roving vehicles, are also not desirable collateral because finding a buyer for them could be difficult. When evaluating inventory as possible loan collateral, the lender looks for items with very stable market prices that have ready markets and that lack undesirable physical properties.

Floating Inventory Liens

floating inventory lien
A secured short-term loan against inventory under which the lender's claim is on the borrower's inventory in general.

A lender may be willing to secure a loan under a **floating inventory lien,** which is a claim on inventory in general. This arrangement is most attractive when the firm has a stable level of inventory that consists of a diversified group of relatively inexpensive merchandise. Inventories of items such as auto tires, screws and bolts, and shoes are candidates for floating-lien loans. Because it is difficult for a lender to verify the presence of the inventory, the lender generally advances less than 50 percent of the book value of the average inventory. The interest charge on a floating lien is 3 to 5 percent above the prime rate. Commercial banks often require floating liens as extra security on what would otherwise be an unsecured loan. Floating lien inventory loans may also be available from commercial finance companies.

Trust Receipt Inventory Loans

trust receipt inventory loan
A secured short-term loan against inventory under which the lender advances 80 to 100 percent of the cost of the borrower's relatively expensive inventory items in exchange for the borrower's promise to repay the lender, with accrued interest, immediately after the sale of each item of collateral.

A **trust receipt inventory loan** often can be made against relatively expensive automotive, consumer durable, and industrial goods that can be identified by serial number. Under this agreement, the borrower keeps the inventory, and the lender may advance 80 to 100 percent of its cost. The lender files a *lien* on all the items financed. The borrower is free to sell the merchandise but is *trusted* to remit the amount lent, along with accrued interest, to the lender immediately after the sale. The lender then releases the lien on the item. The lender makes periodic checks of the borrower's inventory to make sure that the required collateral remains in the hands of the borrower. The interest charge to the borrower is normally 2 percent or more above the prime rate.

Trust receipt loans are often made by manufacturers' wholly owned financing subsidiaries, known as *captive finance companies,* to their customers. Captive finance companies are especially popular in industries that manufacture consumer durable goods because they provide the manufacturer with a useful sales tool. For example, General Motors Acceptance Corporation, the financing subsidiary of General Motors, grants these types of loans to its dealers. Trust receipt loans are also available through commercial banks and commercial finance companies.

Warehouse Receipt Loans

warehouse receipt loan
A secured short-term loan against inventory under which the lender receives control of the pledged inventory collateral, which is stored by a designated warehousing company on the lender's behalf.

A **warehouse receipt loan** is an arrangement whereby the lender, which may be a commercial bank or finance company, receives control of the pledged inventor collateral, which is stored by a designated agent on the lender's behalf. After selecting acceptable collateral, the lender hires a warehousing company to act as its agent and take possession of the inventory.

Two types of warehousing arrangements are possible. A *terminal warehouse* is a central warehouse that is used to store the merchandise of various customers. The lender normally uses such a warehouse when the inventory is easily transported and can be delivered to the warehouse relatively inexpensively. Under a *field warehouse* arrangement, the lender hires a field-warehousing company to set up a warehouse on the borrower's premises or to lease part of the borrower's warehouse to store the pledged collateral. Regardless of the type of warehouse, the warehousing company places a guard over the inventory. Only on written approval of the lender can any portion of the secured inventory be released by the warehousing company.

The actual lending agreement specifically states the requirements for the release of inventory. As with other secured loans, the lender accepts only collateral that it believes to be readily marketable and advances only a portion—generally 75 to 90 percent—of the collateral's value. The specific costs of warehouse receipt loans are generally higher than those of any other secured lending arrangements because of the need to hire and pay a warehousing company to guard and supervise the collateral. The basic interest charged on warehouse receipt loans is higher than that charged on unsecured loans, generally ranging from 3 to 5 percent above the prime rate. In addition to the interest charge, the borrower must absorb the costs of warehousing by paying the warehouse fee, which is generally between 1 and 3 percent of the amount of the loan. The borrower is normally also required to pay the insurance costs on the warehoused merchandise.

→ REVIEW QUESTIONS

15–11 Are secured short-term loans viewed as more risky or less risky than unsecured short-term loans? Why?

15–12 In general, what interest rates and fees are levied on secured short-term loans? Why are these rates generally *higher* than the rates on unsecured short-term loans?

15–13 Describe and compare the basic features of the following methods of using *accounts receivable* to obtain short-term financing: (a) pledging accounts receivable and (b) factoring accounts receivable. Be sure to mention the institutions that offer each of them.

15–14 For the following methods of using *inventory* as short-term loan collateral, describe the basic features of each, and compare their use: (a) floating lien, (b) trust receipt loan, and (c) warehouse receipt loan.

Summary

FOCUS ON VALUE

Current liabilities represent an important and generally inexpensive source of financing for a firm. The level of short-term (current liabilities) financing employed by a firm affects its profitability and risk. Accounts payable and accruals are spontaneous liabilities that should be carefully managed because they represent free financing. Notes payable, which represent negotiated short-term financing, should be obtained at the lowest cost under the best possible terms. Large, well-known firms can obtain unsecured short-term financing through the sale of commercial paper. On a secured basis, the firm can obtain loans from banks or commercial finance companies, using either accounts receivable or inventory as collateral.

The financial manager must obtain the right quantity and form of current liabilities financing to provide the lowest-cost funds with the least risk. Such a strategy should positively contribute to the firm's goal of **maximizing the stock price.**

REVIEW OF LEARNING GOALS

LG 1 **Review accounts payable, the key components of credit terms, and the procedures for analyzing those terms.** The major spontaneous source of short-term financing is accounts payable. They are the primary source of short-term funds. Credit terms may differ with respect to the credit period, cash discount, cash discount period, and beginning of the credit period. Cash discounts should be given up only when a firm in need of short-term funds must pay an interest rate on borrowing that is greater than the cost of giving up the cash discount.

LG 2 **Understand the effects of stretching accounts payable on their cost and the use of accruals.** Stretching accounts payable can lower the cost of giving up a cash discount. Accruals, which result primarily from wage and tax obligations are virtually free.

LG 3 **Describe interest rates and the basic types of unsecured bank sources of short-term loans.** Banks are the major source of unsecured short-term loans to businesses. The interest rate on these loans is tied to the prime rate of interest by a risk premium and may be fixed or floating. It should be evaluated by using the effective annual rate. Whether interest is paid when the loan matures or in advance affects the rate. Bank loans may take the form of a single-payment note, a line of credit, or a revolving credit agreement.

LG 4 **Discuss the basic features of commercial paper and the key aspects of international short-term loans.** Commercial paper is an unsecured IOU issued by firms with a high credit standing. International sales and purchases expose firms to exchange rate risk. Such transactions are larger and of longer maturity than domestic transactions, and they can be financed by using a letter of credit, by borrowing in the local market, or through dollar-denominated loans from international banks. On transactions between subsidiaries, "netting" can be used to minimize foreign exchange fees and other transaction costs.

LG 5 **Explain the characteristics of secured short-term loans and the use of accounts receivable as short-term-loan collateral.** Secured short-term loans are those for which the lender requires collateral, which are usually current assets such as accounts receivable or inventory. Only a percentage of the book value of acceptable collateral is advanced by the lender. These loans are more expensive than unsecured loans. Commercial banks and commercial finance companies make secured short-term loans. Both pledging and factoring involve the use of accounts receivable to obtain needed short-term funds.

LG 6 **Describe the various ways in which inventory can be used as short-term-loan collateral.** Inventory can be used as short-term-loan collateral under a floating lien, a trust receipt arrangement, or a warehouse receipt loan.

Self-Test Problem (Solutions in Appendix)

  ST15–1 **Cash discount decisions** The credit terms for each of three suppliers are shown in the following table. (*Note:* Assume a 365-day year.)

Supplier	Credit terms
X	1/10 net 55 EOM
Y	2/10 net 30 EOM
Z	2/20 net 60 EOM

a. Determine the *approximate* cost of giving up the cash discount from each supplier.

b. Assuming that the firm needs short-term financing, indicate whether it would be better to give up the cash discount or take the discount and borrow from a bank at 15% annual interest. Evaluate each supplier *separately* using your findings in part **a**.

c. Now assume that the firm could stretch its accounts payable (net period only) by 20 days from supplier Z. What impact, if any, would that have on your answer in part **b** relative to this supplier?

Warm-Up Exercises All problems are available in MyFinanceLab.

LG 1 **E15–1** Lyman Nurseries purchased seeds costing $25,000 with terms of 3/15 net 30 EOM on January 12. How much will the firm pay if it takes the cash discount? What is the *approximate cost of giving up the cash discount,* using the simplified formula?

LG 2 **E15–2** Cleaner's, Inc., is switching to paying employees every 2 weeks rather than weekly and will therefore "skip" 1 week's pay. The firm has 25 employees who work a 60-hour week and earn an average wage of $12.50 per hour. Using a 10% rate of interest, how much will this change save the firm annually?

LG 3 **E15–3** Jasmine Scents has been given two competing offers for short-term financing. Both offers are for borrowing $15,000 for 1 year. The first offer is a *discount loan* at 8%, and the second offer is for interest to be paid *at maturity* at a stated interest rate of 9%. Calculate the *effective annual rates* for each loan, and indicate which loan offers the better terms.

LG 3   **E15–4**   Jackson Industries has borrowed $125,000 under a line-of-credit agreement. Although the company normally maintains a checking account balance of $15,000 in the lending bank, this credit line requires a 20% compensating balance. The stated interest rate on the borrowed funds is 10%. What is the *effective annual rate of interest* on the line of credit?

LG 4   **E15–5**   Horizon Telecom sold $300,000 worth of 120-day commercial paper for $298,000. What is the dollar amount of interest paid on the commercial paper? What is the *effective 120-day rate* on the paper?

Problems   All problems are available in MyFinanceLab.

LG 1   **P15–1**   **Payment dates**   Determine when a firm must pay for purchases made and invoices dated on November 25 under each of the following credit terms:
   a. net 30 date of invoice
   b. net 30 EOM
   c. net 45 date of invoice
   d. net 60 EOM

LG 1   **P15–2**   **Cost of giving up cash discounts**   Determine the *cost of giving up the cash discount* under each of the following terms of sale. (*Note:* Assume a 365-day year.)
   a. 2/10 net 30
   b. 1/10 net 30
   c. 1/10 net 45
   d. 3/10 net 90
   e. 1/10 net 60
   f. 3/10 net 30
   g. 4/10 net 180

LG 1   **P15–3**   **Credit terms**   Purchases made on credit are due in full by the end of the billing period. Many firms extend a discount for payment made in the first part of the billing period. The original invoice contains a type of shorthand notation that explains the credit terms that apply. (*Note:* Assume a 365-day year.)
   a. Write the shorthand expression of credit terms for each of the following:

Cash discount	Cash discount period	Credit period	Beginning of credit period
1%	15 days	45 days	date of invoice
2	10	30	end of month
2	7	28	date of invoice
1	10	60	end of month

   b. For each of the sets of credit terms in part **a**, calculate the number of days until full payment is due for invoices dated March 12.
   c. For each of the sets of credit terms, calculate the *cost of giving up the cash discount.*
   d. If the firm's cost of short-term financing is 8%, what would you recommend in regard to taking the discount or giving it up in each case?

P15–4 **Cash discount versus loan** Joanne Germano works in an accounts payable department of a major retailer. She has attempted to convince her boss to take the discount on the 1/15 net 65 credit terms most suppliers offer, but her boss argues that giving up the 1% discount is less costly than a short-term loan at 7%. Prove to whoever is wrong that the other is correct. (*Note:* Assume a 365-day year.)

Personal Finance Problem

 P15–5 **Borrow or pay cash for an asset** Bob and Carol Gibbs are set to move into their first apartment. They visited Furniture R'Us, looking for a dining room table and buffet. Dining room sets are typically one of the more expensive home furnishing items, and the store offers financing arrangements to customers. Bob and Carol have the cash to pay for the furniture, but it would definitely deplete their savings, so they want to look at all their options.

The dining room set costs $3,000, and Furniture R'Us offers a financing plan that would allow them to either (1) put 10% down and finance the balance at 4% annual interest over 24 months or (2) receive an immediate $200 cash rebate, thereby paying only $2,800 cash to buy the furniture.

Bob and Carol currently earn 5.2% annual interest on their savings.
a. Calculate the cash down payment for the loan.
b. Calculate the monthly payment on the available loan. (*Hint:* Treat the current loan as an annuity and solve for the monthly payment.)
c. Calculate the initial cash outlay under the cash purchase option.
d. Assuming that they can earn a simple interest rate of 5.2% on savings, what will Bob and Carol give up (opportunity cost) over the 2 years if they pay cash?
e. What is the cost of the cash alternative at the end of 2 years?
f. Should Bob and Carol choose the financing or the cash alternative?

P15–6 **Cash discount decisions** Prairie Manufacturing has four possible suppliers, all of which offer different credit terms. Except for the differences in credit terms, their products and services are virtually identical. The credit terms offered by these suppliers are shown in the following table. (*Note:* Assume a 365-day year.)

Supplier	Credit terms
J	1/5 net 30 EOM
K	2/20 net 80 EOM
L	1/15 net 60 EOM
M	3/10 net 90 EOM

a. Calculate the *approximate cost of giving up the cash discount* from each supplier.
b. If the firm needs short-term funds, which are currently available from its commercial bank at 9%, and if each of the suppliers is viewed *separately*, which, if any, of the suppliers' cash discounts should the firm give up? Explain why.
c. Now assume that the firm could stretch by 30 days its accounts payable (net period only) from supplier M. What impact, if any, would that have on your answer in part **b** relative to this supplier?

LG2   **P15–7**   **Changing payment cycle**   On accepting the position of chief executive officer and chairman of Muse, Inc., Dominic Howard changed the firm's weekly payday from Monday afternoon to the following Friday afternoon. The firm's weekly payroll was $100 million, and the cost of short-term funds was 5%. If the effect of this change was to delay check clearing by 1 week, what *annual* savings, if any, were realized?

LG2   **P15–8**   **Spontaneous sources of funds, accruals**   When Tallman Haberdashery, Inc., merged with Meyers Men's Suits, Inc., Tallman's employees were switched from a weekly to a biweekly pay period. Tallman's weekly payroll amounted to $750,000. The cost of funds for the combined firms is 11%. What annual savings, if any, are realized by this change of pay period?

LG3   **P15–9**   **Cost of bank loan**   Data Back-Up Systems has obtained a $10,000, 90-day bank loan at an annual interest rate of 15%, payable at maturity. (*Note:* Assume a 365-day year.)
a. How much interest (in dollars) will the firm pay on the 90-day loan?
b. Find the *90-day rate* on the loan.
c. Annualize your result in part **b** to find the *effective annual rate* for this loan, assuming that it is rolled over every 90 days throughout the year under the same terms and circumstances.

Personal Finance Problem

LG3   **P15–10**   **Unsecured sources of short-term loans**   John Savage has obtained a short-term loan from First Carolina Bank. The loan matures in 180 days and is in the amount of $45,000. John needs the money to cover start-up costs in a new business. He hopes to have sufficient backing from other investors in 6 months. First Carolina Bank offers John two financing options for the $45,000 loan: a *fixed-rate loan* at 2.5% above prime rate or a *variable-rate loan* at 1.5% above prime.

Currently, the prime rate of interest is 6.5%, and the consensus interest rate forecast of a group of economists is as follows: Sixty days from today the prime rate will rise by 0.5%; 90 days from today the prime rate will rise another 1%; 180 days from today the prime rate will drop by 0.5%.

Using the forecast prime rate changes, answer the following questions.
a. Calculate the total interest cost over 180 days for a *fixed-rate loan*.
b. Calculate the total interest cost over 180 days for a *variable-rate loan*.
c. Which is the lower-interest-cost loan for the next 180 days?

LG3   **P15–11**   **Effective annual rate**   A financial institution made a $4 million, 1-year discount loan at 6% interest, requiring a compensating balance equal to 5% of the face value of the loan. Determine the *effective annual rate* associated with this loan. (*Note:* Assume that the firm currently maintains $0 on deposit in the financial institution.)

LG3   **P15–12**   **Compensating balances and effective annual rates**   Lincoln Industries has a line of credit at Bank Two that requires it to pay 11% interest on its borrowing and to maintain a compensating balance equal to 15% of the amount borrowed. The firm has borrowed $800,000 during the year under the agreement.
a. Calculate the *effective annual rate* on the firm's borrowing if the firm normally maintains no deposit balances at Bank Two.

b. Calculate the *effective annual rate* on the firm's borrowing if the firm normally maintains $70,000 in deposit balances at Bank Two.

c. Calculate the *effective annual rate* on the firm's borrowing if the firm normally maintains $150,000 in deposit balances at Bank Two.

d. Compare, contrast, and discuss your findings in parts **a**, **b**, and **c**.

LG 3 **P15–13** **Compensating balance versus discount loan** Weathers Catering Supply, Inc., needs to borrow $150,000 for 6 months. State Bank has offered to lend the funds at a 9% annual rate subject to a 10% compensating balance. (*Note:* Weathers currently maintains $0 on deposit in State Bank.) Frost Finance Co. has offered to lend the funds at a 9% annual rate with discount-loan terms. The principal of both loans would be payable at maturity as a single sum.

a. Calculate the *effective annual rate of interest* on each loan.

b. What could Weathers do that would reduce the effective annual rate on the State Bank loan?

LG 3 **P15–14** **Integrative: Comparison of loan terms** Cumberland Furniture wishes to establish a prearranged borrowing agreement with a local commercial bank. The bank's terms for a line of credit are 3.30% over the prime rate, and each year the borrowing must be reduced to zero for a 30-day period. For an equivalent revolving credit agreement, the rate is 2.80% over prime with a commitment fee of 0.50% on the average unused balance. With both loans, the required compensating balance is equal to 20% of the amount borrowed. (*Note:* Cumberland currently maintains $0 on deposit at the bank.) The prime rate is currently 8%. Both agreements have $4 million borrowing limits. The firm expects on average to borrow $2 million during the year no matter which loan agreement it decides to use.

a. What is the *effective annual rate* under the line of credit?

b. What is the *effective annual rate* under the revolving credit agreement? (*Hint:* Compute the ratio of the dollars that the firm will pay in interest and commitment fees to the dollars that the firm will effectively have use of.)

c. If the firm does expect to borrow an average of half the amount available, which arrangement would you recommend for the borrower? Explain why.

LG 4 **P15–15** **Cost of commercial paper** Commercial paper is usually sold at a discount. Fan Corporation has just sold an issue of 90-day commercial paper with a face value of $1 million. The firm has received initial proceeds of $978,000. (*Note:* Assume a 365-day year.)

a. What *effective annual rate* will the firm pay for financing with commercial paper, assuming that it is rolled over every 90 days throughout the year?

b. If a brokerage fee of $9,612 was paid from the initial proceeds to an investment banker for selling the issue, what *effective annual rate* will the firm pay, assuming that the paper is rolled over every 90 days throughout the year?

LG 5 **P15–16** **Accounts receivable as collateral** Kansas City Castings (KCC) is attempting to obtain the maximum loan possible using accounts receivable as collateral. The firm extends net-30-day credit. The amounts that are owed KCC by its 12 credit customers, the average age of each account, and the customer's average payment period are as shown in the following table.

Customer	Account receivable	Average age of account	Average payment period of customer
A	$37,000	40 days	30 days
B	42,000	25	50
C	15,000	40	60
D	8,000	30	35
E	50,000	31	40
F	12,000	28	30
G	24,000	30	70
H	46,000	29	40
I	3,000	30	65
J	22,000	25	35
K	62,000	35	40
L	80,000	60	70

a. If the bank will accept all accounts that can be collected in 45 days or less as long as the customer has a history of paying within 45 days, which accounts will be acceptable? What is the total dollar amount of accounts receivable collateral? (*Note:* Accounts receivable that have an average age greater than the customer's average payment period are also excluded.)

b. In addition to the conditions in part **a**, the bank recognizes that 5% of credit sales will be lost to returns and allowances. Also, the bank will lend only 80% of the acceptable collateral (after adjusting for returns and allowances). What level of funds would be made available through this lending source?

 P15–17 **Accounts receivable as collateral** Springer Products wishes to borrow $80,000 from a local bank using its accounts receivable to secure the loan. The bank's policy is to accept as collateral any accounts that are normally paid within 30 days of the end of the credit period as long as the average age of the account is not greater than the customer's average payment period. Springer's accounts receivable, their average ages, and the average payment period for each customer are shown in the following table. The company extends terms of net 30 days.

Customer	Account receivable	Average age of account	Average payment period of customer
A	$20,000	10 days	40 days
B	6,000	40	35
C	22,000	62	50
D	11,000	68	65
E	2,000	14	30
F	12,000	38	50
G	27,000	55	60
H	19,000	20	35

a. Calculate the dollar amount of acceptable accounts receivable collateral held by Springer Products.
b. The bank reduces collateral by 10% for returns and allowances. What is the level of acceptable collateral under this condition?
c. The bank will advance 75% against the firm's acceptable collateral (after adjusting for returns and allowances). What amount can Springer borrow against these accounts?

LG 3 **LG 5** **P15–18** **Accounts receivable as collateral, cost of borrowing** Maximum Bank has analyzed the accounts receivable of Scientific Software, Inc. The bank has chosen eight accounts totaling $134,000 that it will accept as collateral. The bank's terms include a lending rate set at prime plus 3% and a 2% commission charge. The prime rate currently is 8.5%.
a. The bank will adjust the accounts by 10% for returns and allowances. It then will lend up to 85% of the adjusted acceptable collateral. What is the maximum amount that the bank will lend to Scientific Software?
b. What is Scientific Software's *effective annual rate of interest* if it borrows $100,000 for 12 months? For 6 months? For 3 months? (*Note:* Assume a 365-day year and a prime rate that remains at 8.5% during the life of the loan.)

LG 5 **P15–19** **Factoring** Blair Finance factors the accounts of the Holder Company. All eight factored accounts are shown in the following table, with the amount factored, the date due, and the status on May 30. Indicate the amounts that Blair should have remitted to Holder as of May 30 and the dates of those remittances. Assume that the factor's commission of 2% is deducted as part of determining the amount of the remittance.

Account	Amount	Date due	Status on May 30
A	$200,000	May 30	Collected May 15
B	90,000	May 30	Uncollected
C	110,000	May 30	Uncollected
D	85,000	June 15	Collected May 30
E	120,000	May 30	Collected May 27
F	180,000	June 15	Collected May 30
G	90,000	May 15	Uncollected
H	30,000	June 30	Collected May 30

LG 1 **LG 6** **P15–20** **Inventory financing** Raymond Manufacturing faces a liquidity crisis: It needs a loan of $100,000 for 1 month. Having no source of additional unsecured borrowing, the firm must find a secured short-term lender. The firm's accounts receivable are quite low, but its inventory is considered liquid and reasonably good collateral. The book value of the inventory is $300,000, of which $120,000 is finished goods. (*Note:* Assume a 365-day year.)
(1) City-Wide Bank will make a $100,000 *trust receipt* loan against the finished goods inventory. The annual interest rate on the loan is 12% on the outstanding loan balance plus a 0.25% administration fee levied against the $100,000 initial loan amount. Because it will be liquidated as inventory is sold, the average amount owed over the month is expected to be $75,000.

(2) Sun State Bank will lend $100,000 against a *floating lien* on the book value of inventory for the 1-month period at an annual interest rate of 13%.

(3) Citizens' Bank and Trust will lend $100,000 against a *warehouse receipt* on the finished goods inventory and charge 15% annual interest on the outstanding loan balance. A 0.5% warehousing fee will be levied against the average amount borrowed. Because the loan will be liquidated as inventory is sold, the average loan balance is expected to be $60,000.

a. Calculate the dollar cost of each of the proposed plans for obtaining an initial loan amount of $100,000.

b. Which plan do you recommend? Why?

c. If the firm had made a purchase of $100,000 for which it had been given terms of 2/10 net 30, would it increase the firm's profitability to give up the discount and not borrow as recommended in part **b**? Why or why not?

 P15–21 **ETHICS PROBLEM** Rancco, Inc., reported total sales of $73 million last year, including $13 million in revenue (labor, sales to tax-exempt entities) exempt from sales tax. The company collects sales tax at a rate of 5%. In reviewing its information as part of its loan application, you notice that Rancco's sales tax payments show a total of $2 million in payments over the same time period. What are your conclusions regarding the financial statements that you are reviewing? How might you verify any discrepancies?

Spreadsheet Exercise

Your company is considering manufacturing protective cases for a popular new smartphone. Management decides to borrow $200,000 from each of two banks, First American and First Citizen. On the day that you visit both banks, the quoted prime interest rate is 7%. Each loan is similar in that each involves a 60-day note, with interest to be paid at the end of 60 days.

The interest rate was set at 2% above the prime rate on First American's *fixed-rate note*. Over the 60-day period, the rate of interest on this note will remain at the 2% premium over the prime rate regardless of fluctuations in the prime rate.

First Citizen sets its interest rate at 1.5% above the prime rate on its *floating-rate note*. The rate charged over the 60 days will vary directly with the prime rate.

TO DO

Create a spreadsheet to calculate and analyze the following for the First American loan:

a. Calculate the total dollar interest cost on the loan. Assume a 365-day year.

b. Calculate the *60-day rate* on the loan.

c. Assume that the loan is rolled over each 60 days throughout the year under identical conditions and terms. Calculate the *effective annual rate of interest* on the fixed-rate, 60-day First American note.

Next, create a spreadsheet to calculate the following for the First Citizen loan:

d. Calculate the initial interest rate.

e. Assuming that the prime rate immediately jumps to 7.5% and after 30 days it drops to 7.25%, calculate the interest rate for the first 30 days and the second 30 days of the loan.

f. Calculate the total dollar interest cost.

g. Calculate the *60-day rate of interest*.

h. Assume that the loan is rolled over each 60 days throughout the year under the same conditions and terms. Calculate the *effective annual rate of interest*.

i. Which loan would you choose, and why?

MyFinanceLab Visit www.myfinancelab.com for **Chapter Case: *Selecting Kanton Company's Financing Strategy and Unsecured Short-Term Borrowing Arrangement,*** Group Exercises, and numerous online resources.

Chapter 1

ST1–1

Accounting view (accrual basis)		Financial view (cash basis)	
Worldwide Rugs income statement for the year ended 12/31		Worldwide Rugs cash flow statement for the year ended 12/31	
Sales revenue	$3,000,000	Cash inflow	$2,550,000
Less: Costs	2,500,000	Less: Cash outflow	2,500,000
Net profit	$ 500,000	Net cash flow	$ 50,000

a. $3,000,000 − $2,500,000 = $500,000

b. Yes, from an accounting perspective Worldwide Rug was profitable. It generated a 20% profit ($500,000/$2,500,000 = 0.20) on its investment.

c. $2,550,000 − $2,500,000 = $50,000

d. It generated a positive cash flow, but it only represents a 2% return on investment ($50,000/$2,500,000 = 0.02), and it may not be enough to cover operating costs.

e. Given the risk associated with importing and Worldwide Rug's ability to collect on its accounts receivables, a 2% return on investment seems unlikely to lead to long-term success. Without adequate cash inflows to meet its obligations, the firm will not survive, regardless of its level of profits.

Chapter 2

ST2–1

a. Capital gains = $180,000 sale price − $150,000 original purchase price = $30,000

b. Total taxable income = $280,000 operating earnings + $30,000 capital gain = $310,000

   c. Firm's tax liability:

   Using Table 2.1:

$$\text{Total taxes due} = \$22{,}250 + [0.39 \times (\$310{,}000 - \$100{,}000)]$$
$$= \$22{,}250 + (0.39 \times \$210{,}000) = \$22{,}250 + \$81{,}900$$
$$= \underline{\$104{,}150}$$

   d. $\text{Average tax rate} = \dfrac{\$104{,}150}{\$310{,}000} = \underline{33.6\%}$

     $\text{Marginal tax rate} = \underline{39\%}$

Chapter 3

ST3–1

Ratio	Too high	Too low
Current ratio = current assets/ current liabilities	May indicate that the firm is holding excessive cash, accounts receivable, or inventory.	May indicate poor ability to satisfy short-term obligations.
Inventory turnover = CGS/inventory	May indicate lower level of inventory, which may cause stockouts and lost sales.	May indicate poor inventory management, excessive inventory, or obsolete inventory.
Times interest earned = earnings before interest and taxes/interest		May indicate poor ability to pay contractual interest payments.
Gross profit margin = gross profits/sales	Indicates the low cost of merchandise sold relative to the sales price; may indicate non-competitive pricing and potential lost sales.	Indicates the high cost of the merchandise sold relative to the sales price; may indicate either a low sales price or a high cost of goods sold.
Return on total assets = profits after taxes/ total assets		Indicates ineffective management in generating profits with the available assets.
Price/earnings (P/E) ratio = market price per share of common stock/earnings per share	Investors may have an excessive degree of confidence in the firm's future and underestimate its risk.	Investors lack confidence in the firm's future outcomes and believe that the firm has an excessive level of risk.

ST3–2

O'Keefe Industries
Balance Sheet
December 31, 2015

Assets		Liabilities and stockholders' equity	
Cash	$ 32,720	Accounts payable	$ 120,000
Marketable securities	25,000	Notes payable	160,000[e]
Accounts receivable	197,280[a]	Accruals	20,000
Inventories	225,000[b]	Total current liabilities	$ 300,000[d]
Total current assets	$ 480,000	Long-term debt	$ 600,000[f]
Net fixed assets	$1,020,000[c]	Stockholders' equity	$ 600,000
Total assets	$1,500,000	Total liabilities and stockholders' equity	$1,500,000

[a]Average collection period (ACP) = 40 days
ACP = Accounts receivable/Average sales per day
$40 = $ Accounts receivable/($1,800,000/365)
$40 = $ Accounts receivable/$4,932
$197,280 = $ Accounts receivable

[b]Inventory turnover = 6.0
Inventory turnover = Cost of goods sold/Inventory
$6.0 = [$Sales $\times$ (1 − Gross profit margin)]/Inventory
$6.0 = [$1,800,000 \times (1 − 0.25)]/$Inventory
$225,000 = $ Inventory

[c]Total asset turnover = 1.20
Total asset turnover = Sales/Total assets
$1.20 = $1,800,000/$Total assets
$1,500,000 = $ Total assets
Total assets = Current assets + Net fixed assets
$1,500,000 = $480,000 + $ Net fixed assets
$1,020,000 = $ Net fixed assets

[d]Current ratio = 1.60
Current ratio = Current assets/Current liabilities
$1.60 = $480,000/$Current liabilities
$300,000 = $ Current liabilities

[e]Notes Payable $=$ Total current liabilities $-$ Accounts payable $-$ Accruals
$= $300,000 − $120,000 − $20,000$
$= $160,000$

[f]Debt ratio = 0.60
Debt ratio = Total liabilities/Total assets
$0.60 = $ Total liabilities/$1,500,000
$900,000 = $ Total liabilities

Total liabilities $=$ Current liabilities $+$ Long-term debt
$900,000 = $300,000 + $ Long-term debt
$600,000 = $ Long-term debt

Chapter 4

ST4–1 a. Depreciation schedule:

Year	Cost[a] (1)	Percentages (from Table 4.2) (2)	Depreciation [(1)×(2)] (3)
1	$150,000	20%	$ 30,000
2	150,000	32	48,000
3	150,000	19	28,500
4	150,000	12	18,000
5	150,000	12	18,000
6	150,000	5	7,500
Totals		100%	$150,000

[a]$140,000 asset cost + $10,000 installation cost.

b. Operating cash flow:

Year	EBIT (1)	NOPAT [(1) × (1 − 0.40)] (2)	Depreciation (3)	Operating cash flows [(2) + (3)] (4)
1	$160,000	$96,000	$30,000	$126,000
2	160,000	96,000	48,000	144,000
3	160,000	96,000	28,500	124,500
4	160,000	96,000	18,000	114,000
5	160,000	96,000	18,000	114,000
6	160,000	96,000	7,500	103,500

c. Change in net fixed assets in year 6 = $0 − $7,500 = −$7,500

NFAI in year 6 = −$7,500 + $7,500 = $0

Change in current assets in year 6 = $110,000 − $90,000 = $20,000

Change in (Accounts payable + Accruals) in year 6 = ($ 45,000 + $7,000) − ($40,000 + $8,000) = $52,000 − $48,000 = $4,000

NCAI in year 6 = $20,000 − $4,000 = $16,000

For year 6

FCF = OCF − NFAI − NCAI

     = $103,500* − $0 − $16,000 = <u>$87,500</u>

*From part **b,** column 4 value for year 6.

d. In part **b,** we can see that, in each of the 6 years, the operating cash flow is positive, which means that the firm is generating cash that it could use to invest in fixed assets or working capital, or it could distribute some of the cash flow to investors by paying interest or dividends. The free cash flow (FCF) calculated in part **c** for year 6 represents the cash flow available to investors—providers of debt and equity—after covering all operating needs and paying for net fixed asset investment (NFAI) and net current asset investment (NCAI) that occurred during the year.

ST4–2 a.

	Carroll Company Cash Budget April–June					Accounts receivable at end of June	
	February	March	April	May	June	July	August
Forecast sales	$500	$600	$400	$200	$200		
Cash sales (0.30)	$150	$180	$120	$60	$60		
Collections of A/R							
Lagged 1 month [(0.7 × 0.7) = 0.49]		245	294	196	98	$98	
Lagged 2 months [(0.3 × 0.7) = 0.21]			105	126	84	42	$42
						$140 + $42 = $182	
Total cash receipts			$519	$382	$242		
Less: Total cash disbursements			600	500	200		
Net cash flow			($81)	($118)	$42		
Add: Beginning cash			115	34	(84)		
Ending cash			$34	($84)	($42)		
Less: Minimum cash balance			25	25	25		
Required total financing (notes payable)			—	$109	$67		
Excess cash balance (marketable securities)			$9	—	—		

b. Carroll Company would need a maximum of $109 in financing over the 3-month period.

c.

Account	Amount	Source of amount
Cash	$25	Minimum cash balance—June
Notes payable	67	Required total financing—June
Marketable securities	0	Excess cash balance—June
Accounts receivable	182	Calculation at right of cash budget statement

ST4–3 a.

Euro Designs, Inc., Pro Forma Income Statement for the Year Ended December 31, 2016	
Sales revenue (given)	$3,900,000
Less: Cost of goods sold (0.55)[a]	2,145,000
Gross profits	$1,755,000
Less: Operating expenses (0.12)[b]	468,000
Operating profits	$1,287,000
Less: Interest expense (given)	325,000
Net profits before taxes	$962,000
Less: Taxes (0.40 × $962,000)	384,800
Net profits after taxes	$577,200
Less: Cash dividends (given)	320,000
To retained earnings	$257,200

[a]From 2012: CGS/Sales = $1,925,000/$3,500,000 = 0.55.
[b]From 2012: Oper. Exp./Sales = $420,000/$3,500,000 = 0.12.

b. The percent-of-sales method may underestimate actual 2016 pro forma income by assuming that all costs are variable. If the firm has fixed costs, which by definition would not increase with increasing sales, the 2016 pro forma income would probably be underestimated.

Chapter 5

ST5–1 a. *Bank A:*

$$FV_3 = \$10,000 \times (1 + 0.04)^3 = \$10,000 \times 1.125 = \underline{\$11,250}$$

(Calculator solution = $11,248.64)

Bank B:

$$FV_3 = \$10,000 \times (1 + 0.04/2)^6 = \$10,000 \times 1.126 = \underline{\$11,260}$$

(Calculator solution = $11,261.62)

Bank C:

$$FV_3 = \$10,000 \times (1 + 0.04/4)^{12} = \$10,000 \times 1.127 = \underline{\$11,270}$$

(Calculator solution = $11,268.25)

b. *Bank A:*

$$EAR = (1 + 0.04/1)^1 - 1 = (1 + 0.04)^1 - 1 = 1.04 - 1 = 0.04 = \underline{4\%}$$

Bank B:

$$EAR = (1 + 0.04/2)^2 - 1 = (1 + 0.02)^2 - 1$$
$$= 1.0404 - 1 = 0.0404 = \underline{4.04\%}$$

Bank C:

$$EAR = (1 + 0.04/4)^4 - 1 = (1 + 0.01)^4 - 1 = 1.0406 - 1$$
$$= 0.0406 = \underline{4.06\%}$$

c. Ms. Martin should deal with Bank C: The quarterly compounding of interest at the given 4% rate results in the highest future value as a result of the corresponding highest effective annual rate.

d. *Bank D:*

$$FV_3 = \$10,000 \times e^{0.04 \times 3} = \$10,000 \times e^{0.12}$$
$$= \$10,000 \times 1.127497 = \underline{\$11,274.97}$$

This alternative is better than Bank C; it results in a higher future value because of the use of continuous compounding, which with otherwise identical cash flows always results in the highest future value of any compounding period.

ST5–2 a. On the surface, annuity Y looks more attractive than annuity X because it provides $1,000 more each year than does annuity X. Of course, X being an annuity due means that the $9,000 would be received at the beginning of each year, unlike the $10,000 at the end of each year, and this fact makes annuity X more appealing than it otherwise would be.

b. *Annuity X:*

$$FV_6 = \$9,000 \times \{ [(1 + 0.15)^6 - 1]/0.15 \} \times (1 + 0.15)$$
$$= \$9,000 \times 8.754 \times 1.15 = \underline{\$90,603.90}$$

(Calculator solution = $90,601.19)

Annuity Y:

$$FV_6 = \$10,000 \times \{[(1 + 0.15)^6 - 1]/0.15\}$$
$$= \$10,000 \times 8.754 = \underline{\$87,540.00}$$

(Calculator solution = $87,537.38)

c. Annuity X is more attractive because its future value at the end of year 6, FV_6, of $90,603.90 is greater than annuity Y's end-of-year-6 future value, FV_6, of $87,540.00. The subjective assessment in part a was incorrect. The benefit of receiving annuity X's cash inflows at the beginning of each year appears to have outweighed the fact that annuity Y's annual cash inflow, which occurs at the end of each year, is $1,000 larger ($10,000 vs. $9,000) than annuity X's.

ST5–3   *Alternative A:*

Cash flow stream:

$$PV_5 = \$700/0.09 \times [1 - 1/(1 + 0.09)^5]$$
$$= \$700/0.09 \times 0.350 = \underline{\$2,723}$$

(Calculator solution = $2,722.76)

Single amount: $\underline{\$2,825}$

Alternative B:

Cash flow stream:

Year (n)	Present value calculation	Present value
1	$1,100/(1 + 0.09) =	$1,009.17
2	900/(1 + 0.09)² =	757.51
3	700/(1 + 0.09)³ =	540.53
4	500/(1 + 0.09)⁴ =	354.21
5	300/(1 + 0.09)⁵ =	194.98
	Present value	$2,856.40

(Calculator solution = $2,856.41)

Single amount: $\underline{\$2,800}$

Conclusion: Alternative B in the form of a cash flow stream is preferred because its present value of $2,856.40 is greater than the other three values.

ST5–4

$$CF = \$8,000/\{[(1 + 0.07)^5 - 1]/0.07\}$$
$$CF = \$8,000/5.751$$
$$CF = \$1,391.06$$

(Calculator solution = $1,391.13)

Judi should deposit $1,391.06 at the end of each of the 5 years to meet her goal of accumulating $8,000 at the end of the fifth year.

Chapter 6

ST6–1 **a.** $B_0 = I/r_d \times [1 - 1/(1 + r_d)^n] + M \times 1/(1 + r_d)^n$

$I = 0.08 \times \$1,000 = \$80$

$M = \$1,000$

$n = 12$ yrs

1. $r_d = 7\%$

$B_0 = \$80/0.07 \times [1 - 1/(1 + 0.07)^{12}] + \$1,000 \times 1/(1 + 0.07)^{12}$

$\qquad = (\$1,142.86 \times 0.556) + (\$1,000 \times 0.444)$

$\qquad = \$635.43 + \$444.00 = \underline{\$1,079.43}$

(Calculator solution = $1,079.43)

2. $r_d = 8\%$

$B_0 = \$80/0.08 \times [1 - 1/(1 + 0.08)^{12}] + \$1,000 \times 1/(1 + 0.08)^{12}$

$\qquad = (\$1,000 \times 0.603) + (\$1,000 \times 0.397)$

$\qquad = \$603.00 + \$397.00 = \underline{\$1,000.00}$

(Calculator solution = $1,000.00)

3. $r_d = 10\%$

$B_0 = \$80/0.10 \times [1 - 1/(1 + 0.10)^{12}] + \$1,000 \times 1/(1 + 0.10)^{12}$

$\qquad = (\$800 \times 0.681) + (\$1,000 \times 0.319)$

$\qquad = \$544.80 + \$319.00 = \underline{\$863.80}$

(Calculator solution = $863.73)

b. **1.** $r_d = 7\%$, $B_0 = \$1,079.43$; sells at a *premium*

2. $r_d = 8\%$, $B_0 = \$1,000.00$; sells at its *par value*

3. $r_d = 10\%$, $B_0 = \$863.80$; sells at a *discount*

c. $B_0 = (I/2)/r_d \times [1 - 1/(1 + r_d/2)^{2n}] + M \times 1/(1 + r_d/2)^{2n}$

$\qquad = (\$80/2)/(0.10/2) \times [1 - 1/(1 + 0.10/2)^{24}]$

$\qquad\quad + \$1,000 \times 1/(1 + 0.10/2)^{24}$

$\qquad = \$800 \times 0.690 + \$1,000 \times 0.310$

$\qquad = \$552.00 + \$310.00 = \underline{\$862.00}$

(Calculator solution = $862.01)

ST6–2 **a.** $B_0 = \$1,150$

$I = 0.11 \times \$1,000 = \$110$ $\qquad$ Current yield $= \dfrac{\text{annual interest}}{\text{current price}}$

$M = \$1,000$

$n = 18$ yrs $\qquad\qquad\qquad\qquad\qquad = \dfrac{\$110}{\$1,150} = 9.57\%$

b. $1,150 = \$110/r_d \times [1 - 1/(1 + r_d)^{18}] + \$1,000 \times 1/(1 + r_d)^{18}$

Because if $r_d = 11\%$, $B_0 = \$1,000 = M$, try $r_d = 10\%$.

$$B_0 = \$110/0.10 \times [1 - 1/(1 + 0.10)^{18}] + \$1,000 \times 1/(1 + 0.10)^{18}$$
$$= (\$1,100 \times 0.820) + (\$1,000 \times 0.180)$$
$$= \$902.00 + \$180.00 = \$1,082.00$$

Because $1,082.00 < \$1,150$, try $r_d = 9\%$.

$$B_0 = \$110/0.09 \times [1 - 1/(1 + 0.09)^{18}] + \$1,000 \times 1/(1 + 0.09)^{18}$$
$$= (\$1,222.22 \times 0.788) + (\$1,000 \times 0.212)$$
$$= \$963.11 + \$212.00 = \$1,175.11$$

Because the $1,175.11 value at 9% is higher than $1,150 and the $1,082.00 value at the 10% rate is lower than $1,150, the bond's yield to maturity must be between 9% and 10%. Because the $1,175.11 value is closer to $1,150, by rounding to the nearest whole percent, the YTM is 9%. (By using interpolation, the more precise YTM value is 9.27%.)

(Calculator solution = 9.26%)

c. The YTM of 9.27% is below both the bond's 11% coupon interest rate and its current yield of 9.57% calculated in part **a** because the bond's market value of $1,150 is above its $1,000 par value. Whenever a bond's market value is above its par value (it sells at a *premium*), its YTM and current yield will be below its coupon interest rate; when a bond sells at *par*, the YTM and current yield will equal its coupon interest rate; and when the bond sells for less than par (at a *discount*), its YTM and current yield will be greater than its coupon interest rate. Observe also that the current yield measures the bond's coupon payment relative to its current price. When the bond sells at a premium, its YTM will be below its current yield because the YTM also takes into account that the bondholder will receive just $1,000 back at maturity, which represents a loss relative to the bond's current market price. In other words, the YTM is measuring both the value of the coupon payment that the investor receives (just like the current yield does) and the "loss" that the bondholder endures when the bond matures.

Chapter 7

ST7–1 $D_0 = \$1.80/\text{share}$

$r_s = 12\%$

a. *Zero growth:*
$$P_0 = \frac{D_1}{r_s} = \frac{D_1 = D_0 = \$1.80}{0.12} = \$15/\text{share}$$

b. *Constant growth, g = 5%:*

$D_1 = D_0 \times (1 + g) = \$1.80 \times (1 + 0.05) = \$1.89/\text{share}$

$$P_0 = \frac{D_1}{r_s - g} = \frac{\$1.89}{0.12 - 0.05} = \frac{\$1.89}{0.07} = \underline{\$27/\text{share}}$$

c. *Variable growth, N = 3, g_1 = 5% for years 1 to 3 and g_2 = 4% for years 4 to ∞:*

$$D_1 = D_0 \times (1 + g_1)^1 = \$1.80 \times (1 + 0.05)^1 = \$1.89/\text{share}$$
$$D_2 = D_0 \times (1 + g_1)^2 = \$1.80 \times (1 + 0.05)^2 = \$1.98/\text{share}$$
$$D_3 = D_0 \times (1 + g_1)^3 = \$1.80 \times (1 + 0.05)^3 = \$2.08/\text{share}$$
$$D_4 = D_3 \times (1 + g_2) = \$2.08 \times (1 + 0.04) = \$2.16/\text{share}$$

$$P_0 = \sum_{t=1}^{N} \frac{D_0 \times (1 + g_1)^t}{(1 + r_s)^t} + \left(\frac{1}{(1 + r_s)^N} \times \frac{D_{N+1}}{r_s - g_2} \right)$$

$$\sum_{t=1}^{N} \frac{D_0 \times (1 + g_1)^t}{(1 + r_s)^t} = \frac{1.89}{(1 + 0.12)^1} + \frac{1.98}{(1 + 0.12)^2} + \frac{2.08}{(1 + 0.12)^3}$$

$$= \$1.69 + \$1.58 + \$1.48 = \$4.75$$

$$\left[\frac{1}{(1 + r_s)^N} \times \frac{D_{N+1}}{r_s - g_2} \right] = \frac{1}{(1 + 0.12)^3} \times \frac{D_4 = \$2.16}{0.12 - 0.04}$$

$$= 0.712 \times \$27.00 = \$19.22$$

$$P_0 = \sum_{t=1}^{N} \frac{D_0 \times (1 + g_1)^t}{(1 + r_s)^t} + \left[\frac{1}{(1 + r_s)^N} \times \frac{D_{N+1}}{r_s - g_2} \right] = \$4.75 + \$19.22$$

$$= \$23.97/\text{share}$$

ST7–2 a. **Step 1:** Present value of free cash flow from end of 2020 to infinity measured at the end of 2019:

$$FCF_{2020} = \$1,500,000 \times (1 + 0.04) = \$1,560,000$$

$$\text{Value of } FCF_{2020 \to \infty} = \frac{\$1,560,000}{0.10 - 0.04} = \frac{\$1,560,000}{0.06} = \$26,000,000$$

Step 2: Add the value found in Step 1 to the 2019 FCF.

Total FCF_{2019} = \$1,500,000 + \$26,000,000 = $\underline{\$27,500,000}$

Step 3: Find the sum of the present values of the FCFs for 2016 through 2019 to determine company value, VC.

Year (*t*)	Present value calculation	Present value of FCF_t
2016	$ 800,000/(1 + 0.10) =	$ 727,272.73
2017	1,200,000/(1 + 0.10)² =	991,735.54
2018	1,400,000/(1 + 0.10)³ =	1,051,840.72
2019	27,500,000/(1 + 0.10)⁴ =	18,782,870.02
	Value of entire company, V_C =	$21,553,719.01

(Calculator solution = \$21,553,719.01)

b. Common Stock value, $V_S = V_C - V_D - V_P$

V_C = \$21,553,719.01 (calculated in part **a**)

V_D = \$12,500,000 (given)

$V_P = \$0$ (given)

$V_S = \$21,553,719.01 - \$12,500,000 - \$0 = \underline{\$9,053,719.01}$

(Calculator solution $= \$9,053,719.01$)

c. Price per share $= \dfrac{\$9,053,719.01}{500,000} = \underline{\$18.11/\text{share}}$

(Calculator solution $= \$18.11/\text{share}$)

Chapter 8

ST8–1 a. Expected return, $\bar{r} = \dfrac{\sum \text{Returns}}{3}$

$\bar{r}_A = \dfrac{12\% + 14\% + 16\%}{3} = \dfrac{42\%}{3} = \underline{\underline{14\%}}$

$\bar{r}_B = \dfrac{16\% + 14\% + 12\%}{3} = \dfrac{42\%}{3} = \underline{\underline{14\%}}$

$\bar{r}_C = \dfrac{12\% + 14\% + 16\%}{3} = \dfrac{42\%}{3} = \underline{\underline{14\%}}$

b. Standard deviation, $\sigma_r = \sqrt{\dfrac{\sum\limits_{j=1}^{n}(r_i - \bar{r})^2}{n-1}}$

$\sigma_{r_A} = \sqrt{\dfrac{(12\% - 14\%)^2 + (14\% - 14\%)^2 + (16\% - 14\%)^2}{3-1}}$

$= \sqrt{\dfrac{4\% + 0\% + 4\%}{2}} = \sqrt{\dfrac{8\%}{2}} = \underline{\underline{2\%}}$

$\sigma_{r_B} = \sqrt{\dfrac{(16\% - 14\%)^2 + (14\% - 14\%)^2 + (12\% - 14\%)^2}{3-1}}$

$= \sqrt{\dfrac{4\% + 0\% + 4\%}{2}} = \sqrt{\dfrac{8\%}{2}} = \underline{\underline{2\%}}$

$\sigma_{r_C} = \sqrt{\dfrac{(12\% - 14\%)^2 + (14\% - 14\%)^2 + (16\% - 14\%)^2}{3-1}}$

$= \sqrt{\dfrac{4\% + 0\% + 4\%}{2}} = \sqrt{\dfrac{8\%}{2}} = \underline{\underline{2\%}}$

c.

	Annual expected returns	
Year	Portfolio AB	Portfolio AC
2016	$(0.50 \times 12\%) + (0.50 \times 16\%) = 14\%$	$(0.50 \times 12\%) + (0.50 \times 12\%) = 12\%$
2017	$(0.50 \times 14\%) + (0.50 \times 14\%) = 14\%$	$(0.50 \times 14\%) + (0.50 \times 14\%) = 14\%$
2018	$(0.50 \times 16\%) + (0.50 \times 12\%) = 14\%$	$(0.50 \times 16\%) + (0.50 \times 16\%) = 16\%$

Over the 3-year period:

$$\bar{r}_{AB} = \frac{14\% + 14\% + 14\%}{3} = \frac{42\%}{3} = \underline{\underline{14\%}}$$

$$\bar{r}_{AC} = \frac{12\% + 14\% + 16\%}{3} = \frac{42\%}{3} = \underline{\underline{14\%}}$$

d. AB is perfectly negatively correlated.

AC is perfectly positively correlated.

e. Standard deviation of the portfolios:

$$\sigma_{r_{AB}} = \sqrt{\frac{(14\% - 14\%)^2 + (14\% - 14\%)^2 + (14\% - 14\%)^2}{3 - 1}}$$

$$= \sqrt{\frac{(0\% + 0\% + 0\%)}{2}} = \sqrt{\frac{0\%}{2}} = \underline{\underline{0\%}}$$

$$\sigma_{r_{AC}} = \sqrt{\frac{(12\% - 14\%)^2 + (14\% - 14\%)^2 + (16\% - 14\%)^2}{3 - 1}}$$

$$= \sqrt{\frac{4\% + 0\% + 4\%}{2}} = \sqrt{\frac{8\%}{2}} = \underline{\underline{2\%}}$$

f. Portfolio AB is preferred because it provides the same return (14%) as AC but with less risk $[(\sigma_{r_{AB}} = 0\%) < (\sigma_{r_{AC}} = 2\%)]$.

ST8–2 a. When the market return increases by 10%, the investment's return would be expected to increase by 15% (1.50 × 10%). When the market return decreases by 10%, the investment's return would be expected to decrease by 15% [1.50 × (−10%)].

b. $r_j = R_F + [\beta_j \times (r_m - R_F)]$

   $= 7\% + [1.50 \times (10\% - 7\%)]$

   $= 7\% + 4.5\% = \underline{\underline{11.5\%}}$

c. No, the investment should be rejected because its *expected* return of 11% is less than the 11.5% return *required* from the investment.

d. $r_j = 7\% + [1.50 \times (9\% - 7\%)]$

   $= 7\% + 3\% = \underline{\underline{10\%}}$

   The investment would now be acceptable because its *expected* return of 11% is now in excess of the *required* return, which has declined to 10% as a result of investors in the marketplace becoming less risk averse.

Chapter 9

ST9–1 a. Cost of debt, r_i (using approximation formula)

$$r_d = \frac{I + \dfrac{\$1,000 - N_d}{n}}{\dfrac{N_d + \$1,000}{2}}$$

$I = 0.10 \times \$1,000 = \$100$

$N_d = \$1,000 - \$30$ discount $- \$20$ flotation cost $= \$950$

$n = 10$ years

$$r_d = \frac{\$100 + \dfrac{\$1{,}000 - \$950}{10}}{\dfrac{\$950 + \$1{,}000}{2}} = \frac{\$100 + \$5}{\$975} = 10.8\%$$

(Calculator solution $= 10.8\%$)

$r_i = r_d \times (1 - T)$

$T = 0.40$

$r_i = 10.8\% \times (1 - 0.40) = \underline{6.5\%}$

Cost of preferred stock, r_p

$$r_p = \frac{D_p}{N_p}$$

$D_p = 0.11 \times \$100 = \$11$

$N_p = \$100 - \$4$ flotation cost $= \$96$

$$r_p = \frac{\$11}{\$96} = \underline{11.5\%}$$

Cost of retained earnings, r_r

$$r_r = r_s = \frac{D_1}{P_0} + g$$

$$= \frac{\$6}{\$80} + 6.0\% = 7.5\% + 6.0\% = \underline{13.5\%}$$

Cost of new common stock, r_n

$$r_n = \frac{D_1}{N_n} + g$$

$D_1 = \$6$

$N_n = \$80 - \$4$ underpricing $- \$4$ flotation cost $= \$72$

$g = 6.0\%$

$$r_n = \frac{\$6}{\$72} + 6.0\% = 8.3\% + 6.0\% = \underline{14.3\%}$$

b. WACC for total new financing $< \$500{,}000$. This level of new financing is obtained by using retained earnings, so the cost of common equity is equal to the cost of retained earnings.

Source of capital	Weight (1)	Cost (2)	Weighted cost [(1) × (2)] (3)
Long-term debt	0.40	6.5%	2.6%
Preferred stock	0.15	11.5	1.7
Common stock equity	0.45	13.5	6.1
Totals	1.00		10.4

Weighted average cost of capital $= 10.4\%$

WACC for total new financing > $500,000. This level of new financing requires the use of new common stock, so the cost of common equity is equal to the cost of new common stock.

Source of capital	Weight (1)	Cost (2)	Weighted cost [(1) × (2)] (3)
Long-term debt	0.40	6.5%	2.6%
Preferred stock	0.15	11.5	1.7
Common stock equity	0.45	14.3	6.4
Totals	1.00		10.7%

Weighted average cost of capital = 10.7%

c.

Investment opportunity	Internal rate of return (IRR)	Initial investment	Cumulative investment
D	16.5%	$200,000	$ 200,000
C	12.9	150,000	350,000
E	11.8	450,000	800,000
A	11.2	100,000	900,000
G	10.5	300,000	1,200,000
F	10.1	600,000	1,800,000
B	9.7	500,000	2,300,000

Projects D, C, E, and A should be accepted because their respective IRRs exceed the WMCC. They will require $900,000 of total new financing.

Chapter 10

ST10–1   a. Payback period:

Project M: $\dfrac{\$28,500}{\$10,000} = \underline{2.85}$ years

Project N:

Year (t)	Cash inflows (CF_t)	Cumulative cash inflows
1	$11,000	$11,000
2	10,000	21,000 ←
3	9,000	30,000
4	8,000	38,000

$2 + \dfrac{\$27,000 - \$21,000}{\$9,000}$ years

$2 + \dfrac{\$6,000}{\$9,000}$ years $= \underline{2.67}$ years

b. Net present value (NPV):

Project M: NPV = $\$10,000/0.14 \times [1 - 1/(1 + 0.14)^4] - \$28,500$
$= (\$71,428.57 \times 0.408) - \$28,500$
$= \$29,142.86 - \$28,500 = \underline{\$642.86}$

(Calculator solution = $637.12)
Project N:

Year (t)	Present value	Present values
1	$\$11,000/(1 + 0.14) =$	$ 9,649.12
2	$10,000/(1 + 0.14)^2 =$	7,694.68
3	$9,000/(1 + 0.14)^3 =$	6,074.74
4	$8,000/(1 + 0.14)^4 =$	4,736.64
	Present value of cash inflows	28,155.18
	− Initial investment	27,000.00
	Net present value (NPV)	$ 1,155.18

(Calculator solution = $1,155.18)

c. Internal rate of return (IRR):

Project M: NPV $= 0 = \$10,000/IRR \times [1 - 1/(1 + IRR)^4] - \$28,500$

Because a 14% discount rate results in a positive NPV of $637.12, the IRR must be greater than 14%, but not a lot greater. Guess 15%.

Project M: NPV $= \$10,000/0.15 \times [1 - 1/(1 + 0.15)^4] - \$28,500$
$= (\$66,666.67 \times 0.428) - \$28,500$
$= \$28,533.34 - \$28,500 = \underline{\$33.34}$
IRR $\approx \underline{15\%}$

(Calculator solution = 15.09%)

Project N: NPV $= 0 = 11,000/(1 + IRR) + 10,000/(1 + IRR)^2$
$+ 9,000/(1 + IRR)^3 + 8,000/(1 + IRR)^4 - 27,000$

Because a 14% discount rate results in a positive NPV of $1,155.18, the IRR must be greater than 14%. Guess 15%.

Project N: NPV $= 11,000/(1 + 0.15) + 10,000/(1 + 0.15)^2$
$+ 9,000/(1 + 0.15)^3 + 8,000/(1 + 0.15)^4 - 27,000$
$= 9,565.22 + 7,561.44 + 5,917.65 + 4,574.03 - 27,000$
$= \$618.34$

Because a 15% discount rate results in a positive NPV of $618.34, the IRR must be greater than 15%. Guess 16%.

Project N: NPV $= 11,000/(1 + 0.16) + 10,000/(1 + 0.16)^2$
$+ 9,000/(1 + 0.16)^3 + 8,000/(1 + 0.16)^4 - 27,000$
$= 9,482.76 + 7,431.63 + 5,765.92 + 4,418.33 - 27,000$
$= \$98.64$
IRR $\approx \underline{16\%}$

(Calculator solution = 16.19%)

d.

	Project	
	M	**N**
Payback period	2.85 years	2.67 years[a]
NPV	$642.86	$1,155.18[a]
IRR	15%	16%[a]

[a]Preferred project.

Project N is recommended because it has the shorter payback period and the higher NPV, which is greater than zero, and the larger IRR, which is greater than the 14% cost of capital.

e. Net present value profiles:

	NPV	
Discount rate	**Project M**	**Project N**
0%	$11,500[a]	$11,000[b]
14	642.86	1,155.18
15	0	—
16	—	0

[a]($10,000 + $10,000 + $10,000 + $ 10,000) − $ 28,500
= $40,000 − $28,500
= $ 11,500
[b]($11,000 + $10,000 + $9,000 + $8,000) − $27,000
= $38,000 − $ 27,000
= $11,000

From the NPV profile that follows, it can be seen that if the firm has a cost of capital below approximately 6% (exact value is 5.75%), conflicting rankings of the projects would exist using the NPV and IRR decision techniques. Because the firm's cost of capital is 14%, it can be seen in part **d** that no conflict exists.

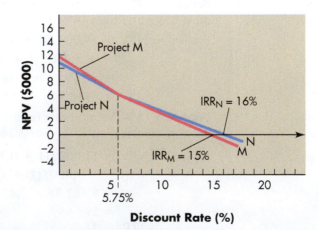

Chapter 11

ST11–1 a. Initial investment:

Installed cost of new machine	
Cost of new machine	$140,000
+ Installation costs	10,000
Total installed cost—new	$150,000
(depreciable value)	
− After-tax proceeds from sale of old machine	
Proceeds from sale of old machine	42,000
− Taxes on sale of old machine[1]	9,120
Total after-tax proceeds—old	$ 32,880
+ Change in net working capital[2]	20,000
Initial investment	$137,120

---

[1]Book value of old machine $= \$40,000 - (0.20 + 0.32) \times \$40,000$
$$= \$40,000 - (0.52 \times \$40,000)$$
$$= \$40,000 - \$20,800 = \$19,200$$

Gain on sale $= \$42,000 - \$19,200 = \$22,800$
    Taxes $= 0.40 \times \$22,800 = \underline{\$9,120}$

[2]Change in net working capital $= \$10,000 + \$25,000 - \$15,000$
$$= \$35,000 - \$15,000 = \underline{\$20,000}$$

b. Incremental operating cash inflows:

Calculation of Depreciation Expense

Year	Cost (1)	Applicable MACRS depreciation percentages (from Table 4.2) (2)	Depreciation [(1) × (2)] (3)
With new machine			
1	$150,000	33%	$ 49,500
2	150,000	45	67,500
3	150,000	15	22,500
4	150,000	7	10,500
		Totals 100%	$150,000
With old machine			
1	$ 40,000	19% (year-3 depreciation)	$ 7,600
2	40,000	12 (year-4 depreciation)	4,800
3	40,000	12 (year-5 depreciation)	4,800
4	40,000	5 (year-6 depreciation)	2,000
			Total $19,200[a]

[a]The total of $19,200 represents the book value of the old machine at the end of the second year, which was calculated in part a.

Calculation of Operating Cash Inflows

	Year			
	1	2	3	4
With new machine				
Earnings before depr., int., and taxes[a]	$120,000	$130,000	$130,000	$ 0
− Depreciation[b]	49,500	67,500	22,500	10,500
Earnings before int. and taxes	$ 70,500	$ 62,500	$107,500	($10,500)
− Taxes (rate, $T=40\%$)	28,200	25,000	43,000	(4,200)
Net operating profit after taxes	$ 42,300	$ 37,500	$ 64,500	($ 6,300)
+ Depreciation[b]	49,500	67,500	22,500	10,500
Operating cash inflows	$191,800	$105,000	$ 87,000	$ 4,200
With old machine				
Earnings before depr., int., and taxes[a]	$ 70,000	$ 70,000	$ 70,000	$ 0
− Depreciation[c]	7,600	4,800	4,800	2,000
Earnings before int. and taxes	$ 62,400	$ 65,200	$ 65,200	($ 2,000)
− Taxes (rate, $T = 40\%$)	24,960	26,080	26,080	(800)
Net operating profit after taxes	$ 37,440	$ 39,120	$ 39,120	($ 1,200)
+ Depreciation	7,600	4,800	4,800	2,000
Operating cash inflows	$ 45,040	$ 43,920	$ 43,920	$ 800

[a]Given in the problem.
[b]From column 3 of the preceding table, top.
[c]From column 3 of the preceding table, bottom.

Calculation of Incremental Operating Cash Inflows
Operating cash inflows

Year	New machine[a] (1)	Old machine[a] (2)	Incremental (relevant) [(1) − (2)] (3)
1	$ 91,800	$45,040	$46,760
2	105,000	43,920	61,080
3	87,000	43,920	43,080
4	4,200	800	3,400

[a]From the final row for the respective machine in the preceding table.

c. Terminal cash flow (end of year 3):

After-tax proceeds from sale of new machine	
Proceeds from sale of new machine	$35,000
Taxes on sale of new machine[3]	9,800
Total after-tax proceeds—new	$25,200
− After-tax proceeds from sale of old machine	
Proceeds from sale of old machine	0
− Tax on sale of old machine[4]	−800
Total after-tax proceeds—old	$ 800
+ Change in net working capital	20,000
Terminal cash flow	$44,400

---

[3]Book value of new machine at end of year 3
= $150,000 − [(0.33 + 0.45 + 0.15) × $150,000] = $150,000 − (0.93 × $150,000)
= $150,000 − $139,500 = $10,500
Tax on sale = 0.40 × ($35,000 sale price − $10,500 book value)
= 0.40 × $24,500 = $9,800

[4]Book value of old machine at end of year 3
= $40,000 − [(0.20 + 0.32 + 0.19 + 0.12 + 0.12) × $40,000] = $40,000 − (0.95 × $40,000)
= $40,000 − $38,000 = $2,000
Tax on sale = 0.40 × ($0 sale price − $2,000 book value)
= 0.40 × − $2,000 = −$800 (i.e., $800 tax saving)

d.

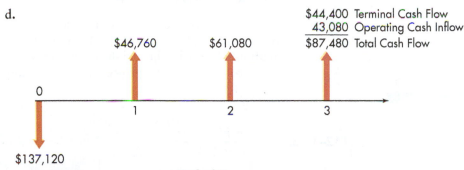

$44,400	Terminal Cash Flow
43,080	Operating Cash Inflow
$87,480	Total Cash Flow

End of Year

Note: The year-4 incremental operating cash inflow of $3,400 is not directly included; it is instead reflected in the book values used to calculate the taxes on sale of the machines at the end of year 3 and is therefore part of the terminal cash flow.

ST11–2   a. Net present value (NPV) using a 10% cost of capital:

Project A: NPV = $7,000/0.10 × [1 − 1/(1 + 0.10)³] − $15,000
= ($70,000.00 × 0.249) − $15,000
= $17,430.00 − $15,000 = $2,430

(Calculator solution = $2,407.96)

Project B:

$$NPV = \$10,000/0.10 \times [1 - 1/(1 + 0.10)^3] - \$20,000$$
$$= (\$100,000.00 \times 0.249) - \$20,000$$
$$= \$24,900.00 - \$20,000 = \underline{\$4,900}^*$$

(Calculator solution = $4,868.52)

---

*Preferred project, because higher NPV.

b. Net present value (NPV) using the risk-adjusted discount rate (*RADR*) for project A of 9% and for project B of 16%.

Project A:

$$NPV = \$7,000/0.09 \times [1 - 1/(1 + 0.09)^3] - \$15,000$$
$$= (\$77,777.78 \times 0.228) - \$15,000$$
$$= \$17,733.33 - \$15,000 = \underline{\$2,733.33}^*$$

(Calculator solution = $2,719.06)

Project B:

$$NPV = \$10,000/0.16 \times [1 - 1/(1 + 0.16)^3] - \$20,000$$
$$= (\$62,500.00 \times 0.359) - \$20,000$$
$$= \$22,437.50 - \$20,000 = \underline{\$2,437.50}$$

(Calculator solution = $2,458.90)

---

*Preferred project, because higher NPV.

c. When the differences in risk were ignored in part **a,** project B was preferred over project A, but when the higher risk of project B is incorporated into the analysis using risk-adjusted discount rates in part **b,** *project A is preferred over project B.* Clearly, project A should be implemented.

Chapter 12

ST12–1   a. $Q = \dfrac{FC}{P - VC}$

$$= \frac{\$250,000}{\$7.50 - \$3.00} = \frac{\$250,000}{\$4.50} = \underline{55,556} \text{ units}$$

b.

	+20%	
Sales (in units)	100,000	120,000
Sales revenue (units × $7.50/unit)	$750,000	$900,000
Less: Variable operating costs (units × $3.00/unit)	300,000	360,000
Less: Fixed operating costs	250,000	250,000
Earnings before interest and taxes (EBIT)	$200,000	$290,000

+45%

Less: Interest	80,000	80,000
Net profits before taxes	$120,000	$210,000
Less: Taxes ($T = 0.40$)	48,000	84,000
Net profits after taxes	$ 72,000	$126,000
Less: Preferred dividends (8,000 shares × $5.00/share)	40,000	40,000
Earnings available for common	$132,000	$ 86,000
Earnings per share (EPS)	$32,000/20,000 = $1.60/share	$86,000/20,000 = $4.30/share

+169%

c. $\text{DOL} = \dfrac{\% \text{ change in EBIT}}{\% \text{ change in sales}} = \dfrac{+45\%}{+20\%} = \underline{2.25}$

d. $\text{DFL} = \dfrac{\% \text{ change in EPS}}{\% \text{ change in EBIT}} = \dfrac{+169\%}{+45} = \underline{3.76}$

e. $\text{DTL} = \text{DOL} \times \text{DFL}$

$= 2.25 \times 3.76 = \underline{8.46}$

Using the other DTL formula:

$\text{DTL} = \dfrac{\% \text{ change in EPS}}{\% \text{ change in sales}}$

$8.46 = \dfrac{\% \text{ change in EPS}}{50\%}$

$\% \text{ change in EPS} = 8.46 \times 0.50 = 4.23 = \underline{+423\%}$

ST12–2

Data summary for alternative plans		
Source of capital	**Plan A (bond)**	**Plan B (stock)**
Long-term debt	$60,000 at 12% annual interest	$50,000 at 12% annual interest
Annual interest =	0.12 × $60,000 = $7,200	0.12 × $50,000 = $6,000
Common stock	10,000 shares	11,000 shares

a.

	Plan A (bond)		Plan B (stock)	
EBIT[a]	$30,000	$40,000	$30,000	$40,000
Less: Interest	7,200	7,200	6,000	6,000
Net profits before taxes	$22,800	$32,800	$24,000	$34,000
Less: Taxes ($T = 0.40$)	9,120	13,120	9,600	13,600
Net profits after taxes	$13,680	$19,680	$14,400	$20,400
EPS (10,000 shares)	$1.37	$1.97		
(11,000 shares)			$1.31	$1.85

[a]Values were arbitrarily selected; other values could have been used.

	Coordinates	
	EBIT	
	$30,000	$40,000
Financing plan	Earnings per share (EPS)	
A (Bond)	$1.37	$1.97
B (Stock)	1.31	1.85

b.

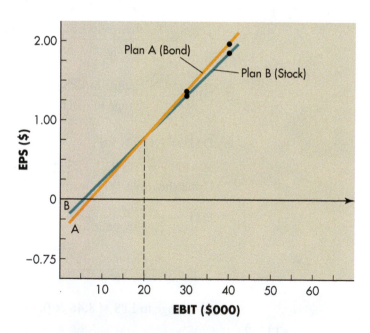

c. The bond plan (Plan A) becomes superior to the stock plan (Plan B) at *around $20,000* of EBIT, as represented by the dashed vertical line in the figure in part **b.** (*Note:* The actual point is $19,200, which was determined algebraically by using the technique described in footnote 18.)

ST12–3 a.

Capital structure debt ratio	Expected EPS (1)	Required return, r_s (2)	Estimated share value [(1) ÷ (2)] (3)
0%	$3.12	0.13	$24.00
10	3.90	0.15	26.00
20	4.80	0.16	30.00
30	5.44	0.17	32.00
40	5.51	0.19	29.00
50	5.00	0.20	25.00
60	4.40	0.22	20.00

b. Using the table in part a:

1. Maximization of EPS: *40% debt ratio,* EPS = $5.51/share (see column 1).
2. Maximization of share value: *30% debt ratio,* share value = $32.00 (see column 3).

c. Recommend *30% debt ratio* because it results in the maximum share value and is therefore consistent with the firm's goal of owner wealth maximization.

Chapter 13

ST13–1 a. Earnings per share (EPS) $= \dfrac{\$2,000,000 \text{ earnings available}}{500,000 \text{ shares of common outstanding}}$

$= \$4.00/\text{share}$

Price/earnings (P/E) ratio $= \dfrac{\$60 \text{ market price}}{\$4.00 \text{ EPS}} = 15$

b. Proposed dividends = 500,000 shares × $2 per share = $1,000,000

Shares that can be repurchased $= \dfrac{\$1,000,000}{\$62} = 16,129 \text{ shares}$

c. *After proposed repurchase:*

Shares outstanding = 500,000 − 16,129 = 483,871

EPS $= \dfrac{\$2,000,000}{483,871} = \$4.13/\text{share}$

d. Market price = $4.13/share × 15 = $61.95/share

e. The earnings per share (EPS) are higher after the repurchase because there are fewer shares of stock outstanding (483,871 shares versus 500,000 shares) to divide up the firm's $2,000,000 of available earnings.

f. In both cases, the stockholders would receive $2 per share: a $2 cash dividend in the dividend case or an approximately $2 increase in share price ($60.00 per share to $61.95 per share) in the repurchase case. [*Note:* The difference of $0.05 per share ($2.00 − $1.95) is due to rounding.]

Chapter 14

ST14–1

Basic data		
Time component	Current	Proposed
Average payment period (APP)	10 days	30 days
Average collection period (ACP)	30 days	30 days
Average age of inventory (AAI)	40 days	40 days

$$\text{Cash conversion cycle (CCC)} = \text{AAI} + \text{ACP} - \text{APP}$$
$$\text{CCC}_{current} = 40 \text{ days} + 30 \text{ days} - 10 \text{ days} = 60 \text{ days}$$
$$\text{CCC}_{proposed} = 40 \text{ days} + 30 \text{ days} - 30 \text{ days} = \underline{40} \text{ days}$$
$$\text{Reduction in CCC} \quad \underline{20} \text{days}$$

Old accounts payable $= 10 \text{ days} \times (\$14,000,000 \div 360 \text{ days}) = \$388,889$
New accounts payable $= 30 \text{ days} \times (\$14,000,000 \div 360 \text{ days}) = \$1,166,667$

Change in accounts payable $= \$1,166,667 - \$388,889 = \$777,778$

Because accounts payable has increased, the amount represents a decrease in net working capital.

Reduction in resource investment $= \$777,778$

Annual profit increase $= 0.12 \times \$777,778 = \underline{\$93,333}$

ST14–2   **a.** *Data:*

$S = 60,000$ gallons
$O = \$200$ per order
$C = \$1$ per gallon per year

Calculation:

$$EOQ = \sqrt{\frac{2 \times S \times O}{C}}$$
$$= \sqrt{\frac{2 \times 60,000 \times \$200}{\$1}}$$
$$= \sqrt{24,000,000}$$
$$= \underline{4,899} \text{ gallons}$$

b. *Data:*

Lead time = 20 days
Daily usage = 60,000 gallons/365 days
$= 164.38$ gallons/day

Calculation:

Reorder point = lead time in days × daily usage
$= 20 \text{ days} \times 164.38 \text{ gallons/day}$
$= \underline{3,287.6} \text{ gallons}$

ST14–3   Tabular calculation of the effects of relaxing credit standards on Regency Rug Repair Company:

Additional profit contribution from sales		
[4,000 rugs × ($32 avg. sale price − $28 var. cost)]		$16,000
Cost of marginal investment in accounts receivable		
Average investment under proposed plan:		
$\dfrac{(\$28 \times 76,000 \text{ rugs})}{365/48} = \dfrac{\$2,128,000}{7.6}$	$280,000	
Average investment under present plan:		
$\dfrac{(\$28 \times 72,000 \text{ rugs})}{365/40} = \dfrac{\$2,016,000}{9.1}$	221,538	
Marginal investment in A/R	$ 58,462	
Cost of marginal investment in A/R (0.14 × $58,462)		($ 8,185)
Cost of marginal bad debts		
Bad debts under proposed plan		
(0.015 × $32 × 76,000 rugs)	$ 36,480	
Bad debts under present plan		
(0.010 × $32 × 72,000 rugs)	23,040	
Cost of marginal bad debts		($13,440)
Net loss from implementation of proposed plan		($ 5,625)

Recommendation: Because a net loss of $5,625 is expected to result from relaxing credit standards, *the proposed plan should not be implemented.*

Chapter 15

ST15–1   **a.**

Supplier	Approximate cost of giving up cash discount
X	1% × [365/(55 − 10)] = 1% × 365/45 = 1% × 8.1 = 8.1%
Y	2% × [365/(30 − 10)] = 2% × 365/20 = 2% × 18.25 = 36.5%
Z	2% × [365/(60 − 20)] = 2% × 365/40 = 2% × 9.125 = 18.25%

b.

Supplier	Recommendation
X	8.1% cost of giving up discount < 15% interest cost from bank; therefore, *give up discount.*
Y	36.5% cost of giving up discount > 15% interest cost from bank; therefore, *take discount and borrow from bank.*
Z	18.25% cost of giving up discount > 15% interest cost from bank; therefore, *take discount and borrow from bank.*

c. Stretching accounts payable for supplier Z would change the cost of giving up the cash discount to

$$2\% \times [365/(60 + 20) - 20]) = 2\% \times 365/60 = 2\% \times 6.1 = \underline{\underline{12.2\%}}$$

In this case, in light of the 15% interest cost from the bank, the recommended strategy in part **b** would be to *give up the discount* because the 12.2% cost of giving up the discount would be less than the 15% interest cost from the bank.

Glossary

ABC inventory system
Inventory management technique that divides inventory into three groups—A, B, and C, in descending order of importance and level of monitoring—on the basis of the dollar investment in each. (Chapter 14)

ability to service debts
The ability of a firm to make the payments required on a scheduled basis over the life of a debt. (Chapter 3)

accept–reject approach
The evaluation of capital expenditure proposals to determine whether they meet the firm's minimum acceptance criterion. (Chapter 10)

accounts payable management
Management by the firm of the time that elapses between its purchase of raw materials and its mailing payment to the supplier. (Chapter 15)

accrual basis
In preparation of financial statements, recognizes revenue at the time of sale and recognizes expenses when they are incurred. (Chapter 1)

accruals
Liabilities for services received for which payment has yet to be made. (Chapter 15)

ACH (automated clearinghouse) transfer
Preauthorized electronic withdrawal from the payer's account and deposit into the payee's account via a settlement among banks by the *automated clearinghouse, or ACH.* (Chapter 14)

activity ratios
Measure the speed with which various accounts are converted into sales or cash or inflows or outflows. (Chapter 3)

after-tax proceeds from sale of old asset
The difference between the old asset's sale proceeds and any applicable taxes or tax refunds related to its sale. (Chapter 11)

agency costs
Costs arising from agency problems that are borne by shareholders and represent a loss of shareholder wealth. (Chapter 1)

agency problems
Problems that arise when managers place personal goals ahead of the goals of shareholders. (Chapter 1)

aggressive funding strategy
A funding strategy under which the firm funds its seasonal requirements with short-term debt and its permanent requirements with long-term debt. (Chapter 14)

aging schedule
A credit-monitoring technique that breaks down accounts receivable into groups on the basis of their time of origin; it indicates the percentages of the total accounts receivable balance that have been outstanding for specified periods of time. (Chapter 14)

American depositary receipts (ADRs)
Securities, backed by *American depositary shares (ADSs),* that permit U.S. investors to hold shares of non-U.S. companies and trade them in U.S. markets. (Chapter 7)

American depositary shares (ADSs)
Dollar-denominated receipts for the stocks of foreign companies that are held by a U.S. financial institution overseas. (Chapter 7)

angel capitalists (angels)
Wealthy individual investors who do not operate as a business but invest in promising early-stage companies in exchange for a portion of the firm's equity. (Chapter 7)

annual cleanup
The requirement that for a certain number of days during the year borrowers under a line of credit carry a zero loan balance (that is, owe the bank nothing). (Chapter 15)

annualized net present value (ANPV) approach
An approach to evaluating unequal-lived projects that converts the net present value of unequal-lived, mutually exclusive projects into an equivalent annual amount (in NPV terms). (Chapter 11)

annual percentage rate (APR)
The *nominal annual rate* of interest, found by multiplying the periodic rate by the number of periods

in one year, that must be disclosed to consumers on credit cards and loans as a result of "truth-in-lending laws." (Chapter 5)

annual percentage yield (APY)
The *effective annual rate* of interest that must be disclosed to consumers by banks on their savings products as a result of "truth-in-savings laws." (Chapter 5)

annuity
A stream of equal periodic cash flows over a specified time period. These cash flows can be *inflows* of returns earned on investments or *outflows* of funds invested to earn future returns. (Chapter 5)

annuity due
An annuity for which the cash flow occurs at the *beginning* of each period. (Chapter 5)

articles of partnership
The written contract used to formally establish a business partnership. (Chapter 1)

ask price
The lowest price at which a security is offered for sale. (Chapter 2)

asymmetric information
The situation in which managers of a firm have more information about operations and future prospects than do investors. (Chapter 12)

authorized shares
Shares of common stock that a firm's corporate charter allows it to issue. (Chapter 7)

average age of inventory
Average number of days' sales in inventory. (Chapter 3)

average collection period
The average amount of time needed to collect accounts receivable. (Chapter 3)

average payment period
The average amount of time needed to pay accounts payable. (Chapter 3)

average tax rate
A firm's taxes divided by its taxable income. (Chapter 2)

balance sheet
Summary statement of the firm's financial position at a given point in time. (Chapter 3)

bar chart
The simplest type of probability distribution; shows only a limited number of outcomes and associated probabilities for a given event. (Chapter 8)

behavioral finance
A growing body of research that focuses on investor behavior and its impact on investment decisions and stock prices. Advocates are commonly referred to as "behaviorists." (Chapter 7)

benchmarking
A type of *cross-sectional analysis* in which the firm's ratio values are compared with those of a key competitor or with a group of competitors that it wishes to emulate. (Chapter 3)

beta coefficient (β)
A relative measure of nondiversifiable risk. An index of the degree of movement of an asset's return in response to a change in the *market return*. (Chapter 8)

bid price
The highest price offered to purchase a security. (Chapter 2)

bird-in-the-hand argument
The belief, in support of *dividend relevance theory*, that investors see current dividends as less risky than future dividends or capital gains. (Chapter 13)

board of directors
Group elected by the firm's stockholders and typically responsible for approving strategic goals and plans, setting general policy, guiding corporate affairs, and approving major expenditures. (Chapter 1)

bond
Long-term debt instrument used by business and government to raise large sums of money, generally from a diverse group of lenders. (Chapter 2)

bond indenture
A legal document that specifies both the rights of the bondholders and the duties of the issuing corporation. (Chapter 6)

book value
The strict accounting value of an asset, calculated by subtracting its accumulated depreciation from its installed cost. (Chapter 11)

book value per share
The amount per share of common stock that would be received if all of the firm's assets were sold for

their exact book *(accounting)* value and the proceeds remaining after paying all liabilities (including preferred stock) were divided among the common stockholders. (Chapter 7)

book value weights
Weights that use accounting values to measure the proportion of each type of capital in the firm's financial structure. (Chapter 9)

breakeven analysis
Used to indicate the level of operations necessary to cover all costs and to evaluate the profitability associated with various levels of sales; also called *cost-volume-profit analysis*. (Chapter 12)

breakeven cash inflow
The minimum level of cash inflow necessary for a project to be acceptable, that is, NPV > $0. (Chapter 11)

broker market
The securities exchanges on which the two sides of a transaction, the buyer and seller, are brought together to trade securities. (Chapter 2)

business ethics
Standards of conduct or moral judgment that apply to persons engaged in commerce. (Chapter 1)

callable feature (preferred stock)
A feature of *callable preferred stock* that allows the issuer to retire the shares within a certain period of time and at a specified price. (Chapter 7)

call feature
A feature included in nearly all corporate bond issues that gives the issuer the opportunity to repurchase bonds at a stated call price prior to maturity. (Chapter 6)

call premium
The amount by which a bond's *call price* exceeds its par value. (Chapter 6)

call price
The stated price at which a bond may be repurchased, by use of *a call feature*, prior to maturity. (Chapter 6)

capital asset pricing model (CAPM)
The basic theory that links risk and return for all assets. (Chapter 9)

capital asset pricing model (CAPM)
Describes the relationship between the required return, r_s, and the nondiversifiable risk of the firm as measured by the beta coefficient, β. (Chapter 8)

capital budgeting
The process of evaluating and selecting long-term investments that are consistent with the firm's goal of maximizing owners' wealth. (Chapter 10)

capital budgeting process
Five distinct but interrelated steps: *proposal generation, review and analysis, decision making, implementation,* and *follow-up.* (Chapter 10)

capital expenditure
An outlay of funds by the firm that is expected to produce benefits over a period of time greater than 1 year. (Chapter 10)

capital gain
The amount by which the sale price of an asset exceeds the asset's purchase price. (Chapter 2)

capital market
A market that enables suppliers and demanders of *long-term funds* to make transactions. (Chapter 2)

capital rationing
The financial situation in which a firm has only a fixed number of dollars available for capital expenditures and numerous projects compete for these dollars. (Chapter 10)

capital structure
The mix of long-term debt and equity maintained by the firm. (Chapter 12)

carrying costs
The variable costs per unit of holding an item in inventory for a specific period of time. (Chapter 14)

cash basis
Recognizes revenues and expenses only with respect to actual inflows and outflows of cash. (Chapter 1)

cash bonuses
Cash paid to management for achieving certain performance goals. (Chapter 1)

cash budget (cash forecast)
A statement of the firm's planned inflows and outflows of cash that is used to estimate its short-term cash requirements. (Chapter 4)

cash concentration
The process used by the firm to bring lockbox and other deposits together into one bank, often called the *concentration bank.* (Chapter 14)

cash conversion cycle (CCC)
The length of time required for a company to convert cash invested in its operations to cash received as a result of its operations. (Chapter 14)

cash discount
A percentage deduction from the purchase price; available to the credit customer who pays its account within a specified time. (Chapter 14)

cash discount period
The number of days after the beginning of the credit period during which the cash discount is available. (Chapter 14)

cash flow from financing activities
Cash flows that result from debt and equity financing transactions; include incurrence and repayment of debt, cash inflow from the sale of stock, and cash outflows to repurchase stock or pay cash dividends. (Chapter 4)

cash flow from investment activities
Cash flows associated with purchase and sale of both fixed assets and equity investments in other firms. (Chapter 4)

cash flow from operating activities
Cash flows directly related to sale and production of the firm's products and services. (Chapter 4)

catering theory
A theory that says firms cater to the preferences of investors, initiating or increasing dividend payments during periods in which high-dividend stocks are particularly appealing to investors. (Chapter 13)

change in net working capital
The difference between a change in current assets and a change in current liabilities. (Chapter 11)

clearing float
The time between deposit of a payment and when spendable funds become available to the firm. (Chapter 14)

clientele effect
The argument that different payout policies attract different types of investors but still do not change the value of the firm. (Chapter 13)

closely owned (stock)
The common stock of a firm is owned by an individual or a small group of investors (such as a family); they are usually privately owned companies. (Chapter 7)

coefficient of variation (*CV*)
A measure of relative dispersion that is useful in comparing the risks of assets with differing expected returns. (Chapter 8)

collateral trust bonds
See Table 6.4.

commercial banks
Institutions that provide savers with a secure place to invest their funds and that offer loans to individual and business borrowers. (Chapter 2)

commercial finance companies
Lending institutions that make only secured loans—both short-term and long-term—to businesses. (Chapter 15)

commercial paper
A form of financing consisting of short-term, unsecured promissory notes issued by firms with a high credit standing. (Chapter 15)

commitment fee
The fee that is normally charged on a *revolving credit agreement;* it often applies to the *average unused portion* of the borrower's credit line. (Chapter 15)

common-size income statement
An income statement in which each item is expressed as a percentage of sales. (Chapter 3)

common stock
The purest and most basic form of corporate ownership. (Chapter 1)

compensating balance
A required checking account balance equal to a certain percentage of the amount borrowed from a bank under a line-of-credit or revolving credit agreement. (Chapter 15)

compound interest
Interest that is earned on a given deposit and has become part of the *principal* at the end of a specified period. (Chapter 5)

conflicting rankings
Conflicts in the ranking given a project by NPV and IRR, resulting from *differences in the magnitude and timing of cash flows.* (Chapter 10)

conservative funding strategy
A funding strategy under which the firm funds both its seasonal and its permanent requirements with long-term debt. (Chapter 14)

constant-growth model
A widely cited dividend valuation approach that assumes that dividends will grow at a constant rate, but a rate that is less than the required return. (Chapter 7)

constant-growth valuation (Gordon growth) model
Assumes that the value of a share of stock equals the present value of all future dividends (assumed to grow at a constant rate) that it is expected to provide over an infinite time horizon. (Chapter 9)

constant-payout-ratio dividend policy
A dividend policy based on the payment of a certain percentage of earnings to owners in each dividend period. (Chapter 13)

continuous compounding
Compounding of interest an infinite number of times per year at intervals of microseconds. (Chapter 5)

continuous probability distribution
A probability distribution showing all the possible outcomes and associated probabilities for a given event. (Chapter 8)

controlled disbursing
The strategic use of mailing points and bank accounts to lengthen mail float and clearing float, respectively. (Chapter 14)

controller
The firm's chief accountant, who is responsible for the firm's accounting activities, such as corporate accounting, tax management, financial accounting, and cost accounting. (Chapter 1)

conversion feature
A feature of convertible bonds that allows bondholders to change each bond into a stated number of shares of common stock. (Chapter 6)

conversion feature
An option that is included as part of a bond or a preferred stock issue and allows its holder to change the security into a stated number of shares of common stock. (Chapter 6)

conversion feature (preferred stock)
A feature of *convertible preferred stock* that allows holders to change each share into a stated number of shares of common stock. (Chapter 7)

corporate bond
A long-term debt instrument indicating that a corporation has borrowed a certain amount of money and promises to repay it in the future under clearly defined terms. (Chapter 6)

corporate governance
The rules, processes, and laws by which companies are operated, controlled, and regulated. (Chapter 1)

corporation
An entity created by law. (Chapter 1)

correlation
A statistical measure of the relationship between any two series of numbers. (Chapter 8)

correlation coefficient
A measure of the degree of correlation between two series. (Chapter 8)

cost of a new issue of common stock, r_n
The cost of common stock, net of underpricing and associated flotation costs. (Chapter 9)

cost of capital
Represents the firm's cost of financing and is the minimum rate of return that a project must earn to increase firm value. (Chapter 9)

cost of common stock equity, r_s
The rate at which investors discount the expected dividends of the firm to determine its share value. (Chapter 9)

cost of giving up a cash discount
The implied rate of interest paid to delay payment of an account payable for an additional number of days. (Chapter 15)

cost of long-term debt
The financing cost associated with new funds raised through long-term borrowing. (Chapter 9)

cost of new asset
The net outflow necessary to acquire a new asset. (Chapters 9 and 11)

cost of preferred stock, r_p
The ratio of the preferred stock dividend to the firm's net proceeds from the sale of preferred stock. (Chapter 9)

cost of retained earnings, r_r
The same as the cost of an *equivalent fully subscribed issue of additional common stock*, which is equal to the cost of common stock equity, r_s. (Chapter 9)

coupon interest rate
The percentage of a bond's par value that will be paid annually, typically in two equal semiannual payments, as interest. (Chapter 6)

coverage ratios
Ratios that measure the firm's ability to pay certain fixed charges. (Chapter 3)

credit monitoring
The ongoing review of a firm's accounts receivable to determine whether customers are paying according to the stated credit terms. (Chapter 14)

credit period
The number of days after the beginning of the credit period until full payment of the account is due. (Chapter 14)

credit scoring
A credit selection method commonly used with high-volume/small-dollar credit requests; relies on a credit score determined by applying statistically derived weights to a credit applicant's scores on key financial and credit characteristics. (Chapter 14)

credit standards
The firm's minimum requirements for extending credit to a customer. (Chapter 14)

credit terms
The terms of sale for customers who have been extended credit by the firm. (Chapter 14)

cross-sectional analysis
Comparison of different firms' financial ratios at the same point in time; involves comparing the firm's ratios with those of other firms in its industry or with industry averages. (Chapter 3)

cumulative (preferred stock)
Preferred stock for which all passed (unpaid) dividends in arrears, along with the current dividend, must be paid before dividends can be paid to common stockholders. (Chapter 7)

current assets
Short-term assets, expected to be converted into cash within 1 year or less. (Chapter 3)

current liabilities
Short-term liabilities, expected to be paid within 1 year or less. (Chapter 3)

current rate (translation) method
Technique used by U.S.–based companies to translate their foreign-currency-denominated assets and liabilities into U.S. dollars, for consolidation with the parent company's financial statements, using the year-end (current) exchange rate. (Chapter 3)

current ratio
A measure of liquidity calculated by dividing the firm's current assets by its current liabilities. (Chapter 3)

current yield
A measure of a bond's cash return for the year; calculated by dividing the bond's annual interest payment by its current price. (Chapter 6)

date of record (dividends)
Set by the firm's directors, the date on which all persons whose names are recorded as stockholders receive a declared dividend at a specified future time. (Chapter 13)

dealer market
The market in which the buyer and seller are not brought together directly but instead have their orders executed by securities dealers that "make markets" in the given security. (Chapter 2)

debentures
See Table 6.4.

debt
Includes borrowing incurred by a firm, including bonds, and is repaid according to a fixed schedule of payments. (Chapter 7)

debt ratio
Measures the proportion of total assets financed by the firm's creditors. (Chapter 3)

debt-to-equity ratio
Measures the relative proportion of total liabilities and common stock equity used to finance the firm's total assets. (Chapter 3)

deflation
A general trend of falling prices. (Chapter 6)

degree of financial leverage (DFL)
The numerical measure of the firm's financial leverage. (Chapter 12)

degree of indebtedness
Measures the amount of debt relative to other significant balance sheet amounts. (Chapter 3)

degree of operating leverage (DOL)
The numerical measure of the firm's operating leverage. (Chapter 12)

degree of total leverage (DTL)
The numerical measure of the firm's total leverage. (Chapter 12)

depository transfer check (DTC)
An unsigned check drawn on one of a firm's bank accounts and deposited in another. (Chapter 14)

depreciable life
Time period over which an asset is depreciated. (Chapter 4)

depreciation
A portion of the costs of fixed assets charged against annual revenues over time. (Chapter 4)

dilution of earnings
A reduction in each previous shareholder's fractional claim on the firm's earnings resulting from the issuance of additional shares of common stock. (Chapter 7)

dilution of ownership
A reduction in each previous shareholder's fractional ownership resulting from the issuance of additional shares of common stock. (Chapter 7)

discount
The amount by which a bond sells at a value that is less than its par value. (Chapter 6)

discounting cash flows
The process of finding present values; the inverse of compounding interest. (Chapter 5)

discount loan
Loan on which interest is paid in advance by being deducted from the amount borrowed. (Chapter 15)

diversifiable risk
The portion of an asset's risk that is attributable to firm-specific, random causes; can be eliminated through diversification. Also called *unsystematic risk*. (Chapter 8)

divestiture
The selling of some of a firm's assets for various strategic reasons. (Chapter 8)

dividend irrelevance theory
Miller and Modigliani's theory that, in a perfect world, the firm's value is determined solely by the earning power and risk of its assets (investments) and that the manner in which it splits its earnings stream between dividends and internally retained (and reinvested) funds does not affect this value. (Chapter 13)

dividend payout ratio
Indicates the percentage of each dollar earned that a firm distributes to the owners in the form of cash. It is calculated by dividing the firm's cash dividend per share by its earnings per share. (Chapter 13)

dividend per share (DPS)
The dollar amount of cash distributed during the period on behalf of each outstanding share of common stock. (Chapter 3)

dividend policy
The firm's plan of action to be followed whenever it makes a dividend decision. (Chapter 13)

dividend reinvestment plans (DRIPs)
Plans that enable stockholders to use dividends received on the firm's stock to acquire additional shares—even fractional shares—at little or no transaction cost. (Chapter 13)

dividend relevance theory
The theory, advanced by Gordon and Lintner, that there is a direct relationship between a firm's dividend policy and its market value. (Chapter 13)

dividends
Periodic distributions of cash to the stockholders of a firm. (Chapter 1)

double taxation
Situation that occurs when after-tax corporate earnings are distributed as cash dividends to stockholders, who then must pay personal taxes on the dividend amount. (Chapter 2)

DuPont formula
Multiplies the firm's *net profit margin* by its *total asset turnover* to calculate the firm's *return on total assets (ROA)*. (Chapter 3)

DuPont system of analysis
System used to dissect the firm's financial statements and to assess its financial condition. (Chapter 3)

Dutch auction repurchase
A repurchase method in which the firm specifies how many shares it wants to buy back and a range of prices at which it is willing to repurchase shares. Investors specify how many shares they will sell at each price in the range, and the firm determines the minimum price required to repurchase its target number of shares. All investors who tender receive the same price. (Chapter 13)

earnings per share (EPS)
The amount earned during the period on behalf of each outstanding share of common stock, calculated by dividing the period's total earnings available for the firm's common stockholders by the number of shares of common stock outstanding. (Chapter 1)

EBIT–EPS approach
An approach for selecting the capital structure that maximizes earnings per share (EPS) over the expected range of earnings before interest and taxes (EBIT). (Chapter 12)

economic order quantity (EOQ) model
Inventory management technique for determining an item's optimal order size, which is the size that minimizes the total of its *order costs* and *carrying costs*. (Chapter 14)

effective (true) annual rate (EAR)
The annual rate of interest actually paid or earned. (Chapter 5)

efficient market
A market that establishes correct prices for the securities that firms sell and allocates funds to their most productive uses. (Chapter 2)

efficient-market hypothesis (EMH)
Theory describing the behavior of an assumed "perfect" market in which (1) securities are in equilibrium, (2) security prices fully reflect all available information and react swiftly to new information, and (3), because stocks are fully and fairly priced, investors need not waste time looking for mispriced securities. (Chapter 7)

efficient portfolio
A portfolio that maximizes return for a given level of risk. (Chapter 8)

ending cash
The sum of the firm's beginning cash and its net cash flow for the period. (Chapter 4)

enterprise resource planning (ERP)
A computerized system that electronically integrates external information about the firm's suppliers and customers with the firm's departmental data so that information on all available resources—human and material—can be instantly obtained in a fashion that eliminates production delays and controls costs. (Chapter 14)

equipment trust certificates
See Table 6.4.

equity
Funds provided by the firm's owners (investors or stockholders) that are repaid subject to the firm's performance. (Chapter 7)

Eurobond
A bond issued by an international borrower and sold to investors in countries with currencies other than the currency in which the bond is denominated. (Chapter 2)

Eurobond market
The market in which corporations and governments typically issue bonds denominated in dollars and sell them to investors located outside the United States. (Chapter 2)

Eurocurrency market
International equivalent of the domestic money market. (Chapter 2)

excess cash balance
The (excess) amount available for investment by the firm if the period's ending cash is greater than the desired minimum cash balance; assumed to be invested in marketable securities. (Chapter 4)

excess earnings accumulation tax
The tax the IRS levies on retained earnings above $250,000 for most businesses when it determines that the firm has accumulated an excess of earnings to allow owners to delay paying ordinary income taxes on dividends received. (Chapter 13)

ex dividend
A period beginning 2 *business days* prior to the date of record, during which a stock is sold without the right to receive the current dividend. (Chapter 13)

expectations theory
The theory that the yield curve reflects investor expectations about future interest rates; an expectation of rising interest rates results in an upward-sloping yield curve, and an expectation of declining rates results in a downward-sloping yield curve. (Chapter 6)

expected value of a return ($\bar{r}$)
The average return that an investment is expected to produce over time. (Chapter 8)

extendible notes
See Table 6.5.

external financing required ("plug" figure)
Under the judgmental approach for developing a pro forma balance sheet, the amount of external financing needed to bring the statement into balance. It can be either a positive or a negative value. (Chapter 4)

external forecast
A sales forecast based on the relationships observed between the firm's sales and certain key external economic indicators. (Chapter 4)

extra dividend
An additional dividend optionally paid by the firm when earnings are higher than normal in a given period. (Chapter 13)

factor
A financial institution that specializes in purchasing accounts receivable from businesses. (Chapter 15)

factoring accounts receivable
The outright sale of accounts receivable at a discount to a *factor* or other financial institution. (Chapter 15)

Federal Deposit Insurance Corporation (FDIC)
An agency created by the Glass-Steagall Act that provides insurance for deposits at banks and monitors banks to ensure their safety and soundness. (Chapter 2)

finance
The science and art of managing money. (Chapter 1)

Financial Accounting Standards Board (FASB)
The accounting profession's rule-setting body, which authorizes *generally accepted accounting principles (GAAP)*. (Chapter 3)

Financial Accounting Standards Board (FASB) Standard No. 52
Mandates that U.S.–based companies translate their foreign-currency-denominated assets and liabilities into U.S. dollars, for consolidation with the parent company's financial statements. This process is done by using the *current rate (translation) method*. (Chapter 3)

financial breakeven point
The level of EBIT necessary to just cover all *fixed financial costs;* the level of EBIT for which EPS = $0. (Chapter 12)

financial institution
An intermediary that channels the savings of individuals, businesses, and governments into loans or investments. (Chapter 2)

financial leverage
The magnification of risk and return through the use of fixed-cost financing, such as debt and preferred stock. (Chapter 3)

financial leverage
The use of *fixed financial costs* to magnify the effects of changes in earnings before interest and taxes on the firm's earnings per share. (Chapter 12)

financial leverage multiplier (FLM)
The ratio of the firm's total assets to its common stock equity. (Chapter 3)

financial manager
Actively manages the financial affairs of all types of businesses, whether private or public, large or small, profit seeking or not for profit. (Chapter 1)

financial markets
Forums in which suppliers of funds and demanders of funds can transact business directly. (Chapter 2)

financial planning process
Planning that begins with long-term, or *strategic,* financial plans that in turn guide the formulation of short-term, or *operating,* plans and budgets. (Chapter 4)

financial services
The area of finance concerned with the design and delivery of advice and financial products to individuals, businesses, and governments. (Chapter 1)

five C's of credit
The five key dimensions—character, capacity, capital, collateral, and conditions—used by credit analysts to provide a framework for in-depth credit analysis. (Chapter 14)

fixed-payment coverage ratio
Measures the firm's ability to meet all fixed-payment obligations. (Chapter 3)

fixed-rate loan
A loan with a rate of interest that is determined at a set increment above the prime rate and remains unvarying until maturity. (Chapter 15)

flat yield curve
A yield curve that indicates that interest rates do not vary much at different maturities. (Chapter 6)

float
Funds that have been sent by the payer but are not yet usable funds to the payee. (Chapter 14)

floating inventory lien
A secured short-term loan against inventory under which the lender's claim is on the borrower's inventory in general. (Chapter 15)

floating-rate bonds
See Table 6.5.

floating-rate loan
A loan with a rate of interest initially set at an increment above the prime rate and allowed to "float," or vary, above prime *as the prime rate varies* until maturity. (Chapter 15)

flotation costs
The total costs of issuing and selling a security. (Chapter 9)

foreign bond
A bond that is issued by a foreign corporation or government and is denominated in the investor's home currency and sold in the investor's home market. (Chapters 2 and 6)

foreign direct investment (FDI)
The transfer of capital, managerial, and technical assets to a foreign country. (Chapters 11)

foreign exchange manager
The manager responsible for managing and monitoring the firm's exposure to loss from currency fluctuations. (Chapter 1)

free cash flow (FCF)
The amount of cash flow available to investors (creditors and owners) after the firm has met all operating needs and paid for investments in net fixed assets and net current assets. (Chapter 4)

free cash flow valuation model
A model that determines the value of an entire company as the present value of its expected *free cash flows* discounted at the firm's *weighted average cost of capital,* which is its expected average future cost of funds over the long run. (Chapter 7)

future value
The value at a given future date of an amount placed on deposit today and earning interest at a specified rate. Found by applying *compound interest* over a specified period of time. (Chapter 5)

General Agreement on Tariffs and Trade (GATT)
A treaty that has governed world trade throughout most of the postwar era; it extends free-trading rules to broad areas of economic activity and is policed by the *World Trade Organization (WTO).* (Chapter 3)

generally accepted accounting principles (GAAP)
The practice and procedure guidelines used to prepare and maintain financial records and reports; authorized by the *Financial Accounting Standards Board (FASB).* (Chapter 3)

Glass-Steagall Act
An act of Congress in 1933 that created the federal deposit insurance program and separated the activities of commercial and investment banks. (Chapter 2)

Gordon growth model
A common name for the *constant-growth model* that is widely cited in dividend valuation. (Chapter 7)

Gramm-Leach-Bliley Act
An act that allows business combinations (that is, mergers) between commercial banks, investment banks, and insurance companies and thus permits these institutions to compete in markets that prior regulations prohibited them from entering. (Chapter 2)

gross profit margin
Measures the percentage of each sales dollar remaining after the firm has paid for its goods. (Chapter 3)

historical weights
Either book or market value weights based on *actual* capital structure proportions. (Chapter 9)

incentive plans
Management compensation plans that tie management compensation to share price; one example involves the granting of *stock options.* (Chapter 1)

income bonds
See Table 6.4.

income statement
Provides a financial summary of the firm's operating results during a specified period. (Chapter 3)

incremental cash flows
The *additional* cash flows—outflows or inflows—expected to result from a proposed capital expenditure. (Chapter 11)

independent projects
Projects whose cash flows are unrelated to (or independent of) one another; the acceptance of one does not *eliminate* the others from further consideration. (Chapter 10)

individual investors
Investors who own relatively small quantities of shares so as to meet personal investment goals. (Chapter 1)

inflation
A rising trend in the prices of most goods and services. (Chapter 6)

informational content
The information provided by the dividends of a firm with respect to future earnings, which causes owners to bid up or down the price of the firm's stock. (Chapter 13)

initial investment
The relevant cash outflow for a proposed project at time zero. (Chapter 11)

initial public offering (IPO)
The first public sale of a firm's stock. (Chapter 7)

insolvent
Describes a firm that is unable to pay its bills as they come due. (Chapter 14)

installation costs
Any added costs that are necessary to place an asset into operation. (Chapter 11)

installed cost of new asset
The *cost of new asset* plus its *installation costs;* equals the asset's depreciable value. (Chapter 11)

institutional investors
Investment professionals such as banks, insurance companies, mutual funds, and pension funds that are paid to manage and hold large quantities of securities on behalf of others. (Chapter 1)

interest rate
Usually applied to debt instruments such as bank loans or bonds; the compensation paid by the borrower of funds to the lender; from the borrower's point of view, the cost of borrowing funds. (Chapter 6)

interest rate risk
The chance that interest rates will change and thereby change the required return and bond value. Rising rates, which result in decreasing bond values, are of greatest concern. (Chapter 6)

intermediate cash inflows
Cash inflows received prior to the termination of a project. (Chapter 10)

internal forecast
A sales forecast based on a buildup, or consensus, of sales forecasts through the firm's own sales channels. (Chapter 4)

internal rate of return approach
An approach to capital rationing that involves graphing project IRRs in descending order against the total dollar investment to determine the group of acceptable projects. (Chapter 11)

internal rate of return (IRR)
The discount rate that equates the NPV of an investment opportunity with $0 (because the present value of cash inflows equals the initial investment); it is the rate of return that the firm will earn if it invests in the project and receives the given cash inflows. (Chapter 10)

international equity market
A market that allows corporations to sell blocks of shares to investors in a number of different countries simultaneously. (Chapter 2)

inventory turnover
Measures the activity, or liquidity, of a firm's inventory. (Chapter 3)

inverted yield curve
A *downward-sloping* yield curve indicates that short-term interest rates are generally higher than long-term interest rates. (Chapter 6)

investment bankers
Financial intermediary that specializes in selling new security issues and advising firms with regard to major financial transactions. (Chapter 7)

investment banks
Institutions that assist companies in raising capital, advise firms on major transactions such as mergers or financial restructurings, and engage in trading and market making activities. (Chapter 2)

investment opportunities schedule (IOS)
The graph that plots project IRRs in descending order against the total dollar investment. (Chapter 11)

issued shares
Shares of common stock that have been put into circulation; the sum of *outstanding shares* and *treasury stock.* (Chapter 7)

judgmental approach
A simplified approach for preparing the pro forma balance sheet under which the firm estimates the values of certain balance sheet accounts and uses its external financing as a balancing, or "plug," figure. (Chapter 4)

junk bonds
See Table 6.5.

just-in-time (JIT) system
Inventory management technique that minimizes inventory investment by having materials arrive at exactly the time they are needed for production. (Chapter 14)

letter of credit
A letter written by a company's bank to the company's foreign supplier, stating that the bank guarantees payment of an invoiced amount if all the underlying agreements are met. (Chapter 15)

letter to stockholders
Typically, the first element of the annual stockholders' report and the primary communication from management. (Chapter 3)

leverage
Refers to the effects that fixed costs have on the returns that shareholders earn; higher leverage generally results in higher but more volatile returns. (Chapter 12)

lien
A publicly disclosed legal claim on loan collateral. (Chapter 15)

limited liability
A legal provision that limits stockholders' liability for a corporation's debt to the amount they initially invested in the firm by purchasing stock. (Chapter 1)

limited liability company (LLC)
Permitted in most states, the LLC gives its owners limited liability and taxation as a partnership. But unlike an S corp, the LLC can own more than 80% of another corporation, and corporations, partnerships, or non-U.S. residents can own LLC shares. (Chapter 1)

limited liability partnership (LLP)
Permitted in most states, LLP partners are liable for their own acts of malpractice, but not for those of other partners. The LLP is taxed as a partnership and is frequently used by legal and accounting professionals. (Chapter 1)

limited partnership (LP)
A partnership in which one or more partners have limited liability as long as at least one partner (the general partner) has unlimited liability. The limited partners are passive investors that cannot take an active role in the firm's management. (Chapter 1)

line of credit
An agreement between a commercial bank and a business specifying the amount of unsecured short-term borrowing the bank will make available to the firm over a given period of time. (Chapter 15)

liquidation value per share
The *actual amount* per share of common stock that would be received if all of the firm's assets were sold for their market value, liabilities (including preferred stock) were paid, and any remaining money were divided among the common stockholders. (Chapter 7)

liquidity
A firm's ability to satisfy its short-term obligations *as they come due*. (Chapter 3)

liquidity preference
A general tendency for investors to prefer short-term (that is, more liquid) securities. (Chapter 6)

liquidity preference theory
Theory suggesting that long-term rates are generally higher than short-term rates (hence, the yield curve is upward sloping) because investors perceive short-term investments to be more liquid and less risky than long-term investments. Borrowers must offer higher rates on long-term bonds to entice investors away from their preferred short-term securities. (Chapter 6)

loan amortization
The determination of the equal periodic loan payments necessary to provide a lender with a specified interest return and to repay the loan principal over a specified period. (Chapter 5)

loan amortization schedule
A schedule of equal payments to repay a loan. It shows the allocation of each loan payment to interest and principal. (Chapter 5)

lockbox system
A collection procedure in which customers mail payments to a post office box that is emptied regularly by the firm's bank, which processes the payments and deposits them in the firm's account. This system speeds up collection time by reducing processing time as well as mail and clearing time. (Chapter 14)

long-term debt
Debt for which payment is not due in the current year. (Chapter 3)

long-term (strategic) financial plans
Plans that lay out a company's planned financial actions and the anticipated impact of those actions over periods ranging from 2 to 10 years. (Chapter 4)

low-regular-and-extra dividend policy
A dividend policy based on paying a low regular dividend, supplemented by an additional ("extra") dividend when earnings are higher than normal in a given period. (Chapter 13)

mail float
The time delay between when payment is placed in the mail and when it is received. (Chapter 14)

managerial finance
Concerns the duties of the *financial manager* in a business. (Chapter 1)

manufacturing resource planning II (MRP II)
A sophisticated computerized system that integrates data from numerous areas such as finance, accounting, marketing, engineering, and manufacturing and

generates production plans as well as numerous financial and management reports. (Chapter 14)

marginal cost–benefit analysis
Economic principle that states that financial decisions should be made and actions taken only when the added benefits exceed the added costs. (Chapter 1)

marginal tax rate
The rate at which *additional income* is taxed. (Chapter 2)

marketable securities
Short-term debt instruments, such as U.S. Treasury bills, commercial paper, and negotiable certificates of deposit issued by government, business, and financial institutions, respectively. (Chapter 2)

market/book (M/B) ratio
Provides an assessment of how investors view the firm's performance. Firms expected to earn high returns relative to their risk typically sell at higher M/B multiples. (Chapter 3)

market makers
Securities dealers who "make markets" by offering to buy or sell certain securities at stated prices. (Chapter 2)

market ratios
Relate a firm's market value, as measured by its current share price, to certain accounting values. (Chapter 3)

market return
The return on the market portfolio of all traded securities. (Chapter 8)

market segmentation theory
Theory suggesting that the market for loans is segmented on the basis of maturity and that the supply of and demand for loans within each segment determine its prevailing interest rate; the slope of the yield curve is determined by the general relationship between the prevailing rates in each market segment. (Chapter 6)

market value weights
Weights that use market values to measure the proportion of each type of capital in the firm's financial structure. (Chapter 9)

materials requirement planning (MRP) system
Inventory management technique that applies EOQ concepts and a computer to compare production needs to available inventory balances and determine when orders should be placed for various items on a product's *bill of materials*. (Chapter 14)

mixed stream
A stream of unequal periodic cash flows that reflect no particular pattern. (Chapter 5)

modified accelerated cost recovery system (MACRS)
System used to determine the depreciation of assets for tax purposes. (Chapter 4)

modified DuPont formula
Relates the firm's *return on total assets (ROA)* to its *return on equity (ROE)* using the *financial leverage multiplier (FLM)*. (Chapter 3)

money market
A financial relationship created between suppliers and demanders of *short-term funds*. (Chapter 2)

mortgage-backed securities
Securities that represent claims on the cash flows generated by a pool of mortgages. (Chapter 2)

mortgage bonds
See Table 6.4.

multiple IRRs
More than one IRR resulting from a capital budgeting project with a *nonconventional cash flow pattern*; the maximum number of IRRs for a project is equal to the number of sign changes in its cash flows. (Chapter 10)

mutually exclusive projects
Projects that compete with one another so that the acceptance of one *eliminates* from further consideration all other projects that serve a similar function. (Chapter 10)

Nasdaq market
An all-electronic trading platform used to execute securities trades. (Chapter 2)

negatively correlated
Describes two series that move in opposite directions. (Chapter 8)

net cash flow
The mathematical difference between the firm's cash receipts and its cash disbursements in each period. (Chapter 4)

net operating profits after taxes (NOPAT)
A firm's earnings before interest and after taxes, $EBIT \times (1 - T)$. (Chapter 4)

net present value approach
An approach to capital rationing that is based on the use of present values to determine the group of projects that will maximize owners' wealth. (Chapter 11)

net present value (NPV)
A sophisticated capital budgeting technique; found by subtracting a project's initial investment from the present value of its cash inflows discounted at a rate equal to the firm's cost of capital. (Chapter 10)

net present value profile
Graph that depicts a project's NPVs for various discount rates. (Chapter 10)

net proceeds
Funds actually received by the firm from the sale of a security. (Chapter 9)

net profit margin
Measures the percentage of each sales dollar remaining after all costs and expenses, *including* interest, taxes, and preferred stock dividends, have been deducted. (Chapter 3)

net working capital
The difference between the firm's current assets and its current liabilities. (Chapters 11 and 14)

nominal rate of interest
The actual rate of interest charged by the supplier of funds and paid by the demander. (Chapter 6)

nominal (stated) annual rate
Contractual annual rate of interest charged by a lender or promised by a borrower. (Chapter 5)

noncash charge
An expense that is deducted on the income statement but does not involve the actual outlay of cash during the period; includes depreciation, amortization, and depletion. (Chapter 4)

noncumulative (preferred stock)
Preferred stock for which passed (unpaid) dividends do not accumulate. (Chapter 7)

nondiversifiable risk
The relevant portion of an asset's risk attributable to market factors that affect all firms; cannot be eliminated through diversification. Also called *systematic risk*. (Chapter 8)

nonnotification basis
The basis on which a borrower, having pledged an account receivable, continues to collect the account payments without notifying the account customer. (Chapter 15)

nonrecourse basis
The basis on which accounts receivable are sold to a factor with the understanding that the factor accepts all credit risks on the purchased accounts. (Chapter 15)

nonvoting common stock
Common stock that carries no voting rights; issued when the firm wishes to raise capital through the sale of common stock but does not want to give up its voting control. (Chapter 7)

no-par preferred stock
Preferred stock with no stated face value but with a stated annual dollar dividend. (Chapter 7)

normal probability distribution
A symmetrical probability distribution whose shape resembles a "bell-shaped" curve. (Chapter 8)

normal yield curve
An *upward-sloping* yield curve indicates that long-term interest rates are generally higher than short-term interest rates. (Chapter 6)

notes to the financial statements
Explanatory notes keyed to relevant accounts in the statements; they provide detailed information on the accounting policies, procedures, calculations, and transactions underlying entries in the financial statements. (Chapter 3)

notification basis
The basis on which an account customer whose account has been pledged (or factored) is notified to remit payment directly to the lender (or factor). (Chapter 15)

open-market share repurchase
A share repurchase program in which firms simply buy back some of their outstanding shares on the open market. (Chapter 13)

operating breakeven point
The level of sales necessary to cover all *operating costs;* the point at which EBIT = $0. (Chapter 12)

operating cash flow (OCF)
The cash flow a firm generates from its normal operations; calculated as *net operating profits after taxes (NOPAT)* plus depreciation. (Chapter 4)

operating cash flows
The incremental after-tax cash flows resulting from implementation of a project during its life. (Chapter 11)

operating-change restrictions
Contractual restrictions that a bank may impose on a firm's financial condition or operations as part of a line-of-credit agreement. (Chapter 15)

operating cycle (OC)
The time from the beginning of the production process to collection of cash from the sale of the finished product. (Chapter 14)

operating expenditure
An outlay of funds by the firm resulting in benefits received *within* 1 year. (Chapter 10)

operating leverage
The use of *fixed operating costs* to magnify the effects of changes in sales on the firm's earnings before interest and taxes. (Chapter 12)

operating profit margin
Measures the percentage of each sales dollar remaining after all costs and expenses *other than* interest, taxes, and preferred stock dividends are deducted; the "pure profits" earned on each sales dollar. (Chapter 3)

opportunity costs
Cash flows that could be realized from the best alternative use of an owned asset. (Chapter 11)

optimal capital structure
The capital structure at which the weighted average cost of capital is minimized, thereby maximizing the firm's value. (Chapter 12)

order costs
The fixed clerical costs of placing and receiving an inventory order. (Chapter 14)

ordinary annuity
An annuity for which the cash flow occurs at the *end* of each period. (Chapter 5)

ordinary income
Income earned through the sale of a firm's goods or services. (Chapter 2)

outstanding shares
Issued shares of common stock held by investors, including both private and public investors. (Chapter 7)

over-the-counter (OTC) market
Market where smaller, unlisted securities are traded. (Chapter 2)

paid-in capital in excess of par
The amount of proceeds in excess of the par value received from the original sale of common stock. (Chapter 3)

partnership
A business owned by two or more people and operated for profit. (Chapter 1)

par-value common stock
An arbitrary value established for legal purposes in the firm's corporate charter and which can be used to find the total number of shares outstanding by dividing it into the book value of common stock. (Chapter 7)

par-value preferred stock
Preferred stock with a stated face value that is used with the specified dividend percentage to determine the annual dollar dividend. (Chapter 7)

payback period
The amount of time required for a firm to recover its initial investment in a project as calculated from cash *inflows*. (Chapter 10)

payment date
Set by the firm's directors, the actual date on which the firm mails the dividend payment to the holders of record. (Chapter 13)

payout policy
Decisions that a firm makes regarding whether to distribute cash to shareholders, how much cash to distribute, and the means by which cash should be distributed. (Chapter 13)

pecking order
A hierarchy of financing that begins with retained earnings, which is followed by debt financing and finally external equity financing. (Chapter 12)

percentage advance
The percentage of the book value of the collateral that constitutes the principal of a secured loan. (Chapter 15)

percent-of-sales method
A simple method for developing the pro forma income statement; it forecasts sales and then expresses the various income statement items as percentages of projected sales. (Chapter 4)

perfectly negatively correlated
Describes two *negatively correlated* series that have a *correlation coefficient* of −1. (Chapter 8)

perfectly positively correlated
Describes two *positively correlated* series that have a *correlation coefficient* of +1. (Chapter 8)

performance plans
Plans that tie management compensation to measures such as EPS or growth in EPS. *Performance shares, cash bonuses,* or both are used as compensation under these plans. (Chapter 1)

performance shares
Shares of stock given to management for meeting stated performance goals. (Chapter 1)

permanent funding requirement
A constant investment in operating assets resulting from constant sales over time. (Chapter 14)

perpetuity
An annuity with an infinite life, providing continual annual cash flow. (Chapter 5)

pledge of accounts receivable
The use of a firm's accounts receivable as security, or collateral, to obtain a short-term loan. (Chapter 15)

political risk
Risk that arises from the possibility that a host government will take actions harmful to foreign investors or that political turmoil will endanger investments. (Chapter 8)

portfolio
A collection, or group, of assets. (Chapter 8)

positively correlated
Describes two series that move in the same direction. (Chapter 8)

preemptive right
Allows common stockholders to maintain their proportionate ownership in the corporation when new shares are issued, thus protecting them from dilution of their ownership. (Chapter 7)

preferred stock
A special form of ownership having a fixed periodic dividend that must be paid prior to payment of any dividends to common stockholders. (Chapter 2)

premium
The amount by which a bond sells at a value that is greater than its par value. (Chapter 6)

present value
The current dollar value of a future amount: the amount of money that would have to be invested today at a given interest rate over a specified period to equal the future amount. (Chapter 5)

president or chief executive officer (CEO)
Corporate official responsible for managing the firm's day-to-day operations and carrying out

the policies established by the board of directors. (Chapter 1)

price/earnings multiple approach
A popular technique used to estimate the firm's share value; calculated by multiplying the firm's expected earnings per share (EPS) by the average price/earnings (P/E) ratio for the industry. (Chapter 7)

price/earnings (P/E) ratio
Measures the amount that investors are willing to pay for each dollar of a firm's earnings; the higher the P/E ratio, the greater the investor confidence. (Chapter 3)

primary market
Financial market in which securities are initially issued; the only market in which the issuer is directly involved in the transaction. (Chapter 2)

prime rate of interest (prime rate)
The lowest rate of interest charged by leading banks on business loans to their most important business borrowers. (Chapter 15)

principal
The amount of money on which interest is paid. (Chapter 5)

principal–agent relationship
An arrangement in which an agent acts on the behalf of a principal. For example, shareholders of a company (principals) elect management (agents) to act on their behalf. (Chapter 1)

privately owned (stock)
The common stock of a firm is owned by private investors; this stock is not publicly traded. (Chapter 7)

private placement
The sale of a new security directly to an investor or group of investors. (Chapter 2)

probability
The *chance* that a given outcome will occur. (Chapter 8)

probability distribution
A model that relates probabilities to the associated outcomes. (Chapter 8)

proceeds from sale of old asset
The cash inflows, net of any removal or cleanup costs, resulting from the sale of an existing asset. (Chapter 11)

processing float
The time between receipt of a payment and its deposit into the firm's account. (Chapter 14)

profitability
The relationship between revenues and costs generated by using the firm's assets—both current and fixed—in productive activities. (Chapter 14)

pro forma statements
Projected, or forecast, income statements and balance sheets. (Chapter 4)

prospectus
A portion of a security registration statement that describes the key aspects of the issue, the issuer, and its management and financial position. (Chapter 7)

proxy battle
The attempt by a nonmanagement group to gain control of the management of a firm by soliciting a sufficient number of proxy votes. (Chapter 7)

proxy statement
A statement transferring the votes of a stockholder to another party. (Chapter 7)

**Public Company Accounting Oversight Board
'CAOB)**
∩ not-for-profit corporation established by the *Sarbanes-Oxley Act of 2002* to protect the interests of investors and further the public interest in the preparation of informative, fair, and independent audit reports. (Chapter 3)

publicly owned (stock)
The common stock of a firm is owned by public investors; this stock is publicly traded. (Chapter 7)

public offering
The sale of either bonds or stocks to the general public. (Chapter 2)

pure economic profit
A profit above and beyond the normal competitive rate of return in a line of business. (Chapter 10)

putable bonds
See Table 6.5.

quarterly compounding
Compounding of interest over four periods within the year. (Chapter 5)

quick (acid-test) ratio
A measure of liquidity calculated by dividing the firm's current assets minus inventory by its current ibilities. (Chapter 3)

range
A measure of an asset's risk, which is found by subtracting the return associated with the pessimistic (worst) outcome from the return associated with the optimistic (best) outcome. (Chapter 8)

ranking approach
The ranking of capital expenditure projects on the basis of some predetermined measure, such as the rate of return. (Chapter 10)

ratio analysis
Involves methods of calculating and interpreting financial ratios to analyze and monitor the firm's performance. (Chapter 3)

real options
Opportunities that are embedded in capital projects that enable managers to alter their cash flows and risk in a way that affects project acceptability (NPV). Also called *strategic options*. (Chapter 11)

real rate of interest
The rate that creates equilibrium between the supply of savings and the demand for investment funds in a perfect world, without inflation, where suppliers and demanders of funds have no liquidity preferences and there is no risk. (Chapter 6)

recaptured depreciation
The portion of an asset's sale price that is above its book value and below its initial purchase price. (Chapter 11)

recovery period
The appropriate depreciable life of a particular asset as determined by MACRS. (Chapter 4)

red herring
A preliminary prospectus made available to prospective investors during the waiting period between the registration statement's filing with the SEC and its approval. (Chapter 7)

regular dividend policy
A dividend policy based on the payment of a fixed-dollar dividend in each period. (Chapter 13)

relevant cash flows
The *incremental cash outflow (investment) and resulting subsequent inflows* associated with a proposed capital expenditure. (Chapter 11)

reorder point
The point at which to reorder inventory, expressed as days of lead time × daily usage. (Chapter 14)

required return
Usually applied to equity instruments such as common stock; the cost of funds obtained by selling an ownership interest. (Chapter 6)

required total financing
Amount of funds needed by the firm if the ending cash for the period is less than the desired minimum cash balance; typically represented by notes payable. (Chapter 4)

residual theory of dividends
A school of thought that suggests that the dividend paid by a firm should be viewed as a *residual,* the amount left over after all acceptable investment opportunities have been undertaken. (Chapter 13)

restrictive covenants
Provisions in a bond indenture that place operating and financial constraints on the borrower. (Chapter 6)

retained earnings
The cumulative total of all earnings, net of dividends, that have been retained and reinvested in the firm since its inception. (Chapter 3)

return on equity (ROE)
Measures the return earned on the common stockholders' investment in the firm. (Chapter 3)

return on total assets (ROA)
Measures the overall effectiveness of management in generating profits with its available assets; also called the *return on investment (ROI).* (Chapter 3)

reverse stock split
A method used to raise the market price of a firm's stock by exchanging a certain number of outstanding shares for one new share. (Chapter 13)

revolving credit agreement
A line of credit *guaranteed* to a borrower by a commercial bank regardless of the scarcity of money. (Chapter 15)

rights
Financial instruments that allow stockholders to purchase additional shares at a price below the market price, in direct proportion to their number of owned shares. (Chapter 7)

risk
The chance that actual outcomes may differ from those expected. (Chapter 1)

risk
A measure of the uncertainty surrounding the return that an investment will earn or, more formally, *the variability of returns associated with a given asset.* (Chapter 8)

risk-adjusted discount rate (RADR)
The rate of return that must be earned on a given project to compensate the firm's owners adequately, that is, to maintain or improve the firm's share price. (Chapter 11)

risk averse
Requiring compensation to bear risk. (Chapter 1)

risk averse
The attitude toward risk in which investors require an increased return as compensation for an increase in risk. (Chapter 8)

risk-free rate of return (R_F)
The required return on a *risk-free asset,* typically a 3-month *U.S. Treasury bill.* (Chapter 8)

risk (in capital budgeting)
The uncertainty surrounding the cash flows that a project will generate or, more formally, the degree of variability of cash flows. (Chapter 11)

risk neutral
The attitude toward risk in which investors choose the investment with the higher return regardless of its risk. (Chapter 8)

risk (of insolvency)
The probability that a firm will be unable to pay its bills as they come due. (Chapter 14)

risk seeking
The attitude toward risk in which investors prefer investments with greater risk even if they have lower expected returns. (Chapter 8)

safety stock
Extra inventory that is held to prevent stockouts of important items. (Chapter 14)

sales forecast
The prediction of the firm's sales over a given period, based on external and/or internal data; used as the key input to the short-term financial planning process. (Chapter 4)

Sarbanes-Oxley Act of 2002 (SOX)
An act aimed at eliminating corporate disclosure and conflict of interest problems. Contains provisions about corporate financial disclosures and the relationships

among corporations, analysts, auditors, attorneys, directors, officers, and shareholders. (Chapter 1)

scenario analysis
An approach for assessing risk that uses several possible alternative outcomes (scenarios) to obtain a sense of the variability among returns. (Chapter 8)

S corporation (S corp)
A tax-reporting entity that allows certain corporations with 100 or fewer stockholders to choose to be taxed as partnerships. Its stockholders receive the organizational benefits of a corporation and the tax advantages of a partnership. (Chapter 1)

seasonal funding requirement
An investment in operating assets that varies over time as a result of cyclic sales. (Chapter 14)

secondary market
Financial market in which preowned securities (those that are not new issues) are traded. (Chapter 2)

secured short-term financing
Short-term financing (loan) that has specific assets pledged as collateral. (Chapter 15)

Securities Act of 1933
An act that regulates the sale of securities to the public via the primary market. (Chapter 2)

Securities and Exchange Commission (SEC)
The primary government agency responsible for enforcing federal securities laws. (Chapter 2)

Securities Exchange Act of 1934
An act that regulates the trading of securities such as stocks and bonds in the secondary market. (Chapter 2)

securities exchanges
Organizations that provide the marketplace in which firms can raise funds through the sale of new securities and purchasers can resell securities. (Chapter 2)

securitization
The process of pooling mortgages or other types of loans and then selling claims or securities against that pool in the secondary market. (Chapter 2)

security agreement
The agreement between the borrower and the lender that specifies the collateral held against a secured loan. (Chapter 15)

security market line (SML)
The depiction of the *capital asset pricing model (CAPM)* as a graph that reflects the required return in the marketplace for each level of nondiversifiable risk (beta). (Chapter 8)

selling group
A large number of brokerage firms that join the originating investment banker(s); each accepts responsibility for selling a certain portion of a new security issue on a commission basis. (Chapter 7)

semiannual compounding
Compounding of interest over two periods within the year. (Chapter 5)

shadow banking system
A group of institutions that engage in lending activities, much like traditional banks, but do not accept deposits and therefore are not subject to the same regulations as traditional banks. (Chapter 2)

short-term (operating) financial plans
Specify short-term financial actions and the anticipated impact of those actions. (Chapter 4)

short-term, self-liquidating loan
An unsecured short-term loan in which the use to which the borrowed money is put provides the mechanism through which the loan is repaid. (Chapter 15)

signal
A financing action by management that is believed to reflect its view of the firm's stock value; generally, debt financing is viewed as a *positive signal* that management believes the stock is "undervalued," and a stock issue is viewed as a *negative signal* that management believes the stock is "overvalued." (Chapter 12)

simulation
A statistics-based behavioral approach that applies predetermined probability distributions and random numbers to estimate risky outcomes. (Chapter 11)

single-payment note
A short-term, one-time loan made to a borrower who needs funds for a specific purpose for a short period. (Chapter 15)

sinking-fund requirement
A restrictive provision often included in a bond indenture, providing for the systematic retirement of bonds prior to their maturity. (Chapter 6)

small (ordinary) stock dividend
A stock dividend representing less than 20 percent to 25 percent of the common stock outstanding when the dividend is declared. (Chapter 13)

sole proprietorship
A business owned by one person and operated for his or her own profit. (Chapter 1)

spontaneous liabilities
Financing that arises from the normal course of business; the two major short-term sources of such liabilities are accounts payable and accruals. (Chapter 15)

stakeholders
Groups such as employees, customers, suppliers, creditors, owners, and others who have a direct economic link to the firm. (Chapter 1)

standard debt provisions
Provisions in a *bond indenture* specifying certain record-keeping and general business practices that the bond issuer must follow; normally, they do not place a burden on a financially sound business. (Chapter 6)

standard deviation (σ_r)
The most common statistical indicator of an asset's risk; it measures the dispersion around the expected value. (Chapter 8)

statement of cash flows
Provides a summary of the firm's operating, investment, and financing cash flows and reconciles them with changes in its cash and marketable securities during the period. (Chapter 3)

statement of retained earnings
Reconciles the net income earned during a given year, and any cash dividends paid, with the change in retained earnings between the start and the end of that year. An abbreviated form of the *statement of stockholders' equity*. (Chapter 3)

statement of stockholders' equity
Shows all equity account transactions that occurred during a given year. (Chapter 3)

stock dividend
The payment, to existing owners, of a dividend in the form of stock. (Chapter 13)

stockholders
The owners of a corporation, whose ownership, or equity, takes the form of common stock, or less frequently, preferred stock. (Chapter 1)

stockholders' report
Annual report that publicly owned corporations must provide to stockholders; it summarizes and documents the firm's financial activities during the past year. (Chapter 3)

stock options
Options extended by the firm that allow management to benefit from increases in stock prices over time. (Chapter 1)

stock purchase warrants
Instruments that give their holders the right to purchase a certain number of shares of the issuer's common stock at a specified price over a certain period of time. (Chapter 6)

stock split
A method commonly used to lower the market price of a firm's stock by increasing the number of shares belonging to each shareholder. (Chapter 13)

stretching accounts payable
Paying bills as late as possible without damaging the firm's credit rating. (Chapter 15)

subordinated debentures
See Table 6.4.

subordination
In a bond indenture, the stipulation that subsequent creditors agree to wait until all claims of the *senior debt* are satisfied. (Chapter 6)

sunk costs
Cash outlays that have already been made (past outlays) and therefore have no effect on the cash flows relevant to a current decision. (Chapter 11)

supervoting shares
Stock that carries with it multiple votes per share rather than the single vote per share typically given on regular shares of common stock. (Chapter 7)

target dividend-payout ratio
A dividend policy under which the firm attempts to pay out a certain percentage of earnings as a stated dollar dividend and adjusts that dividend toward a target payout as proven earnings increases occur. (Chapter 13)

target weights
Either book or market value weights based on *desired* capital structure proportions. (Chapter 9)

tax on sale of old asset
Tax that depends on the relationship between the old asset's sale price and book value and on existing government tax rules. (Chapter 11)

tender offer repurchase
A repurchase program in which a firm offers to repurchase a fixed number of shares, usually at a premium relative to the market value, and shareholders decide whether or not they want to sell back their shares at that price. (Chapter 13)

terminal cash flow
The after-tax nonoperating cash flow occurring in the final year of a project. It is usually attributable to liquidation of the project. (Chapter 11)

term structure of interest rates
The relationship between the maturity and rate of return for bonds with similar levels of risk. (Chapter 6)

time line
A horizontal line on which time zero appears at the leftmost end and future periods are marked from left to right; can be used to depict investment cash flows. (Chapter 5)

time-series analysis
Evaluation of the firm's financial performance over time using financial ratio analysis. (Chapter 3)

times interest earned ratio
Measures the firm's ability to make contractual interest payments; sometimes called the *interest coverage ratio*. (Chapter 3)

total asset turnover
Indicates the efficiency with which the firm uses its assets to generate sales. (Chapter 3)

total cash disbursements
All outlays of cash by the firm during a given financial period. (Chapter 4)

total cash receipts
All a firm's inflows of cash during a given financial period. (Chapter 4)

total cost of inventory
The sum of order costs and carrying costs of inventory. (Chapter 14)

total leverage
The use of *fixed costs, both operating and financial*, to magnify the effects of changes in sales on the firm's earnings per share. (Chapter 12)

total rate of return
The total gain or loss experienced on an investment over a given period of time; calculated by dividing the asset's cash distributions during the period, plus change in value, by its beginning-of-period investment value. (Chapter 8)

total risk
The combination of a security's *nondiversifiable risk* and *diversifiable risk*. (Chapter 8)

treasurer
The firm's chief financial manager, who manages the firm's cash, oversees its pension plans, and manages key risks. (Chapter 1)

treasury stock
Issued shares of common stock held by the firm; often these shares have been repurchased by the firm. (Chapter 7)

trustee
A paid individual, corporation, or commercial bank trust department that acts as the third party to a *bond indenture* and can take specified actions on behalf of the bondholders if the terms of the indenture are violated. (Chapter 6)

trust receipt inventory loan
A secured short-term loan against inventory under which the lender advances 80 to 100 percent of the cost of the borrower's relatively expensive inventory items in exchange for the borrower's promise to repay the lender, with accrued interest, immediately after the sale of each item of collateral. (Chapter 15)

two-bin method
Unsophisticated inventory-monitoring technique that is typically applied to C group items and involves reordering inventory when one of two bins is empty. (Chapter 14)

uncorrelated
Describes two series that lack any interaction and therefore have a *correlation coefficient* close to zero. (Chapter 8)

underpriced
Stock sold at a price below its current market price, P_0. (Chapter 9)

underwriting
The role of the investment banker in bearing the risk of reselling, at a profit, the securities purchased from an issuing corporation at an agreed-on price. (Chapter 7)

underwriting syndicate
A group of other bankers formed by an *investment banker* to share the financial risk associated with underwriting new securities. (Chapter 7)

unlimited funds
The financial situation in which a firm is able to accept all independent projects that provide an acceptable return. (Chapter 10)

unlimited liability
The condition of a sole proprietorship (or general partnership), giving creditors the right to make claims against the owner's personal assets to recover debts owed by the business. (Chapter 1)

unsecured short-term financing
Short-term financing obtained without pledging specific assets as collateral. (Chapter 15)

U.S. Treasury bills (T-bills)
Short-term IOUs issued by the U.S. Treasury; considered the *risk-free asset*. (Chapter 8)

valuation
The process that links risk and return to determine the worth of an asset. (Chapter 6)

variable-growth model
A dividend valuation approach that allows for a change in the dividend growth rate. (Chapter 7)

venture capital
Privately raised external equity capital used to fund early-stage firms with attractive growth prospects. (Chapter 7)

venture capitalists (VCs)
Providers of venture capital; typically, formal businesses that maintain strong oversight over the firms they invest in and that have clearly defined exit strategies. (Chapter 7)

warehouse receipt loan
A secured short-term loan against inventory under which the lender receives control of the pledged inventory collateral, which is stored by a designated warehousing company on the lender's behalf. (Chapter 15)

weighted average cost of capital (WACC), r_a
Reflects the expected average future cost of capital over the long run; found by weighting the cost of each specific type of capital by its proportion in the firm's capital structure. (Chapter 9)

widely owned (stock)
The common stock of a firm is owned by many unrelated individual or institutional investors. (Chapter 7)

wire transfer
An electronic communication that, via bookkeeping entries, removes funds from the payer's bank and deposits them in the payee's bank. (Chapter 14)

working capital
Current assets, which represent the portion of investment that circulates from one form to another in the ordinary conduct of business. (Chapter 14)

working capital (or short-term financial) management
Management of current assets and current liabilities. (Chapter 14)

yield curve
A graphic depiction of the term structure of interest rates. (Chapter 6)

yield to maturity
Compound annual rate of return earned on a debt security purchased on a given day and held to maturity. (Chapter 6)

zero-balance account (ZBA)
A disbursement account that always has an end-of-day balance of zero because the firm deposits money to cover checks drawn on the account only as they are presented for payment each day. (Chapter 14)

zero-growth model
An approach to dividend valuation that assumes a constant, nongrowing dividend stream. (Chapter 7)

zero- (or low-) coupon bonds
See Table 6.5.

Index

Note: Boldface page numbers indicate pages where terms are defined.

The Key to Your Success in Three Easy Steps!

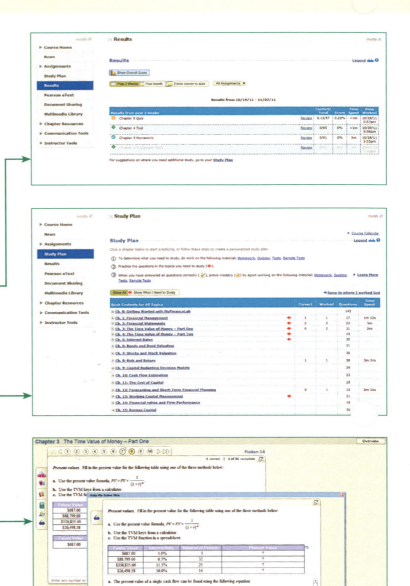

1. Take a Sample Test to assess your knowledge.

2. Review your personalized Study Plan to see where you need more work.

3. Use the Study Plan exercises and step-by-step tutorials to get practice—and individualized feedback—where you need it.

If your instructor assigns homework and tests using MyFinanceLab

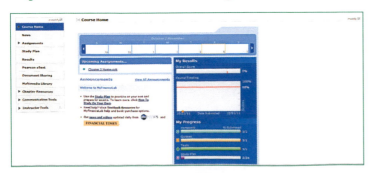

The MyFinanceLab Course Home page uses graphs to let students know their current progress in the course and it has a detailed calendar that not only displays due dates, but allows instructors to add entries.

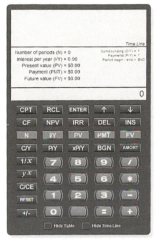

View the Financial Calculator Tutorials

Use the Financial Calculator to solve math problems right in MyFinanceLab! The Financial Calculator is available as a smartphone application as well as on a computer and includes important functions such as future and present value.

Fifteen helpful tutorials show instructors and students the many ways to use the Financial Calculator in MyFinanceLab. Tutorials include lessons on calculator ctions such as IRR and bond valuation.

Select end-of-chapter problems are now available in MyFinanceLab as simulated Excel problems. Each problem has algorithmically generated values and allows students to solve the problem as they would in Excel. Each problem is autograded and has both Excel and problem-specific Learning Aids.

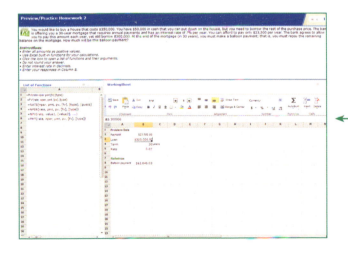